ISSUES AND IMAGES
AN ARGUMENT READER

Dedication

To Vincent E. Miller and Constance Dean Antonsen,
who taught me to see through literature and art;

And especially to

Alicia
Lorrie
Evan
Ashleigh

who daily show me much that delights and challenges.

ISSUES AND IMAGES
AN ARGUMENT READER

WILLIAM E. RIVERS

Harcourt Brace Jovanovich College Publishers

Fort Worth Philadelphia San Diego New York Orlando Austin San Antonio
Toronto Montreal London Sydney Tokyo

Publisher:	Ted Buchholz
Acquisitions Editor:	Michael Rosenberg
Developmental Editor:	Helen Triller
Project Editor:	Barbara Moreland/Dawn Youngblood
Production Manager:	J. Montgomery Shaw
Book Designer:	Priscilla Mingus

Cover Image: René Magritte, *LA LUNETTE D'APPROCHE* (The Telescope) 1963 oil on canvas 69⅓ × 45¼ inches. Courtesy The Menil Collection, Houston, Texas.
© 1992 C. Herscovici/ARS, New York.
Text Illustrations: Lamberto Alvarez

Acknowledgments continue on page 650, which constitutes a continuation of this copyright page.

ISBN: 0-03-055157-9

Library of Congress Cataloging-in-Publication Number:
92-07124-7

Address for editorial correspondence:
301 Commerce Street, Suite 3700
Fort Worth, TX 76102

Address for orders:
6277 Sea Harbor Drive
Orlando FL 32887
1-800-782-4479 outside Florida
1-800-433-0001 inside Florida

PRINTED IN THE UNITED STATES OF AMERICA
3 4 5 6 7 8 9 0 1 2 016 9 8 7 6 5 4 3 2 1

Preface

This text book contains not only essays to help you meet the basic objectives of an argument-based composition course, but also additional essays and other materials not usually found in an argument reader. The idea for an argument reader with a broader than usual selection of materials evolved over several years of teaching, while I was directing a large Freshman Composition program. During this time my talks with other instructors revealed that they, too, were looking for a more varied collection of readings. We wanted a book that would

1. hold students' interest by having them examine a range of materials that vary in purpose, subject matter, and approach;
2. show students that all public writing (including descriptive or personal essays, fiction, and even poetry) involves argument and that studying examples of both explicit and implicit argument could enhance their overall understanding of persuasive writing;
3. introduce students to visual argument (the "images" of the book's title);
4. help students develop stronger reading and writing skills by exposing them to different organizational schemes and stylistic patterns used by writers working in different genres and different rhetorical situations; and
5. challenge students intellectually with essays and materials that are longer and more sophisticated than those usually anthologized.

Although this reader does have brief appendixes on argument and on writing from sources, it was conceived as a reader that would be used in conjunction with a handbook and therefore does not contain an elaborate introduction to argument. The goal is to provide students and instructors easy access to essays and other materials so they can get at the essential business of a composition course based on a reader—reading and writing. The apparatus in this book is therefore restricted to brief introductions (which provide overviews of the materials in major units or give biographical information on authors and artists) and questions after entries. The questions are designed to push students to examine the thesis or argument, the evidence offered (its strengths and weaknesses), and the organizational patterns in each essay, as well as, when appropriate, to compare arguments offered in different essays. Guiding questions are provided for almost all of the reproduced paintings and editorial cartoons. Some of the editorial cartoons are unaccompanied by questions so that students must deal with them solely on the basis of their impact as visual arguments, helped only by contrast or comparison with the essays and other materials in that section of the reader.

The organizational pattern in this reader is pedagogical, not rhetorical, and generally reflects the sequence of reading and writing assignments I follow when teaching the course for which this text was designed. Basically, the pattern moves from shorter, more accessible reading and writing assignments to more challenging assignments that require students to read and incorporate more information into their writing. The goal of this series of assignments is to move students toward being able to present a wide range of opinions on a topic while also clearly articulating their own opinions in their own voice.

Issues and Images begins and ends with materials not usually found in an argument reader. PART I, IMPLICIT AND EXPLICIT ARGUMENTS, is divided into two subsections. The first subsection, *Implicit Arguments,* contains essays that are personal, descriptive, and reflective in nature. These attempts by various writers to make sense of the world, our society, and human experience all demonstrate the importance and effectiveness of implicit argument. The essays provide interesting points of departure for assignments that require students to write from their own personal experience. I have placed them at the beginning of the book because I prefer to start a freshman-level composition course—even one that emphasizes argument—by having students write personal essays. This kind of assignment can also be used later in the semester to provide a welcome break from the more rigid analytical, argumentative writing and thinking typical of an argument-based writing course. The second subsection, *Explicit Arguments,* contains examples of straightforwardly argumentative essays more typical of those found in argument readers.

PART II, CONTRASTING VIEWS, offers contrasting opinions on difficult social, ethical, or intellectual issues. The goal is to give students a clear sense of how writers on opposite sides of an issue present their arguments and to increase students' awareness of the need to anticipate counter arguments. In the last three units I have included a third essay that defines a middle-ground position between the two more extreme positions. These middle-ground essays (and others like them in PART III) help students see the problems in logic often inherent in the arguments of writers who take clear-cut pro or con positions on an issue. These essays also help students realize that a balanced compromise, though not always possible and often very difficult to articulate, is frequently the most reasonable, attractive, and practical approach to many issues. The *Paired Paintings* section in PART II (as well as other paintings and editorial cartoons scattered throughout the text) are included to expand students' intellectual and semantic experience by having them think about visual argument and the vocabulary they must use to talk about it. The paired paintings challenge students to think and write about how artists from different cultures and different times reveal their attitudes about life and society through their art.

PART III, PRIVATE OPINION AND PUBLIC POLICY, contains essays and other materials on four contemporary public policy issues. I have tried to include essays that argue all sides of the issue as well as selections that provide different ways of viewing and responding to that issue. For example, in each grouping you will find some or all of the following: literary works that provide more personal, subjective, and often very powerful emotional perspectives on issues we usually try to debate on logical and legal grounds; essays that provide historical perspective on contemporary issues; and editorial cartoons that illustrate the power of visual argument. Many of these essays contain political, religious, or philosophical biases that students must learn to recognize and take into account as they analyze what they read and develop their own opinions.

Finally, PART IV, PERSISTENT HUMAN PROBLEMS, contains essays and other materials on four problems that have perplexed humankind for centuries: racial injustice, gender differences, war, and cultural misunderstandings. These units provide a special and important alternative not found in most argument readers in that they deal with problems not easily reducible to either/or analysis and discussion. The goal here is to give students the challenge of formulating and presenting their own analysis of a very complex human problem and push them to consider how that problem might be solved or at least minimized. The focus in each of these groupings is on recent manifestations of the problems; however, for three of the topics I have tried to provide readings that will give students a clear sense of how these problems have changed (or not changed) over time.

The Instructor's Manual that accompanies this reader contains a brief analysis of each essay cartoon, and painting in *Issues and Images.* Each entry focuses on how that specific work might be presented in class. Special attention is placed on elements that enhance or detract from the persuasiveness of the work, including special perspectives or biases, unusual features of language, or interesting organizational strategies. In some cases, suggestions for comparisons with other essays and for assignments are presented.

Acknowledgments

Completing this project has made me again acutely aware of how much my ability to get things done depends on the help and encouragement of many people. During the early planning and proposal stage of the project Ruth Strickland offered many suggestions that helped shape and improve this book. Jean Wyrick (Colorado State University) and Erica Lindemann (University of North Carolina) shared their experience with textbook publishing; the advice and the encouragement of Karen Moore (one of the best book reps in the business) helped me settle on Holt, Rinehart & Winston—now Harcourt Brace Jovanovich. In the process of gathering ideas and information I talked with many people who shared their expertise and recommended materials; among these people I owe special thanks to Nora Bell, Jan Love, Bruce Pearson, Leah Lake, and Greta Little. Melissa Walker Heidari and Guy Litton, research assistants for this project, worked hard and well to find materials for the text and offered valuable suggestions about what to include. Guy also allowed me to adapt his class handout on MLA documentation for Appendix B. Elizabeth Ellison, Norah Grimball, Greta Little, Todd Stebbins, Gloria Underwood, and many others provided the encouragement and direct help necessary for me to complete other projects and meet other responsibilities. Throughout the project Maxine James offered suggestions for readings and was always a reliable source of wisdom about how to improve the writing in the introductions. Elizabeth Smith took on most of the responsibility for seeking permissions and worked wonders on the telephone in the last stages of the project. Without her persistence and patience (which usually were strongest when I had none), the project would not have been completed. Finally, thanks to my family, who often had to do without me or (what was probably worse) had to deal with me over the term of this project. Although she had more than enough of her own writing and editing to do, Alicia came to my rescue a number of times. Her proofreading helped me eliminate not only typographical errors but also phrasing and logic problems. The text and the instructor's manual are much stronger because of her careful reading and thoughtful advice. My girls provided hugs when I needed them. The "worry stone" my son gave me for Christmas 1991 ("to help you with the book") captured for me the concern and patience they all demonstrated.

The advice offered by reviewers at several stages in the development of this project was invaluable. They were encouraging when encouragement was justified, but were (thankfully) candid about what should be omitted or changed. My gratitude goes to John G. Bayer, St. Louis Community College at Meramee; Carolyn Channell, Southern Methodist University; Stanley Coberly, West Virginia University at Parkersburg, Ane Ipsen, California State University, Fullerton; Carol V. Johnson, Virginia Wesleyan College, Norfolk; Kimberly Miller, Colorado State University.

At Harcourt Brace Jovanovich I have many people to thank. Without their patience, encouragement, and advice the job could not have been done. Michael Rosenberg had the courage to sign me on and the patience to endure my slowness. Helen Triller took over as Development Editor late in the life of the project and in a few short months made several years' worth of improvements. Barbara Moreland and Dawn Youngblood, Project Editors, turned a messy manuscript into a real book. The professionalism of these and many others at HBJ repeatedly renewed my energy when it flagged, especially toward the end.

One other group deserves a special mention: the graduate students who teach in the Freshman Composition Program at the University of South Carolina. Watching them in the classroom and talking with them about their work has been an enlightening and inspiring experience. Much of what they have taught me is reflected in this book.

Introduction for Students

On Reading and Writing

Reading is potentially one of the most productive ways to improve your writing skills. Think about it. There are only two ways we as human beings have to acquire and to improve our facility with language: conversation and reading. Conversation is important. Most of us first learn language by conversing, and conversation can continue all our lives to be an excellent way to expand our vocabulary and to improve our sense of sentence structure and flow.

But conversation cannot offer the potential to improve your writing that comes from reading a wide variety of materials on a regular basis over a long period of time. Reading serves to improve your writing in four ways: it expands your vocabulary and your sense of sentence structure; it enlarges your knowledge of the world; it teaches you to be more aware of what to expect in writing; and it helps you develop a sense of how to structure your own writing.

First, reading helps you become a better writer by expanding your vocabulary and enlarging your sense of what sentence patterns and organizational structures are available to you as a writer. Unless you are extraordinarily lucky, your conversation will be limited to a relatively small number of people. You will probably find, if you think about those with whom you converse, that most of them fall into a few groups who have common interests and experiences and thus use basically the same vocabulary and sentence patterns. Linguists call these groups discourse communities. Although you can enlarge the number of discourse communities you deal with as a speaker (going to college is an excellent way to do this), the best way to diversify your experience and thus to strengthen your facility with language is through reading. Reading what many different writers have to say about a broad range of subjects brings you into contact with vocabulary, sentence structures, and rhetorical strategies you simply cannot encounter in any other way. Because you absorb vocabulary and semantic patterns unconsciously anytime you read, even reading for pleasure is valuable. When you approach a reading task with an active, inquisitive mind, you will find your ability to recognize, appreciate, and incorporate new words and patterns improving in a steady and very satisfying way.

Second, reading will enlarge your knowledge of the world and give you more facts, ideas, and opinions to draw upon when you write. The effectiveness of any piece of writing is not determined just by how well the words are put together. Effectiveness in writing is measured by how well the words, sentences, and paragraphs work together to communicate what you the writer *have to say.* What you have to say is your personal opinion about our world and our society, and your place in them. Reading can provide new information and perspectives that you can use (sometimes directly, sometimes indirectly) to further your thinking and support your opinions. What you have to say when you write (or speak) always goes into a context determined by an ongoing conversation of speakers and writers. Broad-based reading provides your easiest access to this conversation—a conversation that goes on constantly and is essential to the exchange of ideas in a free society.

Third, reading helps you become a better reader, which in turn helps you become a better writer. The more you read, the more you become aware of what to expect in a piece of writing. You will get better at recognizing a writer's thesis and organizational strategy; at defining words by their context; at realizing what information or steps of logic are missing; at recognizing and appreciating a writer's skillful effort. The reading skills you build will help you read faster and with greater comprehension. Furthermore, the more you read, especially if you read with an active mind, the more you become aware of what readers look for in a piece of writing. That awareness of a reader's wants and needs can, if you make it a part of your writing process, allow you to constantly improve as a writer.

Remember that every piece of writing is written for someone else to *read.* Your writing will be more effective if you are aware of

- what your reader might look for in a piece of writing;
- what questions your reader might ask; and
- what information and linguistic signals might help your reader better understand your message.

Awareness of your reader will also help you become more focused on the message you want to convey.

Finally, reading helps you gain a better sense of how writing can be structured. One of the biggest problems any writer has is deciding how to order information and ideas on paper. If you read widely, and especially if you consistently try to raise questions about how each piece of writing is organized, you will improve your sense of what organizational schemes might fit the writing task before you.

Writing is not a concern you can dismiss after a few semesters. Writing will continue to be an important part of your academic and professional life. Therefore, developing broad-based reading habits can be an integral part of your ongoing professional success, not to mention your personal and intellectual growth, which is, after all, a process that should continue the rest of your life.

On the Importance and Nature of Argument

Argument is one of the fundamental ways we as individuals and as a society have to work out what we think. We debate about whether information is reliable, about what information and ideas are important, about what values we espouse, about what policies we will pursue, and about what actions we should take. We are constantly talking, writing, listening, and reading in an attempt to understand and persuade. This dialogue—this constant exchange of opinions, ideas, information, and observation—is essential to a diverse and progressive society. We find this dialogue in politics, religion, science, business, and law; in newspapers, scientific journals, literary magazines, business reports and letters, legal briefs, political speeches, sermons, and college essays.

Seen in this way, argument is a crucial human activity that does not so much imply discord and rancor (as many assume) as it shows human beings attempting

- to agree on common intellectual, moral, and ethical grounds;
- to find workable solutions to difficult problems; and
- to determine what we agree might be true about our beautiful, complex, baffling, and sometimes frightening world.

Argument does not always lead to agreement; disagreement and compromise are important parts of the process.

Your participation in this argument—this pervasive dialogue that defines our society—is both an intellectual challenge and a means of defining yourself as an individual.

On Issues and Images

Good persuasive writing—even writing about very abstract, non-visual issues—has a visual element. Effective writers help us see their points by using examples, metaphors, similes, analogies, and anecdotes. In fact, human beings link seeing so closely with thinking that we quite regularly use the verb "to see" to indicate understanding or insight. Our ability to visualize—to "see" relationships, patterns, information, ideas, and facts—is one of the most powerful mental tools we have because it pushes us to think in a more specific, tangible way. As you read the essays in this book, watch for the strategies authors use to engage your mind's eye. Consider how you as a writer can incorporate these strategies into your writing.

When we think of images, most of us do not think first of written discourse; we think first of what we see in the world around us and then of the images visual artists create based on that world. Works of art, because they convey artists' perceptions of the world and how it works, are arguments and thus quite appropriate for inclusion in this textbook. (They can also provide refreshing breaks from prose arguments.) The visual arguments in this book include both paintings and editorial cartoons.

A brief introduction to paintings appears in the Paired Paintings section that begins Part II. That introduction stresses the need to linger over a painting to assess its full impact as a work of art. A slightly different approach, however, is more appropriate for editorial cartoons. They are designed for immediate, satiric impact and thus require less time for analysis. However, editorial cartoons can be quite sophisticated and thought-provoking arguments. Cartoon art is especially effective at revealing contradictions in human behavior and within human institutions. As you evaluate the cartoons scattered throughout this textbook, look for the contrasts within the cartoon. Those contrasts may be between two or more visual elements, between the image in the cartoon and the words of the title or the words spoken by a character in the cartoon, or between the image of the cartoon and a familiar image from our common experience outside the cartoon. All the editorial cartoons are presented with a single essay or a group of essays that deal with the same issue. First look for the contrasts that reveal the cartoon's argument and then consider how the cartoon reinforces or contradicts the arguments you find in the essays.

Reading Critically

Reading critically is essential if you are to understand information and arguments and if you wish to improve your skills as a writer. Following the suggestions listed below can help you become a more careful, more active, and more critical reader.

1. Before You Read, Look Around, Look Ahead, and Ask Questions
   Who wrote the selection? What else has she or he written? Where and when did the article originally appear? Does anything you find suggest a bias or special interest? What is the author's thesis? Can you tell from the title? From the first paragraph or an early thesis paragraph? How long is the selection? How is the selection organized? (If it has headings, its organization should be obvious. If it doesn't have headings, look for transition sentences and paragraphs.) Where is the author going? What is the author's conclusion? (There's no rule against peeking, so read the final paragraph if you wish.)
2. While You Read, Stay Involved
   Always read with a pencil in your hand. Place checks in margins by key points (e.g., thesis statements, good ideas, new information, good material for quotations). If you know the selection is one you will use as a source for your essay, annotate it. (Use the margins to write in your reactions to the author's comments and/or to outline the piece.) Underline or highlight key passages. (This is best done on second reading, but if you feel you must mark it on first reading, be judicious and don't overmark material. Too much underlining keeps you and your eye from finding the really important stuff later.)
3. After You Read, Review
   Look back over the thesis statement and key arguments. This review can help you remember the essay and better assess its value to you. Write a short response/evaluation. This activity gives you invaluable practice in writing about your subject. Consider these questions: What is your opinion of the whole piece? Of its thesis? Of its key points? Can you use anything from it to support your argument? Does it help you identify arguments you must refute?

Contents

Part I

IMPLICIT AND EXPLICIT ARGUMENTS

The dialogue that goes on within our society takes many written forms. Some pieces of writing are what you might expect to find in an argument reader—they are explicit, direct attempts to persuade readers to agree with the writer and, in some cases, to take action. For example, Susan B. Anthony's "On Women's Right to Suffrage" (Part IV) straightforwardly argues that she and every other woman should have the right to vote. Since women at the time that Anthony wrote were by law not allowed to vote and many men did not believe that women should be given that right, she was arguing hoping to change both attitudes and laws.

Other writers, because of their temperament, the issue they are addressing, or their assessment of their audience, will produce documents that have more restricted goals but are nevertheless explicit arguments. These writers may seek only to persuade their readers to accept their positions as reasonable, even if the reader does not agree. These writers are not directly seeking a change in policy or asking for action; they are simply asking for understanding or tolerance. However, in a society as diverse as ours, these goals are often very difficult to achieve. Sometimes only a modicum of understanding and the beginnings of tolerance are achieved. In "To Blacks and Jews: Hab Rachmones" (Part IV), James A. McPherson examines in detail the relationship between Blacks and Jews in order to build understanding and thus reduce tensions. His assumption is that if these two groups remember how they have worked together for their common good in the past and better understand the sources of their present differences, they can avoid conflict. Understanding can bring tolerance even if it does not bring a change in attitude.

Other pieces of writing may not seem to have persuasive goals at all. Many just present information or make observations that do not require a direct response. Essayists, poets, and writers of fiction will often share their perceptions or their puzzlement about life and the world. In these cases the argument is implicit. The implied assertion may simply be that the information being presented is accurate and important or that the writer and his or her opinions are worthy of being heard. In fact, some of the most dramatic and arresting contributions to our social dialogue fall into this category. Lance Morrow's essay "Kidnapping the Brainchildren" (Part I) is a rambling (though not illogically arranged) piece that comes to no clear conclusion as he ponders the question of why people are willing to plagiarize the work of others. His implicit argument is a commonplace: Human beings are flawed, paradoxical creatures. He presents his insight as a puzzle he must learn to accept (even though he does not like it), not as a situation that action or understanding can change. James Baldwin's short story "Sonny's Blues" (Part III) chronicles the interactions of a number of people who influence and are influenced by Sonny. The implications (implicit arguments) we can see in the story are many; they have to do with race relations, drugs, family dynamics, friendship, and music. The appeal here is for our interest, concern, and understanding. And even if Baldwin does not directly argue for certain changes in attitude, he certainly provides insights that we can build on to support explicit arguments.

In this reader you will find materials that illustrate this range of purposes and techniques within argumentation. Most of the essays argue explicitly for a position or policy or are appeals for understanding. However, throughout the reader you will find examples of implicit argument in essays, poems, and short stories. This diversity challenges us to look at issues from different perspectives.

In Part I you will find implicit and explicit arguments grouped into separate subsections to help you more easily identify the similarities and differences between these two kinds of arguments. The first subsection, ''Implicit Arguments,'' contains essays that are personal, descriptive, and reflective in nature. These attempts by various writers to make sense of the world, society, and human experience all demonstrate the importance and effectiveness of implicit argument. The second subsection, ''Explicit Arguments,'' contains examples of straightforwardly argumentative essays more typical of what you would expect in an argument reader.

Implicit Arguments

Ray Bradbury

Summer Rituals

(1953)

Best known for his science fiction, Ray Bradbury (b. 1920) has also published poetry, short stories, novels, and essays. This piece comes from *Dandelion Wine*, a collection of essays first published in 1953.

1 Yes, summer was rituals, each with its natural time and place. The ritual of lemonade or ice-tea making, the ritual of wine, shoes, or no shoes, and at last, swiftly following the others, with quiet dignity, the ritual of the front-porch swing.

2 On the third day of summer in the late afternoon Grandfather reappeared from the front door to gaze serenely at the two empty eye rings in the ceiling of the porch. Moving to the geranium-pot-lined rail like Ahab surveying the mild mild day and the mild-looking sky, he wet his finger to test the wind, and shucked his coat to see how shirt sleeves felt in the westering hours. He acknowledged the salutes of other captains on yet other flowered porches, out themselves to discern the gentle ground swell of weather, oblivious to their wives chirping or snapping like fuzzball hand dogs hidden behind black porch screens.

3 "All right, Douglas, let's let it up."

4 In the garage they found, dusted, and carried forth the howdah, as it were, for the quiet summer-night festivals, the swing chair which Grandpa chained to the porch-ceiling eyelets.

5 Douglas, being lighter, was first to sit in the swing. Then, after a moment, Grandfather gingerly settled his pontifical weight beside the boy. Thus they sat, smiling at each other, nodding, as they swung silently back and forth, back and forth.

6 Ten minutes later Grandma appeared with water buckets and brooms to wash down and sweep off the porch. Other chairs, rockers and straight-backs, were summoned from the house.

7 "Always like to start sitting early in the season," said Grandpa, "before the mosquitoes thicken."

8 About seven o'clock you could hear the chairs scraping back from the tables, someone experimenting with a yellow-toothed piano, if you stood outside the dining-room

window and listened. Matches being struck, the first dishes bubbling in the suds and tinkling on the wall racks, somewhere, faintly, a phonograph playing. And then as the evening changed the hour, at house after house on the twilight streets, under the immense oaks and elms, on shady porches, people would begin to appear, like those figures who tell good or bad weather in rain-or-shine clocks.

9 Uncle Bert, perhaps Grandfather, then Father, and some of the cousins; the men all coming out first into the syrupy evening, blowing smoke, leaving the women's voices behind in the cooling-warm kitchen to set their universe aright. Then the first male voices under the porch brim, the feet up, the boys fringed on the worn steps or wooden rails where sometime during the evening something, a boy or a geranium pot, would fall off.

10 At last, like ghosts hovering momentarily behind the door screen, Grandma, Great-grandma, and Mother would appear, and the men would shift, move, and offer seats. The women carried varieties of fans with them, folded newspapers, bamboo whisks, or perfumed kerchiefs, to start the air moving about their faces as they talked.

11 What they talked of all evening long, no one remembered next day. It wasn't important to anyone what the adults talked about; it was only important that the sounds came and went over the delicate ferns that bordered the porch on three sides; it was only important that the darkness filled the town like black water being poured over the houses, and that the cigars glowed and that the conversations went on, and on. The female gossip moved out, disturbing the first mosquitoes so they danced in frenzies on the air. The male voices invaded the old house timbers; if you closed your eyes and put your head down against the floor boards you could hear the men's voices rumbling like a distant, political earthquake, constant, unceasing, rising or falling a pitch.

12 Douglas sprawled back on the dry porch planks, completely contented and reassured by these voices, which would speak on through eternity, flow in a stream of murmurings over his body, over his closed eyelids, into his drowsy ears, for all time. The rocking chairs sounded like crickets, the crickets sounded like rocking chairs, and the moss-covered rain barrel by the dining-room window produced another generation of mosquitoes to provide a topic of conversation through endless summers ahead.

13 Sitting on the summer-night porch was so good, so easy and so reassuring that it could never be done away with. These were rituals that were right and lasting; the lighting of pipes, the pale hands that moved knitting needles in the dimness, the eating of foil-wrapped, chill Eskimo Pies, the coming and going of all the people. For at some time or other during the evening, everyone visited here; the neighbors down the way, the people across the street; Miss Fern and Miss Roberta humming by in their electric runabout, giving Tom or Douglas a ride around the block and then coming up to sit down and fan away the fever in their cheeks; or Mr. Jonas, the junkman, having left his horse and wagon hidden in the alley, and ripe to bursting with words, would come up the steps looking as fresh as if his talk had never been said before, and somehow it never had. And last of all, the children, who had been off squinting their way through a last hide-and-seek or kick-the-can, panting, glowing, would sickle quietly back like boomerangs along the soundless lawn, to sink beneath the talking talking talking of the porch voices which would weigh and gentle them down. . . .

14 Oh, the luxury of lying in the fern night and the grass night and the night of susurrant, slumbrous voices weaving the dark together. The grownups had forgotten he was there, so still, so quiet Douglas lay, noting the plans they were making for his and their own futures. And the voices chanted, drifted, in moonlit clouds of cigarette smoke while the moths, like late appleblossoms come alive, tapped faintly about the far street lights, and the voices moved on into the coming years. . . .

Questions for Analysis

1. Bradbury's essay is a short description of one very simple ritual in the life of a family and town. Notice the details that Bradbury uses to create this description. Does any sense dominate? Seeing? Hearing? Touch or feeling? Enumerate those details and others so that you can see how Bradbury put this description together.
2. Describe the details concerning what the men do and what the women do. Do these differences reveal anything about the culture and ritual Bradbury describes?
3. From what point of view is the essay written? Is there one character in the essay who seems closer to the center of the story's significance than the others? Who? Explain.
4. What is the significance of the ritual Bradbury describes? How does time operate in the story? How does time connect to the significance of the ritual?
5. List some rituals important to your family or to you and a group of friends. Choose one that has special significance for you and enumerate details (people; places; things seen, smelled, heard, and felt) that you associate with that ritual. How would you order those details to convey to a reader the significance of the ritual (your argument) without saying something obvious like "The significance of this ritual is. . . ."?

John McPhee

The Pines

(1967)

A writer for *The New Yorker,* John McPhee (b. 1931) has written about people and places in over 20 books and numerous essays. "The Pines" is part of a longer essay, *The Pine Barrens,* which describes the land and people of southern New Jersey.

1 Fred Brown's house is on an unpaved road that curves along the edge of a wide cranberry bog. What attracted me to it was the pump that stands in his yard. It was

something of a wonder that I noticed the pump, because there were, among other things, eight automobiles in the yard, two of them on their sides and one of them upside down, all ten years old or older. Around the cars were old refrigerators, vacuum cleaners, partly dismantled radios, cathode-ray tubes, a short wooden ski, a large wooden mallet, dozens of cranberry picker's boxes, many tires, an orange crate dated 1946, a cord or so of firewood, mandolins, engine heads, and maybe a thousand other things. The house itself, two stories high, was covered with tarpaper that was peeling away in some places, revealing its original shingles, made of Atlantic white cedar from the stream courses of the surrounding forest. I called out to ask if anyone was home, and a voice inside called back, "Come in. Come in. Come on the hell in."

2 I walked through a vestibule that had a dirt floor, stepped up into a kitchen, and went on into another room that had several overstuffed chairs in it and a porcelain-topped table, where Fred Brown was seated, eating a pork chop. He was dressed in a white sleeveless shirt, ankle-top shoes, and undershorts. He gave me a cheerful greeting and, without asking why I had come or what I wanted, picked up a pair of khaki trousers that had been tossed onto one of the overstuffed chairs and asked me to sit down. He set the trousers on another chair, and he apologized for being in the middle of his breakfast, explaining that he seldom drank much but the night before he had had a few drinks and this had caused his day to start slowly. "I don't know what's the matter with me, but there's got to be something the matter with me, because drink don't agree with me anymore," he said. He had a raw onion in one hand, and while he talked he shaved slices from the onion and ate them between bites of the chop. He was a muscular and well-built man, with short, bristly white hair, and he had bright, fast-moving eyes in a wide-open face. His legs were trim and strong, with large muscles in the calves. I guessed that he was about sixty, and for a man of sixty he seemed to be in remarkably good shape. He was actually seventy-nine. "My rule is: Never eat except when you're hungry," he said, and he ate another slice of the onion.

3 In a straight-backed chair near the doorway to the kitchen sat a young man with long black hair, who wore a visored red leather cap that had darkened with age. His shirt was coarse-woven and had eyelets down a V neck that was laced with a thong. His trousers were made of canvas, and he was wearing gum boots. His arms were folded, his legs were stretched out, he had one ankle over the other, and as he sat there he appeared to be sighting carefully past his feet, as if his toes were the outer frame of a gunsight and he could see some sort of target in the floor. When I had entered, I had said hello to him, and he had nodded without looking up. He had a long, straight nose and high cheekbones, in a deeply tanned face that was, somehow, gaunt. I had no idea whether he was shy or hostile. Eventually, when I came to know him, I found him to be as shy a person as I have ever had a chance to know. His name is Bill Wasovwich, and he lives alone in a cabin about half a mile from Fred. First his father, then his mother left him when he was a young boy, and he grew up depending on the help of various people in the pines. One of them, a cranberry grower, employs him and has given him some acreage, in which Bill is building a small cranberry bog of his own, "turfing it out" by hand. When he is not working in the bogs, he goes roaming, as he

puts it, setting out cross-country on long, looping journeys, hiking about thirty miles in a typical day, in search of what he calls "events"—surprising a buck, or a gray fox, or perhaps a poacher or a man with a still. Almost no one who is not native to the pines could do this, for the woods have an undulating sameness, and the understory—huckleberries, sheep laurel, sweet fern, high-bush blueberry—is often so dense that a wanderer can walk in a fairly tight circle and think that he is moving in a straight line. State forest rangers spend a good part of their time finding hikers and hunters, some of whom have vanished for days. In his long, pathless journeys, Bill always emerges from the woods near his cabin—and about when he plans to. In the fall, when thousands of hunters come into the pines, he sometimes works as a guide. In the evenings, or in the daytime when he is not working or roaming, he goes to Fred Brown's house and sits there for hours. The old man is a widower whose seven children are long since gone from Hog Wallow, and he is as expansively talkative and worldly as the young one is withdrawn and wild. Although there are fifty-three years between their ages, it is obviously fortunate for each of them to be the other's neighbor.

4 That first morning, while Bill went on looking at his outstretched toes, Fred got up from the table, put on his pants, and said he was going to cook me a pork chop, because I looked hungry and ought to eat something. It was about noon, and I was even hungrier than I may have looked, so I gratefully accepted his offer, which was a considerable one. There are two or three small general stores in the pines, but for anything as fragile as a fresh pork chop it is necessary to make a round trip from Fred's place of about fifty miles. Fred went into the kitchen and dropped a chop into a frying pan that was crackling with hot grease. He has a fairly new four-burner stove that uses bottled gas. He keeps water in a large bowl on a table in the kitchen and ladles some when he wants it. While he cooked the meat, he looked out a window through a stand of pitch pines and into the cranberry bog. "I saw a big buck out here last night with velvet on his horns," he said. "Them horns is soft when they're in velvet." On a nail high on one wall of the room that Bill and I were sitting in was a large meat cleaver. Next to it was a billy club. The wall itself was papered in a flower pattern, and the wallpaper continued out across the ceiling and down the three other walls, lending the room something of the appearance of the inside of a gift box. In some parts of the ceiling, the paper had come loose. "I didn't paper this year," Fred said. "For the last couple months, I've had sinus." The floor was covered with old rugs. They had been put down in random pieces, and in some places as many as six layers were stacked up. In winter, when the temperature approaches zero, the worst cold comes through the floor. The only source of heat in the house is a wood-burning stove in the main room. There were seven calendars on the walls, all current and none with pictures of nudes. Fading into pastel on one wall was a rotogravure photograph of President and Mrs. Eisenhower. A framed poem read:

God hath not promised
Sun without rain
Joy without sorrow
Peace without pain.

5 Noticing my interest in all this, Fred reached into a drawer and showed me what appeared to be a postcard. On it was a photograph of a woman, and Fred said with a straight face that she was his present girl, adding that he meets her regularly under a juniper tree on a road farther south in the pines. The woman, whose appearance suggested strongly that she had never been within a great many miles of the Pine Barrens, was wearing nothing at all.

6 I asked Fred what all those cars were doing in his yard, and he said that one of them was in running condition and the rest were its predecessors. The working vehicle was a 1956 Mercury. Each of the seven others had at one time or another been his best car, and each, in turn, had lain down like a sick animal and had died right there in the yard, unless it had been towed home after a mishap elsewhere in the pines. Fred recited, with affection, the history of each car. Of one old Ford, for example, he said, “I upset that up to Speedwell in the creek.” And of an even older car, a station wagon, he said, “I busted that one up in the snow. I met a car on a little hill, and hit the brake, and hit a tree.” One of the cars had met its end at a narrow bridge about four miles from Hog Wallow, where Fred had hit a state trooper, head on.

7 The pork was delicious and almost crisp. Fred gave me a potato with it, and a pitcher of melted grease from the frying pan to pour over the potato. He also handed me a loaf of bread and a dish of margarine, saying, “Here's your bread. You can have one piece or two. Whatever you want.”

8 Fred apologized for not having a phone, after I asked where I would have to go to make a call, later on. He said, “I don't have no phone because I don't have no electric. If I had electric, I would have had a phone in here a long time ago.” He uses a kerosene lamp, a propane lamp, and two flashlights.

9 He asked where I was going, and I said that I had no particular destination, explaining that I was in the pines because I found it hard to believe that so much unbroken forest could still exist so near the big Eastern cities, and I wanted to see it while it was still there. “Is that so?” he said, three times. Like many people in the pines, he often says things three times. “Is that so? Is *that* so?”

10 I asked him what he thought of a plan that has been developed by Burlington and Ocean Counties to create a supersonic jetport in the pines, connected by a spur of the Garden State Parkway to a new city of two hundred and fifty thousand people, also in the pines.

11 “They've been talking about that for three years, and they've never given up,” Fred said.

12 “It'd be the end of these woods,” Bill said. This was the first time I heard Bill speak. I had been there for an hour, and he had not said a word. Without looking up, he said again, “It'd be the end of these woods, I can tell you that.”

13 Fred said, “They could build ten jetports around me. I wouldn't give a damn.”

14 “You ain't going to be around very long,” Bill said to him. “It would be the end of these woods.”

15 Fred took that as a fact, and not as an insult. “Yes, it would be the end of these woods,” he said. “But there'd be people here you could do business with.”

16 Bill said, "There ain't no place like this left in the country, I don't believe—and I travelled around a little bit, too."

17 Eventually, I made the request I had intended to make when I walked in the door. "Could I have some water?" I said to Fred. "I have a jerry can and I'd like to fill it at the pump."

18 "Hell, yes," he said. "That isn't my water. That's God's water. That's God's water. That right, Bill?"

19 "I *guess* so," Bill said, without looking up. "It's good water, I can tell you that."

20 "That's God's water," Fred said again. "Take all you want."

Questions for Analysis

1. How do the things around and in Fred's house reveal what he is like?
2. How does McPhee learn about Bill? Do we know? What is his life like? Is it full? Is it limited? How do the "events" of his life determine its quality? Can we judge its quality by our standards?
3. What is the organizing principle McPhee uses in this essay? How is Paragraph 3 an exception to this pattern? Why did he place this information here?
4. What things make the pines a special place? Why does McPhee end this piece with the emphasis Fred places on "God's water"?

Joan Didion

Los Angeles Notebook

(1968)

Joan Didion (b. 1934) is a writer and novelist whose stories and essays are often set in her native California. This short piece, taken from her very successful early collection of essays called *Slouching Toward Bethlehem,* reveals her ability to weave together details about people, places, and actions to define the society before her.

1 There is something uneasy in the Los Angeles air this afternoon, some unnatural stillness, some tension. What it means is that tonight a Santa Ana will begin to blow, a hot wind from the northeast whining down through the Cajon and San Gorgonio Passes, blowing up sandstorms out along Route 66, drying the hills and the nerves to the flash point. For a few days now we will see smoke back in the canyons, and hear

sirens in the night. I have neither heard nor read that a Santa Ana is due, but I know it, and almost everyone I have seen today knows it too. We know it because we feel it. The baby frets. The maid sulks. I rekindle a waning argument with the telephone company, then cut my losses and lie down, given over to whatever it is in the air. To live with the Santa Ana is to accept, consciously or unconsciously, a deeply mechanistic view of human behavior.

2 I recall being told, when I first moved to Los Angeles and was living on an isolated beach, that the Indians would throw themselves into the sea when the bad wind blew. I could see why. The Pacific turned ominously glossy during a Santa Ana period, and one woke in the night troubled not only by the peacocks screaming in the olive trees but by the eerie absence of surf. The heat was surreal. The sky had a yellow cast, the kind of light sometimes called "earthquake weather." My only neighbor would not come out of her house for days, and there were no lights at night, and her husband roamed the place with a machete. One day he would tell me that he had heard a trespasser, the next a rattlesnake.

3 "On nights like that," Raymond Chandler once wrote about the Santa Ana, "every booze party ends in a fight. Meek little wives feel the edge of the carving knife and study their husbands' necks. Anything can happen." That was the kind of wind it was. I did not know then that there was any basis for the effect it had on all of us, but it turns out to be another of these cases in which science bears out folk wisdom. The Santa Ana, which is named for one of the canyons it rushes through, is a *foehn* wind, like the *foehn* of Austria and Switzerland and the *hamsin* of Israel. There are a number of persistent malevolent winds, perhaps the best known of which are the mistral of France and the Mediterranean sirocco, but a *foehn* wind has distinct characteristics: it occurs on the leeward slope of a mountain range and, although the air begins as a cold mass, it is warmed as it comes down the mountain and appears finally as a hot dry wind. Whenever and wherever a *foehn* blows, doctors hear about headaches and nausea and allergies, about "nervousness," about "depression." In Los Angeles some teachers do not attempt to conduct formal classes during a Santa Ana, because the children become unmanageable. In Switzerland the suicide rate goes up during the *foehn,* and in the courts of some Swiss cantons the wind is considered a mitigating circumstance for crime. Surgeons are said to watch the wind, because blood does not clot normally during a *foehn.* A few years ago an Israeli physicist discovered that not only during such winds, but for the ten or twelve hours which precede them, the air carries an unusually high ratio of positive to negative ions. No one seems to know exactly why that should be; some talk about friction and others suggest solar disturbances. In any case the positive ions are there, and what an excess of positive ions does, in the simplest terms, is make people unhappy. One cannot get much more mechanistic than that.

4 Easterners commonly complain that there is no "weather" at all in Southern California, that the days and the seasons slip by relentlessly, numbingly bland. That is quite misleading. In fact the climate is characterized by infrequent but violent extremes: two periods of torrential subtropical rains which continue for weeks and wash out the hills and send subdivisions sliding toward the sea; about twenty scattered days a year of the

Santa Ana, which, with its incendiary dryness, invariably means fire. At the first prediction of a Santa Ana, the Forest Service flies men and equipment from northern California into the southern forests, and the Los Angeles Fire Department cancels its ordinary non-firefighting routines. The Santa Ana caused Malibu to burn the way it did in 1956, and Bel Air in 1961, and Santa Barbara in 1964. In the winter of 1966–67 eleven men were killed fighting a Santa Ana fire that spread through the San Gabriel Mountains.

5 Just to watch the front-page news out of Los Angeles during a Santa Ana is to get very close to what it is about the place. The longest single Santa Ana period in recent years was in 1957, and it lasted not the usual three or four days but fourteen days, from November 21 until December 4. On the first day 25,000 acres of the San Gabriel Mountains were burning, with gusts reaching 100 miles an hour. In town, the wind reached Force 12, or hurricane force, on the Beaufort Scale; oil derricks were toppled and people ordered off the downtown streets to avoid injury from flying objects. On November 22 the fire in the San Gabriels was out of control. On November 24 six people were killed in automobile accidents, and by the end of the week the Los Angeles *Times* was keeping a box score of traffic deaths. On November 26 a prominent Pasadena attorney, depressed about money, shot and killed his wife, their two sons, and himself. On November 27 a South Gate divorcée, twenty-two, was murdered and thrown from a moving car. On November 30 the San Gabriel fire was still out of control, and the wind in town was blowing eighty miles an hour. On the first day of December four people died violently, and on the third the wind began to break.

6 It is hard for people who have not lived in Los Angeles to realize how radically the Santa Ana figures in the local imagination. The city burning is Los Angeles's deepest image of itself: Nathanael West perceived that, in *The Day of the Locust;* and at the time of the 1965 Watts riots what struck the imagination most indelibly were the fires. For days one could drive the Harbor Freeway and see the city on fire, just as we had always known it would be in the end. Los Angeles weather is the weather of catastrophe, of apocalypse, and, just as the reliably long and bitter winters of New England determine the way life is lived there, so the violence and the unpredictability of the Santa Ana affect the entire quality of life in Los Angeles, accentuate its impermanence, its unreliability. The wind shows us how close to the edge we are.

Questions for Analysis

1. Didion here is describing weather and people. What is the thesis (argument) of her description?
2. Look carefully at what Didion presents in her first two paragraphs. Why does she start this way?

3. After quoting a dramatic passage from Chandler, Didion defines a *foehm* wind in Paragraph 3. Describe the techniques she uses in this definition. How does her definition make the essay more effective?
4. Examine the last sentence in the essay. Is this a thesis statement? Do the examples and definitions she has provided in earlier passages support this claim?

Lewis Thomas

The Medusa and the Snail

(1979)

Lewis Thomas (b. 1913) is a medical doctor and scientist who has specialized in cancer research. He has for a number of years been director of the prestigious Sloan-Kettering Cancer Institute in New York City. During the 1970s, at the request of the editors of the *New England Journal of Medicine,* Thomas began writing personal/scientific essays that were later collected into several books. This piece is the title essay from *The Medusa and the Snail* (1979).

1 We've never been so self-conscious about our selves as we seem to be these days. The popular magazines are filled with advice on things to do with a self: how to find it, identify it, nurture it, protect it, even, for special occasions, weekends, how to lose it transiently. There are instructive books, best sellers on self-realization, self-help, self-development. Groups of self-respecting people pay large fees for three-day sessions together, learning self-awareness. Self-enlightenment can be taught in college electives.

2 You'd think, to read about it, that we'd only just now discovered selves. Having long suspected that there was *something alive* in there, running the place, separate from everything else, absolutely individual and independent, we've celebrated by giving it a real name. My self.

3 It is an interesting word, formed long ago in much more social ambiguity than you'd expect. The original root was *se* or *seu*, simply the pronoun of the third person, and most of the descendant words, except "self" itself, were constructed to allude to other, somehow connected people; "sibs" and "gossips," relatives and close acquaintances, came from *seu. Se* was also used to indicate something outside or apart, hence words like "separate," "secret," and "segregate." From an extended root *swedh* it moved into Greek as *ethnos*, meaning people of one's own sort, and *ethos*, meaning the customs of such people. "Ethics" means the behavior of people like one's self, one's own ethics.

4 We tend to think of our selves as the only wholly unique creations in nature, but it is not so. Uniqueness is so commonplace a property of living things that there is really

nothing at all unique about it. A phenomenon can't be unique and universal at the same time. Even individual, free-swimming bacteria can be viewed as unique entities, distinguishable from each other even when they are the progeny of a single clone. Spudich and Koshland have recently reported that motile microorganisms of the same species are like solitary eccentrics in their swimming behavior. When they are searching for food, some tumble in one direction for precisely so many seconds before quitting, while others tumble differently and for different, but characteristic, periods of time. If you watch them closely, tethered by their flagellae to the surface of an antibody-coated slide, you can tell them from each other by the way they twirl, as accurately as though they had different names.

5 Beans carry self-labels, and are marked by these as distinctly as a mouse by his special smell. The labels are glycoproteins, the lectins, and may have something to do with negotiating the intimate and essential attachment between the bean and the nitrogen-fixing bacteria which live as part of the plant's flesh, embedded in root nodules. The lectin from one line of legume has a special affinity for the surfaces of the particular bacteria which colonize that line, but not for bacteria from other types of bean. The system seems designed for the maintenance of exclusive partnerships. Nature is pieced together by little snobberies like this.

6 Coral polyps are biologically self-conscious. If you place polyps of the same genetic line together, touching each other, they will fuse and become a single polyp, but if the lines are different, one will reject the other.

7 Fish can tell each other apart as individuals, by the smell of self. So can mice, and here the olfactory discrimination is governed by the same H_2 locus which contains the genes for immunologic self-marking.

8 The only living units that seem to have no sense of privacy at all are the nucleated cells that have been detached from the parent organism and isolated in a laboratory dish. Given the opportunity, under the right conditions, two cells from wildly different sources, a yeast cell, say, and a chicken erythrocyte, will touch, fuse, and the two nuclei will then fuse as well, and the new hybrid cell will now divide into monstrous progeny. Naked cells, lacking self-respect, do not seem to have any sense of self.

9 The markers of self, and the sensing mechanisms responsible for detecting such markers, are conventionally regarded as mechanisms for maintaining individuality for its own sake, enabling one kind of creature to defend and protect itself against all the rest. Selfness, seen thus, is for self-preservation.

10 In real life, though, it doesn't seem to work this way. The self-marking of invertebrate animals in the sea, who must have perfected the business long before evolution got around to us, was set up in order to permit creatures of one kind to locate others, not for predation but to set up symbiotic households. The anemones who live on the shells of crabs are precisely finicky; so are the crabs. Only a single species of anemone will find its way to only a single species of crab. They sense each other exquisitely, and live together as though made for each other.

11 Sometimes there is such a mix-up about selfness that two creatures, each attracted by the molecular configuration of the other, incorporate the two selves to make a single

organism. The best story I've ever heard about this is the tale told of the nudibranch and medusa living in the Bay of Naples. When first observed, the nudibranch, a common sea slug, was found to have a tiny vestigial parasite, in the form of a jellyfish, permanently affixed to the ventral surface near the mouth. In curiosity to learn how the medusa got there, some marine biologists began searching the local waters for earlier developmental forms, and discovered something amazing. The attached parasite, although apparently so specialized as to have given up living for itself, can still produce offspring, for they are found in abundance at certain seasons of the year. They drift through the upper waters, grow up nicely and astonishingly, and finally become full-grown, handsome, normal jellyfish. Meanwhile, the snail produces snail larvae, and these too begin to grow normally, but not for long. While still extremely small, they become entrapped in the tentacles of the medusa and then engulfed within the umbrella-shaped body. At first glance, you'd believe the medusae are now the predators, paying back for earlier humiliations, and the snails the prey. But no. Soon the snails, undigested and insatiable, begin to eat, browsing away first at the radial canals, then the borders of the rim, finally the tentacles, until the jellyfish becomes reduced in substance by being eaten while the snail grows correspondingly in size. At the end, the arrangement is back to the first scene, with a full-grown nudibranch basking, and nothing left of the jellyfish except the round, successfully edited parasite, safely affixed to the skin near the mouth.

12 It is a confusing tale to sort out, and even more confusing to think about. Both creatures are designed for this encounter, marked as selves so that they can find each other in the waters of the Bay of Naples. The collaboration, if you want to call it that, is entirely specific; it is only this species of medusa and only this kind of nudibranch that can come together and live this way. And, more surprising, they cannot live in any other way; they depend for their survival on each other. They are not really selves, they are specific others.

13 The thought of these creatures gives me an odd feeling. They do not remind me of anything, really. I've never heard of such a cycle before. They are bizarre, that's it, unique. And at the same time, like a vaguely remembered dream, they remind me of the whole earth at once. I cannot get my mind to stay still and think it through.

Questions for Analysis

1. Thomas is writing in this essay first about words and then about animals. How is it, then, a personal essay?
2. Explain the opposition and similarity Thomas sets up between self and other. How is this link seen in the animals he chooses to include? How does the discussion of the roots of self (Paragraph 3) show both self and other?
3. What does Thomas mean when he says that "They [the medusa and the snail] are not really selves, they are specific others"?

4. What does Thomas mean in his last sentence? Why the reference to "the whole earth at once"? Why can't he get his "mind to stay still and think"? What is his "argument" in this essay?

Lance Morrow

Kidnapping the Brainchildren

(1990)

An editor for *Time*, Lance Morrow (b. 1939) frequently writes essays that appear in that magazine. He has also written several books of nonfiction, including a biography of his father, *The Chief* (1981). This essay appeared in the *Time* issue for December 3, 1990.

1 A story that haunts me:

The book critic for a newspaper plagiarized an old essay of mine. Someone sent the thing to me. There on the page, under another man's name, my words had taken up a new life—clause upon clause, whole paragraphs transplanted. My phrases ambled along dressed in the same meanings. The language gesticulated as before. It argued and whistled and waved to friends. It acted very much at home. My sentences had gone over into a parallel universe, which was another writer's work. The words mocked me across the distance, like an ex-wife who shows up years later looking much the same but married to a gangster. The thoughts were mine, all right. But they were tricked up as another man's inner life, a stranger's.

2 Coming upon my own words, now alienated, I was amused, amazed, flattered, outraged, spooked—and in a moment, simply pained: I learned that after the article was published, the plagiarist had been found out, by someone else, not me, and had committed suicide.

3 I do not know what to make of his death, or of my bizarre and passive implication in it: the man died of the words that he stole from me, or he died of shame. Or something more complex; I cannot say. Maybe he killed himself for other reasons entirely. But his death has a sad phosphorescence in my mind.

4 Strange: we know that plagiarism may be fatal to reputation. But it is seldom so savage that it actually kills the writer. Plagiarism is usually too squalid and minor to take a part in tragedy; maybe that was the suicide's true shame, the grubbiness. Plagiarism proclaims no majestic flaw of character but a trait, pathetic, that makes you turn aside in embarrassment. It belongs to the same rundown neighborhood as obscene phone calls or shoplifting.

5 That is why it is hard to make sense of the information that Martin Luther King Jr. was guilty of plagiarism a number of times in the course of his academic career. How could it be that King, with his extraordinary moral intelligence, the man who sought the transformation of the American soul at the level of its deepest wrong (race), could commit that trashy offense, not once but many times?

6 Character is unexpected mystery. King wrote his doctoral dissertation about the theologians Henry Nelson Wieman and Paul Tillich and plagiarized passages from an earlier student's dissertation. Tillich, one of the great theologians of the 20th century, also had secrets, including a taste for pornography and many women not his wife.

7 I believe in the Moping Dog doctrine. Ralph Waldo Emerson wrote about the inconsistencies of human behavior: "It seems as if heaven had sent its insane angels into our world as to an asylum, and here they will break out in their native music and utter at intervals the words they have heard in heaven; then the mad fit returns and they mope and wallow like dogs."

8 Part of the mystery is that King had no need to plagiarize. He dealt himself a gratuitous wound. And what he lifted from others, or failed to attribute, tended to be pedestrian—a moping prose.

9 Plagiarism at least proclaims that some written words are valuable enough to steal. If the language is magnificent, the sin is comprehensible: the plagiarist could not resist. But what if the borrowed stuff is a flat, lifeless mess—the road kill of passing ideas? In that case there is less risk, but surely no joy at all. (Does the plagiarist ever feel joy?) Safer to steal the duller stones. None but the dreariest specialists will remember them or sift for them in the muck.

10 The Commandments warn against stealing, against bearing false witness, against coveting. *Plagiarius* is kidnapper in Latin, The plagiarist snatches the writer's brain-children, pieces of his soul. Plagiarism gives off a shabby metaphysic. Delaware's Senator Joseph Biden, during the 1988 presidential primaries, expanded the conceptual frontier by appropriating not just the language of British Labour Party leader Neil Kinnock but also of his poignant Welsh coal-mining ancestors. Biden transplanted [his] mythic forebears to northeastern Pennsylvania. He conjured them coming up out of the mines to play football. "They read poetry and wrote poetry and taught me how to sing verse." A fascinating avenue: the romantic plagiarist reinvented himself and his heritage entirely. He jumped out of his own skin and evicted his ancestors from theirs as well.

11 Why plagiarize? Out of some clammy hope for fame, for a grade, for a forlorn fix of approbation. Out of dread of a deadline, or out of sheer neurotic compulsion. Plagiarism is a specialized mystery. Or the mystery may be writing itself. Many people cannot manage it. They borrow. Or they call up a term-paper service.

12 The only charming plagiarism belongs to the young. Schoolchildren shovel information out of an encyclopedia. Gradually they complicate the burglary, taking from two or three reference books instead of one. The mind (still on the wrong side of the law) then deviously begins to intermingle passages, reshuffle sentences, disguise raw chunks from the Britannica, find synonyms, reshape information until it becomes something like the student's own. A writer, as Saul Bellow has said, "is a reader moved to

emulation.'' Knowledge transforms theft. An autonomous mind emerges from the sloughed skin of the plagiarist.

13 There is a certain symmetry of the childish in the King case. Something childish in King's student mind was still copying out of encyclopedias, just as something immature in his sexual development had him going obsessively after women. And something childish in every mind rejects imperfection in heroes. King's greatness came from somewhere else entirely, a deeper part of the forest. No character is flawless, and if it were flawless, that would be its flaw. Everything in nature, Emerson wrote, is cracked.

Questions for Analysis

1. Why does Morrow begin his essay with the story of the man who plagiarized his old essay?
2. What do you learn about plagiarism from Morrow's essay? Does it help you to think more clearly about what plagiarism involves and why (in some cases) it occurs?
3. How does Morrow organize his essay? Does it seem to move along a clear path of logic or does it seem to wander in almost a stream-of-consciousness manner? Is the essay's organizational pattern effective?
4. What is Morrow's purpose in writing this essay? Is he trying to define plagiarism? Is he merely condemning those who plagiarize? Is he trying to understand why plagiarism occurs?
5. Morrow ends his essay by saying that ''no character is flawless, and if it were flawless, that would be its flaw.'' Explain that statement. Does he think flaws are good? Necessary?

E. B. White

Once More to the Lake

(1941)

E. B. White (1899–1985) has for decades been one of America's most popular and most anthologized essayists. During his career, he was a regular contributor to *The New Yorker* and other popular periodicals. This essay is taken from *One Man's Meat* (1941). Should his reputation as an essayist ever diminish, he will no doubt be fondly remembered by many generations to come as the author of the children's classic, *Charlotte's Web* (1952).

1 One summer, along about 1904, my father rented a camp on a lake in Maine and took us all there for the month of August. We all got ringworm from some kittens and

had to rub Pond's Extract on our arms and legs night and morning, and my father rolled over in a canoe with all his clothes on; but outside of that the vacation was a success and from then on none of us ever thought there was any place in the world like that lake in Maine. We returned summer after summer—always on August 1st for one month. I have since become a salt-water man, but sometimes in summer there are days when the restlessness of the tides and the fearful cold of the sea water and the incessant wind which blows across the afternoon and into the evening make me wish for the placidity of a lake in the woods. A few weeks ago this feeling got so strong I bought myself a couple of bass hooks and a spinner and returned to the lake where we used to go, for a week's fishing and to revisit old haunts.

2 I took along my son, who had never had any fresh water up his nose and who had seen lily pads only from train windows. On the journey over to the lake I began to wonder what it would be like. I wondered how time would have marred this unique, this holy spot—the coves and streams, the hills that the sun set behind, the camps and the paths behind the camps. I was sure the tarred road would have found it out and I wondered in what other ways it would be desolated. It is strange how much you can remember about places like that once you allow your mind to return into the grooves which lead back. You remember one thing, and that suddenly reminds you of another thing. I guess I remembered clearest of all the early mornings, when the lake was cool and motionless, remembered how the bedroom smelled of the lumber it was made of and of the wet woods whose scent entered through the screen. The partitions in the camp were thin and did not extend clear to the top of the rooms, and as I was always the first up I would dress softly so as not to wake the others, and sneak out into the sweet outdoors and start out in the canoe, keeping close along the shore in the long shadows of the pines. I remembered being very careful never to rub my paddle against the gunwale for fear of disturbing the stillness of the cathedral.

3 The lake had never been what you would call a wild lake. There were cottages sprinkled around the shores, and it was in farming country although the shores of the lake were quite heavily wooded. Some of the cottages were owned by nearby farmers, and you would live at the shore and eat your meals at the farmhouse. That's what our family did. But although it wasn't wild, it was a fairly large and undisturbed lake and there were places in it which, to a child at least, seemed infinitely remote and primeval.

4 I was right about the tar: it led to within half a mile of the shore. But when I got back there, with my boy, and we settled into a camp near a farmhouse and into the kind of summertime I had known, I could tell that it was going to be pretty much the same as it had been before—I knew it, lying in bed the first morning, smelling the bedroom, and hearing the boy sneak quietly out and go off along the shore in a boat. I began to sustain the illusion that he was I, and therefore, by simple transposition, that I was my father. This sensation persisted, kept cropping up all the time we were there. It was not an entirely new feeling, but in this setting it grew much stronger. I seemed to be living a dual existence. I would be in the middle of some simple act, I would be picking up a bait box or laying down a table fork, or I would be saying something, and

suddenly it would be not I but my father who was saying the words or making the gesture. It gave me a creepy sensation.

5 We went fishing the first morning. I felt the same damp moss covering the worms in the bait can, and saw the dragonfly alight on the tip of my rod as it hovered a few inches from the surface of the water. It was the arrival of this fly that convinced me beyond any doubt that everything was as it always had been, that the years were a mirage and there had been no years. The small waves were the same, chucking the rowboat under the chin as we fished at anchor, and the boat was the same boat, the same color green and the ribs broken in the same places, and under the floor-boards the same fresh-water leavings and débris—the dead helgramite, the wisps of moss, the rusty discarded fishook, the dried blood from yesterday's catch. We stared silently at the tips of our rods, at the dragonflies that came and went. I lowered the tip of mine into the water tentatively, pensively dislodging the fly, which darted two feet away, poised, darted two feet back, and came to rest again a little farther up the rod. There had been no years between the ducking of this dragonfly and the other one—the one that was part of memory. I looked at the boy, who was silently watching his fly, and it was my hands that held his rod, my eyes watching. I felt dizzy and didn't know which rod I was at the end of.

6 We caught two bass, hauling them in briskly as though they were mackerel, pulling them over the side of the boat in a businesslike manner without any landing net, and stunning them with a blow on the back of the head. When we got back for a swim before lunch, the lake was exactly where we had left it, the same number of inches from the dock, and there was only the merest suggestion of a breeze. This seemed an utterly enchanted sea, this lake you could leave to its own devices for a few hours and come back to, and find that it had not stirred, this constant and trustworthy body of water. In the shallows, the dark, water-soaked sticks and twigs, smooth and old, were undulating in clusters on the bottom against the clean ribbed sand, and the track of the mussel was plain. A school of minnows swam by, each minnow with its small individual shadow, doubling the attendance, so clear and sharp in the sunlight. Some of the other campers were in swimming, along the shore, one of them with a cake of soap, and the water felt thin and clear and unsubstantial. Over the years there had been this person with the cake of soap, this cultist, and here he was. There had been no years.

7 Up to the farmhouse to dinner through the teeming, dusty field, the road under our sneakers was only a two-track road. The middle track was missing, the one with the marks of the hooves and the splotches of dried, flaky manure. There had always been three tracks to choose from in choosing which track to walk in; now the choice was narrowed down to two. For a moment I missed terribly the middle alternative. But the way led past the tennis court, and something about the way it lay there in the sun reassured me; the tape had loosened along the backline, the alleys were green with plantains and other weeds, and the net (installed in June and removed in September) sagged in the dry noon, and the whole place steamed with midday heat and hunger and emptiness. There was a choice of pie for dessert, and one was blueberry and one was apple, and the waitresses were the same country girls, there having been no passage of

time, only the illusion of it as in a dropped curtain—the waitresses were still fifteen; their hair had been washed, that was the only difference—they had been to the movies and seen the pretty girls with the clean hair.

8 Summertime, oh summertime, pattern of life indelible, the fade-proof lake, the woods unshatterable, the pasture with the sweetfern and the juniper forever and ever, summer without end; this was the background, and the life along the shore was the design, the cottagers with their innocent and tranquil design, their tiny docks with the flagpole and the American flag floating against the white clouds in the blue sky, the little paths over the roots of the trees leading from camp to camp and the paths leading back to the outhouses and the can of lime for sprinkling, and at the souvenir counters at the store the miniature birch-bark canoes and the post cards that showed things looking a little better than they looked. This was the American family at play, escaping the city heat, wondering whether the newcomers in the camp at the head of the cove were "common" or "nice," wondering whether it was true that the people who drove up for Sunday dinner at the farmhouse were turned away because there wasn't enough chicken.

9 It seemed to me, as I kept remembering all this, that those times and those summers had been infinitely precious and worth saving. There had been jollity and peace and goodness. The arriving (at the beginning of August) had been so big a business in itself, at the railway station the farm wagon drawn up, the first smell of the pine-laden air, the first glimpse of the smiling farmer, and the great importance of the trunks and your father's enormous authority in such matters, and the feel of the wagon under you for the long ten-mile haul, and at the top of the last long hill catching the first view of the lake after eleven months of not seeing this cherished body of water. The shouts and cries of the other campers when they saw you, and the trunks to be unpacked, to give up their rich burden. (Arriving was less exciting nowadays, when you sneaked up in your car and parked it under a tree near the camp and took out the bags and in five minutes it was all over, no fuss, no loud wonderful fuss about trunks.)

10 Peace and goodness and jollity. The only thing that was wrong now, really, was the sound of the place, an unfamiliar nervous sound of the outboard motors. This was the note that jarred, the one thing that would sometimes break the illusion and set the years moving. In those other summertimes all motors were inboard; and when they were at a little distance, the noise they made was a sedative, an ingredient of summer sleep. They were one-cylinder and two-cylinder engines, and some were make-and-break and some were jump-spark, but they all made a sleepy sound across the lake. The one-lungers throbbed and fluttered, and the twin-cylinder ones purred and purred, and that was a quiet sound too. But now the campers all had outboards. In the daytime, in the hot mornings, these motors made a petulant, irritable sound; at night, in the still evening when the afterglow lit the water, they whined about one's ears like mosquitoes. My boy loved our rented outboard, and his great desire was to achieve singlehanded mastery over it, and authority, and he soon learned the trick of choking it a little (but not too much), and the adjustment of the needle valve. Watching him I would remember the things you could do with the old one-cylinder engine with the heavy flywheel, how you could have it eating out of your hand if you got really close to it spiritually. Motor

boats in those days didn't have clutches, and you would make a landing by shutting off the motor at the proper time and coasting in with a dead rudder. But there was a way of reversing them, if you learned the trick, by cutting the switch and putting it on again exactly on the final dying revolution of the flywheel, so that it would kick back against compression and begin reversing. Approaching a dock in a strong following breeze, it was difficult to slow up sufficiently by the ordinary coasting method, and if a boy felt he had complete mastery over his motor, he was tempted to keep it running beyond its time and then reverse it a few feet from the dock. It took a cool nerve, because if you threw the switch a twentieth of a second too soon you would catch the flywheel when it still had speed enough to go up past center, and the boat would leap ahead, charging bull-fashion at the dock.

11 We had a good week at the camp. The bass were biting well and the sun shone endlessly, day after day. We would be tired at night and lie down in the accumulated heat of the little bedrooms after the long hot day and the breeze would stir almost imperceptibly outside and the smell of the swamp drift in through the rusty screens. Sleep would come easily and in the morning the red squirrel would be on the roof, tapping out his gay routine. I kept remembering everything, lying in bed in the mornings—the small steamboat that had a long rounded stern like the lip of a Ubangi, and how quietly she ran on the moonlight sails, when the older boys played their mandolins and the girls sang and we ate doughnuts dipped in sugar, and how sweet the music was on the water in the shining night, and what it had felt like to think about girls then. After breakfast we would go up to the store and the things were in the same place—the minnows in a bottle, the plugs and spinners disarranged and pawed over by the youngsters from the boys' camp, the fig newtons and the Beeman's gum. Outside, the road was tarred and cars stood in front of the store. Inside, all was just as it had always been, except there was more Coca-Cola and not so much Moxie and root beer and birch beer and sarsaparilla. We would walk out with a bottle of pop apiece and sometimes the pop would backfire up our noses and hurt. We explored the streams, quietly, where the turtles slid off the sunny logs and dug their way into the soft bottom; and we lay on the town wharf and fed worms to the tame bass. Everywhere we went I had trouble making out which was I, the one walking at my side, the one walking in my pants.

12 One afternoon while we were there at that lake a thunderstorm came up. It was like the revival of an old melodrama that I had seen long ago with childish awe. The second-act climax of the drama of the electrical disturbance over a lake in America had not changed in any important respect. This was the big scene, still the big scene. The whole thing was so familiar, the first feeling of oppression and heat and a general air around camp of not wanting to go very far away. In midafternoon (it was all the same) a curious darkening of the sky, and a lull in everything that had made life tick; and then the way the boats suddenly swung the other way at their moorings with the coming of a breeze out of the new quarter, and the premonitory rumble. Then the kettle drum, then the snare, then the bass drum and cymbals, then crackling light against the dark, and the gods grinning and licking their chops in the hills. Afterward the calm, the rain steadily rustling in the calm lake, the return of light and hope and spirits, and the campers

running out in joy and relief to go swimming in the rain, their bright cries perpetuating the deathless joke about how they were getting simply drenched, and the children screaming with delight at the new sensation of bathing in the rain, and the joke about getting drenched linking the generations in a strong indestructible chain. And the comedian who waded in carrying an umbrella.

13 When the others went swimming my son said he was going in too. He pulled his dripping trunks from the line where they had hung all through the shower, and wrung them out. Languidly, and with no thought of going in, I watched him, his hard little body, skinny and bare, saw him wince slightly as he pulled up around his vitals the small, soggy, icy garment. As he buckled the swollen belt suddenly my groin felt the chill of death.

Questions for Analysis

1. In the first paragraph White says that in the time since he last was at the lake in Maine, he had become a "salt-water man." What are the special characteristics of a freshwater lake that make it attractive to White? How do these characteristics help him echo his thesis throughout his essay?
2. How has the lake changed since he was there as a boy? How has it remained the same? What things would be similar and different today?
3. Why is his son's presence important to the essay? Could he have written the essay without his son's being there?
4. Explain the significance of the last sentence in the essay. How has all the detail he has offered up to this point contributed to the effect of this sentence? Despite the "chill of death" White felt and expressed in this the climax of his piece, do you think White enjoyed thinking about and writing this essay? Explain.

Explicit Arguments

Mark Twain

Two Ways of Seeing a River

(1883)

Perhaps the best-known and best-loved American author, Mark Twain (pen name of Samuel Clemens, 1835–1910) is remembered for many works, especially *The Adventures of Huckleberry Finn.* This piece is from "Old Times on the Mississippi," a work that was later expanded into *Life on the Mississippi* (1883).

1 Now when I had mastered the language of this water and had come to know every trifling feature that bordered the great river as familiarly as I knew the letters of the alphabet, I had made a valuable acquisition. But I had lost something, too. I had lost something which could never be restored to me while I lived. All the grace, the beauty, the poetry, had gone out of the majestic river! I still kept in mind a certain wonderful sunset which I witnessed when steamboating was new to me. A broad expanse of the river was turned to blood; in the middle distance the red hue brightened into gold, through which a solitary log came floating, black and conspicuous; in one place a long, slanting mark lay sparkling upon the water; in another the surface was broken by boiling, tumbling rings, that were as many-tinted as an opal; where the ruddy flush was faintest, was a smooth spot that was covered with graceful circles and radiating lines, ever so delicately traced; the shore on our left was densely wooded and the somber shadow that fell from this forest was broken in one place by a long, ruffled trail that shone like silver; and high above the forest wall a clean-stemmed dead tree waved a single leafy bough that glowed like a flame in the unobstructed splendor that was flowing from the sun. There were graceful curves, reflected images, woody heights, soft distances, and over the whole scene, far and near, the dissolving lights drifted steadily, enriching it every passing moment with new marvels of coloring.

2 I stood like one bewitched. I drank it in, in a speechless rapture. The world was new to me and I had never seen anything like this at home. But as I have said, a day came when I began to cease from noting the glories and the charms which the moon and the sun and the twilight wrought upon the river's face; another day came when I ceased

altogether to note them. Then, if that sunset scene had been repeated, I should have looked upon it without rapture, and should have commented upon it inwardly after this fashion: "This sun means that we are going to have wind to-morrow; that floating log means that the river is rising, small thanks to it; that slanting mark on the water refers to a bluff reef which is going to kill somebody's steamboat one of these nights, if it keeps on stretching out like that; those tumbling 'boils' show a dissolving bar and a changing channel there; the lines and circles in the slick water over yonder are a warning that that troublesome place is shoaling up dangerously; that silver streak in the shadow of the forest is the 'break' from a new snag and he has located himself in the very best place he could have found to fish for steamboats; that tall dead tree, with a single living branch, is not going to last long, and then how is a body ever going to get through this blind place at night without the friendly old landmark?"

3 No, the romance and beauty were all gone from the river. All the value any feature of it had for me now was the amount of usefulness it could furnish toward compassing the safe piloting of a steamboat. Since those days, I have pitied doctors from my heart. What does the lovely flush in a beauty's cheek mean to a doctor but a "break" that ripples above some deadly disease? Are not all her visible charms sown thick with what are to him the signs and symbols of hidden decay? Does he ever see her beauty at all, or doesn't he simply view her professionally and comment upon her unwholesome condition all to himself? And doesn't he sometimes wonder whether he has gained most or lost most by learning his trade?

Questions for Analysis

1. Twain begins this piece by saying that he gained and lost something when he "mastered the language of this water." In the two descriptions of the same stretch of river seen at sunset, he shows us what he lost and gained. Does it balance? Does Twain feel he lost more than he gained? Explain. Did you think he really lost the ability to see the beauty in the river?
2. Why did Twain organize his comparison as he did? Would the essay be as effective if he had compared each detail before and after his mastery, rather than describing the entire scene as he saw it when he first started working on the river and then the entire scene as he saw it after working as a riverboat pilot?
3. Does the last paragraph's description of a physician's view of patients help make his point? Do you agree with Twain's assertion that professionals always lose the ability to see the beauty in whatever they study?

Mary Field Belenky, Blythe McVicker Clinchy, Nancy Rule Goldberger, and Jill Mattuck Tarule

Two Attitudes Toward Knowing

(1986)

The following piece is from *Women's Ways of Knowing* (1986), a study of women's intellectual and emotional development based on interviews with a number of women from different social and economic situations. The authors, all researchers and/or professors (Belenky [b. 1933] at the University of Vermont; Clinchy [b. 1934] at Wellesley College; Goldberger [b. 1934] at New York University; Tarule [b. 1943] at Lesley College Graduate School), conducted the interviews with these women and from them derived the patterns that are presented in this very influential study. The title of this piece, which comes from their chapter "Toward an Education for Women," is mine.

1 We begin with the reminiscences of two ordinary women, each recalling an hour during her first year at college. One of them, now middle aged, remembered the first meeting of an introductory science course. The professor marched into the lecture hall, placed upon his desk a large jar filled with dried beans, and invited the students to guess how many beans the jar contained. After listening to an enthusiastic chorus of wildly inaccurate estimates the professor smiled a thin, dry smile, revealed the correct answer, and announced, "You have just learned an important lesson about science. Never trust the evidence of your own senses."

2 Thirty years later, the woman could guess what the professor had in mind. He saw himself, perhaps, as inviting his students to embark upon an exciting voyage into a mysterious underworld invisible to the naked eye, accessible only through scientific method and scientific instruments. But the seventeen-year-old girl could not accept or even hear the invitation. Her sense of herself as a knower was shaky, and it was based on the belief that she could use her own firsthand experience as a source of truth. This man was saying that this belief was fallacious. He was taking away her only tool for knowing and providing her with no substitute. "I remember feeling small and scared," the woman says, "and I did the only thing I could do. I dropped the course that afternoon, and I haven't gone near science since."

3 The second woman, in her first year at college, told a superficially similar but profoundly different story about a philosophy class she had attended just a month or two before the interview. The teacher came into class carrying a large cardboard cube. She placed it on the desk in front of her and asked the class what it was. They said it was a cube. She asked what a cube was, and they said a cube contained six equal square sides. She asked how they knew that this object contained six equal square sides. By

looking at it, they said. "But how do you know?" the teacher asked again. She pointed to the side facing her and, therefore, invisible to the students; then she lifted the cube and pointed to the side that had been face down on the desk, and, therefore, also invisible. "We can't look at all six sides of a cube at once, can we? So we can't exactly *see* a cube. And yet, you're right. You know it's a cube. But you know it not just because you have eyes but because you have intelligence. You invent the sides you cannot see. You use your intelligence to create the 'truth' about cubes."

4 The student said to the interviewer,

> It blew my mind. You'll think I'm nuts, but I ran back to the dorm and I called my boyfriend and I said, "Listen, this is just incredible," and I told him all about it. I'm not sure he could see why I was so excited. I'm not sure I understand it myself. But I really felt, for the first time, like I was really in college, like I was—I don't know—sort of *grown up.*

5 Both stories are about the limitations of firsthand experience as a source of knowledge—we cannot simply see the truth about either the jar of beans or the cube—but there is a difference. We can know the truth about cubes. Indeed, the students did know it. As the science professor pointed out, the students were wrong about the beans; their senses had deceived them. But, as the philosophy teacher pointed out, the students were right about the cube; their minds had served them well.

6 The science professor was the only person in the room who knew how many beans were in that jar. Theoretically, the knowledge was available to the students; they could have counted the beans. But faced with that tedious prospect, most would doubtless take the professor's word for it. He is authority. They had to rely upon his knowledge rather than their own. On the other hand, every member of the philosophy class knew that the cube had six sides. They were all colleagues.

7 The science professor exercised his authority in a benign fashion, promising the students that he would provide them with the tools they needed to excavate invisible truths. Similarly, the philosophy teacher planned to teach her students the skills of philosophical analysis, but she was at pains to assure them that they already possessed the tools to construct some powerful truths. They had built cubes on their own, using only their own powers of inference, without the aid of elaborate procedures or fancy apparatus or even a teacher. Although a teacher might have told them once that a cube contained six equal square sides, they did not have to take the teacher's word for it; they could have easily verified it for themselves.

8 The lesson the science professor wanted to teach is that experience is a source of error. Taught in isolation, this lesson diminished the student, rendering her dumb and dependent. The philosophy teacher's lesson was that although raw experience is insufficient, by reflecting upon it the student could arrive at truth. It was a lesson that made the student feel more powerful ("sort of grown up").

9 No doubt it is true that, as the professor in May Sarton's novel *The Small Room* says, the "art" of being a student requires humility. But the woman we interviewed

did not find the science lesson humbling; she found it humiliating. Arrogance was not then and is not now her natural habitat. Like most of the women in our sample she lacked confidence in herself as a thinker; and the kind of learning the science teacher demanded was not only painful but crippling.

10 In thinking about the education of women, Adrienne Rich writes, "Suppose we were to ask ourselves, simply: What does a woman need to know?" ([*On Lies, Secrets and Silence; Selected Prose—1966–78,* New York: Norton] 1979, p. 240). A woman, like any other human being, does need to know that the mind makes mistakes; but our interviews have convinced us that every woman, regardless of age, social class, ethnicity, and academic achievement, needs to know that she is capable of intelligent thought, and she needs to know it right away. Perhaps men learn this lesson before going to college, or perhaps they can wait until they have proved themselves to hear it; we do not know. We do know that many of the women we interviewed had not yet learned it.

Questions for Analysis

1. This essay is built, first, on two experiences by women as they began their college educations and, second, on the writers' assessment of what these experiences show. Describe the differences and similarities in the two women's experiences.
2. Do you think the second woman would have reacted as the first woman did had she been in the science class? Would the first woman have been enthusiastic about the philosophy teacher's approach? Explain.
3. Do you agree with the authors' assessment of the two experiences? Explain.
4. Is the conclusion the authors draw about these two experiences applicable only to women? Do all men know they are "capable of intelligent thought"? Do your own study: Examine your own experience and ask your friends about their experiences. Do they correspond to the conclusions presented here?

Peter Passell

Lotto is Financed by the Poor and Won by the States

(1989)

Peter Passell (b. 1974) is an economist. His essay on the lottery appeared in *The New York Times* on May 21, 1989.

1 The happiest person in Pennsylvania last month may have been Alverta Handel, a housekeeper from the town of Portage who beat 9.6 million-to-one odds to win an $8.2

million share of the record-breaking $115 million lotto jackpot. But the biggest winner by far in Pennsylvania's lottery is the state treasury, which last year netted $593 million from ticket sales.

2 Boosted by ultra-high-stakes lotto games, lotteries have been transformed from a small-change alternative to illegal numbers games into a $16 billion cash cow for financially pressed states. From Maine to California, legislators have stopped worrying about the wages of sin and learned to love the tax that millions wait patiently in line to pay each day.

3 Even the Bible Belt is succumbing to the lure of easy government revenue. Last September, Virginia became the twenty-eighth state to go into the lottery business. And just last month opponents of a property and gasoline tax increase in Louisiana convinced the voters that a lottery could fill the gap left by evaporating oil royalties.

4 Not everyone, though, believes that this form of revenue-gathering is painless. In a book to be published this fall, two Duke University economists, Charles Clotfelter and Philip Cook, offer evidence that the states' share of the lottery amounts to a heavy tax, levied in part on people who can ill afford to pay it. And they raise less tangible, but arguably more troubling questions about the impact of state-sponsored lotteries on public attitudes toward work and thrift.

5 Last year 48 cents of every dollar bet on the state lotteries went for prizes, while another 15 cents covered the cost of promotion, sales, and administration. That left 37 percent of the $16 billion pot, or $5.7 billion, for government.

6 To grateful state officials, the 37 percent is a free lunch. To economists, it is a levy on a product that people plainly want and can only buy legally from the government. The fact that so many people prefer to pay the premium rather than do without the product makes it no more voluntary than the tax on airline tickets.

7 Moreover, unlike the tax on air travel, the tax on lottery tickets is sharply regressive. According to Mr. Clotfelter and Mr. Cook's study of the Maryland lottery, people earning less than $10,000 buy more tickets than any other income group.

8 Even in states like California, where evidence suggests that the rich and poor spend roughly the same amount on lottery tickets, those at the low end of the income scale spend a far higher percentage of their incomes on lottery games. And though almost anyone can afford the occasional $1 flyer, some people bet far more. While the average Californian shelled out just $75 last year for lottery tickets, a 1986 poll by the *Los Angeles Times* showed that just 10 percent of adults made 65 percent of the wagers.

9 Taxes on alcohol and tobacco are almost as regressive as the lottery tax, Mr. Clotfelter and Mr. Cook point out. But the tax rates on these products are generally much lower. In any case, taxes on drinking and smoking are usually justified as a means of discouraging consumption or covering the costs of related, antisocial behavior like drunken driving.

"A Dollar and a Dream"

10 But if the states still view gambling as an antisocial activity to be discouraged through taxation, the message is not getting through to lottery managers. Most lotteries advertise

heavily (''All you need is a dollar and a dream''). And most aggressively market the product, tinkering with the frequency of drawings and the mechanics of the game to maintain a sense of novelty and excitement. When it became clear, for example, that huge payouts were the key to lotto's success, New York increased the odds against winning from 1 in 6 million to 1 in 12.9 million.

11 Of course, it would hardly matter who bought tickets if the lottery merely diverted revenues and profits from illegal gambling to worthy government activities. The daily three-digit games may indeed be displacing some betting on illegal numbers. But Mr. Clotfelter and Mr. Cook find no evidence of such substitution in the high-stakes lotto games, which now absorb almost half of all lottery dollars. Lotto fever, it seems, is a brand new disease.

12 Nor is it always clear that lottery earnings are financing good government. Where states earmark lottery revenues for specific purposes, it may be possible to figure out who actually benefits. Kansas, for example, uses the lottery to finance technical assistance to small businesses.

Where the Money Goes

13 More typically, the money amounts to seasoning in the stewpot of ever-changing state appropriations and taxes, leaving each observer free to speculate about how budget priorities would be altered if the lottery lagniappe were to vanish. As Bill Honig, California's public school superintendent, complained to an *Atlanta Constitution* reporter, ''For every $5 the lottery gives to the schools, the state takes away $4.''

14 Betting on the lotteries is still modest compared to sports and casino wagering, and it is probably less regressive and poses fewer temptations to problem gamblers.

15 But these are private (and often illegal) activities, tolerated by government. The fact that states promote and celebrate the lottery games may increase their impact on public attitudes to work and saving.

16 A survey of Southern California high school students found that the percentage who participate in any form of gambling went up by 40 percent after the state lottery was introduced in 1985. And according to an article in *Forbes* magazine last October, many manufacturers of supermarket products are abandoning ''cents-off'' coupons for big-prize sweepstakes promotions.

17 To Mr. Clotfelter and Mr. Cook, the lottery is ''a risky experiment to determine whether a system that allocates rewards on the basis of luck will undermine a parallel system that allocates . . . on the basis of effort and skill.'' For many people, however, it remains the only imaginable way to become filthy rich.

Questions for Analysis

1. Passell provides factual evidence in the form of statistics to show that the poor are the major source of lottery revenue. Is that statistical evidence convincing?

2. An important part of Passell's argument is that the lottery is a "regressive tax." Define that term. He compares the lottery to a regressive tax on two products, tobacco and alcohol. What's the difference that he sees?
3. In addition to factual evidence, Passell offers a claim of value—that the lottery is morally wrong and yet is sponsored by the states. Explain this argument as he applies it to both individuals and the states.
4. Passell uses two headings in his essay. One—"Where the Money Goes"—is a straightforward description; the other—"A Dollar and a Dream"—is a quotation from a lottery advertisement. Is it effective? Explain.
5. The headings also outline the essay's organizational plan. Is that plan logical? Is it effective?
6. Do you find Passell's argument convincing? Can you think of reasons for a state keeping or starting a lottery? Are there ways to avoid any of the problems Passell points out, such as by changing the way lotteries are conducted or how the state uses the money they generate?
7. Passell ends his essay with a very provocative comparison. What do you think about it? Is a system based on luck replacing one based on "effort and skill"? Are there other indicators that suggest our society is moving away from our traditional emphasis on "effort and skill"?

Florence King

I'd Rather Smoke than Kiss

(1990)

Florence King (b. 1936) is a free-lance writer whose latest book, *Lump It or Leave It,* was published in 1990. This essay originally appeared in the July 9, 1990, issue of the *National Review.*

1 I am a woman of 54 who started smoking at the late age of 26. I had no reason to start earlier; smoking as a gesture of teenage rebellion would have been pointless in my family. My mother started at 12. At first her preferred brands were the Fatimas and Sweet Caporals that were all the rage during World War I. Later she switched to Lucky Strike Greens and smoked four packs a day.

2 She made no effort to cut down while she was pregnant with me, but I was not a low-birth-weight baby. The Angel of Death saw the nicotine stains on our door and passed over; I weighed nine pounds. My smoke-filled childhood was remarkably healthy and safe except for the time Mama set fire to my Easter basket. That was all right, however, because I was not the Easter-basket type.

3 I probably wouldn't have started smoking if I had not been a writer. One day in the drugstore I happened to see a display of Du Maurier English cigarettes in pretty red boxes with a tray that slid out like a little drawer. I thought the boxes would be ideal for keeping my paperclips in, so I brought two.

4 When I got home, I emptied out the cigarettes and replaced them with paperclips, putting the loose cigarettes in the desk drawer where the loose paperclips had been scattered. Now the cigarettes were scattered. One day, spurred by two of my best traits, neatness and thrift, I decided that the cigarettes were messing up the desk and going to waste, so I tried one.

5 It never would have happened if I had been able to offer the Du Mauriers to a lover who smoked, but I didn't get an addicted one until after I had become addicted myself. When he entered my life it was the beginning of a uniquely pleasurable footnote to sex: the post-coital cigarette.

6 Today when I see the truculent, joyless faces of anti-tobacco Puritans, I remember those easy-going smoking sessions with that man: the click of the lighter, the brief orange glow in the darkness, the ashtray between us—spilling sometimes because we laughed so much together that the bed shook.

7 A cigarette ad I remember from my childhood said: "One of life's great pleasures is smoking. Camels give you all of the enjoyment of choice tobaccos. Is enjoyment good for you? You just bet it is." My sentiments exactly. I believe life should be savored rather than lengthened, and I am ready to fight the misanthropes among us who are trying to make me switch.

8 A *misanthrope* is someone who hates people. Hatred of smokers is the most popular form of closet misanthropy in America today. Smokists don't hate the sin, they hate the sinner, and they don't care who knows it.

9 Their campaign never would have succeeded so well if the alleged dangers of smoking had remained a problem for smokers alone. We simply would have been allowed to invoke the Right to Die, always a favorite with democratic lovers of mankind, and that would have been that. To put a real damper on smoking and make it stick, the right of others not to die had to be invoked somehow, so "passive smoking" was invented.

10 The name was a stroke of genius. Just about everybody in America is passive. Passive Americans have been taking it on the chin for years, but the concept of passive smoking offered them a chance to hate in the land of compulsory love, a chance to dish it out for a change with no fear of being called a bigot. The right of self-defense, long since gone up in smoke, was back.

Smokers on the Run

11 The big, brave Passive Americans responded with a vengeance. They began shouting at smokers in restaurants. They shuddered and grimaced and said "Ugh!" as they waved away the impure air. They put up little signs in their cars and homes: at first they said, "Thank You for Not Smoking," but now they feature a cigarette in a circle slashed with a red diagonal. Smokists even issue conditional invitations. I know—I got one. The woman said, "I'd love to have you to dinner, but I don't allow smoking in my

home. Do you think you could refrain for a couple of hours?'' I said, ''Go ---- yourself,'' and she told everybody I was the rudest person she had ever met.

12 Smokists practice a sadistic brutality that would have done Vlad the Impaler proud. *Washington Times* columnist and smoker Jeremiah O'Leary was the target of two incredibly baleful letters to the editor after he defended the habit. The first letter said, ''Smoke yourself to death, but please don't smoke me to death,'' but it was only a foretaste of the letter that followed:

> Jeremiah O'Leary's March 1 column, ''Perilous persuaders . . . tenacious zealots,'' is a typical statement of a drug addict trying to defend his vice.
>
> To a cigarette smoker, all the world is an ashtray. A person who would never throw a candy wrapper or soda can will drop a lit cigarette without a thought.
>
> Mr. O'Leary is mistaken that nonsmokers are concerned about the damage smokers are inflicting on themselves. What arrogance! We care about living in a pleasant environment without the stench of tobacco smoke or the litter of smokers' trash.
>
> If Mr. O'Leary wants to kill himself, that is his choice. I ask only that he do so without imposing his drug or discarded filth on me. *It would be nice if he would die in such a way that would not increase my health-insurance rates* [my italics].

13 The expendability of smokers has also aroused the tender concern of the Federal Government. I was taking my first drag of the morning when I opened the *Washington Post* and found myself staring at this headline: NOT SMOKING COULD BE HAZARDOUS TO PENSION SYSTEM. MEDICARE, SOCIAL SECURITY MAY BE PINCHED IF ANTI-TOBACCO CAMPAIGN SUCCEEDS, REPORT SAYS.

14 The article explained that since smokers die younger than non-smokers, the Social Security we don't live to collect is put to good use, because we subsidize the pensions of our fellow citizens like a good American should. However, this convenient arrangement could end, for if too many smokers heed the Surgeon General's warnings and stop smoking, they will live too long and break the budget.

15 That, of course, is not how the government economists phrased it. They said:

> The implications of our results are that smokers ''save'' the Social Security system hundreds of billions of dollars. Certainly this does not mean that decreased smoking would not be socially beneficial. In fact, it is probably one of the most cost-effective ways of increasing average longevity. It does indicate, however, that if people alter their behavior in a manner which extends life expectancy, then this must be recognized by our national retirement program.

16 At this point the reporter steps in with the soothing reminder that ''the war on tobacco is more appropriately cast as a public-health crusade than as an attempt to save money.'' But then we hear from Health Policy Center economist Gio Gori, who says: ''Prevention

of disease is obviously something we should strive for. But it's not going to be cheap. We will have to pay for those who survive.”

17 Something darkling crawls out of that last sentence. The whole article has a die-damn-you undertow that would make an honest misanthrope wonder if perhaps a cure for cancer was discovered years ago, but due to cost-effectiveness considerations . . .

18 But honest misanthropes are at a premium that no amount of Raleigh coupons can buy. Instead we have tinpot Torquemadas like Ahron Leichtman, president of Citizens against Tobacco Smoke, who announced after the airline smoking ban: “CATS will next launch its smoke-free airports project, which is the second phase of our smoke-free skies campaign.” Representative Richard J. Durbin (D., Ill.) promised the next target will be “other forms of public transportation such as Amtrak, the inter-city bus system, and commuter lines that receive federal funding.” His colleague, Senator Frank Lautenberg (D., N.J.), confessed, “We *are* gloating a little bit,” and Fran Du Melle of the Coalition on Smoking OR Health, gave an ominous hint of things to come when she heralded the airline ban as “only one encouraging step on the road to a smoke-free society.”

Health Nazis

19 These remarks manifest a sly, cowardly form of misanthropy that the Germans call *Schadenfreude:* pleasure in the unhappiness of others. It has always been the chief subconscious motivation of Puritans, but the smokists harbor several other subconscious motivations that are too egregious to bear close examination—which is precisely what I will now conduct.

20 Study their agitprop and you will find the same theme of pitiless revulsion running through nearly all of their so-called public-service ads. One of the earliest showed Brooke Shields toweling her wet hair and saying disgustedly, “I hate it when somebody smokes after I've just washed my hair. Yuk!” Another proclaimed, “Kissing a smoker is like licking an ashtray.” The latest, a California radio spot, asks: “Why sell cigarettes? Why not just sell phlegm and cut out the middle man?”

21 Fear of being physically disgusting and smelling bad is the American's worst nightmare, which is why bathsoap commercials never include the controlled-force shower nozzles recommended by environmentalists in *their* public-service ads. The showering American uses oceans of hot water to get “ZESTfully clean” in a sudsy deluge that is often followed by a deodorant commercial.

22 “Raise your hand, raise your hand, raise your hand if you're SURE!” During this jingle we see an ecstatically happy assortment of people from all walks of life and representing every conceivable national origin, all obediently raising their hands, until the ad climaxes with a shot of the Statue of Liberty raising hers.

The New Greenhorns

23 The Statue of Liberty has become a symbol of immigration, the first aspect of American life the huddled masses experienced. The second was being called a “dirty little” something-or-other as soon as they got off the boat. Deodorant companies see the

wisdom in reminding their descendants of the dirty-little period. You can sell a lot of deodorant that way. Ethnics get the point directly; WASPs get it by default in the subliminal reminder that, historically speaking, there is no such thing as a dirty little WASP.

24 Smokers have become the new greenhorns in the land of sweetness and health, scapegoats for a quintessentially American need, rooted in our fabled Great Diversity, to identify and punish the undesirables among us. Ethnic tobacco haters can get even for past slurs on their fastidiousness by refusing to inhale around dirty little smokers; WASP tobacco haters can once again savor the joys of being the "real Americans" by hurling with impunity the same dirty little insults their ancestors hurled with impunity.

25 The tobacco pogrom serves additionally as the basis for a class war in a nation afraid to mention the word "class" aloud. Hating smokers is an excellent way to hate the white working class without going on record as hating the white working class.

26 The anti-smoking campaign has enjoyed thumping success among the "data-receptive," a lovely euphemism describing the privilege of spending four years sitting in a classroom. The ubiquitous statistic that college graduates are two-and-a-half times as likely to be non-smokers as those who never went beyond high school is balm to the data-receptive, many of whom are only a generation or two removed from the lunch-bucket that smokers represent. Haunted by a fear of falling back down the ladder, and half-believing that they deserve to, they soothe their anxiety by kicking a smoker as the proverbial hen-pecked husband soothed his by kicking the dog.

27 The earnest shock that greeted the RJR Reynolds Uptown marketing scheme aimed at blacks cramped the vituperative style of the data-receptive. Looking down on blacks as smokers might be interpreted as looking down on blacks as blacks, so they settled for aping the compassionate concern they picked up from the media.

28 They got their sadism-receptive bona fides back when the same company announced plans to target Dakota cigarettes at a fearsome group called "virile females."

29 When I first saw the headline I thought surely they meant me: what other woman writer is sent off to a book-and-author luncheon with the warning, "Watch your language and don't wear your Baltimore Orioles warm-up jacket"? But they didn't. Virile females are "Caucasian females, 18 to 24, with no education beyond high school and entry-level service or factory jobs."

30 Commentators could barely hide their smirks as they listed the tractor pulls, motorcycle races, and macho-man contests that comprise the leisure activities of the target group. Crocodile tears flowed copiously. "It's blue-collar people without enough education to understand what is happening to them," mourned Virginia Ernster of the University of California School of Medicine. "It's pathetic that these companies would work so hard to get these women who may not feel much control over their lives." George Will, winner of the metaphor-man contest, wrote: "They use sophisticated marketing like a sniper's rifle, drawing beads on the most vulnerable, manipulable Americans." (I would walk a mile to see Virginia Ernster riding on the back of George Will's motorcycle.)

31 Hating smokers is also a guiltless way for a youth-worshipping country to hate old people, as well as those who are merely over the hill—especially middle-aged women. Smokers predominate in both groups because we saw Bette Davis's movies the same year they were released. Now we catch *Dark Victory* whenever it comes on television just for the pleasure of watching the scene in the staff lounge at the hospital when Dr. George Brent and all the other doctors light up.

32 Smoking is the only thing that the politically correct can't blame on white males. Red men started it, but the cowardly cossacks of the anti-tobacco crusade don't dare say so because it would be too close for comfort. They see no difference between tobacco and hard drugs like cocaine and crack because they don't wish to see any. Never mind that you will never be mugged by someone needing a cigarette; hatred of smokers is the conformist's substitute for the hatred that dare not speak its name. Condemning ''substance abuse'' out of hand, without picking and choosing or practicing discrimination, produces lofty sensations of democratic purity in those who keep moving farther and farther out in the suburbs to get away from . . . smokers.

Questions for Analysis

1. King's essay is a defense of smoking. How does she support her position? What reasons does she advance to justify smoking?
2. Evaluate King's analysis of the antismoking groups. Does she use *ad hominem* arguments? Do her explanations for the reasons these people attack smoking and smokers seem reasonable? Are we as a nation unnaturally preoccupied with cleanliness? Is the pressure now placed on smokers a manifestation of our desire to ''identify and punish undesirables''?
3. In the last section of her essay, King mentions the tobacco industry's ad campaigns for Uptown and Dakota cigarettes and the anti-tobacco commentators' response to them to support her assertion that these people are engaging in a ''class war.'' Explain her point. Do you agree with her? Is there a basis for claiming that the ad campaigns are morally questionable? Compare King's point of view with that expressed in Kevin Siers's cartoon, ''Updown Rap,'' which follows.
4. Did you find King's essay fun to read? Is her tone serious? Find places where her word choice, phrasing, and attitude are meant to amuse. Why did she write the essay this way? Does her tone undercut her argument or help it?

Kevin Siers

Uptown Rap

(1990)

Kevin Siers (b. 1954) is the editorial cartoonist for *The Charlotte Observer* in Charlotte, North Carolina. This cartoon appeared soon after R. J. Reynolds Tobacco Company began its advertising campaign for "Uptown" cigarettes.

Kevin Siers, *The Charlotte Observer*

Robert L. Wolke

A Message to Students: If You Have a Lawyer Handy, Go Ahead and Cheat Like Crazy

(1991)

Robert L. Wolke (b. 1928) is Professor Emeritus of Chemistry at the University of Pittsburgh and founding director of its Office of Faculty Development. This essay appeared in *The Chronicle of Higher Education,* May 15, 1991.

1 In a sort of subdued chaos, 210 students filed into the cavernous lecture hall to take their final examination in freshman chemistry. One student—I'll call him Jones—stood out like a sore thumb. My students knew from the previous two exams that semester that they were supposed to take seats in every other front-to-back row during an exam—ahead of or behind another student, but with an empty seat on each side. I had found that this arrangement minimized the visibility of neighboring papers. Jones, however, had taken a seat right next to a classmate. He grudgingly moved only after I had told him twice to do so.

2 The examination began, and before long a proctor whispered to me that Jones was trying to look at his nearest neighbor's paper. When I myself saw him acting suspiciously, I decided to check his answer sheet against the other student's, when the answer sheets came back from the scoring machine.

3 When I did so, I found that the answers to 29 of 30 questions were identical (of 404 possible multiple-choice responses to the 30 questions, the two students had chosen or rejected the same responses in 403 cases). I dug further and uncovered evidence that Jones had been copying exams, quizzes, and lab reports from the day the course began. Never in my 33 years of teaching had I seen such a flagrant case of premeditated cheating.

4 Like most universities, mine has prescribed procedures for charging a student with dishonesty. I followed them carefully—suspended his grade, apprised him of the charges, notified the dean, obtained a written statement from the proctor—in preparation for a formal hearing before the Academic Integrity Board.

5 Then began a flood of irate telephone calls and letters from Jones's father, a lawyer, who was determined to get his boy "off." I handled as many as I could before turning everything over to the dean's office in accordance with university procedures—but not until I had complied with the father's request for copies of all my evidence. He was engaging in what lawyers call "discovery."

6 He kept threatening to sue, and the dean's office turned the case over to the university's lawyer. I soon found myself being "asked" to give Jones a respectable grade in exchange for his father's promise not to sue. It turned out that when I had copied

students' answer sheets in providing the evidence for him, I had inadvertently failed to block out the names of the students from whom Jones had copied, thereby running afoul of the so-called Buckley Amendment, which makes it illegal for universities to divulge any student's academic records without his or her consent. The university's lawyer apparently figured that it was safer to let the matter drop than to risk a lawsuit or problems with the federal government, which can cut off funds to institutions that violate the Buckley Amendment.

7 Our lawyer asked me what grade Jones would have received on the basis of the exams and other papers that bore his name. The average for this "work" was 69 percent, missing a B by only one percentage point, which I refused to throw in, although it is my usual practice to do so. The lawyer then wanted to know why, if I had ever given a B to someone with a 69-per-cent average, I wouldn't do the same for Jones? What were my grading practices, anyway? Could I defend in court the contention that I was totally consistent? If someone else had gotten a B for a 69, why shouldn't Jones? After all, the father might sue us for prejudicial grading.

8 Appalled that I actually was being asked to defend my professional judgment to a university lawyer, and even more appalled that the dean's office had been cowed into bypassing its own adjudication procedures, I decided to retract my charges against Jones. I sent the dean the following retraction:

- "I retract my first charge against student John M. Jones, to the effect that he copied from another student's paper on the first exam in Chemistry 12 during the 1990 Winter Term. This charge was based on the fact that all his answers were identical to those of another student from whose paper a teaching assistant saw him copying.
- "I retract my second charge, to the effect that Mr. Jones copied from another student's paper on the second examination. This charge was based on the fact that all of his answers were identical to those of a student sitting next to him and the fact that a teaching assistant said she saw him looking at the other student's paper and warned him about it.
- "I retract my third charge, to the effect that on the final examination Mr. Jones copied from the same student as in the first examination. This charge was based on four facts: (a) that 29 out of 30 of Mr. Jones's answers were identical to those of the other student; (b) that a proctor said she saw him looking at the other student's paper; (c) that I myself saw him deliberately choose a seat next to the other student and act suspiciously throughout the examination; and (d) that on Mr. Jones's answer sheets, several of the responses had apparently been erased and changed to conform to those of the student next to him.
- "I retract my fourth and fifth charges, to the effect that Mr. Jones copied from other students' papers on the weekly quizzes and that he copied his lab reports from other students. I have no firsthand evidence of these purported actions; the student who reported them to me has chosen not to pursue the matter after having been contacted by Mr. Jones's father.

9 "I now realize that my suspicions of dishonesty on Mr. Jones's part were unjustified.

10 "By way of apology, however, I must explain what led me to the unfortunate suspicion that Mr. Jones had been cheating.

11 "The machine-scored answer sheets show that on the three exams, Mr. Jones selected or rejected 624 multiple-choice answers, out of a possible 625, identical to those of a nearby student.

12 "An average of 214 students took the three examinations. Using a printout of all the answer sheets, I determined for each question the likelihood that any two students would come up with identical responses. (Each multiple-choice question offered between 5 and 10 alternative responses.) In consultation with a mathematics professor who is an expert in probability, I used the class's *actual* identical-response statistics, rather than a mathematically calculated (random chance) probability of agreement. This takes into account the rightness or wrongness of the answers, a correct response presumably being more probable than any given incorrect one.

13 "The odds against Mr. Jones's responses being identical to those of his neighbors turned out to be 260,000 to one on the first exam; 90,000,000,000 to one on the second; and 1,200,000,000 to one on the final exam. (The respective probabilities are 0.000,003,9; 0.000,000,000,011; and 0.000,000,000,81.) On the three exams taken together, the odds against Mr. Jones's responding just as his neighbors did turns out to be 29 trillion trillion to one. A probability of this magnitude is roughly comparable to the chance that a brick will spontaneously jump up into the air because all of its molecules happen to be vibrating in the same direction at the same instant.

14 "However, these are mere probabilities. As the associate dean (a mathematics professor) has pointed out to me, there is still a perfectly good one in 29 trillion trillion chance that Mr. Jones's answers were the same as those of the students seated near him purely by accident. I cannot, therefore, continue to accuse him of such an egregious offense as cheating his way through an entire course.

15 "I wish Mr. Jones the best of success in his expressed intention of entering the priesthood following his graduation from college. I am assigning him a grade of A+ in Chemistry 12."

16 Why the A+? Because travesty begets travesty. Except for a very supportive department chairman, my university's timorous administration gave me no support whatsoever in my attempt to uphold the integrity of the academic enterprise or the institution's own established procedures. Instead, I was asked to give an undeserved grade to avoid trouble—even the trouble of a formal airing of my charges. They wanted an undeserved grade; that's what they got.

17 Of course, the dean's office screamed. ("That isn't fair to the other students." I replied, "No. Nor is it fair to give Jones a stolen C when other students worked hard to get an honest one.")

18 The university's lawyer screamed. ("Now I'll have to check to see if they can sue us for giving too high a grade." I replied, "That'll be the day.")

19 The student's father screamed. (He thought my retraction was "nasty.")

20 I haven't heard from Jones himself. But let him gloat. The A+ proclaiming him a whiz in chemistry will be on his transcript—and his conscience—forever.

21 And the moral for students? If you have a lawyer handy, go ahead and cheat like crazy. Universities are pushovers.

Questions for Analysis

1. Explain the irony in the title. Is Wolke really advising students to cheat? What is the purpose (the argument) of Wolke's essay?
2. In a sense this essay contains two separate arguments: the one you defined in response to Question 1 and the one inherent in the "retraction" of his charges against Jones that Wolke sent his dean. Though it does retract his charges, Wolke's letter also argues that Jones is guilty of cheating. Is it effective? Describe the argument, its organization, and logic.
3. Does the reference to Jones entering the priesthood in the last paragraph of the retraction help or hurt Wolke's argument? Explain.
4. Evaluate Wolke's logic in giving Jones an "A+." Was that grade assignment appropriate? Will it accomplish anything? What alternatives did Wolke have? Would any of them have been preferable?
5. The willingness of students to cheat on academic work is a problem that has attracted growing attention over the last few years. What does that trend say about our society? What can or cannot be done? Should the expense of possible litigation prevent universities from upholding basic principles of personal and academic integrity? What is the value of personal and academic integrity?

Joshua Adler

Our Alarmist Society

(1990)

Now a student at Yale University, Joshua Adler (b. 1972) wrote this essay when he was a senior at Walt Whitman High School in Bethesda, Maryland. His essay won First Prize in the ages-19-and-under category of the Eighth Annual North American Essay Contest sponsored by *The Humanist* and was published in the July/August 1990 issue of that magazine.

1 In the spring of 1989, the Natural Resources Defense Council campaigned to eliminate the use of Alar, which was sprayed on apples to promote crispness and redness.

The NRDC emphasized U.S. Environmental Protection Agency studies indicating that a chemical byproduct of decomposed Alar caused cancer in laboratory rodents. Newspapers gave the finding front-page billing across the country, ostensibly to protect the nation's children, many of whom would carry a Red Delicious to school in a brown paper bag as a (formerly) healthy part of lunch.

2 The EPA noted weakly in the face of public outrage that Alar itself was not dangerous and that the byproduct, UDMH, existed in quantities that were barely measurable, much less harmful. In addition, only 5 percent of the nation's apple produce carried Alar. But the damage had already been done. Hundreds of small, independent orchards went out of business; nationally, apple sales declined by over 12 percent.

3 By late 1990, the concern had disappeared. Alar has long since passed out of the headlines; meanwhile, however, the bankrupted farmers are still bankrupt, as real human problems do not vanish with the daily paper.

4 Scientific alarmism is becoming a way of life in the United States. A research group releases a study announcing the discovery of a new carcinogen in an everyday product, and the press pounds the news into our collective consciousness. We swallow new information without chewing because we live in an age of information flow far greater than any individual can digest.

5 Alarmism can have a tremendous negative impact by shutting down entire sections of the economy. It can seriously affect our quality of life by inducing people to avoid basically healthy products and by deterring people from taking advantage of potentially helpful scientific advances out of fear. Eventually, alarmism will inure the public to valuable scientific wisdom by blurring the distinction between distortion and truth.

6 We can avert this problem only by closely examining the facts and by learning how they can be skewed by various self-interested groups with their own agendas manipulating the public's ignorance. Our goal must always be to find a solution that treats all parties with compassion and fairness—a process that demands deliberation.

7 In the summer of 1989, an anonymous caller informed U.S. Customs officers that a shipment of grapes from Chile was poisoned. Customs officials examined incoming grape shipments and, despite the fact that the department was—and still is—severely understaffed, one inspector found two damaged grapes that had been injected with enough cyanide to sicken an adult.

8 From that point on, events followed a predictably alarmist course. The public, particularly phobic of fruit related dangers, put massive pressure on the U.S. Customs Service to ban South American grapes. There was no reason to believe that there were any more contaminated grapes than the two found in that one shipment, and yet, with the continuing support of the sensationalist press, Americans stopped buying grapes already available.

9 As a result, we nearly destroyed the Peruvian and Chilean economies. Both are struggling nations that need U.S. business to maintain even the most basic quality of life, and the United States is their primary grape market. Although the grape scare is long past, the Chilean economy has not completely recovered. Another unintended effect of the grape scare: when farmers in South America cannot make enough money

to live through legal crops, they often turn to producing illegal crops, like the coca leaves which feed America's drug addiction.

10 The grape scare was based upon emotionalism—not scientific inquiry. This case shows, in fact, how pervasive alarmism can be; the grape scare was treated by the mass media with the same sensationalism without evaluation that supermarket tabloids employ to influence us. Brighter photographs and taller headlines overpower us at the same time that individual stories are growing in magnitude. In recent decades, the news has gone from being usually of only local significance to being often global in scale.

11 Perhaps there was never a time when significant events appeared manageable to the average citizen. But today, any event is significant if the press says it is, and nearly every event seems to be out of anyone's control.

12 A personal anecdote: last spring break, I was returning home from visiting colleges in the northeastern United States with my father and little sister. We stopped at a Denny's in Poughkeepsie, New York, for breakfast. Near us, an elderly couple waited for their food. A waitress delivered some pancakes to the old man and sunny-side-up eggs to the old woman. The old woman became outraged, insisting that she had ordered scrambled eggs. The waitress promised to bring scrambled eggs immediately. The old man said to the woman, "Come on, honey, one time won't hurt you." The woman responded, "No, no. You know what they say—even one time and you never know what could happen. Those yolks will kill you for sure with a heart attack. That's why I always eat scrambled eggs."

13 This scene really happened. The woman accepted what "they" said without ever applying reason. What she couldn't see—the obscured yolk in the scrambled eggs, as opposed to the obvious yolk in the sunny-side-up eggs—simply did not exist for her. She never pondered why scrambled eggs were yellow or, for that matter, how so many people can eat eggs without immediately dying of a heart attack. Imagine what would happen to egg-producing farms if everyone believed as she did. Imagine even how much time each one of us could spend worrying that a bit of yolk was in a meal as an emulsifier or to add flavor; imagine the unquantifiable quality of life lost. It is exactly this lack of critical thinking that alarmism encourages.

14 In this case, of course, the alarmists were certain members of the health professions on the issue of cholesterol. Since the Korean war, we have found cholesterol blocking the coronary arteries of people who have died of heart attacks. What is not clear, even after dozens of studies, is that this cholesterol builds up in any relationship with cholesterol consumed. Thomas J. Moore in the September 1989 issue of the *Atlantic* and in his book *Heart Failure* argues that evidence indicates that there is almost no correlation between diet and cholesterol buildup or elimination and that using drugs which lower cholesterol levels is at least as dangerous as having a high cholesterol level. Nonetheless, the National Cholesterol Education Program's anti-cholesterol media blitz has provoked public fear and convinced most Americans that cholesterol is just plain bad.

15 "Bad" and "good," without qualifications, are powerful descriptors that are used mainly by persons who do not analyze. It is very easy to rank things according to some

binary system of description; if something matters at all, it can be "bad" or "good." Cholesterol is bad; fiber is good. Chemicals are bad; organic food is good.

16 Take the case of the spotted owl in the Pacific Northwest forests. The owl is endangered because of massive logging in these forests. Environmental alarmists argue that protecting the environment is an unconditional good and, since owls are part of the environment, they must be preserved at all costs. Alarmists ignore the benefits that the logging industry confers upon the general populace—and the lives that depend upon logging jobs.

17 I do not argue that environmentalism is negative; no reasonable person can doubt that a course of uninhibited industrialism will destroy us and our planet. But we cannot make decisions about when to protect the environment and when to develop natural resources (and, most importantly, when we can do both simultaneously, an option whose existence is denied by alarmism) by shutting down thought and compassion out of fear that the world will end. Instead we must work together and negotiate between countervailing interests; no issue is a zero-sum game unless we set up a competition that *makes* it so.

18 Attempting to persuade people by appealing to absolutes tends to coarsen the delicate intellectual skills we need to draw fine lines between shades of grey. It also drives rational, moderate arguments out of existence in the competition for attention.

19 The side that yells the loudest usually gets all the attention. Advocates for any position quickly move to the lowest common denominator in making their point—as we saw in "negative" political advertising during the 1988 presidential election. No one is willing to admit that a compromise might be a superior alternative to either side, rather than a mere expedient.

20 When persuasion through absolutes becomes the dominant mode of communication in a society, then alarmism is inevitable. Alarmism tells us that we are in immediate danger from something evil—that we do not have the time to think, only to act. Combine this alarmist tendency with our modern mass media and our very real global problems and alarmism in our society achieves near-omnipotence.

21 Only through thoughtful responsibility can we uphold the values of reason and compassion. Promoting this sense of responsibility must be the work of every individual in the media (especially) and in the political and business ranks. Obviously, there is no legitimate way to police people's thoughts to ensure that each person is being responsible; we can turn only to education. Of course, that is no small power. Education exists everywhere, not just in school or books. All communication teaches us *something;* the question is, what messages are we sending each other?

22 The fight against alarmism—scientific or otherwise—is not one that I expect us to win unconditionally. Moral progress is always undercut by people who are willing to use an immoral expedient to achieve their ends. I am also by no means certain what specific direction "moral progress" requires. No one is—that's why discussion is imperative. But by recognizing that alarmism in our society has become a real threat, and by developing our capacity for reason and critical thinking, each of us can shift the social scale in humanity's favor.

Questions for Analysis

1. Adler's most obvious argument in this essay is that ours is an alarmist society. He also defines alarmist thinking and proposes that we as a society need to change that thinking. Describe the kind of thinking he advocates.
2. Evaluate the evidence Adler presents to support his claims and proposal. Does the evidence support his claim that we are an alarmist society? Does it clearly show the presence of the kind of thinking that Adler asserts we must change?
3. Most of Adler's examples concern food (e.g., alar on apples, poisoned grapes, cholesterol in eggs). Should he have spent more space on environmental issues, political campaigns, or other kinds of examples?
4. Adler criticizes the media for its contribution to our tendency toward alarmism. Is his charge valid? Explain.
5. Adler seems to think that we can become less of an alarmist society by "developing our capacity for reason and critical thinking." What do you think? Can most people change? Can enough people change?

Norman Cousins

How to Make People Smaller Than They Are

(1978)

Norman Cousins (1915–1991) was for over 30 years editor of the influential *Saturday Review,* a magazine devoted to the arts and civic affairs. For many years a champion of education, Cousins spent the last years of his life encouraging medical schools to place more emphasis on the humanities in their curricula so that physicians could respond better to their patients as people. This essay originally appeared in the *Saturday Review* in 1978.

1 Three months ago in this space we wrote about the costly retreat from the humanities on all the levels of American education. Since that time, we have had occasion to visit a number of campuses and have been troubled to find that the general situation is even more serious than we had thought. It has become apparent to us that one of the biggest problems confronting American education today is the increasing vocationalization of our colleges and universities. Throughout the country, schools are under pressure to become job-training centers and employment agencies.

2 The pressure comes mainly from two sources. One is the growing determination of many citizens to reduce taxes—understandable and even commendable in itself, but

irrational and irresponsible when connected to the reduction or dismantling of vital public services. The second source of pressure comes from parents and students who tend to scorn courses of study that do not teach people how to become attractive to employers in a rapidly tightening job market.

3 It is absurd to believe that the development of skills does not also require the systematic development of the human mind. Education is being measured more by the size of the benefits the individual can extract from society than by the extent to which the individual can come into possession of his or her full powers. The result is that the life-giving juices are in danger of being drained out of education.

4 Emphasis on "practicalities" is being characterized by the subordination of words to numbers. History is seen not as essential experience to be transmitted to new generations, but as abstractions that carry dank odors. Art is regarded as something that calls for indulgence or patronage and that has no place among the practical realities. Political science is viewed more as a specialized subject for people who want to go into politics than as an opportunity for citizens to develop a knowledgeable relationship with the systems by which human societies are governed. Finally, literature and philosophy are assigned the role of add-ons—intellectual adornments that have nothing to do with "genuine" education.

5 Instead of trying to shrink the liberal arts, the American people ought to be putting pressure on colleges and universities to increase the ratio of the humanities to the sciences. Most serious studies of medical-school curricula in recent years have called attention to the stark gaps in the liberal education of medical students. The experts agree that the schools shouldn't leave it up to students to close those gaps.

6 We must not make it appear, however, that nothing is being done. In the past decade, the National Endowment for the Humanities has been a prime mover in infusing the liberal arts into medical education and other specialized schools. During this past year alone, NEH has given 108 grants to medical schools and research organizations in the areas of ethics and human values. Some medical schools, like the one at Pennsylvania State University, have led the way in both the number and the depth of courses offered in the humanities. Penn State has been especially innovative in weaving literature and philosophy into the full medical course of study. It is ironical that the pressure against the humanities should be manifesting itself at precisely the time when so many medical schools are at long last moving in this direction.

7 The irony of the emphasis being placed on careers is that nothing is more valuable for anyone who has had a professional or vocational education than to be able to deal with abstractions or complexities, or to feel comfortable with subtleties of thought or language, or to think sequentially. The doctor who knows only disease is at a disadvantage alongside the doctor who knows at least as much about people as he does about pathological organisms. The lawyer who argues in court from a narrow legal base is no match for the lawyer who can connect legal precedents to historical experience and who employs wide-ranging intellectual resources. The business executive whose competence in general management is bolstered by an artistic ability to deal with people is of prime value to his company. For the technologist, the engineering of consent can be

just as important as the engineering of moving parts. In all these respects, the liberal arts have much to offer. Just in terms of career preparation, therefore, a student is shortchanging himself by shortcutting the humanities.

8 But even if it could be demonstrated that the humanities contribute nothing directly to a job, they would still be an essential part of the educational equipment of any person who wants to come to terms with life. The humanities would be expendable only if human beings didn't have to make decisions that affect their lives and the lives of others; if the human past never existed or had nothing to tell us about the present; if thought processes were irrelevant to the achievement of purpose; if creativity was beyond the human mind and had nothing to do with the joy of living; if human relationships were random aspects of life; if human beings never had to cope with panic or pain, or if they never had to anticipate the connection between cause and effect; if all the mysteries of mind and nature were fully plumbed; and if no special demands arose from the accident of being born a human being instead of a hen or a hog.

9 Finally, there would be good reason to eliminate the humanities if a free society were not absolutely dependent on a functioning citizenry. If the main purpose of a university is job training, then the underlying philosophy of our government has little meaning. The debates that went into the making of American society concerned not just institutions or governing principles but the capacity of humans to sustain those institutions. Whatever the disagreements were over other issues at the American Constitutional Convention, the fundamental question sensed by everyone, a question that lay over the entire assembly, was whether the people themselves would understand what it meant to hold the ultimate power of society, and whether they had enough of a sense of history and destiny to know where they had been and where they ought to be going.

10 Jefferson was prouder of having been the founder of the University of Virginia than of having been President of the United States. He knew that the educated and developed mind was the best assurance that a political system could be made to work—a system based on the informed consent of the governed. If this idea fails, then all the saved tax dollars in the world will not be enough to prevent the nation from turning on itself.

Questions for Analysis

1. Gary Trudeau's cartoon (which follows this reading) and Cousins's essay are arguments that focus on higher education. How are their claims similar? How are their claims very different? (Notice that the course being taught in Trudeau's cartoon is either history or political science.) How does Trudeau's cartoon both support Cousins's essay and illustrate a problem with his argument?
2. What evidence does Cousins present to support his argument for the importance of the humanities? Is his evidence quantitative or qualitative? Explain. (Notice that

in his first sentence Cousins speaks of "the *costly* retreat from the humanities." What kind of "cost" does he have in mind?)

3. Examine the organization of Cousins's essay. Why did he order it as he did? Why does he end with the point about Thomas Jefferson?
4. This essay first appeared in 1978. In your opinion, have things changed? Is the emphasis on vocational studies still too strong? What do you think is the purpose of a university education? Why are you attending college?

Garry B. Trudeau

Teaching Is Dead

(1985)

Garry Trudeau's (b. 1948) comic strip "Doonesbury" appears in over 850 newspapers. That wide readership makes him one of the most influential commentators on America's social and political life. The strip reproduced here originally appeared in 1985.

Michael Pollan,

Why Mow: The Case Against Lawns

(1990)

Michael Pollan (b. 1955) is executive editor of *Harpers Magazine*. This essay, which appeared originally in *The New York Times Magazine*, was selected for inclusion in *The Best American Essays: 1990*. It is also a chapter in Pollan's book-length study of nature and gardening, *Second Nature: A Gardener's Education* (Atlantic Monthly Press, 1991).

1 Anyone new to the experience of owning a lawn, as I am, soon figures out that there is more at stake here than a patch of grass. A lawn immediately establishes a certain relationship with one's neighbors and, by extension, the larger American landscape. Mowing the lawn, I realized the first time I gazed into my neighbor's yard and imagined him gazing back into mine, is a civic responsibility.

2 For no lawn is an island, at least in America. Starting at my front stoop, this scruffy green carpet tumbles down a hill and leaps across a one-lane road into my neighbor's yard. From there it skips over some wooded patches and stone walls before finding its way across a dozen other unfenced properties that lead down into the Housatonic Valley, there to begin its march south to the metropolitan area. Once below Danbury, the lawn—now purged of weeds and meticulously coiffed—races up and down the suburban lanes, heedless of property lines. It then heads west, crossing the New York border; moving now at a more stately pace, it strolls beneath the maples of Scarsdale, unfurls across a dozen golf courses, and wraps itself around the pale blue pools of Bronxville before pressing on toward the Hudson. New Jersey next is covered, an emerald postage stamp laid down front and back of ten thousand split levels, before the broadening green river divides in two.

3 One tributary pushes south, and does not pause until it has colonized the thin, sandy soils of Florida. The other dilates and spreads west, easily overtaking the Midwest's vast grid before running up against the inhospitable western states. But neither flinty soil nor obdurate climate will impede the lawn's march to the Pacific: it vaults the Rockies and, abetted by a monumental irrigation network, proceeds to green great stretches of western desert.

4 Nowhere in the world are lawns as prized as in America. In little more than a century, we've rolled a green mantle of grass across the continent, with scarcely a thought to the local conditions or expense. America has more than fifty thousand square *miles* of lawn under cultivation, on which we spend an estimated $30 billion a year—this according to the Lawn Institute, a Pleasant Hill, Tennessee, outfit devoted to publicizing the benefits of turf to Americans (surely a case of preaching to the converted).

5 Like the interstate highway system, like fast-food chains, like television, the lawn has served to unify the American landscape; it is what makes the suburbs of Cleveland and Tucson, the streets of Eugene and Tampa, look more alike than not. According to Ann Leighton, the late historian of gardens, America has made essentially one important contribution to world garden design: the custom of "uniting the front lawns of however many houses there may be on both sides of a street to present an untroubled aspect of expansive green to the passer-by." France has its formal, geometric gardens, England its picturesque parks, and America this unbounded democratic river of manicured lawn along which we array our houses.

6 It is not easy to stand in the way of such a powerful current. Since we have traditionally eschewed fences and hedges in America (looking on these as Old World vestiges), the suburban vista can be marred by the negligence—or dissent—of a single property owner. This is why lawn care is regarded as such an important civic responsibility in the suburbs, and why the majority will not tolerate the laggard. I learned this at an early age, growing up in a cookie-cutter subdivision in Farmingdale, Long Island.

7 My father, you see, was a lawn dissident. Whether owing to laziness or contempt for his neighbors I was never sure, but he could not see much point in cranking up the Toro more than once a month or so. The grass on our quarter-acre plot towered over the crew-cut lawns on either side of us and soon disturbed the peace of the entire neighborhood.

8 That subtle yet unmistakable frontier, where the closely shaved lawn rubs up against a shaggy one, is a scar on the face of suburbia, an intolerable hint of trouble in paradise. The scar shows up in *The Great Gatsby,* when Nick Carraway rents the house next to Gatsby's and fails to maintain his lawn according to West Egg standards. The rift between the two lawns so troubles Gatsby that he dispatches his gardener to mow Nick's grass and thereby erase it.

9 Our neighbors in Farmingdale displayed somewhat less class. "Lawn mower on the fritz?" they'd ask. "Want to borrow mine?" But the more heavily they leaned on my father, the more recalcitrant he became, until one summer—probably 1959, or 1960—he let the lawn go altogether. The grass plants grew tall enough to flower and set seed; the lawn rippled in the breeze like a flag. There was beauty here, I'm sure, but it was not visible in this context. Stuck in the middle of a row of tract houses on Long Island, our lawn said *turpitude* rather than *meadow,* even though strictly speaking that is what it had become.

10 That summer I felt the hot breath of the majority's tyranny for the first time. No one said anything now, but you could hear it all the same: *Mow your lawn or get out.* Certain neighbors let it be known to my parents that I was not to play with their children. Cars would slow down as they drove by. Probably some of the drivers were merely curious: they saw the unmowed lawn and wondered if someone had left in a hurry, or perhaps died. But others drove by in a manner that was unmistakably expressive, slowing down as they drew near and then hitting the gas angrily as they passed—pithy driving, the sort of move that is second nature to a Klansman.

11 We got the message by other media, too. Our next-door neighbor, a mild engineer who was my father's last remaining friend in the development, was charged with the unpleasant task of conveying the sense of the community to my father. It was early on a summer evening that he came to deliver his message. I don't remember it all (I was only four or five at the time), but I can imagine him taking a highball glass from my mother, squeaking out what he had been told to say about the threat to property values, and then waiting for my father—who next to him was a bear—to respond.

12 My father's reply could not have been more eloquent. Without a word he strode out to the garage and cranked up the rusty old Toro for the first time since fall; it's a miracle the thing started. He pushed it out to the curb and then started back across the lawn to the house, but not in a straight line: he swerved right, then left, then right again. He had cut an *S* in the high grass. Then he made an *M,* and finally a *P.* These are his initials, and as soon as he finished writing them he wheeled the lawn mower back to the garage, never to start it up again.

13 I wasn't prepared to take such a hard line on my new lawn, at least not right off. So I bought a lawn mower, a Toro, and started mowing. Four hours every Saturday. At first I tried for a kind of Zen approach, clearing my mind of everything but the task at hand, immersing myself in the lawn-mowing here-and-now. I liked the idea that my weekly sessions with the grass would acquaint me with the minutes details of my yard. I soon knew by heart the exact location of every stump and stone, the tunnel route of each resident mole, the address of every anthill. I noticed that where rain collected white clover flourished, that it was on the drier rises that crabgrass thrived. After a few weekends I had a map of the lawn in my head as precise and comprehensive as the mental map one has of the back of one's hand.

14 The finished product pleased me too, the fine scent and the sense of order restored that a new-cut lawn exhales. My house abuts woods on two sides, and mowing the lawn is, in both a real and metaphorical sense, how I keep the forest at bay and preserve my place in this landscape. Much as we've come to distrust it, the urge to dominate nature is a deeply human one, and lawn mowing answers to it. I thought of the lawn mower as civilization's knife and my lawn as the hospitable plane it carved out of the wilderness. My lawn was a part of nature made fit for human habitation.

15 So perhaps the allure of lawns is in the genes. The sociobiologists think so: they've gone so far as to propose a "Savanna Syndrome" to explain our fondness for grass. Encoded in our DNA is a preference for an open grassy landscape resembling the short-grass savannas of Africa on which we evolved and spent our first few million years. This is said to explain why we have remade the wooded landscapes of Europe and North America in the image of East Africa.

16 Such theories go some way toward explaining the widespread appeal of grass, but they don't really account for the American Lawn. They don't, for instance, account for the keen interest Jay Gatsby takes in Nick Carraway's lawn, or the scandal my father's lawn sparked in Farmingdale. Or the fact that, in America, we have taken down our fences and hedges in order to combine our lawns. And they don't even begin to account

for the unmistakable odor of virtue that hovers in this country over a scrupulously maintained lawn.

17 If any individual can be said to have invented the American lawn, it is Frederick Law Olmsted. In 1868, he received a commission to design Riverside, outside Chicago, one of the first planned suburban communities in America. Olmsted's design stipulated that each house be set back thirty feet from the road and it proscribed walls. He was reacting against the "high deadwalls" of England, which he felt made a row of homes there seem "as of a series of private madhouses." In Riverside, each owner would maintain one or two trees and a lawn that would flow seamlessly into his neighbors', creating the impression that all lived together in a single park.

18 Olmsted was part of a generation of American landscape designer-reformers who set out at midcentury to beautify the American landscape. That it needed beautification may seem surprising to us today, assuming as we do that the history of the landscape is a story of decline, but few at the time thought otherwise. William Cobbett, visiting from England, was struck at the "out-of-door slovenliness" of American homesteads. Each farmer, he wrote, was content with his "shell of boards, while all around him is as barren as the sea beach . . . though there is no English shrub, or flower, which will not grow and flourish here."

19 The land looked as if it had been shaped and cleared in a great hurry—as indeed it had: the landscape largely denuded of trees, makeshift fences outlining badly plowed fields, tree stumps everywhere one looked. As Cobbett and many other nineteenth-century visitors noted, hardly anyone practiced ornamental gardening; the typical yard was "landscaped" in the style southerners would come to call "white trash"—a few chickens, some busted farm equipment, mud and weeds, an unkempt patch of vegetables.

20 This might do for farmers, but for the growing number of middle-class city people moving to the "borderland" in the years following the Civil War, something more respectable was called for. In 1870, Frank J. Scott, seeking to make Olmsted's ideas accessible to the middle class, published the first volume ever devoted to "suburban home embellishment": *The Art of Beautifying Suburban Home Grounds,* a book that probably did more than any other to determine the look of the suburban landscape in America. Like so many reformers of his time, Scott was nothing if not sure of himself: "A smooth, closely shaven surface of grass is by far the most essential element of beauty on the grounds of a suburban house."

21 Americans like Olsmted and Scott did not invent the lawn; lawns had been popular in England since Tudor times. But in England, lawns were usually found only on estates; the Americans democratized them, cutting the vast manorial greenswards into quarter-acre slices everyone could afford. Also, the English never considered the lawn an end in itself: it served as a setting for lawn games and as a backdrop for flower beds and trees. Scott subordinated all other elements of the landscape to the lawn; flowers were permissible, but only on the periphery of the grass: "Let your lawn be your home's velvet robe, and your flowers its not too promiscuous decoration."

22 But Scott's most radical departure from Old World practice was to dwell on the individual's responsibility to his neighbors. “It is unchristian,” he declared, “to hedge from the sight of others the beauties of nature which it has been our good fortune to create or secure.” One's lawn, Scott held, should contribute to the collective landscape. “The beauty obtained by throwing front grounds open together, is of that excellent quality which enriches all who take part in the exchange, and makes no man poorer.” Like Olsmted before him, Scott sought to elevate an unassuming patch of turfgrass into an institution of democracy.

23 With our open-faced front lawns we declare our like-mindedness to our neighbors—and our distance from the English, who surround their yards with “inhospitable brick wall, topped with broken bottles,” to thwart the envious gaze of the lower orders. The American lawn is an egalitarian conceit, implying that there is no reason to hide behind fence or hedge since we all occupy the same middle class. We are all property owners here, the lawn announces, and that suggests its other purpose: to provide a suitably grand stage for the proud display of one's own house. Noting that our yards were organized “to capture the admiration of the street,” one garden writer in 1921 attributed the popularity of open lawns to our “infantile instinct to cry 'hello!' to the passer-by, to lift up our possessions to his gaze.”

24 Of course the democratic front yard has its darker, more coercive side, as my family learned in Farmingdale. In specifying the “plain style” of an unembellished lawn for American front yards, the midcentury designer-reformers were, like Puritan ministers, laying down rigid conventions governing our relationship to the land, our observance of which would henceforth be taken as an index of our character. And just as the Puritans would not tolerate any individual who sought to establish his or her own back-channel relationship with the divinity, the members of the suburban utopia do not tolerate the homeowner who establishes a relationship with the land that is not mediated by the group's conventions.

25 The parallel is not as farfetched as it might sound, when you recall that nature in America has often been regarded as divine. Think of nature as Spirit, the collective suburban lawn as the Church, and lawn mowing as a kind of sacrament. You begin to see why ornamental gardening would take so long to catch on in America, and why my father might seem an antinomian in the eyes of his neighbors. Like Hester Prynne, he claimed not to need their consecration for his actions, perhaps his initials in the front lawn were a kind of Emerald Letter.

26 Possibly because it is this common land, rather than race or tribe, that makes us all Americans, we have developed a deep distrust of individualistic approaches to the landscape. The land is too important to our identity as Americans to simply allow everyone to have his own way with it. And once we decide that the land should serve as a vehicle of consensus, rather than an arena of self-expression, the American lawn—collective, national, ritualized, and plain—begins to look inevitable.

27 After my first season of lawn mowing, the Zen approach began to wear thin. I had taken up flower and vegetable gardening, and soon came to resent the four hours that

my lawn demanded of me each week. I tired of the endless circuit, pushing the howling mower back and forth across the vast page of my yard, recopying the same green sentences over and over: "I am a conscientious homeowner. I share your middle-class values." Lawn care was gardening aimed at capturing "the admiration of the street," a ritual of consensus I did not have my heart in. I began to entertain idle fantasies of rebellion: Why couldn't I plant a hedge along the road, remove my property from the national stream of greensward and do something else with it?

28 The third spring I planted fruit trees in the front lawn, apple, peach, cherry, and plum, hoping these would relieve the monotony and begin to make the lawn productive. Behind the house, I put in a perennial border. I built three raised beds out of old chestnut barnboards and planted two dozen different vegetable varieties. Hard work though it was, removing the grass from the site of my new beds proved a keen pleasure. First I outlined the beds with string. Then I made an incision in the lawn with the sharp edge of a spade. Starting at one end, I pried the sod from the soil and slowly rolled it up like a carpet. The grass made a tearing sound as I broke its grip on the earth. I felt a little like a pioneer subduing the forest with his ax; I daydreamed of scalping the entire yard. But I didn't do it—I continued to observe front-yard conventions, mowing assiduously and locating all my new garden beds in the back yard.

29 The more serious about gardening I became, the more dubious lawns seemed. The problem for me was not, as it was for my father, the relation to my neighbors that a lawn implied; it was the lawn's relationship to nature. For however democratic a lawn may be with respect to one's neighbors, with respect to nature it is authoritarian. Under the mower's brutal indiscriminate rotor, the landscape is subdued, homogenized, dominated utterly. I became convinced that lawn care had about as much to do with gardening as floor waxing or road paving. Gardening was a subtle process of give and take with the landscape, a search for some middle ground between culture and nature. A lawn was nature under culture's boot.

30 Mowing the lawn, I felt that I was battling the earth rather than working it; each week it sent forth a green army and each week I beat it back with my infernal machine. Unlike every other plant in my garden, the grasses were anonymous, massified, deprived of any change or development whatsoever, not to mention any semblance of self-determination. I ruled a totalitarian landscape.

31 Hot, monotonous hours behind the mower gave rise to existential speculations. I spent part of one afternoon trying to decide who, in the absurdist drama of lawn mowing, was Sisyphus. Me? A case could certainly be made. Or was it the grass, pushing up through the soil every week, one layer of cells at a time, only to be cut down and then, perversely, encouraged (with fertilizer, lime, etc.) to start the whole doomed process over again? Another day it occurred to me that time as we know it doesn't exist in the lawn, since grass never dies or is allowed to flower and set seed. Lawns are nature purged of sex and death. No wonder Americans like them so much.

32 And just where *was* my lawn, anyway? The answer's not as obvious as it seems. Gardening, I had come to appreciate, is a painstaking exploration of place; everything that happens in my garden—the thriving and dying of particular plants, the maraudings

of various insects and other pests—teaches me to know this patch of land intimately, its geology and microclimate, the particular ecology of its local weeds and animals and insects. My garden prospers to the extent I grasp these particularities and adapt to them.

33 Lawns work on the opposite principle. They depend for their success on the *overcoming* of local conditions. Like Jefferson superimposing one great grid over the infinitely various topography of the Northwest Territory, we superimpose our lawns on the land. And since the geography and climate of much of this country is poorly suited to turfgrasses (none of which are native), this can't be accomplished without the tools of twentieth-century industrial civilization—its chemical fertilizers, pesticides, herbicides, and machinery. For we won't settle for the lawn that will grow here; we want the one that grows *there,* that dense springy supergreen and weed-free carpet, that Platonic ideal of a lawn we glimpse in the ChemLawn commercials, the magazine spreads, the kitschy sitcom yards, the sublime links and pristine diamonds. Our lawns exist less here than there; they drink from the national stream of images, lift our gaze from the real places we live and fix it on unreal places elsewhere. Lawns are a form of television.

34 Need I point out that such an approach to "nature" is not likely to be environmentally sound? Lately we have begun to recognize that we are poisoning ourselves with our lawns, which receive, on average, more pesticide and herbicide per acre than just about any crop grown in this country. Suits fly against the national lawn-care companies, and interest is kindled in "organic" methods of lawn care. But the problem is larger than this. Lawns, I am convinced, are a symptom of, and a metaphor for, our skewed relationship to the land. They teach us that, with the help of petrochemicals and technology, we can bend nature to our will. Lawns stoke our hubris with regard to the land.

35 What is the alternative? To turn them into gardens. I'm not suggesting that there is no place for lawns *in* these gardens or that gardens by themselves will right our relationship to the land, but the habits of thought they foster can take us some way in that direction.

36 Gardening, as compared to lawn care, tutors us in nature's ways, fostering an ethic of give and take with respect to the land. Gardens instruct us in the particularities of place. They lessen our dependence on distant sources of energy, technology, food, and, for that matter, interest.

37 For if lawn mowing feels like copying the same sentence over and over, gardening is like writing out new ones, an infinitely variable process of invention and discovery. Gardens also teach the necessary if rather un-American lesson that nature and culture can be compromised, that there might be some middle ground between the lawn and the forest—between those who would complete the conquest of the planet in the name of progress and those who believe it's time we abdicated our rule and left the earth in the care of its more innocent species. The garden suggests there might be a place where we can meet nature halfway.

38 Probably you will want to know if I have begun to practice what I'm preaching. Well, I have not ripped out my lawn entirely. But each spring larger and larger tracts of it give way to garden. Last year I took a half acre and planted a meadow of black-eyed

Susans and oxeye daisies. In return for a single annual scything, I am rewarded with a field of flowers from May until frost.

39 The lawn is shrinking, and I've hired a neighborhood kid to mow what's left of it. Any Saturday that Bon Jovi, Twisted Sister, or Van Halen isn't playing the Hartford Civic Center, this large blond teenaged being is apt to show up with a forty-eight-inch John Deere mower that shears the lawn in less than an hour. It's $30 a week, but he's freed me from my dark musings about the lawn and so given me more time in the garden.

40 Out in front, along the road where my lawn overlooks my neighbors', and in turn the rest of the country's, I have made my most radical move. I built a split rail fence and have begun to plant a hedge along it—a rough one made up of forsythia, lilac, bittersweet, and bridal wreath. As soon as this hedge grows tall and thick, my secession from the national lawn will be complete.

41 Anything then is possible. I *could* let it all revert to meadow, or even forest, except that I don't go in for that sort of self-effacement. I could put in a pumpkin patch, a lily pond, or maybe an apple orchard. And I could even leave an area of grass. But even if I did, this would be a very different lawn from the one I have now. For one thing, it would have a frame, which means it could accommodate plants more subtle and various than the screaming marigolds, fierce red salvias, and musclebound rhododendrons that people usually throw into the ring against a big unfenced lawn. Walled off from the neighbors, no longer a tributary of the national stream, my lawn would now form a distinct and private space—become part of a garden rather than a substitute for one.

42 Yes, there might well be a place for a small lawn in my new garden. But I think I'll wait until the hedge fills in before I make a decision. It's a private matter, and I'm trying to keep politics out of it.

Questions for Analysis

1. Pollan's argument against lawns involves much more than just his distaste for mowing. He is objecting to a social, cultural phenomenon. Explain and analyze this part of his claim.
2. Pollan includes in his essay personal narrative, personal history (his father's attitude and actions), and historical background. What do each of these accounts contribute to his argument? How do they work together?
3. Much of Pollan's essay is built around a comparison between lawns and gardens. Explain the significant difference he sees. How does this contrast help his argument?
4. Review Pollan's essay to determine its structure noting especially the divisions marked by an extra space. What heading would you write for each section?

5. Pollan's essay is much more than an argument against lawns: It is also a statement of personal independence and an analysis of one example of social conformity in this country. Do you agree with his analysis? Can you think of other things that we do (or do not do) that are dictated more by social expectation than personal interest?
6. Although he does not pursue it, Pollan touches on evidence that could be used to support a claim of value: that we in America are investing precious resources (e.g., water, fertilizer) on a crop (our lawns) that has only ornamental value, while millions are starving who might be saved if we invested those same resources in a food crop. How would you incorporate this claim into Pollan's argument? If you disagree with Pollan, how would you respond to this claim of value? In other words, how can we justify the time and resources we invest in lawns?
7. The cartoon by Tom Toles, which follows this reading, focuses on yet another argument one could present in the case against lawns. What is Toles's argument? Based on what Pollan says in Paragraph 34, do you think he would agree with Toles?

Tom Toles

What Could They Have Been Thinking?

(1991)

Tom Toles (b. 1951) is editorial cartoonist for *The Buffalo News,* Buffalo, New York.

Tom Toles in *The Buffalo News*

James Shreeve

Machiavellian Monkeys

(1991)

James Shreeve (b. 1951) is a freelance science writer who frequently contributes to *Discover*. This article appeared in that magazine in June of 1991.

1 This is a story about frauds, cheats, liars, faithless lovers, incorrigible con artists, and downright thieves. You're gonna love 'em.

2 Let's start with a young rascal named Paul. You'll remember his type from your days back in the playground. You're minding your own business, playing on the new swing set, when along comes Paul, such a little runt that you hardly notice him sidle up to you. All of a sudden he lets out a scream like you've run him through with a white-hot barbed harpoon or something. Of course the teacher comes running, and the next thing you know you're being whisked inside with an angry finger shaking in your face. That's the end of recess for you. But look out the window: there's Paul, having a great time on *your* swing. Cute kid.

3 Okay, you're a little older now and a little smarter. You've got a bag of chips stashed away in your closet, where for once your older brother won't be able to find them. You're about to open the closet door when he pokes his head in the room. Quickly you pretend to be fetching your high tops; he gives you a look, but he leaves. You wait a couple of minutes, lacing up the sneakers in case he walks back in, then you dive for the chips. Before you can get the bag open, he's over your shoulder, snatching it out of your hands. "Nice try, punk," he says through a mouthful, "but I was hiding outside your room the whole time."

4 This sort of trickery is such a common part of human interaction that we hardly notice how much time we spend defending ourselves against it or perpetrating it ourselves. What's so special about the fakes and cheaters here, however, is that they're not human. Paul is a young baboon, and your big brother is, well, a chimpanzee. With some admittedly deceptive alterations of scenery and props, the situations have been lifted from a recent issue of *Primate Report*. The journal is the work of Richard Byrne and Andrew Whiten, two psychologists at the University of St. Andrews in Scotland, and it is devoted to cataloging the petty betrayals of monkeys and apes as witnessed by primatologists around the world. It is a testament to the evolutionary importance of what Byrne and Whiten call Machiavellian intelligence—a facility named for the famed sixteenth-century author of *The Prince,* the ultimate how-to guide to prevailing in a complex society through the judicious application of cleverness, deceit, and political acumen.

5 Deception is rife in the natural world. Stick bugs mimic sticks. Harmless snakes resemble deadly poisonous ones. When threatened, blowfish puff themselves up and

cats arch their backs and bristle their hair to seem bigger than they really are. All these animals could be said to practice deception because they fool other animals—usually members of other species—into thinking they are something that they patently are not. Even so, it would be overreading the situation to attribute Machiavellian cunning to a blow-fish, or to accuse a stick bug of being a lying scoundrel. Their deceptions, whether in their looks or in their actions, are programmed genetic responses. Biology leaves them no choice but to dissemble: they are just being true to themselves.

6 The kind of deception that interests Byrne and Whiten—what they call tactical deception—is a different kettle of blowfish altogether. Here an animal has the mental flexibility to take an "honest" behavior and use it in such a way that another animal—usually a member of the deceiver's own social group—is misled, thinking that a normal, familiar state of affairs is under way, while, in fact, something quite different is happening.

7 Take Paul, for example. The real Paul is a young chacma baboon that caught Whiten's attention in 1983, while he and Byrne were studying foraging behavior among the chacma in the Drakensberg Mountains of southern Africa. Whiten saw a member of Paul's group, an adult female named Mel, digging in the ground, trying to extract a nutritious plant bulb. Paul approached and looked around. There were no other baboons within sight. Suddenly he let out a yell, and within seconds his mother came running, chasing the startled Mel over a small cliff. Paul then took the bulb for himself.

8 In this case the deceived party was Paul's mother, who was misled by his scream into believing that Paul was being attacked, when actually no such attack was taking place. As a result of her apparent misinterpretation Paul was left alone to eat the bulb that Mel had carefully extracted—a morsel, by the way, that he would not have had the strength to dig out on his own.

9 If Paul's ruse had been an isolated case, Whiten might have gone on with his foraging studies and never given it a second thought. But when he compared his field notes with Byrne's, he noticed that both their notebooks were sprinkled with similar incidents and had been so all summer long. After they returned home to Scotland, they boasted about their "dead smart" baboons to their colleagues in pubs after conferences, expecting them to be suitably impressed. Instead the other researchers countered with tales about their own shrewd vervets or Machiavellian macaques.

10 "That's when we realized that a whole phenomenon might be slipping through a sieve," says Whiten. Researchers had assumed that this sort of complex trickery was a product of the sophisticated human brain. After all, deceitful behavior seemed unique to humans, and the human brain is unusually large, even for primates—"three times as big as you would expect for a primate of our size," notes Whiten, if you're plotting brain size against body weight.

11 But if primates other than humans deceived one another on a regular basis, the two psychologists reasoned, then it raised the extremely provocative possibility that the primate brain, and ultimately the human brain, is an instrument crafted for social manipulation. Humans evolved from the same evolutionary stock as apes, and if tactical deception was an important part of the lives of our evolutionary ancestors, then the

sneakiness and subterfuge that human beings are so manifestly capable of might not be simply a result of our great intelligence and oversize brain, but a driving force behind their development.

12 To Byrne and Whiten these were ideas worth pursuing. They fit in with a theory put forth some years earlier by English psychologist Nicholas Humphrey. In 1976 Humphrey had eloquently suggested that the evolution of primate intelligence might have been spurred not by the challenges of environment, as was generally thought, but rather by the complex cognitive demands of living with one's own companions. Since then a number of primatologists had begun to flesh out his theory with field observations of politically astute monkeys and apes.

13 Deception, however, had rarely been reported. And no wonder: If chimps, baboons, and higher primates generally are skilled deceivers, how could one ever know it? The best deceptions would by their very nature go undetected by the other members of the primate group, not to mention by a human stranger. Even those ruses that an observer could see through would have to be rare, for if used too often, they would lose their effectiveness. If Paul always cried wolf, for example, his mother would soon learn to ignore his ersatz distress. So while the monkey stories swapped over beers certainly suggested that deception was widespread among higher primates, it seemed unlikely that one or even a few researchers could observe enough instances of it to scientifically quantify how much, by whom, when, and to what effect.

14 Byrne and Whiten's solution was to extend their pub-derived data base with a more formal survey. In 1985 they sent a questionnaire to more than 100 primatologists working both in the field and in labs, asking them to report back any incidents in which they felt their subjects had perpetrated deception on one another. The questionnaire netted a promising assortment of deceptive tactics used by a variety of monkeys and all the great apes. Only the relatively small-brained and socially simple lemur family, which includes bush babies and lorises, failed to elicit a single instance. This supported the notion that society, sneakiness, brain size, and intelligence are intimately bound up with one another. The sneakier the primate, it seemed, the bigger the brain.

15 Byrne and Whiten drew up a second, much more comprehensive questionnaire in 1989 and sent it to hundreds more primatologists and animal behaviorists, greatly increasing the data base. Once again, when the results were tallied, only the lemur family failed to register a single case of deception.

16 All the other species, however, represented a simian rogues' gallery of liars and frauds. Often deception was used to distract another animal's attention. In one cartoonish example, a young baboon, chased by some angry elders, suddenly stopped, stood on his hind legs, and stared at a spot on the horizon, as if he noticed the presence of a predator or a foreign troop of baboons. His pursuers braked to a halt and looked in the same direction, giving up the chase. Powerful field binoculars revealed that no predator or baboon troop was anywhere in sight.

17 Sometimes the deception was simply a matter of one animal hiding a choice bit of food from the awareness of those strong enough to take it away. One of Jane Goodall's

chimps, for example, named Figan, was once given some bananas after the more dominant members of the troop had wandered off. In the excitement, he uttered some loud "food barks"; the others quickly returned and took the bananas away. The next day Figan again waited behind the others and got some bananas. This time, however, he kept silent, even though the human observers, Goodall reported, "could hear faint choking sounds in his throat."

18 Concealment was a common ruse in sexual situations as well. Male monkeys and chimpanzees in groups have fairly strict hierarchies that control their access to females. Animals at the top of the order intimidate those lower down, forcing them away from females. Yet one researcher reported seeing a male stump-tailed macaque of a middle rank leading a female out of sight of the more dominant males and then mating with her silently, his climax unaccompanied by the harsh, low-pitched grunts that the male stump-tailed normally makes. At one point during the tryst the female turned and stared into his face, then covered his mouth with her hand. In another case a subordinate chimpanzee, aroused by the presence of a female in estrus, covered his erect penis with his hand when a dominant male approached, thus avoiding a likely attack.

19 In one particularly provocative instance a female hamadryas baboon slowly shuffled toward a large rock, appearing to forage, all the time keeping an eye on the most dominant male in the group. After 20 minutes she ended up with her head and shoulders visible to the big, watchful male, but with her hands happily engaged in the illicit activity of grooming a favorite subordinate male, who was hidden from view behind the rock.

20 Baboons proved singularly adept at a form of deception that Byrne and Whiten call "using a social tool." Paul's scam is a perfect example: he fools his mother into acting as a lever to pry the plant bulb away from the adult female, Mel. But can it be said unequivocally that he intended to deceive her? Perhaps Paul had simply learned through trial and error that letting out a yell brought his mother running and left him with food, in which case there is no reason to endow his young baboon intellect with Machiavellian intent. How do we know that Mel didn't actually threaten Paul in some way that Byrne and Whiten, watching, could not comprehend? While we're at it, how do we know that any of the primate deceptions reported here were really deliberate, conscious acts?

21 "It has to be said that there is a whole school of psychology that would deny such behavior even to humans," says Byrne. The school in question—strict behaviorism—would seek an explanation for the baboons' behavior not by trying to crawl inside their head but by carefully analyzing observable behaviors and the stimuli that might be triggering them. Byrne and Whiten's strategy against such skepticism was to be hyper-skeptical themselves. They accepted that trial-and-error learning or simple conditioning, in which an animal's actions are reinforced by a reward, might account for a majority of the incidents reported to them—even when they believed that tactical deception was really taking place. But when explaining things "simply" led to a maze of extraordinary coincidences and tortuous logic, the evidence for deliberate deception seemed hard to dismiss.

22 Paul, for instance, *might* have simply learned that screaming elicits the reward of food, via his mother's intervention. But Byrne witnessed him using the same tactic several times, and in each case his mother was out of sight, able to hear his yell but not able to see what was really going on. If Paul was simply conditioned to scream, why would he do so only when his mother could not see who was—or was not—attacking her son?

23 Still, it is possible that she was not intentionally deceived. But in at least one other, similar case there is virtually no doubt that the mother was responding to a bogus attack, because the alleged attacker was quite able to verbalize his innocence. A five-year-old male chimp named Katabi, in the process of weaning, had discovered that the best way to get his reluctant mother to suckle him was to convince her he needed reassurance. One day Katabi approached a human observer—Japanese primatologist Toshisada Nishida—and began to screech, circling around the researcher and waving an accusing hand at him. The chimp's mother and her escort immediately glared at Nishida, their hair erect. Only by slowly backing away from the screaming youngster did Nishida avoid a possible attack from the two adult chimps.

24 "In fact I did nothing to him," Nishida protested. It follows that the adults were indeed misled by Katabi's hysterics—unless there was some threat in Nishida unknown even to himself.

25 "If you try hard enough," says Byrne, "you can explain every single case without endowing the animal with the ability to deceive. But if you look at the whole body of work, there comes a point where you have to strive officiously to deny it."

26 The cases most resistant to such officious denials are the rarest—and the most compelling. In these interactions the primate involved not only employed tactical deception but clearly understood the concept. Such comprehension would depend upon one animal's ability to "read the mind" of another: to attribute desires, intentions, or even beliefs to the other creature that do not necessarily correspond to its own view of the world. Such mind reading was clearly evident in only 16 out of 253 cases in the 1989 survey, all of them involving great apes.

27 For example, consider Figan again, the young chimp who suppressed his food barks in order to keep the bananas for himself. In his case, mind reading is not evident: he might simply have learned from experience that food barks in certain contexts result in a loss of food, and thus he might not understand the nature of his own ruse, even if the other chimps are in fact deceived.

28 But contrast Figan with some chimps observed by Dutch primatologist Frans Plooij. One of these chimps was alone in a feeding area when a metal box containing food was opened electronically. At the same moment another chimp happened to approach. (Sound familiar? It's your older brother again.) The first chimp quickly closed the metal box (that's you hiding your chips), walked away, and sat down, looking around as if nothing had happened. The second chimp departed, but after going some distance away he hid behind a tree and peeked back at the first chimp. When the first chimp thought the coast was clear, he opened the box. The second chimp ran out, pushed the other aside, and ate the bananas.

29 Chimp One might be a clever rogue, but Chimp Two, who counters his deception with a ruse of his own, is the true mind reader. The success of his ploy is based on his insight that Chimp One was trying to deceive *him* and on his ability to adjust his behavior accordingly. He has in fact performed a prodigious cognitive leap—proving himself capable of projecting himself into another's mental space, and becoming what Humphrey would call a natural psychologist.

30 Niccolò Machiavelli might have called him good raw material. It is certainly suggestive that only the great apes—our closest relatives—seem capable of deceits based on such mind reading, and chimpanzees most of all. This does not necessarily mean that chimps are inherently more intelligent: the difference may be a matter of social organization. Orangutans live most of their lives alone, and thus they would not have much reason to develop such a complex social skill. And gorillas live in close family groups, whose members would be more familiar, harder to fool, and more likely to punish an attempted swindle. Chimpanzees, on the other hand, spend their lives in a shifting swirl of friends and relations, where small groups constantly form and break apart and reform with new members.

31 "What an opportunity for lying and cheating!" muses Byrne. Many anthropologists now believe that the social life of early hominids—our first nonape ancestors—was much like that of chimps today, with similar opportunities to hone their cognitive skills on one another. Byrne and Whiten stop just short of saying that mind reading is the key to understanding the growth of human intelligence. But it would be disingenuous to ignore the possibility. If you were an early hominid who could comprehend the subjective impressions of others and manipulate them to your own ends, you might well have a competitive advantage over those less psychosocially nimble, perhaps enjoying slightly easier access to food and to the mating opportunities that would ensure your genetic survival.

32 Consider too how much more important your social wits would be in a world where the targets of your deceptions were constantly trying to outsmart *you.* After millennia of intrigue and counterintrigue, a hominid species might well evolve a brain three times bigger than it "should" be—and capable of far more than deceiving other hominids. "The ability to attribute other intentions to other people could have been an enormous building block for many human achievements, including language," says Whiten. "That this leap seems to have been taken by chimps and possibly the other great apes puts that development in human mentality quite early."

33 So did our intellect rise to its present height on a tide of manipulation and deceit? Some psychologists, even those who support the notion that the evolution of intelligence was socially driven, think that Byrne and Whiten's choice of the loaded adjective *Machiavellian* might be unnecessarily harsh.

34 "In my opinion," says Humphrey, "the word gives too much weight to the hostile use of intelligence. One of the functions of intellect in higher primates and humans is to keep the social unit together and make it able to successfully exploit the environment. A lot of intelligence could better be seen as driven by the need for cooperation and

compassion.'' To that, Byrne and Whiten only point out that cooperation is itself an excellent Machiavellian strategy—sometimes.

The Scottish researchers are not, of course, the first to have noticed this. ''It is good to appear clement, trustworthy, humane, religious, and honest, and also to be so,'' Machiavelli advised his aspiring Borgia prince in 1513. ''But always with the mind so disposed that, when the occasion arises not to be so, you can become the opposite.''

Questions for Analysis

1. As a writer for *Discover,* James Shreeve takes very technical articles produced by scientists for professional journals and rewrites them so that they are intelligible to a lay audience. In this essay can you pick out any material that you are reasonably sure was not in Richard Byrne and Andrew Whiten's original article in *Primate Report?* Does this additional information make the essay more interesting and persuasive?
2. Do you think that Shreeve interviewed Byrne and Whiten before writing this article? What evidence in the article suggests that an interview did or did not occur?
3. To support the claim about monkey behavior, Shreeve presents a number of examples. Do you find this evidence convincing? Explain.
4. Shreeve offers and rejects alternative explanations for several incidents with monkeys. Does this strategy strengthen his argument? Point out the places where he does this and explain how his discussion helps to make his case.
5. If Byrne and Whiten are right and the evolution of the human brain was accelerated in large part by the need to deceive, is there such a thing as altruism? Can you find evidence (as Shreeve does) in the human behavior you see to support your thesis?

Part II

CONTRASTING VIEWS

Paired Paintings

Painters, like writers, are active and important participants in the dialogue we pursue as we try to define and understand our world, our society, and ourselves. Paintings are often powerful arguments about the way things are. They can provoke both an aesthetic response—in the moods and emotions their images evoke—and an intellectual response to the artists' statements about life and the world.

Paintings have a direct impact that prose cannot attain. While this impact is one of the special strengths of art, it can also be a liability: If we don't look carefully, we can miss details that might give us a fuller, more accurate understanding of the artist's vision and message. Learning to look carefully at art can thus teach us much about looking at life: Our reliance on first impressions may not give us all the information we need to fully understand what is happening.

The questions after each of the following pairs of paintings direct your attention to special aspects of each painting, and challenge you to consider the implications of the artists' choices about subject matter, perspective, style, and composition. That process should help you develop your sense of what the artist is showing and help you find the details you will need to support your opinion of what the artist's message is. The paintings are presented in pairs, for comparison forces us to look carefully to understand why different paintings on the same or similar subjects convey very different impressions.

Remember that while paintings are contributions to our culture's intellectual dialogue, they are also aesthetic creations. Try to enjoy their beauty as you try to understand and explain their arguments.

The Broken Pitcher,
Greuze, 1725–1805,
Louvre, Paris

Woman, I, de Kooning (1950–52)
Oil on canvas, 6′3⅞″ × 58″.
Collection, The Museum of
Modern Art, New York. Purchase.

Women

Jean Greuze
The Broken Pitcher

(1773)

Jean Greuze (1725–1805) was a French genre and portrait painter. (Genre paintings take as their subject matter scenes from everyday life.) Although he was never admitted to the French Academy of Art, Greuze's work, especially his genre paintings, were very popular before the French Revolution. *The Broken Pitcher* (1773) is one of many genre paintings he produced that depicted young girls at that point in life when youthful innocence must deal with the realities of the world.

Willem de Kooning
Woman, I

(1950–1952)

Willem de Kooning (b. 1904) is a Dutch-born painter who, after studying and working in Europe, settled permanently in the United States in 1926. Although his work had been realistic before his arrival, he quickly became a leader of the abstract art movement in the United States. Between about 1945 and 1955, his works dealt almost entirely with the human figure depicted in raw, abstract, sometimes brutally bold forms. During that period he painted *Woman, I* (1950–1952), the most intense and disturbing painting in a famous series focusing on the female form.

Questions for Analysis

1. Describe as accurately as possible Greuze's painting. Pay particular attention to the girl (her facial expression, her clothing, her hair), but also notice the pitcher and the fountain in the right background. What has happened? Why is the pitcher broken?
2. Describe as accurately as possible the woman in de Kooning's painting. Pay particular attention to the expression on her face (notice her eyes, her mouth, her nose) and the shape and presentation of her body. How would you describe the brush strokes de Kooning uses in various parts of this painting? How do they help convey the impression this painting conveys? How does the image of the woman fit into the background of the painting? How does the background help convey the message of the painting? Can you tell what has happened in this painting?
3. Compare the two paintings. How do you react to each? Explain how the subject matter and the techniques used by these two artists convey different impressions.
4. What do these two paintings suggest to you about these artists' attitudes toward women? About the place of women in eighteenth-century France and twentieth-century America? About how women in these different times might respond to similar situations?

View of Toledo, El Greco. The Metropolitan Museum of Art, Bequest of Mrs. H.O. Havemeyer, 1929. The H.O. Havemeyer Collection, 1929 (29-100-6)

Bare Willows and Distant Mountains, Ma Yuan, China, Southern Sung Dynasty, about 1200. Round album leaf; ink and colors on silk, 23.8 × 21.2 cm. *Chinese and Japanese Special Fund. Courtesy, Museum of Fine Arts, Boston*

Landscapes

El Greco
A View of Toledo

(ca. 1607–1610)

El Greco (1541–1614) is the name commonly given to Domenico Theotocopuli, a painter, born in Crete, who studied and worked in Venice and Rome before moving to Spain between about 1575 and his death. While in Spain, El Greco developed a dynamic, emotional style that quickly separated him from the more sedate and realistic style he left behind in Italy. It was his unique approach that established his fame as an innovative, powerful artist. The *View of Toledo* (ca. 1607–1610) is an excellent example of the energy and drama he conveyed through his paintings, including, as in this case, his landscapes.

Ma Yüan
Bare Willows and Distant Mountains

(ca. 1220)

Ma Yüan (ca. 1190–1225) was the most famous member of the Ma family of painters who, for at least five generations, made important contributions to China's artistic heritage. Considered one of the two leading masters of his time, Ma Yüan's influence was felt not only in China but also in Japan, where he was regarded as one of the foremost of all Chinese painters. Along with Hsia Kuei, the other master of his time, Ma Yüan became famous for developing the asymmetrical ("one-cornered") style in which an area of great detail, usually in one corner of the work, resides in contrast to open areas of paper or silk. Ma Yüan, however, also produced many paintings which demonstrate his interest in balanced composition. *Bare Willows and Distant Mountains* demonstrates this style even as it reveals his interest in setting areas of high detail against open spaces.

Questions for Analysis

1. Describe each painting. Consider the following aspects of each:
    a. the presentation of detail and of open space (space in the paintings without lines or paint);
    b. the placement of mountains;
    c. the treatment of the sky; and
    d. the placement of structures created by people
2. Consider the very different technical approaches used by these two artists. Notice and describe, for example, their use of line and brush stroke as well as the different ways they fill space in their paintings.
3. Using details to support your statements, describe the mood conveyed by each painting. What feeling or mood do you think each artist was trying to convey? Are those different moods indicative of the difference in the two cultures out of which these two paintings come? Explain.
4. Consider how these paintings convey a different attitude toward the relationship between human beings and nature. Again, are these different attitudes indicative of differences between Oriental and Occidental ways of viewing the world? Explain.

Edward Hopper, American, 1882–1967, *Nighthawks*, oil on canvas, 1942, 76.2 × 144 cm. Friends of American Art Collection, 1942.51 photograph © 1992, The Art Institute of Chicago. All Rights Reserved.

Edvard Munch *The Dance of Life* (1899–1900). Nasjonalgalleriet, Oslo, Kommune Kunstsamlingene, Munch-Museet, Oslo.

Social Scenes

Edward Hopper

Night Hawks

(1942)

Edward Hopper (1882–1967) was an American painter who supported himself as a commercial artist and illustrator until the 1920s, when his paintings gradually began to find an audience. Hopper's paintings focus on architectural and engineering structures such as bridges, buildings, or highways and usually contain few, if any, people. He frequently painted public places (theaters, lunch counters, gas stations, etc.) at times of day when few people would be there (e.g., late at night, early in the morning). His approach tended to isolate human figures and set them starkly against their surroundings as seen in *Night Hawks* (1942).

Edvard Munch

The Dance of Life

(1899–1900)

Edvard Munch (1863–1944) was a Norwegian painter whose emotional, expressionistic painting was very influential in Eastern Europe, especially Germany. His paintings often contain distressing, but fascinating scenes that reflect his own unhappiness and the anxiety and loneliness of modern life. The women who frequently appear in his art are often hauntingly beautiful and realistic, despite his expressionist bent. *The Dance of Life* (1899–1900) is indicative of his interest in the relationships between men and women and the symbolic style he often employed.

Questions for Analysis

1. Describe each painting. In *Night Hawks* pay particular attention to the relationships between the inside and outside of the cafe, between the people in the painting, and between the architectural space and the people. How does setting people in this scene affect the way they might react to each other and you to them? In *The Dance of Life* consider carefully the relationship between the three main female figures (including the female figure who is dancing with the man in the center foreground), but also consider the relationships between the man and woman dancing in the center foreground and between the foreground and background figures.
2. Based on your analysis of the relationships in each painting, what do you think is happening in each? Do you sense that the relationships between the people in one painting are more complex than those in the other? Explain your answer. Would this difference make one painting better than the other or just different? Explain.
3. Describe the differences in artistic technique and style used by Hopper and Munch. Pay particular attention to line, shadow, contrast, and to how realistic a representation of reality you find in each painting. How do these differences in style help to convey the mood and message these artists wish to convey?
4. What are, in your opinion, the messages about people, social relationships, and life that these two artists are trying to convey?

Persuasive Writing

One of the best ways to learn about persuasive writing is to examine essays that take opposing positions on an issue. Head-to-head comparison allows you to see more clearly the strategies writers use to present their positions, the information they include, the information they omit, and the ways they deal with (or avoid) the opposition's arguments. Reading essays that take opposing positions can also help you sort out your own thinking on an important issue or find more arguments to support an opinion you have already formed.

The first four essays in this section are contrasting views on two difficult, but very important issues in medical ethics. The first two essays deal with euthanasia. Although the ethical and legal ramifications of enthuanasia have been debated for years, Dr. Jack Kavorkian's recent use of his ''suicide machine'' has pushed the issue into the courts and the news. The two essays reprinted here are classic arguments on the still unresolved euthanasia issue. Both focus on distinctions between active and passive euthanasia (or, in more direct language, ''killing'' or ''letting die'') and, in the process, touch on most of the ethical and personal rights questions.

The second pair of essays deals with another painfully difficult issue in medical ethics: Do parents have the right to reject treatment for infants with severe birth defects? As with euthanasia, the arguments here focus on ''quality of life'' (a concept that is very difficult for people to agree on because of different professional, religious, social, and cultural perspectives), the morality of a decision to withhold treatment, and our willingness as a society to accept decisions that we might not agree with. Even though Earl E. Shelp and C. Everett Koop take fundamentally different stances on this issue, they each also reveal a range of tolerance, which suggests they might agree on many individual cases.

In the last three subsections of Part II, you will find, in addition to the essays that take pro and con sides of the issue, a third essay that defines a middle ground between the more extreme pro or con positions. These additional essays are there to emphasize that most issues are not as clear-cut as many advocates on either side would often have us believe. Compromise positions are usually more difficult to understand and to argue because they are more complex. Despite their complexity, they should be carefully considered: they frequently, though not always, offer the most practical and intellectually satisfying option.

In the sub-section on animal rights and scientific research, Cleveland Amory in ''The Trials of Animals'' is sharply critical of researchers who test animals and accuses them of feeling that they are above the law. In his essay ''The Animal Rights 'War' on Medicine,'' John G. Hubbell enumerates incidents in which valuable research has been disrupted by animal-rights activists and warns that their activities and the legislation they support may ''put an end to progress in medical research.'' Sneed B. Collard III, however, in ''Refocusing Animal Rights'' argues that scientists and animal-rights activists have many compatible goals and should re-examine their thinking and subsequently redirect their efforts to counter some major threats to the well-being of all animals, including human beings. The fourth item in this section is a cartoon series by Garry B. Trudeau. His message, "live and live," refocuses the issue in a comic yet emphatic way.

The three essays on the responsibilities of rich nations in a world of starving people are among the longest in this reader; they may also be the most important. The shortages of food, water, and essential medical supplies caused by natural disaster, political turmoil, and overpopulation simply do not go away. Because the issue has political ramifications that can obscure the moral issues, the essays chosen for inclusion here are older than most in the text and deal only with the moral questions. In "Lifeboat Ethics: The Case Against Helping the Poor," Garrett Hardin argues the isolationist position (a stance popular with some politicians and voters). Peter Singer, on the other hand, argues in "Famine, Affluence, and Morality" for the other extreme when he suggests that we should share our resources even if it means we too must starve (a position that few politicans have endorsed). In "Reason and Morality in a World of Limited Food," Richard A. Watson tries to articulate a more reasonable approach that calls for finding the point at which we can give the most help without risking our own stability.

The final sub-section deals with the debate that began in the nineteenth century between those who supported the theory of evolution and those who opposed it on religious grounds. In recent years the debate has been stirred by "scientific creationists." Their protests have actually led publishers to modify the treatment of evolution in the biology textbooks used in public schools and thus, in the eyes of many, including Stephen Jay Gould, to weaken those texts. Gould, one of the most articulate and productive of the many scientist–writers now writing for lay audiences, emphatically defends evolution against attacks from scientific creationists in his essay "Evolution As Fact and Theory." Duane T. Gish, another scientist and one of the most vocal advocates of scientific creationism, wrote "A Response to Gould's Argument" to refute Gould's arguments. The last essay in this section, "Biblical Fundamentalists vs. Scientific Ones: The Creationism Controversy," is an analysis by Anne Marie Brennan that reveals problems with the arguments on both sides. She believes the solution lies in a higher level of both scientific and religious literacy.

As you read, discuss, and write about the issues in Part II, keep in mind that it is your responsibility to decide what is the most reasonable and, in many cases, the most ethical position on each issue. Compromise positions are sometimes the most practical and fairest choices. Sometimes, however, compromises require us to give up more than we should; sometimes they are cop-outs. Sometimes maintaining an extreme position is the right thing to do and may even require a little old-fashioned heroism. But extreme positions also can be wrong-headed, can impede progress, and can cause needless pain. It is up to you to make a decision and to defend it. The conflicting views in this section as well as essays on the controversial topics in Parts III and IV will give you plenty of practice in this difficult but essential task.

Euthanasia: When Should It Be Allowed? How Should It Be Done?

James Rachels

Active and Passive Euthanasia

(1975)

Although this essay originally appeared in *The New England Journal of Medicine* in 1975, it is still cited and anthologized frequently. James Rachels (b. 1941) teaches philosophy and ethics at the University of Alabama.

The distinction between active and passive euthanasia is thought to be crucial for medical ethics. The idea is that it is permissible, at least in some cases, to withhold treatment and allow a patient to die, but it is never permissible to take any direct action designed to kill the patient. This doctrine seems to be accepted by most doctors, and it is endorsed in a statement adopted by the House of Delegates of the American Medical Association on December 4, 1973:

> The intentional termination of the life of one human being by another—mercy killing—is contrary to that for which the medical profession stands and is contrary to the policy of the American Medical Association.
>
> The cessation of the employment of extraordinary means to prolong the life of the body when there is irrefutable evidence that biological death is imminent is the decision of the patient and/or his immediate family. The advice and judgment of the physician should be freely available to the patient and/or his immediate family.

However, a strong case can be made against this doctrine. In what follows I will set out some of the relevant arguments, and urge doctors to reconsider their views on this matter.

To begin with a familiar type of situation, a patient who is dying of incurable cancer of the throat is in terrible pain, which can no longer be satisfactorily alleviated. He is certain to die within a few days, even if present treatment is continued, but he does not want to go on living for those days since the pain is unbearable. So he asks the doctor for an end to it, and his family joins in the request.

4 Suppose the doctor agrees to withhold treatment, as the conventional doctrine says he may. The justification for his doing so is that the patient is in terrible agony, and since he is going to die anyway, it would be wrong to prolong his suffering needlessly. But now notice this. If one simply withholds treatment, it may take the patient longer to die, and so he may suffer more than he would if more direct action were taken and a lethal injection given. This fact provides strong reason for thinking that, once the initial decision not to prolong his agony has been made, active euthanasia is actually preferable to passive euthanasia, rather than the reverse. To say otherwise is to endorse the option that leads to more suffering rather than less, and is contrary to the humanitarian impulse that prompts the decision not to prolong his life in the first place.

5 Part of my point is that the process of being "allowed to die" can be relatively slow and painful, whereas being given a lethal injection is relatively quick and painless. Let me give a different sort of example. In the United States about one in 600 babies is born with Down's syndrome. Most of these babies are otherwise healthy—that is, with only the usual pediatric care, they will proceed to an otherwise normal infancy. Some, however, are born with congenital defects such as intestinal obstructions that require operations if they are to live. Sometimes, the parents and the doctor will decide not to operate, and let the infant die. Anthony Shaw describes what happens then:

> . . . When surgery is denied [the doctor] must try to keep the infant from suffering while natural forces sap the baby's life away. As a surgeon whose natural inclination is to use the scalpel to fight off death, standing by and watching a salvageable baby die is the most emotionally exhausting experience I know. It is easy at a conference, in a theoretical discussion, to decide that such infants should be allowed to die. It is altogether different to stand by in the nursery and watch as dehydration and infection wither a tiny being over hours and days. This is a terrible ordeal for me and the hospital staff—much more so than for the parents who never set foot in the nursery.[1]

6 I can understand why some people are opposed to all euthanasia, and insist that such infants must be allowed to live. I think I can also understand why other people favor destroying these babies quickly and painlessly. But why should anyone favor letting "dehydration and infection wither a tiny being over hours and days"? The doctrine that says that a baby may be allowed to dehydrate and wither, but may not be given an injection that would end its life without suffering, seems so patently cruel as to require no further refutation. The strong language is not intended to offend, but only to put the point in the clearest possible way.

7 My second argument is that the conventional doctrine leads to decisions concerning life and death made on irrelevant grounds.

8 Consider again the case of the infants with Down's syndrome who need operations for congenital defects unrelated to the syndrome to live. Sometimes, there is no operation, and the baby dies, but when there is no such defect, the baby lives on. Now, an operation such as that to remove an intestinal obstruction is not prohibitively difficult. The reason why such operations are not performed in these cases is, clearly, that the child has Down's syndrome and the parents and the doctor judge that because of that fact it is better for the child to die.

9 But notice that this situation is absurd, no matter what view one takes of the lives and potentials of such babies. If the life of such an infant is worth preserving, what does it matter if it needs a simple operation? Or, if one thinks it better that such a baby should not live on, what difference does it make that it happens to have an obstructed intestinal tract? In either case, the matter of life and death is being decided on irrelevant grounds. It is the Down's syndrome, and not the intestines, that is the issue. The matter should be decided, if at all, on that basis, and not be allowed to depend on the essentially irrelevant question of whether the intestinal tract is blocked.

10 What makes this situation possible, of course, is the idea that when there is an intestinal blockage, one can ''let the baby die,'' but when there is no such defect there is nothing that can be done, for one must not ''kill'' it. The fact that this idea leads to such results as deciding life or death on irrelevant grounds is another good reason why the doctrine should be rejected.

11 One reason why so many people think that there is an important moral difference between active and passive euthanasia is that they think killing someone is morally worse than letting someone die. But is it? Is killing, in itself, worse than letting die? To investigate this issue, two cases may be considered that are exactly alike except that one involves killing whereas the other involves letting someone die. Then, it can be asked whether this difference makes any difference to the moral assessments. It is important that the cases be exactly alike, except for this one difference, since otherwise one cannot be confident that it is this difference and not some other that accounts for any variation in the assessment of the two cases. So, let us consider this pair of cases:

12 In the first, Smith stands to gain a large inheritance if anything should happen to his six-year-old cousin. One evening while the child is taking his bath, Smith sneaks into the bathroom and drowns the child, and then arranges things so that it will look like an accident.

13 In the second, Jones also stands to gain if anything should happen to his six-year-old cousin. Like Smith, Jones sneaks in planning to drown the child in his bath. However, just as he enters the bathroom Jones sees the child slip and hit his head, and fall face down in the water. Jones is delighted; he stands by ready to push the child's head back under if it is necessary, but it is not necessary. With only a little thrashing about, the child drowns all by himself, ''accidentally'' as Jones watches and does nothing.

14 Now Smith killed the child, whereas Jones ''merely'' let the child die. That is the only difference between them. Did either man behave better, from a moral point of view? If the difference between killing and letting die were in itself a morally important matter, one should say that Jones's behavior was less reprehensible than Smith's. But

does one really want to say that? I think not. In the first place, both men acted from the same motive, personal gain, and both had exactly the same end in view when they acted. It may be inferred from Smith's conduct that he is a bad man, although that judgment may be withdrawn or modified if certain further facts are learned about him—for example, that he is mentally deranged. But would not the very same thing be inferred about Jones from his conduct? And would not the same further considerations also be relevant to any modification of this judgment? Moreover, suppose Jones pleaded in his own defense, "After all, I didn't do anything except just stand there and watch the child drown. I didn't kill him. I only let him die." Again, if letting die were in itself less bad than killing, the defense should have at least some insight. But it does not. Such a "defense" can only be regarded as a grotesque perversion of moral reasoning. Morally speaking, it is no defense at all.

15 Now it may be pointed out, quite properly, that the cases of euthanasia with which doctors are concerned are not like this at all. They do not involve personal gain or the destruction of normal healthy children. Doctors are concerned only with cases in which the patient's life is of no further use of him, one in which the patient's life has become or will soon become a terrible burden. However, the point is the same in these cases: the bare difference between killing and letting die does not, in itself, make a moral difference. If a doctor lets a patient die for humane reasons, he is in the same moral position as if he had given the patient a lethal injection for humane reasons. If his decision was wrong—if, for example, the patient's illness was in fact curable—the decision would be equally regrettable no matter which method was used to carry it out. And if the doctor's decision was the right one, the method used is not in itself important.

16 The AMA policy statement isolates the crucial issue very well: the crucial issue is "the intentional termination of the life of one human being by another." But after identifying this issue, and forbidding "mercy killing," the statement goes on to say that the cessation of treatment is the intentional termination of life. This is where the mistake comes in, for what is the cessation of treatment, in these circumstances, if it is not "the intentional termination of the life of one human being by another"? Of course it is exactly that and if it were not, there would be no point to it.

17 Many people find this judgment hard to accept. One reason, I think, is that it is very easy to conflate the question of whether killing is, in itself, worse than letting die, with the very different question of whether most actual cases of killing are more reprehensible than most actual cases of letting die. Most actual cases of killing are clearly terrible (think, for example, of all the murders reported in the newspapers), and one hears of such cases every day. On the other hand, one hardly ever hears of a case of letting die, except for the action of doctors who are motivated by humanitarian reasons. So one learns to think of killing in a much worse light than of letting die. But this does not mean that there is something about killing that makes it in itself worse than letting die, for it is not the bare difference between killing and letting die that makes the difference in these cases. Rather, the other factors—the murderer's motive of personal gain, for example, contrasted with the doctor's humanitarian motivation—account for different reactions to the different cases.

18 I have argued that killing is not in itself any worse than letting die; if my contention is right, it follows that active euthanasia is not any worse than passive euthanasia. What arguments can be given on the other side? The most common, I believe, is the following:

19 "The important difference between active and passive euthanasia is that, in passive euthanasia, the doctor does not do anything to bring about the patient's death. The doctor does nothing, and the patient dies of whatever ills already afflict him. In active euthanasia, however, the doctor does something to bring about the patient's death: he kills him. The doctor who gives that patient with cancer a lethal injection has himself caused the patient's death; whereas if he merely ceases treatment, the cancer is the cause of the death."

20 A number of points need to be made here. The first is that it is not exactly correct to say that in passive euthanasia the doctor does nothing, for he does do one thing that is very important: he lets the patient die. "Letting someone die" is certainly different, in some respects, from other types of action—mainly in that it is a kind of action that one may perform by way of not performing certain other actions. For example, one may let a patient die by way of not giving medication, just as one may insult someone by way of not shaking his hand. But for any purpose of moral assessment, it is a type of action nonetheless. The decision to let a patient die is subject to moral appraisal in the same way that a decision to kill him would be subject to moral appraisal: it may be assessed as wise or unwise, compassionate or sadistic, right or wrong. If a doctor deliberately let a patient die who was suffering from a routinely curable illness, the doctor would certainly be to blame for what he had done, just as he would be to blame if he had needlessly killed the patient. Charges against him would then be appropriate. If so, it would be no defense at all for him to insist that he didn't "do anything." He would have done something very serious indeed, for he let his patient die.

21 Fixing the cause of death may be very important from a legal point of view, for it may determine whether criminal charges are brought against the doctor. But I do not think that this notion can be used to show a moral difference between active and passive euthanasia. The reason why it is considered bad to be the cause of someone's death is that death is regarded as a great evil—and so it is. However, if it has been decided that euthanasia—even passive euthanasia—is desirable in a given case, it has also been decided that in this instance death is no greater an evil than the patient's continued existence. And if this is true, the usual reason for not wanting to be the cause of someone's death simply does not apply.

22 Finally, doctors may think that all of this is only of academic interest—the sort of thing that philosophers may worry about but that has no practical bearing on their own work. After all, doctors must be concerned about the legal consequences of what they do, and active euthanasia is clearly forbidden by law. But even so, doctors should also be concerned with the fact that the law is forcing upon them a moral doctrine that may well be indefensible, and has a considerable effect on their practices. Of course, most doctors are not now in the position of being coerced in this matter, for they do not regard themselves as merely going along with what the law requires. Rather, in statements such as the AMA policy statement that I have quoted, they are endorsing this

doctrine as a central point of medical ethics. In that statement, active euthanasia is condemned not merely as illegal but as "contrary to that for which the medical profession stands," whereas passive euthanasia is approved. However, the preceding considerations suggest that there is really no moral difference between the two, considered in themselves (there may be important moral differences in some cases in their *consequences,* but as I pointed out, these differences may make active euthanasia, and not passive euthanasia, the morally preferable option). So, whereas doctors may have to discriminate between active and passive euthanasia to satisfy the law, they should not do any more than that. In particular, they should not give the distinction any added authority and weight by writing it into official statements of medical ethics.

Notes

1. A. Shaw, "Doctor, Do We Have a Choice?" *The New York Times Magazine,* January 30, 1972, p. 59.

Questions for Analysis

1. What is Rachels's position on the difference between active and passive euthanasia?
2. If we accept the premise that active and passive euthanasia are the same, we could then argue against both forms of euthanasia or for both. Which route does Rachels take? Why?
3. Rachels uses examples and an analogy in his essay. Point them out. Do they help make his argument less abstract and thus more powerful? Explain.
4. In his final paragraph Rachels says there is no moral difference in active and passive euthanasia, but does assert there may be important moral differences in their consequences. What does he mean by "consequences"?

Tom L. Beauchamp and James F. Childress

The Distinction Between Killing and Letting Die

(1989)

This essay comes from *Principles of Biomedical Ethics* published by Oxford University Press. Beauchamp (b. 1939) and Childress (b. 1940) have established this text, now in its third edition, as an important source of information on the ethical problems faced by professionals in medicine and medical research.

1 In a well-known case, a sixty-eight-year-old doctor who suffered severely from terminal carcinoma of the stomach collapsed with a massive pulmonary embolism. He

survived because one of his young colleagues performed a pulmonary embolectomy. Upon recovery, the doctor-patient requested that no steps be taken to prolong his life if he suffered another cardiovascular collapse. He wrote an authorization to this effect for the hospital records. Viewing his pain as too much to bear given his dismal prospects, he asked to be allowed to die, under specified conditions. However, he did not ask to be killed.[1]

2 In [another case] a newborn with Down syndrome needed an operation to correct a tracheoesophageal fistula. The parents and physicians determined that survival was not in this infant's best interests and decided to allow the infant to die rather than to perform an operation. In these and other cases, we need to ask whether certain actions, such as intentionally not attempting to save the patient after a cardiovascular collapse and not performing an operation, can legitimately be described as ''allowing to die'' or ''letting die'' rather than ''killing,'' and whether such actions are justifiable.

3 For many people, it is important both to distinguish between killing and letting die and to prohibit the former while authorizing the latter in some cases. After prohibiting ''mercy killing'' or the ''intentional termination of the life of one human being by another,'' the American Medical Association House of Delegates in 1973 held that cessation of treatment is morally justified when the patient or the patient's immediate family, with the advice and judgment of the physician, decides to withhold or withdraw ''extraordinary means to prolong the life of the body when there is irrefutable evidence that biological death is imminent.''[2] Although several terms in this statement, including *extraordinary, irrefutable,* and *imminent,* need careful examination, the statement clearly permits some instances of intentional allowing to die by withholding or stopping treatment, but it excludes killing. Whether letting particular patients die is morally acceptable depends in this policy on several factors. But if their deaths in identical circumstances were to involve killing rather than being merely allowed to die, they are never justifiable, according to the guidelines.

Attacks on the Distinction Between Killing and Letting Die

4 In recent years, the distinction between killing and letting die has come under frequent attack. Some critics focus on developments in biomedical technology that appear to make it conceptually difficult to classify acts as instances either of killing or of letting die. Stopping a respirator is a standard example of this problem. Other critics dismiss the distinction as a conceptual quibble without moral significance.

5 Before we explore and assess the arguments for and against this distinction, we note that acceptance or rejection of the conceptual distinction does not by itself determine moral conclusions about particular cases. For instance, one might deny that there is a clear conceptual difference between killing and letting die, while at the same time holding either that some cases of so-called killing and letting die are morally permissible or that all cases are morally impermissible. It is also possible to affirm the distinction and yet to hold that many cases of letting die and all cases of killing are morally wrong. Even if the distinction is morally significant, the labels ''killing'' and ''letting die''

should not be used to dictate moral conclusions about particular cases. For example, it would be absurd to affirm the moral significance of the distinction and then to accept all cases of letting die as morally fitting. Even instances of letting die must meet other criteria such as the balance of benefits over burdens to the patient, and some cases of allowed death involve egregious negligence.

6 In a widely discussed argument for rejecting both the distinction between active and passive euthanasia and the AMA policy statement, James Rachels contends that killing is not, in itself, worse than letting die.[3] [This article appears on p. 80 of this book.] That is, the "bare difference" between acts of killing and acts of letting die is not in itself a morally relevant difference. Rachels argues that if it is morally permissible to act intentionally so that a person dies, then the only morally significant question about how death may occur concerns which method will minimize the person's suffering. Part of Rachels's strategy is to sketch two cases that differ only in that one involves killing while the other involves allowing to die. He contends that if there is no morally relevant difference between these cases, the bare difference between acts of killing and allowing to die cannot be morally relevant. In his two cases, two young men, Smith and Jones, want their six-year-old cousins dead so that they can gain inheritances. Smith drowns his cousin while the boy is taking a bath. Jones plans to drown his cousin, but as he enters the bathroom he sees the boy slip and hit his head. Jones stands by, doing nothing, while the boy drowns. Thus, Smith killed his cousin, but Jones merely allowed his cousin to die.

7 While we agree with Rachels that these acts are equally reprehensible because of the agents' motives and actions, we do not accept his conclusion that these examples show that the distinction between killing and letting die is morally irrelevant. Several rejoinders to Rachels are in order. First, Rachels's cases and the cessations of treatment envisioned by the AMA are so markedly disanalogous that Rachels's argument is misdirected. In some cases of unjustified acts, including both of Rachels's examples, we are not interested in moral distinctions per se. As Richard Trammell points out, some examples have a "masking" or "sledgehammer" effect; the fact that "one cannot distinguish the taste of two wines when both are mixed with green persimmon juice, does not imply that there is no distinction between the wines."[4] Because Rachels's examples involve two morally unjustified acts by agents whose motives and intentions are despicable, it is not surprising that some other features of their situations, such as killing and letting die, do not seem morally compelling considerations in the circumstances.

8 Second, in Rachels's cases Smith and Jones are morally responsible and morally blameworthy for the deaths of their respective cousins, even if Jones, who allowed his cousin to drown, is not causally responsible. The law might find only Smith, who killed his cousin, guilty of homicide (because of the law's theory of proximate cause), but morality condemns both actions alike because of the agents' commissions and omissions. We find Jones's actions reprehensible because he could and morally should have rescued the child. Even if he had no other special duties to the child, the obligation of beneficence requires affirmative action in such a case.

9 Third, the point of the cases envisioned by the AMA is not inconsistent with Rachels's points. The AMA's central claim is that the physician is always morally prohibited from killing patients but is not morally bound to preserve life in all cases. According to the AMA, the physician has a right and perhaps a duty to stop treatment if and only if three conditions are met: (1) the life of the body is being preserved by extraordinary means, (2) there is irrefutable evidence that biological death is imminent, and (3) the patient or the family consents. While Rachels's cases involve two unjustified actions, one of killing and the other of letting die, the AMA statement distinguishes cases of unjustified killing from cases of justified letting die. The AMA statement does not claim that the moral difference is entirely predicated on the distinction between killing and letting die. It also does not imply that the bare difference between (passive) letting die and (active) killing is the major difference or a morally sufficient difference to distinguish the justified from the unjustified cases. The point is rather that the justified actions in medicine are confined to (passive) letting die.

10 The AMA statement holds that ''mercy killing'' in medicine is unjustified in all circumstances, but it holds neither that letting die is right in all circumstances nor that killing outside medicine is always wrong. For an act that results in an earlier death for the patient to be justified, it is necessary that it be an act of letting die, but this condition is not sufficient to justify the act; nor is the bare fact of an act's being a killing sufficient to make the act wrong. This AMA declaration is meant to control conduct exclusively in the context of the physician-patient relationship.

11 Even if the distinction between killing and letting die is morally irrelevant in some contexts, it does not follow that it is morally irrelevant in all contexts. Although Rachels does effectively undermine all attempts to rest moral judgments about ending life on the ''bare difference'' between killing and letting die, his target may nonetheless be made of straw. Many philosophers and theologians have argued that there are independent moral, religious, and other reasons both for defending the distinction and for prohibiting killing while authorizing allowing to die in some circumstances or based on some motives.

12 One theologian has argued, for example, that we can discern the moral significance of the distinction between killing and letting die by ''placing it in the religious context out of which it grew.''[5] That context is the biblical story of God's actions toward his creatures. In that context it makes sense to talk about ''placing patients in God's hands,'' just as it is important not to usurp God's prerogatives by desperately struggling to prolong life when the patient is irreversibly dying. But even if the distinction between killing and letting die originated within a religious context, and even if it makes more sense in that context than in some others, it can be defended on nontheological grounds without being reduced to a claim about a ''bare difference.'' We turn next to this defense of the distinction.

A Defense of the Distinction Between Killing and Letting Die

13 Even if there are sufficient reasons in some cases to warrant mercy killing, there may also be good reasons to retain the distinction between killing and letting die and to

maintain our current practices against killing *in medicine,* albeit with some clarifications and modifications. We defend this perspective in this section.

14 ***Acts and Practices.*** The most important arguments for the distinction between killing and letting die depend on a distinction between acts and practices.[6] It is one thing to justify an act; it is another to justify a general practice. As we saw in our examination of rule utilitarianism and rule deontology, many beliefs about principles and consequences are applied to rules rather than directly to acts. For example, we might justify a rule of confidentiality because it encourages people to seek therapy and because it promotes respect for persons and their privacy, although such a rule might lead to undesirable results in particular cases. Likewise, a rule that prohibits ''active killing'' while permitting some ''allowed deaths'' may be justifiable, even if it excludes some particular acts of killing that in themselves are justifiable. For example, the rule would not permit us to kill a patient who suffers from terrible pain, who will probably die within three weeks, and who rationally asks for a merciful assisted death. In order to maintain a viable practice that expresses our principles and avoids seriously undesirable consequences, it may be necessary to prohibit some acts that would not otherwise be wrong. Thus, although particular acts of killing may not violate the obligation of nonmaleficence and may be humane and compassionate, a policy that authorizes killing in medicine—in even a few cases—stands to violate the obligation of nonmaleficence by creating a grave risk of harm in many cases.

15 The prohibition of killing even for ''mercy'' expresses principles and supports practices that provide a basis of trust between patients and health-care professionals. When we trust such professionals, we expect them to promote our welfare and to do us no harm without a prospect of benefit as well as our consent. Trust, or the attitude of confidence and reliance placed in persons and institutions, can exist with little actual evidence of real trustworthiness (the quality or character trait of reliability, which is closely associated with fidelity and loyalty). The prohibition of killing is an attempt to promote a solid basis for trust in the role of caring for patients and protecting them from harm. This prohibition is both instrumentally and symbolically important, and its removal could weaken a set of practices and restraints that we cannot easily replace.[7]

16 ***Wedge or Slippery Slope Arguments.*** This last argument—a wedge or slippery slope argument—is plausible but needs to be stated carefully. Because of the widespread misuses of such arguments in biomedical ethics (and perhaps because of their heavily metaphorical character—''the leading, entering, or thin edge of the wedge,'' ''the first step on the slippery slope,'' ''the foot in the door,'' and ''the camel's nose under the tent''), there is a tendency to dismiss them whenever they are offered. However, as expressions of the principle of nonmaleficence, they are defensible in some cases.[8] They also force us to consider whether unacceptable harms may result from attractive and apparently innocent first steps. All of the metaphors invoked in this connection are used to express the conviction that legitimation of some forms of action, such as active voluntary euthanasia, will lead to other acts or practices that are morally objectionable

even if some individual acts of this type are acceptable in themselves. The claim is that accepting the act in question would cross a line that has already been drawn against killing; and once that line has been crossed, it will not be possible to draw it again to preclude unacceptable acts or practices.

17 Wedge or slippery slope arguments appear in two versions: *logical-conceptual* and *psychological-sociological.* The first version maintains that there is no defensible line between acts leading to legitimate deaths and those leading to illegitimate deaths, unless there is a clear distinction sustained by moral reasons. A justification offered for one sort of act that strikes us as right may logically support another sort of act that strikes us as wrong. For example, some justifications offered for abortion logically imply a justification of infanticide under relevantly similar circumstances, and yet the act of infanticide seems wrong (to defenders of the similar act of abortion).

18 This first version of the wedge argument derives its power from the principle of universalizability discussed [elsewhere]. That principle commits us to ethical consistency and thus to judging relevantly similar cases in a similar way. If we judge X to be right, and we can point to no morally relevant dissimilarities between X and Y, then we logically cannot judge Y to be wrong. This first version of the wedge argument focuses on how support for one sort of action that seems acceptable logically implies support for another unacceptable action, where it is not possible in principle to identify morally relevant differences.[9]

19 Defenders of the prohibition of mercy killing sometimes appeal to this version of the wedge argument in the following way. Whereas we morally justify killing aggressors in self-defense and war, these killings do not threaten the following rule, which is derived from the principle of nonmaleficence: Do not directly kill innocent persons. Killing in self-defense or war is justified because the persons killed are not innocent. By contrast, if we once support the killing of innocent persons in medical settings, there is no clear way to limit the killing to legitimate cases of mercy directed at appropriate parties, because there will be no way to distinguish these parties from the vulnerable, the defenseless, the socially nonproductive, and the like.

20 Wedge arguments of this type may not be as damaging as they may seem at first. As Rachels correctly contends, "there obviously are good reasons for objecting to killing patients in order to get away for the weekend—or for even more respectable purposes, such as securing organs for transplantation—which do not apply to killing in order to put the patient out of extreme agony."[10] In other words, the counterreply is that relevant distinctions can be drawn, and we are not subject to uncontrollable implications from general principles. This first version of the wedge argument thus does not assist supporters of the distinction between killing and letting die as much as they might suppose. Indeed, it can be used against them: If it is rational and morally defensible to allow patients to die under conditions X, Y, and Z, it is rational and morally defensible to kill them under those same conditions. If it is in their best interests to die, it is (prima facie) irrelevant how death is brought about. Rachels makes a similar point when he argues that reliance on the distinction between killing and letting die may lead to decisions about life and death made on irrelevant grounds—such as whether the patient will

or will not die without certain forms of treatment—instead of being made in terms of the patient's best interests.[11]

21 For example, [the Down syndrome baby mentioned above] suffering from several defects needs an operation to correct a tracheoesophageal fistula; otherwise the baby will die. A baby suffering from those same defects but without the fistula may be kept alive, while the baby who needs the operation may be allowed to die. It is possible to argue that we need to determine the conditions under which death is in the baby's best interests and then choose to kill or to let die by determining which means would be more humane and compassionate in the circumstances. In the now famous Johns Hopkins Hospital case, an infant with Down syndrome and duodenal atresia was placed in a back room and died eleven days later of dehydration and starvation. This process of dying, which senior physicians had recommended against, was extremely difficult for all the parties involved, particularly the nurses. If the decision makers legitimately determine that a patient would be better off dead (we think the parties mistakenly came to this conclusion in these two cases), how could an act of killing violate the patient's interests if the patient will not die when artificial treatment is discontinued? A morally irrelevant factor would be allowed to dictate the outcome, and this would violate the rule of universalizability. This first version of the wedge or slippery slope argument, then, does not offer a clear and compelling reason to oppose mercy killing.

22 By contrast, the causal-empirical version does offer a strong reason for maintaining the distinction between killing and letting die. This psychological-sociological version focuses on what the wedge is driven into by examining the society and culture in order to determine the probable impact of making exceptions to rules or changing rules in a more permissive direction. If certain restraints against killing are removed, a moral decline might result, because various psychological or social forces make it unlikely that people will draw distinctions that are, in principle, clear and defensible. For example, in some settings it is plausible to argue that (1) to authorize killing patients for their own benefit when they are suffering excruciating pain or have a bleak future could open the door to a policy of killing patients for the sake of social benefits such as reducing financial burdens, and that (2) voluntary euthanasia might open the door to nonvoluntary and perhaps involuntary euthanasia.

23 These arguments do not depend on the conceptual version of the wedge or slippery slope arguments, because there are clear and defensible distinctions, rooted in moral principles, between voluntary and involuntary euthanasia and between killing patients at their request for their own benefit and killing them without their request for social benefits. Nevertheless, if there are psychological and social forces such as racism, an increasing number of handicapped newborns who survive at large expense to the public, or a growing number of aging persons with medical problems that require larger and larger proportions of a society's financial resources, this wedge argument becomes more compelling. We acknowledge that the success or failure of the argument depends on admittedly speculative predictions of a progressive erosion of moral restraints because of psychological or sociological forces; those, including the present authors, who accept

this causal version of the wedge argument need a premise on the order of "better safe than sorry."

24 The main reservation expressed in this argument is the following. If rules permitting mercy killing were once introduced, society might gradually move in the direction of nonvoluntary and perhaps involuntary euthanasia—for example, in the form of killing handicapped newborns to avoid social and familial burdens. There could be a general reduction of respect for human life as a result of the official removal of barriers to killing. Rules against killing in a moral code are not isolated fragments; they are threads in a fabric of rules, drawn in part from nonmaleficence, that support respect for human life. The more threads we remove, the weaker the fabric becomes. If we focus on attitudes and not merely rules, the general attitude of respect for life may be eroded by shifts in particular areas. Determination of the likelihood of such an erosion depends not only on the connectedness of rules and attitudes but also on operative forces in the society.

25 ***The Nazi Analogy.*** In debates about euthanasia, the holocaust under Nazi rule continues to serve as a powerful vision of the bottom of the slippery slope for a society that adopts mercy killing. Although the analogies are sometimes overplayed, this period left a string of inadequately answered questions about euthanasia. After the Nuremberg trial of German physicians, an American physician, Leo Alexander, argued that the Nazis started by accepting euthanasia for the incurably ill and then moved on to their policies of genocide:

> Whatever proportions [the Nazi] crimes finally assumed, it became evident to all who investigated them that they had started from small beginnings. The beginnings at first were merely a subtle shift in emphasis in the basic attitude of the physicians. It started with the acceptance of the attitude, basic in the euthanasia movement, that there is such a thing as life not worthy to be lived. This attitude in its early stages concerned itself merely with the severely and chronically sick. Gradually the sphere of those to be included in this category was enlarged to encompass the socially unproductive, the ideologically unwanted, the racially unwanted and finally all non-Germans. But it is important to realize that the infinitely small wedged-in lever from which this entire trend of mind received its impetus was the attitude toward the nonrehabilitatable sick.[12]

26 This image of "small beginnings" also appears in Robert Lifton's study of Nazi physicians, which describes the first steps as well as the final horror of implementing the general principle of "life unworthy of life" in an effort to "uncover psychological conditions conducive to evil."[13] Lifton notes that "prior to Auschwitz and the other death camps, the Nazis established a policy of direct medical killing: that is, killing arranged within medical channels, by means of medical decisions, and carried out by doctors and their assistants." Crucial to the program was the removal of a social and psychological barrier against killing through the "medicalization of killing," where

killing was justified in the name of healing the society, a "therapeutic imperative." Lifton argues that although this program was called euthanasia, the term simply "camouflaged mass murder."

27 Contemporary proponents of mercy killing often properly insist that the rationale of the Nazi program was racist ideology, not respect for personal wishes and interests. They dispute the appropriateness of the Nazi analogy, because the Nazis concentrated on nonvoluntary and especially involuntary killing against the wishes of the victims—a program inappropriately labeled euthanasia, or good death. Thus, many argue, it is not the case that the Nazis took one step on the slippery slope and then could not stop. Rather, their ideology drove them to extremes.[14] Even if they had not changed their social and legal rules against killing innocent persons, their ideology encouraged redefining the "innocent" to exclude people they viewed as social threats. Hence, critics of the Nazi analogy contend, rules against mercy killing are neither necessary nor sufficient to prevent such a horrible state of affairs.

28 We accept this argument, but we also maintain that rules against killing, including mercy killing, are important in order to protect vital social practices and to maintain attitudes of respect for life, even if it is difficult to determine the degree of risk. This argument is not meant to suggest that mercy killing is always wrong. Rules against killing, like all moral rules, are prima facie, not absolute. We are now concentrating on rules at the level of social policy, professional ethics, and institutional directives. At this level, traditional restraints against killing are justifiable and appropriate.[15] In a particular case, the prima facie duty to refrain from killing may be outweighed by the prima facie duties to relieve suffering or to respect patients' autonomous wishes. Nevertheless, the empirical version of the wedge argument, in combination with some elements of the conceptual version and with other considerations of consequences, supports a strong rule of practice against mercy killing, backed by legal, social, and professional sanctions designed to caution health professionals and family members against expedient or ill-considered resort to killing.

29 An example of mercy killing that prohibitory rules should help deter was reported in the *Journal of the American Medical Association* in January 1988 under the provocative title "It's Over, Debbie."[16] A gynecology resident rotating through a large private hospital was awakened by a telephone call from a nurse who told him that a patient on the gynecologic-oncology unit, not the resident's usual duty station, was having difficulty getting rest. The chart at the nurses' station provided some details. A twenty-year-old woman named Debbie who was dying of ovarian cancer was experiencing unrelenting vomiting, apparently as a result of the alcohol drip administered for sedation (a procedure that some have criticized). The woman was emaciated, weighed eighty pounds, had an intravenous line, was receiving nasal oxygen, and was sitting in bed suffering from severe air hunger. She had not eaten or slept in two days, and she was receiving only supportive care because she had not responded to chemotherapy. The patient's only words to the resident were, "Let's get this over with." It was not reported whether the middle-aged female visitor in the room made any comments. After having the nurse draw twenty milligrams of morphine sulfate into a syringe, the resident took

it into the room and injected it intravenously into the patient after telling the two women that it ''would let her rest'' and ''to say good-bye.'' The patient died within a few minutes.

30 If this is an actual case—and doubts have been voiced about its authenticity—the resident acted rashly. Other medications could perhaps have relieved the patient's pain and suffering and enabled her to rest comfortably. The resident's intention was to kill the patient out of ''mercy,'' not simply to provide comfort at the risk of hastening her death. But in the absence of any previous contact with the patient, the resident had no basis for interpreting her words as a request to be killed, and he or she (the gender of the resident was not reported) did not consult with anyone else before making a quick, momentous, and irreversible decision.

31 ***Mercy Killing and the Practice of Medicine.*** In addition to fears of abuse of individuals such as the mentally disabled who cannot consent, there are other legitimate fears. Consider the following two types of wrongly diagnosed patients:[17]

1. Patients who are wrongly diagnosed as hopeless and who will survive if a treatment is ceased (in order to allow a natural death)
2. Patients who are wrongly diagnosed as hopeless and who will survive only if the treatment is *not* ceased (in order to allow a natural death)

If a social rule that allows some patients to die were in effect, doctors and families who followed it would only lose patients in the second category. But if killings were permitted, at least some of the patients in the first category would be needlessly lost. Thus, a rule prohibiting killing would save some more lives that would be lost if both killing and allowing to die were permitted. Such a consequence is not a decisive reason for a policy of (only) allowing to die, because the numbers in categories 1 and 2 are likely to be small, and other reasons for killing, such as extreme pain and autonomous choice, might be weighty. But it is a morally relevant reason for the policy.

32 Proponents of the practice of killing certain patients sometimes appeal to a range of exceptional cases that override normal constraints against killing. Among the strongest reasons for killing some patients is to relieve unbearable and uncontrollable pain and suffering. No one would deny that pain and suffering can so ravage and dehumanize patients that death appears to be in their best interests. Prolonging life and refusing to kill in such circumstances may appear to be cruel and to violate the obligation of nonmaleficence. Often proponents of mercy killing appeal to nonmedical situations to show that killing may be more humane and compassionate than letting die—as, for example, in the case of a soldier mortally wounded on the battlefield or an accident victim inextricably trapped in a burning vehicle who cries out for a merciful death. In such tragic situations the present authors are reluctant to say that those who kill at the behest of the victim act wrongly. At least some such persons act justifiably and commendably.

33 There are, nevertheless, serious objections to building into medical practice an explicit exception that licenses physicians to kill their patients in order to relieve uncontrollable pain and suffering. It is not clear that many, if any, cases in medical practice are relevantly similar to the person trapped in a burning wreck. In medical practice the physician can usually relieve pain and make a patient comfortable without killing, or intending to kill, the patient, even if the medications may hasten death. We agree that clinicians have a moral obligation, based on nonmaleficence, beneficence, and autonomy, to relieve patients' pain in accord with their wishes and interests. However, it is important to preserve the distinction between the intention to relieve pain at the risk of hastening death and the intention to kill in order to relieve pain, however difficult it will be in borderline cases to apply the distinction. In the case of Debbie presented above, the medical resident intended to kill Debbie through the large dose of morphine sulfate in order to relieve her pain and give her rest. He or she failed to pursue other available measures that could have relieved Debbie's pain and enabled her to rest with the risk of hastened death.

34 Clinicians also have a moral obligation to inform patients of alternative approaches, such as a hospice, which assign a high priority to the relief of pain and suffering. The increased risk of addiction has often been overestimated and unduly feared in the care of terminally ill patients.[18] However, public policy-makers in the United States have resisted legalizing heroin, a powerful pain-killer, even in the care of terminally ill cancer patients, because of their fear of the harmful consequences that might flow from such an act, including not only addiction of surviving patients but also the legitimation of heroin and the possibility of abuses. Yet heroin has been used for terminally ill cancer patients for several years in Great Britain without evidence of uncontrollable problems. We thus see no merit in the societal prohibition of the use of heroin to relieve pain in terminally ill cancer patients. However, the main point is that clinicians already have under their control measures of pain relief that are both legal and generally effective. If clinicians took more seriously their obligation to relieve pain, the arguments for mercy killing from unbearable pain would be less powerful.[19]

35 Another reason for not giving physicians a license to kill is that we should be reluctant to construct a social or professional ethic on borderline situations and emergency cases, even if medical practitioners do confront some cases of unmanageable pain and suffering. It is dangerous to generalize from emergencies, because hard cases may make bad social and professional ethics as well as bad law. As Charles Fried writes,

> The concept of emergency is only a tolerable moral concept if somehow we can truly think of it as exceptional, if we can truly think of it as a circumstance that, far from defying our usual moral universe, suspends it for a limited time and thus suspends usual moral principles. It is when emergencies become usual that we are threatened with moral disintegration, dehumanization.[20]

36 ***Exceptional Cases.*** There are, we believe, ways to accept acts of killing in exceptional circumstances without altering the rules of practice in order to accommodate

them. Juries often find those who kill their suffering relatives not guilty by reason of temporary insanity. Consider a famous case in New Jersey.[21] In June 1973, George Zygmaniak was in a motorcycle accident that left him paralyzed from the neck down. The paralysis was considered to be irreversible, and Zygmaniak begged his brother to kill him. Three days later, his brother brought a sawed-off shotgun to the hospital and shot Zygmaniak in the head, after having said, "Close your eyes now, I'm going to shoot you." A judgment of temporary insanity in this case springs from the lack of a legal channel to say the act was, under the circumstances, justifiable. Verdicts such as "not guilty by reason of temporary insanity" function under law to excuse the agent by finding (somewhat implausibly) that he or she lacked the conditions of responsibility necessary to be legally guilty.

37 The legal rule against killing can be maintained even if physicians and others sometimes find that it is morally permissible to engage in justified conscientious or civil disobedience against those rules. This is another way of acknowledging that there can be justified exceptions to enforceable rules against killing.[22] The conditions that justify conscientious refusals to follow the rule against killing patients are too complex and diverse to be considered here, but the important point is that if pain and suffering of a certain magnitude can in principle justify active killing, then only acts of conscientious refusal to follow the rule of practice will be justified (as long as certain other conditions are met), not fundamental changes in the rule itself. We do not invoke the language of "conscientious refusal" to evade acceptance of the justifiability of active killing in the difficult cases. [Elsewhere], we present an actual case of nonvoluntary active killing by a physician that we believe was justified. We also do not believe that our position commits us to side primarily with utilitarians against deontological constraints on killing. Nothing in deontological rules of prima facie obligation prohibits killing under all possible circumstances, even for health-care professionals.

38 Finally, we need to ask which side in the debate has the burden of proof—the proponents or the opponents of a practice of selective killing. One prominent view is that supporters of the current practice of prohibiting killing bear the burden of proof because the prohibition of voluntary euthanasia infringes liberty and autonomy.[23] However, a policy of voluntary euthanasia, based on either a negative right to die (a right to noninterference) or a positive right to die (a right to be killed), would involve such a change in society's vision of the medical profession and in medical attitudes that a shift in the burden of proof to the proponents of change seems to us essential. We have argued that the prohibition of killing expresses important moral principles and attitudes whose loss, or serious alteration, could have major negative consequences. Because the current practice of prohibiting killing while accepting some "allowed deaths" has served us well, if not perfectly, it should be altered only with the utmost caution. Lines are not easy to draw and maintain, but in general we have been able to respect the line between killing and letting die in medical practice. Before we undertake any major changes, we need more evidence than we now have that the changes are needed in order to avoid important harms or secure important benefits and that the good effects will outweigh the bad effects.

Notes

1. See W. St. C. Symmers, Sr., ''Not Allowed to Die,'' *British Medical Journal* 1 (1968): 442.
2. This 1973 statement, which was distributed by the AMA in reproduced typescript, is reprinted in James Rachels, *The End of Life: Euthanasia and Morality* (Oxford: Oxford University Press, 1986), pp. 88, 192–93.
3. James Rachels, ''Active and Passive Euthanasia,'' *New England Journal of Medicine* 292 (1975): 78–80. For valuable articles on the distinction between killing and letting die, see Steinbock, *Killing and Letting Die;* and John Ladd, ed., *Ethical Issues Relating to Life and Death* (New York: Oxford University Press, 1979).
4. Richard L. Trammell, ''Saving Life and Taking Life,'' *Journal of Philosophy* 72 (1975): 131–37.
5. Gilbert Meilaender, ''The Distinction between Killing and Allowing to Die,'' *Theological Studies* 37 (1976): 467–70.
6. This distinction and our arguments are indebted to John Rawls, ''Two Concepts of Rules,'' *Philosophical Review* 64 (1955): 3–32.
7. See G. J. Hughes, S. J., ''Killing and Letting Die,'' *The Month* 236 (1975): 42–45; and David Louisell, ''Euthanasia and Biothanasia: On Dying and Killing.'' *Linacre Quarterly* 40 (1973): 234–58.
8. For fuller discussions, see Sissela Bok, ''The Leading Edge of the Wedge,'' *Hastings Center Report* 1 (December 1971): 8–10; Paul Ramsey, ''The Wedge: Not So Simple,'' *Hastings Center Report* 1 (December 1971): 11–12; Trudy Govier, ''What's Wrong with Slippery Slope Arguments?'' *Canadian Journal of Philosophy* 12 (June 1982): 303–16; Frederick Schauer, ''Slippery Slopes,'' *Harvard Law Review* 99 (1985): 361–83; and Bernard Williams, ''Which Slopes are Slippery?'' in *Moral Dilemmas in Modern Medicine,* ed. Michael Lockwood (Oxford: Oxford University Press, 1985), pp. 126–37. Williams further distinguishes two types of slippery slope argument: the *horrible result* argument objects to what is at the bottom of the slope; the *arbitrary result* argument objects to the fact that it is a slope and that there is no nonarbitrary way to get off. Even critics of the application of the slippery slope argument in debates about euthanasia may recognize that it has what James Rachels calls a ''grain of truth,'' in that the reasons that support voluntary euthanasia may also support some forms of nonvoluntary euthanasia. However, he insists that they do not push toward acceptance of involuntary euthanasia. Rachels, *The End of Life,* chap. 10.
9. See Paul Ramsey, *Ethics at the Edges of Life* (New Haven: Yale University Press, 1978), pp. 306–7.
10. James Rachels, ''Medical Ethics and the Rule against Killing: Comments on Professor Hare's Paper,'' in *Philosophical Medical Ethics,* ed. Spicker and Engelhardt, p. 65.
11. Rachels, ''Active and Passive Euthanasia.''
12. Leo Alexander, ''Medical Science under Dictatorship,'' *New England Journal of Medicine* 241 (1949): 39–47.
13. Robert Jay Lifton, *The Nazi Doctors: Medical Killing and the Psychology of Genocide* (New York: Basic Books, 1986).
14. See Rachels, *The End of Life.* For the controversy about the appropriateness of the Nazi analogy, see the special supplement on ''Biomedical Ethics and the Shadow of Nazism,'' *Hastings Center Report* 6 (1976), esp. the article by Lucy Dawidowicz.
15. For an important debate about these issues, see Yale Kamisar, ''Some Non-religious Views against Proposed 'Mercy-Killing' Legislation,'' *Minnesota Law Review* 42 (1958); and Glanville Williams, ''Mercy-Killing' Legislation—A Rejoinder,'' *Minnesota Law Review* 43 (1958). For the movement to legalize active, voluntary euthanasia in the Netherlands, see ''Final Report of the Netherlands State Commission on Euthanasia: An English Summary,'' *Bioethics* 1 (1987): 156–62; and J. K. M. Gevers, ''Legal Developments Concerning Active Euthanasia on Request in the Netherlands,'' *Bioethics* 1 (1987): 163–74.
16. ''It's Over, Debbie,'' *Journal of the American Medical Association* 259 (1988): 272.
17. We owe most of this argument to James Rachels.
18. Marcia Angell, ''The Quality of Mercy,'' *New England Journal of Medicine* 306 (1982): 98–99.
19. Eric J. Cassell, ''The Nature of Suffering and the Goods of Medicine,'' *New England Journal of Medicine* 306 (1982): 639–45.
20. Charles Fried, ''Rights and Health Care—Beyond Equity and Efficiency,'' *New England Journal of Medicine* 293 (1975): 245.
21. For a discussion of this case, see Paige Mitchell, *Act of Love: The Killing of George Zygmaniak* (New York: Knopf, 1976).

22. See Ramsey, *Ethics at the Edges of Life,* p. 217; and Robert Veatch, *Death, Dying, and the Biological Revolution* (New Haven: Yale University Press, 1976), p. 97.
23. See Antony Flew, "The Principle of Euthanasia," in *Euthanasia and the Right to Death: The Case of Voluntary Euthanasia,* ed. A. B. Downing (London: Peter Owen, 1969), pp. 30–48; and H. Tristram Engelhardt, Jr., *The Foundations of Bioethics* (New York: Oxford University Press, 1986), esp. chap. 7.

Questions for Analysis

1. In their analysis of the ethical problems associated with the distinction between killing and letting die, Beauchamp and Childress responded to James Rachels's essay (p. 80) and in particular to his analogy based on the stories of Smith and Jones. How do they counter Rachels's use of this analogy? Is their objection persuasive? Do they call attention to both the power and the weakness of analogies? Explain.
2. Beauchamp and Childress argue that there is a distinction between killing and letting die. What arguments do they offer to defend that position? Do you find their arguments persuasive? Easy to follow?
3. Beauchamp and Childress devote major sections of this essay to "Wedge or Slippery Slope Arguments" and "The Nazi Analogy." What position do they take in these sections? Do they fully accept or reject the wedge or slippery slope argument or the Nazi analogy? Do their discussions in these sections help make their entire essay more persuasive? Explain.
4. Explain the "concept of emergency" as it is used by Beauchamp and Childress (and by Charles Fried in Paragraph 35) and the distinction between "acts" and "rules of practice." How do they use these concepts to argue against the practice of active euthanasia and yet allow for the possibility that it might be the right thing to do?
5. Carefully reconsider the position taken by both Rachels and by Beauchamp and Childress. Are their attitudes toward life and death very far apart? On what do they agree? On what do they disagree?

Do Parents Have the Right to Reject Treatment for Infants with Birth Defects?

Earl E. Shelp

Deciding the Fate of Critically Ill Newborns

(1986)

Earl E. Shelp (b. 1947) is a theologian and author of *Born to Die: Deciding the Fate of Critically Ill Newborns.* The essay printed here is taken from that book published by The Free Press.

1 Parents of severely diseased or defective newborns may reasonably choose not to authorize life-prolonging interventions when one of several conditions obtain: (1) extended life is reasonably judged not to constitute a net benefit to the infant; (2) it is reasonably believed that the infant's condition is such that the capacities sufficient for a minimal independent existence of personhood in a strict sense cannot be attained; or (3) the costs to other persons, especially parents and family, are sufficient to defeat customary duties of beneficence toward a particular human infant.

2 Moral support for parental discretion in these matters is further strengthened by an understanding of human neonates as persons in a social sense, rather than as persons in a strict sense. Persons in a strict sense are moral agents, morally self-determining, unqualified members of the moral community, subjects of duties of beneficence, and bearers of rights to forebearance. Newborn human infants, normal or impaired, do not possess the properties or capacities sufficient for unqualified membership in the moral community, are not morally self-determining, or bearers of rights and duties, including those of forebearance and beneficence. Nevertheless, newborn infants can be understood as persons in a social sense because of their role in the moral order. The rights and duties they will bear when they become persons are held in trust for them and exercised in their behalf by parents, in normal circumstances, until a future time and for a future person yet to develop.

3 This view of parental responsibility and the moral status of newborn humans entails a commensurate understanding of parental authority. This is to say that parents are presumed to be authorities and to have authority to determine the care and nurture of their incompetent children. This authority would encompass judgments regarding the medical care of imperiled newborns that are reasonable under the circumstances and guided by relevant moral principles as interpreted by the particular moral community of which the parents are a part. These decisions warrant respect within a society that acknowledges its pluralism and protects the freedom of particular moral communities and agents to create, discover, and pursue their concrete view of the good. In these situations of reproductive tragedy, parents may conclude, on the basis of their competent understanding of the relevant medical facts, and in accord with their particular moral commitments, that death for an imperiled newborn would be a grace or otherwise morally justified. As the analysis of the alleged moral distinction between killing and letting die showed, a merciful and aesthetic death brought about by direct human intervention is as morally licit in these circumstances as standing by while the mortal process continues unhindered. The role of neonatologists and other members of the neonatal team is that of a sustaining presence, providing competent diagnoses and prognoses based on the best available medical evidence. Understood in this fashion, the neonatal medical team is free to cooperate with parental decisions to the degree that their cooperation does not violate their own moral commitments. Further, public policies that endeavor to override reasonable parental decisions in these matters are unjustified. They misperceive the proper role of the state with regard to parents and this class of infants, and the legal protections appropriate to the moral status of imperiled neonates.

4 These arguments support a general policy of tolerance of and respect for reasonable parental decisions regarding the treatment, nontreatment, or means of death for that class of severely diseased or defective newborns who satisfy at least one of the several conditions identified above. More specific policies are not morally justified according to the arguments provided here. Neither are they practical. The relevant circumstances of all possible cases are not predictable. Further, it would be difficult to keep them current with the ever-changing capacities of medicine to alter nature's course in these instances.

5 The defense of parental responsibility and authority with regard to treatment decisions for severely diseased or defective newborns provided here is not intended to disregard or disrespect the value of newborn human life. Neither have I intended to demean or ridicule moral senses and commitments different from those defended [elsewhere]. Rather, the analyses of dilemmas in neonatology provided here are intended to place them in a moral perspective grounded in an understanding of relevant moral principles, informed by relevant research in custom, medicine, and law, and sensitive to the emotional dimensions of these tragic events.

6 These analyses and conclusions surely are controversial, but, in my judgment, they are defensible and superior to proposals to deprive parents of the responsibility and authority to make reasonable decisions regarding the medical care of their threatened infant. Specific counsel about what to do with very low birth weight, premature, Down syndrome, or spina bifida infants, for example, has not been provided. The burden of

decisions in these cases rests properly on responsible parents who are free to make reasonable decisions consistent with their particular moral commitments. Neither has specific direction been given to medical personnel. As a sustaining presence they are enabled to sojourn with parents and newborn down a path often marked by ambivalence, uncertainty, and, perhaps paradoxically, loyalty to the good and the right as it is reasonably discerned by parents in complex and vexing circumstances. In short, the general policy advocated [here] is one that respects and defends the freedom of present moral agents, regardless of their specific role in situations of reproductive tragedy, to make reasonable decisions and to act in accord with the vision and norms of the particular moral community of which they are a part.

7 The moral issues and questions related to the medical treatment of imperiled newborn infants will not be settled for everyone by the positions taken [here]. Further, new dilemmas will emerge as the present limits of neonatal medicine to rescue anomalous newborns are broken. The moral question of whether we ought to do what we can do in every instance of reproductive tragedy will be asked again and again: at times for infants and conditions to which we have become accustomed, (e.g., Down syndrome with operable congenital defects); at other times, for treatments that are novel or new (e.g., cross-species transplantation of vital organs). No effort has been made to specify answers for either class of cases. Rather, as I have maintained throughout these pages, the wisdom of particular moral communities and agents are the places to turn for specific guidance. The approach taken here is one in which freedom for moral agents is a value and a constraint upon what may be forced upon present persons without their consent. The moral visions and derived norms of particular communities that generate reasonable choices and conduct in response to complex and perplexing instances of human reproduction warrant respect in a moral pluralism where a single, compelling, concrete view of the good for a particular infant, family, community, and society is lacking. Where moral certainty is missing, where moral judgments are not universally agreed upon, where a moral pluralism is acknowledged and protected, tolerance and respect for considered differences should prevail while an analysis of vexing moral disagreements is sustained. This view holds not only for controversies in neonatology but for every area of moral decision making in which the pluralistic character of the moral community is made manifest by the disagreements that emerge. May we have the wisdom, patience, and courage to perceive the limitations of our particular moral visions and derived norms. And may we have the wisdom, patience, and courage to respect similar limitations that we perceive in the particular moral visions and derived norms of persons with whom we disagree.

Questions for Analysis

1. Shelp argues that under certain conditions parents have the moral right to choose not to prolong the life of an infant. What are the conditions? Are they clear? Are they reasonable?

2. What arguments does Shelp present to justify his position?
3. What is the purpose of Paragraph 5?
4. In Shelp's argument, especially at the end of this essay, he emphasizes the "pluralistic nature of the moral community." Explain what he means by the term "pluralistic" and how it affects his argument.
5. In the last two sentences of his essay, Shelp eloquently calls for tolerance. Analyze and explain the reasons for his appeal. Do you agree that our tolerance for the reasonable decisions of others in these cases is needed even when those decisions violate our moral standards? When should our moral standards be seen as those that should apply to all?

C. Everett Koop

Ethical and Surgical Considerations in the Care of the Newborn with Congenital Abnormalities

(1982)

C. Everett Koop (b. 1916) was trained and practiced for years as a pediatric surgeon. He served as surgeon general for the Reagan Administration. This essay is taken from his book *Infanticide and the Handicapped Newborn* published by Brigham Young University Press in 1982.

1 Infanticide is the killing of a born infant by direct means or by withholding something necessary for its survival. This practice in the United States is extraordinarily important to those who are interested in the sanctity of human life because infanticide might never have come about had it not been for abortion on demand. When I read, in the months following the January 22, 1973 decision of the Supreme Court in *Roe v. Wade,* various references to Justice Blackmun's majority opinion in that case, my blood ran cold. You will remember that he considered the Hippocratic Oath which forbids abortion to be irrelevant. He spurned whatever morality he might have gleaned from the Judeo-Christian heritage of this country and turned instead to the pagan religions of Rome, of Greece, and of Persia. Although those countries practiced abortion, it was infanticide and euthanasia which were more important inhumanities in their cultures.

2 The second important thing to remember about infanticide is that it is euthanasia in an age group. There are many semantic differences in the English language on both sides of the Atlantic and infanticide is one of them. Infanticide in Great Britain usually means killing of a born infant by the infant's mother. Infanticide in this country is the killing of a born infant by the medical personnel in a hospital either by a direct act or much more commonly by the withholding of something necessary for the survival of

that infant. Its hidden importance in reference to our concerns in the future is that I am certain the day will come when the euthanasia forces will say, "Why are you concerned about euthanasia? We have had euthanasia of infants for a long time and there has been no outcry."

3 The third important thing concerning infanticide is that it is being practiced by a segment of the medical profession from whom we have traditionally expected more—pediatricians and pediatric surgeons—and it is being ignored by a segment of our society from whom the victim has a right to expect more—namely, the law.

4 The medical profession has slipped its anchor and drifted away from the commitment which put the patient first in the recognition of the fact that he needed the help a physician could provide. This principle was rather universally understood in medicine not too long ago when morality was based on certain absolutes that the individual perceived as right or wrong. I am distressed that in an era of moral relativism, the life of a handicapped child can be forfeited to alleviate suffering in the family. If the practice of infanticide is a perversion of the former morality in medicine, that is bad enough. But if the situation is compounded by the fact that the law has turned its back as though infanticide did not exist, then we are indeed in trouble, for who knows the direction the extension of this philosophy will take next?

5 For almost thirty-five years now I have devoted the major part of my professional life to the management of children born with a congenital defect. I was, however, a surgeon of the skin and its contents in my early years. Therefore, my experience with congenital defects is broader than just the field that ordinarily is now called general pediatric surgery. Although in my more recent years my interests have been confined to those congenital anomalies incompatible with life but nevertheless amenable to surgical correction, there was a day when I was concerned with the management of cleft lips and palates, orthopedic defects, spina bifida and its complications, congenital heart disease, and major urologic defects.

6 I know what can be accomplished in the habilitation of a child born less than perfect. I know what can be done with that child's family. I know that these children become loved and loving, that they are creative, and that their entrance into a family is frequently looked back upon in subsequent years as an extraordinarily positive experience. Those who never have had the privilege of working with handicapped children who are being habilitated into our society after the correction of a congenital defect frequently tell me that such a child should be allowed to die or even encouraged to die because its life could obviously be nothing but unhappy and miserable. Yet it has been my constant experience that disability and unhappiness do not go hand in hand. The most unhappy children I have known have been completely normal. On the other hand, there is remarkable joy and happiness in the lives of most handicapped children; yet some have borne burdens that I would have indeed found very difficult to endure.

7 The first medical effort I know of in this country to educate the profession in the management of a defective newborn where death was one of the options in treatment is the film *Who Shall Survive?* produced by the Joseph P. Kennedy Foundation.[1] It depicts the manner in which a child with both Down's syndrome and duodenal atresia

was given nothing by mouth until it expired from dehydration and starvation fifteen days later. Whatever was the intent of those who produced and financed this film, when it is seen during orientation week by new medical students across the country it is interpreted as an acceptable example of the management of a difficult problem in neonatology.

8 The first medical article along these lines to attract wide attention is entitled "Dilemmas of the Newborn Intensive Care Nursery," by Drs. Raymond S. Duff and A. G. M. Campbell of Yale University School of Medicine.[2] They acknowledge that over a two-year period about 14 percent of the deaths in their special care unit were those they permitted to happen because it was their considered judgment after discussion with the family that these children's lives were not worth living. It is impossible for the physician not to influence the family by innuendo alone; how much more if he counsels: "If this were my own child. . . ." The written word can never truly compete with the spoken word in matters such as this. I have to acknowledge that when I read the Duff and Campbell report, my emotions were a combination of fury and frustration. Yet, when I talk with Dr. Duff, I recognize that we have different concerns, and probably different understandings, of the ethics of the situation. My focus is on the life of the child; his is on the well-being of the family. My ethics might be said to be based on moral rules concerning absolutes of right and wrong, whereas I would suspect that his ethical principles are based more on a balance between the advantages to the patient and the disadvantages to the family.

9 My concerns about death as an option in the management of a handicapped newborn are centered not only on withholding treatment from the patient, but also on the implications of this form of management when extended to other children and to adults. This is because I believe in the "thin edge of the wedge" theory and in the dangers of the "slippery slope," whereas Dr. Duff does not see the slippery slope in the same light.

10 Drs. Duff and Campbell state in their article: "Survivors of these neonatal intensive care units may be healthy and their parents grateful, but in some instances continue to suffer from such conditions as chronic pulmonary disease, short bowel syndrome or various manifestations of brain damage. Others are severely handicapped by a myriad of congenital malformations that in previous times have resulted in death."[3] Because a newborn child has the possibility of having dyspnea, oxygen dependence, incontinence, paralysis, a contracture, or a sexual handicap does not necessarily entitle the physician to decide that the child's life is not worth living. If we decide that this is a reason for terminating a child's life, how long will it be before the same thinking is extended to adults who already have these same signs and symptoms and might be considered candidates for some type of euthanasia program?

11 Drs. Duff and Campbell also state: "Often too, the parents' or siblings' rights to relief from the seemingly pointless, crushing burdens were important considerations."[4] It seems to me that this is solving a social problem by inattention to a newborn handicapped child resulting in his death. I do not think this is the proper use of medical expertise. As stated previously, society is the loser when the patient becomes the impersonal consumer and the profession is delivering a service.

12 When a double standard exists for the management of the newborn with a handicap, one can expect a double standard to follow for the care of the nonhandicapped newborns and for older patients as well. . . .

13 I have recently written the script for, acted in, and narrated several documentary films, collectively entitled *Whatever Happened to the Human Race?,* that I have undertaken with Francis A. Schaeffer, an American-born theologian-philosopher who lives in Switzerland.[5] The second of these films is on the subject of infanticide. I think one of the most compelling scenes in any of the films is one held in my livingroom where four of my patients born with defects incompatible with life and who were operated upon by me on the first day or two of life were assembled with four other patients who had developed lethal problems in early childhood. They were not coached in any way concerning what answer they were to give to my questions. They were told we were making some documentary movies and were writing a book on the general topic of *Whatever Happened to the Human Race?* We allowed time for them to talk to each other for about an hour in order to feel comfortable before being asked to participate in the film.

14 The patients at the time ranged in age from eleven to thirty-three years. One patient had been born with a number of major congenital anomalies down the midline of his body requiring, up to then, thirty-seven operative procedures for correction. Another was born without an esophagus, requiring transplantation of the colon to replace that absent organ. Still another was born with a tumor of the tongue necessitating almost total amputation of that structure in a series of operations. The fourth youngster with congenital defects was born with no rectum, no innervation of the bladder, and with major defects of the esophagus.

15 The other four children all had tumors. One was a benign tumor of the bones of the face, which had required a number of operations for correction and we still had not achieved perfection. The other three had cancers of the adrenal gland, of the parotid gland, and of the uterus, respectively. There can be no doubt about how such young people feel concerning the joy of living, despite the time-consuming and usually painful medical and surgical procedures they have endured to correct birth defects or situations discovered in early childhood. Here are samples of their comments:

> Because the start was a little abnormal, it doesn't mean you're going to finish that way. I'm a normal, functioning human being, capable of doing anything anybody else can.
>
> At times it got very hard, but life is certainly worth living. I married a wonderful guy and I'm just so happy.
>
> At the beginning it was a little difficult going back to school after surgery, but then things started looking up, with a little perseverance and support. I am an anesthetist and I'm happily married. Things are going great for me.
>
> I really think that all my operations and all the things I had wrong with me were worth it, because I really enjoy life and I don't really let the things that are wrong with me bother me.

> If anything, I think I've had an added quality to my life—an appreciation of life. I look forward to every single morning.
>
> Most of the problems are what my parents went through with the surgery. I've now been teaching high school for eight years and it's a great joy.
>
> They spend millions of dollars to send men to the moon. I think they can spend any amount necessary to save someone's life. A human life is so important because it's a gift—not something you can give, so you really don't have the right to take it either.
>
> I really don't consider myself handicapped. Life is just worth living. What else can I say?[6]

16 In another part of the film we talk to a young man who is now a graduate student. He was a thalidomide baby, born without a left leg and without arms below the elbows. When we asked this young man what he thought about those who say that people born with such serious birth defects should be eliminated, this, in part, was his reply.

> They don't really see that what they are talking about is murder. I know, when I was born, the first thing my dad said to my mom was that "this one needs our love more." An individual with a handicap needs our love and needs us to help him grow into the being that God has made him to be. They are advocating that we destroy these children before they're even given a chance to live and to conquer their handicaps.
>
> I'm very glad to be alive. I live a full, meaningful life. I have many friends and many things that I want to do in life. I think the secret of living with a handicap is realizing who you are—that you are a human being, somebody who is very special—looking at the things that you *can* do in spite of your handicap, and maybe even through your handicap.[7]

17 Anxious to know in my own patients what perceptions parents had years after their encounter with a surgical procedure to save a handicapped newborn's life, a study was done on thirty-one families in which I personally had operated on a child more than fifteen years before for the correction of esophageal atresia.[8] When fifty-three parents were asked what type of overall effect the situation had on the family, only two said the effect was strong and negative. Seven said the effect was mild and negative, ten said it was strong and positive, and fourteen claimed the effect was mild and positive. Eighteen parents thought there was *no* impact on the family. . . .

18 If any group of physicians knows what can be accomplished by surgery on the handicapped newborn—and the proper support of the patient and his family in subsequent years—it is pediatric surgeons. Drs. Anthony Shaw, Judson G. Randolph, and Barbara Manard surveyed members of the surgical section of the American Academy of Pediatrics in reference to the management of newborns with handicaps.[9] Of the 400 pediatric surgeons queried, 267 (67 percent) completed questionnaires. A separate group of 308 pediatricians completed 190 questionnaires (62 percent). The first question was,

"Do you believe that the life of each and every newborn infant should be saved if it is within our ability to do so?" Eighty percent of those surgeons with my kind of background answered no.[10]

19 Here are some other readily remembered statistics. Seventy-six percent of the pediatric surgeons would acquiesce in the parents' decision to refuse consent for surgery in a newborn with intestinal obstruction if the infant also had Down's syndrome, or mongolism.[11] An almost unbelievable fact is that 8 percent of the surgeons (respondents) said they would acquiesce to the parents' wishes if the child had nothing other than simple intestinal atresia, the operation which is almost 100 percent successful and life after which is completely normal.[12]

20 To return to the infant with duodenal obstruction, which is fatal but easily correctable, and Down's syndrome, the following percentages are significant. Twenty-three percent of the pediatric surgeons group would move the parents in the direction of not signing a consent for surgery and an operative permit making it the physician's decision whether or not to let the baby die; nevertheless, if the family desired surgery the surgeon would perform it.[13] Over half of the same group said they would provide the parents with all known facts and make the decision completely the parents'. (Surely the bias of the doctor would show through.) Only 16 percent would try to persuade the parents to allow surgery but would not take them to court on refusal. Three percent would get a court order if the parents refused consent for operation.[14]

21 The schizophrenic nature of these replies is indicated by the fact that if they acquiesce to the parents' decision to withhold lifesaving surgery 63 percent would have stopped all supportive treatment, 30 percent would have given oral feedings which of course would be vomited immediately, but less than .05 percent would have terminated the infant's life by an injection of a drug such as morphine. . . .[15]

22 I practice medicine in the realm of trust between my patient's family and me. I do withhold treatment from patients under certain circumstances, but if I do, I have to know three things: an extraordinary amount about the disease process in question, an extraordinary amount about my patient, and an extraordinary amount about the relationship of my patient to the disease process in question. If I do not know all of these three, then I must, as an ethical physician, in any decision process come down on the side of life.

References

1. *Report of the Joseph R. Kennedy Foundation Int'l Symposium on Human Rights, Retardation and Research,* Oct. 16, 1971. For an extended version of the Johns Hopkins case study, *see* Gustafson, "Mongolism, Parental Desires and the Right to Life," 16 *Perspectives in Biology & Med.* 529 (1973).
2. Duff & Campbell, "Moral and Ethical Dilemmas In The Special-Care Nursery," 289 *New Eng. J. Med.* 890 (1973).
3. *Id.* at 890.
4. *Id.* at 891.
5. F. Schaeffer & C. E. Koop, *Whatever Happened to the Human Race?* (1979).
6. *Id.* at 64–65.
7. *Id.* at 65.

8. Koop et al., ''The Social, Psychological and Economic Problems of the Patient's Family After Secondary Repair of Esophageal Atresia,'' 17 *Kinderchirurgie* (Supp. July, 1975).
9. Shaw, Randolph, & Manard, ''Ethical Issues in Pediatrics Surgery: A National Survey of Pediatricians and Pediatric Surgeons,'' *60 Pediatric 588* (1977).
10. *Id.* at 589. Of 259 responses from pediatric surgeons, 17 percent said yes and 83 percent said no. ''Because the respondents [were] not a random sample of either [pediatric surgeons or pediatricians] but represented self-selected subgroups of entire populations, the use of inferential statistics is inappropriate.'' *Id.*
11. *Id.* at 590. Fifty percent of the pediatricians' group responded that they would acquiesce in such a decision.
12. *Id.* at 590–91. The authors note, however, that these respondents' answers to other questions indicated that most had read the question too hastily. These were not more likely than others to refuse to operate on a baby with Down's syndrome. *Id.* at 591.
13. *Id.* at 591–92.
14. *Id.* Several of those who responded checked more than one option. (The pediatric surgeons usually chose to move the parents in the direction of not signing, and also to provide the parents with information and make the decision completely theirs.)
15. *Id.* at 592–93. It is interesting to note the difference between the responses of the pediatric surgeons and the pediatricians. Generally, the pediatricians were more willing to attempt to save the infant's life.

Questions for Analysis

1. What is Koop's position on infanticide? How does his position differ from Shelp's? Were you surprized when you read Koop's statement in his final paragraph that he does withhold treatment in some cases? Explain.
2. From his first paragraph through much of his essay, Koop argues that infanticide is part of a very ''slippery slope.'' What is the slippery slope he sees? ''Slippery slope'' is the name often used for a particular type of logical fallacy. Is it a fallacy here?
3. A major part of the evidence Koop presents to support his position is drawn from interviews he conducted as a part of a film series entitled *Whatever Happened to the Human Race?* Do these interviews effectively support his point? Is there a bias in his choice of subjects that might weaken their authority?
4. How would you characterize the differences between Shelp's and Koop's writing style? Which writer is more persuasive? Why?
5. Koop stresses in his first paragraph the connection he sees between abortion and infanticide. What parallels and what differences do you see? Do you know of practices in any countries today that might illustrate some of Koop's fears about where infanticide as it is practiced in this country might lead?

Animal Rights and Scientific Research

Cleveland Amory

The Trials of Animals

(1989)

Cleveland Amory (b. 1917) has for years been a prominent advocate for animal rights and has written several books on the topic, including *The Cat Who Came for Christmas*. This piece originally appeared on the Op-Ed page of the September 17, 1989, issue of *The New York Times*.

1 Ask an experimenter about the animals in his laboratory. Nine times out of ten he will tell you that they are well cared for and that he abides by the Animal Welfare Act passed by Congress in 1966.

2 What he will not say is that both he and his colleagues fought the act and the amendments to it every step of the way; that, under the act, his laboratory is inspected at most (if at all) once a year; that when his animals are under experimentation, the act doesn't apply. Nor will he say that many laboratories ignore the act's most important amendment, passed in 1986, which mandates that at least one member of the public vote on the laboratory's animal-care committee.

3 Your experimenter is not a scoff-law. Having been for so long sole judge and jury of what he does, he believes that he is above the law. A prime example is that of the monkeys in Silver Spring, Maryland.

4 The monkeys were used in experiments in which, first, nerves in their limbs were removed and then stimuli—including electrical shocks and flames—were applied to see if they could still use their appendages.

5 Dr. Edward Taub, who ran the laboratory, was eventually tried and found guilty, not of cruelty to animals but of maintaining a filthy lab. Maryland is one of many states that exempts federally funded experiments from cruelty charges.

6 Dr. Taub is today a free man. His monkeys, however, are not. They are still in a laboratory under the jurisdiction of the National Institutes of Health, which first funded these cruel experiments. Three hundred members of Congress have asked the NIH to release the monkeys; the NIH says it does not want them; two animal sanctuaries have

offered to take them. Why can't they live what remains of their lives receiving the first evidence of human kindness they have ever known?

7 In the overcrowded field of cat experimentation, researchers at Louisiana State University, under an eight-year, $2 million Department of Defense contract, put cats in vises, remove part of their skulls, and then shoot them in the head.

8 More than two hundred doctors and Senator Daniel Inouye, chairman of the Defense Appropriations Subcommittee, have protested this cruelty. The experimenters say that their purpose is to find a way to return brain-wounded soldiers to active duty.

9 "Basic training for an Army infantryman costs $9,000" one experimenter argued. "If our research allows only 170 additional men to return to active duty . . . it will have paid for itself." But Dr. Donald Doll of Truman Veterans Hospital in Columbia, Missouri, said of these experiments: "I can find nothing which supports applying any of this data to humans."

10 At the University of Oregon, under a seventeen-year, $1.5 million grant, psychologists surgically rotated the eyes of kittens, implanted electrodes in their brains, and forced them to jump onto a block in a pan of water to test their equilibrium. These experiments resulted in a famous laboratory break-in in 1986, and the subsequent trial and conviction of one of the animals' liberators.

11 During the trial, experimenters were unable to cite a single case in which their research had benefited humans. Additional testimony revealed instances of cats being inadequately anesthetized while having their eye muscles cut, untrained and unlicensed personnel performing the surgery, and mother cats suffering such stress that they ate their babies.

12 The trial judge, Edwin Allen, stated that the testimony was "disturbing to me as a citizen of this state and as a graduate of the University of Oregon. It would be highly appropriate to have these facilities opened to the public."

Questions for Analysis

1. What is Amory's argument? What policy is he arguing should be changed?
2. What pieces of evidence does he use to support his argument? Do these items get your attention and (important in this case) your sympathy as well?
3. What impression does this presentation give you of the scientists involved in this experimentation? Do you believe it is an accurate, balanced depiction? Why or why not?
4. Explain what Amory is asking for in the last paragraph of his essay.

John G. Hubbell

The Animal Rights "War" on Medicine

(1990)

John G. Hubbell is a roving editor on the staff of *The Reader's Digest,* where this essay appeared in the June 1990 issue.

1 In the predawn hours of July 4, 1989, members of the Animal Liberation Front (ALF), an "animal rights" organization, broke into a laboratory at Texas Tech University in Lubbock. Their target: Prof. John Orem, a leading expert on sleep-disordered breathing.

2 The invaders vandalized Orem's equipment, breaking recorders, oscilloscopes and other instruments valued at some $70,000. They also stole five cats, halting his work in progress—work that could lead to an understanding of disorders such as Sudden Infant Death Syndrome (SIDS), or crib death, which kills over 5000 infants every year.

3 An organization known as People for the Ethical Treatment of Animals (PETA), which routinely issues press releases on ALF activities, quoted ALF claims that biomedical scientists are "animal-Nazis" and that Orem "abuses, mutilates and kills animals as part of the federal grant gravy train."

4 That was only the beginning of the campaign. A month later, on August 18, animal-rights activists held statewide demonstrations against Orem, picketing federal buildings in several Texas cities. The result: a flood of hate mail to the scientist and angry letters to the National Institutes of Health (NIH), which had awarded Orem more than $800,000 in grants. Finally PETA, quoting 16 "experts," filed a formal complaint with the NIH which called Orem's work "cruel" and without "scientific significance." The public had no way of knowing that none of the 16 had any expertise in sleep-disordered breathing or had ever been in Orem's lab.

5 NIH dispatched a team of authorities in physiology, neuroscience and pulmonary and veterinary medicine who, on September 18, reported back. Not only did they find the charges against Orem to be unfounded, but they judged him an exemplary researcher and his work "important and of the highest scientific quality."

6 PETA first intruded on the public consciousness in 1981, during a notorious episode in Silver Spring, Md. That May, a personable college student named Alex Pacheco went to research psychologist Edward Taub for a job. Taub was studying monkeys under an NIH grant, searching for ways to help stroke victims regain use of paralyzed limbs. Pacheco said he was interested in gaining laboratory experience. Taub offered him a position as a volunteer, which Pacheco accepted.

7 Late that summer, Taub took a vacation, leaving his lab in the care of his assistants. As he was about to return to work on September 11, an assistant called. Police, armed with a search warrant, were confiscating the monkeys: there was also a crowd of reporters on hand.

8 To his amazement, Taub was charged with 119 counts of cruelty to animals—most based on information provided to the police by Alex Pacheco, who, it turned out, was one of PETA's founders.

9 After five years in the courts, Taub was finally cleared of all charges. Yet the animal-rights movement never ceased vilifying him, producing hate mail and death threats. Amid the controversy the NIH suspended and later terminated Taub's grant (essentially for not buying new cages, altering the ventilation system or providing regular visits by a veterinarian). Thorough investigations by the American Physiological Society and the Society for Neuroscience determined that, in the words of the latter, the NIH decision was ''incommensurate with the deficiencies cited.'' Yet a program that could have benefited many of the 2.5 million Americans now living with the debilitating consequences of stroke came to a screeching halt.

10 Wiped out financially, Taub lost his laboratory, though the work of this gifted researcher had already helped rewrite accepted beliefs about the nervous system.

11 ***Dramatic Progress.*** The animal-rights movement has its roots in Europe, where antivivisectionists have held the biomedical research community under siege for years. In 1875, Britain's Sir George Duckett of the Society for the Abolition of Vivisection declared: ''Vivisection is monstrous. Medical science has little to learn, and nothing can be gained by repetition of experiments on living animals.''

12 This sentiment is endlessly parroted by contemporary ''activists.'' It is patently false. Since Duckett's time, animal research has led to vaccines against diphtheria, polio, measles, mumps, whooping cough, rubella. It has meant eradication of smallpox, effective treatment for diabetes and control of infection with powerful antibiotics.

13 The cardiac pacemaker, microsurgery to reattach severed limbs, and heart, kidney, lung, liver and other transplants are all possible because of animal research. In the early 1960s, the cure rate for acute lymphocytic leukemia in a child was four percent. Today, because of animal research, the cure rate exceeds 70 percent. Since the turn of the century, animal research has helped increase our life-span by nearly 28 years. And now animal research is leading to dramatic progress against AIDS and Alzheimer's disease.

14 Animals themselves have benefited. We are now able to extend and improve the lives of our pets and farm animals through cataract surgery, open-heart surgery and cardiac pacemakers, and can immunize them against rabies, distemper, anthrax, tetanus and feline leukemia. Animal research is an unqualified success story.

15 We should see even more spectacular medical breakthroughs in the coming decades. But not if today's animal-rights movement has its way.

16 ***Anti-Human Absurdities.*** In the United States, the movement is spearheaded by PETA, whose leadership insists that animals are the moral equivalent of human beings.

Any differentiation between people and animals constitutes "speciesism," as unethical as racism. Says PETA co-founder and director Ingrid Newkirk, "There really is no rational reason for saying a human being has special rights. . . . A rat is a pig is a dog is a boy." She compares the killing of chickens with the Nazi Holocaust. "Six million people died in concentration camps," she told the *Washington Post,* "but six billion broiler chickens will die this year in slaughterhouses."

17 Newkirk has been quoted as saying that meat-eating is "primitive, barbaric, arrogant," that humans have "grown like a cancer. We're the biggest blight on the face of the earth," and that if her father had a heart attack, "it would give me no solace at all to know his treatment was first tried on a dog."

18 The movement insists that animal research is irrelevant, that researchers simply refuse to move on to modern techniques. "The movement's big buzzword is 'alternatives,' meaning animals can now be replaced by computers and tissue cultures," says Bessie Borwein, associate dean for research-medicine at the University of Western Ontario. "That is nonsense. You cannot study kidney transplantation or diarrhea or high blood pressure on a computer screen."

19 "A tissue culture cannot replicate a complex organ," echoes Frederick Goodwin, head of the U.S. Alcohol, Drug Abuse and Mental Health Administration (ADAMHA).

20 What do the nation's 570,000 physicians feel about animal research? A 1988 American Medical Association survey found that 97 percent of doctors support it, despite the animal-rights movement's propaganda to the contrary.

21 "Without animal research, medical science would come to a total standstill," says Dr. Lewis Thomas, best-selling author and scholar-in-residence at New York's Cornell University Medical College.

22 "As a human being and physician, I cannot conceive of telling parents their sick child will die because we cannot use all the tools at our disposal," says pioneering heart surgeon Dr. Michael E. DeBakey of Houston's Baylor College of Medicine. "How will they feel about a society that legislates the rights of animals above those of humans?"

23 "The power of today's medical practice is based on research—and that includes crucial research involving animals," adds Dr. Louis W. Sullivan, Secretary of the U.S. Department of Health and Human Services.

24 ***Radical Infiltration.*** How then have the animal-rights activists achieved respectability? By exploiting the public's rightful concern for humane treatment of animals. ADAMHA's Goodwin explains: "They have gradually taken over highly respectable humane societies by using classic radical techniques: packing memberships and steering committees and electing directors. They have insidiously gained control of one group after another."

25 The average supporter has no idea that societies which traditionally promoted better treatment for animals, taught pet care, built shelters and cared for strays are now dedicated to ending the most effective kind of medical research. For example, the Humane Society of the United States (HSUS) insists it is not anti-vivisectionist; yet it has

persistently stated that animal research is often unnecessary. It published an editorial by animal-rights proponent Tom Regan endorsing civil disobedience for the cause. Says Frederick A. King, director of the Yerkes Regional Primate Center of Emory University, "HSUS flies a false flag. It is part of the same group that has attempted to do severe damage to research."

26 PETA's chairman, Alex Pacheco, says that it is best to be "strategically assertive" in seeking reforms while never losing sight of the ultimate goal: "total abolition" of "animal exploitation." This strategy has worked. It has taken the research community about ten years to realize that it is not dealing with moderates. It is dealing with organizations like ALF, which since 1988 has been on the FBI's list of domestic terrorist organizations. And with Trans-Species Unlimited, which trumpets: "The liberation of animal life can only be achieved through the radical transformation of human consciousness and the overthrow of the existing power structures in which human and animal abuse are entrenched."

27 Consider some of the movement's "liberation activities":

28 ■ In the early hours of April 3, 1989, hooded animal-rights activists broke into four buildings at the University of Arizona at Tucson. They smashed expensive equipment, spray-painted messages such as "Scum" and "Nazis" and stole 1231 animals. They set fire to two of the four buildings.

29 ALF took credit for the destruction, the cost of which amounted to more than $200,000. Fifteen projects were disrupted. One example: 30 of 1160 mice taken by ALF were infected with Cryptosporidium, a parasite that can cause severe intestinal disease in humans. The project's aim was to develop an effective disinfectant for Cryptosporidium-contaminated water. Now, not only is the work halted but researchers warn that, with less than expert handling, the stolen mice could spread cryptosporidiosis, which remains untreatable.

30 ■ On October 26, 1986, an ALF contingent broke into two facilities at the University of Oregon at Eugene. The equipment the intruders smashed and soaked with red paint included a $10,000 microscope, an electrocardiogram machine, an X-ray machine, an incubator and a sterilizer. At least 150 research animals were taken. As a result, more than a dozen projects were seriously delayed, including research by neuroscientist Barbara Gordon-Lickey on visual defects in newborns. An ALF statement called the neuroscientist a "butcher" and claimed that the animals had found new homes through "an intricate underground railroad network, much like the one used to transport fugitive slaves to the free states of the North in the last century."

31 Police caught up with one of the thieves: Roger Troen, 56, of Portland, Ore., a member of PETA. He was tried and convicted. PETA denied complicity, but Ingrid Newkirk said that PETA would pay Troen's legal expenses, including an appeal of his conviction. PETA then alleged to the NIH that the university was guilty of 12 counts of noncompliance with Public Health Service policy on humane care and use of laboratory animals.

32 Following a lengthy investigation, investigators found all PETA's charges groundless. "To the contrary," their report to the NIH stated, "evidence suggests a firm commitment to the appropriate care and use of laboratory animals."

33 But animal-rights extremists continued their campaign against Gordon-Lickey. They posted placards urging students not to take her courses because she tortured animals. As Nobel Laureate Dr. David H. Hugel of Harvard University, a pioneer in Gordon-Lickey's field, says, "Their tactics are clear. Work to increase the costs of research, and stop its progress with red tape and lawsuits."

34 ■ Dr. Herbert Pardes, president of the American Psychiatric Association, arrived in New York City in 1984 to take over as chairman of psychiatry at Columbia University. His office was in the New York State Psychiatric Institute, part of the Columbia Presbyterian Medical Center complex. Soon after, he noticed that people were handing out leaflets challenging the value of animal research. They picketed Dr. Pardes's home and sent him envelopes containing human feces.

35 Another Columbia scientist received a phone call on December 1, 1988, from someone who said, "We know where you live. How much insurance do you have?" A few mornings later, he found a pool of red paint in front of his house. On January 4, 1989, a guest cottage at his country home burned down.

36 ***Devastating Results.*** How effective has the animal-rights movement been? Very. Although recent polls reveal that more than 70 percent of Americans support animal research, about the same number believe the lie that medical researchers torture their animals.

37 According to ADAMHA's Frederick Goodwin, the movement has at its disposal at least $50 million annually, millions of which it dedicates to stopping biomedical research. It has been especially successful in pressuring state legislatures, as well as Congress, which in turn has pressured the federal health establishment. As a result, new regulations are demoralizing many scientists and driving up the cost of research. (For fiscal 1990, an estimated $1.5 billion—approximately 20 percent of the entire federal biomedical-research budget—may be needed to cover the costs of proposed regulation changes and increased security.)

38 At Stanford University, a costly security system has had to be installed and 24-hour guards hired to protect the animal-research facilities. As a consequence of the April 1989 raid at the University of Arizona at Tucson, the school must now spend $10,000 per week on security, money that otherwise could have been used for biomedical research.

39 Threats of violence to researchers and their families are having an effect as well. "It's hard to measure," says Charles R. McCarthy, director of the Office for Protection from Research Risks at the NIH. "But all of a sudden there is a hole in the kind of research being done."

40 In the past two years, for instance, there has been a 50- to 60-percent drop in the number of reports published by scientists using primates to study drug abuse. Reports on the use of primates to learn about severe depression have ended altogether.

41 And what of our future researchers? Between 1977 and 1987 there was a 28-percent drop in the number of college students graduating with degrees in biomedical science, and the growing influence of the animal-rights movement may add to that decline.

42 ***Stop the Fanatics.*** How are we to ensure that the animal-rights movement does not put an end to progress in medical research?

43 1. Don't swallow whole what the movement says about horrors in our biomedical-research laboratories. With rare exceptions, experimental animals are treated humanely. Biomedical researchers know that an animal in distress is simply not a good research subject. Researchers are embarked on an effort to alleviate misery, not cause it.

44 2. There are many humane societies that are truly concerned with animal welfare and oppose the animal-rights movement. They deserve your support. But before you contribute, make sure the society has not been taken over by animal-rights extremists. If you are not sure, contact iiFAR (incurably ill For Animal Research), P.O. Box 1873, Bridgeview, Ill. 60455. This organization is one of medical research's most effective allies.

45 3. Oppose legislation at local, state and federal levels that is designed to hamper biomedical research or price it out of business. Your representatives in government are lobbied by the animal-rights movement all the time. Let them know how *you* feel.

46 4. Support HR 3270, the "Farm Animal and Research Animal Facilities Protection Act of 1989," introduced by Rep. Charles Stenholm (D., Texas). This bill would make the kinds of break-ins and vandalism ALF has been perpetrating a federal offense subject to a maximum of three years in prison and/or a fine of up to $10,000. Also support HR 3349, the "Health Facilities Protection and Primate Center Rehabilitation Act of 1989," introduced by Rep. Henry A. Waxman (D., Calif.). This bill makes criminal assaults on federally funded facilities a federal offense.

47 If we want to defeat the killer diseases that still confront us—AIDS, Alzheimer's, cancer, heart disease and many others, the misguided fanatics of the animal-rights movement must be stopped.

Questions for Analysis

1. What is the thesis of Hubbell's essay? Is his supporting evidence persuasive?
2. Why does Hubbell start his essay with accounts of the problems encountered by two medical research scientists who use animals in their work?
3. Both Hubbell and Amory write about Dr. Edward Taub and his use of animals. Whose account do you believe is more accurate? Why?
4. Both Hubbell and Amory use quotations from authorities to support their conclusions. Whose use of authorities do you find more effective? Why?
5. Does Hubbell's essay alarm and/or anger you? Why? Do you detect a bias in Hubbell's essay? If you do, what is it and does it make you feel you should distrust his argument?

6. Why does Hubbell end his essay with a list of things you, the reader, can do to help support animal research?

Sneed B. Collard III

Refocusing Animal Rights

(1990)

Sneed B. Collard (b. 1959) is a free-lance writer who specializes in natural history and the environment. He is also a computer consultant at the University of California at Santa Barbara. This essay was a second-place winner in the ages twenty to twenty-nine category of the Eighth Annual North American Essay Contest sponsored by *The Humanist* magazine. It appeared in the July/August 1990 issue of that periodical.

1 I first collided with the animal rights movement in 1983, while I was a senior studying marine biology at the University of California at Berkeley. The campus *Daily Californian* had published an article covering a recent protest at the U.C. Davis Primate Center, an article seething with unanswered assertions by animal rights activists that biology buildings were ''torture labs'' and that biologists saw animals as nothing more than ''research tools.''

2 Reading that story filled me with rage. After all, I was studying biology because I *loved* animals and all life. Where were these animal rights people getting off?

3 Hands trembling, I powered up my Selectric typewriter and unleashed a scathing, emotional denunciation of animal rights activists as elitist animal lovers, and a defense of biologists as the people who care most about animals. My letter—also published in the *Daily Californian*—was to spark an intense editorial debate between animal rights activists and those defending animal research.

4 Over the next five years, while pursuing avocational passions for environmental protection and writing, I forged a career helping scientists at U.C. Santa Barbara utilize computers in research—much of it involving animal experimentation. All during that time, I stayed away from the animal rights movement while subconsciously hoping that they would stay away from me.

5 They didn't.

6 Some months ago, I was confronted by over thirty animal rights demonstrators besieging the building in which I work. Armed with walkie-talkies and signs, and accompanied by cameramen from regional television stations, the protesters had climbed five flights of stairs to the U.C. Santa Barbara's main vivarium and proceeded to chant for the halt of animal experimentation, the firing of neurobiology professors, and various other demands.

7 My first impulse was to race home and go another round on the letters to the editor page with these myopic fanatics who were disrupting pure research and contributing to mass anti-intellectualism. But I resisted. Instead of attacking the demonstrators, I began talking with them. After they'd been escorted from the building, I also began poring over the reams of literature for and against the animal rights movement. It's time, I decided, to stop shouting and find out what this movement is all about.

8 The first thing I learned was that there are dozens of groups working for animals in a myriad of ways and with a score of different emphases. In the back of a magazine called the *Animals' Voice,* almost two hundred organizations from around the world were listed as the "Animal's Allies." Many specialized in particular species, such as wolves or horses; others in the humane treatment of pets.

9 But the groups that interested me most were clustered under such categories as "Lab Animal Protection," "Animal Liberation," and "Animal Rights." These groups generally insist that animals deserve the same rights as humans and therefore should not be subjected to any "trivial human uses." According to Peter Singer in his book *Animal Liberation,* "trivial human uses" include laboratory research and the domestic raising of animals. Singer argues that to use animals in these ways constitutes speciesism, "a form of prejudice no less objectionable than prejudice about a person's race or sex."

10 As I began my inquiries into the animal rights controversy, I was surprised to find myself agreeing with much of what I read. After reading about the animal experiments of the 1960s and 1970s, for instance, I agreed that many animals were indeed killed for trivial purposes. It was also clear that many of the research animals were subjected to brutal conditions. Both the drop in the number of research animals and the increase in the quality of their care since the late 1960s are no doubt results of the efforts of animal rights activists—results which I applauded.

11 I was even more impressed by the arguments against the domestic use of animals, especially as food sources. Particularly persuasive were the statistics showing how many more resources are required to raise *animals* for protein than to extract the same protein directly from *vegetable* sources, and how much environmental damage results from raising domestic animals, especially grazing livestock.

12 Despite my enthusiasm for these animal rights issues, however, I soon confronted aspects of the movement which proved harder to accept. As a human being and an environmentalist, I balked at the movement's demand to totally abandon animal research, as well as its black-and-white portrayal of what constitutes the moral use of animals and the extreme priority it places on saving or protecting individual animals, rather than entire *ecosystems.*

13 As I discovered, it is clear that much past animal research has been unnecessary: for example, the use of animals in testing cosmetics. But what about medical research? Although some of this research is undoubtedly needless and wasteful, the simple fact that there's a good chance I'd be dead without past animal experimentation makes me think long and hard about the topic. The cure for polio and the treatment of diabetes are both well-known medical advances which extensively employed animal research.

And while I personally agree with animal rights philosophers that humans are not inherently better than other living things, my own sense of survival says differently. Others may disagree, and I respect them for it; but for me, if there's no other way to discover and test some medicine or procedure that has a good chance of saving my life (and, despite animal rights groups' claims, there often is no other way), I say, "Kill the animal."

14 My second area of conflict with animal rights activists involves their black-and-white treatment of complex issues. While they maintain that any harming of animals is immoral—period—they generally refuse to acknowledge that even they draw the line somewhere. One group of animal rights protesters I talked to was surprised to learn that they were probably crushing thousands of microscopic worms called nematodes by standing on the grass in front of our building. Obviously, to avoid crushing such creatures would be impossible for anyone. But other protesters draw other lines without realizing it. Some wore leather shoes. Even the leader of the group that stormed my building depended on drugs primarily extracted from animals to treat her diabetes. My point isn't that lines shouldn't be drawn—they must be—but that an open dialogue about drawing them is a prerequisite for honestly dealing with legitimate animal rights issues.

15 My biggest problem with the animal rights movement, however, stems from a philosophy I share with many other environmentalists. I feel that a large part of the animal rights movement's energy is misdirected. While superfluous animal research and the domestic use of animals are certainly worthy subjects, by far the greatest harm to animals is caused by the destruction of habitat due to human overpopulation.

16 In the United States, animal research utilizes and kills approximately 17 to 22 million animals per year—a staggering sum. Far more animals die, however, from bulldozing or burning or logging a single acre of pristine forest. Granted, the forest animals include invertebrates as well as the more cuddly species commonly featured on the covers of animal rights magazines—but they are all animals and they are all precious.

17 If you consider that an acre of tropical rainforest disappears approximately every two seconds, it soon becomes clear that the animal death toll from habitat destruction is horrifying—undoubtedly in the trillions each year. And, of course, what fuels this destruction is *people*—too many people competing for too few resources.

18 I asked several protesters how they justified expending their energy attacking research that might possibly prove beneficial to humans while so many more animals died needlessly as a result of habitat destruction. None provided a direct answer.

19 Some, though, asserted that just because environmental destruction also kills animals doesn't mean research abuses should be ignored. I agreed. But one must ask, "Are the millions destroyed for potentially beneficial research equivalent to the trillions (including billions of mammals) dying from habitat destruction? Are they equivalent to the fifty to one hundred species going extinct *per day* in the rainforests?" Not to me, and not to anyone else who seriously considers the problem. That's why I choose, along with many others, to devote my energies and resources to groups working to control

human population and prevent the destruction of forests, wetlands, and other habitats disappearing worldwide.

20 Having raised the previous objections, I wish to emphasize that my purpose is not to blow the environmentalist horn or discredit the animal rights movement. My purpose is to help join two broad classes of activists—the environmentalists and the animal rights groups—which should be pooling their resources. Without claiming to have all the answers, I thought of several ideas that could raise the animal rights movement's acceptability with the public—particularly the environmental community, whose support would advance its cause tremendously—and increase its effectiveness in saving animals' lives.

21 The first thing the movement needs to do is to acknowledge that the boundaries of reasonable animal use are not absolute. This issue is well discussed in Singer's *Animal Liberation,* but virtually ignored in all the other popular literature I reviewed, probably because it isn't reducible to black-and-white terms. But precisely because animal use lines vary for everyone, groups need to formulate a concerted approach to what reasonable lines are—lines which allow individual flexibility but reject merely convenient practices. For instance, I think the public can eventually be persuaded to accept vegetarianism because it is clearly practicable and because it clearly benefits the planet and all its inhabitants. In research, however, I doubt that humans will ever opt to accept AIDS to save animals' lives as long as there's a tiny chance to discover an AIDS cure via animal research.

22 Second, animal rights activists need to educate themselves more about ecological and environmental issues—particularly the effects of human civilization on animals in the wild. While it appears that animal rights groups are gradually developing a more sophisticated awareness of the importance of *all* animals to the planet, the majority of animal rights articles presents the cases of individual, mostly cute animals that have been mistreated.

23 A recent headline in the *Animals' Voice,* for instance, declared "Hungry Coyotes Get Zapped." Reading the article, I learned that an electric fence had been installed to keep coyotes from eating California least terns, an endangered species. Sure, some coyotes were zapped—but that electric fence was protecting an entire species that is in danger of becoming extinct. Animal rights activists must deemphasize heartstring-yanking and start focusing on entire ecosystems—not because individuals aren't important, but because without healthy ecosystems *nothing* will survive, including individual animals.

24 By learning how all plants and animals fit into food chains, as well as how the destruction of habitat affects everything from earthworms to elephants, animal rights activists will accomplish several things. First, they will redirect their efforts to the roots of the problem instead of the symptoms. Second, they will gain the support of a much larger slice of the public—and much more influence as a result. Third, they will make themselves less vulnerable to critics' attacks by having considered all sides of these

complex issues. Fourth (and most important), they will save the lives of many more animals than they are presently doing.

25 Fortunately, the seeds of this process have already been planted. At recent demonstrations, I was very impressed by several of the animal rights activists that I spoke with. Many of them already supported a number of broader environmental issues, and they were open to learning about more. In turn, they taught me about many environmental facets of the domestic use and abuse of animals that I had not fully considered. Such a dialogue between the scientific community (particularly environmentalists) and those within the animal rights movement can only benefit both sides—as well as society as a whole. After all, one doesn't have to look too hard to see that we're all really fighting the same battle: the battle to preserve our planet for both ourselves and our fellow species.

Questions for Analysis

1. Although Collard has found himself at odds with animal-rights activists on several occasions, his argument is not a total rejection of their aims. Define Collard's position in this essay.
2. What is the major criticism Collard directs toward most of the animal-rights activists he has met and most of the articles on animal rights he has read? What logical fallacy is he, in effect, saying these people commit?
3. What evidence does Collard present to support his position on how animals should be used for research and how they should be protected?
4. The first section of Collard's essay is a personal narrative presented in chronological order. Why did Collard organize and present that section as he did? Does it help establish his *ethos*—our sense of his reliability and believability as a writer? How does he organize material in the subsequent parts of his essay?
5. Has Collard achieved the goal of his essay with you? Have you rethought your position on the rights of animals? What is it?
6. With whom would Collard be more likely to agree, Amory or Hubbell? Would he agree with aspects of the other's essay? Explain.

Garry B. Trudeau

Live and Let Live

(1989)

These three installments in the often controversial comic strip by Garry Trudeau (b. 1948) originally appeared just after Christmas 1989 (December 26, 27, and 29).

Doonesbury BY GARRY TRUDEAU

Doonesbury BY GARRY TRUDEAU

Doonesbury BY GARRY TRUDEAU

Questions for Analysis

1. Which side of the animal-rights controversy presented in the essays by Amory, Hubbell, and Collard do you think Trudeau would be on? Why?
2. What is the point Trudeau is making through the conversation between Marcia and the store clerk in the first strip? How is Marcia's attitude similar to many people's attitude toward medical research with animals?

The Responsibilities of Rich Nations in a World of Starving People: Three Views

Garrett Hardin

Lifeboat Ethics: The Case Against Helping the Poor

(1974)

A biologist willing to venture into considerations of the practicalities and ethics of our obligations to the poor of the world, Garrett Hardin (b. 1915) wrote this essay for *Psychology Today* magazine where it first appeared in 1974.

Environmentalists use the metaphor of the earth as a ''spaceship'' in trying to persuade countries, industries and people to stop wasting and polluting our natural resources. Since we all share life on this planet, they argue, no single person or institution has the right to destroy, waste or use more than a fair share of its resources.

But does everyone on earth have an equal right to an equal share of its resources? The spaceship metaphor can be dangerous when used by misguided idealists to justify suicidal policies for sharing our resources through uncontrolled immigration and foreign aid. In their enthusiastic but unrealistic generosity, they confuse the ethics of a spaceship with those of a lifeboat.

A true spaceship would have to be under the control of a captain, since no ship could possibly survive if its course were determined by committee. Spaceship Earth certainly has no captain; the United Nations is merely a toothless tiger, with little power to enforce any policy upon its bickering members.

If we divide the world crudely into rich nations and poor nations, two thirds of them are desperately poor, and only one third comparatively rich, with the United States the wealthiest of all. Metaphorically each rich nation can be seen as a lifeboat full of comparatively rich people. In the ocean outside each lifeboat swim the poor of the world, who would like to get in, or at least to share some of the wealth. What should the lifeboat passengers do?

5 First, we must recognize the limited capacity of any lifeboat. For example, a nation's land has a limited capacity to support a population and as the current energy crisis has shown us, in some ways we have already exceeded the carrying capacity of our land.

Adrift in a Moral Sea

6 So here we sit, say fifty people in our lifeboat. To be generous, let us assume it has room for ten more, making a total capacity of sixty. Suppose the fifty of us in the lifeboat see 100 others swimming in the water outside, begging for admission to our boat or for handouts. We have several options: We may be tempted to try to live by the Christian ideal of being "our brother's keeper," or by the Marxist ideal of "to each according to his needs." Since the needs of all in the water are the same, and since they can all be seen as "our brothers," we could take them all into our boat, making a total of 150 in a boat designed for sixty. The boat swamps, everyone drowns. Complete justice, complete catastrophe.

7 Since the boat has an unused excess capacity of ten more passengers, we could admit just ten more to it. But which ten do we let in? How do we choose? Do we pick the best ten, the neediest ten, "first come, first served"? And what do we say to the ninety we exclude? If we do let an extra ten into our lifeboat, we will have lost our "safety factor," an engineering principle of critical importance. For example, if we don't leave room for excess capacity as a safety factor in our country's agriculture, a new plant disease or a bad change in the weather could have disastrous consequences.

8 Suppose we decide to preserve our small safety factor and admit no more to the lifeboat. Our survival is then possible, although we shall have to be constantly on guard against boarding parties.

9 While this last solution clearly offers the only means of our survival, it is morally abhorrent to many people. Some say they feel guilty about their good luck. My reply is simple: "Get out and yield your place to others." This may solve the problem of the guilt-ridden person's conscience, but it does not change the ethics of the lifeboat. The needy person to whom the guilt-ridden person yields his place will not himself feel guilty about his good luck. If he did, he would not climb aboard. The net result of conscience-stricken people giving up their unjustly held seats is the elimination of that sort of conscience from the lifeboat.

10 This is the basic metaphor within which we must work out our solutions. Let us now enrich the image, step by step, with substantive additions from the real world, a world that must solve real and pressing problems of overpopulation and hunger.

11 The harsh ethics of the lifeboat become even harsher when we consider the reproductive differences between the rich nations and the poor nations. The people inside the lifeboats are doubling in numbers every eighty-seven years; those swimming around outside are doubling, on the average, every thirty-five years, more than twice as fast as the rich. And since the world's resources are dwindling, the difference in prosperity between the rich and the poor can only increase.

12 As of 1973, the U.S. had a population of 210 million people, who were increasing by 0.8 percent per year. Outside our lifeboat, let us imagine another 210 million people

(say the combined populations of Colombia, Ecuador, Venezuela, Morocco, Pakistan, Thailand and the Philippines), who are increasing at a rate of 3.3 percent per year. Put differently, the doubling time for this aggregate population is twenty-one years, compared to eighty-seven years for the U.S.

Multiplying the Rich and the Poor

13 Now suppose the U.S. agreed to pool its resources with those seven countries, with everyone receiving an equal share. Initially the ratio of Americans to non-Americans in this model would be one-to-one. But consider what the ratio would be after eighty-seven years, by which time the Americans would have doubled to a population of 420 million. By then, doubling every twenty-one years, the other group would have swollen to 354 billion. Each American would have to share the available resources with more than eight people.

14 But, one could argue, this discussion assumes that current population trends will continue, and they may not. Quite so. Most likely the rate of population increase will decline much faster in the U.S. than it will in the other countries, and there does not seem to be much we can do about it. In sharing with "each according to his needs," we must recognize that needs are determined by population size, which is determined by the rate of reproduction, which at present is regarded as a sovereign right of every nation, poor or not. This being so, the philanthropic load created by the sharing ethic of the spaceship can only increase.

The Tragedy of the Commons

15 The fundamental error of spaceship ethics, and the sharing it requires, is that it leads to what I call "the tragedy of the commons." Under a system of private property, the men who own property recognize their responsibility to care for it, for if they don't they will eventually suffer. A farmer, for instance, will allow no more cattle in a pasture than its carrying capacity justifies. If he overloads it, erosion sets in, weeds take over, and he loses the use of the pasture.

16 If a pasture becomes a commons open to all, the right of each to use it may not be matched by a corresponding responsibility to protect it. Asking everyone to use it with discretion will hardly do, for the considerate herdsman who refrains from overloading the commons suffers more than a selfish one who says his needs are greater. If everyone would restrain himself, all would be well; but it takes only one less than everyone to ruin a system of voluntary restraint. In a crowded world of less than perfect human beings, mutual ruin is inevitable if there are no controls. This is the tragedy of the commons.

17 One of the major tasks of education today should be the creation of such an acute awareness of the dangers of the commons that people will recognize its many varieties. For example, the air and water have become polluted because they are treated as commons. Further growth in the population or per-capita conversion of natural resources into pollutants will only make the problem worse. The same holds true for the fish of the oceans. Fishing fleets have nearly disappeared in many parts of the world; tech-

nological improvements in the art of fishing are hastening the day of complete ruin. Only the replacement of the system of the commons with a responsible system of control will save the land, air, water and oceanic fisheries.

The World Food Bank

18 In recent years there has been a push to create a new commons called a World Food Bank, an international depository of food reserves to which nations would contribute according to their abilities and from which they would draw according to their needs. This humanitarian proposal has received support from many liberal international groups, and from such prominent citizens as Margaret Mead, U.N. Secretary General Kurt Waldheim, and Senators Edward Kennedy and George McGovern.

19 A world food bank appeals powerfully to our humanitarian impulses. But before we rush ahead with such a plan, let us recognize where the greatest political push comes from, lest we be disillusioned later. Our experience with the ''Food for Peace program,'' or Public Law 480, gives us the answer. This program moved billions of dollars' worth of U.S. surplus grain to food-short, population-long countries during the past two decades. But when P.L. 480 first became law, a headline in the business magazine *Forbes* revealed the real power behind it: ''Feeding the World's Hungry Millions: How It Will Mean Billions for U.S. Business.''

20 And indeed it did. In the years 1960 to 1970, U.S. taxpayers spent a total of $7.9 billion on the Food for Peace program. Between 1948 and 1970, they also paid an additional $50 billion for other economic-aid programs, some of which went for food and food-producing machinery and technology. Though all U.S. taxpayers were forced to contribute to the cost of P.L. 480, certain special interest groups gained handsomely under the program. Farmers did not have to contribute the grain; the Government, or rather the taxpayers, bought it from them at full market prices. The increased demand raised prices of farm products generally. The manufacturers of farm machinery, fertilizers and pesticides benefited by the farmers' extra efforts to grow more food. Grain elevators profited from storing the surplus until it could be shipped. Railroads made money hauling it to ports, and shipping lines profited from carrying it overseas. The implementation of P.L. 480 required the creation of a vast Government bureaucracy, which then acquired its own vested interest in continuing the program regardless of its merits.

Extracting Dollars

21 Those who proposed and defended the Food for Peace program in public rarely mentioned its importance to any of these special interests. The public emphasis was always on its humanitarian effects. The combination of silent selfish interests and highly vocal humanitarian apologists made a powerful and successful lobby for extracting money from taxpayers. We can expect the same lobby to push now for the creation of a World Food Bank.

22 However great the potential benefit to selfish interests, it should not be a decisive argument against a truly humanitarian program. We must ask if such a program would

actually do more good than harm, not only momentarily but also in the long run. Those who propose the food bank usually refer to a current "emergency" or "crisis" in terms of world food supply. But what is an emergency? Although they may be infrequent and sudden, everyone knows that emergencies will occur from time to time. A well-run family, company, organization or country prepares for the likelihood of accidents and emergencies. It expects them, it budgets for them, it saves for them.

Learning the Hard Way

23 What happens if some organizations or countries budget for accidents and others do not? If each country is solely responsible for its own well-being, poorly managed ones will suffer. But they can learn from experience. They may mend their ways, and learn to budget for infrequent but certain emergencies. For example, the weather varies from year to year, and periodic crop failures are certain. A wise and competent government saves out of the production of the good years in anticipation of bad years to come. Joseph taught this policy to Pharaoh in Egypt more than 2,000 years ago. Yet the great majority of the governments in the world today do not follow such a policy. They lack either the wisdom or the competence, or both. Should those nations that do manage to put something aside be forced to come to the rescue each time an emergency occurs among the poor nations?

24 "But it isn't their fault!" some kindhearted liberals argue. "How can we blame the poor people who are caught in an emergency? Why must they suffer for the sins of their governments?" The concept of blame is simply not relevant here. The real question is, what are the operational consequences of establishing a world food bank? If it is open to every country every time a need develops, slovenly rulers will not be motivated to take Joseph's advice. Someone will always come to their aid. Some countries will deposit food in the world food bank, and others will withdraw it. There will be almost no overlap. As a result of such solutions to food shortage emergencies, the poor countries will not learn to mend their ways, and will suffer progressively greater emergencies as their populations grow.

Population Control the Crude Way

25 On the average, poor countries undergo a 2.5 percent increase in population each year; rich countries, about 0.8 percent. Only rich countries have anything in the way of food reserves set aside, and even they do not have as much as they should. Poor countries have none. If poor countries received no food from the outside, the rate of their population growth would be periodically checked by crop failures and famines. But if they can always draw on a world food bank in time of need, their population can continue to grow unchecked, and so will their "need" for aid. In the short run, a world food bank may diminish that need, but in the long run it actually increases the need without limit.

26 Without some system of worldwide food sharing, the proportion of people in the rich and poor nations might eventually stabilize. The overpopulated poor countries would decrease in numbers, while the rich countries that had room for more people

would increase. But with a well-meaning system of sharing, such as a world food bank, the growth differential between the rich and the poor countries will not only persist, it will increase. Because of the higher rate of population growth in the poor countries of the world, 88 percent of today's children are born poor, and only 12 percent rich. Year by year the ratio becomes worse, as the fast-reproducing poor outnumber the slow-reproducing rich.

27 A world food bank is thus a commons in disguise. People will have more motivation to draw from it than to add to any common store. The less provident and less able will multiply at the expense of the abler and more provident, bringing eventual ruin upon all who share in the commons. Besides, any system of "sharing" that amounts to foreign aid from the rich nations to the poor nations will carry the taint of charity, which will contribute little to the world peace so devoutly desired by those who support the idea of a world food bank.

28 As past U.S. foreign-aid programs have amply and depressingly demonstrated, international charity frequently inspires mistrust and antagonism rather than gratitude on the part of the recipient nation.

Chinese Fish and Miracle Rice

29 The modern approach to foreign aid stresses the export of technology and advice, rather than money and food. As an ancient Chinese proverb goes: "Give a man a fish and he will eat for a day; teach him how to fish and he will eat for the rest of his days." Acting on this advice, the Rockefeller and Ford Foundations have financed a number of programs for improving agriculture in the hungry nations. Known as the "Green Revolution," these programs have led to the development of "miracle rice" and "miracle wheat," new strains that offer bigger harvests and greater resistance to crop damage. Norman Borlaug, the Nobel Prize winning agronomist who, supported by the Rockefeller Foundation, developed "miracle wheat," is one of the most prominent advocates of a world food bank.

30 Whether or not the Green Revolution can increase food production as much as its champions claim is a debatable but possibly irrelevant point. Those who support this well-intended humanitarian effort should first consider some of the fundamentals of human ecology. Ironically, one man who did was the late Alan Gregg, a vice president of the Rockefeller Foundation. Two decades ago he expressed strong doubts about the wisdom of such attempts to increase food production. He likened the growth and spread of humanity over the surface of the earth to the spread of cancer in the human body, remarking that "cancerous growths demand food; but, as far as I know, they have never been cured by getting it."

Overloading the Environment

31 Every human born constitutes a draft on all aspects of the environment: food, air, water, forests, beaches, wildlife, scenery and solitude. Food can, perhaps, be significantly increased to meet a growing demand. But what about clean beaches, unspoiled forests,

and solitude? If we satisfy a growing population's need for food, we necessarily decrease its per-capita supply of the other resources needed by men.

32 India, for example, now has a population of 600 million, which increases by 15 million each year. This population already puts a huge load on a relatively impoverished environment. The country's forests are now only a small fraction of what they were three centuries ago, and floods and erosion continually destroy the insufficient farmland that remains. Every one of the 15 million new lives added to India's population puts an additional burden on the environment, and increases the economic and social costs of crowding. However humanitarian our intent, every Indian life saved through medical or nutritional assistance from abroad diminishes the quality of life for those who remain, and for subsequent generations. If rich countries make it possible, through foreign aid, for 600 million Indians to swell to 1.2 billion in a mere twenty-eight years, as their current growth rate threatens, will future generations of Indians thank us for hastening the destruction of their environment? Will our good intentions be sufficient excuse for the consequences of our actions?

33 My final example of a commons in action is one for which the public has the least desire for rational discussion—immigration. Anyone who publicly questions the wisdom of current U.S. immigration policy is promptly charged with bigotry, prejudice, ethnocentrism, chauvinism, isolationism or selfishness. Rather than encounter such accusations, one would rather talk about other matters, leaving immigration policy to wallow in the crosscurrents of special interests that take no account of the good of the whole, or the interest of posterity.

34 Perhaps we still feel guilty about things we said in the past. Two generations ago the popular press frequently referred to Dagos, Wops, Polacks, Chinks and Krauts, in articles about how America was being "overrun" by foreigners of supposedly inferior genetic stock. But because the implied inferiority of foreigners was used then as justification for keeping them out, people now assume that restrictive policies could only be based on such misguided notions. There are other grounds.

A Nation of Immigrants

35 Just consider the numbers involved. Our Government acknowledges a net inflow of 400,000 immigrants a year. While we have no hard data on the extent of illegal entries, educated guesses put the figure at about 600,000 a year. Since the natural increase (excess of births over deaths) of the resident population now runs about 1.7 million per year, the yearly gain from immigration amounts to at least 19 percent of the total annual increase, and may be as much as 37 percent if we include the estimate for illegal immigrants. Considering the growing use of birth-control devices, the potential effect of educational campaigns by such organizations as Planned Parenthood Federation of America and Zero Population Growth, and the influence of inflation and the housing shortage, the fertility rate of American women may decline so much that immigration could account for all the yearly increase in population. Should we not at least ask if that is what we want?

36 For the sake of those who worry about whether the ''quality'' of the average immigrant compares favorably with the quality of the average resident, let us assume that immigrants and nativeborn citizens are of exactly equal quality, however one defines that term. We will focus here only on quantity; and since our conclusions will depend on nothing else, all charges of bigotry and chauvinism become irrelevant.

Immigration vs. Food Supply

37 World food banks *move food to the people,* hastening the exhaustion of the environment of the poor countries. Unrestricted immigration, on the other hand, *moves people to the food,* thus speeding up the destruction of the environment of the rich countries. We can easily understand why poor people should want to make this latter transfer, but why should rich hosts encourage it?

38 As in the case of foreign-aid programs, immigration receives support from selfish interests and humanitarian impulses. The primary selfish interest in unimpeded immigration is the desire of employers for cheap labor, particularly in industries and trades that offer degrading work. In the past, one wave of foreigners after another was brought into the U.S. to work at wretched jobs for wretched wages. In recent years the Cubans, Puerto Ricans and Mexicans have had this dubious honor. The interests of the employers of cheap labor mesh well with the guilty silence of the country's liberal intelligentsia. White Anglo-Saxon Protestants are particularly reluctant to call for a closing of the doors to immigration for fear of being called bigots.

39 But not all countries have such reluctant leadership. Most educated Hawaiians, for example, are keenly aware of the limits of their environment, particularly in terms of population growth. There is only so much room on the islands, and the islanders know it. To Hawaiians, immigrants from the other forty-nine states present as great a threat as those from other nations. At a recent meeting of Hawaiian government officials in Honolulu, I had the ironic delight of hearing a speaker, who like most of his audience was of Japanese ancestry, ask how the country might practically and constitutionally close its doors to further immigration. One member of the audience countered: ''How can we shut the doors now? We have many friends and relatives in Japan that we'd like to bring here someday so that they can enjoy Hawaii too.'' The Japanese-American speaker smiled sympathetically and answered: ''Yes, but we have children now, and someday we'll have grandchildren too. We can bring more people here from Japan only by giving away some of the land that we hope to pass on to our grandchildren some day. What right do we have to do that?''

40 At this point, I can hear U.S. liberals asking: ''How can you justify slamming the door once you're inside? You say that immigrants should be kept out. But aren't we all immigrants, or the descendants of immigrants? If we insist on staying, must we not admit all others?'' Our craving for intellectual order leads us to seek and prefer symmetrical rules and morals: a single rule for me and everybody else; the same rule yesterday, today, and tomorrow. Justice, we feel, should not change with time and place.

41 We Americans of non-Indian ancestry can look upon ourselves as the descendants of thieves who are guilty morally, if not legally, of stealing this land from its Indian

owners. Should we then give back the land to the now living American descendants of those Indians? However morally or logically sound this proposal may be, I, for one, am unwilling to live by it and I know no one else who is. Besides, the logical consequence would be absurd. Suppose that, intoxicated with a sense of pure justice, we should decide to turn our land over to the Indians. Since all our wealth has also been derived from the land, wouldn't we be morally obliged to give that back to the Indians too?

Pure Justice vs. Reality

42 Clearly, the concept of pure justice produces an infinite regression to absurdity. Centuries ago, wise men invented statutes of limitations to justify the rejection of such pure justice, in the interest of preventing continual disorder. The law zealously defends property rights, but only relatively recent property rights. Drawing a line after an arbitrary time has elapsed may be unjust, but the alternatives are worse.

43 We are all descendants of thieves, and the world's resources are inequitably distributed. But we must begin the journey to tomorrow from the point where we are today. We cannot remake the past. We cannot safely divide the wealth equitably among all peoples so long as people reproduce at different rates. To do so would guarantee that our grandchildren, and everyone else's grandchildren, would have only a ruined world to inhabit.

44 To be generous with one's own possessions is quite different from being generous with those of posterity. We should call this point to the attention of those who, from a commendable love of justice and equality, would institute a system of the commons, either in the form of a world food bank, or of unrestricted immigration. We must convince them if we wish to save at least some parts of the world from environmental ruin.

45 Without a true world government to control reproduction and the use of available resources, the sharing ethic of the spaceship is impossible. For the foreseeable future, our survival demands that we govern our actions by the ethics of a lifeboat, harsh though they may be. Posterity will be satisfied with nothing less.

Questions for Analysis

1. Hardin begins his essay by rejecting the earth-as-spaceship metaphor and substituting the metaphor of rich nation as lifeboat. Explain the reasons for his move with metaphors. Does his discussion illustrate both the power and limitations of metaphors? Do you see any limitations or weaknesses in his lifeboat metaphor?
2. In Paragraph 6, Hardin rejects both Christian and Marxist ideas by asserting that they both will bring "complete justice, complete catastrophe." What is Hardin's reason for including this assessment and assertion? Does it help or hurt his essay?

3. Define what Hardin means by "the tragedy of the commons" and explain how that concept fits into his argument.
4. In Paragraph 42, Hardin rejects "pure justice" as "an infinite regression into absurdity" that is incompatible with the survival of human society. Explain Hardin's reasoning.
5. Hardin places a great deal of emphasis on our obligations to future generations. Is this a persuasive argument? Explain.
6. Do you find Hardin's insistence on following the dictates of what he calls "reality" over ideas such as "justice" and "equality" distressing? Necessary? Unavoidable? Does his argument leave us any ways we can help disadvantaged, poor nations?

Peter Singer

Famine, Affluence, and Morality

(1972)

Well known for his writings on various issues including world hunger and animal rights, Peter Singer (b. 1946) teaches philosophy at Monash University in Australia. This essay originally appeared in the journal *Philosophy and Public Affairs*.

1 As I write this, in November 1971, people are dying in East Bengal from lack of food, shelter, and medical care. The suffering and death that are occurring there now are not inevitable, not unavoidable in any fatalistic sense of the term. Constant poverty, a cyclone, and a civil war have turned at least nine million people into destitute refugees; nevertheless, it is not beyond the capacity of the richer nations to give enough assistance to reduce any further suffering to very small proportions. The decisions and actions of human beings can prevent this kind of suffering. Unfortunately, human beings have not made the necessary decisions. At the individual level, people have, with very few exceptions, not responded to the situation in any significant way. Generally speaking, people have not given large sums to relief funds; they have not written to their parliamentary representatives demanding increased government assistance; they have not demonstrated in the streets, held symbolic fasts, or done anything else directed toward providing the refugees with the means to satisfy their essential needs. At the government level, no government has given the sort of massive aid that would enable the refugees to survive for more than a few days. Britain, for instance, has given rather more than most countries. It has, to date, given £14,750,000. For comparative purposes, Britain's share of the nonrecoverable development costs of the Anglo-French Concorde project is already in excess of £275,000,000, and on present estimates will reach £440,000,000.

The implication is that the British government values a supersonic transport more than thirty times as highly as it values the lives of the nine million refugees. Australia is another country which, on a per capita basis, is well up in the "aid to Bengal" table. Australia's aid, however, amounts to less than one-twelfth of the cost of Sydney's new opera house. The total amount given, from all sources, now stands at about £65,000,000. The estimated cost of keeping the refugees alive for one year is £464,000,000. Most of the refugees have now been in the camps for more than six months. The World Bank has said that India needs a minimum of £300,000,000 in assistance from other countries before the end of the year. It seems obvious that assistance on this scale will not be forthcoming. India will be forced to choose between letting the refugees starve or diverting funds from her own development program, which will mean that more of her own people will starve in the future.[1]

2 These are the essential facts about the present situation in Bengal. So far as it concerns us here, there is nothing unique about this situation except its magnitude. The Bengal emergency is just the latest and most acute of a series of major emergencies in various parts of the world, arising both from natural and from man-made causes. There are also many parts of the world in which people die from malnutrition and lack of food independent of any special emergency. I take Bengal as my example only because it is the present concern, and because the size of the problem has ensured that it has been given adequate publicity. Neither individuals nor governments can claim to be unaware of what is happening there.

3 What are the moral implications of a situation like this? In what follows, I shall argue that the way people in relatively affluent countries react to a situation like that in Bengal cannot be justified; indeed, the whole way we look at moral issues—our moral conceptual scheme—needs to be altered, and with it, the way of life that has come to be taken for granted in our society.

4 In arguing for this conclusion I will not, of course, claim to be morally neutral. I shall, however, try to argue for the moral position that I take, so that anyone who accepts certain assumptions, to be made explicit, will, I hope, accept my conclusion.

5 I begin with the assumption that suffering and death from lack of food, shelter, and medical care are bad. I think most people will agree about this, although one may reach the same view by different routes. I shall not argue for this view. People can hold all sorts of eccentric positions, and perhaps from some of them it would not follow that death by starvation is in itself bad. It is difficult, perhaps impossible, to refute such positions, and so for brevity. I will henceforth take this assumption as accepted. Those who disagree need read no further.

6 My next point is this: If it is in our power to prevent something bad from happening, without thereby sacrificing anything of comparable moral importance, we ought, morally, to do it. By "without sacrificing anything of comparable moral importance" I mean without causing anything else comparably bad to happen, or doing something that is wrong in itself, or failing to promote some moral good, comparable in significance to the bad thing that we can prevent. This principle seems almost as uncontrov-

ersial as the last one. It requires us only to prevent what is bad, and not to promote what is good, and it requires this of us only when we can do it without sacrificing anything that is, from the moral point of view, comparably important. I could even, as far as the application of my argument to the Bengal emergency is concerned, qualify the point so as to make it: If it is in our power to prevent something very bad from happening, without thereby sacrificing anything morally significant, we ought, morally, to do it. An application of this principle would be as follows: If I am walking past a shallow pond and see a child drowning in it, I ought to wade in and pull the child out. This will mean getting my clothes muddy, but this is insignificant, while the death of the child would presumably be a very bad thing.

7 The uncontroversial appearance of the principle just stated is deceptive. If it were acted upon, even in its qualified form, our lives, our society, and our world would be fundamentally changed. For the principle takes, firstly, no account of proximity or distance. It makes no moral difference whether the person I can help is a neighbor's child ten yards from me or a Bengali whose name I shall never know, ten thousand miles away. Secondly, the principle makes no distinction between cases in which I am the only person who could possibly do anything and cases in which I am just one among millions in the same position.

8 I do not think I need to say much in defense of the refusal to take proximity and distance into account. The fact that a person is physically near to us, so that we have personal contact with him, may make it more likely that we *shall* assist him, but this does not show that we *ought* to help him rather than another who happens to be further away. If we accept any principle of impartiality, universalizability, equality, or whatever, we cannot discriminate against someone merely because he is far away from us (or we are far away from him). Admittedly, it is possible that we are in a better position to judge what needs to be done to help a person near to us than one far away, and perhaps also to provide the assistance we judge to be necessary. If this were the case, it would be a reason for helping those near to us first. This may once have been a justification for being more concerned with the poor in one's town than with famine victims in India. Unfortunately for those who like to keep their moral responsibilities limited, instant communication and swift transportation have changed the situation. From the moral point of view, the development of the world into a "global village" has made an important, though still unrecognized, difference to our moral situation. Expert observers and supervisors, sent out by famine relief organizations or permanently stationed in famine-prone areas, can direct our aid to a refugee in Bengal almost as effectively as we could get it to someone in our own block. There would seem, therefore, to be no possible justification for discriminating on geographical grounds.

9 There may be a greater need to defend the second implication of my principle—that the fact that there are millions of other people in the same position, in respect to the Bengali refugees, as I am, does not make the situation significantly different from a situation in which I am the only person who can prevent something very bad from occurring. Again, of course, I admit that there is a psychological difference between the cases; one feels less guilty about doing nothing if one can point to others, similarly

placed, who have also done nothing. Yet this can make no real difference to our moral obligations.[2] Should I consider that I am less obliged to pull the drowning child out of the pond if on looking around I see other people, no further away than I am, who have also noticed the child but are doing nothing? One has only to ask this question to see the absurdity of the view that numbers lessen obligation. It is a view that is an ideal excuse for inactivity; unfortunately most of the major evils—poverty, overpopulation, pollution—are problems in which everyone is almost equally involved.

10 The view that numbers do make a difference can be made plausible if stated in this way: If everyone in circumstances like mine gave £5 to the Bengal Relief Fund, there would be enough to provide food, shelter, and medical care for the refugees; there is no reason why I should give more than anyone else in the same circumstances as I am; therefore I have no obligation to give more than £5. Each premise in this argument is true, and the argument looks sound. It may convince us, unless we notice that it is based on a hypothetical premise, although the conclusion is not stated hypothetically. The argument would be sound if the conclusion were: if everyone in circumstances like mine were to give £5, I would have no obligation to give more than £5. If the conclusion were so stated, however, it would be obvious that the argument has no bearing on a situation in which it is not the case that everyone else gives £5. This, of course, is the actual situation. It is more or less certain that not everyone in circumstances like mine will give £5. So there will not be enough to provide the needed food, shelter, and medical care. Therefore by giving more than £5 I will prevent more suffering than I would if I gave just £5.

11 It might be thought that this argument has an absurd consequence. Since the situation appears to be that very few people are likely to give substantial amounts, it follows that I and everyone else in similar circumstances ought to give as much as possible, that is, at least up to the point at which by giving more one would begin to cause serious suffering for oneself and one's dependents—perhaps even beyond this point to the point of marginal utility, at which by giving more one would cause oneself and one's dependents as much suffering as one would prevent in Bengal. If everyone does this, however, there will be more than can be used for the benefit of the refugees, and some of the sacrifice will have been unnecessary. Thus, if everyone does what he ought to do, the result will not be as good as it would be if everyone did a little less than he ought to do, or if only some do all that they ought to do.

12 The paradox here arises only if we assume that the actions in question—sending money to the relief funds—are performed more or less simultaneously, and are also unexpected. For if it is to be expected that everyone is going to contribute something, then clearly each is not obliged to give as much as he would have been obliged to had others not been giving too. And if everyone is not acting more or less simultaneously, then those giving later will know how much more is needed, and will have no obligation to give more than is necessary to reach this amount. To say this is not to deny the principle that people in the same circumstances have the same obligations, but to point out that the fact that others have given, or may be expected to give, is a relevant circumstance: Those giving after it has become known that many others are giving and

those giving before are not in the same circumstances. So the seemingly absurd consequence of the principle I have put forward can occur only if people are in error about the actual circumstances—that is, if they think they are giving when others are not, but in fact they are giving when others are. The result of everyone doing what he really ought to do cannot be worse than the result of everyone doing less than he ought to do, although the result of everyone doing what he reasonably believes he ought to do could be.

13 If my argument so far has been sound, neither our distance from a preventable evil nor the number of other people who, in respect to that evil, are in the same situation as we are, lessens our obligation to mitigate or prevent that evil. I shall therefore take as established the principle I asserted earlier. As I have already said, I need to assert it only in its qualified form: If it is in our power to prevent something very bad from happening, without thereby sacrificing anything else morally significant, we ought, morally, to do it.

14 The outcome of this argument is that our traditional moral categories are upset. The traditional distinction between duty and charity cannot be drawn, or at least, not in the place we normally draw it. Giving money to the Bengal Relief Fund is regarded as an act of charity in our society. The bodies which collect money are known as "charities." These organizations see themselves in this way—if you send them a check, you will be thanked for your "generosity." Because giving money is regarded as an act of charity, it is not thought that there is anything wrong with not giving. The charitable man may be praised, but the man who is not charitable is not condemned. People do not feel in any way ashamed or guilty about spending money on new clothes or a new car instead of giving it to a famine relief. (Indeed, the alternative does not occur to them.) This way of looking at the matter cannot be justified. When we buy new clothes not to keep ourselves warm but to look "well-dressed" we are not providing for any important need. We would not be sacrificing anything significant if we were to continue to wear our old clothes, and give the money to famine relief. By doing so, we would be preventing another person from starving. It follows from what I have said earlier that we ought to give money away, rather than spend it on clothes which we do not need to keep us warm. To do so is not charitable, or generous. Nor is it the kind of act which philosophers and theologians have called "supererogatory"—an act which it would be good to do, but not wrong not to do. On the contrary, we ought to give the money away, and it is wrong not to do so.

15 I am not maintaining that there are no acts which are charitable, or that there are no acts which it would be good to do but not wrong not to do. It may be possible to redraw the distinction between duty and charity in some other place. All I am arguing here is that the present way of drawing the distinction, which makes it an act of charity for a man living at the level of affluence which most people in the "developed nations" enjoy to give money to save someone else from starvation, cannot be supported. It is beyond the scope of my argument to consider whether the distinction should be redrawn or abolished altogether. There would be many other possible ways of drawing the

distinction—for instance, one might decide that it is good to make other people as happy as possible, but not wrong not to do so.

16 Despite the limited nature of the revision in our moral conceptual scheme which I am proposing, the revision would, given the extent of both affluence and famine in the world today, have radical implications. These implications may lead to further objections, distinct from those I have already considered. I shall discuss two of these.

17 One objection to the position I have taken might be simply that it is too drastic a revision of our moral scheme. People do not ordinarily judge in the way I have suggested they should. Most people reserve their moral condemnation for those who violate some moral norm, such as the norm against taking another person's property. They do not condemn those who indulge in luxury instead of giving to famine relief. But given that I did not set out to present a morally neutral description of the way people make moral judgments, the way people do in fact judge has nothing to do with the validity of my conclusion. My conclusion follows from the principle which I advanced earlier, and unless that principle is rejected, or the arguments shown to be unsound, I think the conclusion must stand, however strange it appears.

18 It might, nevertheless, be interesting to consider why our society, and most other societies, do judge differently from the way I have suggested they should. In a well-known article, J. O. Urmson suggests that the imperatives of duty, which tell us what we must do, as distinct from what it would be good to do but not wrong not to do, function so as to prohibit behavior that is intolerable if men are to live together in society.[3] This may explain the origin and continued existence of the present division between acts of duty and acts of charity. Moral attitudes are shaped by the needs of society, and no doubt society needs people who will observe the rules that make social existence tolerable. From the point of view of a particular society, it is essential to prevent violations of norms against killing, stealing, and so on. It is quite inessential, however, to help people outside one's own society.

19 If this is an explanation of our common distinction between duty and supererogation, however, it is not a justification of it. The moral point of view requires us to look beyond the interests of our own society. Previously, as I have already mentioned, this may hardly have been feasible, but it is quite feasible now. From the moral point of view, the prevention of the starvation of millions of people outside our society must be considered at least as pressing as the upholding of property norms within our society.

20 It has been argued by some writers, among them Sidgwick and Urmson, that we need to have a basic moral code which is not too far beyond the capacities of ordinary man, for otherwise there will be a general breakdown of compliance with the moral code. Crudely stated, this argument suggests that if we tell people that they ought to refrain from murder and give everything they do not really need to famine relief, they will do neither, whereas if we tell them that they ought to refrain from murder and that it is good to give to famine relief but not wrong not to do so, they will at least refrain from murder. The issue here is: Where should we draw the line between conduct that is required and conduct that is good although not required, so as to get the best possible result? This would seem to be an empirical question, although a very difficult one. One

objection to the Sidgwick-Urmson line of argument is that it takes insufficient account of the effect that moral standards can have on the decisions we make. Given a society in which a wealthy man who gives 5 percent of his income to famine relief is regarded as most generous, it is not surprising that a proposal that we all ought to give away half our incomes will be thought to be absurdly unrealistic. In a society which held that no man should have more than enough while others have less than they need, such a proposal might seem narrow-minded. What it is possible for a man to do and what he is likely to do are both, I think, very greatly influenced by what people around him are doing and expecting him to do. In any case, the possibility that by spreading the idea that we ought to be doing very much more than we are to relieve famine we shall bring about a general breakdown of moral behavior seems remote. If the stakes are an end to widespread starvation, it is worth the risk. Finally, it should be emphasized that these considerations are relevant only to the issue of what we should require from others, and not to what we ourselves ought to do.

21 The second objection to my attack on the present distinction between duty and charity is one which has from time to time been made against utilitarianism. It follows from some forms of utilitarian theory that we all ought, morally, to be working full time to increase the balance of happiness over misery. The position I have taken here would not lead to this conclusion in all circumstances, for if there were no bad occurrences that we could prevent without sacrificing something of comparable moral importance, my argument would have no application. Given the present conditions in many parts of the world, however, it does follow from my argument that we ought, morally, to be working full time to relieve great suffering of the sort that occurs as a result of famine or other disasters. Of course, mitigating circumstances can be adduced—for instance, that if we wear ourselves out through overwork, we shall be less effective than we would otherwise have been. Nevertheless, when all considerations of this sort have been taken into account, the conclusion remains: We ought to be preventing as much suffering as we can without sacrificing something else of comparable moral importance. This conclusion is one which we may be reluctant to face. I cannot see, though, why it should be regarded as a criticism of the position for which I have argued, rather than a criticism of our ordinary standards of behavior. Since most people are self-interested to some degree, very few of us are likely to do everything that we ought to do. It would, however, hardly be honest to take this as evidence that it is not the case that we ought to do it.

22 It may still be thought that my conclusions are so wildly out of line with what everyone else thinks and has always thought that there must be something wrong with the argument somewhere. In order to show that my conclusions, while certainly contrary to contemporary Western moral standards, would not have seemed so extraordinary at other times and in other places, I would like to quote a passage from a writer not normally thought of as a way-out radical, Thomas Aquinas.

> Now, according to the natural order instituted by divine providence, material goods are provided for the satisfaction of human needs. Therefore the division

and appropriation of property, which proceeds from human law, must not hinder the satisfaction of man's necessity from such goods. Equally, whatever a man has in superabundance is owed, of natural right, to the poor for their sustenance. So Ambrosius says, and it is also to be found in the *Decretum Gratiani:* "The bread which you withhold belongs to the hungry; the clothing you shut away, to the naked; and the money you bury in the earth is the redemption and freedom of the penniless."[4]

23 I now want to consider a number of points, more practical than philosophical, which are relevant to the application of the moral conclusion we have reached. These points challenge not the idea that we ought to be doing all we can to prevent starvation, but the idea that giving away a great deal of money is the best means to this end.

24 It is sometimes said that overseas aid should be a government responsibility, and that therefore one ought not to give to privately run charities. Giving privately, it is said, allows the government and the noncontributing members of society to escape their responsibilities.

25 This argument seems to assume that the more people there are who give to privately organized famine relief funds, the less likely it is that the government will take over full responsibility for such aid. This assumption is unsupported, and does not strike me as at all plausible. The opposite view—that if no one gives voluntarily, a government will assume that its citizens are uninterested in famine relief and would not wish to be forced into giving aid—seems more plausible. In any case, unless there were a definite probability that by refusing to give one would be helping to bring about massive government assistance, people who do refuse to make voluntary contributions are refusing to prevent a certain amount of suffering without being able to point to any tangible beneficial consequence of their refusal. So the onus of showing how their refusal will bring about government action is on those who refuse to give.

26 I do not, of course, want to dispute the contention that governments of affluent nations should be giving many times the amount of genuine, no-strings-attached aid that they are giving now. I agree, too, that giving privately is not enough, and that we ought to be campaigning actively for entirely new standards for both public and private contributions to famine relief. Indeed, I would sympathize with someone who thought that campaigning was more important than giving oneself, although I doubt whether preaching what one does not practice would be very effective. Unfortunately, for many people the idea that "it's the government's responsibility" is a reason for not giving which does not appear to entail any political action either.

27 Another, more serious reason for not giving to famine relief funds is that until there is effective population control, relieving famine merely postpones starvation. If we save the Bengal refugees now, others, perhaps the children of these refugees, will face starvation in a few years' time. In support of this, one may cite the now well-known facts about the population explosion and the relatively limited scope for expanded production.

28 This point, like the previous one, is an argument against relieving suffering that is happening now, because of a belief about what might happen in the future; it is unlike the previous point in that very good evidence can be adduced in support of this belief about the future. I will not go into the evidence here. I accept that the earth cannot support indefinitely a population rising at the present rate. This certainly poses a problem for anyone who thinks it important to prevent famine. Again, however, one could accept the argument without drawing the conclusion that it absolves one from any obligation to do anything to prevent famine. The conclusion that should be drawn is that the best means of preventing famine, in the long run, is population control. It would then follow from the position reached earlier that one ought to be doing all one can to promote population control (unless one held that all forms of population control were wrong in themselves, or would have significantly bad consequences). Since there are organizations working specifically for population control, one would then support them rather than more orthodox methods of preventing famine.

29 A third point raised by the conclusion reached earlier relates to the question of just how much we all ought to be giving away. One possibility, which has already been mentioned, is that we ought to give until we reach the level of marginal utility—that is, the level at which, by giving more, I would cause as much suffering to myself or my dependents as I would relieve by my gift. This would mean, of course, that one would reduce oneself to very near the material circumstances of a Bengali refugee. It will be recalled that earlier I put forward both a strong and a moderate version of the principle of preventing bad occurrences. The strong version, which required us to prevent bad things from happening unless in doing so we would be sacrificing something of comparable moral significance, does seem to require reducing ourselves to the level of marginal utility. I should also say that the strong version seems to me to be the correct one. I proposed the more moderate version—that we should prevent bad occurrences unless, to do so, we had to sacrifice something morally significant—only in order to show that even on this surely undeniable principle a great change in our way of life is required. On the more moderate principle, it may not follow that we ought to reduce ourselves to the level of marginal utility, for one might hold that to reduce oneself and one's family to this level is to cause something significantly bad to happen. Whether this is so I shall not discuss, since, as I have said, I can see no good reason for holding the moderate version of the principle rather than the strong version. Even if we accepted the principle only in its moderate form, however, it should be clear that we would have to give away enough to ensure that the consumer society, dependent as it is on people spending on trivia rather than giving to famine relief, would slow down and perhaps disappear entirely. There are several reasons why this would be desirable in itself. The value and necessity of economic growth are now being questioned not only by conservationists, but by economists as well.[5] There is no doubt, too, that the consumer society has had a distorting effect on the goals and purposes of its members. Yet looking at the matter purely from the point of view of overseas aid, there must be a limit to the extent to which we should deliberately slow down our economy; for it might be the case that if we gave away, say, 40 percent of our Gross National Product, we would

slow down the economy so much that in absolute terms we would be giving less than if we gave 25 percent of the much larger GNP that we would have if we limited our contribution to this smaller percentage.

30 I mention this only as an indication of the sort of factor that one would have to take into account in working out an ideal. Since Western societies generally consider one percent of the GNP an acceptable level for overseas aid, the matter is entirely academic. Nor does it affect the question of how much an individual should give in a society in which very few are giving substantial amounts.

31 It is sometimes said, though less often now than it used to be, that philosophers have no special role to play in public affairs, since most public issues depend primarily on an assessment of facts. On questions of fact, it is said, philosophers as such have no special expertise, and so it has been possible to engage in philosophy without committing oneself to any position on major public issues. No doubt there are some issues of social policy and foreign policy about which it can truly be said that a really expert assessment of the facts is required before taking sides or acting, but the issue of famine is surely not one of these. The facts about the existence of suffering are beyond dispute. Nor, I think, is it disputed that we can do something about it, either through orthodox methods of famine relief or through population control or both. This is therefore an issue on which philosophers are competent to take a position. The issue is one which faces everyone who has more money than he needs to support himself and his dependents, or who is in a position to take some sort of political action. These categories must include practically every teacher and student of philosophy in the universities of the Western world. If philosophy is to deal with matters that are relevant to both teachers and students, this is an issue that philosophers should discuss.

32 Discussion, though, is not enough. What is the point of relating philosophy to public (and personal) affairs if we do not take our conclusions seriously? In this instance, taking our conclusion seriously means acting upon it. The philosopher will not find it any easier than anyone else to alter his attitudes and way of life to the extent that, if I am right, is involved in doing everything that we ought to be doing. At the very least, though, one can make a start. The philosopher who does so will have to sacrifice some of the benefits of the consumer society, but he can find compensation in the satisfaction of a way of life in which theory and practice, if not yet in harmony, are at least coming together.

Postscript

33 The crisis in Bangladesh that spurred me to write the above article is now of historical interest only, but the world food crisis is, if anything, still more serious. The huge grain reserves that were then held by the United States have vanished. Increased oil prices have made both fertilizer and energy more expensive in developing countries, and have made it difficult for them to produce more food. At the same time, their population has continued to grow. Fortunately, as I write now, there is no major famine anywhere in the world; but poor people are still starving in several countries, and malnutrition

remains very widespread. The need for assistance is, therefore, just as great as when I first wrote, and we can be sure that without it there will, again, be major famines.

34 The contrast between poverty and affluence that I wrote about is also as great as it was then. True, the affluent nations have experienced a recession, and are perhaps not as prosperous as they were in 1971. But the poorer nations have suffered at least as much from the recession, in reduced government aid (because if governments decide to reduce expenditure, they regard foreign aid as one of the expendable items, ahead of, for instance, defense or public construction projects) and in increased prices for goods and materials they need to buy. In any case, compared to the difference between the affluent nations and the poor nations, the whole recession was trifling; the poorest in the affluent nations remained incomparably better off than the poorest in the poor nations.

35 So the case for aid, on both a personal and a governmental level, remains as great now as it was in 1971, and I would not wish to change the basic argument that I put forward then.

36 There are, however, some matters of emphasis that I might put differently if I were to rewrite the article, and the most important of these concerns the population problem. I still think that, as I wrote then, the view that famine relief merely postpones starvation unless something is done to check population growth is not an argument against aid, it is only an argument against the *type* of aid that should be given. Those who hold this view have the same obligation to give to prevent starvation as those who do not; the difference is that they regard assisting population control schemes as a more effective way of preventing starvation in the long run. I would now, however, have given greater space to the discussion of the population problem; for I now think that there is a serious case for saying that if a country refuses to take any steps to slow the rate of its population growth, we should not give it aid. This is, of course, a very drastic step to take, and the choice it represents is a horrible choice to have to make, but if, after a dispassionate analysis of all the available information, we come to the conclusion that without population control we will not, in the long run, be able to prevent famine or other catastrophes, then it may be more humane in the long run to aid those countries that are prepared to take strong measures to reduce population growth, and to use our aid policy as a means of pressuring other countries to take similar steps.

37 It may be objected that such a policy involves an attempt to coerce a sovereign nation. But since we are not under an obligation to give aid unless that aid is likely to be effective in reducing starvation or malnutrition, we are not under an obligation to give aid to countries that make no effort to reduce a rate of population growth that will lead to catastrophe. Since we do not force any nation to accept our aid, simply making it clear that we will not give aid where it is not going to be effective cannot properly be regarded as a form of coercion.

38 I should also make it clear that the kind of aid that will slow population growth is not just assistance with the setting up of facilities for dispensing contraceptives and performing sterilizations. It is also necessary to create the conditions under which people do not wish to have so many children. This will involve, among other things, providing

greater economic security for people, particularly in their old age, so that they do not need the security of a large family to provide for them. Thus, the requirements of aid designed to reduce population growth and aid designed to eliminate starvation are by no means separate; they overlap, and the latter will often be a means to the former. The obligation of the affluent is, I believe, to do both. Fortunately, there are now so many people in the foreign aid field, including those in the private agencies, who are aware of this.

39 One other matter that I should now put forward slightly differently is that my argument does, of course, apply to assistance with development, particularly agricultural development, as well as to direct famine relief. Indeed, I think the former is usually the better long-term investment. Although this was my view when I wrote the article, the fact that I started from a famine situation, where the need was for immediate food, has led some readers to suppose that the argument is only about giving food and not about other types of aid. This is quite mistaken, and my view is that the aid should be of whatever type is most effective.

40 On a more philosophical level, there has been some discussion of the original article which has been helpful in clarifying the issues and pointing to the areas in which more work on the argument is needed. In particular, as John Arthur has shown in ''Rights and the Duty to Bring Aid'' . . . something more needs to be said about the notion of ''moral significance.'' The problem is that to give an account of this notion involves nothing less than a full-fledged ethical theory; and while I am myself inclined toward a utilitarian view, it was my aim in writing ''Famine, Affluence, and Morality'' to produce an argument which would appeal not only to utilitarians, but also to anyone who accepted the initial premises of the argument, which seemed to me likely to have a very wide acceptance. So I tried to get around the need to produce a complete ethical theory by allowing my readers to fill in their own version—within limits—of what is morally significant, and then see what the moral consequences are. This tactic works reasonably well with those who are prepared to agree that such matters as being fashionably dressed are not really of moral significance; but Arthur is right to say that people could take the opposite view without being obviously irrational. Hence, I do not accept Arthur's claim that the weak principle implies little or no duty of benevolence, for it will imply a significant duty of benevolence for those who admit, as I think most nonphilosophers and even off-guard philosophers will admit, that they spend considerable sums on items that by their own standards are of no moral significance. But I do agree that the weak principle is nonetheless too weak, because it makes it too easy for the duty of benevolence to be avoided.

41 On the other hand, I think the strong principle will stand, whether the notion of moral significance is developed along utilitarian lines, or once again left to the individual reader's own sincere judgment. In either case, I would argue against Arthur's view that we are morally entitled to give greater weight to our own interests and purposes simply because they are our own. This view seems to me contrary to the idea, now widely shared by moral philosophers, that some element of impartiality or universalizability is inherent in the very notion of a moral judgment. (For a discussion of the

different formulations of this idea, and an indication of the extent to which they are in agreement, see R. M. Hare, ''Rules of War and Moral Reasoning,'' *Philosophy and Public Affairs* I, no. 2 [1972].) Granted, in normal circumstances, it may be better for everyone if we recognize that each of us will be primarily responsible for running our own lives and only secondarily responsible for others. This, however, is not a moral ultimate, but a secondary principle that derives from consideration of how a society may best order its affairs, given the limits of altruism in human beings. Such secondary principles are, I think, swept aside by the extreme evil of people starving to death.

Notes

1. There was also a third possibility: that India would go to war to enable the refugees to return to their lands. Since I wrote this paper, India has taken this way out. The situation is no longer that described above, but this does not affect my argument, as the next paragraph indicates.
2. In view of the special sense philosophers often give to the term, I should say that I use ''obligation'' simply as the abstract noun derived from ''ought,'' so that ''I have an obligation to'' means no more, and no less, than ''I ought to.'' This usage is in accordance with the definition of ''ought'' given by the *Shorter Oxford English Dictionary:* ''the general verb to express duty or obligation.'' I do not think any issue of substance hangs on the way the term is used; sentences in which I use ''obligation'' could be all rewritten, although somewhat clumsily, as sentences in which a clause containing ''ought'' replaces the term ''obligation.''
3. J. O. Urmson, ''Saints and Heroes,'' in *Essays in Moral Philosophy,* ed. Abraham I. Melden (Seattle: University of Washington Press, 1958), p. 214. For a related but significantly different view see also Henry Sidgwick, *The Methods of Ethics,* 7th edn. (London: Dover Press, 1907), pp. 220–21, 492–93.
4. *Summa Theologica,* II-II, Question 66, Article 7, in *Aquinas, Selected Political Writings,* ed. A. P. d'Entreves, trans. J. G. Dawson (Oxford: Basil Blackwell, 1948), p. 171.
5. See, for instance, John Kenneth Galbraith, *The New Industrial State* (Boston: Houghton Mifflin, 1967); and E. J. Mishan, *The Costs of Economic Growth* (New York: Praeger, 1967).

Questions for Analysis

1. What is the purpose of the first paragraph in Singer's essay? Even though he speaks of events (and monetary values) of over 20 years ago, have conditions in this world changed much? Is this issue still one we must face?
2. In paragraphs 8 through 13, Singer deals with arguments people often present when they do not wish to give much if anything to relieve the suffering of others. Explain in your own words these two lines of reasoning and Singer's response to them. Have you heard (or used yourself) either of these reasons?
3. Explain the distinction Singer makes between charity and duty. Which term does he use when discussing world famine?
4. Singer's view of moral behavior would require each of us to sacrifice. In your opinion, is the sacrifice he calls for reasonable? Is that sacrifice possible, given what you know about human nature?

5. Singer added his ''Postscript'' several years after he wrote this essay in 1971. Does he moderate his position by adding the ''Postscript''? Explain.
6. In Paragraph 38, Singer talks of the need not just to make available the means to control population growth but also to ''create the conditions under which people do not wish to have so many children.'' He goes on to mention the ''economic security'' provided by large families. Are economic changes enough? Can we, and should we, change cultural traditions that favor large families? Can we, and should we, change cultural traditions that favor male children?
7. Despite his call for actions that are dramatically out of the mainstream in current Western cultures, could you argue that Singer's position is the moderate one between Hardin's and Watson's (see next essay) views? If not, define and justify what you think would be a middle-of-the-road position on this issue.

Richard A. Watson

Reason and Morality in a World of Limited Food

(1977)

Richard Watson (b. 1931) is a philosopher who takes a radically moral position on world hunger. His essay first appeared in a collection of essays by a number of authors entitled *World Hunger and Moral Obligation,* which was published in 1977.

1 A few years ago, President Johnson said:

> There are 200 million of us and 3 billion of them and they want what we've got, but we're not going to give it to them.

2 In this essay I examine the conflict between reasonable and moral behavior in a world of limited food. It appears to be unreasonable—and conceivably immoral—to share all food equally when this would result in everyone's being malnourished. Arguments for the morality of unequal distribution are presented from the standpoint of the individual, the nation, and the human species. These arguments fail because, although it is unreasonable to share limited food when sharing threatens survival, the moral principle of equity ranks sharing above survival. I accept the principle of equity, and conclude by challenging the ideological basis that makes sharing unreasonable.

3 The contrast of the moral with the reasonable depends on distinguishing people from things. Moral considerations pertain to behavior of individuals that affects other people

by acting on them directly or by acting on things in which they have an interest. The moral context is broad, for people have interests in almost everything, and almost any behavior may affect someone.

4 If reasonable and moral behavior were coextensive, then there would be no morality. Thus, there is no contrast at the extremes that bound the moral milieu, reason and morality being the same at one pole, and morality not existing at the other. These extremes meet in evolutionary naturalism: If it is moral to treat people as animals surviving, then reason augmenting instinct is the best criterion for behavior, and a separate discipline of morality is extraneous. Only between the extremes can reason and morality conflict.

5 Between the extremes, some moralists use "rational" to indicate conclusions that tend toward moral behavior, and "practical" for conclusions that excusably do not. The use of these terms often constitutes special pleading, either to gain sympathy for a position that is not strictly reasonable but is "rational" (because it is "right"), or that is not strictly moral but is "practical" (because it "should" be done). These hedges hide the sharp distinction between people and things in the context of reason and morality. The rational and the practical are obviously reasonable in a way that they are not obviously either moral or immoral. Reasonable behavior is either moral, immoral, or amoral. When reason and morality conflict, there can be confusion, but no compromise.

6 Attacks on morality by reason disguised in practical dress are so common as to go almost without notice. The practical ousts morality as a determinant of behavior, particularly in industrialized nations. Many argue that the practical imperatives of survival preclude moral behavior even by those who want to be moral. If only it were practical to be moral, then all would gladly be so.

7 It is difficult to be moral in a world of limited food because the supreme moral principle is that of equity. The principle of equity is based on the belief that all human beings are moral equals with equal rights to the necessities of life. Differential treatment of human beings thus should be based only on their freely chosen actions and not on accidents of their birth and environment. Specific to this discussion, everyone has a right to an equal share of available food.

8 However, we find ourselves in a world about which many food and population experts assert the following:

1. One-third of the world's people (the West) consume two-thirds of the world's resources.
2. Two-thirds of the world's people (the Third World) are malnourished.
3. Equal distribution of the world's resources would result in everyone's being malnourished.

There is ample evidence that these statements are true, but for this discussion it is enough that many people in the West—particularly those who occupy positions of responsibility and power—understand and accept them.

9 These moral and factual beliefs drive one to this practical conclusion: Although morally we should share all food equally, and we in the West eat more than we need, equal sharing would be futile (unreasonable), for then no one would be well nourished. Thus, any food sharing is necessarily symbolic, for no practical action would alleviate the plight of the malnourished.

10 For example, practical action—moral as far as it goes—might be to reduce food consumption until every Westerner is just well nourished. But if the surplus were distributed equally to the other two-thirds of the world's people, they would still be malnourished. Thus, an easy excuse for not sharing at all is that it would neither solve the nourishment problem nor change the moral situation. Two-thirds would still be malnourished, and one-third would still be consuming more than equal shares of the world's food, to which everyone has equal rights.

11 Another argument for unequal distribution is as follows: All people are moral equals. Because everyone has a right to be well nourished, it would be immoral to take so much food from someone who has enough as to leave him without enough. Anyone who takes the food would be acting immorally, even if the taker is starving. This argument can go two ways. One could simply say that it would be immoral to deprive oneself of what one has. But if one wanted to discredit morality itself, one could claim that morality in this instance is self-contradictory. For if I behave morally by distributing food equally, I behave immorally by depriving someone (myself) of enough food to remain well nourished. And noticing that if all food were shared equally, everyone would be malnourished instead of just some, one might argue that it cannot be moral to deprive one person of his right to enough food so that two people have less than enough. Proper moral action must be to maintain the inequity, so at least one person can enjoy his rights.

12 Nevertheless, according to the highest principles of traditional (Western) morality, available food should be distributed equally even if everyone then will be malnourished. This is belabored by everyone who compares the earth to a lifeboat, a desert island, or a spaceship. In these situations, the strong are expected to take even a smaller share than the weak. There is no need for us to go overboard, however. We shall soon be as weak as anyone else if we just do our moral duty and distribute the food equally.

13 Given this, the well-nourished minority might try to buttress its position morally by attempting to solve the nourishment problem for everyone, either by producing enough food for everyone, or by humanely reducing the world's population to a size at which equal distribution of food would nourish everyone adequately. The difficulty with this is that national survival for the food-favored industrial nations requires maintenance of political and economic systems that depend on unequal distribution of limited goods.[1] In the present world context, it would be unreasonable (disastrous) for an industrialized nation to attempt to provide food for everybody. Who would pay for it? And after all, well-nourished citizens are obviously important to the survival of the nation. As for humanely reducing the world's population, there are no practical means for doing it. Thus, the practical expediencies of national survival preclude actions that might justify temporary unequal distribution with the claim that it is essential for solving the nour-

ishment problem. Equal distribution is impossible without total (impractical) economic and political revolution.

14 These arguments are morally spurious. That food sufficient for well-nourished survival is the equal right of every human individual or nation is a specification of the higher principle that everyone has equal right to the necessities of life. The moral stress of the principle of equity is primarily on equal sharing, and only secondarily on what is being shared. The higher moral principle is of human *equity per se.* Consequently, the moral action is to distribute all food equally, *whatever the consequences.* This is the hard line apparently drawn by such moralists as Immanuel Kant and Noam Chomsky—but then, morality is hard. The conclusion may be unreasonable (impractical and irrational in conventional terms), but it is obviously moral. Nor should anyone purport surprise; it has always been understood that the claims of morality—if taken seriously—supersede those of conflicting reason.

15 One may even have to sacrifice one's life or one's nation to be moral in situations where practical behavior would preserve it. For example, if a prisoner of war undergoing torture is to be a (perhaps dead) patriot even when reason tells him that collaboration will hurt no one, he remains silent. Similarly, if one is to be moral, one distributes available food in equal shares (even if everyone then dies). That an action is necessary to save one's life is no excuse for behaving unpatriotically or immorally if one wishes to be a patriot or moral. No principle of morality absolves one of behaving immorally simply to save one's life or nation. There is a strict analogy here between adhering to moral principles for the sake of being moral, and adhering to Christian principles for the sake of being Christian. The moral world contains pits and lions, but one looks always to the highest light. The ultimate test always harks to the highest principle—recant or die—and it is pathetic to profess morality if one quits when the going gets rough.

16 I have put aside many questions of detail—such as the mechanical problems of distributing food—because detail does not alter the stark conclusion. If every human life is equal in value, then the equal distribution of the necessities of life is an extremely high, if not the highest, moral duty. It is at least high enough to override the excuse that by doing it one would lose one's own life. But many people cannot accept the view that one must distribute equally even if the nation collapses or all people die.

17 If everyone dies, then there will be no realm of morality. Practically speaking, sheer survival comes first. One can adhere to the principle of equity only if one exists. So it is rational to suppose that the principle of survival is morally higher than the principle of equity. And though one might not be able to argue for unequal distribution of food to save a nation—for nations can come and go—one might well argue that unequal distribution is necessary for the survival of the human species. That is, some large group—say one-third of the present world population—should be a least well-nourished for human survival.

18 However, from an individual standpoint, the human species—like the nation—is of no moral relevance. From a naturalistic standpoint, survival does come first; from a moralistic standpoint—as indicated above—survival may have to be sacrificed. In the

milieu of morality, it is immaterial whether or not the human species survives as a result of individual moral behavior.

19 A possible way to resolve this conflict between reason and morality is to challenge the view that morality pertains only to the behavior of individual human beings. One way to do this is to break down the distinction between people and things. It would have to be established that such abstract things as "the people," "the nation," and "the human species" in themselves have moral status. Then they would have a right to survival just as human beings have a right to life: We should be concerned about the survival of these things not merely because human beings have an interest in them, but because it would be immoral *per se* to destroy them.

20 In the West, corporation law provides the theoretical basis for treating things as people.[2] Corporate entities such as the State, the Church, and trading companies have long enjoyed special status in Western society. The rights of corporate entities are precisely defined by a legal fiction, the concept of the corporate person. Christopher D. Stone says that corporate persons enjoy as many legal rights as, and sometimes more than, do individual human persons.[3] Thus, while most of us are not tempted to confuse ordinary things like stones and houses with people, almost everyone concurs with a legal system that treats corporate entities as people. The great familiarity and usefulness of this system supports the delusion that corporate entities have rights in common with, and are the moral equals of, individual human beings.

21 On these grounds, some argue that because of size, importance, and power of corporate entities, institutional rights have priority over the rights of individuals. Of course, to the extent that society is defined by the economy or the State, people are dependent on and subordinate to these institutions. Practically speaking, institutional needs come first; people's needs are satisfied perhaps coextensively with, but secondarily to, satisfying institutional needs. It is argued that to put individual human needs first would be both illogical and impractical, for people and their needs are defined only in the social context. Institutions come first because they are prerequisite to the very existence of people.

22 A difficulty with the above argument as a support for any given institution is that it provides merely for the priority of *some* institutions over human individuals, not, say, for the priority of the United States or the West. But it does appear to provide an argument for the priority of the human species.

23 Given that the human species has rights as a fictional person on the analogy of corporate rights, it would seem to be rational to place the right of survival of the species above that of individuals. Unless the species survives, no individual will survive, and thus an individual's right to life is subordinate to the species' right to survival. If species survival depends on the unequal distribution of food to maintain a healthy breeding stock, then it is morally right for some people to have plenty while others starve. Only if there is enough food to nourish everyone well does it follow that food should be shared equally.

24 This might be true if corporate entities actually do have moral status and moral rights. But obviously, the legal status of corporate entities as fictional persons does not

make them moral equals or superiors of actual human persons. Legislators might profess astonishment that anyone would think that a corporate person is a *person* as people are, let alone a moral person. However, because the legal rights of corporate entities are based on individual rights, and because corporate entities are treated so much like persons, the transition is often made.

25 Few theorists today would argue that the state or the human species is a personal agent.[4] But all this means is that idealism is dead in theory. Unfortunately, its influence lives, so it is worth giving an argument to show that corporate entities are not real persons.

26 Corporate entities are not persons as you and I are in the explicit sense that we are self-conscious agents and they are not. Corporate entities are not *agents* at all, let alone moral agents. This is a good reason for not treating corporate entities even as fictional persons. The distinction between people and other things, to generalize, is that people are self-conscious agents, whereas things are not.

27 The possession of rights essentially depends on an entity's being self-conscious, i.e., on its actually being a person. If it is self-conscious, then it has a right to life. Self-consciousness is a necessary, but not sufficient, condition for an entity's also being a responsible moral agent as most human beings are. A moral agent must have the capacity to be responsible, i.e., the capacity to choose and to act freely with respect to consequences that the agent does or can recognize and accept as its own choice and doing. Only a being who knows himself as a person, and who can effect choices and accept consequences, is a responsible moral agent.

28 On these grounds, moral equality rests on the actuality of moral agency based on reciprocal rights and responsibilities. One is responsible to something only if it can be responsible in return. Thus, we have responsibilities to other people, and they have reciprocal rights. We have no responsibilities to things as such, and they have no rights. If we care for things, it is because people have interests in them, not because things in themselves impose responsibilities on us.

29 That is, as stated early in this essay, morality essentially has to do with relations among people, among persons. It is nonsense to talk of things that cannot be moral agents as having responsibilities; consequently, it is nonsense to talk of whatever is not actually a person as having rights. It is deceptive even to talk of legal rights of a corporate entity. Those rights (and reciprocal responsibilities) actually pertain to individual human beings who have an interest in the corporate entity. The State or the human species have no rights at all, let alone rights superior to those of individuals.

30 The basic reason given for preserving a nation or the human species is that otherwise the milieu of morality would not exist. This is false so far as specific nations are concerned, but it is true that the existence of individuals depends on the existence of the species. However, although moral behavior is required of each individual, no principle requires that the realm of morality itself be preserved. Thus, we are reduced to the position that people's interest in preserving the human species is based primarily on the interest of each in individual survival. Having shown above that the principle of

equity is morally superior to the principle of survival, we can conclude again that food should be shared equally even if this means the extinction of the human race.

31 Is there no way to produce enough food to nourish everyone well? Besides cutting down to the minimum, people in the West might quit feeding such nonhuman animals as cats and dogs. However, some people (e.g., Peter Singer) argue that mere sentience—the capacity to suffer pain—means that an animal is the moral equal of human beings.[5] I argue that because nonhuman animals are not moral agents, they do not share the rights of self-conscious responsible persons. And considering the profligacy of nature, it is rational to argue that if nonhuman animals have any rights at all, they include not the right to life, but merely the right to fight for life. In fact, if people in the West did not feed grain to cattle, sheep, and hogs, a considerable amount of food would be freed for human consumption. Even then, there might not be enough to nourish everyone well.

32 Let me remark that Stone and Singer attempt to break down the distinction between people on the one hand, and certain things (corporate entities) and nonhuman animals on the other, out of moral concern. However, there is another, profoundly antihumanitarian movement also attempting to break down the distinction. All over the world, heirs of Gobineau, Goebbels, and Hitler practice genocide and otherwise treat people as nonhuman animals and things in the name of the State. I am afraid that the consequences of treating entities such as corporations and nonhuman animals—that are not moral agents—as persons with rights will not be that we will treat national parks and chickens the way we treat people, but that we will have provided support for those who treat people the way we now treat nonhuman animals and things.

33 The benefits of modern society depend in no small part on the institution of corporation law. Even if the majority of these benefits are to the good—of which I am by no means sure—the legal fiction of corporate personhood still elevates corporate needs above the needs of people. In the present context, reverence for corporate entities leads to the spurious argument that the present world imbalance of food and resources is morally justified in the name of the higher rights of sovereign nations, or even of the human species, the survival of which is said to be more important than the right of any individual to life.

34 This conclusion is morally absurd. This is not, however, the fault of morality. We *should* share all food equally, at least until everyone is well-nourished. Besides food, *all* the necessities of life should be shared, at least until everyone is adequately supplied with a humane minimum. The hard conclusion remains that we should share all food equally even if this means that everyone starves and the human species becomes extinct. But, of course, the human race would survive even equal sharing, for after enough people died, the remainder could be well-nourished on the food that remained. But this grisly prospect does not show that anything is wrong with the principle of equity. Instead, it shows that something is profoundly wrong with the social institutions in which sharing the necessities of life equally is ''impractical'' and ''irrational.''

35 In another ideological frame, moral behavior might also be practical and rational. As remarked above, equal sharing can be accomplished only through total economic and political revolution. Obviously, this is what is needed.

Notes

1. See Richard Watson, "The Limits of World Order," *Alternatives: A Journal of World Policy,* I (1975), 487–513.
2. See Christopher D. Stone, *Should Trees Have Standing? Toward Legal Rights for Natural Objects* (Los Altos, Calif.: William Kaufman, 1974). Stone proposes that to protect such things as national parks, we should give them legal personhood as we do corporations.
3. Ibid., p. 47: "It is more and more the individual human being, with his consciousness, that is the legal fiction." Also: "The legal system does the best it can to maintain the illusion of the reality of the individual human being." (footnote 125) Many public figures have discovered that they have a higher legal status if they incorporate themselves than they do as individual persons.
4. Stone (ibid., p. 47) does say that "institutions . . . have wills, minds, purposes, and inertias that are in very important ways their own, i.e., that can transcend and survive changes in the consciousness of the individual humans who supposedly comprise them, and whom they supposedly serve," but I do not think Stone actually believes that corporate entities are persons like you and me.
5. See Peter Singer, *Animal Liberation* (New York: The New York Review of Books/Random House, 1975).

Questions for Analysis

1. Why does Watson begin his essay with a quotation from President Johnson?
2. What are the key differences between Watson's position and Singer's position? How would Watson argue against Singer's position?
3. Explain Watson's argument against considering corporate entities (e.g., "the state," "the human species") as having rights equal to or greater than individual human beings. Why does he present this argument?
4. Watson admits that his argument for equity, while being absolutely moral, would be open to being called "impractical" or "irrational." How does he counter these possible objections? Is there a difference between "impractical" and "impossible" that Watson fails to take into account? What would he say to that distinction?
5. What do you think of Watson's view of morality? Does he have a standard that human beings can meet? Is it one we should strive for? Does it violate the instinct of self-preservation? Should morality take priority over self-preservation?

Evolution vs. Scientific Creationism

Stephen Jay Gould

Evolution as Fact and Theory

(1981)

Stephen Jay Gould (b. 1941) is Professor of Geology at Harvard University and one of the leading contributors to the study of human evolution. He has also written essays on widely ranging topics in science for the magazine *Natural History*. Many of his essays have been collected into books. This essay first appeared in *Discover* magazine.

1 Kirtley Mather, who died last year at age eighty-nine, was a pillar of both science and the Christian religion in America and one of my dearest friends. The difference of half a century in our ages evaporated before our common interests. The most curious thing we shared was a battle we each fought at the same age. For Kirtley had gone to Tennessee with Clarence Darrow to testify for evolution at the Scopes trial of 1925.[1] When I think that we are enmeshed again in the same struggle for one of the best documented, most compelling and exciting concepts in all of science, I don't know whether to laugh or cry.

2 According to idealized principles of scientific discourse, the arousal of dormant issues should reflect fresh data that give renewed life to abandoned notions. Those outside the current debate may therefore be excused for suspecting that creationists have come up with something new, or that evolutionists have generated some serious internal trouble. But nothing has changed; the creationists have not a single new fact or argument. Darrow and Bryan were at least more entertaining than we lesser antagonists today. The rise of creationism is politics, pure and simple; it represents one issue (and by no means the major concern) of the resurgent evangelical right. Arguments that seemed kooky just a decade ago have reentered the mainstream.

3 The basic attack of the creationists falls apart on two general counts before we even reach the supposed factual details of their complaints against evolution. First, they play

[1]AUTHOR'S NOTE: The Scopes "Monkey Trial" occurred in Tennessee when John Scopes, a high-school science teacher, was accused of teaching evolution in violation of a 1925 Tennessee law. Despite the brilliance of his defense attorney (Clarence Darrow), Scopes was convicted. The law was not repealed until 1967.

upon a vernacular misunderstanding of the word ''theory'' to convey the false impression that we evolutionists are covering up the rotten core of our edifice. Second, they misuse a popular philosophy of science to argue that they are behaving scientifically in attacking evolution. Yet the same philosophy demonstrates that their own belief is not science, and that ''scientific creationism'' is therefore meaningless and self-contradictory, a superb example of what Orwell[2] called ''newspeak.''

4 In the American vernacular, ''theory'' often means ''imperfect fact''—part of a hierarchy of confidence running downhill from fact to theory to hypothesis to guess. Thus the power of the creationist argument: Evolution is ''only'' a theory, and intense debate now rages about many aspects of the theory. If evolution is less than a fact, and scientists can't even make up their minds about the theory, then what confidence can we have in it? Indeed, President Reagan echoed this argument before an evangelical group in Dallas when he said (in what I devoutly hope was campaign rhetoric): ''Well, it is a theory. It is a scientific theory only, and it has in recent years been challenged in the world of science—that is, not believed in the scientific community to be as infallible as it once was.''

5 Well, evolution *is* a theory. It is also a fact. And facts and theories are different things, not rungs in a hierarchy of increasing certainty. Facts are the world's data. Theories are structures of ideas that explain and interpret facts. Facts do not go away when scientists debate rival theories to explain them. Einstein's theory of gravitation replaced Newton's, but apples did not suspend themselves in mid-air pending the outcome. And human beings evolved from apelike ancestors whether they did so by Darwin's proposed mechanism or by some other, yet to be discovered.

6 Moreover, ''fact'' does not mean ''absolute certainty.'' The final proofs of logic and mathematics flow deductively from stated premises and achieve certainty only because they are *not* about the empirical world. Evolutionists make no claim for perpetual truth, though creationists often do (and then attack us for a style of argument that they themselves favor). In science, ''fact'' can only mean ''confirmed to such a degree that it would be perverse to withhold provisional assent.'' I suppose that apples might start to rise tomorrow, but the possibility does not merit equal time in physics classrooms.

7 Evolutionists have been clear about this distinction between fact and theory from the very beginning, if only because we have always acknowledged how far we are from completely understanding the mechanisms (theory) by which evolution (fact) occurred. Darwin continually emphasized the difference between his two great and separate accomplishments: establishing the fact of evolution, and proposing a theory—natural selection—to explain the mechanism of evolution. He wrote in *The Descent of Man:* ''I had two distinct objects in view; firstly, to show that species had not been separately created, and secondly, that natural selection had been the chief agent of change. . . . Hence If I have erred in . . . having exaggerated its natural selection's power. . . . I have

[2]AUTHOR'S NOTE: George Orwell (1903–1950) was an English essayist and novelist best known for his novel *1984.* The rulers in *1984* create a language called ''newspeak,'' a confusing, ultimately meaningless way of speaking that interferes with clear thought.

at least, as I hope, done good service in aiding to overthrow the dogma of separate creations.''

8 Thus Darwin acknowledged the provisional nature of natural selection while affirming the fact of evolution. The fruitful theoretical debate that Darwin initiated has never ceased. From the 1940s through the 1960s, Darwin's own theory of natural selection did achieve a temporary hegemony that it never enjoyed in his lifetime. But renewed debate characterizes our decade, and, while no biologist questions the importance of natural selection, many now doubt its ubiquity. In particular, many evolutionists argue that substantial amounts of genetic change may not be subject to natural selection and may spread through populations at random. Others are challenging Darwin's linking of natural selection with gradual, imperceptible change through all intermediary degrees; they are arguing that most evolutionary events may occur far more rapidly than Darwin envisioned.

9 Scientists regard debates on fundamental issues of theory as a sign of intellectual health and a source of excitement. Science is—and how else can I say it?—most fun when it plays with interesting ideas, examines their implications, and recognizes that old information may be explained in surprisingly new ways. Evolutionary theory is now enjoying this uncommon vigor. Yet amidst all this turmoil no biologist has been led to doubt the fact that evolution occurred; we are debating *how* it happened. We are all trying to explain the same thing: the tree of evolutionary descent linking all organisms by ties of genealogy. Creationists pervert and caricature this debate by conveniently neglecting the common conviction that underlies it, and by falsely suggesting that we now doubt the very phenomenon we are struggling to understand.

10 Using another invalid argument, creationists claim that ''the dogma of separate creations,'' as Darwin characterized it a century ago, is a scientific theory meriting equal time with evolution in high school biology curricula. But a prevailing viewpoint among philosophers of science belies this creationist argument. Philosopher Karl Popper has argued for decades that the primary criterion of science is the falsifiability of its theories. We can never prove absolutely, but we can falsify. A set of ideas that cannot, in principle, be falsified is not science.

11 The entire creationist argument involves little more than a rhetorical attempt to falsify evolution by presenting supposed contradictions among its supporters. Their brand of creationism, they claim, is ''scientific'' because it follows the Popperian model in trying to demolish evolution. Yet Popper's argument must apply in both directions. One does not become a scientist by the simple act of trying to falsify another scientific system; one has to present an alternative system that also meets Popper's criterion—it too must be falsifiable in principle.

12 ''Scientific creationism'' is a self-contradictory, nonsense phrase precisely because it cannot be falsified. I can envision observations and experiments that would disprove any evolutionary theory I know, but I cannot imagine what potential data could lead creationists to abandon their beliefs. Unbeatable systems are dogma, not science. Lest I seem harsh or rhetorical, I quote creationism's leading intellectual, Duane Gish, Ph.D., from his recent (1978) book *Evolution? The Fossils Say No!* ''By creation we mean

the bringing into being by a supernatural Creator of the basic kinds of plants and animals by the process of sudden, or fiat, creation. We do not know how the Creator created, what processes He used, *for He used processes which are not now operating anywhere in the natural universe* [Gish's italics]. This is why we refer to creation as special creation. We cannot discover by scientific investigations anything about the creative processes used by the Creator.'' Pray tell, Dr. Gish, in the light of your last sentence, what then is ''scientific'' creationism?

The Fact of Evolution

13 Our confidence that evolution occurred centers upon three general arguments. First, we have abundant, direct, observational evidence of evolution in action, from both the field and the laboratory. It ranges from countless experiments on change in nearly everything about fruit flies subjected to artificial selection in the laboratory to the famous British moths that turned black when industrial soot darkened the trees upon which they rest. (The moths gain protection from sharp-sighted bird predators by blending into the background.) Creationists do not deny these observations; how could they? Creationists have tightened their act. They now argue that God only created ''basic kinds,'' and allowed for limited evolutionary meandering within them. Thus toy poodles and Great Danes come from the dog kind and moths can change color, but nature cannot convert a dog to a cat or a monkey to a man.

14 The second and third arguments for evolution—the case for major changes—do not involve direct observation of evolution in action. They rest upon inference, but are no less secure for that reason. Major evolutionary change requires too much time for direct observation on the scale of recorded human history. All historical sciences rest upon inference, and evolution is no different from geology, cosmology, or human history in this respect. In principle, we cannot observe processes that operated in the past. We must infer them from results that still survive: living and fossil organisms for evolution, documents and artifacts for human history, strata and topography for geology.

15 The second argument—that the imperfection of nature reveals evolution—strikes many people as ironic, for they feel that evolution should be most elegantly displayed in the nearly perfect adaptation expressed by some organisms—the chamber of a gull's wing, or butterflies that cannot be seen in ground litter because they mimic leaves so precisely. But perfection could be imposed by a wise creator or evolved by natural selection. Perfection covers the tracks of past history. And past history—the evidence of descent—is our mark of evolution.

16 Evolution lies exposed in the *imperfections* that record a history of descent. Why should a rat run, a bat fly, a porpoise swim, and I type this essay with structures built of the same bones unless we all inherited them from a common ancestor? An engineer, starting from scratch, could design better limbs in each case. Why should all the large native mammals of Australia be marsupials, unless they descended from a common ancestor isolated on this island continent? Marsupials are not ''better,'' or ideally suited for Australia; many have been wiped out by placental mammals imported by man from other continents. This principle of imperfection extends to all historical sciences. When

we recognize the etymology of September, October, November, and December (seventh, eight, ninth, and tenth, from the Latin), we know that two additional items (January and February) must have been added to an original calendar of ten months.

17 The third argument is more direct: Transitions are often found in the fossil record. Preserved transitions are not common—and should not be, according to our understanding of evolution (see next section)—but they are not entirely wanting, as creationists often claim. The lower jaw of reptiles contains several bones, that of mammals only one. The non-mammalian jawbones are reduced, step by step, in mammalian ancestors until they become tiny nubbins located at the back of the jaw. The "hammer" and "anvil" bones of the mammalian ear are descendants of these nubbins. How could such a transition be accomplished? the creationists ask. Surely a bone is either entirely in the jaw or in the ear. Yet paleontologists have discovered two transitional lineages or therapsids (the so-called mammal-like reptiles) with a double jaw joint—one composed of the old quadrate and articular bones (soon to become the hammer and anvil), the other of the squamosal and dentary bones (as in modern mammals). For that matter, what better transitional form could we desire than the oldest human, *Australopithecus afarensis,* with its apelike palate, its human upright stance, and a cranial capacity larger than any ape's of the same body size but a full 1,000 cubic centimeters below ours? If God made each of the half dozen human species discovered in ancient rocks, why did he create in an unbroken temporal sequence of progressively more modern features—increasing cranial capacity, reduced face and teeth, larger body size? Did he create to mimic evolution and test our faith thereby?

An Example of Creationist Argument

18 Faced with these facts of evolution and the philosophical bankruptcy of their own position, creationists rely upon distortion and innuendo to buttress their rhetorical claim. If I sound sharp or bitter, indeed I am—for I have become a major target of these practices.

19 I count myself among the evolutionists who argue for a jerky, or episodic, rather than a smoothly gradual, pace of change. In 1972 my colleague Niles Eldredge and I developed the theory of punctuated equilibrium [*Discover,* October]. We argued that two outstanding facts of the fossil record—geologically "sudden" origin of new species and failure to change thereafter (stasis)—reflect the predictions of evolutionary theory, not the imperfections of the fossil record. In most theories, small isolated populations are the source of new species, and the process of speciation takes thousands or tens of thousands of years. This amount of time, so long when measured against our lives, is a geological microsecond. It represents much less than 1 per cent of the average life span for a fossil invertebrate species—more than 10 million years. Large, widespread, and well-established species, on the other hand, are not expected to change very much. We believe that the inertia of large populations explains the stasis of most fossil species over millions of years.

20 We proposed the theory of punctuated equilibrium largely to provide a different explanation for pervasive trends in the fossil record. Trends,we argued, cannot be attrib-

uted to gradual transformation within lineages, but must arise from the differential success of certain kinds of species. A trend, we argued, is more like climbing a flight of stairs (punctuations and stasis) than rolling up an inclined plane.

21 Since we proposed punctuated equilibria to explain trends, it is infuriating to be quoted again and again by creationists—whether through design or stupidity, I do not know—as admitting that the fossil record includes no transitional forms. Transitional forms are generally lacking at the species level, but are abundant between larger groups. The evolution from reptiles to mammals, as mentioned earlier, is well documented. Yet a pamphlet entitled "Harvard Scientists Agree Evolution Is a Hoax" states: "The facts of punctuated equilibrium which Gould and Eldredge . . . are forcing Darwinists to swallow fit the picture that Bryan insisted on, and which God has revealed to us in the Bible."

22 Continuing the distortion, several creationists have equated the theory of punctuated equilibrium with a caricature of the beliefs of Richard Goldschmidt, a great early geneticist. Goldschmidt argued, in a famous book published in 1940, that new groups can arise all at once through major mutations. He referred to these suddenly transformed creatures as "hopeful monsters." (I am attracted to some aspects of the non-caricatured version, but Goldschmidt's theory still has nothing to do with punctuated equilibrium.) Creationist Luther Sunderland talks of the "punctuated equilibrium hopeful monster theory" and tells his hopeful readers that "it amounts to tacit admission that anti-evolutionists are correct in asserting there is no fossil evidence supporting the theory that all life is connected to a common ancestor." Duane Gish writes, "According to Goldschmidt, and now apparently according to Gould, a reptile laid an egg from which the first bird, feathers and all, was produced." Any evolutionist who believed such nonsense would rightly be laughed off the intellectual stage; yet the only theory that could ever envision such a scenario for the evolution of birds is creationism—God acts in the egg.

Conclusion

23 I am both angry at and amused by the creationists; but mostly I am deeply sad. Sad for many reasons. Sad because so many people who respond to creationist appeals are troubled for the right reason, but venting their anger at the wrong target. It is true that scientists have often been dogmatic and elitist. It is true that we have often allowed the white-coated, advertising image to represent us—"Scientists say that Brand X cures bunions ten times faster than. . . ." We have not fought it adequately because we derive benefits from appearing as a new priesthood. It is also true that faceless bureaucratic state power intrudes more and more into our lives and removes choices that should belong to individuals and communities. I can understand that requiring that evolution be taught in the schools might be seen as one more insult on all these grounds. But the culprit is not, and cannot be, evolution or any other fact of the natural world. Identify and fight your legitimate enemies by all means, but we are not among them.

24 I am sad because the practical result of this brouhaha will not be expanded coverage to include creationism (that would also make me sad), but the reduction or excision of

evolution from high school curricula. Evolution is one of the half dozen "great ideas" developed by science. It speaks to the profound issues of genealogy that fascinate all of us—the "roots" phenomenon writ large. Where did we come from? Where did life arise? How did it develop? How are organisms related? It forces us to think, ponder, and wonder. Shall we deprive millions of this knowledge and once again teach biology as a set of dull and unconnected facts, without the thread that weaves diverse material into a supple unity?

25 But most of all I am saddened by a trend I am just beginning to discern among my colleagues. I sense that some now wish to mute the healthy debate about theory that has brought new life to evolutionary biology. It provides grist for creationist mills, they say, even if only by distortion. Perhaps we should lie low and rally round the flag of strict Darwinism, at least for the moment—a kind of old-time religion on our part.

26 But we should borrow another metaphor and recognize that we too have to tread a straight and narrow path, surrounded by roads to perdition. For if we ever begin to suppress our search to understand nature, to quench our own intellectual excitement in a misguided effort to present a united front where it does not and should not exist, then we are truly lost.

Questions for Analysis

1. What is the purpose of Gould's first paragraph?
2. Explain the distinction between fact and theory that Gould offers. How does it differ from that offered by creationists?
3. Toward the end of his essay Gould admits that he is "angry at . . . the creationists." Do you see evidence of his anger in Gould's choice of words or phrasing at times? Do these choices hurt or help his argument? Do you think Gould's anger is justified based on the information he presents in Paragraph 21?
4. Summarize the arguments Gould presents that support the theory of evolution. Are they clear? Persuasive?

Duane T. Gish

A Response to Gould's Argument

(1981)

Duane T. Gish (b. 1921) is one of the most active and influential advocates of creationism. He holds impressive credentials in science—a Ph.D. in biochemistry from the University of California, Berkeley, and research positions at Cornell and Berkeley. His most recent professional work, however, has been as Professor of Natural Science at Christian Heritage College in San Diego. His book *Evolution? The Fossils Say No!* is an explanation of the creationist position written for adults and school-age children. This piece appeared in *Discover* magazine in response to Gould's essay. The title is mine.

To the Editors:

1 In his Essay "Evolution as Fact and Theory" [May], Stephen Jay Gould states that creationists claim creation is a scientific theory. This is a false accusation. Creationists have repeatedly stated that neither creation nor evolution is a scientific theory (and each is equally religious). Gould in fact quotes from my book, *Evolution? The Fossils Say No!,* in which I state that both concepts of origins fail the criteria of a scientific theory.

2 Gould uses the argument of Sir Karl Popper that the primary criterion of a scientific theory is its potential falsifiability, and then uses this sword to strike down creation as a scientific theory. Fine. Gould surely realizes, however, that this is a two-edged sword. Sir Karl has used it to strike down evolution as a scientific theory, stating that Darwinism is not a testable scientific theory, but a metaphysical research program (*Unended Quest,* 1976).

3 Another criterion that must apply to a scientific theory is the ability to repeatedly observe the events, processes, or properties used to support the theory. There were obviously no human witnesses to the origin of the universe, the origin of life, or in fact to the origin of a single living thing, and even if evolution were occurring today, the process would require far in excess of all recorded history to produce sufficient change to document evolution. Evolution has not and cannot be observed any more than creation.

4 Gould states, "Theories are structures of ideas that explain and interpret facts." Certainly, creation and evolution can both be used as theories in that sense. Furthermore, one or the other must be true, since ultimately they are the only two alternatives we have to explain origins.

5 Gould charges creationists with dogma. Please note, however, Gould's own dogmatism. His use of the term "fact of evolution" appears throughout his paper. Furthermore, Gould seems to have a strange view of the relationship of fact and theory. He says, "Facts do not go away when scientists debate rival theories to explain them. Einstein's theory of gravitation replaced Newton's, but apples did not suspend them-

selves in mid-air pending the outcome. And human beings evolved from apelike ancestors whether they did so by Darwin's proposed mechanism or by some other, yet to be discovered.'' Well, evolutionists believe indeed that both apes and hydrogen evolved into people (the latter just took longer), but neither has ever been observed. All of us, however, have seen apples fall off trees.

6 Gould's ''fact of evolution'' immediately deteriorates into ''three general arguments,'' two of which quickly deteriorate further into mere inferences. Gould's only direct observational evidence for evolution (his first argument) is experiments on fruit flies and observations on peppered moths in Britain. Neither, of course, offers evidence for evolution, for from beginning to end fruit flies remain fruit flies and peppered moths remain peppered moths. The task of the evolutionist is to answer the question how moths came to be moths, tigers came to be tigers, and people came to be people. In fact, this type of evidence is what Gould himself has sought in recent years to discredit as an explanation for the origin of higher categories.

7 Gould's second argument is an inference based on *imperfections.* He mentions homologous structures as evidence for evolution from a common ancestor. Gould should know first that many, if not most, homologous structures are not even possessed by the assumed common ancestor and secondly that the actual evidence (particularly that from genetics) is so contradictory to what is predicted by evolution that Sir Gavin de Beer titled his Oxford biology reader (1971) on that subject *Homology, an Unsolved Problem.* Sir Gavin, along with S. C. Harland, felt compelled to suggest that organs, such as the eye, remain unchanged while the genes governing these structures become wholly altered during the evolutionary process! The whole Darwinian edifice collapses if that is true.

8 Gould's third argument is based on inferences drawn from the fossil record. The fossil record, with its ''explosive appearance'' (the term often used by geologists) of the highly complex creatures found in Cambrian rocks, for which no ancestors have been found, and the systematic absence of transitional forms between all higher categories of plants and animals, has proven an embarrassment to evolutionists ever since Darwin. Gould's argument, however, is that ''transitions are often found in the fossil record.'' That is surprising indeed, since he seems intent in other publications to convey just the opposite opinion.

9 For example, in his 1977 *Natural History* essay ''The Return of Hopeful Monsters,'' after recounting the derision meted out to Richard Goldschmidt for his hopeful-monster mechanism of evolution, Gould says, ''I do, however, predict that during the next decade Goldschmidt will be largely vindicated in the world of evolutionary biology.'' Why? Among others, ''The fossil record with its abrupt transitions offers no support for gradual change.'' A bit later: ''All paleontologists know that the fossil record contains precious little in the way of intermediate forms; transitions between major groups are characteristically abrupt.'' Many similar statements by Gould and others could be cited.

10 Finally, Gould assails Sunderland and me for linking him to a hopeful-monster mechanism whereby a reptile laid an egg and a bird was hatched. He says an evolutionist

who believed such nonsense would rightly be laughed off the intellectual stage. Let's see, then, what Goldschmidt really did say. In *The Material Basis of Evolution,* Goldschmidt says, "I need only quote Schindewolf (1936), the most progressive investigator known to me. He shows by examples from fossil material that the major evolutionary advances must have taken place in single large steps. . . . He shows that the many missing links in the paleontological record are sought for in vain because they have never existed: 'The first bird hatched from a reptilian egg.' " By Gould's own testimony, then, Goldschmidt, Gould's hero of the next decade, should be laughed off the intellectual stage.

11 Along with thousands of other creation scientists, in view of a wealth of evidence from thermodynamics, probability relationships, biology, molecular biology, paleontology, and cosmology, I have become convinced that evolution theory is scientifically untenable and that the concept of direct, special creation is a far more credible explanation.

Duane T. Gish
Vice President
Institute for Creation Research
El Cajon, California

Questions for Analysis

1. Gish states in his first paragraph that "neither creation nor evolution is a scientific theory (and each is equally religious)." How does Gish support his assertions, especially the assertion that evolution is a "religious" theory?
2. Both Gould and Gish use Sir Karl Popper to support their arguments. How is it that both writers can do this? What does "falsifiability" mean?
3. Gish accuses Gould of "dogmatism." What evidence does he use to support this assertion?
4. Evaluate Gish's analysis of Gould's arguments, in particular his attack on Gould's statements about transitions. Has Gish misrepresented Gould? Is this another example of the misrepresentation Gould claims in his essay (Paragraphs 21 and 22) that the creationists perpetrate?

Anne Marie Brennan

Biblical Fundamentalists vs. Scientistic Ones: The Creationism Controversy

(1982)

Anne Marie Brennan (b. 1935) holds a Ph.D. in religion granted by both Columbia University and Union Theological Seminary. A teacher with experience in elementary, high-school, and college classrooms, she now directs an adult religious-education program. This essay originally appeared in *Commonweal.*

1 The Institute for Creation Research and the Creation Research Society, with the support of the Moral Majority and similar religio-political groups, have been waging a nationwide campaign to require the teaching of creationism alongside evolution in public school biology classes. Last year, Florida's Hillsborough County School Board voted in favor of such a requirement. This was a regrettable decision, one that will cost a lot in time, energy, and taxpayers' dollars, not to mention student confusion, before it is inevitably reversed. It does reveal how prevalent are popular misconceptions about religion and science. But it obscures the real concerns at the heart of the fundamentalist attack on contemporary culture, and so delays any rational attempts to resolve the deeper issues.

2 Evolution is not a religious issue any more than creation is a proper object of scientific investigation. Evolution is a scientific theory. This doesn't mean that it's a guess which will become a fact when we're absolutely sure of it. A fact is merely a description of something we have observed. A theory is a tentative explanation of how a lot of facts are related. After repeated observations and debates, scientists may accept a theory as a reasonably sound and useful explanation of the available facts, knowing that the theory may have to be revised in light of future discoveries. The scientific academy is currently debating the mechanism of evolution, but it is unanimous in its acceptance of the theory of evolution, on the basis of an overwhelming body of confirming evidence.

3 Creation names a divine activity which is certainly beyond our powers of observation. Religious belief in creation is rooted in an awareness of our dependence on mysterious powers that shape our origin and destiny. This sense of radical dependence has found expression in myth and ritual, belief systems, and moral codes. Myth is the language proper to religious experience. It expresses in drama and imagery the otherwise inexpressible awareness of a transcendent Other just beyond the reach of our imagination.

4 The Judeo/Christian belief in our absolute dependence on the God of Abraham and Jesus is beautifully expressed in the ancient Hebrew creation myths. The discovery in the past century of languages and texts from the biblical cultures gave scholars the tools they needed to unlock, at last, the meanings intended by the authors of Genesis. Their profound religious insights and literary genius had been obscured by centuries of mistaking superb poetic drama for something akin to the Congressional Record.

5 Faith in the biblical Creator is not based on such misinterpretation of Genesis. Nor is it based on scientific evidence, but on the religious experience of our contingency. The faith in creation expressed in Genesis does not answer our scientific questions about how things in the universe work, but our deeper questions about why there is anything at all, and why we assume it makes sense and is worth mastering.

6 It follows that a term like "scientific creationism" is self-contradictory, and about as meaningful as "mathematical love-making." Its widespread use is yet one more indication of what we might boldly call the scientific and religious illiteracy of the products of our nation's educational system. Equally revealing are debates entitled "Evolution vs. Creationism," which promise as much enlightenment as might debates entitled "Statistical Probability vs. Divine Providence," or "Penicillin vs. Prayer," or "Love vs. Vitamins."

7 Creationists and evolutionists often argue their cases like opponents in a lawsuit. Each claims to have an authentic photo of, say, an accident, while charging that the other's contradictory picture has been fraudulently touched up. The crucial insight that is missing is that science and religion are different but complementary ways of knowing, each with its own language and rules. They function not so much like contradictory pictures of the world, but more like different kinds of lenses through which we can view the world from different angles or in different lights. The discovery and growing ability to use both kinds of lenses is the story of civilization.

8 Primitive peoples saw their world through the single lens of their tribal myth. It was an all-encompassing view which fused the practical knowledge of common sense with a religious awareness of transcendent mystery. It provided an integrated system of answers to two basic kinds of questions: how do things in our world work relative to our survival; and why are so many things beyond our control? The tribal myth, fundamentally religious, indeed religious fundamentalism in its origins, was the certain and secure basis for tribal culture. It dictated the rituals and customs, the values and lifestyle, that insured tribal uniformity and survival.

9 The needs of critical thought eventually broke through the hard ground of tribal conformity, raising doubts about the adequacy of the myths to explain recurring natural events. As thinking developed and people began asking how things work in themselves, apart from practical or religious concerns, science was born. Centuries of theoretical questioning produced the various branches of science we have today. The twentieth-century mind is the product of a long, irreversible process of development of what we might call its multiple-lens approach to reality. It is a regression for us to be arguing religion vs. science, creation vs. evolution at this stage of our civilization, as though we could only see through a single lens.

10 Evolution has been made to appear a religious issue by two opposing groups of religious fundamentalists, each proposing a single-lens view of reality. The biblical fundamentalists, interpreting the creation narratives in Genesis as historical and scientific records dictated by God, are compelled to reject any scientific theory which, like evolution, appears to contradict what God said. Never mind that their biblicism flies in the face of a century of biblical scholarship and is rejected by the majority of religious

denominations whose traditions stem from the same biblical witness. This only reinforces their conviction that they are the righteous few who will be saved. Never mind that, like the churchmen who refused to look through Galileo's telescope, they must deny an enormous body of scientific evidence for evolution. This only proves that scientists are the tools of Satan, using the theory of evolution to spread vice and corruption everywhere. Never mind that many scientists see an evolving universe as an even more magnificent tribute to a Creator than a static one. They are lying, for only atheists ''believe in'' evolution. Salvation for us all lies in conversion to, or legal enforcement of, the biblical fundamentalists' tribal myth, with its unquestionable morals and mores.

11 The opposite extreme of religious fundamentalism is represented by the ''secular humanists.'' Their creed is the Humanist Manifesto, I and II. Since they are neither secular nor humanistic, in the traditional sense, and their basic premise seems to be that science has displaced religion as the only valid way of acquiring knowledge of the real world, a better name for them might be ''scientistic fundamentalists.'' This group does not seem bent on proselytizing, perhaps because it assumes that those who can leave behind the religious myths (read ''fantasies'') of mankind's childhood will be limited to the enlightened few. Their biases appear as gratuitous snipes at religion, such as sometimes mar the otherwise lucid writings of Isaac Asimov.

12 A perfect metaphor for scientistic fundamentalism is the TV program, *Cosmos.* Carl Sagan has managed to take good scientific material and present it as a religious trip through the heavens, in a cathedral-like ship, enveloped in ethereal lighting and filled with hushed, tremulous tones, interspersed with sophistic sneers at those religious myths of our ancestors which science has displaced. Here is the reverse image of biblical fundamentalism. In place of the biblical myth, the scientistic fundamentalists propose the ''science-is-all'' myth. Instead of denying the evidence for evolution, they would deny the evidence for the validity of religious experience and knowledge. They would reject the deepest realm of human inquiry. But the religious quest can no more be extinguished by their sneers than can the scientific quest by religious dogmatism.

13 Religious Fundamentalism, whether biblical, scientistic, or any other variety, will be ever with us. It is rooted in the fundamentally religious nature of human persons. Our most primitive religious impulse is to get some measure of control over the mystery that surrounds our existence. We are frightened by our vulnerability. We want to be sure about our ultimate well-being, however we imagine our salvation. By contrast, the message of the Bible is that we are called to go beyond our fear-ridden religious impulses and surrender in faith to the God who made us. That God promises light and life at the end of our quest.

14 Religious leaders of the Judeo/Christian tradition would do the public a service by speaking out clearly against these false prophets, who offer certitudes and guarantees of salvation in place of that relationship with God, full of risk and uncertainty, that is biblical faith. They also might remind everyone that fidelity to the biblical Creator inspires an enthusiastic pursuit of scientific enquiry, not suspicion and condemnation.

15 Scientists, in turn, would be doing everyone a service if they would find ways to help the public understand just what it is they are doing and not doing when they are doing science. They need to make very clear which kinds of questions they can hope to answer and which they cannot, and why. They should refrain from giving the impression that scientific theories can prove religious beliefs, theistic or atheistic. And, they might caution those who would suggest that religious belief is necessarily opposed to science or is an outmoded approach which science has supplanted.

16 Religious fundamentalism is flourishing in our land, as elsewhere, because of the insecurity we are feeling in the wake of profound cultural changes. The information explosion of this century and rapid technological advances have made us unsure of things we once thought were unquestionable—and this at a time when we are challenged with increasingly complex kinds of ethical decisions. At the edge of our religious faith are some anxious doubts awakened by the new knowledge and by traumatic experience of evil on a global scale. And, beneath the excitement of our new conquests in science, there are some disquieting questions about whether our pursuits of meaning and happiness are absurd flounderings in a meaningless world, or whether there might, after all, be some ultimate source of meaning and value outside ourselves.

17 The fundamentalist grasp for absolutes is an understandable regression to the mythological security of the primitive tribe. It is a little like the ten-year-old, the first night in the new house, who clutches the old teddy bear to assuage his reawakened fears of the dark. We are all afraid of the dark. We need to stop whistling dissonant tunes at each other and turn on some lights!

18 Religious leaders, humanists, scientists, educators—all have a responsibility to help create a more intelligent and better informed American society. We cannot afford to lose our own or future generations to ignorance and bigotry. The challenge facing us in this age is to integrate a vast amount of new knowledge with authentic religious and moral values. We need to develop a new, rich self-image, one that can permeate the "brave new world" of our technology with human intelligence, freedom, and compassion. One powerful model for such an endeavor is the late French paleontologist theologian, Pierre Teilhard de Chardin, who presented cosmic evolution as an illuminating framework for science, humanism, and Christianity. "Scientific creationism," however, is a facile attempt at the needed integration. It will inevitably fail, because it is true neither to the new knowledge nor to the biblical faith it is trying to preserve. But, it will have a far longer day in court because our schools have not produced citizens who can understand and think critically about the issues involved.

19 Rather than mandate the teaching of religion in science classes, school boards would better serve our society by adopting more fruitful policies, such as: (1) making comparative religion a required subject rather than an elective; (2) insuring that scientific method be clearly explained in all science courses from the earliest grades; (3) incorporating into the curriculum at every level exercises in critical thinking and problem-solving. What is at stake is our survival and growth as a free, pluralistic society, dedicated to the cause of advancing humanity on this planet and beyond, without fear, in the presence of the living God.

Questions for Analysis

1. Review Brennan's definition of "fact" and "theory." Are her definitions consistent with Gould's? Would Gish agree?
2. Brennan uses facetious comparisons in several places in her essay. (See Paragraphs 4 and 6.) Do these funny, but gratuitous, comparisons help or hurt her argument? What segments of her potential audience might like them? What segments might find them offensive?
3. Explain Brennan's purpose in her discussion of the single vs. multiple lens.
4. Brennan criticizes the "two opposing groups of religious fundamentalists" for making evolution appear to be a religious issue. The biblical fundamentalists are more familiar to us than the "scientistic fundamentalists." Who are these people? What is their agenda? Is Gould one of them?
5. Brennan says the whole debate over evolution is the product of widespread "scientific and religious illiteracy." She ends her essay calling for reforms in our educational programs that would combat this illiteracy. She wrote her essay in the early 1980s. Have things changed for the better in the 10 years since she published her essay? Explain.

Part III

PRIVATE OPINION AND PUBLIC POLICY

Should Drugs Be Legalized?

For decades the United States has been the world's largest consumer of illegal drugs. Despite intense efforts to suppress the drug trade through force of law, it still flourishes, spawning violence and corruption. The debate over how to deal with the wide range of problems associated with drug use has tended to focus on two opposing solutions: wage the war on drugs even more intensely than we do now through stricter laws and tighter enforcement; or legalize drugs, sell them at low cost through government operated clinics, and divert money currently spent on drug enforcement to education and rehabilitation.

As with any question of public policy, the issue is much more complex than these two options of legalization or stiffer laws imply. Any policy argument on this issue should take into account the many individuals (some innocent, some guilty, some simply unfortunate and weak) effected by drug law and policy; the various drugs currently being used and their differing effects on human behavior and health; and the willingness of our society to accept radical changes of policy or even more stringent application of present policy.

The selections that follow provide a sense of the extremes on the issue of drug legalization, as well as some knowledge of the possible moderating choices. While all of the selections in this section were published in or after 1989, they include references to earlier essays and provide a sense of the duration of concern over this issue.

The essays are presented in chronological order. James Ostrowski in "Thinking about Drug Legalization" argues that "the war on drugs is immoral as well as impractical." He lays out the propositions that he thinks demonstrate that drugs should be legalized. The next essay, "Legalization Holds No Answer to Drugs," by Marianne Means, argues the opposite position, relying heavily on parallels and nonparallels to the effects of alcohol prohibition on consumption.

As the federal government's chief representative for the war on drugs during the first few years of the Bush administration, William J. Bennett was responsible for establishing and articulating that administration's tough stance on drugs. His *Reader's Digest* essay "Should Drugs Be Legalized?" is a point-by-point response to the main arguments offered by those who say that we have lost the war on drugs. Next Lewis Lapham's, "A Political Opiate: The War on Drugs Is a Folly and a Menace" strongly attacks the war on drugs and on the politicization of the war by the Bush administration; note, however, that Lapham seems to have his own political agenda. Both essays demonstrate how firmly the drug war has insinuated itself into the political rhetoric of our country.

Walter Wink in "Biting the Bullet: The Case for Legalizing Drugs" brings a unique Christian interpretation to bear in his nonpolitical, pragmatic criticism of the war on drugs. James Q. Wilson's "Against the Legalization of Drugs" has a measured, reasonable tone similar to that in Wink's essay, yet argues the opposite position. And, despite Wilson's years of working for the government as Chairman of the National Advisory Council for Drug Abuse Prevention, his stance, like Wink's, seems not to convey an overtly political position.

The final essay in this collection, Diana R. Gordon's "Europe's Kinder, Gentler Approach," examines the European approach, which emphasizes helping addicts ("harm reduction") rather than prosecuting them. The European view of our attitudes and policies provides a fresh, informative perspective.

The literary piece in this section is "Sonny's Blues" by James Baldwin. This powerful short story, written and set in the 1950s in New York City, vividly depicts one young man's struggle with heroin. The story, however, goes well beyond simple drug use to deal with the family and social forces that drove Sonny to drugs, and to suggest the concern for the individual that is necessary to retrieve an addict from a drug habit.

James Ostrowski

Thinking about Drug Legalization

(1989)

James Ostrowski is an attorney and past vice chairman of the New York County Lawyers Association Committee on Law Reform. This article appeared in the *Cato Institute Policy Analysis* dated May 25, 1989.

Defining the Issue

1 Much of the confusion surrounding drug policy discussions could be alleviated by asking the right question initially. The question that must be addressed in determining whether to legalize drugs is this: Do drug laws do more harm than good?

2 The focus here is not how dangerous drugs are or how much damage drug users inflict upon themselves. If these factors were decisive, then surely alcohol and tobacco would be banned. Rather, the proper focus is how effective drug laws are in preventing damage from drugs, compared with the amount of injury the laws themselves cause.

3 With this emphasis in mind, the respective burdens of proof resting upon the parties to the debate can now be specified. Supporters of prohibition must demonstrate *all* of the following:

1. that drug use would increase substantially after legalization;

2. that the harm caused by any increased use would not be offset by the increased safety of legal drug use;
3. that the harm caused by any increased use would not be offset by a reduction in the use of dangerous drugs that are already legal (e.g., alcohol and tobacco); and
4. that the harm caused by any increased drug use not offset by (2) or (3) would exceed the harm now caused by the side effects of prohibition (e.g., crime and corruption).

In the absence of data supporting these propositions, neither the theoretical danger of illegal drugs nor their actual harmful effects can be sufficient basis for prohibition. Neither can the bare fact, if proven, that illegal drug use would rise under legalization.

4 Prohibitionists face a daunting task—one that no one has yet accomplished or, apparently, even attempted. It might be noted, parenthetically, that a 1984 study by the Research Triangle Institute on the economic costs of drug abuse has been erroneously cited in support of drug prohibition. This report, which estimates the cost of drug abuse at $60 billion for 1983, is not, and was not intended to be, an evaluation of the efficacy of prohibition or the wisdom of legalization. It does not mention the terms "legalization" and "decriminalization" and makes no attempt to separate the costs attributable to drug use per se from the costs attributable to the illegality of drug use. In fact, the study seems to include some costs of *legal* drugs in its estimates. Many of the costs cited are clearly the result of prohibition, for example, interdiction costs ($677 million). Furthermore, the report considers only costs that prohibition has failed to prevent, making no attempt to measure the costs prevented—or caused—by prohibition. In its present form, the study is therefore almost entirely irrelevant to the issue of legalizing drugs.

5 The case for legalization is sustained if *any* of the following propositions is true:

1. prohibition has no substantial impact on the level of illegal drug use;
2. prohibition increases illegal drug use;
3. prohibition merely redistributes drug use from illegal drugs to harmful legal drugs; or
4. even though prohibition might decrease the use of illegal drugs, the negative effects of prohibition outweigh the beneficial effects of reduced illegal drug use.

6 This paper relies primarily upon point (4) and secondarily upon points (1) and (3). The paper does not rely upon point (2), but Edward Brecher presented much historical evidence for that point in his masterly work *Licit and Illicit Drugs,* coauthored by the editors of *Consumer Reports.*

Street Crime by Drug Users

7 Drug laws greatly increase the price of illegal drugs, often forcing users to steal to get the money to obtain them. Although difficult to estimate, the black market prices of heroin and cocaine appear to be about 100 times greater than their pharmaceutical prices. For example, a hospital-dispensed dose of morphine (a drug from which heroin

is relatively easily derived) costs only pennies; legal cocaine costs about $20 per ounce. It is frequently estimated that at least 40 percent of all property crime in the United States is committed by drug users so that they can maintain their habits. That amounts to about 4 million crimes per year and $7.5 billion in stolen property.

8 Supporters of prohibition have traditionally used drug-related crime as a simplistic argument for enforcement: Stop drug use to stop drug-related crime. They have even exaggerated the amount of such crime in the hopes of demonstrating a need for larger budgets and greater powers. But in recent years, the more astute prohibitionists have noticed that drug-related crime is in fact drug-*law*-related. Thus, in many cases they have begun to argue that even if drugs were legal and thus relatively inexpensive, drug users would still commit crimes simply because they are criminals at heart.

9 The fact is, while some researchers have questioned the causal connection between illegal drugs and street crime, many studies over a long period have confirmed what every inner-city dweller already knows: Drug users steal to get the money to buy expensive illegal drugs. These studies were reviewed in 1985 in an article entitled "Narcotics and Crime: An Analysis of Existing Evidence for a Causal Relationship." The authors conclude:

> Heroin addiction can be shown to dramatically increase property crime levels. . . . A high proportion of addicts' preaddiction criminality consists of minor and drug offenses, while postaddiction criminality is characterized much more by property crime.

Moreover, prohibition also stimulates crime by

- criminalizing users of illegal drugs, creating disrespect for the law;
- forcing users into daily contact with professional criminals, which often leads to arrest and prison records that make legitimate employment difficult to obtain;
- discouraging legitimate employment because of the need to "hustle" for drug money;
- encouraging young people to become criminals by creating an extremely lucrative black market in drugs;
- destroying, through drug crime, the economic viability of low-income neighborhoods, leaving young people fewer alternatives to working in the black market; and
- removing the settling of drug-related disputes from the legal process, creating a context of violence for the buying and selling of drugs.

10 Every property crime committed by a drug user is potentially a violent crime. Many victims are beaten and severely injured, and 1,600 are murdered each year. Last year, a sixteen-year-old boy murdered thirty-nine-year-old Eli Wald of Brooklyn, father of a baby girl, taking $200 to buy crack. Another New York City crack user murdered five people in an eight-day period to get the money to buy crack. The user survived the crack, but his victims did not survive the user.

Black Market Violence

11 Prohibition also causes what the media and police misname ''drug-related violence.'' This *prohibition*-related violence includes all the random shootings and murders associated with black market drug transactions: ripoffs, eliminating the competition, killing informers, and killing suspected informers.

12 Those who doubt that prohibition is responsible for this violence need only note the absence of violence in the legal drug market. For example, there is no violence associated with the production, distribution, and sale of alcohol. Such violence was ended by the repeal of Prohibition.

13 The President's Commission on Organized Crime estimates a total of about seventy drug-market murders yearly in Miami alone. Based on that figure and FBI data, a reasonable nationwide estimate would be at least 750 such murders each year. Recent estimates from New York and Washington would suggest an even higher figure.

14 Since the black market in illegal drugs is the source of most drug-related problems, that market must be eliminated to the greatest extent possible. The most efficient means of doing so is legalization.

Hope for the Future

15 It is clear that most of the serious problems the public associates with illegal drug use are, in reality, caused directly or indirectly by drug prohibition.

16 Let's assume the war on drugs was given up as the misguided enterprise that it is. What would happen? The day after legalization went into effect, the streets of America would be safer. The drug dealers would be gone. The shootouts between drug dealers would end. Innocent bystanders would not be murdered anymore. Hundreds of thousands of drug ''addicts'' would no longer roam the streets, shoplifting, mugging, breaking into homes in the middle of the night to steal, and dealing violently with those who happened to wake up. One year after prohibition was repealed, 1,600 innocent people who would otherwise have been dead at the hands of drug criminals would be alive.

17 Within days of prohibition repeal, thousands of judges, prosecutors, and police would be freed up to catch, try, and imprison violent career criminals—criminals who commit fifty to one hundred serious crimes per year when on the loose, including robbery, rape, and murder. For the first time in years, our overcrowded prisons would have room for them. Ultimately, repeal of prohibition would open up *75,000* jail cells.

18 The day after repeal, organized crime would get a big pay cut—$80 billion a year.

19 How about those slick young drug dealers who are the new role models for the youth of the inner cities, with their designer clothes and Mercedes convertibles, always wearing a broad, smug smile that says crime pays? They snicker at the honest kids going to school or to work at the minimum wage. The day after repeal, the honest kids will have the last laugh. The dealers will be out of a job, unemployed.

20 The day after repeal, real drug education can begin and, for the first time in history, it can be honest. No more need to prop up the failed war on drugs.

21 The year before repeal, 500,000 Americans would have died from illnesses related to overeating and lack of exercise; 390,000, from smoking; and 150,000, from drinking alcohol. About 3,000 would have died from cocaine, heroin, and marijuana combined, with many of these deaths the result of the lack of quality control in the black market. The day after repeal, cocaine, heroin, and marijuana would, by and large, do no harm to those who chose not to consume them. In contrast, the day before prohibition repeal, all Americans, whether or not they chose to use illegal drugs, were forced to endure the violence, street crime, erosion of civil liberties, corruption, and social and economic decay caused by the war on drugs.

22 That is why, at this point in the argument, drug legalization unavoidably becomes a moral issue. The war on drugs is immoral as well as impractical. It imposes enormous costs, including the ultimate cost of death, on large numbers of non-drug-abusing citizens in the failed attempt to save a relatively small group of hard-core drug abusers from themselves. It is immoral and absurd to *force* some people to bear costs so that others might be prevented from *choosing* to do harm to themselves. This crude utilitarian sacrifice—so at odds with traditional American values—has never been, and can never be, justified. That is why the war on drugs must end and why it *will* be ended once the public comes to understand the truth about this destructive policy.

Questions for Analysis

1. In Paragraphs 3 and 5, Ostrowski uses two lists of propositions. Do you find these lists effective ways of conveying Ostrowski's position? Explain.
2. In at least two places, Ostrowski changes *received terms* (terms commonly used in discussions of drug problems). In Paragraph 8, he makes a distinction between "drug-related crime" and "drug-law–related crime." In Paragraph 11, he wants to reject "drug-related violence" for "prohibition-related violence." What are the reasons behind these changes? Are they valid? What is the point of the last sentence in Paragraph 8—the one that follows and builds on the point about drug-law–related crime? Could you rephrase it to make his point clearer?
3. Could the examples in Paragraph 10 be used by those who argue for strict prohibitions to support their position? Explain.
4. Evaluate the comparison in Paragraph 21 and explain how the pre-repeal and post-repeal statistics support Ostrowski's point. How would a prohibitionist respond?

Marianne Means

Legalization Holds No Answer to Drugs

(1989)

Marianne Means (b. 1934) is a print and broadcast journalist whose syndicated column on national politics appears in newspapers across the country. She lives and works in Washington, DC.

1 Since President Bush outlined his modest skirmish against drugs, an astonishing phenomenon has been taking root among intellectuals of both the right and left.

2 Increasingly, respected voices are raised to advocate the legalization of drugs, arguing that the violence accompanying the spread of crack, crank, cocaine and other substances is due mostly to corruption spawned by the huge profits of peddling a product that is against the law. The notion is that if selling drugs were legal, crime would go down, drugs would lose some of their allure and the government could both regulate and tax the stuff.

3 Proponents point to Prohibition, a nationwide ban on alcoholic beverages a half century ago that made Al Capone's gang rich and created criminals of millions of otherwise law-abiding citizens who were stubbornly devoted to their nightly toddy. Totally unenforceable, it was repealed by popular demand. Gin went from the bathtub to the store shelves and consumption of liquor soared by 350 percent.

4 No national public official has yet bought the spurious reasoning for legalization; it remains a distinctly minority view. But the administration underestimates the smooth simplicity of the argument and the rapidity with which it is becoming a subject of serious public and private debate.

5 Legalization appeals to those who despair that drug abuse can ever be controlled; ironically, the president fueled this pessimism with a drug strategy so financially limited that its goal is only a 50 percent reduction in the use of drugs over the next 10 years.

6 It also appeals to those who disagree with the administration's insistence that social users of marijuana are as guilty as crack addicts. Middle-class casual users do not want to admit they are doing anything wrong.

7 This is a frightening trend. It is a cruel hoax to suggest that the problem with drugs is their illegality rather than their addictive nature and their disastrous chemical impact upon both mind and body.

8 Comparisons between alcohol abuse and serious drug addiction are dangerously misleading. The former can create health and social problems but the latter is virtually guaranteed to do so and do it in a terrifying way that is likely to injure others.

9 Crack and crank are relatively new drugs for which we have no long-term health statistics. It would be playing with fire to approve of something about which we know so little. Thus far, there is no proven treatment.

10 There are few reliable, current figures reflecting the full scope of the present drug epidemic, in part because it has hit hardest among the poor, for whom it is only one of many problems.

11 But 85 percent of those who drink alcohol rarely become intoxicated and 90 percent never become addicted. The opposite is true of cocaine and crack. Surveys indicate 70 percent of users who experiment with cocaine become addicted. Heroin and crack, which can hook victims after only one or two uses, are worse.

12 A new study shows that 51 percent of high school students who drank liquor reported they had experienced "very high" levels of intoxication whereas 75 percent of those who used cocaine reported being similarly bombed.

13 Too much liquor may lead to accidents and abusive behavior but it does not regularly trigger violence, paranoia and insanity to the extent that crack and cocaine do. Shootings and beatings among crack users are not entirely due to criminals fighting over profits. A simple family quarrel can set off murder and mayhem. The president's Office of National Drug Control Policy describes a typical reaction as "quick resort to violence on minimal provocation."

14 Hospital emergencies for overdoses, injuries and other problems due to crack went up 121 percent between 1985 and 1987. Intensive care for babies born with AIDS or crack addictions passed on by their mothers runs to $2.5 billion a year and is mounting. Intravenous drug use is now the single largest source of new HIV-AIDS virus infections; about one-half of all AIDS deaths are drug-related.

15 Legalization would make drugs cheaper and more readily available, easily tripling their usage just as alcohol consumption shot up after Prohibition. In fact, there would be nothing financial, moral or legally punitive to stop their spread.

16 This would be a social disaster. Capitulating to drugs would be appallingly dangerous. With ever-expanding usage, none of us would be safe from the consequences of highway, airplane and job accidents and random street violence. Yet without criminal sanctions prevention would be impossible; we have enough difficulty trying to prevent such problems now.

17 We would be recklessly jeopardizing our future. It would become morally difficult to teach youngsters to avoid drugs. If society endorsed addictive drugs as insufficiently harmful to be sold over the counter, how would children be motivated to stay away? Would taxpayers bother to pay for treatment and education centers?

18 The Food and Drug Administration forbids the marketing of foodstuffs that tests indicate can cause cancer in rats. History would have nothing good to say about a society that found drugs a lesser threat.

19 The way to fight drug crime is not to make it legal. The way to fight it is to fight it.

Questions for Analysis

1. In Paragraph 3, as an argument against the legalization of drugs, means uses the fact that consumption of alcoholic beverages went up by 350 percent after the repeal

of Prohibition. What additional information about this figure would you wish to know? What information would render this figure less effective as an argument? What information would make it more effective? Why might the percentage be more impressive than the actual numbers?

2. Does the second sentence in Paragraph 7 accurately state the position of those who argue for legalization of drugs? Does it involve a false dilemma (in other words, does it unfairly suggest that those who argue for legalization must necessarily accept only one of two very narrow positions)?
3. Means argues that comparisons between drugs and alcohol are "dangerously misleading." How does she support this assertion? What are her most convincing arguments?

William J. Bennett

Should Drugs Be Legalized?

(1990)

William J. Bennett (b. 1943), who holds a PhD in philosophy, has served as Secretary of Education in the Reagan administration and as "Drug Czar" in the Bush administration. He wrote this essay for *Reader's Digest* while he was still the Bush administration's coordinator and spokesman for the war on drugs.

1 Since I took command of the war on drugs, I have learned from former secretary of state George Shultz that our concept of fighting drugs is "flawed." The only thing to do, he says, is to "make it possible for addicts to buy drugs at some regulated place." Conservative commentator William F. Buckley, Jr., suggests I should be "fatalistic" about the flood of cocaine from South America and simply "let it in." Syndicated columnist Mike Royko contends it would be easier to sweep junkies out of the gutters "than to fight a hopeless war" against the narcotics that send them there. Labeling our efforts "bankrupt," federal judge Robert W. Sweet opts for legalization, saying, "If our society can learn to stop using butter, it should be able to cut down on cocaine."

2 Flawed, fatalistic, hopeless, bankrupt! I never realized surrender was so fashionable until I assumed this post.

3 Though most Americans are overwhelmingly determined to go toe-to-toe with the foreign drug lords and neighborhood pushers, a small minority believe that enforcing drug laws imposes greater costs on society than do drugs themselves. Like addicts seeking immediate euphoria, the legalizers want peace at any price, even though it means the inevitable proliferation of a practice that degrades, impoverishes, and kills.

4 I am acutely aware of the burdens drug enforcement places upon us. It consumes economic resources we would like to use elsewhere. It is sometimes frustrating,

thankless, and often dangerous. But the consequences of *not* enforcing drug laws would be far more costly. Those consequences involve the intrinsically destructive nature of drugs and the toll they exact from our society in hundreds of thousands of lost and broken lives . . . human potential never realized . . . time stolen from families and jobs . . . precious spiritual and economic resources squandered.

5 That is precisely why virtually every civilized society has found it necessary to exert some form of control over mind-altering substances and why this war is so important. Americans feel up to their hips in drugs now. They would be up to their necks under legalization.

6 Even limited experiments in drug legalization have shown that when drugs are more widely available, addiction skyrockets. In 1975 Italy liberalized its drug law and now has one of the highest heroin-related death rates in Western Europe. In Alaska, where marijuana was decriminalized in 1975, the easy atmosphere has increased usage of the drug, particularly among children. Nor does it stop there. Some Alaskan schoolchildren now tout "coco puffs," marijuana cigarettes laced with cocaine.

7 Many legalizers concede that drug legalization might increase use, but they shrug off the matter. "It may well be that there would be more addicts, and I would regret that result," says Nobel laureate economist Milton Friedman. The late Harvard Medical School psychiatry professor Norman Zinberg, a longtime proponent of "responsible" drug use, admitted that "use of now-illicit drugs would certainly increase. Also casualties probably would increase."

8 In fact, Dr. Herbert D. Kleber of Yale University, my deputy in charge of demand reduction, predicts legalization might cause a "five-to-sixfold increase" in cocaine use. But legalizers regard this as a necessary price for the "benefits" of legalization. What benefits?

9 1. *Legalization will take the profit out of drugs.* The result supposedly will be the end of criminal drug pushers and the big foreign drug wholesalers, who will turn to other enterprises because nobody will need to make furtive and dangerous trips to his local pusher.

10 But what, exactly, would the brave new world of legalized drugs look like? Buckley stresses that "adults get to buy the stuff at carefully regulated stores." (Would you want one in *your* neighborhood?) Others, like Friedman, suggest we sell the drugs at "ordinary retail outlets."

11 Former City University of New York sociologist Georgette Bennett assures us that "brand-name competition will be prohibited" and that strict quality control and proper labeling will be overseen by the Food and Drug Administration. In a touching egalitarian note, she adds that "free drugs will be provided at government clinics" for addicts too poor to buy them.

12 Almost all legalizers point out that the price of drugs will fall, even though the drugs will be heavily taxed. Buckley, for example, argues that somehow federal drugstores will keep the price "low enough to discourage a black market but high enough to accumulate a surplus to be used for drug education."

13 Supposedly, drug sales will generate huge amounts of revenue, which will then be used to tell the public not to use drugs and to treat those who don't listen.

14 In reality, this tax would only allow government to *share* the drug profits now garnered by criminals. Legalizers would have to tax drugs heavily in order to pay for drug education and treatment programs. Criminals could undercut the official price and still make huge profits. What alternative would the government have? Cut the price until it was within the lunch-money budget of the average sixth-grade student?

15 2. *Legalization will eliminate the black market.* Wrong. And not just because the regulated prices could be undercut. Many legalizers admit that drugs such as crack or PCP are simply too dangerous to allow the shelter of the law. Thus criminals will provide what the government will not. ''As long as drugs that people very much want remain illegal, a black market will exist,'' says legalization advocate David Boaz of the libertarian Cato Institute.

16 Look at crack. In powdered form, cocaine was an expensive indulgence. But street chemists found that a better and far less expensive—and far more dangerous—high could be achieved by mixing cocaine with baking soda and heating it. Crack was born, and ''cheap'' coke invaded low-income communities with furious speed.

17 An ounce of powdered cocaine might sell on the street for $1200. That same ounce can produce 370 vials of crack at $10 each. Ten bucks seems like a cheap hit, but crack's intense ten- to fifteen-minute high is followed by an unbearable depression. The user wants more crack, thus starting a rapid and costly descent into addiction.

18 If government drugstores do not stock crack, addicts will find it in the clandestine market or simply bake it themselves from their legally purchased cocaine.

19 Currently crack is being laced with insecticides and animal tranquilizers to heighten its effect. Emergency rooms are now warned to expect victims of ''sandwiches'' and ''moon rocks,'' life-threatening smokable mixtures of heroin and crack. Unless the government is prepared to sell these deadly variations of dangerous drugs, it will perpetuate a criminal black market by default.

20 And what about children and teenagers? They would obviously be barred from drug purchases, just as they are prohibited from buying beer and liquor. But pushers will continue to cater to these young customers with the old, favorite come ons a couple of free fixes to get them hooked. And what good will antidrug education be when these youngsters observe their older brothers and sisters, parents, and friends lighting up and shooting up with government permission?

21 Legalization will give us the worst of both worlds: millions of *new* drug users *and* a thriving criminal black market.

22 3. *Legalization will dramatically reduce crime.* ''It is the high price of drugs that leads addicts to robbery, murder, and other crimes,'' says Ira Glasser, executive director of the American Civil Liberties Union. A study by the Cato Institute concludes: ''Most, if not all 'drug-related murders' are the result of drug prohibition.''

23 But researchers tell us that many drug-related felonies are committed by people involved in crime *before* they started taking drugs. The drugs, so routinely available in criminal circles, make the criminals more violent and unpredictable.

24 Certainly there are some kill-for-a-fix crimes, but does any rational person believe that a cut-rate price for drugs at a government outlet will stop such psychopathic behavior? The fact is that under the influence of drugs, normal people do not act normally, and abnormal people behave in chilling and horrible ways. DEA agents told me about a teenage addict in Manhattan who was smoking crack when he sexually abused and caused permanent internal injuries to his one-month-old daughter.

25 Children are among the most frequent victims of violent, drug-related crimes that have nothing to do with the cost of acquiring the drugs. In Philadelphia in 1987 more than half the child-abuse fatalities involved at least one parent who was a heavy drug user. Seventy-three percent of the child-abuse deaths in New York City in 1987 involved parental drug use.

26 In my travels to the ramparts of the drug war, I have seen nothing to support the legalizers' argument that lower drug prices would reduce crime. Virtually everywhere I have gone, police and DEA agents have told me that crime rates are highest where crack is cheapest.

27 4. *Drug use should be legal since users only harm themselves.* Those who believe this should stand beside the medical examiner as he counts the thirty-six bullet wounds in the shattered corpse of a three-year-old who happened to get in the way of his mother's drug-crazed boyfriend. They should visit the babies abandoned by cocaine-addicted mothers—infants who already carry the ravages of addiction in their own tiny bodies. They should console the devastated relatives of the nun who worked in a homeless shelter and was stabbed to death by a crack addict enraged that she would not stake him to a fix.

28 Do drug addicts only harm themselves? Here is a former cocaine addict describing the compulsion that quickly draws even the most "responsible" user into irresponsible behavior: "Everything is about getting high, and any means necessary to get there becomes rational. If it means stealing something from somebody close to you, lying to your family, borrowing money from people you know you can't pay back, writing checks you know you can't cover, you do all those things—things that are totally against everything you have ever believed in."

29 Society pays for this behavior, and not just in bigger insurance premiums, losses from accidents, and poor job performance. We pay in the loss of a priceless social currency as families are destroyed, trust between friends is betrayed, and promising careers are never fulfilled. I cannot imagine sanctioning behavior that would increase that toll.

30 I find no merit in the legalizers' case. The simple fact is that drug use is wrong. And the moral argument, in the end, is the most compelling argument. A citizen in a drug-induced haze, whether on his backyard deck or on a mattress in a ghetto crack house, is not what the founding fathers meant by the "pursuit of happiness." Despite the

legalizers' argument that drug use is a matter of "personal freedom," our nation's notion of liberty is rooted in the ideal of a self-reliant citizenry. Helpless wrecks in treatment centers, men chained by their noses to cocaine—these people are slaves.

31 Imagine if, in the darkest days of 1940, Winston Churchill had rallied the West by saying, "This war looks hopeless, and besides, it will cost too much. Hitler can't be *that* bad. Let's surrender and see what happens." That is essentially what we hear from the legalizers.

32 This war *can* be won. I am heartened by indications that education and public revulsion are having an effect on drug use. The National Institute on Drug Abuse's latest survey of current users shows a 37-percent *decrease* in drug consumption since 1985. Cocaine is down 50 percent; marijuana use among young people is at its lowest rate since 1972. In my travels I've been encouraged by signs that Americans are fighting back.

33 I am under no illusion that such developments, however hopeful, mean the war is over. We need to involve more citizens in the fight, increase pressure on drug criminals, and build on antidrug programs that have proved to work. This will not be easy. But the moral and social costs of surrender are simply too great to contemplate.

Questions for Analysis

1. What is the purpose of the first paragraph in Bennett's essay? How do the quotations from proponents of drug legalization work to make the point Bennett wishes to make?
2. Reread the first sentence in Paragraph 3. What does "going toe-to-toe with the foreign drug lords and neighborhood pushers" really mean? Is the distinction between "most Americans" who are "overwhelmingly determined to go toe-to-toe" and "a small minority" who "believe that enforcing drug laws imposes greater costs on society than do drugs themselves" clear? Is it a false distinction? In other words, might people fall into neither group, or into both groups simultaneously?
3. Bennett's organizational strategy corresponds to four benefits claimed by advocates of drug legalization. Is this strategy effective? What are its strengths and weaknesses? Which section in Bennett's response is most effective? Which is least effective?
4. One critic of Bennett's drug policy (Diana Gordon in this section "Europe's Kindler, Gentler Approach") has called attention to Bennett's "moral fundamentalism about drug taking" and his "demonization of drug takers." Can you find places in this essay where Bennett's words convey these messages? How does that language (and attitude) generate the reaction Gordon and others see? Try to rephrase

some of Bennett's sentences to soften his tone. Can you come up with rewrites that change his tone without changing his meaning?

Lewis Lapham

A Political Opiate: The War on Drugs Is a Folly and a Menace

(1989)

Lewis Lapham (b. 1935) is editor of *Harper's Magazine* and a frequent contributor to its pages. This essay appeared in the December 1989 issue.

1 If President Bush's September address to the nation on the topic of drugs can be taken as an example of either his honesty or his courage, I see no reason why I can't look forward to hearing him declare a war against cripples, or one-eyed people, or red geraniums. It was a genuinely awful speech, rooted at the beginning in a lie, directed at an imaginary enemy, sustained by false argument, proposing a policy that already had failed, playing to the galleries of prejudice and fear. The first several sentences of the speech established its credentials as a fraud. "Drugs," said Bush, "are sapping our strength as a nation." "The gravest domestic threat facing our nation," said Bush, "is drugs." "Our most serious problem today," said Bush, "is cocaine." None of the statements meets the standards either of minimal analysis or casual observation. The government's own figures show that the addiction to illegal drugs troubles a relatively small number of Americans, and the current generation of American youth is the strongest and healthiest in the nation's history.[1]

2 In the sixth paragraph of his speech, the President elaborated his fraud by holding up a small plastic bag, as distastefully as if he were holding a urine specimen. "This is crack cocaine," he said, "seized a few days ago by Drug Enforcement Administration agents in a park just across the street from the White House. It could easily have been heroin or PCP." But since nobody, ever, has been known to sell any kind of drug in Lafayette Park, it couldn't possibly have been heroin or PCP. The bag of cocaine wasn't anything other than a stage prop: The DEA was put to considerable trouble and expense to tempt a dealer into the park in order to make the arrest at a time and place convenient to the President's little dramatic effect.

3 Bush's speechwriters ordered the staging of the "buy" because they wanted to make a rhetorical point about the dark and terrible sea of drugs washing up on the innocent, sun-dappled lawns of the White House. The sale was difficult to arrange because the

drug dealer in question had never heard of Lafayette Park, didn't know how to find the place on a map, and couldn't imagine why anybody would want to make such complicated travel arrangements in order to buy rocks of low-grade crack.

4 Two days later, confronted by the press with the mechanics of his sleight of hand, Bush said, "I don't understand. I mean, has somebody got some advocates here for this drug guy?" The surprised and petulant tone of his question gave away the nature of the political game that he was playing, playing on what he assumed was the home field of the nation's best-loved superstitions. After seven months in office, he had chosen to make his first televised address on a topic that he thought was as safe as mother and the undesecrated flag. He had politely avoided any and all of the "serious problems facing our nation today" (the deficit, say, or the environment, or the question of race) and he had done what he could to animate a noncontroversial platitude with a good visual. He expected people to be supportive and nice.

5 Apparently it never occurred to him that anybody would complain about his taking a few minor liberties with the facts. Nor did he seem to notice that he had seized upon the human suffering implicit in the drug trade as an occasion for a shabby political trick. He had exploited exactly the same device in his election campaign by transforming the image of Willie Horton, a black convict who committed violent crimes after being released on furlough from a Massachusetts prison, into a metaphor for all the world's wickedness. I can imagine his speechwriters explaining to him that the war on drugs was nothing more than Willie Horton writ large.

6 The premise of the war is so patently false, and the hope for victory so obviously futile, that I can make sense of it only by asking the rhetorical question *cui bono?* Who stands to gain by virtue of Bush's lovely little war, and what must the rest of us pay as tribute?

7 The question is a political one. But, then, the war on drugs is a political war, waged not by scientists and doctors but by police officers and politicians. Under more fortunate circumstances, the prevalence of drugs in American society—not only cocaine and heroin and marijuana but also alcohol and tobacco and sleeping pills—would be properly addressed as a public-health question. The American Medical Association classifies drug addiction as a disease, not as a crime or a moral defeat. Nor is addiction contagious, like measles and the flu. Given the folly and expense of the war on drugs (comparable to the folly and expense of the war in Vietnam), I expect that the United States eventually will arrive at some method of decriminalizing the use of all drugs. The arguments in favor of decriminalization seem to me irrefutable, as do the lessons of experience taught by the failed attempt at the prohibition of alcohol.[2]

8 But for the time being, as long as the question remains primarily political, the war on drugs serves the purposes of the more reactionary interests within our society (i.e., the defenders of the imagined innocence of a nonexistent past) and transfers the costs of the war to precisely those individuals whom the promoters of the war say they wish to protect. I find it difficult to believe that the joke, although bitter, is unintended.

9 To politicians in search of sound opinions and sustained applause, the war on drugs presents itself as a gift from heaven. Because the human craving for intoxicants cannot

be suppressed—not by priests or jailers or acts of Congress—the politicians can bravely confront an allegorical enemy rather than an enemy that takes the corporeal form of the tobacco industry, say, or the Chinese, or the oil and banking lobbies.[3] The war against drugs provides them with something to say that offends nobody, requires them to do nothing difficult, and allows them to postpone, perhaps indefinitely, the more urgent and specific questions about the state of the nation's schools, housing, employment opportunities for young black men—i.e., the conditions to which drug addiction speaks as a tragic symptom, not a cause. They remain safe in the knowledge that they might as well be denouncing Satan or the rain, and so they can direct the voices of prerecorded blame at metaphors and apparitions who, unlike Senator Jesse Helms and his friends at the North Carolina tobacco auctions, can be transformed into demonic spirits riding north across the Caribbean on an evil wind. The war on drugs thus becomes the perfect war for people who would rather not fight a war, a war in which the politicians who stand so fearlessly on the side of the good, the true, and the beautiful need do nothing else but strike noble poses as protectors of the people and defenders of the public trust.

10 Their cynicism is implicit in the arithmetic. President Bush in his September speech asked for $7.9 billion to wage his ''assault on every front'' of the drug war, but the Pentagon allots $5 billion a year to the B-2 program—i.e., to a single weapon. Expressed as a percentage of the federal budget, the new funds assigned to the war on drugs amount to .065 percent. Nor does the government offer to do anything boldly military about the legal drugs, principally alcohol and tobacco, that do far more damage to the society than all the marijuana and all the cocaine ever smuggled into Florida or California.[4]

11 The drug war, like all wars, sells papers, and the media, like the politicians, ask for nothing better than a safe and profitable menace. The campaign against drugs involves most of the theatrical devices employed by *Miami Vice*—scenes of crimes in progress (almost always dressed up, for salacious effect, with the cameo appearances of one or two prostitutes), melodramatic villains in the Andes, a vocabulary of high-tech military jargon as reassuring as the acronyms in a Tom Clancy novel, the specter of a crazed lumpenproletariat rising in revolt in the nation's cities.

12 Like camp followers trudging after an army of crusader knights on its way to Jerusalem, the media have in recent months displayed all the garish colors of the profession. Everybody who was anybody set up a booth and offered his or her tears for sale—not only Geraldo and Maury Povich but also, in much the same garish language, Dan Rather (on *48 Hours*), Ted Koppel (on *Nightline*), and Sam Donaldson (on *Prime Time Live*). In the six weeks between August 1 and September 13, the three television networks combined with the *New York Times* and the *Washington Post* to produce 347 reports from the frontiers of the apocalypse—crack in the cities, cocaine in the suburbs, customs agents seizing pickup trucks on the Mexican border, smugglers named Julio arriving every hour on the hour at Key West.

13 Most of the journalists writing the dispatches, like most of the columnists handing down the judgments of conscience, knew as much about crack or heroin or cocaine as

they knew about the molecular structure of the moons of Saturn. Their ignorance didn't prevent them from coming to the rescue of their own, and the President's, big story. On *World News Tonight* a few days after the President delivered his address, Peter Jennings in a tone of voice that was as certain as it was silly (as well as being characteristic of the rest of the propaganda being broadcast over the other networks), said, "Using it even once can make a person crave cocaine for as long as they [*sic*] live."

14 So great was the media's excitement, and so determined their efforts to drum up a paying crowd, that hardly anybody bothered to question the premises of the drug war, and several of the more senior members of the troupe took it upon themselves to write diatribes against any dissent from the wisdom in office. A. M. Rosenthal, on the op-ed page of the *New York Times,* denounced even the slightest show of tolerance toward illegal drugs as an act of iniquity deserving comparison to the defense of slavery. William Safire, also writing in the *New York Times,* characterized any argument against the war on drugs as an un-American proof of defeatism. Without notable exception, the chorus of the big media tuned its instruments to the high metallic pitch of zero tolerance, scorned any truth that didn't echo their own, and pasted the smears of derision on the foreheads of the few people, among them Milton Friedman and William Buckley, who had the temerity to suggest that perhaps the war on drugs was both stupid and lost.

15 The story of the drug war plays to the prejudices of an audience only too eager to believe the worst that can be said about people whom they would rather not know. Because most of the killing allied with the drug trade takes place in the inner cities, and because most of the people arrested for selling drugs prove to be either black or Hispanic, it becomes relatively easy for white people living in safe neighborhoods to blur the distinction between crime and race. Few of them have ever seen an addict or witnessed a drug deal, but the newspapers and television networks keep showing them photographs that convey the impression of a class war, and those among them who always worried about driving through Harlem (for fear of being seized by gangs of armed black men) or who always wished that they didn't feel quite so guilty about the socioeconomic distance between East 72nd Street and West 126th Street can comfort themselves, finally, at long last, and with a clear conscience, with the thought that poverty is another word for sin, that their BMW is a proof of their virtue, and that they or, more likely, their mothers were always right to fear the lower classes and the darker races.

16 As conditions in the slums deteriorate, which they inevitably must because the government subtracts money from the juvenile-justice and housing programs to finance its war on drugs, the slums come to look just the way they are supposed to look in the suburban imagination, confirming the fondest suspicions of the governing and possessing classes, justifying the further uses of force and repression. The people who pay the price for the official portrait turn out to be (wonder of wonders) not the members of the prosperous middle class—not the journalists or the academic theorists, not the politicians and government functionaries living behind hedges in Maryland and Virginia—but (*mirabile dictu*) the law-abiding residents of the inner cities living in the only neighborhoods that they can afford.

17 It is in the slums of New York that three people, on average, get killed every day—which, over the course of a year, adds up to a higher casualty rate than pertains in Gaza and the West Bank; it is in the slums that the drug trade recruits children to sell narcotics, which is not the result of indigenous villainy but of the nature of the law; it is in the slums that the drug trade has become the exemplary model of finance capitalism for children aspiring to the success of Donald Trump and Samuel Pierce; and it is in the slums that the police experiment with the practice of apartheid, obliging residents of housing projects to carry identity cards and summarily evicting the residents of apartment houses tainted by the presence of drug dealers.[5]

18 To the extent that the slums can be seen as the locus of the nation's wickedness (i.e., a desolate *mise-en-scène* not unlike the Evil Empire that Ronald Reagan found in the Soviet Union), the crimes allied with the drug traffic can be classified as somebody else's moral problem rather than one's own social or political problem. The slums become foreign, alien nations on the other side of the economic and cultural frontiers. The deliberate confusion of geography with metaphysics turns out, again to nobody's surprise, to be wonderfully convenient for the sponsors of the war on drugs. The politicians get their names in the papers, the media have a story to tell, and the rest of us get off the hooks that otherwise might impale us on the questions of conscience or the obligation of higher taxes. In New York last week, I overheard a woman in an expensive restaurant say that she didn't understand why the government didn't arrange to put "arsenic or something" in a seized shipment of cocaine. If the government (or "the CIA or the FBI or whoever does that sort of thing") allowed the poisoned cocaine to find its way back onto the streets, then "pretty soon we'd be rid of the whole damn thing."

19 If the folly of the war on drugs could be understood merely as a lesson in political cynicism, or simply as an example of the aplomb with which the venal media can play upon the sentiments of a mob, maybe I would rest content with a few last jokes about the foolishness of the age. But the war on drugs also serves the interests of the state, which, under the pretext of rescuing people from incalculable peril, claims for itself enormously enhanced powers of repression and control.

20 An opinion poll conducted during the week following President Bush's September address showed 62 percent of the respondents "willing to give up some freedoms" in order to hold America harmless against the scourge of drugs. The government stands more than willing to take them at their word. The war on drugs becomes a useful surrogate for the obsolescent Cold War, now fading into the realm of warm and nostalgic memory. Under the familiar rubrics of constant terror and ceaseless threat, the government subtracts as much as possible from the sum of the nation's civil liberties and imposes *de facto* martial law on a citizenry that it chooses to imagine as a dangerous rabble.

21 Anybody who doubts this point has only to read the speeches of William Bennett, the commander-in-chief of the Bush administration's war on drugs. Bennett's voice is the voice of an intolerant scold, narrow and shrill and mean-spirited, the voice of a man afraid of liberty and mistrustful of freedom. He believes that it is the government's duty

to impose on people a puritanical code of behavior best exemplified by the discipline in place at an unheated boarding school. He never misses the chance to demand more police, more jails, more judges, more arrests, more punishments, more people serving more millennia of "serious time."

22 Reading Bennett's speeches, I am reminded of the Ayatollah Khalkhali, appointed by the authorities in Iran to the office of executioner without portfolio. Khalkhali was blessed with the power to order the death of anybody whom he found in the company of drugs, and within a period of seven weeks he killed 176 people. Still he failed to suppress the use of opium, and he said, "If we wanted to kill everybody who had five grams of heroin, we would have to kill 5,000 people." And then, after a wistful pause, he said, "And this would be difficult."

23 In line with Bennett's zeal for coercion, politicians of both parties demand longer jail sentences and harsher laws as well as the right to invade almost everybody's privacy; to search, without a warrant, almost anybody's automobile or boat; to bend the rules of evidence, hire police spies, and attach, again without a warrant, the wires of electronic surveillance. The more obviously the enforcement of the law fails to accomplish its nominal purpose (i.e., as more drugs become more accessible at cheaper prices), the more reasons the Supreme Court finds to warrant the invasion of privacy. In recent years, the Court has granted police increasingly autocratic powers—permission (without probable cause) to stop, detain, and question travelers passing through the nation's airports in whom the police can see a resemblance to a drug dealer; permission (again without probable cause) to search barns, stop motorists, inspect bank records, and tap phones.

24 The polls suggest that a majority of the American people accept these measures as right and proper. Of the respondents questioned by an ABC/*Washington Post* poll in September, 55 percent supported mandatory drug testing for all Americans, 82 percent favored enlisting the military in the war on drugs, 52 percent were willing to have their homes searched, and 83 percent favored reporting suspected drug users to the police, even if the suspects happened to be members of their own family. In October, *Newsweek* took note of an inquisition in progress in Clinton, Iowa. The local paper had taken to printing cutout coupons that said, "I've had enough of drugs in my neighborhood! I have reason to believe that (blank) is using/dealing drugs." The paper collected the coupons for the town police, who reported the response as "excellent."

25 The enforcement of more and stricter laws requires additional tiers of expensive government, and of the $7.9 billion that President Bush allotted to the war on drugs in September, the bulk of the money swells the budgets of the fifty-eight federal agencies and seventy-four congressional committees currently engaged, each with its own agenda and armies to feed, on various fronts of the campaign. Which doesn't mean, of course, that the money will be honestly, or even intelligently, spent. As was demonstrated all too plainly by the Reagan administration (cf. the sums misappropriated from HUD and the Pentagon), the government has a talent for theft and fraud barely distinguishable from the criminal virtuosity of the drug syndicates it wishes to destroy.

26 Even so, and notwithstanding its habitual incompetence and greed, the government doesn't lightly relinquish the spoils of power seized under the pretexts of apocalypse. What the government grasps, the government seeks to keep and hold. The militarization of the rhetoric supporting the war on drugs rots the public debate with a corrosive silence. The political weather turns gray and pinched. People who become accustomed to the arbitrary intrusions of the police also learn to speak more softly in the presence of political authority, to bow and smile and fill out the printed forms with the cowed obsequiousness of musicians playing waltzes at a Mafia wedding.

27 And for what? To punish people desperate enough or foolish enough to poison themselves with drugs? To exact vengeance on people afflicted with the sickness of addiction and who, to their grief and shame, can find no other way out of the alleys of their despair?

28 As a consequence of President Bush's war on drugs, society gains nothing except immediate access to an unlimited fund of resentment and unspecific rage. In return for so poor a victory, and in the interests of the kind of people who would build prisons instead of schools, Bush offers the nation the chance to deny its best principles, to corrupt its magistrates and enrich its most vicious and efficient criminals, to repudiate its civil liberties and repent of the habits of freedom. The deal is as shabby as President Bush's trick with the bag of cocaine. For the sake of a vindictive policeman's dream of a quiet and orderly heaven, the country risks losing its constitutional right to its soul.

Notes

1. In 1983, for the first time since anybody began keeping records, the death rate among youths aged fifteen to twenty-four dropped below 100 in 100,000. The truth of the statistic should be apparent to anyone who has taken the trouble to look at the crowd in the stands during a televised broadcast of a college football game.
2. *Harper's Magazine* over the past twenty years has published a fair number of articles and essays arguing the brief for the decriminalization of drugs. For the interested reader who wishes to pursue the subject with more-current writers, I recommend Ethan A. Nadelmann in the Spring 1988 *Foreign Policy* and the interview with Arnold Trebach in last summer's *New Perspectives Quarterly*.
3. Even governments with all the means of fascist repression at their command cannot force human nature into the molds made for prime-time television comedy. In Turkey in the nineteenth century, the authorities slit the nostrils of anybody caught smoking cigarettes. Czarist Russia punished the crime of smoking with death. Although I suspect that both punishments might be heartily endorsed by certain members of the Bush administration, neither of them eliminated the use of tobacco.
4. In 1988, American hospitals counted 3,308 deaths attributed to cocaine, as opposed to 390,000 deaths in some way attributable to the use of tobacco and 100,000 deaths directly related to the excessive use of alcohol.
5. The government's own statistics indicate that the middle classes no longer recognize the drug problem as one of their own. Doing lines of cocaine hasn't been hip for at least five years, and among college and high school students, the use of drugs has declined markedly over the same period of time. In fact, the number of current cocaine users has gone down from 5.8 million in 1985 to 2.9 million in 1988. A July poll conducted by the mayor's office in Washington, D.C., showed that the white residents in town worried more about potholes than about cocaine.

Questions for Analysis

1. In Paragraph one, Lapham attacks President Bush's September 1989 speech on drugs as "a genuinely awful speech, rooted at the beginning in a lie, directed at an imaginary enemy, sustained by false argument. . . ." How does he support these and the following assertions? Is Bush's message undercut by our knowing, for example, that the drug dealer arrested in Lafayette Park was lured there to set up the speech? Why or why not? Were Bush's characterizations of the drug problem overstatements?
2. Lapham says in Paragraph 7 that the question is a political one. How does he say politicians use the war on drugs for political advantage? Do you perceive the political cynicism Lapham describes as characteristic of the politicians you read about and hear? Explain. Should the war on drugs be a political war?
3. What are Lapham's political biases? Point out several places where his language conveys his bias. Do these uses of language enhance or undercut the persuasiveness of his essay? How would different audiences react to his language and tone?
4. In Paragraphs 15–18, Lapham suggests that our drug policy reflects a racial and economic bias. Evaluate his argument here. Is his point clear and his support persuasive?
5. In Paragraph 21, Lapham describes Bennett and his language. Is this characterization consistent with your response to Bennett's essay in this text and with the opinions of other writers who have written about Bennett? Explain.
6. What is your overall response to Lapham's essay? Is his essay effective? Did it make you reconsider your opinions even if it did not change your mind? What parts of his essay did you find effective and persuasive? What parts did you find ineffective and not persuasive?
7. How do you think Lapham would respond to Gordon's essay, later in this chapter, on drug policy and law in Europe?

Walter Wink

Biting the Bullet: The Case for Legalizing Drugs

(1990)

Walter Wink (b. 1935) is a theologian and a regular contributor to *The Christian Century,* in which this essay appeared in August 1990. He teaches at Auburn Theological Seminary in New York City.

1 The drug war is over. We lost it long before the latest declaration of war by President Bush. Whatever the other factors, we lost primarily for spiritual reasons. We merely repeated the mistake of Prohibition: the harder we tried to stamp out the evil, the more lucrative we made it. We should know that prohibition doesn't work. Forcible resistance to evil simply makes it more profitable.

2 Our attempts to stamp out drugs violate a fundamental principle that Jesus articulated in the Sermon on the Mount: "Resist not evil." The Greek term translated "resist" is *antistenai.* When it is used by the Greek Old Testament or by the first-century Jewish historian Josephus, however, the word is usually translated, "to be engaged in a revolt, rebellion, riot, insurrection." It is virtually a synonym for war. It means to stand up against an enemy and fight. So Jesus' words should be translated, "Do not resist evil by violent means. Do not fight evil with evil. Do not mirror evil, do not let evil set the terms of your response." Applied to the drug issue, this means, "Do not resist drugs by violent methods."

3 When we oppose evil with the same weapons that evil employs, we commit the same atrocities, violate the same civil liberties and break the same laws as do those whom we oppose. We become what we hate. Evil makes us over into its mimetic double. If one side prevails, the evil continues by virtue of having been established through the means used. More often, however, both sides grow, fed by their mutual resistance, as in the arms race, the Vietnam war, the Salvadoran civil war and Lebanon. This principle of mimetic opposition is illustrated abundantly in the drug war.

4 Bush's drug-war strategy has three elements. First, it requires cutting off the drug source in Colombia, Peru and Bolivia. Yet this appears to be impossible. Already we see signs that Colombia is collapsing into civil war. Officials and journalists are being gunned down on the streets, civilian homes are being raided and seized, civilian government is increasingly being taken over by the military—and so far the drug lords have only engaged in selective terrorism.

5 Moreover, the Colombian army has seldom confronted the 140 paramilitary private armies of the drug lords, or raided their training bases. For in certain areas of the country the military has formed a marriage of convenience with drug traffickers and landowners

in a common front against a 30-year-old leftist guerilla insurgency. With an income in the billions of dollars, drug leaders are able to buy generals, judges and police. In one week last fall, the Colombian national police fired 2,075 officers for having links with the cartels. The drug lords have also bought limited public acceptance by sponsoring the national soccer league, diversifying into legitimate businesses, supporting charities and offering to pay off the government's $10 billion external debt.

6 To test public reaction, the Bush administration may talk about sending in U.S. troops. But even if only military advisers are sent, they will soon discover in the field what our advisers found in Vietnam: an army not really committed to a fight. And even if those producing countries could be rid of coca tomorrow, production would simply be moved somewhere else, and the eradication effort would have to be started all over again in Southeast Asia, Turkey, Afghanistan and other countries far less likely to let us call the shots. So far, cocaine cultivation uses only 700 square miles of the 2.5 million square miles suitable for its growth in South America. There is simply no way the U.S. can police so vast an area.

7 Second, the Bush strategy calls for interdicting cocaine at our borders. We have been trying that for years, and it simply cannot be done short of militarizing the borders. According to a Government Accounting Office study, the U.S. Air Force spent $3.3 million on drug interdiction, using sophisticated AWACS surveillance planes over a 15-month period ending in 1987. The grand total of drug seizures from that effort was eight. During the same period, the combined efforts of the U.S. Coast Guard and Navy, sailing for 2,512 ship days at a cost of $40 million, resulted in the seizure of a mere 20 drug-carrying vessels. Drugs are easy to smuggle. The entire country's current annual import of cocaine would fit into a single C-5A cargo plane.

8 Even when interdiction works, it does nothing to reduce drug availability. On September 29, 1989, 21.4 tons of cocaine was seized in Los Angeles: within a week nine tons was taken in Harlingen, Texas, and five more at sea off Mexico's Yucatan Peninsula. The almost 36 tons netted in the three seizures was valued at $11 billion. Yet ten days later undercover agents were able to buy cocaine in bulk at the same price as before the seizures.

9 William Bennett, director of the National Office of Drug Control Policy, hopes that interdiction will raise drug prices. In fact, however, cocaine has become more available, while its wholesale price has dropped by 80 percent during the past decade. Increased prices would not deter addicts anyway; it would simply increase their rate of criminal acts. In Dade County, Florida, a mere 254 young addicts accounted for 223,000 crimes in a single year—almost 2.5 per youth per day. Multiply that by a nation and you see why the drug war was lost before it began.

10 As Senator John Kerry's subcommittee on narcotics reported in December 1988, increased cooperation with foreign governments has neither cut the amount of cocaine entering the U.S. nor led to the destruction of the major smuggling organizations. Fifteen percent of the drugs entering this country are being confiscated, but "for the drug cartels, whose production capacities stagger the imagination, a 15 percent loss rate is more than acceptable."

11 Third, the Bush plan calls for arresting drug dealers and casual users. There are already 750,000 drug arrests per year, and the current prison population is overtaxing facilities. At an average of $51,000 per inmate per year, just to incarcerate the 750,000 arrested annually would cost $38 billion. There are 35 to 40 million Americans who have used illegal drugs within the past year. To jail all users would run a tidy $1,785 trillion.

12 As for using the death penalty for deterrence, it seems unlikely that this country is ready to execute drug dealers by the hundreds of thousands. If so many millions are flouting the law, Prohibition style, is there really a political will for harsh enforcement? And how sincere is our antidrug effort going to be when the financial community realizes that the cash flow from the drug trade is the only thing preventing a default by some of the heavily indebted Latin American nations or major money-laundering banks? Cocaine trade brings Bolivia's economy about $600 million per year, a figure equal to the country's total legal export income. Revenues from drug trafficking in Miami are greater than those from tourism, exports, health care and all other legitimate businesses combined.

13 It is not drugs but rather drug laws that have made drug dealing profitable. Drug laws have also fostered drug-related murders and an estimated 40 percent of all property crime in the U.S. Ethan A. Nadelmann, whose article ''Drug Prohibition in the United States'' in the September 1, 1989, issue of *Science* has been a major catalyst for public discussion of legalization, argues that ''the greatest beneficiaries of the drug laws are organized and unorganized drug traffickers. The criminalization of the drug market effectively imposes a de facto value-added tax that is enforced and occasionally augmented by the law enforcement establishment and collected by the drug traffickers.'' Rather than collecting taxes on the sale of drugs, governments at all levels expend billions of dollars in what amounts to a subsidy of organized criminals.

14 The war on drugs creates casualties beyond those arrested. There are those killed in fights over turf, innocents caught in cross fire, citizens terrified of city streets, escalating robberies, children fed free crack to get them addicted and then enlisted as runners and dealers, mothers so crazed for a fix that they abandon their babies, prostitute themselves and their daughters, and addict their unborn. Much of that, too, is the result of the drug laws. Cocaine, after all, has been around a long time and was once sold over the counter in tablet form and consumed in *Coca*-Cola. What makes it so irresistible today is its lucrativeness. And it is lucrative only because it is illegal.

15 The media usually portray cocaine and crack use as a black ghetto phenomenon. This is a racist caricature. The *New York Times* reported on October 1, 1989, that there are more crack addicts among the white middle and upper class than any other segment of the population and far more such occasional cocaine users. The typical user is a single white male 20 to 40 years old who generally obtains his drugs from black dealers. The white demand makes the drugs flow. Americans consume 60 percent of the world's illegal drugs—too profitable a market for dealers to ignore.

16 In the drug war, we are blindly fighting what we have become as a nation. Some observers say that drugs are the ultimate consumer product for people who want to feel

good now without benefit of hard work, social interaction, or making a productive contribution to society. Drug dealers are living out the rags-to-riches American dream as private entrepreneurs trying desperately to become upwardly mobile. That is why we cannot win the war on drugs. We Americans are the enemy, and we cannot face that fact. So we launch a half-hearted, half-funded, half-baked war against a menace that only mirrors what we have ourselves become as a nation.

17 The uproar about drugs is itself odd. In 1987, according to the Kerry subcommittee, there were 1,400 deaths from cocaine; in 1988, that figure had increased to 3,308. Deaths from *all* forms of illegal drugs total under 6,000. By contrast, 320,000 to 390,000 people die prematurely each year from tobacco and 100,000 to 200,000 from misuse of alcohol. Alcohol is associated with 40 percent of all suicide attempts, 40 percent of all traffic deaths, 54 percent of all violent crimes and 10 percent of all work-related injuries.

18 None of the illegal drugs are as lethal as tobacco or alcohol. If anyone has ever died as a direct result of a marijuana overdose, no one seems to know about it. Many people can be addicted to heroin for most of their lives without serious consequences. Cocaine in powder form is not as addictive as nicotine; Nadelmann points out that only 3 percent of those who try it become addicted. Crack is terribly addictive, but its use is a direct consequence of the high cost of powdered cocaine. Crack was a cheap ghetto alternative, and its spread to the middle and upper classes has in part been a function of its low price. Severely addicted humans may in some ways resemble those experimental monkeys who will starve themselves to death if supplied with unlimited cocaine, but the vast majority of users are not in such danger (and alcoholic humans also will drink themselves to death).

19 We must be honest about these facts, because much of the hysteria about illegal drugs has been based on misinformation. All addiction is a serious matter, and the churches are right to be concerned about the human costs. But many of these costs are a consequence of a wrongheaded approach to eradication. Our tolerance of the real killer drugs and our abhorrence of the drugs which are far less lethal is hypocritical, or at best a selective moralism reflecting fashions of indignation.

20 Drug addiction is singled out as evil, yet we are a society of addicts living in an addictive society. We project on the black drug subculture profound anxieties about our own addictions (to wealth, power, sex, food, work, religion, alcohol and tobacco) and attack addiction in others without having to gain insight about ourselves. New York City Councilman Wendell Foster illustrated this scapegoating attitude when he suggested chaining addicts to trees so people could spit on them.

21 I'm not advocating giving up the war on drugs because we cannot win. I am saying that we cannot win as long as we let drugs dictate the means we use to oppose them. The only way to win is to ruin the world market price of drugs by legalizing them. When drug prices plummet, drug profits will collapse—and with them, the drug empire.

22 Some people have called for decriminalization, but they probably mean legalization. Decriminalization would mean no more laws regulating drugs, no governmental restraints on sales to minors, no quality controls to curtail overdose and no prosecution

of the inevitable boot-leggers. Legalization, however, means that the government would maintain regulatory control over drug sales, possibly through state clinics or stores. Advertising would be strictly prohibited, selling drugs to children would continue to be a criminal offense, and other evasions of government regulation would be prosecuted. Driving, flying or piloting a vessel under the influence would still be punished. Taxes on drugs would pay for enforcement, education, rehabilitation and research (Nadelmann estimates a net benefit of at least $10 billion from reduced expenditures on enforcement and new tax revenues). Street users would be picked up and taken to hospitals, like drunks, instead of arrested.

23 Legalization would lead to an immediate decrease in murders, burglaries and robberies, paralleling the end of alcohol prohibition in 1933. Cheap drugs would mean that most addicts would not be driven to crime to support their habit, and that drug lords would no longer have a turf to fight over. Legalization would be a blow to South American peasants, who would need support in switching back to less lucrative crops; but that would be less devastating than destruction of their crops altogether by aerial spraying or biological warfare. Legalization would enable countries like Peru to regularize the cocaine sector and absorb its money-making capacity in the taxable, legal, unionized economic world. Legalization would be a blow to ghetto dealers, who would be deprived of their ticket to riches. It would remove glamorous, Al Capone-type traffickers who are role models for the young, and it would destroy the "cool" status of drug use. It would cancel the corrupting role of the drug cartels in South American politics, a powerful incentive to corruption at all levels of our own government and a dangerous threat to our civil liberties through mistaken enforcement and property confiscation. It would free law-enforcement agencies to focus on other crimes and reduce the strain on the court and prison systems. It would nip in the bud a multibillion-dollar bureaucracy whose prosperity depends on *not* solving the drug problem. It would remove a major cause of public cynicism about obeying the laws of the land.

24 Legalization would also free up money wasted on interdiction of supplies that are needed desperately for treatment, education and research. Clinics in New York have room for only 48,000 of the state's estimated half-million addicts. Only $700 million has been earmarked by the Bush administration for treatment, out of a total expenditure of $8 billion for the drug war. Yet nationally, approximately 90 percent of the addicts who apply to drug treatment and rehabilitation centers are turned away for lack of space, resources and personnel. For those who do persist, the waiting period is six to 18 months. Even then, one-third to one-half of drug abusers turned away do reapply after waiting the extended time.

25 The worst prospect of legalization is that it might lead to a short-term increase in the use of drugs, due to availability, lower prices and the sudden freedom from prosecution. The repeal of Prohibition had that result. Drugs cheap enough to destroy their profitability would also be in the range of any child's allowance, just like beer and cigarettes. Cocaine is easily concealable and its effects less overt than alcohol. The possibility of increased teenage use is admittedly frightening.

26 On the other hand, ending the drug war would free drug control officers to concentrate on protecting children from exploitation, and here stiff penalties would continue to be in effect. The alarmist prediction that cheap available drugs could lead to an addiction rate of 75 percent of regular users simply ignores the fact that 35 to 40 million Americans are already using some drugs and that only 3 percent become addicts. Most people have strong reasons *not* to become addicts. A major educational program would need to be in effect well before drug legalization took effect.

27 Fighting the drug war may appear to hold the high moral ground, but this is only an illusion. And while some have argued that legalization would place the state's moral imprimatur on drugs, we have already legalized the most lethal drugs—and no one argues that this constitutes governmental endorsement. But legalizing would indeed imply that drugs are no longer being satanized like ''demon rum.'' It's time we bit the bullet. Addicts will be healed by care and compassion, not condemnation. Dealers will be cured by a ruined world drug market, not by enforcement that simply escalates the profitability of drugs. Legalization offers a nonviolent, nonreactive, creative alternative that will let the drug menace collapse of its own deadly weight.

Questions for Analysis

1. Wink bases an important part of his argument on the phrase ''Resist not evil'' taken from Christ's ''Sermon on the Mount.'' How does this phrase, as Wink explains it, epitomize the problem he sees in the war on drugs?
2. Throughout his essay Wink uses statistics to support his arguments. How effective are these statistics? Where are they most effective? Where are they least effective?
3. In Paragraph 16, Wink says that in the drug war, we are ''blindly fighting what we have become as a nation.'' What does he mean by this statement? What would proponents of the war on drugs say in response?
4. In Paragraph 25, Wink acknowledges the negative results of legalization of drugs. Then in Paragraph 26 he tries to counter those negative results by calling attention again to the clear benefits he sees in legalization. Is this rhetorical strategy effective? Explain.
5. In Paragraph 22 Wink defines two key terms: decriminalization and legalization. How do his definitions help advance his argument by clarifying his position?
6. Try to block out the major organizational divisions in Wink's essay and then evaluate his overall plan. How does he call attention to his organizational plan in his essay? Try to make the structure of this essay more obvious and effective by writing headings to fit the major divisions of the essay.

James Q. Wilson

Against the Legalization of Drugs

(1990)

James Q. Wilson (b. 1931) is Collins Professor of Management and Public Policy at UCLA. He has authored and co-authored several books on crime. His latest is *Bureaucracy*. This essay appeared in the February 1990 issue of *Commentary*.

1 In 1972, the President appointed me chairman of the National Advisory Council for Drug Abuse Prevention. Created by Congress, the Council was charged with providing guidance on how best to coordinate the national war on drugs. (Yes, we called it a war then, too.) In those days, the drug we were chiefly concerned with was heroin. When I took office, heroin use had been increasing dramatically. Everybody was worried that this increase would continue. Such phrases as "heroin epidemic" were commonplace.

2 That same year, the eminent economist Milton Friedman published an essay in *Newsweek* in which he called for legalizing heroin. His argument was on two grounds: as a matter of ethics, the government has no right to tell people not to use heroin (or to drink or to commit suicide); as a matter of economics, the prohibition of drug use imposes costs on society that far exceed the benefits. Others, such as the psychoanalyst Thomas Szasz, made the same argument.

3 We did not take Friedman's advice. (Government commissions rarely do.) I do not recall that we even discussed legalizing heroin, though we did discuss (but did not take action on) legalizing a drug, cocaine, that many people then argued was benign. Our marching orders were to figure out how to win the war on heroin, not to run up the white flag of surrender.

4 That was 1972. Today, we have the same number of heroin addicts that we had then—half a million, give or take a few thousand. Having that many heroin addicts is no trivial matter; these people deserve our attention. But not having had an increase in that number for over fifteen years is also something that deserves our attention. What happened to the "heroin epidemic" that many people once thought would overwhelm us?

5 The facts are clear: a more or less stable pool of heroin addicts has been getting older, with relatively few new recruits. In 1976 the average age of heroin users who appeared in hospital emergency rooms was about twenty-seven; ten years later it was thirty-two. More than two-thirds of all heroin users appearing in emergency rooms are now over the age of thirty. Back in the early 1970's, when heroin got onto the national political agenda, the typical heroin addict was much younger, often a teenager. Household surveys show the same thing—the rate of opiate use (which includes heroin) has

been flat for the better part of two decades. More fine-grained studies of inner-city neighborhoods confirm this. John Boyle and Ann Brunswick found that the percentage of young blacks in Harlem who used heroin fell from 8 percent in 1970–71 to about 3 percent in 1975–76.

6 Why did heroin lose its appeal for young people? When the young blacks in Harlem were asked why they stopped, more than half mentioned "trouble with the law" or "high cost" (and high cost is, of course, directly the result of law enforcement). Two-thirds said that heroin hurt their health; nearly all said they had had a bad experience with it. We need not rely, however, simply on what they said. In New York City in 1973–75, the street price of heroin rose dramatically and its purity sharply declined, probably as a result of the heroin shortage caused by the success of the Turkish government in reducing the supply of opium base and of the French government in closing down heroin-processing laboratories located in and around Marseilles. These were short-lived gains for, just as Friedman predicted, alternative sources of supply—mostly in Mexico—quickly emerged. But the three-year heroin shortage interrupted the easy recruitment of new users.

7 Health and related problems were no doubt part of the reason for the reduced flow of recruits. Over the preceding years, Harlem youth had watched as more and more heroin users died of overdoses, were poisoned by adulterated doses, or acquired hepatitis from dirty needles. The word got around: heroin can kill you. By 1974 new hepatitis cases and drug-overdose deaths had dropped to a fraction of what they had been in 1970.

8 Alas, treatment did not seem to explain much of the cessation in drug use. Treatment programs can and do help heroin addicts, but treatment did not explain the drop in the number of *new* users (who by definition had never been in treatment) nor even much of the reduction in the number of experienced users.

9 No one knows how much of the decline to attribute to personal observation as opposed to high prices or reduced supply. But other evidence suggests strongly that price and supply played a large role. In 1972 the National Advisory Council was especially worried by the prospect that U.S. servicemen returning to this country from Vietnam would bring their heroin habits with them. Fortunately, a brilliant study by Lee Robins of Washington University in St. Louis put that fear to rest. She measured drug use of Vietnam veterans shortly after they had returned home. Though many had used heroin regularly while in Southeast Asia, most gave up the habit when back in the United States. The reason: here, heroin was less available and sanctions on its use were more pronounced. Of course, if a veteran had been willing to pay enough—which might have meant traveling to another city and would certainly have meant making an illegal contact with a disreputable dealer in a threatening neighborhood in order to acquire a (possibly) dangerous dose—he could have sustained his drug habit. Most veterans were unwilling to pay this price, and so their drug use declined or disappeared.

Reliving the Past

10 Suppose we had taken Friedman's advice in 1972. What would have happened? We cannot be entirely certain, but at a minimum we would have placed the young heroin

addicts (and, above all, the prospective addicts) in a very different position from the one in which they actually found themselves. Heroin would have been legal. Its price would have been reduced by 95 percent (minus whatever we chose to recover in taxes). Now that it could be sold by the same people who make aspirin, its quality would have been assured—no poisons, no adulterants. Sterile hypodermic needles would have been readily available at the neighborhood drugstore, probably at the same counter where the heroin was sold. No need to travel to big cities or unfamiliar neighborhoods—heroin could have been purchased anywhere, perhaps by mail order.

11 There would no longer have been any financial or medical reason to avoid heroin use. Anybody could have afforded it. We might have tried to prevent children from buying it, but as we have learned from our efforts to prevent minors from buying alcohol and tobacco, young people have a way of penetrating markets theoretically reserved for adults. Returning Vietnam veterans would have discovered that Omaha and Raleigh had been converted into the pharmaceutical equivalent of Saigon.

12 Under these circumstances, can we doubt for a moment that heroin use would have grown exponentially? Or that a vastly larger supply of new users would have been recruited? Professor Friedman is a Nobel Prize-winning economist whose understanding of market forces is profound. What did he think would happen to consumption under his legalized regime? Here are his words: "Legalizing drugs might increase the number of addicts, but it is not clear that it would. Forbidden fruit is attractive, particularly to the young."

13 Really? I suppose that we should expect no increase in Porsche sales if we cut the price by 95 percent, no increase in whiskey sales if we cut the price by a comparable amount—because young people only want fast cars and strong liquor when they are "forbidden." Perhaps Friedman's uncharacteristic lapse from the obvious implications of price theory can be explained by a misunderstanding of how drug users are recruited. In his 1972 essay he said that "drug addicts are deliberately made by pushers, who give likely prospects their first few doses free." If drugs were legal it would not pay anybody to produce addicts, because everybody would buy from the cheapest source. But as every drug expert knows, pushers do not produce addicts. Friends or acquaintances do. In fact, pushers are usually reluctant to deal with non-users because a non-user could be an undercover cop. Drug use spreads in the same way any fad or fashion spreads: somebody who is already a user urges his friends to try, or simply shows already-eager friends how to do it.

14 But we need not rely on speculation, however plausible, that lowered prices and more abundant supplies would have increased heroin usage. Great Britain once followed such a policy and with almost exactly those results. Until the mid-1960's British physicians were allowed to prescribe heroin to certain classes of addicts. (Possessing these drugs without a doctor's prescription remained a criminal offense.) For many years this policy worked well enough because the addict patients were typically middle-class people who had become dependent on opiate painkillers while undergoing hospital treatment. There was no drug culture. The British system worked for many years, not

because it prevented drug abuse, but because there was no problem of drug abuse that would test the system.

15 All that changed in the 1960's. A few unscrupulous doctors began passing out heroin in wholesale amounts. One doctor prescribed almost 600,000 heroin tablets—that is, over thirteen pounds—in just one year. A youthful drug culture emerged with a demand for drugs far different from that of the older addicts. As a result, the British government required doctors to refer users to government-run clinics to receive their heroin.

16 But the shift to clinics did not curtail the growth in heroin use. Throughout the 1960's the number of addicts increased—the late John Kaplan of Stanford estimated by fivefold—in part as a result of the diversion of heroin from clinic patients to new users on the streets. An addict would bargain with the clinic doctor over how big a dose he would receive. The patient wanted as much as he could get, the doctor wanted to give as little as was needed. The patient had an advantage in this conflict because the doctor could not be certain how much was really needed. Many patients would use some of their "maintenance" dose and sell the remaining part to friends, thereby recruiting new addicts. As the clinics learned of this, they began to shift their treatment away from heroin and toward methadone, an addictive drug that, when taken orally, does not produce a "high" but will block the withdrawal pains associated with heroin abstinence.

17 Whether what happened in England in the 1960's was a mini-epidemic or an epidemic depends on whether one looks at numbers or at rates of change. Compared to the United States, the numbers were small. In 1960 there were 68 heroin addicts known to the British government; by 1968 there were 2,000 in treatment and many more who refused treatment. (They would refuse in part because they did not want to get methadone at a clinic if they could get heroin on the street.) Richard Hartnoll estimates that the actual number of addicts in England is five times the number officially registered. At a minimum, the number of British addicts increased by thirtyfold in ten years; the actual increase may have been much larger.

18 In the early 1980's the numbers began to rise again, and this time nobody doubted that a real epidemic was at hand. The increase was estimated to be 40 percent a year. By 1982 there were thought to be 20,000 heroin users in London alone. Geoffrey Pearson reports that many cities—Glasgow, Liverpool, Manchester, and Sheffield among them—were now experiencing a drug problem that once had been largely confined to London. The problem, again, was supply. The country was being flooded with cheap, high-quality heroin, first from Iran and then from Southeast Asia.

19 The United States began the 1960's with a much larger number of heroin addicts and probably a bigger at-risk population than was the case in Great Britain. Even though it would be foolhardy to suppose that the British system, if installed here, would have worked the same way or with the same results, it would be equally foolhardy to suppose that a combination of heroin available from leaky clinics and from street dealers who faced only minimal law-enforcement risks would not have produced a much greater increase in heroin use than we actually experienced. My guess is that if we had allowed either doctors or clinics to prescribe heroin, we would have had far worse results than

were produced in Britain, if for no other reason than the vastly larger number of addicts with which we began. We would have had to find some way to police thousands (not scores) of physicians and hundreds (not dozens) of clinics. If the British civil service found it difficult to keep heroin in the hands of addicts and out of the hands of recruits when it was dealing with a few hundred people, how well would the American civil service have accomplished the same tasks when dealing with tens of thousands of people?

Back to the Future

20 Now cocaine, especially in its potent form, crack, is the focus of attention. Now as in 1972 the government is trying to reduce its use. Now as then some people are advocating legalization. Is there any more reason to yield to those arguments today than there was almost two decades ago?*

21 I think not. If we had yielded in 1972 we almost certainly would have had today a permanent population of several million, not several hundred thousand, heroin addicts. If we yield now we will have a far more serious problem with cocaine.

22 Crack is worse than heroin by almost any measure. Heroin produces a pleasant drowsiness and, if hygienically administered, has only the physical side effects of constipation and sexual impotence. Regular heroin use incapacitates many users, especially poor ones, for any productive work or social responsibility. They will sit nodding on a street corner, helpless but at least harmless. By contrast, regular cocaine use leaves the user neither helpless nor harmless. When smoked (as with crack) or injected, cocaine produces instant, intense, and short-lived euphoria. The experience generates a powerful desire to repeat it. If the drug is readily available, repeat use will occur. Those people who progress to ''bingeing'' on cocaine become devoted to the drug and its effects to the exclusion of almost all other considerations—job, family, children, sleep, food, even sex. Dr. Frank Gawin at Yale and Dr. Everett Ellinwood at Duke report that a substantial percentage of all high-dose, binge users become uninhibited, impulsive, hypersexual, compulsive, irritable, and hyperactive. Their moods vacillate dramatically, leading at times to violence and homicide.

23 Women are much more likely to use crack than heroin, and if they are pregnant, the effects on their babies are tragic. Douglas Besharov, who has been following the effects of drugs on infants for twenty years, writes that nothing he learned about heroin prepared him for the devastation of cocaine. Cocaine harms the fetus and can lead to physical deformities or neurological damage. Some crack babies have for all practical purposes suffered a disabling stroke while still in the womb. The long-term consequences of this brain damage are lowered cognitive ability and the onset of mood disorders. Besharov estimates that about 30,000 to 50,000 such babies are born every year, about 7,000 in New York City alone. There may be ways to treat such infants, but from everything we now know the treatment will be long, difficult, and expensive. Worse, the mothers who are most likely to produce crack babies are precisely the ones who, because of poverty or temperament, are least able and willing to obtain such

treatment. In fact, anecdotal evidence suggests that crack mothers are likely to abuse their infants.

24 The notion that abusing drugs such as cocaine is a "victimless crime" is not only absurd but dangerous. Even ignoring the fetal drug syndrome, crack-dependent people are, like heroin addicts, individuals who regularly victimize their children by neglect, their spouses by improvidence, their employers by lethargy, and their co-workers by carelessness. Society is not and could never be a collection of autonomous individuals. We all have a stake in ensuring that each of us displays a minimal level of dignity, responsibility, and empathy. We cannot, of course, coerce people into goodness, but we can and should insist that some standards must be met if society itself—on which the very existence of the human personality depends—is to persist. Drawing the line that defines those standards is difficult and contentious, but if crack and heroin use do not fall below it, what does?

25 The advocates of legalization will respond by suggesting that my picture is overdrawn. Ethan Nadelmann of Princeton argues that the risk of legalization is less than most people suppose. Over 20 million Americans between the ages of eighteen and twenty-five have tried cocaine (according to a government survey), but only a quarter million use it daily. From this Nadelmann concludes that at most 3 percent of all young people who try cocaine develop a problem with it. The implication is clear: make the drug legal and we only have to worry about 3 percent of our youth.

26 The implication rests on a logical fallacy and a factual error. The fallacy is this: the percentage of occasional cocaine users who become binge users *when the drug is illegal* (and thus expensive and hard to find) tells us nothing about the percentage who will become dependent when the drug is legal (and thus cheap and abundant). Drs. Gawin and Ellinwood report, in common with several other researchers, that controlled or occasional use of cocaine changes to compulsive and frequent use "when access to the drug increases" or when the user switches from snorting to smoking. More cocaine more potently administered alters, perhaps sharply, the proportion of "controlled" users who become heavy users.

27 The factual error is this: the federal survey Nadelmann quotes was done in 1985, *before* crack had become common. Thus the probability of becoming dependent on cocaine was derived from the responses of users who snorted the drug. The speed and potency of cocaine's action increases dramatically when it is smoked. We do not yet know how greatly the advent of crack increases the risk of dependency, but all the clinical evidence suggests that the increase is likely to be large.

28 It is possible that some people will not become heavy users even when the drug is readily available in its most potent form. So far there are no scientific grounds for predicting who will and who will not become dependent. Neither socio-economic background nor personality traits differentiate between casual and intensive users. Thus, the only way to settle the question of who is correct about the effect of easy availability on drug use, Nadelmann or Gawin and Ellinwood, is to try it and see. But that social experiment is so risky as to be no experiment at all, for if cocaine is legalized and if

the rate of its abusive use increases dramatically, there is no way to put the genie back in the bottle, and it is not a kindly genie.

Have We Lost?

29 Many people who agree that there are risks in legalizing cocaine or heroin still favor it because, they think, we have lost the war on drugs. "Nothing we have done has worked" and the current federal policy is just "more of the same." Whatever the costs of greater drug use, surely they would be less than the costs of our present, failed efforts.

30 That is exactly what I was told in 1972—and heroin is not quite as bad a drug as cocaine. We did not surrender and we did not lose. We did not win, either. What the nation accomplished then was what most efforts to save people from themselves accomplish: the problem was contained and the number of victims minimized, all at a considerable cost in law enforcement and increased crime. Was the cost worth it? I think so, but others may disagree. What are the lives of would-be addicts worth? I recall some people saying to me then, "Let them kill themselves." I was appalled. Happily, such views did not prevail.

31 Have we lost today? Not at all. High-rate cocaine use is not commonplace. The National Institute of Drug Abuse (NIDA) reports that less than 5 percent of high-school seniors used cocaine within the last thirty days. Of course this survey misses young people who have dropped out of school and miscounts those who lie on the questionnaire, but even if we inflate the NIDA estimate by some plausible percentage, it is still not much above 5 percent. Medical examiners reported in 1987 that about 1,500 died from cocaine use; hospital emergency rooms reported about 30,000 admissions related to cocaine abuse.

32 These are not small numbers, but neither are they evidence of a nationwide plague that threatens to engulf us all. Moreover, cities vary greatly in the proportion of people who are involved with cocaine. To get city-level data we need to turn to drug tests carried out on arrested persons, who obviously are more likely to be drug users than the average citizen. The National Institute of Justice, through its Drug Use Forecasting (DUF) project, collects urinalysis data on arrestees in 22 cities. As we have already seen, opiate (chiefly heroin) use has been flat or declining in most of these cities over the last decade. Cocaine use has gone up sharply, but with great variation among cities. New York, Philadelphia, and Washington, D.C., all report that two-thirds or more of their arrestees tested positive for cocaine, but in Portland, San Antonio, and Indianapolis the percentage was one-third or less.

33 In some neighborhoods, of course, matters have reached crisis proportions. Gangs control the streets, shootings terrorize residents, and drug-dealing occurs in plain view. The police seem barely able to contain matters. But in these neighborhoods—unlike at Palo Alto cocktail parties—the people are not calling for legalization, they are calling for help. And often not much help has come. Many cities are willing to do almost anything about the drug problem except spend more money on it. The federal govern-

ment cannot change that; only local voters and politicians can. It is not clear that they will.

34 It took about ten years to contain heroin. We have had experience with crack for only about three or four years. Each year we spend perhaps $11 billion on law enforcement (and some of that goes to deal with marijuana) and perhaps $2 billion on treatment. Large sums, but not sums that should lead anyone to say, "We just can't afford this any more."

35 The illegality of drugs increases crime, partly because some users turn to crime to pay for their habits, partly because some users are stimulated by certain drugs (such as crack or PCP) to act more violently or ruthlessly than they otherwise would, and partly because criminal organizations seeking to control drug supplies use force to manage their markets. These also are serious costs, but no one knows how much they would be reduced if drugs were legalized. Addicts would no longer steal to pay black-market prices for drugs, a real gain. But some, perhaps a great deal, of that gain would be offset by the great increase in the number of addicts. These people, nodding on heroin or living in the delusion-ridden high of cocaine, would hardly be ideal employees. Many would steal simply to support themselves, since snatch-and-grab, opportunistic crime can be managed even by people unable to hold a regular job or plan an elaborate crime. Those British addicts who get their supplies from government clinics are not models of law-abiding decency. Most are in crime, and though their per-capita rate of criminality may be lower thanks to the cheapness of their drugs, the total volume of crime they produce may be quite large. Of course, society could decide to support all unemployable addicts on welfare, but that would mean that gains from lowered rates of crime would have to be offset by large increases in welfare budgets.

36 Proponents of legalization claim that the costs of having more addicts around would be largely if not entirely offset by having more money available with which to treat and care for them. The money would come from taxes levied on the sale of heroin and cocaine.

37 To obtain this fiscal dividend, however, legalization's supporters must first solve an economic dilemma. If they want to raise a lot of money to pay for welfare and treatment, the tax rate on the drugs will have to be quite high. Even if they themselves do not want a high rate, the politicians' love of "sin taxes" would probably guarantee that it would be high anyway. But the higher the tax, the higher the price of the drug, and the higher the price the greater the likelihood that addicts will turn to crime to find the money for it and that criminal organizations will be formed to sell tax-free drugs at below-market rates. If we managed to keep taxes (and thus prices) low, we would get that much less money to pay for welfare and treatment and more people could afford to become addicts. There may be an optimal tax rate for drugs that maximizes revenue while minimizing crime, bootlegging, and the recruitment of new addicts, but our experience with alcohol does not suggest that we know how to find it.

The Benefits of Illegality

38 The advocates of legalization find nothing to be said in favor of the current system except, possibly, that it keeps the number of addicts smaller than it would otherwise be. In fact, the benefits are more substantial than that.

39 First, treatment. All the talk about providing "treatment on demand" implies that there is a demand for treatment. That is not quite right. There are some drug-dependent people who genuinely want treatment and will remain in it if offered; they should receive it. But there are far more who want only short-term help after a bad crash; once stabilized and bathed, they are back on the street again, hustling. And even many of the addicts who enroll in a program honestly wanting help drop out after a short while when they discover that help takes time and commitment. Drug-dependent people have very short time horizons and a weak capacity for commitment. These two groups—those looking for a quick fix and those unable to stick with a long-term fix—are not easily helped. Even if we increase the number of treatment slots—as we should—we would have to do something to make treatment more effective.

40 One thing that can often make it more effective is compulsion. Douglas Anglin of UCLA, in common with many other researchers, has found that the longer one stays in a treatment program, the better the chances of a reduction in drug dependency. But he, again like most other researchers, has found that drop-out rates are high. He has also found, however, that patients who enter treatment under legal compulsion stay in the program longer than those not subject to such pressure. His research on the California civil-commitment program, for example, found that heroin users involved with its required drug-testing program had over the long term a lower rate of heroin use than similar addicts who were free of such constraints. If for many addicts compulsion is a useful component of treatment, it is not clear how compulsion could be achieved in a society in which purchasing, possessing, and using the drug were legal. It could be managed, I suppose, but I would not want to have to answer the challenge from the American Civil Liberties Union that it is wrong to compel a person to undergo treatment for consuming a legal commodity.

41 Next, education. We are now investing substantially in drug-education programs in the schools. Though we do not yet know for certain what will work, there are some promising leads. But I wonder how credible such programs would be if they were aimed at dissuading children from doing something perfectly legal. We could, of course, treat drug education like smoking education: inhaling crack and inhaling tobacco are both legal, but you should not do it because it is bad for you. That tobacco is bad for you is easily shown; the Surgeon General has seen to that. But what do we say about crack? It is pleasurable, but devoting yourself to so much pleasure is not a good idea (though perfectly legal)? Unlike tobacco, cocaine will not give you cancer or emphysema, but it will lead you to neglect your duties to family, job, and neighborhood? Everybody is doing cocaine, but you should not?

42 Again, it might be possible under a legalized regime to have effective drug-prevention programs, but their effectiveness would depend heavily, I think, on first having decided that cocaine use, like tobacco use, is purely a matter of practical consequences; no fundamental moral significance attaches to either. But if we believe—as I do—that dependency on certain mind-altering drugs *is* a moral issue and that their illegality rests in part on their immorality, then legalizing them undercuts, if it does not eliminate altogether, the moral message.

43 That message is at the root of the distinction we now make between nicotine and cocaine. Both are highly addictive; both have harmful physical effects. But we treat the two drugs differently, not simply because nicotine is so widely used as to be beyond the reach of effective prohibition, but because its use does not destroy the user's essential humanity. Tobacco shortens one's life, cocaine debases it. Nicotine alters one's habits, cocaine alters one's soul. The heavy use of crack, unlike the heavy use of tobacco, corrodes those natural sentiments of sympathy and duty that constitute our human nature and make possible our social life. To say, as does Nadelmann, that distinguishing morally between tobacco and cocaine is "little more than a transient prejudice" is close to saying that morality itself is but a prejudice.

The Alcohol Problem

44 Now we have arrived where many arguments about legalizing drugs begin: is there any reason to treat heroin and cocaine differently from the way we treat alcohol?

45 There is no easy answer to that question because, as with so many human problems, one cannot decide simply on the basis either of moral principles or of individual consequences; one has to temper any policy by a common-sense judgment of what is possible. Alcohol, like heroin, cocaine, PCP, and marijuana, is a drug—that is, a mood-altering substance—and consumed to excess it certainly has harmful consequences: auto accidents, barroom fights, bedroom shootings. It is also, for some people, addictive. We cannot confidently compare the addictive powers of these drugs, but the best evidence suggests that crack and heroin are much more addictive than alcohol.

46 Many people, Nadelmann included, argue that since the health and financial costs of alcohol abuse are so much higher than those of cocaine or heroin abuse, it is hypocritical folly to devote our efforts to preventing cocaine or drug use. But as Mark Kleiman of Harvard has pointed out, this comparison is quite misleading. What Nadelmann is doing is showing that a *legalized* drug (alcohol) produces greater social harm than *illegal* ones (cocaine and heroin). But of course. Suppose that in the 1920's we had made heroin and cocaine legal and alcohol illegal. Can anyone doubt that Nadelmann would now be writing that it is folly to continue our ban on alcohol because cocaine and heroin are so much more harmful?

47 And let there be no doubt about it—widespread heroin and cocaine use are associated with all manner of ills. Thomas Bewley found that the mortality rate of British heroin addicts in 1968 was 28 times as high as the death rate of the same age group of non-addicts, even though in England at the time an addict could obtain free or low-cost heroin and clean needles from British clinics. Perform the following mental experiment: suppose we legalized heroin and cocaine in this country. In what proportion of auto fatalities would the state police report that the driver was nodding off on heroin or recklessly driving on a coke high? In what proportion of spouse-assault and child-abuse cases would the local police report that crack was involved? In what proportion of industrial accidents would safety investigators report that the forklift or drill-press operator was in a drug-induced stupor or frenzy? We do not know exactly what the proportion would be, but anyone who asserts that it would not be much higher than it is

now would have to believe that these drugs have little appeal except when they are illegal. And that is nonsense.

48 An advocate of legalization might concede that social harm—perhaps harm equivalent to that already produced by alcohol—would follow from making cocaine and heroin generally available. But at least, he might add, we would have the problem "out in the open" where it could be treated as a matter of "public health." That is well and good, *if* we knew how to treat—that is, cure—heroin and cocaine abuse. But we do not know how to do it for all the people who would need such help. We are having only limited success in coping with chronic alcoholics. Addictive behavior is immensely difficult to change, and the best methods for changing it—living in drug-free therapeutic communities, becoming faithful members of Alcoholics Anonymous or Narcotics Anonymous—require great personal commitment, a quality that is, alas, in short supply among the very persons—young people, disadvantaged people—who are often most at risk for addiction.

49 Suppose that today we had, not 15 million alcohol abusers, but half a million. Suppose that we already knew what we have learned from our long experience with the widespread use of alcohol. Would we make whiskey legal? I do not know, but I suspect there would be a lively debate. The Surgeon General would remind us of the risks alcohol poses to pregnant women. The National Highway Traffic Safety Administration would point to the likelihood of more highway fatalities caused by drunk drivers. The Food and Drug Administration might find that there is a nontrivial increase in cancer associated with alcohol consumption. At the same time the police would report great difficulty in keeping illegal whiskey out of our cities, officers being corrupted by bootleggers, and alcohol addicts often resorting to crime to feed their habit. Libertarians, for their part, would argue that every citizen has a right to drink anything he wishes and that drinking is, in any event, a "victimless crime."

50 However the debate might turn out, the central fact would be that the problem was still, at that point, a small one. The government cannot legislate away the addictive tendencies in all of us, nor can it remove completely even the most dangerous addictive substances. But it can cope with harms when the harms are still manageable.

Science and Addiction

51 One advantage of containing a problem while it is still containable is that it buys time for science to learn more about it and perhaps to discover a cure. Almost unnoticed in the current debate over legalizing drugs is that basic science has made rapid strides in identifying the underlying neurological processes involved in some forms of addiction. Stimulants such as cocaine and amphetamines alter the way certain brain cells communicate with one another. That alteration is complex and not entirely understood, but in simplified form it involves modifying the way in which a neurotransmitter called dopamine sends signals from one cell to another.

52 When dopamine crosses the synapse between two cells, it is in effect carrying a message from the first cell to activate the second one. In certain parts of the brain that message is experienced as pleasure. After the message is delivered, the dopamine

returns to the first cell. Cocaine apparently blocks this return, or "reuptake," so that the excited cell and others nearby continue to send pleasure messages. When the exaggerated high produced by cocaine-influenced dopamine finally ends, the brain cells may (in ways that are still a matter of dispute) suffer from an extreme lack of dopamine, thereby making the individual unable to experience any pleasure at all. This would explain why cocaine users often feel so depressed after enjoying the drug. Stimulants may also affect the way in which other neurotransmitters, such as serotonin and noradrenaline, operate.

53 Whatever the exact mechanism may be, once it is identified it becomes possible to use drugs to block either the effect of cocaine or its tendency to produce dependency. There have already been experiments using desipramine, imipramine, bromocriptine, carbamazepine, and other chemicals. There are some promising results.

54 Tragically, we spend very little on such research, and the agencies funding it have not in the past occupied very influential or visible posts in the federal bureaucracy. If there is one aspect of the "war on drugs" metaphor that I dislike, it is its tendency to focus attention almost exclusively on the troops in the trenches, whether engaged in enforcement or treatment, and away from the research-and-development efforts back on the home front where the war may ultimately be decided.

55 I believe that the prospects of scientists in controlling addiction will be strongly influenced by the size and character of the problem they face. If the problem is a few hundred thousand chronic, high-dose users of an illegal product, the chances of making a difference at a reasonable cost will be much greater than if the problem is a few million chronic users of legal substances. Once a drug is legal, not only will its use increase but many of those who then use it will prefer the drug to the treatment: they will want the pleasure, whatever the cost to themselves or their families, and they will resist—probably successfully—any effort to wean them away from experiencing the high that comes from inhaling a legal substance.

If I Am Wrong . . .

56 No one can know what our society would be like if we changed the law to make access to cocaine, heroin, and PCP easier. I believe, for reasons given, that the result would be a sharp increase in use, a more widespread degradation of the human personality, and a greater rate of accidents and violence.

57 I may be wrong. If I am, then we will needlessly have incurred heavy costs in law enforcement and some forms of criminality. But if I am right, and the legalizers prevail anyway, then we will have consigned millions of people, hundreds of thousands of infants, and hundreds of neighborhoods to a life of oblivion and disease. To the lives and families destroyed by alcohol we will have added countless more destroyed by cocaine, heroin, PCP, and whatever else a basement scientist can invent.

58 Human character is formed by society; indeed, human character is inconceivable without society, and good character is less likely in a bad society. Will we, in the name of an abstract doctrine of radical individualism, and with the false comfort of suspect

predictions, decide to take the chance that somehow individual decency can survive amid a more general level of degradation?

59 I think not. The American people are too wise for that, whatever the academic essayists and cocktail-party pundits may say. But if Americans today are less wise than I suppose, then Americans at some future time will look back on us now and wonder, what kind of people were they that they could have done such a thing?

Notes

1. I do not here take up the question of marijuana. For a variety of reasons—its widespread use and its lesser tendency to addict—it presents a different problem from cocaine or heroin. For a penetrating analysis, see Mark Kleiman, *Marijuana: Costs of Abuse, Costs of Control* (Greenwood Press, 217 pp., $37.95).

Questions for Analysis

1. What information does Wilson provide early in his essay that establishes his qualifications to speak on this topic?
2. Much of Wilson's argument depends on comparisons: heroin use in the 1970s compared with cocaine use in the late 1980s; the British experience with laws legalizing controlled distribution of heroin compared with what our experience might be if we were to enact a similar policy with cocaine. Are these comparisons logical and effective?
3. Block out and explain the pattern of organization in Wilson's essay. How do the headings help to display this pattern and keep you reading through an essay that is longer than most in this reader?
4. Compare Wilson's tone and rhetorical stance to those in Bennett's and Lapham's essays. What makes Wilson's tone different?
5. In the following essay, Diana Gordon says that many who wish to maintain antidrug laws see the problem as an evil, overstate its dangers, and depict drug users as monsters who should be arrested, not helped. Does Wilson fit into this category? Explain your answer.

Diana R. Gordon

Europe's Kinder, Gentler Approach

(1991)

Diana R. Gordon (b. 1958) teaches political science and criminology at the City College of New York. She is the author of *The Justice Juggernaut* published by Rutgers University Press. This essay appeared in the issue of *The Nation* dated February 4, 1991.

1 National drug policy in this country is a bit like the mirage on the highway: You think there's something there until you get close to it, by which time it has dissolved. Upon taking office George Bush promised an all-out war on drugs but backed away less than a week later, saying the deficit required that he mount "a major educational effort," which would be less expensive than trying to lock up all the dealers or seal the borders to keep drugs out. Then, perhaps figuring that bark could substitute for bite, at least temporarily, he appointed William Bennett as drug czar, who needled his boss into being more overtly punitive, saying, "Should we have drug education programs or should we have tough policy? If I have the choice of only one, I will take policy every time because I know children." And now Bennett's successor is likely to be former Florida Governor Bob Martinez, a hard-line conservative who nevertheless more than doubled funding for drug treatment in Florida during his four-year term and earnestly embraces a "holistic approach" to drugs, whatever that means.

2 In September I spent three weeks in four European countries—Britain, the Netherlands, Germany and Italy—trying to find out if their approaches were as incoherent and cynical as ours. Superficially, the answer is yes. (The exception is the Netherlands, where policy is consistently permissive and prevention-oriented with users but tough on traffickers.) In Britain the Home Secretary warned in 1989 of an impending crack epidemic that has not materialized (although home-made crack has been noted in South London). Margaret Thatcher's rhetoric often sounded a lot like Bush's, but while she praised the police whose drug raid on a pub led to a riot in 1989, the Department of Health and Social Security (D.H.S.S.) substantially increased funding for AIDS prevention that included giving clean needles to addicts. Last summer Italy, a country where previously the possession of small amounts of both hard and soft drugs was not punishable, adopted a new law that theoretically would force any drug user to choose jail or treatment and would punish anyone in possession of more than a "daily dose" of drugs as a dealer. But not to worry, I was repeatedly told; those provisions will rarely be enforced, just as, two and a half years after Italy became the last country in Western Europe to make it illegal to drink and drive, not a single person has been convicted of drunken driving.

3 That's not the whole story, however. Beneath the thin crust of political posturing—the debate over the Italian law was supposedly a means of keeping then-Prime Minister

Bettino Craxi and his Socialist Party on the front pages for a few months—there's a wellspring of serious interest in applying humane and consistent public health and social policies to Europe's drug problem. The concern exists even at the senior political level. "How do we deal with the fact that to experiment with drugs is normal?" a prominent Italian legislator asked me, waving a copy of the recent Berkeley research report that found that adolescents who had used drugs from time to time (mostly marijuana) were better adjusted than their counterparts who were either frequent users or abstainers.

4 It is, of course, difficult to generalize about the perspectives of countries as culturally different as the relaxed, pragmatic Netherlands and its uptight neighbor Germany. Where the former can simply involve the "expediency principle" in its Code of Criminal Procedure to insure that the justice process does not cause more harm to users than drugs do, German law allows no such flexibility.

5 But what can be said generally about Western Europe is that behind whatever policies are being adopted and implemented, there is less moral fundamentalism about drug taking and less demonization of drug takers than in the United States. Most of the Europeans I spoke with—public health officials, youth workers, researchers, politicians, even police—are simply mystified by statements like Bennett's declaration in the March 1990 *Reader's Digest:* "The simple fact is drug use is wrong. And the moral argument, in the end, is the most compelling argument." And they exclaimed in fascinated horror over the political theater of Los Angeles Police Chief Daryl Gates's Senate committee testimony last September to the effect that casual pot users should be "taken out and shot."

6 They're also astonished by the grandiose scale of our aims. "This scourge will stop," said Bush in an inaugural excess that would have surely come back to haunt him if he had meant it seriously in the first place. In Europe more modest aims have taken hold. Acknowledging that illicit drug use is functional for some people in some situations, most countries are turning down the heat on use and possession even as they increase penalties for trafficking. Last June German Chancellor Helmut Kohl unveiled the National Battle Plan Against Narcotics—a German version of our War on Drugs. But even this hard-line plan bows to the reality of rather high pot use among the young by including provisions for decriminalizing possession of small amounts of marijuana.

7 The American aim of eradicating the evil dictates a strategy of exhortation to abstinence. Europeans are less likely to be driven by this logic and often operate on the supposition that policy must develop a variety of approaches for different types of drugs and users. Most interesting, particularly in the Netherlands and Britain (though it's spreading to northern Germany too), is a strategy commonly called "harm reduction." Driven by an awareness that many users of illicit drugs don't want to stop and by a concern that the stigma attached to drug use keeps people from getting medical care and information, public health agencies (and in some cases police) are taking their clients as they find them, helping them become drug-free if they wish and, if they don't, guiding them to drug use that is safer for them and for society as a whole. Dr. John Marks, at his clinic in Widnes, near Liverpool, has revived the "British system" of heroin maintenance and is experimenting with smokable heroin as a safer alternative

to injection, helping some users live productive, settled lives and lowering the incidence of acquisitive crime in the area. The Maryland Training Center in Liverpool (along with many other smaller, less well-known efforts in England) is making clean needles available to intravenous heroin users, helping to keep the HIV-positive rate low in Merseyside as compared with other regions.

8 Without question the advent of AIDS has legitimized the harm-reduction approach. In Britain in 1988 an advisory group of the D.H.S.S. helped it along by concluding flatly, "HIV is a greater danger to individual and public health than drug misuse." The strategy, however, incorporates measures that go beyond the risks of AIDS. A Liverpool clinic, for example, shows addicts who are injecting in the groin (because they have worn out the veins in arms or legs) how to do so safely; hitting the femoral artery, instead of a vein, can be fatal. And harm reduction isn't aimed solely at intravenous users; the core messages of a 1988 Sussex radio campaign aimed at young alcohol and drug users were that mixing alcohol and other drugs is risky, and that drug takers who pass out should be placed in the recovery position and taken to the hospital if they don't soon recover consciousness.

9 An important part of harm-reduction strategy is establishing and maintaining contact with drug users who, with abstinence-oriented approaches, are lost to the health system. The Drop-Inn Center in Hamburg, Germany—a city where the mayor has defied the country's punitive orientation by proposing the legalization of heroin possession—attracts drug users not only with its provision of clean needles and counseling but also by serving free coffee and a cheap lunch. A drug user teetering on the edge of homelessness can spend a few nights there, do a load of laundry and take a shower.

10 At the Drop-Inn Center harm reduction overlaps with another strategy gaining currency in Europe—that of "normalizing" some uses of some drugs. The term has different meanings in different contexts. In Hamburg it simply means that the young users who aren't hassling anyone in the street or spreading AIDS through needle sharing will not only not be arrested but will have a place to hang out where their drug use will be assumed and accepted.

11 In Amsterdam the de facto decriminalization of marijuana and hashish is seen as a kind of affirmative nurturance of youth culture, a part of the larger tolerance that characterizes Dutch society. The coffee-shop scene there (and, to a lesser degree, in Rotterdam and Utrecht) gives these drugs a comfortable niche in modern consumer society. In attractive, brightly lit, individualized surroundings—some coffee shops are aimed at tourists, others at artists or feminists or high school students—the purchaser can drink cannabis tea or munch on "space cake" made with THC-infused oil. Some shops get a jump on their competitors by giving you a free package after you've made your tenth buy. It's all so normalized that one of the shops—actually a small chain—advertises with a billboard in the central railroad station.

12 Normalization in Amsterdam is also evident in the treatment of compulsive use of opiates. Buses cruise the city to provide addicts with maintenance doses of methadone, a normal part of public health routine. The Dutch government is held accountable for

comprehensive drug treatment on demand by interest-group pressure from the junkies' union (''junkiebond'').

13 Although the language of drug policy that I noted in Europe sometimes sounded alarmist in the same ways that ours is, the greater range of aims and strategies in drug policy in general produces a gentler and more varied discourse about drugs. (One fascinating difference is that in Europe one sees earthy humor used in public warning about the dangers of drugs. A poster put out by Britain's D.H.S.S. reads, ''It only takes one prick to give you AIDS.'') Perhaps it's also that in Europe drug use is neither so prevalent nor so entwined with what sociologists call secondary deviance—violent business transactions, child abuse and aggressive panhandling.

14 It is easy to assume that European responses to drugs are irrelevant to the U.S. experience. We tend to think that our druggies are more desperate and dangerous individuals, that the insatiable demand for better living through chemicals is unique to this country. But such conclusions—though they are probably, at the simplest factual level, true—beg the real question, which is why we have become such a drug-dependent society. The European countries that are trying more nuanced drug policies than ours are not only less bedeviled by drug excesses than we are; they are also not gun cultures, and they provide more social and medical supports to their citizens.

15 Harm reduction and normalization may indeed not be meaningful in an American context. If so, however, it is not because our drug users and sellers are beyond the reach of the forgiveness and succor implied by these concepts. Instead, it is because they know that the life into which many would be normalized yields only the minimal rewards of dead-end jobs, atomized social relationships and empty consumerism. That may sound bleak, but welcome to the 1990s.

Questions for Analysis

1. The European laws, policies, and attitudes described by Gordon center on two concepts: harm reduction and normalization. Define those concepts and then compare them with the ''war on drugs'' and the drug legalization approaches discussed in the other pieces in this section. Are these European attitudes compatible with either American position? Explain.
2. One difference Gordon points to when she compares European and American drug policy is the language used to describe drug use and users. What differences does she see? How does language use in this situation both reflect speakers' attitudes and either restrict or open up the possibility of constructive discussion and compromise?
3. Explain the irony in the title. What do that phrase and others Gordon mentions show about our use of language in the political arena?

4. Look again carefully at Gordon's last two paragraphs. Does she seem to think that we in America can implement European policies and attitudes given our social characteristics and problems? What does she advocate we do, if anything? What is her argument?
5. What do you think? Should we study European models and modify our laws and policies to apply forms of harm reduction and normalization? Given our unique problems, can these policies work in America?

James Baldwin

Sonny's Blues

(1953)

James Baldwin (b. 1924) was born in New York City. He served as a minister for three years before moving to Paris and subsequently beginning his literary career. His novels, short stories, and essays eloquently and powerfully illuminate the problems and triumphs of American blacks in our century. "Sonny's Blues" is taken from *Going to Meet the Man* (1965).

1 I read about it in the paper, in the subway, on my way to work. I read it, and I couldn't believe it, and I read it again. Then perhaps I just stared at it, at the newsprint spelling out his name, spelling out the story. I stared at it in the swinging lights of the subway car, and in the faces and bodies of the people, and in my own face, trapped in the darkness which roared outside.

2 It was not to be believed and I kept telling myself that, as I walked from the subway station to the high school. And at the same time I couldn't doubt it. I was scared, scared for Sonny. He became real to me again. A great block of ice got settled in my belly and kept melting there slowly all day long, while I taught my classes algebra. It was a special kind of ice. It kept melting, sending trickles of ice water all up and down my veins, but it never got less. Sometimes it hardened and seemed to expand until I felt my guts were going to come spilling out or that I was going to choke or scream. This would always be at a moment when I was remembering some specific thing Sonny had once said or done.

3 When he was about as old as the boys in my classes his face had been bright and open, there was a lot of copper in it; and he'd had wonderfully direct brown eyes, and great gentleness and privacy. I wondered what he looked like now. He had been picked up, the evening before, in a raid on an apartment downtown, for peddling and using heroin.

4 I couldn't believe it: but what I mean by that is that I couldn't find any room for it anywhere inside me. I had kept it outside me for a long time. I hadn't wanted to know. I had had suspicions, but I didn't name them, I kept putting them away. I told myself

that Sonny was wild, but he wasn't crazy. And he'd always been a good boy, he hadn't ever turned hard or evil or disrespectful, the way kids can, so quick, so quick, especially in Harlem. I didn't want to believe that I'd ever see my brother going down, coming to nothing, all that light in his face gone out, in the condition I'd already seen so many others. Yet it had happened and here I was, talking about algebra to a lot of boys who might, every one of them for all I knew, be popping off needles every time they went to the head. Maybe it did more for them than algebra could.

5 I was sure that the first time Sonny had ever had horse, he couldn't have been much older than these boys were now. These boys, now, were living as we'd been living then, they were growing up with a rush and their heads bumped abruptly against the low ceiling of their actual possibilities. They were filled with rage. All they really knew were two darknesses, the darkness of their lives, which was now closing in on them, and the darkness of the movies, which had blinded them to that other darkness, and in which they now, vindictively, dreamed, at once more together than they were at any other time, and more alone.

6 When the last bell rang, the last class ended, I let out my breath. It seemed I'd been holding it for all that time. My clothes were wet—I may have looked as though I'd been sitting in a steam bath, all dressed up, all afternoon. I sat alone in the classroom a long time. I listened to the boys outside, downstairs, shouting and cursing and laughing. Their laughter struck me for perhaps the first time. It was not the joyous laughter which—God knows why—one associates with children. It was mocking and insular, its intent was to denigrate. It was disenchanted, and in this, also, lay the authority of their curses. Perhaps I was listening to them because I was thinking about my brother and in them I heard my brother. And myself.

7 One boy was whistling a tune, at once very complicated and very simple, it seemed to be pouring out of him as though he were a bird, and it sounded very cool and moving through all that harsh, bright air, only just holding its own through all those other sounds.

I stood up and walked over to the window and looked down into the courtyard. It was the beginning of the spring and the sap was rising in the boys. A teacher passed through them every now and again, quickly, as though he or she couldn't wait to get out of that courtyard, to get those boys out of their sight and off their minds. I started collecting my stuff. I thought I'd better get home and talk to Isabel.

8 The courtyard was almost deserted by the time I got downstairs. I saw this boy standing in the shadow of a doorway, looking just like Sonny. I almost called his name. Then I saw that it wasn't Sonny, but somebody we used to know, a boy from around our block. He'd been Sonny's friend. He'd never been mine, having been too young for me, and, anyway, I'd never liked him. And now, even though he was a grown-up man, he still hung around that block, still spent hours on the street corners, was always high and raggy. I used to run into him from time to time and he'd often work around to asking me for a quarter or fifty cents. He always had some real good excuse, too, and I always gave it to him. I don't know why.

9 But now, abruptly, I hated him. I couldn't stand the way he looked at me, partly like a dog, partly like a cunning child. I wanted to ask him what the hell he was doing in the school courtyard.

10 He sort of shuffled over to me, and he said, “I see you got the papers. So you already know about it.”

11 “You mean about Sonny? Yes, I already know about it. How come they didn't get you?”

12 He grinned. It made him repulsive and it also brought to mind what he'd looked like as a kid. “I wasn't there. I stay away from them people.”

13 “Good for you.” I offered him a cigarette and I watched him through the smoke. “You come all the way down here just to tell me about Sonny?”

14 “That's right.” He was sort of shaking his head and his eyes looked strange, as though they were about to cross. The bright sun deadened his damp dark brown skin and it made his eyes look yellow and showed up the dirt in his kinked hair. He smelled funky. I moved a little away from him and I said, “Well, thanks. But I already know about it and I got to get home.”

15 “I'll walk you a little ways,” he said. We started walking. There were a couple of kids still loitering in the courtyard and one of them said goodnight to me and looked strangely at the boy beside me.

16 “What're you going to do?” he asked me. “I mean, about Sonny?”

17 “Look. I haven't seen Sonny for over a year, I'm not sure I'm going to do anything. Anyway, what the hell *can* I do?”

18 “That's right,” he said quickly, “ain't nothing you can do. Can't much help old Sonny no more, I guess.”

19 It was what I was thinking and so it seemed to me he had no right to say it.

20 “I'm surprised at Sonny, though,” he went on—he had a funny way of talking, he looked straight ahead as though he were talking to himself—“I thought Sonny was a smart boy, I thought he was too smart to get hung.”

21 “I guess he thought so too,” I said sharply, “and that's how he got hung. And how about you? You're pretty goddamn smart, I bet.”

22 Then he looked directly at me, just for a minute. “I ain't smart,” he said. “If I was smart, I'd have reached for a pistol a long time ago.”

23 “Look. Don't tell *me* your sad story, if it was up to me, I'd give you one.” Then I felt guilty—guilty, probably, for never having supposed that the poor bastard *had* a story of his own, much less a sad one, and I asked, quickly, “What's going to happen to him now?”

24 He didn't answer this. He was off by himself some place.

25 “Funny thing,” he said, and from his tone we might have been discussing the quickest way to get to Brooklyn, “when I saw the papers this morning, the first thing I asked myself was if I had anything to do with it. I felt sort of responsible.”

26 I began to listen more carefully. The subway station was on the corner, just before us, and I stopped. He stopped, too. We were in front of a bar and he ducked slightly, peering in, but whoever he was looking for didn't seem to be there. The juke box was

blasting away with something black and bouncy and I half watched the barmaid as she danced her way from the juke box to her place behind the bar. And I watched her face as she laughingly responded to something someone said to her, still keeping time to the music. When she smiled one saw the little girl, one sensed the doomed, still-struggling woman beneath the battered face of the semi-whore.

27 ''I never *give* Sonny nothing,'' the boy said finally, ''but a long time ago I come to school high and Sonny asked me how it felt.'' He paused, I couldn't bear to watch him, I watched the barmaid, and I listened to the music which seemed to be causing the pavement to shake. ''I told him it felt great.'' The music stopped, the barmaid paused and watched the juke box until the music began again. ''It did.''

28 All this was carrying me some place I didn't want to go. I certainly didn't want to know how it felt. It filled everything, the people, the houses, the music, the dark, quicksilver barmaid, with menace; and this menace was their reality.

29 ''What's going to happen to him now?'' I asked again.

30 ''They'll send him away some place and they'll try to cure him.'' He shook his head. ''Maybe he'll even think he's kicked the habit. Then they'll let him loose''—he gestured, throwing his cigarette into the gutter. ''That's all.''

31 ''What do you mean, that's *all?*''

32 But I knew what he meant.

33 ''I *mean,* that's *all.*'' He turned his head and looked at me, pulling down the corners of his mouth. ''Don't you know what I mean?'' he asked, softly.

34 ''How the hell *would* I know what you mean?'' I almost whispered it, I don't know why.

35 ''That's right,'' he said to the air, ''how would *he* know what I mean?'' He turned toward me again, patient and calm, and yet I somehow felt him shaking, shaking as though he were going to fall apart. I felt that ice in my guts again, the dread I'd felt all afternoon; and again I watched the barmaid, moving about the bar, washing glasses, and singing. ''Listen. They'll let him out and then it'll just start all over again. That's what I mean.''

36 ''You mean—they'll let him out. And then he'll just start working his way back in again. You mean he'll never kick the habit. Is that what you mean?''

37 ''That's right,'' he said, cheerfully. ''*You* see what I mean.''

38 ''Tell me,'' I said at last, ''why does he want to die? He must want to die, he's killing himself, why does he want to die?''

39 He looked at me in surprise. He licked his lips. ''He don't want to die. He wants to live. Don't nobody want to die, ever.''

40 Then I wanted to ask him—too many things. He could not have answered, or if he had, I could not have borne the answers. I started walking. ''Well, I guess it's none of my business.''

41 ''It's going to be rough on old Sonny,'' he said. We reached the subway station. ''This is your station?'' he asked. I nodded. I took one step down. ''Damn!'' he said, suddenly. I looked up at him. He grinned again. ''Damn it if I didn't leave all my money home. You ain't got a dollar on you, have you? Just for a couple of days, is all.''

42 All at once something inside gave and threatened to come pouring out of me. I didn't hate him any more. I felt that in another moment I'd start crying like a child.

43 "Sure," I said. "Don't sweat." I looked in my wallet and didn't have a dollar, I only had a five. "Here," I said. "That hold you?"

44 He didn't look at it—he didn't want to look at it. A terrible, closed look came over his face, as though he were keeping the number on the bill a secret from him and me. "Thanks," he said, and now he was dying to see me go. "Don't worry about Sonny. Maybe I'll write him or something."

45 "Sure," I said. "You do that. So long."

46 "Be seeing you," he said. I went on down the steps.

47 And I didn't write Sonny or send him anything for a long time. When I finally did, it was just after my little girl died, and he wrote me back a letter which made me feel like a bastard.

48 Here's what he said:

Dear brother,

You don't know how much I needed to hear from you. I wanted to write you many a time but I dug how much I must have hurt you and so I didn't write. But now I feel like a man who's been trying to climb up out of some deep, real deep and funky hole and just saw the sun up there, outside. I got to get outside.

I can't tell you much about how I got here. I mean I don't know how to tell you. I guess I was afraid of something or I was trying to escape from something and you know I have never been very strong in the head (smile). I'm glad Mama and Daddy are dead and can't see what's happened to their son and I swear if I'd known what I was doing I would never have hurt you so, you and a lot of other fine people who were nice to me and who believed in me.

I don't want you to think it had anything to do with me being a musician. It's more than that. Or maybe less than that. I can't get anything straight in my head down here and I try not to think about what's going to happen to me when I get outside again. Sometime I think I'm going to flip and *never* get outside and sometime I think I'll come straight back. I tell you one thing, though, I'd rather blow my brains out than go through this again. But that's what they all say, so they tell me. If I tell you when I'm coming to New York and if you could meet me, I sure would appreciate it. Give my love to Isabel and the kids and I was sure sorry to hear about little Gracie. I wish I could be like Mama and say the Lord's will be done, but I don't know it seems to me that trouble is the one thing that never does get stopped and I don't know what good it does to blame it on the Lord. But maybe it does some good if you believe it.

Your brother,
Sonny

49 Then I kept in constant touch with him and I sent him whatever I could and I went to meet him when he came back to New York. When I saw him many things I thought

I had forgotten came flooding back to me. This was because I had begun, finally, to wonder about Sonny, about the life that Sonny lived inside. This life, whatever it was, had made him older and thinner and it had deepened the distant stillness in which he had always moved. He looked very unlike my baby brother. Yet, when he smiled, when we shook hands, the baby brother I'd never known looked out from the depths of his private life, like an animal waiting to be coaxed into the light.

50 “How you been keeping?” he asked me.

51 “All right. And you?”

52 “Just fine.” He was smiling all over his face. “It's good to see you again.”

53 “It's good to see you.”

54 The seven years' difference in our ages lay between us like a chasm: I wondered if these years would ever operate between us as a bridge. I was remembering, and it made it hard to catch my breath, that I had been there when he was born; and I had heard the first words he had ever spoken. When he started to walk, he walked from our mother straight to me. I caught him just before he fell when he took the first steps he ever took in this world.

55 “How's Isabel?”

56 “Just fine. She's dying to see you.”

57 “And the boys?”

58 “They're fine, too. They're anxious to see their uncle.”

59 “Oh, come on. You know they don't remember me.”

60 “Are you kidding? Of course they remember you.”

61 He grinned again. We got into a taxi. We had a lot to say to each other, far too much to know how to begin.

62 As the taxi began to move, I asked, “You still want to go to India?”

63 He laughed. “You still remember that. Hell, no. This place is Indian enough for me.”

64 “It used to belong to them,” I said.

65 And he laughed again. “They damn sure knew what they were doing when they got rid of it.”

66 Years ago, when he was around fourteen, he'd been all hipped on the idea of going to India. He read books about people sitting on rocks, naked, in all kinds of weather, but mostly bad, naturally, and walking barefoot through hot coals and arriving at wisdom. I used to say that it sounded to me as though they were getting away from wisdom as fast as they could. I think he sort of looked down on me for that.

67 “Do you mind,” he asked, “if we have the driver drive alongside the park? On the west side—I haven't seen the city in so long.”

68 “Of course not,” I said. I was afraid that I might sound as though I were humoring him, but I hoped he wouldn't take it that way.

69 So we drove along, between the green of the park and the stony, lifeless elegance of hotels and apartment buildings, toward the vivid, killing streets of our childhood. These streets hadn't changed, though housing projects jutted up out of them now like rocks in the middle of a boiling sea. Most of the houses in which we had grown up had

vanished, as had the stores from which we had stolen, the basements in which we had first tried sex, the rooftops from which we had hurled tin cans and bricks. But houses exactly like the houses of our past yet dominated the landscape, boys exactly like the boys we once had been found themselves smothering in these houses, came down into the streets for light and air and found themselves encircled by disaster. Some escaped the trap, most didn't. Those who got out always left something of themselves behind, as some animals amputate a leg and leave it in the trap. It might be said, perhaps, that I had escaped, after all, I was a school teacher; or that Sonny had, he hadn't lived in Harlem for years. Yet, as the cab moved uptown through streets which seemed, with a rush, to darken with dark people, and as I covertly studied Sonny's face, it came to me that what we both were seeking through our separate cab windows was that part of ourselves which had been left behind. It's always at the hour of trouble and confrontation that the missing member aches.

70 We hit 110th Street and started rolling up Lenox Avenue. And I'd known this avenue all my life, but it seemed to me again, as it had seemed on the day I'd first heard about Sonny's trouble, filled with a hidden menace which was its very breath of life.

71 "We almost there," said Sonny.

72 "Almost." We were both too nervous to say anything more.

73 We live in a housing project. It hasn't been up long. A few days after it was up it seemed uninhabitably new, now, of course, it's already rundown. It looks like a parody of the good, clean, faceless life—God knows the people who live in it do their best to make it a parody. The beat-looking grass lying around isn't enough to make their lives green, the hedges will never hold out the streets, and they know it. The big windows fool no one, they aren't big enough to make space out of no space. They don't bother with the windows, they watch the TV screen instead. The playground is most popular with the children who don't play at jacks, or skip rope, or roller skate, or swing, and they can be found in it after dark. We moved in partly because it's not too far from where I teach, and partly for the kids; but it's really just like the houses in which Sonny and I grew up. The same things happen, they'll have the same things to remember. The moment Sonny and I started into the house I had the feeling that I was simply bringing him back into the danger he had almost died trying to escape.

74 Sonny has never been talkative. So I don't know why I was sure he'd be dying to talk to me when supper was over the first night. Everything went fine, the oldest boy remembered him, and the youngest boy liked him, and Sonny had remembered to bring something for each of them; and Isabel, who is really much nicer than I am, more open and giving, had gone to a lot of trouble about dinner and was genuinely glad to see him. And she's always been able to tease Sonny in a way that I haven't. It was nice to see her face so vivid again and to hear her laugh and watch her make Sonny laugh. She wasn't, or, anyway, she didn't seem to be, at all uneasy or embarrassed. She chatted as though there were no subject which had to be avoided and she got Sonny past his first, faint stiffness. And thank God she was there, for I was filled with that icy dread again. Everything I did seemed awkward to me, and everything I said sounded freighted with hidden meaning. I was trying to remember everything I'd heard about dope addiction

and I couldn't help watching Sonny for signs. I wasn't doing it out of malice. I was trying to find out something about my brother. I was dying to hear him tell me he was safe.

75 "Safe!" my father grunted, whenever Mama suggested trying to move to a neighborhood which might be safer for children. "Safe, hell! Ain't no place safe for kids, nor nobody."

76 He always went on like this, but he wasn't, ever, really as bad as he sounded, not even on weekends, when he got drunk. As a matter of fact, he was always on the lookout for "something a little better," but he died before he found it. He died suddenly, during a drunken weekend in the middle of the war, when Sonny was fifteen. He and Sonny hadn't ever got on too well. And this was partly because Sonny was the apple of his father's eye. It was because he loved Sonny so much and was frightened for him, that he was always fighting with him. It doesn't do any good to fight with Sonny. Sonny just moves back, inside himself, where he can't be reached. But the principal reason that they never hit it off is that they were so much alike. Daddy was big and rough and loud-talking, just the opposite of Sonny, but they both had—that same privacy.

77 Mama tried to tell me something about this, just after Daddy died. I was home on leave from the army.

78 This was the last time I ever saw my mother alive. Just the same, this picture gets all mixed up in my mind with pictures I had of her when she was younger. The way I always see her is the way she used to be on a Sunday afternoon, say, when the old folks were talking after the big Sunday dinner. I always see her wearing pale blue. She'd be sitting on the sofa. And my father would be sitting in the easy chair, not far from her. And the living room would be full of church folks and relatives. There they sit, in chairs all around the living room, and the night is creeping up outside, but nobody knows it yet. You can see the darkness growing against the windowpanes and you hear the street noises every now and again, or maybe the jangling beat of a tambourine from one of the churches close by, but it's real quiet in the room. For a moment nobody's talking, but every face looks darkening, like the sky outside. And my mother rocks a little from the waist, and my father's eyes are closed. Everyone is looking at something a child can't see. For a minute they've forgotten the children. Maybe a kid is lying on the rug, half asleep. Maybe somebody's got a kid in his lap and is absent-mindedly stroking the kid's head. Maybe there's a kid, quiet and big-eyed, curled up in a big chair in the corner. The silence, the darkness coming, and the darkness in the faces frighten the child obscurely. He hopes that the hand which strokes his forehead will never stop—will never die. He hopes that there will never come a time when the old folks won't be sitting around the living room, talking about where they've come from, and what they've seen, and what's happened to them and their kinfolk.

79 But something deep and watchful in the child knows that this is bound to end, is already ending. In a moment someone will get up and turn on the light. Then the old folks will remember the children and they won't talk any more that day. And when light fills the room, the child is filled with darkness. He knows that every time this

happens he's moved just a little closer to that darkness outside. The darkness outside is what the old folks have been talking about. It's what they've come from. It's what they endure. The child knows that they won't talk any more because if he knows too much about what's happened to *them,* he'll know too much too soon, about what's going to happen to *him.*

80 The last time I talked to my mother, I remember I was restless. I wanted to get out and see Isabel. We weren't married then and we had a lot to straighten out between us.

81 There Mama sat, in black, by the window. She was humming an old church song, *Lord, you brought me from a long ways off.* Sonny was out somewhere. Mama kept watching the streets.

82 "I don't know," she said, "if I'll ever see you again, after you go off from here. But I hope you'll remember the things I tried to teach you."

83 "Don't talk like that," I said, and smiled. "You'll be here a long time yet."

84 She smiled, too, but she said nothing. She was quiet for a long time. And I said, "Mama, don't you worry about nothing. I'll be writing all the time, and you be getting the checks. . . ."

85 "I want to talk to you about your brother," she said, suddenly. "If anything happens to me he ain't going to have nobody to look out for him."

86 "Mama," I said, "ain't nothing going to happen to you *or* Sonny. Sonny's all right. He's a good boy and he's got good sense."

87 "It ain't a question of his being a good boy," Mama said, "nor of his having good sense. It ain't only the bad ones, nor yet the dumb ones that gets sucked under." She stopped, looking at me. "Your Daddy once had a brother," she said, and she smiled in a way that made me feel she was in pain. "You didn't never know that, did you?"

88 "No," I said, "I never knew that," and I watched her face.

89 "Oh, yes," she said, "your Daddy had a brother." She looked out of the window again. "I know you never saw your Daddy cry. But I did—many a time, through all these years."

90 I asked her, "What happened to his brother? How come nobody's ever talked about him?"

91 This was the first time I ever saw my mother look old.

92 "His brother got killed," she said, "when he was just a little younger than you are now. I knew him. He was a fine boy. He was maybe a little full of the devil, but he didn't mean nobody no harm."

93 Then she stopped and the room was silent, exactly as it had sometimes been on those Sunday afternoons. Mama kept looking out into the streets.

94 "He used to have a job in the mill," she said, "and, like all young folks, he just liked to perform on Saturday nights. Saturday nights, him and your father would drift around to different places, go to dances and things like that, or just sit around with people they knew, and your father's brother would sing, he had a fine voice, and play along with himself on his guitar. Well, this particular Saturday night, him and your father was coming home from some place, and they were both a little drunk and there was a moon that night, it was bright like day. Your father's brother was feeling kind

of good, and he was whistling to himself, and he had his guitar slung over his shoulder. They was coming down a hill and beneath them was a road that turned off from the highway. Well, your father's brother, being always kind of frisky, decided to run down this hill, and he did, with that guitar banging and clanging behind him, and he ran across the road, and he was making water behind a tree. And your father was sort of amused at him and he was still coming down the hill, kind of slow. Then he heard a car motor and that same minute his brother stepped from behind the tree, into the road, in the moonlight. And he started to cross the road. And your father started to run down the hill, he says he don't know why. This car was full of white men. They was all drunk, and when they seen your father's brother they let out a great whoop and holler and they aimed the car straight at him. They was having fun, they just wanted to scare him, the way they do sometimes, you know. But they was drunk. And I guess the boy, being drunk, too, and scared, kind of lost his head. By the time he jumped it was too late. Your father says he heard his brother scream when the car rolled over him, and he heard the wood of that guitar when it give, and he heard them strings go flying, and he heard them white men shouting, and the car kept on a-going and it ain't stopped till this day. And, time your father got down the hill, his brother weren't nothing but blood and pulp."

95 Tears were gleaming on my mother's face. There wasn't anything I could say.

96 "He never mentioned it," she said, "because I never let him mention it before you children. Your Daddy was like a crazy man that night and for many a night thereafter. He says he never in his life seen anything as dark as that road after the lights of that car had gone away. Weren't nothing, weren't nobody on that road, just your Daddy and his brother and that busted guitar. Oh, yes. Your Daddy never did really get right again. Till the day he died he weren't sure but that every white man he saw was the man that killed his brother."

97 She stopped and took out her handkerchief and dried her eyes and looked at me.

98 "I ain't telling you all this," she said, "to make you scared or bitter or to make you hate nobody. I'm telling you this because you got a brother. And the world ain't changed."

99 I guess I didn't want to believe this. I guess she saw this in my face. She turned away from me, toward the window again, searching those streets.

100 "But I praise my Redeemer," she said at last, "that He called your Daddy home before me. I ain't saying it to throw no flowers at myself, but, I declare, it keeps me from feeling too cast down to know I helped your father get safely through this world. Your father always acted like he was the roughest, strongest man on earth. And everybody took him to be like that. But if he hadn't had me there—to see his tears!"

101 She was crying again. Still, I couldn't move. I said, "Lord, Lord, Mama, I didn't know it was like that."

102 "Oh, honey," she said, "there's a lot that you don't know. But you are going to find out." She stood up from the window and came over to me. "You got to hold on to your brother," she said, "and don't let him fall, no matter what it looks like is

happening to him and no matter how evil you gets with him. You going to be evil with him many a time. But don't you forget what I told you, you hear?''

103 ''I won't forget,'' I said. ''Don't you worry, I won't forget. I won't let nothing happen to Sonny.''

104 My mother smiled as though she were amused at something she saw in my face. Then, ''You may not be able to stop nothing from happening. But you got to let him know you's *there.*''

105 Two days later I was married, and then I was gone. And I had a lot of things on my mind and I pretty well forgot my promise to Mama until I got shipped home on a special furlough for her funeral.

106 And, after the funeral, with just Sonny and me alone in the empty kitchen, I tried to find out something about him.

107 ''What do you want to do?'' I asked him.

108 ''I'm going to be a musician,'' he said.

109 For he had graduated, in the time I had been away, from dancing to the juke box to finding out who was playing what, and what they were doing with it, and he had bought himself a set of drums.

110 ''You mean, you want to be a drummer?'' I somehow had the feeling that being a drummer might be all right for other people but not for my brother Sonny.

111 ''I don't think,'' he said, looking at me very gravely, ''that I'll ever be a good drummer. But I think I can play a piano.''

112 I frowned. I'd never played the role of the older brother quite so seriously before, had scarcely ever, in fact, *asked* Sonny a damn thing. I sensed myself in the presence of something I didn't really know how to handle, didn't understand. So I made my frown a little deeper as I asked: ''What kind of musician do you want to be?''

113 He grinned. ''How many kinds do you think there are?''

114 ''Be *serious,*'' I said.

115 He laughed, throwing his head back, and then looked at me. ''I *am* serious.''

116 ''Well, then, for Christ's sake, stop kidding around and answer a serious question. I mean, do you want to be a concert pianist, you want to play classical music and all that, or—or what?'' Long before I finished he was laughing again. ''For Christ's *sake,* Sonny!''

117 He sobered, but with difficulty. ''I'm sorry. But you sound so—*scared!*'' and he was off again.

118 ''Well, you may think it's funny now, baby, but it's not going to be so funny when you have to make your living at it, let me tell you *that.*'' I was furious because I knew he was laughing at me and I didn't know why.

119 ''No,'' he said, very sober now, and afraid, perhaps, that he'd hurt me, ''I don't want to be a classical pianist. That isn't what interests me. I mean''—he paused, looking hard at me, as though his eyes would help me to understand, and then gestured helplessly, as though perhaps his hand would help—''I mean, I'll have a lot of studying to do, and I'll have to study *everything,* but, I mean, I want to play *with*—jazz musicians.'' He stopped. ''I want to play jazz,'' he said.

120 Well, the word had never before sounded as heavy, as real, as it sounded that afternoon in Sonny's mouth. I just looked at him and I was probably frowning a real frown by this time. I simply couldn't see why on earth he'd want to spend his time hanging around nightclubs, clowning around on bandstands, while people pushed each other around a dance floor. It seemed—beneath him, somehow. I had never thought about it before, had never been forced to, but I suppose I had always put jazz musicians in a class with what Daddy called “good-time people.”

121 “Are you *serious?*”

122 “Hell, yes, I'm serious.”

123 He looked more helpless than ever, and annoyed, and deeply hurt.

124 I suggested, helpfully: “You mean—like Louis Armstrong?”

125 His face closed as though I'd struck him. “No. I'm not talking about none of that old-time, down home crap.”

126 “Well, look, Sonny, I'm sorry, don't get mad. I just don't altogether get it, that's all. Name somebody—you know, a jazz musician you admire.”

127 “Bird.”

128 “Who?”

129 “Bird! Charlie Parker! Don't they teach you nothing in the goddamn army?”

130 I lit a cigarette. I was surprised and then a little amused to discover that I was trembling. “I've been out of touch,” I said. “You'll have to be patient with me. Now. Who's this Parker character?”

131 “He's just one of the greatest jazz musicians alive,” said Sonny, sullenly, his hands in his pockets, his back to me. “Maybe *the* greatest,” he added, bitterly, “that's probably why *you* never heard of him.”

132 “All right,” I said, “I'm ignorant. I'm sorry. I'll go out and buy all the cat's records right away, all right?”

133 “It don't,” said Sonny, with dignity, “make any difference to me. I don't care what you listen to. Don't do me no favors.”

134 I was beginning to realize that I'd never seen him so upset before. With another part of my mind I was thinking that this would probably turn out to be one of those things kids go through and that I shouldn't make it seem important by pushing it too hard. Still, I didn't think it would do any harm to ask: “Doesn't all this take a lot of time? Can you make a living at it?”

135 He turned back to me and half leaned, half sat, on the kitchen table. “Everything takes time,” he said, “and—well, yes, sure, I can make a living at it. But what I don't seem to be able to make you understand is that it's the only thing I want to do.”

136 “Well, Sonny,” I said, gently, “you know people can't always do exactly what they *want* to do—”

137 “*No,* I don't know that,” said Sonny, surprising me. “I think people *ought* to do what they want to do, what else are they alive for?”

138 “You getting to be a big boy,” I said desperately, “it's time you started thinking about your future.”

139 “I'm thinking about my future,” said Sonny, grimly. “I think about it all the time.”

140 I gave up. I decided, if he didn't change his mind, that we could always talk about it later. "In the meantime," I said, "you got to finish school." We had already decided that he'd have to move in with Isabel and her folks. I knew this wasn't the ideal arrangement because Isabel's folks are inclined to be dicty and they hadn't especially wanted Isabel to marry me. But I didn't know what else to do. "And we have to get you fixed up at Isabel's."

141 There was a long silence. He moved from the kitchen table to the window. "That's a terrible idea. You know it yourself."

142 "Do you have a *better* idea?"

143 He just walked up and down the kitchen for a minute. He was as tall as I was. He had started to shave. I suddenly had the feeling that I didn't know him at all.

144 He stopped at the kitchen table and picked up my cigarettes. Looking at me with a kind of mocking, amused defiance, he put one between his lips. "You mind?"

145 "You smoking already?"

146 He lit the cigarette and nodded, watching me through the smoke. "I just wanted to see if I'd have the courage to smoke in front of you." He grinned and blew a great cloud of smoke to the ceiling. "It was easy." He looked at my face. "Come on, now. I bet you was smoking at my age, tell the truth."

147 I didn't say anything but the truth was on my face, and he laughed. But now there was something very strained in his laugh.

148 "Sure. And I bet that ain't all you was doing."

149 He was frightening me a little. "Cut the crap," I said. "We already decided that you was going to go and live at Isabel's. Now what's got into you all of a sudden?"

150 "*You* decided it," he pointed out. "*I* didn't decide nothing." He stopped in front of me, leaning against the stove, arms loosely folded. "Look, brother. I don't want to stay in Harlem no more, I really don't." He was very earnest. He looked at me, then over toward the kitchen window. There was something in his eyes I'd never seen before, some thoughtfulness, some worry all his own. He rubbed the muscle of one arm. "It's time I was getting out of here."

151 "Where do you want to *go,* Sonny?"

152 "I want to join the army. Or the navy, I don't care. If I say I'm old enough, they'll believe me."

153 Then I got mad. It was because I was so scared. "You must be crazy. You goddamn fool, what the hell do you want to go and join the *army* for?"

154 "I just told you. To get out of Harlem."

155 "Sonny, you haven't even finished *school.* And if you really want to be a musician, how do you expect to study if you're in the *army?*"

156 He looked at me, trapped, and in anguish. "There's ways. I might be able to work out some kind of deal. Anyway, I'll have the G.I. Bill when I come out."

157 "*If* you come out." We stared at each other. "Sonny, please. Be reasonable. I know the setup is far from perfect. But we got to do the best we can."

158 "I ain't learning nothing in school," he said. "Even when I go." He turned away from me and opened the window and threw his cigarette out into the narrow alley. I

watched his back. ''At least, I ain't learning nothing you'd want me to learn.'' He slammed the window so hard I thought the glass would fly out, and turned back to me. ''And I'm sick of the stink of these garbage cans!''

159 ''Sonny,'' I said, ''I know how you feel. But if you don't finish school now, you're going to be sorry later that you didn't.'' I grabbed him by the shoulders. ''And you only got another year. It ain't so bad. And I'll come back and I swear I'll help you do *whatever* you want to do. Just try to put up with it till I come back. Will you please do that? For me?''

160 He didn't answer and he wouldn't look at me.

161 ''Sonny. You hear me?''

162 He pulled away. ''I hear you. But you never hear anything *I* say.''

163 I didn't know what to say to that. He looked out of the window and then back at me. ''OK,'' he said, and sighed. ''I'll try.''

164 Then I said, trying to cheer him up a little, ''They got a piano at Isabel's. You can practice on it.''

165 And as a matter of fact, it did cheer him up for a minute. ''That's right,'' he said to himself. ''I forgot that.'' His face relaxed a little. But the worry, the thoughtfulness, played on it still, the way shadows play on a face which is staring into the fire.

166 But I thought I'd never hear the end of that piano. At first, Isabel would write me, saying how nice it was that Sonny was so serious about his music and how, as soon as he came in from school, or wherever he had been when he was supposed to be at school, he went straight to that piano and stayed there until suppertime. And, after supper, he went back to that piano and stayed there until everybody went to bed. He was at the piano all day Saturday and all day Sunday. Then he bought a record player and started playing records. He'd play one record over and over again, all day long sometimes, and he'd improvise along with it on the piano. Or he'd play one section of the record, one chord, one change, one progression, then he'd do it on the piano. Then back to the record. Then back to the piano.

167 Well, I really don't know how they stood it. Isabel finally confessed that it wasn't like living with a person at all, it was like living with sound. And the sound didn't make any sense to her, didn't make any sense to any of them—naturally. They began, in a way, to be afflicted by this presence that was living in their home. It was as though Sonny were some sort of god, or monster. He moved in an atmosphere which wasn't like theirs at all. They fed him and he ate, he washed himself, he walked in and out of their door; he certainly wasn't nasty or unpleasant or rude, Sonny isn't any of those things; but it was as though he were all wrapped up in some cloud, some fire, some vision all his own; and there wasn't any way to reach him.

168 At the same time, he wasn't really a man yet, he was still a child, and they had to watch out for him in all kinds of ways. They certainly couldn't throw him out. Neither did they dare to make a great scene about that piano because even they dimly sensed, as I sensed, from so many thousands of miles away, that Sonny was at that piano playing for his life.

169 But he hadn't been going to school. One day a letter came from the school board and Isabel's mother got it—there had, apparently, been other letters but Sonny had torn them up. This day, when Sonny came in, Isabel's mother showed him the letter and asked where he'd been spending his time. And she finally got it out of him that he'd been down in Greenwich Village, with musicians and other characters, in a white girl's apartment. And this scared her and she started to scream at him and what came up, once she began—though she denies it to this day—was what sacrifices they were making to give Sonny a decent home and how little he appreciated it.

170 Sonny didn't play the piano that day. By evening, Isabel's mother had calmed down but then there was the old man to deal with, and Isabel herself. Isabel says she did her best to be calm but she broke down and started crying. She says she just watched Sonny's face. She could tell, by watching him, what was happening with him. And what was happening was that they penetrated his cloud, they had reached him. Even if their fingers had been a thousand times more gentle than human fingers ever are, he could hardly help feeling that they had stripped him naked and were spitting on that nakedness. For he also had to see that his presence, that music, which was life or death to him, had been torture for them and that they had endured it, not at all for his sake, but only for mine. And Sonny couldn't take that. He can take it a little better today than he could then but he's still not very good at it and, frankly, I don't know anybody who is.

171 The silence of the next few days must have been louder than the sound of all the music ever played since time began. One morning, before she went to work, Isabel was in his room for something and she suddenly realized that all of his records were gone. And she knew for certain that he was gone. And he was. He went as far as the navy would carry him. He finally sent me a postcard from some place in Greece and that was the first I knew that Sonny was still alive. I didn't see him any more until we were both back in New York and the war had long been over.

172 He was a man by then, of course, but I wasn't willing to see it. He came by the house from time to time, but we fought almost every time we met. I didn't like the way he carried himself, loose and dreamlike all the time, and I didn't like his friends, and his music seemed to be merely an excuse for the life he led. It sounded just that weird and disordered.

173 Then we had a fight, a pretty awful fight, and I didn't see him for months. By and by I looked him up, where he was living, in a furnished room in the Village, and I tried to make it up. But there were lots of other people in the room and Sonny just lay on his bed, and he wouldn't come downstairs with me, and he treated these other people as though they were his family and I weren't. So I got mad and then he got mad, and then I told him that he might just as well be dead as live the way he was living. Then he stood up and he told me not to worry about him any more in life, that he *was* dead as far as I was concerned. Then he pushed me to the door and the other people looked on as though nothing were happening, and he slammed the door behind me. I stood in the hallway, staring at the door. I heard somebody laugh in the room and then the tears

came to my eyes. I started down the steps, whistling to keep from crying, I kept whistling to myself, *You going to need me, baby, one of these cold, rainy days.*

174 I read about Sonny's trouble in the spring. Little Grace died in the fall. She was a beautiful little girl. But she only lived a little over two years. She died of polio and she suffered. She had a slight fever for a couple of days, but it didn't seem like anything and we just kept her in bed. And we would certainly have called the doctor, but the fever dropped, she seemed to be all right. So we thought it had just been a cold. Then, one day, she was up, playing, Isabel was in the kitchen fixing lunch for the two boys when they'd come in from school, and she heard Grace fall down in the living room. When you have a lot of children you don't always start running when one of them falls, unless they start screaming or something. And, this time, Gracie was quiet. Yet, Isabel says that when she heard that *thump* and then that silence, something happened to her to make her afraid. And she ran to the living room and there was little Grace on the floor, all twisted up, and the reason she hadn't screamed was that she couldn't get her breath. And when she did scream, it was the worst sound, Isabel says, that she'd ever heard in all her life, and she still hears it sometimes in her dreams. Isabel will sometimes wake me up with a low, moaning, strangling sound and I have to be quick to awaken her and hold her to me and where Isabel is weeping against me seems a mortal wound.

175 I think I may have written Sonny the very day that little Grace was buried. I was sitting in the living room in the dark, by myself, and I suddenly thought of Sonny. My trouble made his real.

176 One Saturday afternoon, when Sonny had been living with us, or anyway, been in our house, for nearly two weeks, I found myself wandering aimlessly about the living room, drinking from a can of beer, and trying to work up courage to search Sonny's room. He was out, he was usually out whenever I was home, and Isabel had taken the children to see their grandparents. Suddenly I was standing still in front of the living room window, watching Seventh Avenue. The idea of searching Sonny's room made me still. I scarcely dared to admit to myself what I'd be searching for. I didn't know what I'd do if I found it. Or if I didn't.

177 On the sidewalk across from me, near the entrance to a barbecue joint, some people were holding an old-fashioned revival meeting. The barbecue cook, wearing a dirty white apron, his conked hair reddish and metallic in the pale sun, and a cigarette between his lips, stood in the doorway, watching them. Kids and older people paused in their errands and stood there, along with some older men and a couple of very tough-looking women who watched everything that happened on the avenue, as though they owned it, or were maybe owned by it. Well, they were watching this, too. The revival was being carried on by three sisters in black, and a brother. All they had were their voices and their Bibles and a tambourine. The brother was testifying and while he testified two of the sisters stood together, seeming to say, amen, and the third sister walked around with the tambourine outstretched and a couple of people dropped coins into it. Then the brother's testimony ended and the sister who had been taking up the collection dumped the coins into her palm and transferred them to the pocket of her long black robe. Then she raised both hands, striking the tambourine against the air, and then

against one hand, and she started to sing. And the two other sisters and the brother joined in.

178 It was strange, suddenly, to watch, though I had been seeing these meetings all my life. So, of course, had everybody else down there. Yet, they paused and watched and listened and I stood still at the window. "*'Tis the old ship of Zion,*" they sang, and the sister with the tambourine kept a steady, jangling beat, "*it has rescued many a thousand!*" Not a soul under the sound of their voices was hearing this song for the first time, not one of them had been rescued. Nor had they seen much in the way of rescue work being done around them. Neither did they especially believe in the holiness of the three sisters and the brother, they knew too much about them, knew where they lived, and how. The woman with the tambourine, whose voice dominated the air, whose face was bright with joy, was divided by very little from the woman who stood watching her, a cigarette between her heavy, chapped lips, her hair a cuckoo's nest, her face scarred and swollen from many beatings, and her black eyes glittering like coal. Perhaps they both knew this, which was why, when, as rarely, they addressed each other, they addressed each other as Sister. As the singing filled the air the watching, listening faces underwent a change, the eyes focusing on something within; the music seemed to soothe a poison out of them; and time seemed, nearly, to fall away from the sullen, belligerent, battered faces, as though they were fleeing back to their first condition, while dreaming of their last. The barbecue cook half shook his head and smiled, and dropped his cigarette and disappeared into his joint. A man fumbled in his pockets for change and stood holding it in his hand impatiently, as though he had just remembered a pressing appointment further up the avenue. He looked furious. Then I saw Sonny, standing on the edge of the crowd. He was carrying a wide, flat notebook with a green cover, and it made him look, from where I was standing, almost like a schoolboy. The coppery sun brought out the copper in his skin, he was very faintly smiling, standing very still. Then the singing stopped, the tambourine turned into a collection plate again. The furious man dropped in his coins and vanished, so did a couple of the women, and Sonny dropped some change in the plate, looking directly at the woman with a little smile. He started across the avenue, toward the house. He has a slow, loping walk, something like the way Harlem hipsters walk, only he's imposed on this his own half-beat. I had never really noticed it before.

179 I stayed at the window, both relieved and apprehensive. As Sonny disappeared from my sight, they began singing again. And they were still singing when his key turned in the lock.

180 "Hey," he said.

181 "Hey, yourself. You want some beer?"

182 "No. Well, maybe." But he came up to the window and stood beside me, looking out. "What a warm voice," he said.

183 They were singing *If I could only hear my mother pray again!*

184 "Yes," I said, "and she can sure beat that tambourine."

185 "But what a terrible song," he said, and laughed. He dropped his notebook on the sofa and disappeared into the kitchen. "Where's Isabel and the kids?"

186 ‘‘I think they want to see their grandparents. You hungry?’’

187 ‘‘No.’’ He came back into the living room with his can of beer. ‘‘You want to come some place with me tonight?’’

188 I sensed, I don’t know how, that I couldn’t possibly say no. ‘‘Sure. Where?’’

189 He sat down on the sofa and picked up his notebook and started leafing through it. ‘‘I’m going to sit in with some fellows in a joint in the Village.’’

190 ‘‘You mean, you’re going to play, tonight?’’

191 ‘‘That’s right.’’ He took a swallow of his beer and moved back to the window. He gave me a sidelong look. ‘‘If you can stand it.’’

192 ‘‘I’ll try,’’ I said.

193 He smiled to himself and we both watched as the meeting across the way broke up. The three sisters and the brother, heads bowed, were singing *God be with you till we meet again.* The faces around them were very quiet. Then the song ended. The small crowd dispersed. We watched the three women and the lone man walk slowly up the avenue.

194 ‘‘When she was singing before,’’ said Sonny, abruptly, ‘‘her voice reminded me for a minute of what heroin feels like sometimes—when it’s in your veins. It makes you feel sort of warm and cool at the same time. And distant. And—and sure.’’ He sipped his beer, very deliberately not looking at me. I watched his face. ‘‘It makes you feel—in control. Sometimes you’ve got to have that feeling.’’

195 ‘‘Do you?’’ I sat down slowly in the easy chair.

196 ‘‘Sometimes.’’ He went to the sofa and picked up his notebook again. ‘‘Some people do.’’

197 ‘‘In order,’’ I asked, ‘‘to play?’’ And my voice was very ugly, full of contempt and anger.

198 ‘‘Well’’—he looked at me with great, troubled eyes, as though, in fact, he hoped his eyes would tell me things he could never otherwise say—‘‘they think so. And if they think so—!’’

199 ‘‘And what do *you* think?’’ I asked.

200 He sat on the sofa and put his can of beer on the floor. ‘‘I don’t know,’’ he said, and I couldn’t be sure if he were answering my question or pursuing his thoughts. His face didn’t tell me. ‘‘It’s not so much to *play.* It’s to *stand* it, to be able to make it at all. On any level.’’ He frowned and smiled: ‘‘In order to keep from shaking to pieces.’’

201 ‘‘But these friends of yours,’’ I said, ‘‘they seem to shake themselves to pieces pretty goddamn fast.’’

202 ‘‘Maybe.’’ He played with the notebook. And something told me that I should curb my tongue, that Sonny was doing his best to talk, that I should listen. ‘‘But of course you only know the ones that’ve gone to pieces. Some don’t—or at least they haven’t *yet* and that’s just about all *any* of us can say.’’ He paused. ‘‘And then there are some who just live, really, in hell, and they know it and they see what’s happening and they go right on. I don’t know.’’ He sighed, dropped the notebook, folded his arms. ‘‘Some guys, you can tell from the way they play, they on something *all* the time. And you can see that, well, it makes something real for them. But of course,’’ he picked up his

beer from the floor and sipped it and put the can down again, “they *want* to, too, you've got to see that. Even some of them that say they don't—*some,* not all.”

203 “And what about you?” I asked—I couldn't help it. “What about you? Do *you* want to?”

204 He stood up and walked to the window and I remained silent for a long time. Then he sighed. “Me,” he said. Then: “While I was downstairs before, on my way here, listening to that woman sing, it struck me all of a sudden how much suffering she must have had to go through—to sing like that. It's *repulsive* to think you have to suffer that much.”

205 I said: “But there's no way not to suffer—is there, Sonny?”

206 “I believe not,” he said and smiled, “but that's never stopped anyone from trying.” He looked at me. “Has it?” I realized, with this mocking look, that there stood between us, forever, beyond the power of time or forgiveness, the fact that I had held silence—so long!—when he had needed human speech to help him. He turned back to the window. “No, there's no way not to suffer. But you try all kinds of ways to keep from drowning in it, to keep on top of it, and to make it seem—well, like *you.* Like you did something, all right, and now you're suffering for it. You know?” I said nothing. “Well you know,” he said, impatiently, “why *do* people suffer? Maybe it's better to do something to give it a reason, *any* reason.”

207 “But we just agreed,” I said, “that there's no way not to suffer. Isn't it better, then just to—take it?”

208 “But nobody just takes it.” Sonny cried, “that's what I'm telling you! Everybody tries not to. You're just hung up on the way some people try—it's not your way!”

209 The hair on my face began to itch, my face felt wet. “That's not true,” I said, “that's not true. I don't give a damn what other people do, I don't even care how they suffer. I just care how *you* suffer.” And he looked at me. “Please believe me,” I said, “I don't want to see you—die—trying not to suffer.”

210 “I won't,” he said flatly, “die trying not to suffer. At least, not any faster than anybody else.”

211 “But there's no need,” I said, trying to laugh, “is there? in killing yourself.”

212 I wanted to say more, but I couldn't. I wanted to talk about will power and how life could be—well, beautiful. I wanted to say that it was all within; but was it? or, rather, wasn't that exactly the trouble? And I wanted to promise that I would never fail him again. But it would all have sounded—empty words and lies.

213 So I made the promise to myself and prayed that I would keep it.

214 “It's terrible sometimes, inside,” he said, “that's what's the trouble. You walk these streets, black and funky and cold, and there's not really a living ass to talk to, and there's nothing shaking, and there's no way of getting it out—that storm inside. You can't talk it and you can't make love with it, and when you finally try to get with it and play it, you realize *nobody's* listening. So *you've* got to listen. You got to find a way to listen.”

215 And then he walked away from the window and sat on the sofa again, as though all the wind had suddenly been knocked out of him. ‘‘Sometimes you'll do *anything* to play, even cut your mother's throat.’’ He laughed and looked at me. ‘‘Or your brother's.’’ Then he sobered. ‘‘Or your own.’’ Then: ‘‘Don't worry. I'm all right now and I think I'll be all right. But I can't forget—where I've been. I don't mean just the physical place I've been, I mean where I've been. And what I've been.’’

216 ‘‘What have you been, Sonny?’’ I asked.

217 He smiled—but sat sideways on the sofa, his elbow resting on the back, his fingers playing with his mouth and chin, not looking at me. ‘‘I've been something I didn't recognize, didn't know I could be. Didn't know anybody could be.’’ He stopped, looking inward, looking helplessly young, looking old. ‘‘I'm not talking about it now because I feel *guilty* or anything like that—maybe it would be better if I did, I don't know. Anyway, I can't really talk about it. Not to you, not to anybody,’’ and now he turned and faced me. ‘‘Sometimes, you know, and it was actually when I was most *out* of the world, I felt that I was in it, that I was *with* it, really, and I could play or I didn't really have to *play,* it just came out of me, it was there. And I don't know how I played, thinking about it now, but I know I did awful things, those times, sometimes, to people. Or it wasn't that I *did* anything to them—it was that they weren't real.’’ He picked up the beer can; it was empty; he rolled it between his palms: ‘‘And other times—well, I needed a fix, I needed to find a place to lean, I needed to clear a space to *listen*—and I couldn't find it, and I—went crazy, I did terrible things to *me,* I was terrible *for me.*’’ He began pressing the beer can between his hands, I watched the metal begin to give. It glittered, as he played with it like a knife, and I was afraid he would cut himself, but I said nothing. ‘‘Oh well. I can never tell you. I was all by myself at the bottom of something, stinking and sweating and crying and shaking, and I smelled it, you know? *my* stink, and I thought I'd die if I couldn't get away from it and yet, all the same, I knew that everything I was doing was just locking me in with it. And I didn't know,’’ he paused, still flattening the beer can, ‘‘I didn't know, I still *don't* know, something kept telling me that maybe it was good to smell your own stink, but I didn't think that *that* was what I'd been trying to do—and—who can stand it?’’ and he abruptly dropped the ruined beer can, looking at me with a small, still smile, and then rose, walking to the window as though it were the lodestone rock. I watched his face, he watched the avenue. ‘‘I couldn't tell you when Mama died—but the reason I wanted to leave Harlem so bad was to get away from drugs. And then, when I ran away, that's what I was running from—really. When I came back, nothing had changed, *I* hadn't changed, I was just—older.’’ And he stopped, drumming with his fingers on the windowpane. The sun had vanished, soon darkness would fall. I watched his face. ‘‘It can come again,’’ he said, almost as though speaking to himself. Then he turned to me. ‘‘It can come again,’’ he repeated. ‘‘I just want you to know that.’’

218 ‘‘All right,’’ I said, at last. ‘‘So it can come again. All right.’’

219 He smiled, but the smile was sorrowful. ‘‘I had to try to tell you,’’ he said.

220 ‘‘Yes,’’ I said. ‘‘I understand that.’’

221 ‘‘You're my brother,’’ he said, looking straight at me, and not smiling at all.

222 "Yes," I repeated, "yes. I understand that."

223 "He turned back to the window, looking out. "All that hatred down there," he said, "all that hatred and misery and love. It's a wonder it doesn't blow the avenue apart."

224 We went to the only nightclub on a short, dark street, downtown. We squeezed through the narrow, chattering, jampacked bar to the entrance of the big room, where the bandstand was. And we stood there for a moment, for the lights were very dim in this room and we couldn't see. Then, "Hello, boy," said the voice and an enormous black man, much older than Sonny or myself, erupted out of all that atmospheric lighting and put an arm around Sonny's shoulder. "I been sitting right here," he said, "waiting for you."

He had a big voice, too, and heads in the darkness turned toward us.

225 Sonny grinned and pulled a little away, and said, "Creole, this is my brother. I told you about him."

226 Creole shook my hand. "I'm glad to meet you, son," he said, and it was clear that he was glad to meet me *there,* for Sonny's sake. And he smiled, "You got a real musician in *your* family," and he took his arm from Sonny's shoulder and slapped him, lightly, affectionately, with the back of his hand.

227 "Well. Now I've heard it all," said a voice behind us. This was another musician, and a friend of Sonny's, a coal-black, cheerful-looking man, built close to the ground. He immediately began confiding to me, at the top of his lungs, the most terrible things about Sonny, his teeth gleaming like a lighthouse and his laugh coming up out of him like the beginning of an earthquake. And it turned out that everyone at the bar knew Sonny, or almost everyone; some were musicians, working there, or nearby, or not working, some were simply hangers-on, and some were there to hear Sonny play. I was introduced to all of them and they were all very polite to me. Yet, it was clear that, for them, I was only Sonny's brother. Here, I was in Sonny's world. Or, rather: his kingdom. Here, it was not even a question that his veins bore royal blood.

228 They were going to play soon and Creole installed me, by myself, at a table in a dark corner. Then I watched them, Creole, and the little black man, and Sonny, and the others, while they horsed around, standing just below the bandstand. The light from the bandstand spilled just a little short of them and, watching them laughing and gesturing and moving about, I had the feeling that they, nevertheless, were being most careful not to step into that circle of light too suddenly: that if they moved into the light too suddenly, without thinking, they would perish in flame. Then, while I watched, one of them, the small black man, moved into the light and crossed the bandstand and started fooling around with his drums. Then—being funny and being, also, extremely ceremonious—Creole took Sonny by the arm and led him to the piano. A woman's voice called Sonny's name and a few hands started clapping. And Sonny, also being funny and being ceremonious, and so touched, I think, that he could have cried, but neither hiding it nor showing it, riding it like a man, grinned, and put both hands to his heart and bowed from the waist.

229 Creole then went to the bass fiddle and a lean, very bright-skinned brown man jumped up on the bandstand and picked up his horn. So there they were, and the atmosphere on the bandstand and in the room began to change and tighten. Someone stepped up to the microphone and announced them. Then there were all kinds of murmurs. Some people at the bar shushed others. The waitress ran around, frantically getting in the last orders, guys and chicks got closer to each other, and the lights on the bandstand, on the quartet, turned to a kind of indigo. Then they all looked different there. Creole looked about him for the last time, as though he were making certain that all his chickens were in the coop, and then he—jumped and struck the fiddle. And there they were.

230 All I know about music is that not many people ever really hear it. And even then, on the rare occasions when something opens within, and the music enters, what we mainly hear, or hear corroborated, are personal, private, vanishing evocations. But the man who creates the music is hearing something else, is dealing with the roar rising from the void and imposing order on it as it hits the air. What is evoked in him, then, is of another order, more terrible because it has no words, and triumphant, too, for that same reason. And his triumph, when he triumphs, is ours. I just watched Sonny's face. His face was troubled, he was working hard, but he wasn't with it. And I had the feeling that, in a way, everyone on the bandstand was waiting for him, both waiting for him and pushing him along. But as I began to watch Creole, I realized that it was Creole who held them all back. He had them on a short rein. Up there, keeping the beat with his whole body, wailing on the fiddle with his eyes half closed, he was listening to everything, but he was listening to Sonny. He was having a dialogue with Sonny. He wanted Sonny to leave the shoreline and strike out for the deep water. He was Sonny's witness that deep water and drowning were not the same thing—he had been there, and he knew. And he wanted Sonny to know. He was waiting for Sonny to do the things on the keys which would let Creole know that Sonny was in the water.

231 And, while Creole listened, Sonny moved, deep within, exactly like someone in torment. I had never before thought of how awful the relationship must be between the musician and his instrument. He has to fill it, this instrument, with the breath of life, his own. He has to make it do what he wants it to do. And a piano is just a piano. It's made out of so much wood and wires and little hammers and big ones, and ivory. While there's only so much you can do with it, the only way to find this out is to try; to try and make it do everything.

232 And Sonny hadn't been near a piano for over a year. And he wasn't on much better terms with his life, not the life that stretched before him now. He and the piano stammered, started one way, got scared, stopped; started another way, panicked, marked time, started again; then seemed to have found a direction, panicked again, got stuck. And the face I saw on Sonny I'd never seen before. Everything had been burned out of it, and, at the same time, things usually hidden were being burned in, by the fire and fury of the battle which was occurring in him up there.

233 Yet, watching Creole's face as they neared the end of the first set, I had the feeling that something had happened, something I hadn't heard. Then they finished, there was

scattered applause, and then, without an instant's warning, Creole started into something else, it was almost sardonic, it was *Am I Blue*. And, as though he commanded, Sonny began to play. Something began to happen. And Creole let out the reins. The dry, low, black man said something awful on the drums, Creole answered, and the drums talked back. Then the horn insisted, sweet and high, slightly detached perhaps, and Creole listened, commenting now and then, dry, and driving, beautiful and calm and old. Then they all came together again, and Sonny was part of the family again. I could tell this from his face. He seemed to have found, right there beneath his fingers, a damn brand-new piano. It seemed that he couldn't get over it. Then, for a while, just being happy with Sonny, they seemed to be agreeing with him that brand-new pianos certainly were a gas.

234 Then Creole stepped forward to remind them that what they were playing was the blues. He hit something in all of them, he hit something in me, myself, and the music tightened and deepened, apprehension began to beat the air. Creole began to tell us what the blues were all about. They were not about anything very new. He and his boys up there were keeping it new, at the risk of ruin, destruction, madness, and death, in order to find new ways to make us listen. For, while the tale of how we suffer, and how we are delighted, and how we may triumph is never new, it always must be heard. There isn't any other tale to tell, it's the only light we've got in all this darkness.

235 And this tale, according to that face, that body, those strong hands on those strings, has another aspect in every country, and a new depth in every generation. Listen, Creole seemed to be saying, listen. Now these are Sonny's blues. He made the little black man on the drums know it, and the bright, brown man on the horn. Creole wasn't trying any longer to get Sonny in the water. He was wishing him Godspeed. Then he stepped back, very slowly, filling the air with the immense suggestion that Sonny speak for himself.

236 Then they all gathered around Sonny and Sonny played. Every now and again one of them seemed to say, amen. Sonny's fingers filled the air with life, his life. But that life contained so many others. And Sonny went all the way back, he really began with the spare, flat statement of the opening phrase of the song. Then he began to make it his. It was very beautiful because it wasn't hurried and it was no longer a lament. I seemed to hear with what burning he had made it his, with what burning we had yet to make it ours, how we could cease lamenting. Freedom lurked around us and I understood, at last, that he could help us to be free if we would listen, that he would never be free until we did. Yet, there was no battle in his face now, I heard what he had gone through, and would continue to go through until he came to rest in earth. He had made it his: that long line, of which we knew only Mama and Daddy. And he was giving it back, as everything must be given back, so that, passing through death, it can live forever. I saw my mother's face again, and felt, for the first time, how the stones of the road she had walked on must have bruised her feet. I saw the moonlit road where my father's brother died. And it brought something else back to me, and carried me past it, I saw my little girl again and felt Isabel's tears again, and I felt my own tears begin

to rise. And I was yet aware that this was only a moment, that the world waited outside, as hungry as a tiger, and that trouble stretched above us, longer than the sky.

237 Then it was over. Creole and Sonny let out their breath, both soaking wet, and grinning. There was a lot of applause and some of it was real. In the dark, the girl came by and I asked her to take drinks to the bandstand. There was a long pause, while they talked up there in the indigo light and after awhile I saw the girl put a Scotch and milk on top of the piano for Sonny. He didn't seem to notice it, but just before they started playing again, he sipped from it and looked toward me, and nodded. Then he put it back on top of the piano. For me, then, as they began to play again, it glowed and shook above my brother's head like the very cup of trembling.[1]

Questions for Analysis

1. Sonny's story is a study in the special burdens of being black in America. In another sense his story is one that parallels the experience of people of all races. What aspects of the story convey the problems of being black in America? What aspects are universal?
2. Does "Sonny's Blues" work better to support the argument against or for the legalization of drugs? How might it be used on either side of the argument? How, in your opinion, would the writers of the essays in this section react to this story?
3. Sonny is able to move toward recovery because of support from his family and friends and from his music. What does this part of Sonny's story suggest for our drug policy?

AUTHOR'S NOTE: See *Isaiah* 51:22: ". . . I have taken out of thine hand the cup of trembling . . . thou shalt no more drink it again."

Abortion: A Woman's Choice Or the State's?

Abortion may be the most intensely debated, most complex legal and moral issue to confront Americans in the last quarter of the twentieth century. Abortion has always been a difficult personal decision faced by women with unwanted pregnancies. When it has been illegal in this and other countries, women have had to deal not only with their own private anguish but also, because of abortion's illegality, with additional physical dangers.

Since the 1973 Supreme Court decision *Roe* v. *Wade,* abortion has been legal in the United States. That decision was based on the principle that a woman has the rights of privacy and control over her body and, therefore, the right to choose whether to have a child. *Roe* v. *Wade* has been challenged repeatedly by those who feel that all human life is sacred and that the fetus from the moment of conception is a human being whose life should be recognized, honored, and protected under the law. The debate—always intense—has become more heated in recent years as appointments by Presidents Ronald Reagan and George Bush have made the Supreme Court more conservative and thus more likely to overturn *Roe* v. *Wade* and make abortion illegal. In fact, abortion seems to have been one of the key issues in the appointment and confirmation of the two newest Supreme Court appointees, Judges Souter and Thomas. Several laws have recently been passed by state legislatures to test the Supreme Court's attitude on abortion. These laws are now working their way through the legal system toward the Supreme Court.

The debate has become more visible outside the judicial system as well. Organizations that oppose abortion such as Operation Rescue have sponsored high-profile activities to draw attention to their cause. In the summer and fall of 1991, members of this group blocked entrances to clinics in Witchita, Kansas. Many of them were arrested. Although Operation Rescue is the most militant of the antiabortion groups, its opinions are shared by many other social and religious groups. On the pro-choice side, those concerned with protecting the rights and welfare of women have renewed their efforts to advance their position.

It is difficult to hear rational, thoughtful discourse in such an emotionally charged environment. The extremes, presented by religious fundamentalists on one side and radical feminists on the other, often drown out many others who try to articulate positions that are sensitive to both the needs of women and the sanctity of life. The following selections present the range of arguments on this issue over the past twenty years.

First, the cartoon that begins this section contains a coat hanger, the common household item that has come to symbolize the pain, brutality, and life-threatening injury suffered by women when abortions are illegal. Robert Ariail's 1988 cartoon predicts the "shape of things to come" as the Supreme Court seems to drift further toward reversing *Roe* v. *Wade* with the appointment of each new justice.

Judith Jervis Thomson's "A Defense of Abortion" is considered one of the classic arguments supporting abortion. Writing in 1971, two years before abortion was legalized, Thomson concedes, for argument's sake, that the fetus is a person from conception. She then goes on to argue, through several analogies, that even if we concede that point there are times when abortions are morally permissible.

The next selection was written by Ronald Reagan during his presidency of the United States between 1981 and 1989. His essay reveals the growing conservative pressure to challenge *Roe* v. *Wade* during the 1980s. Furthermore, his appointments to the Supreme Court began the slow but steady tilt of the court toward a conservative view of the law.

The next two essays provide different perspectives on abortion from within the Roman Catholic Church. "Too Many Abortions," written by the editors of the Roman Catholic magazine *Commonweal* argues for more responsible action on the part of adults to prevent unwanted pregnancies. In the next essay Frances Kissling, President of Catholics for a Free Choice, supports abortion but suggests ways to achieve greater consensus for a reasonable middle ground. Her essay, "Ending the Abortion War: A Modest Proposal," appeared in *The Christian Century* in February 1990.

Faye Wattleton, former President of Planned Parenthood Federation of America and a long-time pro-choice activist, wrote the next essay, "Reproductive Rights Are Fundamental Rights." Drawing on recent revelations about the plight of women subjected to the strict antiabortion policies dictated by Nicolae Ceaucescu in Romania, she projects similar problems should the United States again make abortion illegal. Her essay is an interesting recent contribution to the debate over abortion from someone usually thought of (rightly or wrongly) as a radical feminist. Don Wright's cartoon "Woman" (1991) with its question, "Is a woman's body entirely her own?" is especially fitting at this point, since it splices into one picture many of the conflicts and contradictions inherent in the abortion issue.

Two other selections round out this collection. In "Abortion" Richard Seltzer shares with us the horror of abortion through the eyes of a physician and surgeon. We share his struggle as his emotions contend with his knowledge that abortion is often a necessity. It is an exhausting piece that leaves us wondering which side, if either, Seltzer is on. Finally, A. J. Cronin's "Doctor, I Can't . . . I Won't Have a Child" reveals the deception, anger, emotional pain, and physical danger that attended one abortion performed in England during the 1930s, when abortion was illegal.

Robert Ariail

The Shape of Things to Come

1988

Robert Ariail (b. 1955) is a political cartoonist for *The State* newspaper in Columbia, South Carolina.

Robert Ariail, The State *(Columbia, S.C.).*

Judith Jarvis Thomson

A Defense of Abortion

(1971)

Judith Jarvis Thomson (b. 1929), a philosopher, wrote this essay to defend the idea that even if we concede that a fetus is a person from the moment of conception, abortion is, in some situations, a logical and moral choice. Since its original publication in the first issue of *Philosophy & Public Affairs*, it has been one of the most widely reprinted articles on abortion.

1 Most opposition to abortion relies on the premise that the fetus is a human being, a person, from the moment of conception. The premise is argued for, but, as I think, not well. Take, for example, the most common argument. We are asked to notice that the development of a human being from conception through birth into childhood is continuous; then it is said that to draw a line, to choose a point in this development and say "before this point the thing is not a person, after this point it is a person" is to make an arbitrary choice, a choice for which in the nature of things no good reason can be given. It is concluded that the fetus is, or anyway that we had better say it is, a person from the moment of conception. But this conclusion does not follow. Similar things might be said about the development of an acorn into an oak tree, and it does not follow that acorns are oak trees, or that we had better say they are. Arguments of this form are sometimes called "slippery slope arguments"—the phrase is perhaps self-explanatory—and it is dismaying that opponents of abortion rely on them so heavily and uncritically.

2 I am inclined to agree, however, that the prospects for "drawing a line" in the development of the fetus look dim. I am inclined to think also that we shall probably have to agree that the fetus has already become a human person well before birth. Indeed, it comes as a surprise when one first learns how early in its life it begins to acquire human characteristics. By the tenth week, for example, it already has a face, arms and legs, fingers and toes; it has internal organs, and brain activity is detectable.[1] On the other hand, I think that the premise is false, that the fetus is not a person from the moment of conception. A newly fertilized ovum, a newly implanted clump of cells, is no more a person than an acorn is an oak tree. But I shall not discuss any of this. For it seems to me to be of great interest to ask what happens if, for the sake of argument, we allow the premise. How, precisely, are we supposed to get from there to the conclusion that abortion is morally impermissible? Opponents of abortion commonly spend most of their time establishing that the fetus is a person, and hardly any time explaining the step from there to the impermissibility of abortion. Perhaps they think the step too simple and obvious to require much comment. Or perhaps instead they are simply being economical in argument. Many of those who defend abortion rely on the premise that

the fetus is not a person, but only a bit of tissue that will become a person at birth; and why pay out more arguments than you have to? Whatever the explanation, I suggest that the step they take is neither easy nor obvious, that it calls for closer examination than it is commonly given, and that when we do give it this closer examination we shall feel inclined to reject it.

3 I propose, then, that we grant that the fetus is a person from the moment of conception. How does the argument go from here? Something like this, I take it. Every person has a right to life. So the fetus has a right to life. No doubt the mother has a right to decide what shall happen in and to her body; everyone would grant that. But surely a person's right to life is stronger and more stringent than the mother's right to decide what happens in and to her body, and so outweighs it. So the fetus may not be killed; an abortion may not be performed.

4 It sounds plausible. But now let me ask you to imagine this. You wake up in the morning and find yourself back to back in bed with an unconscious violinist. A famous unconscious violinist. He has been found to have a fatal kidney ailment, and the Society of Music Lovers has canvassed all the available medical records and found that you alone have the right blood type to help. They have therefore kidnapped you, and last night the violinist's circulatory system was plugged into yours, so that your kidneys can be used to extract poisons from his blood as well as your own. The director of the hospital now tells you, ''Look, we're sorry the Society of Music Lovers did this to you—we would never have permitted it if we had known. But still, they did it, and the violinist now is plugged into you. To unplug you would be to kill him. But never mind, it's only for nine months. By then he will have recovered from his ailment, and can safely be unplugged from you.'' Is it morally incumbent on you to accede to this situation? No doubt it would be very nice of you if you did, a great kindness. But do you *have* to accede to it? What if it were not nine months, but nine years? Or longer still? What if the director of the hospital says, ''Tough luck, I agree, but you've now got to stay in bed, with the violinist plugged into you, for the rest of your life. Because remember this. All persons have a right to life, and violinists are persons. Granted you have a right to decide what happens in and to your body, but a person's right to life outweighs your right to decide what happens in and to your body. So you cannot ever be unplugged from him.'' I imagine you would regard this as outrageous, which suggests that something really is wrong with that plausible-sounding argument I mentioned a moment ago.

5 In this case, of course, you were kidnapped; you didn't volunteer for the operation that plugged the violinist into your kidneys. Can those who oppose abortion on the ground I mentioned make an exception for a pregnancy due to rape? Certainly. They can say that persons have a right to life only if they didn't come into existence because of rape; or they can say that all persons have a right to life, but that some have less of a right to life than others, in particular, that those who came into existence because of rape have less. But these statements have a rather unpleasant sound. Surely the question of whether you have a right to life at all, or how much of it you have, shouldn't turn on the question of whether or not you are the product of a rape. And in fact the people

who oppose abortion on the ground I mentioned do not make this distinction, and hence do not make an exception in the case of rape.

6 Nor do they make an exception for a case in which the mother has to spend the nine months of her pregnancy in bed. They would agree that would be a great pity, and hard on the mother; but all the same, all persons have a right to life, the fetus is a person, and so on. I suspect, in fact, that they would not make an exception for a case in which, miraculously enough, the pregnancy went on for nine years, or even the rest of the mother's life.

7 Some won't even make an exception for a case in which continuation of the pregnancy is likely to shorten the mother's life; they regard abortion as impermissible even to save the mother's life. Such cases are nowadays very rare, and many opponents of abortion do not accept this extreme view. All the same, it is a good place to begin: A number of points of interest come out in respect to it.

8 **1.** Let us call the view that abortion is impermissible even to save the mother's life "the extreme view." I want to suggest first that it does not issue from the argument I mentioned earlier without the addition of some fairly powerful premises. Suppose a woman has become pregnant, and now learns that she has a cardiac condition such that she will die if she carries the baby to term. What may be done for her? The fetus, being a person, has a right to life, but as the mother is a person too, so has she a right to life. Presumably they have an equal right to life. How is it supposed to come out that an abortion may not be performed? If mother and child have an equal right to life, shouldn't we perhaps flip a coin? Or should we add to the mother's right to life her right to decide what happens in and to her body, which everybody seems to be ready to grant—the sum of her rights now outweighing the fetus' right to life?

9 The most familiar argument here is the following. We are told that performing the abortion would be directly killing[2] the child, whereas doing nothing would not be killing the mother, but only letting her die. Moreover, in killing the child, one would be killing an innocent person, for the child has committed no crime, and is not aiming at his mother's death. And then there are a variety of ways in which this might be continued. (1) But as directly killing an innocent person is always and absolutely impermissible, an abortion may not be performed. Or, (2) as directly killing an innocent person is murder, and murder is always and absolutely impermissible, an abortion may not be performed.[3] Or, (3) as one's duty to refrain from directly killing an innocent person is more stringent than one's duty to keep a person from dying, an abortion may not be performed. Or, (4) if one's only options are directly killing an innocent person or letting a person die, one must prefer letting the person die, and thus an abortion may not be performed.[4]

10 Some people seem to have thought that these are not further premises which must be added if the conclusion is to be reached, but that they follow from the very fact that an innocent person has a right to life.[5] But this seems to me to be a mistake, and perhaps the simplest way to show this is to bring out that while we must certainly grant that innocent persons have a right to life, the theses in (1) through (4) are all false. Take (2), for example. If directly killing an innocent person is murder, and thus is imper-

missible, then the mother's directly killing the innocent person inside her is murder, and thus is impermissible. But it cannot seriously be thought to be murder if the mother performs an abortion on herself to save her life. It cannot seriously be said that she *must* refrain, that she *must* sit passively by and wait for her death. Let us look again at the case of you and the violinist. There you are, in bed with the violinist, and the director of the hospital says to you, "It's all most distressing, and I deeply sympathize, but you see this is putting an additional strain on your kidneys, and you'll be dead within the month. But you *have* to stay where you are all the same. Because unplugging you would be directly killing an innocent violinist, and that's murder, and that's impermissible." If anything in the world is true, it is that you do not commit murder, you do not do what is impermissible, if you reach around to your back and unplug yourself from that violinist to save your life.

11 The main focus of attention in writings on abortion has been on what a third party may or may not do in answer to a request from a woman for an abortion. This is in a way understandable. Things being as they are, there isn't much a woman can safely do to abort herself. So the question asked is what a third party may do, and what the mother may do, if it is mentioned at all, is deduced, almost as an afterthought, from what it is concluded that third parties may do. But it seems to me that to treat the matter in this way is to refuse to grant to the mother that very status of person which is so firmly insisted on for the fetus. For we cannot simply read off what a person may do from what a third party may do. Suppose you find yourself trapped in a tiny house with a growing child. I mean a very tiny house, and a rapidly growing child—you are already up against the wall of the house and in a few minutes you'll be crushed to death. The child on the other hand won't be crushed to death; if nothing is done to stop him from growing he'll be hurt, but in the end he'll simply burst open the house and walk out a free man. Now I could well understand it if a bystander were to say, "There's nothing we can do for you. We cannot choose between your life and his, we cannot be the ones to decide who is to live, we cannot intervene." But it cannot be concluded that you too can do nothing, that you cannot attack it to save your life. However innocent the child may be, you do not have to wait passively while it crushes you to death. Perhaps a pregnant woman is vaguely felt to have the status of house, to which we don't allow the right of self-defense. But if the woman houses the child, it should be remembered that she is a person who houses it.

12 I should perhaps stop to say explicitly that I am not claiming that people have a right to do anything whatever to save their lives. I think, rather, that there are drastic limits to the right of self-defense. If someone threatens you with death unless you torture someone else to death, I think you have not the right, even to save your life, to do so. But the case under consideration here is very different. In our case there are only two people involved, one whose life is threatened, and one who threatens it. Both are innocent. The one who is threatened is not threatened because of any fault, the one who threatens does not threaten because of any fault. For this reason we may feel that we bystanders cannot intervene. But the person threatened can.

13 In sum, a woman surely can defend her life against the threat to it posed by the unborn child, even if doing so involves its death. And this shows not merely that the theses in (1) through (4) are false; it shows also that the extreme view of abortion is false, and so we need not canvass any other possible ways of arriving at it from the argument I mentioned at the outset.

14 **2.** The extreme view could of course be weakened to say that while abortion is permissible to save the mother's life, it may not be performed by a third party, but only by the mother herself. But this cannot be right either. For what we have to keep in mind is that the mother and the unborn child are not like two tenants in a small house which has, by an unfortunate mistake, been rented to both: The mother *owns* the house. The fact that she does adds to the offensiveness of deducing that the mother can do nothing from the supposition that third parties can do nothing. But it does more than this: It casts a bright light on the supposition that third parties can do nothing. Certainly it lets us see that a third party who says "I cannot choose between you" is fooling himself if he thinks this is impartiality. If Jones has found and fastened on a certain coat, which he needs to keep him from freezing, but which Smith also needs to keep him from freezing, then it is not impartiality that says "I cannot choose between you" when Smith owns the coat. Women have said again and again "This body is *my* body!" and they have reason to feel angry, reason to feel that it has been like shouting into the wind. Smith, after all, is hardly likely to bless us if we say to him, "Of course it's your coat, anybody would grant that it is. But no one may choose between you and Jones who is to have it."

15 We should really ask what it is that says "no one may choose" in the face of the fact that the body that houses the child is the mother's body. It may be simply a failure to appreciate this fact. But it may be something more interesting, namely the sense that one has a right to refuse to lay hands on people, even where it would be just and fair to do so, even where justice seems to require that somebody do so. Thus justice might call for somebody to get Smith's coat back from Jones, and yet you have a right to refuse to be the one to lay hands on Jones, a right to refuse to do physical violence to him. This, I think, must be granted. But then what should be said is not "no one may choose," but only "I cannot choose," and indeed not even this, but "I will not *act,*" leaving it open that somebody else can or should, and in particular that anyone in a position of authority, with the job of securing people's rights, both can and should. So this is no difficulty. I have not been arguing that any given third party must accede to the mother's request that he perform an abortion to save her life, but only that he may.

16 I suppose that in some views of human life the mother's body is only on loan to her, the loan not being one which gives her any prior claim to it. One who held this view might well think it impartiality to say "I cannot choose." But I shall simply ignore this possibility. My own view is that if a human being has any just, prior claim to anything at all, he has a just, prior claim to his own body. And perhaps this needn't be argued for here anyway, since, as I mentioned, the arguments against abortion we are looking at do grant that the woman has a right to decide what happens in and to her body.

17 But although they do grant it, I have tried to show that they do not take seriously what is done in granting it. I suggest the same thing will reappear even more clearly when we turn away from cases in which the mother's life is at stake, and attend, as I propose we now do, to the vastly more common cases in which a woman wants an abortion for some less weighty reason than preserving her own life.

18 **3.** Where the mother's life is not at stake, the argument I mentioned at the outset seems to have a much stronger pull. "Everyone has a right to life, so the unborn person has a right to life." And isn't the child's right to life weightier than anything other than the mother's own right to life, which she might put forward as ground for an abortion?

19 This argument treats the right to life as if it were unproblematic. It is not, and this seems to me to be precisely the source of the mistake.

20 For we should now, at long last, ask what it comes to, to have a right to life. In some views having a right to life includes having a right to be given at least the bare minimum one needs for continued life. But suppose that what in fact *is* the bare minimum a man needs for continued life is something he has no right at all to be given? If I am sick unto death, and the only thing that will save my life is the touch of Henry Fonda's cool hand on my fevered brow, then all the same, I have no right to be given the touch of Henry Fonda's cool hand on my fevered brow. It would be frightfully nice of him to fly in from the West Coast to provide it. It would be less nice, though no doubt well meant, if my friends flew out to the West Coast and carried Henry Fonda back with them. But I have no right at all against anybody that he should do this for me. Or again, to return to the story I told earlier, the fact that for continued life that violinist needs the continued use of your kidneys does not establish that he has a right to be given the continued use of your kidneys. He certainly has no right against you that *you* should give him continued use of your kidneys. For nobody has any right to use your kidneys unless you give him such a right; and nobody has the right against you that you shall give him this right—if you do allow him to go on using your kidneys, this is a kindness on your part, and not something he can claim from you as his due. Nor has he any right against anybody else that *they* should give him continued use of your kidneys. Certainly he had no right against the Society of Music Lovers that they should plug him into you in the first place. And if you now start to unplug yourself, having learned that you will otherwise have to spend nine years in bed with him, there is nobody in the world who must try to prevent you, in order to see to it that he is given something he has a right to be given.

21 Some people are rather stricter about the right to life. In their view, it does not include the right to be given anything, but amounts to, and only to, the right not to be killed by anybody. But here a related difficulty arises. If everybody is to refrain from killing that violinist, then everybody must refrain from doing a great many different sorts of things. Everybody must refrain from slitting his throat, everybody must refrain from shooting him—and everybody must refrain from unplugging you from him. But does he have a right against everybody that they shall refrain from unplugging you from him? To refrain from doing this is to allow him to continue to use your kidneys. It could be argued that he has a right against us that *we* should allow him to continue

to use your kidneys. That is, while he had no right against us that we should give him the use of your kidneys, it might be argued that he anyway has a right against us that we shall not now intervene and deprive him of the use of your kidneys. I shall come back to third-party interventions later. But certainly the violinist has no right against you that *you* shall allow him to continue to use your kidneys. As I said, if you do allow him to use them, it is a kindness on your part, and not something you owe him.

22 The difficulty I point to here is not peculiar to the right of life. It reappears in connection with all the other natural rights; and it is something which an adequate account of rights must deal with. For present purposes it is enough just to draw attention to it. But I would stress that I am not arguing that people do not have a right to life—quite to the contrary, it seems to me that the primary control we must place on the acceptability of an account of rights is that it should turn out in that account to be a truth that all persons have a right to life. I am arguing only that having a right to life does not guarantee having either a right to be given the use of or a right to be allowed continued use of another person's body—even if one needs it for life itself. So the right to life will not serve the opponents of abortion in the very simple and clear way in which they seem to have thought it would.

23 **4.** There is another way to bring out the difficulty. In the most ordinary sort of case, to deprive someone of what he has a right to is to treat him unjustly. Suppose a boy and his small brother are jointly given a box of chocolates for Christmas. If the older boy takes the box and refuses to give his brother any of the chocolates, he is unjust to him, for the brother has been given a right to half of them. But suppose that, having learned that otherwise it means nine years in bed with that violinist, you unplug yourself from him. You surely are not being unjust to him, for you gave him no right to use your kidneys, and no one else can have given him any such right. But we have to notice that in unplugging yourself, you are killing him; and violinists, like everybody else, have a right to life, and thus in the view we were considering just now, the right not to be killed. So here you do what he supposedly has a right you shall not do, but you do not act unjustly to him in doing it.

24 The emendation which may be made at this point is this: The right to life consists not in the right not to be killed, but rather in the right not to be killed unjustly. This runs a risk of circularity, but never mind: It would enable us to square the fact that the violinist has a right to life with the fact that you do not act unjustly toward him in unplugging yourself, thereby killing him. For if you do not kill him unjustly, you do not violate his right to life, and so it is no wonder you do him no injustice.

25 But if this emendation is accepted, the gap in the argument against abortion stares us plainly in the face: It is by no means enough to show that the fetus is a person, and to remind us that all persons have a right to life—we need to be shown also that killing the fetus violates its right to life, i.e., that abortion is unjust killing. And is it?

26 I suppose we may take it as a datum that in the case of pregnancy due to rape the mother has not given the unborn person a right to the use of her body for food and shelter. Indeed, in what pregnancy should it be supposed that the mother has given the

unborn person such a right? It is not as if there were unborn persons drifting about the world, to whom a woman who wants a child says "I invite you in."

27 But it might be argued that there are other ways one can have acquired a right to the use of another person's body than by having been invited to use it by that person. Suppose a woman voluntarily indulges in intercourse, knowing of the chance it will issue in pregnancy, and then she does become pregnant; is she not in part responsible for the presence, in fact the very existence, of the unborn person inside? No doubt she did not invite it in. But doesn't her partial responsibility for its being there itself give it a right to the use of her body?[6] If so, then her aborting it would be more like the boy's taking away the chocolates, and less like your unplugging yourself from the violinist—doing so would be depriving it of what it does have a right to, and thus would be doing it an injustice.

28 And then, too, it might be asked whether or not she can kill it even to save her own life: If she voluntarily called it into existence, how can she now kill it, even in self-defense?

29 The first thing to be said about this is that it is something new. Opponents of abortion have been so concerned to make out the independence of the fetus, in order to establish that it has a right to life, just as its mother does, that they have tended to overlook the possible support they might gain from making out that the fetus is *dependent* on the mother, in order to establish that she has a special kind of responsibility for it, a responsibility that gives it rights against her which are not possessed by any independent person—such as an ailing violinist who is a stranger to her.

30 On the other hand, this argument would give the unborn person a right to its mother's body only if her pregnancy resulted from a voluntary act, undertaken in full knowledge of the chance a pregnancy might result from it. It would leave out entirely the unborn person whose existence is due to rape. Pending the availability of some further argument, then, we would be left with the conclusion that unborn persons whose existence is due to rape have no right to the use of their mothers' bodies, and thus that aborting them is not depriving them of anything they have a right to and hence is not unjust killing.

31 And we should also notice that it is not at all plain that this argument really does go even as far as it purports to. For there are cases and cases, and the details make a difference. If the room is stuffy, and I therefore open a window to air it, and a burglar climbs in, it would be absurd to say, "Ah, now he can stay, she's given him a right to the use of her house—for she is partially responsible for his presence there, having voluntarily done what enabled him to get in, in full knowledge that there are such things as burglars, and that burglars burgle." It would be still more absurd to say this if I had had bars installed outside my windows, precisely to prevent burglars from getting in, and a burglar got in only because of a defect in the bars. It remains equally absurd if we imagine it is not a burglar who climbs in, but an innocent person who blunders or falls in. Again, suppose it were like this: Peopleseeds drift about in the air like pollen, and if you open your windows, one may drift in and take root in your carpets or upholstery. You don't want children, so you fix up your windows with fine mesh

screens, the very best you can buy. As can happen, however, and on very, very rare occasions does happen, one of the screens is defective; and a seed drifts in and takes root. Does the personplant who now develops have a right to the use of your house? Surely not—despite the fact that you voluntarily opened your windows, you knowingly kept carpets and upholstered furniture, and you knew that screens were sometimes defective. Someone may argue that you are responsible for its rooting, that it does have a right to your house, because after all you *could* have lived out your life with bare floors and furniture, or with sealed windows and doors. But this won't do—for by the same token anyone can avoid a pregnancy due to rape by having a hysterectomy, or anyway by never leaving home without a (reliable!) army.

32 It seems to me that the argument we are looking at can establish at most that there are *some* cases in which the unborn person has a right to the use of its mother's body, and therefore *some* cases in which abortion is unjust killing. There is room for much discussion and argument as to precisely which, if any. But I think we should sidestep this issue and leave it open, for at any rate the argument certainly does not establish that all abortion is unjust killing.

33 **5.** There is room for yet another argument here, however. We surely must grant that there may be cases in which it would be morally indecent to detach a person from your body at the cost of his life. Suppose you learn that what the violinist needs is not nine years of your life, but only one hour: All you need do to save his life is spend one hour in that bed with him. Suppose also that letting him use your kidneys for that one hour would not affect your health in the slightest. Admittedly you were kidnapped. Admittedly you did not give anyone permission to plug him into you. Nevertheless it seems to me plain you *ought* to allow him to use your kidneys for that hour—it would be indecent to refuse.

34 Again, suppose pregnancy lasted only an hour, and constituted no threat to life or death [sic]. And suppose that a woman becomes pregnant as a result of rape. Admittedly she did not voluntarily do anything to bring about the existence of a child. Admittedly she did nothing at all which would give the unborn person a right to the use of her body. All the same it might well be said, as in the newly emended violinist story, that she *ought* to allow it to remain for that hour—that it would be indecent in her to refuse.

35 Now some people are inclined to use the term "right" in such a way that it follows from the fact that you ought to allow a person to use your body for the hour he needs, that he has a right to use your body for the hour he needs, even though he has not been given that right by any person or act. They may say that it follows also that if you refuse, you act unjustly toward him. This use of the term is perhaps so common that it cannot be called wrong; nevertheless it seems to me to be an unfortunate loosening of what we would do better to keep a tight rein on. Suppose that box of chocolates I mentioned earlier had not been given to both boys jointly, but was given only to the older boy. There he sits, stolidly eating his way through the box, his small brother watching enviously. Here we are likely to say "You ought not to be so mean. You ought to give your brother some of those chocolates." My own view is that it just does not follow from the truth of this that the brother has any right to any of the chocolates.

If the boy refuses to give his brother any, he is greedy, stingy, callous—but not unjust. I suppose that the people I have in mind will say it does follow that the brother has a right to some of the chocolates, and thus that the boy does act unjustly if he refuses to give his brother any. But the effect of saying this is to obscure what we should keep distinct, namely the difference between the boy's refusal in this case and the boy's refusal in the earlier case, in which the box was given to both boys jointly, and in which the small brother thus had what was from any point of view clear title to half.

36 A further objection to so using the term "right" that from the fact that A ought to do a thing for B, it follows that B has a right against A that A do it for him, is that it is going to make the question of whether or not a man has a right to a thing turn on how easy it is to provide him with it; and this seems not merely unfortunate, but morally unacceptable. Take the case of Henry Fonda again. I said earlier that I had no right to the touch of his cool hand on my fevered brow, even though I needed it to save my life. I said it would be frightfully nice of him to fly in from the West Coast to provide me with it, but that I had no right against him that he should do so. But suppose he isn't on the West Coast. Suppose he has only to walk across the room, place a hand briefly on my brow—and lo, my life is saved. Then surely he ought to do it, it would be indecent to refuse. Is it to be said, "Ah, well, it follows that in this case she has a right to the touch of his hand on her brow, and so it would be an unjustice in him to refuse"? So that I have a right to it when it is easy for him to provide it, though no right when it's hard? It's rather a shocking idea that anyone's rights should fade away and disappear as it gets harder and harder to accord them to him.

37 So my own view is that even though you ought to let the violinist use your kidneys for the one hour he needs, we should not conclude that he has a right to do so—we should say that if you refuse, you are, like the boy who owns all the chocolates and will give none away, self-centered and callous, indecent in fact, but not unjust. And similarly, that even supposing a case in which a woman pregnant due to rape ought to allow the unborn person to use her body for the hour he needs, we should not conclude that he has a right to do so; we should conclude that she is self-centered, callous, indecent, but not unjust, if she refuses. The complaints are no less grave; they are just different. However, there is no need to insist on this point. If anyone does wish to deduce "he has a right" from "you ought," then all the same he must surely grant that there are cases in which it is not morally required of you that you allow that violinist to use your kidneys, and in which he does not have a right to use them, and in which you do not do him an injustice if you refuse. And so also for mother and unborn child. Except in such cases as the unborn person has a right to demand it—and we were leaving open the possibility that there may be such cases—nobody is morally *required* to make large sacrifices, of health, of all other interests and concerns, of all other duties and commitments, for nine years, or even for nine months, in order to keep another person alive.

38 **6.** We have in fact to distinguish between the two kinds of Samaritan: the Good Samaritan and what we might call the Minimally Decent Samaritan. The story of the Good Samaritan, you will remember, goes like this:

> A certain man went down from Jerusalem to Jericho, and fell among thieves, which stripped him of his raiment, and wounded him, and departed, leaving him half dead.
>
> And by chance there came down a certain priest that way; and when he saw him, he passed by on the other side.
>
> And likewise a Levite, when he was at the place, came and looked on him, and passed by on the other side.
>
> But a certain Samaritan, as he journeyed, came where he was; and when he saw him he had compassion on him.
>
> And went to him, and bound up his wounds, pouring in oil and wine, and set him on his own beast, and brought him to an inn, and took care of him.
>
> And on the morrow, when he departed, he took out two pence, and gave them to the host, and said unto him, "Take care of him; and whatsoever thou spendest more, when I come again, I will repay thee."
>
> (Luke 10:30–35)

The Good Samaritan went out of his way, at somc cost to himself, to help one in necd of it. We are not told what the options were, that is, whether or not the priest and the Levite could have helped by doing less than the Good Samaritan did, but assuming they could have, then the fact they did nothing at all shows they were not even Minimally Decent Samaritans, not because they were not Samaritans, but because they were not even minimally decent.

39 These things are a matter of degree, of course, but there is a difference, and it comes out perhaps most clearly in the story of Kitty Genovese, who, as you will remember, was murdered while thirty-eight people watched or listened, and did nothing at all to help her. A Good Samaritan would have rushed out to give direct assistance against the murderer. Or perhaps we had better allow that it would have been a Splendid Samaritan who did this, on the ground that it would have involved a risk of death for himself. But the thirty-eight not only did not do this, they did not even trouble to pick up a phone to call the police. Minimally Decent Samaritanism would call for doing at least that, and their not having done it was monstrous.

40 After telling the story of the Good Samaritan, Jesus said, "Go, and do thou likewise." Perhaps he meant that we are morally required to act as the Good Samaritan did. Perhaps he was urging people to do more than is morally required of them. At all events it seems plain that it was not morally required of any of the thirty-eight that he rush out to give direct assistance at the risk of his own life, and that it is not morally required of anyone that he give long stretches of his life—nine years or nine months—to sustaining the life of a person who has no special right (we were leaving open the possibility of this) to demand it.

41 Indeed, with one rather striking class of exceptions, no one in any country in the world is *legally* required to do anywhere near as much as this for anyone else. The

class of exceptions is obvious. My main concern here is not the state of the law in respect to abortion, but it is worth drawing attention to the fact that in no state in this country is any man compelled by law to be even a Minimally Decent Samaritan to any person; there is no law under which charges could be brought against the thirty-eight who stood by while Kitty Genovese died. By contrast, in most states in this country women are compelled by law to be not merely Minimally Decent Samaritans, but Good Samaritans to unborn persons inside them. This doesn't by itself settle anything one way or the other, because it may well be argued that there should be laws in this country—as there are in many European countries—compelling at least Minimally Decent Samaritanism.[7] But it does show that there is a gross injustice in the existing state of the law. And it shows also that the groups currently working against liberalization of abortion laws, in fact working toward having it declared unconstitutional for a state to permit abortion, had better start working for the adoption of Good Samaritan laws generally, or earn the charge that they are acting in bad faith.

42 I should think, myself, that Minimally Decent Samaritan laws would be one thing, Good Samaritan laws quite another, and in fact highly improper. But we are not here concerned with the law. What we should ask is not whether anybody should be compelled by law to be a Good Samaritan, but whether we must accede to a situation in which somebody is being compelled—by nature, perhaps—to be a Good Samaritan. We have, in other words, to look now at third-party interventions. I have been arguing that no person is morally required to make large sacrifices to sustain the life of another who has no right to demand them, and this even where the sacrifices do not include life itself; we are not morally required to be Good Samaritans or anyway Very Good Samaritans to one another. But what if a man cannot extricate himself from such a situation? What if he appeals to us to extricate him? It seems to me plain that there are cases in which we can, cases in which a Good Samaritan would extricate him. There you are, you were kidnapped, and nine years in bed with that violinist lie ahead of you. You have your own life to lead. You are sorry, but you simply cannot see giving up so much of your life to the sustaining of his. You cannot extricate yourself, and ask us to do so. I should have thought that—in light of his having no right to the use of your body—it was obvious that we do not have to accede to your being forced to give up so much. We can do what you ask. There is no injustice to the violinist in our doing so.

43 **7.** Following the lead of the opponents of abortion, I have throughout been speaking of the fetus merely as a person, and what I have been asking is whether or not the argument we began with, which proceeds only from the fetus' being a person, really does establish its conclusion. I have argued that it does not.

44 But of course there are arguments and arguments, and it may be said that I have simply fastened on the wrong one. It may be said that what is important is not merely the fact that the fetus is a person, but that it is a person for whom the woman has a special kind of responsibility issuing from the fact that she is its mother. And it might be argued that all my analogies are therefore irrelevant—for you do not have that special kind of responsibility for that violinist, Henry Fonda does not have that special kind of

responsibility for me. And our attention might be drawn to the fact that men and women both *are* compelled by law to provide support for their children.

45 I have in effect dealt (briefly) with this argument in section 4 above; but a (still briefer) recapitulation now may be in order. Surely we do not have any such "special responsibility" for a person unless we have assumed it, explicitly or implicitly. If a set of parents do not try to prevent pregnancy, do not obtain an abortion, but rather take it home with them, then they have assumed responsibility for it, they have given it rights, and they cannot *now* withdraw support from it at the cost of its life because they now find it difficult to go on providing for it. But if they have taken all reasonable precautions against having a child, they do not simply by virtue of their biological relationship to the child who comes into existence have a special responsibility for it. They may wish to assume responsibility for it, or they may not wish to. And I am suggesting that if assuming responsibility for it would require large sacrifices, then they may refuse. A Good Samaritan would not refuse—or anyway, a Splendid Samaritan, if the sacrifices that had to be made were enormous. But then so would a Good Samaritan assume responsibility for that violinist; so would Henry Fonda, if he is a Good Samaritan, fly in from the West Coast and assume responsibility for me.

46 **8.** My argument will be found unsatisfactory on two counts by many of those who want to regard abortion as morally permissible. First, while I do argue that abortion is not impermissible, I do not argue that it is always permissible. There may well be cases in which carrying the child to term requires only Minimally Decent Samaritanism of the mother, and this is a standard we must not fall below. I am inclined to think it a merit of my account precisely that it does *not* give a general yes or a general no. It allows for and supports our sense that, for example, a sick and desperately frightened fourteen-year-old schoolgirl, pregnant due to rape, may of *course* choose abortion, and that any law which rules this out is an insane law. And it also allows for and supports our sense that in other cases resort to abortion is even positively indecent. It would be indecent in the woman to request an abortion, and indecent in a doctor to perform it, if she is in her seventh month, and wants the abortion just to avoid the nuisance of postponing a trip abroad. The very fact that the arguments I have been drawing attention to treat all cases of abortion, or even all cases of abortion in which the mother's life is not at stake, as morally on a par ought to have made them suspect at the outset.

47 Secondly, while I am arguing for the permissibility of abortion in some cases, I am not arguing for the right to secure the death of the unborn child. It is easy to confuse these two things in that up to a certain point in the life of the fetus it is not able to survive outside the mother's body; hence removing it from her body guarantees its death. But they are importantly different. I have argued that you are not morally required to spend nine months in bed, sustaining the life of that violinist; but to say this is by no means to say that if, when you unplug yourself, there is a miracle and he survives, you then have a right to turn around and slit his throat. You may detach yourself even if this costs him his life; you have no right to be guaranteed his death, by some other means, if unplugging yourself does not kill him. There are some people who will feel dissatisfied by this feature of my argument. A woman may be utterly devastated by the

thought of a child, a bit of herself, put out for adoption and never seen or heard of again. She may therefore want not merely that the child be detached from her, but more, that it die. Some opponents of abortion are inclined to regard this as beneath contempt—thereby showing insensitivity to what is surely a powerful source of despair. All the same, I agree that the desire for the child's death is not one which anybody may gratify, should it turn out to be possible to detach the child alive.

48 At this place, however, it should be remembered that we have only been pretending throughout that the fetus is a human being from the moment of conception. A very early abortion is surely not the killing of a person, and so is not dealt with by anything I have said here.

Notes

1. Daniel Callahan, *Abortion: Law, Choice and Morality* (New York, 1970), p. 373. This book gives a fascinating survey of the available information on abortion. The Jewish tradition in David M. Feldman, *Birth Control in Jewish Law* (New York, 1963), part 5; the Catholic tradition in John T. Noonan, Jr., "An Almost Absolute Value in History," in *The Morality of Abortion,* ed. John T. Noonan, Jr. (Cambridge, Mass., 1970).
2. The term "direct" in the arguments I refer to is a technical one. Roughly, what is meant by "direct killing" is either killing as an end in itself, or killing as a means to some end, for example, the end of saving someone else's life. See note 5 . . . for an example of its use.
3. Cf. *Encyclical Letter of Pope Pius XI on Christian Marriage,* St. Paul Editions (Boston, n.d.), p. 32: "However much we may pity the mother whose health and even life is gravely imperiled in the performance of the duty allotted to her by nature, nevertheless what could ever be a sufficient reason for excusing in any way the direct murder of the innocent? This is precisely what we are dealing with here." Noonan (*The Morality of Abortion,* p. 43) reads this as follows: "What cause can ever avail to excuse in any way the direct killing of the innocent? For it is a question of that."
4. The thesis in (4) is in an interesting way weaker than those in (1), (2), and (3): They rule out abortion even in cases in which both mother *and* child will die if the abortion is not performed. By contrast, one who held the view expressed in (4) could consistently say that one needn't prefer letting two persons die to killing one.
5. Cf. the following passage from Pius XII, *Address to the Italian Catholic Society of Midwives:* "The baby in the maternal breast has the right to life immediately from God.—Hence there is no man, no human authority, no science, no medical, eugenic, social, economic or moral "indication" which can establish or grant a valid juridical ground for a direct deliberate disposition of an innocent human life, that is a disposition which looks to its destruction either as an end or as a means to another end perhaps in itself not illicit.—The baby, still not born, is a man in the same degree and for the same reason as the mother" (quoted in Noonan, *The Morality of Abortion,* p. 45).
6. The need for a discussion of this argument was brought home to me by members of the Society for Ethical and Legal Philosophy, to whom this paper was originally presented.
7. For a discussion of the difficulties involved, and a survey of the European experience with such laws, see *The Good Samaritan and the Law,* ed. James M. Ratcliffe (New York, 1966).

Questions for Analysis

1. If Thomson does not believe that life begins at conception (that the fetus is a person from the moment the egg is fertilized), why does she argue in this essay as if it did?

2. Explain the analogy of the violinist. Is this analogy an effective way for Thomson to convey her arguments about the rights individuals have to determine how their bodies and lives are spent? Discuss.
3. Does Thomson argue that abortion is permissible in all cases? Explain her position and the distinction she makes between a Good Samaritan and a Minimally Decent Samaritan.
4. After such a long (and difficult) series of arguments to justify abortion in some cases, even if we assume that the fetus is a person from conception, what is the effect in the last paragraph of Thomson's saying "A very early abortion is surely not the killing of a person, and so is not dealt with by anything I have said here"?
5. At what point might strong *pro-choice* advocates take issue with Thomson's essay?

Ronald Reagan

Abortion and the Conscience of the Nation

(1984)

Elected President of the United States in 1981, Ronald Reagan (b. 1911) was a movie actor before becoming active in politics and serving two terms as Governor of California. The following piece was taken from his book *Abortion and the Conscience of the Nation,* published in 1984 by the Human Life Foundation.

1 The tenth anniversary of the Supreme Court decision in *Roe v. Wade* is a good time for us to pause and reflect. Our nationwide policy of abortion-on-demand through all nine months of pregnancy was neither voted for by our people nor enacted by our legislators—not a single state had such unrestricted abortion before the Supreme Court decreed it to be national policy in 1973. But the consequences of this judicial decision are now obvious: Since 1973, more than 15 million unborn children have had their lives snuffed out by legalized abortions. That is over ten times the number of Americans lost in all our nation's wars.

2 Make no mistake, abortion-on-demand is not a right granted by the Constitution. No serious scholar, including one disposed to agree with the Court's result, has argued that the framers of the Constitution intended to create such a right. Shortly after the *Roe v. Wade* decision, Professor John Hart Ely, now Dean of Stanford Law School, wrote that the opinion "is not constitutional law and gives almost no sense of an obligation to try to be." Nowhere do the plain words of the Constitution even hint at a "right" so sweeping as to permit abortion up to the time the child is ready to be born. Yet that is what the Court ruled.

3 As an act of ''raw judicial power'' (to use Justice White's biting phrase), the decision by the seven-man majority in *Roe v. Wade* has so far been made to stick. But the Court's decision has by no means settled the debate. Instead, *Roe v. Wade* has become a continuing prod to the conscience of the nation.

4 Abortion concerns not just the unborn child, it concerns every one of us. The English poet, John Donne, wrote: ''. . . any man's death diminishes me, because I am involved in mankind; and therefore never send to know for whom the bell tolls; it tolls for thee.''

5 We cannot diminish the value of one category of human life—the unborn—without diminishing the value of all human life. We saw tragic proof of this truism last year when the Indiana courts allowed the starvation death of ''Baby Doe'' in Bloomington because the child had Down's Syndrome.

6 Many of our fellow citizens grieve over the loss of life that has followed *Roe v. Wade.* Margaret Heckler, soon after being nominated to head the largest department of our government, Health and Human Services, told an audience that she believed abortion to be the greatest moral crisis facing our country today. And the revered Mother Teresa, who works in the streets of Calcutta ministering to dying people in her world-famous mission of mercy, has said that ''the greatest misery of our time is the generalized abortion of children.''

7 Over the first two years of my Administration I have closely followed and assisted efforts in Congress to reverse the tide of abortion—efforts of Congressmen, Senators and citizens responding to an urgent moral crisis. Regrettably, I have also seen the massive efforts of those who, under the banner of ''freedom of choice,'' have so far blocked every effort to reverse nationwide abortion-on-demand.

8 Despite the formidable obstacles before us, we must not lose heart. This is not the first time our country has been divided by a Supreme Court decision that denied the value of certain human lives. The *Dred Scott* decision of 1857 was not overturned in a day, or a year, or even a decade. At first, only a minority of Americans recognized and deplored the moral crisis brought about by denying the full humanity of our black brothers and sisters; but that minority persisted in their vision and finally prevailed. They did it by appealing to the hearts and minds of their countrymen, to the truth of human dignity under God. From their example, we know that respect for the sacred value of human life is too deeply engrained in the hearts of our people to remain forever suppressed. But the great majority of the American people have not yet made their voices heard, and we cannot expect them to—any more than the public voice arose against slavery—*until* the issue is clearly framed and presented.

9 What, then, is the real issue? I have often said that when we talk about abortion, we are talking about two lives—the life of the mother and the life of the unborn child. Why else do we call a pregnant woman a mother? I have also said that anyone who doesn't feel sure whether we are talking about a second human life should clearly give life the benefit of the doubt. If you don't know whether a body is alive or dead, you would never bury it. I think this consideration itself should be enough for all of us to insist on protecting the unborn.

10 The case against abortion does not rest here, however, for medical practice confirms at every step the correctness of these moral sensibilities. Modern medicine treats the unborn child as a patient. Medical pioneers have made great breakthroughs in treating the unborn—for genetic problems, vitamin deficiencies, irregular heart rhythms, and other medical conditions. Who can forget George Will's moving account of the little boy who underwent brain surgery six times during the nine weeks before he was born? Who is the *patient* if not that tiny unborn human being who can feel pain when he or she is approached by doctors who come to kill rather than to cure?

11 The real question today is not when human life begins, but, *What is the value of human life?* The abortionist who reassembles the arms and legs of a tiny baby to make sure all its parts have been torn from its mother's body can hardly doubt whether it is a human being. The real question for him and for all of us is whether that tiny human life has a God-given right to be protected by the law—the same right we have.

12 What more dramatic confirmation could we have of the real issue than the Baby Doe case in Bloomington, Indiana? The death of that tiny infant tore at the hearts of all Americans because the child was undeniably a live human being—one lying helpless before the eyes of the doctors and the eyes of the nation. The real issue for the courts was *not* whether Baby Doe was a human being. The real issue was whether to protect the life of a human being who had Down's Syndrome, who would probably be mentally handicapped, but who needed a routine surgical procedure to unblock his esophagus and allow him to eat. A doctor testified to the presiding judge that, even with his physical problem corrected, Baby Doe would have a ''nonexistent'' possibility for ''a minimally adequate quality of life''—in other words, that retardation was the equivalent of a crime deserving the death penalty. The judge let Baby Doe starve and die, and the Indiana Supreme Court sanctioned his decision.

13 Federal law does not allow federally assisted hospitals to decide that Down's Syndrome infants are not worth treating, much less to decide to starve them to death. Accordingly, I have directed the Departments of Justice and HHS to apply civil rights regulations to protect handicapped newborns. All hospitals receiving federal funds must post notices which will clearly state that failure to feed handicapped babies is prohibited by federal law.[1] The basic issue is whether to value and protect the lives of the handicapped, whether to recognize the sanctity of human life. This is the same basic issue that underlies the question of abortion.

14 The 1981 Senate hearings on the beginning of human life brought out the basic issue more clearly than ever before. The many medical and scientific witnesses who testified disagreed on many things, but not on the *scientific* evidence that the unborn child is alive, is a distinct individual, or is a member of the human species. They did disagree over the *value* question, whether to give value to a human life at its early and most vulnerable stages of existence.

1. AUTHOR'S NOTE: In a decision handed down June 9, 1986, the Supreme Court ruled that the federal government cannot regulate parental decisions concerning the treatment or nontreatment of severely handicapped newborns. For arguments on both sides of this issue, see the essays by Earl E. Shelp and C. Everett Koop in Part II of this text.

15 Regrettably, we live at a time when some persons do *not* value all human life. They want to pick and choose which individuals have value. Some have said that only those individuals with "consciousness of self" are human beings. One such writer has followed this deadly logic and concluded that "shocking as it may seem, a newly born infant is not a human being."

16 A Nobel Prize winning scientist has suggested that if a handicapped child "were not declared fully human until three days after birth, then all parents could be allowed the choice." In other words, "quality control" to see if newly born human beings are up to snuff.

17 Obviously, some influential people want to deny that every human life has intrinsic, sacred worth. They insist that a member of the human race must have certain qualities before they accord him or her status as a "human being."

18 Events have borne out the editorial in a California medical journal which explained three years before *Roe v. Wade* that the social acceptance of abortion is a "defiance of the long-held Western ethic of intrinsic and equal value for every human life regardless of its stage, condition, or status."

19 Every legislator, every doctor, and every citizen needs to recognize that the real issue is whether to affirm and protect the sanctity of all human life, or to embrace a social ethic where some human lives are valued and others are not. As a nation, we must choose between the sanctity of life ethic and the "quality of life" ethic.

20 I have no trouble identifying the answer our nation has always given to this basic question, and the answer that I hope and pray it will give in the future. America was founded by men and women who shared a vision of the value of each and every individual. They stated this vision clearly from the very start in the Declaration of Independence, using words that every schoolboy and schoolgirl can recite:

> We hold these truths to be self-evident, that all men are created equal, that they are endowed by their Creator with certain unalienable rights, that among these are life, liberty, and the pursuit of happiness.

21 We fought a terrible war to guarantee that one category of mankind—black people in America—could not be denied the inalienable rights with which their Creator endowed them. The great champion of the sanctity of all human life in that day, Abraham Lincoln, gave us his assessment of the Declaration's purpose. Speaking of the framers of that noble document, he said:

> This was their majestic interpretation of the economy of the Universe. This was their lofty, and wise, and noble understanding of the justice of the Creator to His creatures. Yes, gentlemen, to all His creatures, to the whole great family of man. In their enlightened belief, nothing stamped with the divine image and likeness was sent into the world to be trodden on. . . . They grasped not only the whole race of man then living, but they reached forward and seized upon the farthest

> posterity. They erected a beacon to guide their children and their children's children, and the countless myriads who should inhabit the earth in other ages.

He warned also of the danger we would face if we closed our eyes to the value of life in any category of human beings:

> I should like to know if taking this old Declaration of Independence, which declares that all men are equal upon principle and making exceptions to it where will it stop. If one man says it does not mean a Negro, why not another say it does not mean some other man?

22 When Congressman John A. Bingham of Ohio drafted the Fourteenth Amendment to guarantee the rights of life, liberty, and property to all human beings, he explained that *all* are ''entitled to the protection of American law, because its divine spirit of equality declares that all men are created equal.'' He said the rights guaranteed by the amendment would therefore apply to ''any human being.'' Justice William Brennan, writing in another case decided only the year before *Roe v. Wade,* referred to our society as one that ''strongly affirms the sanctity of life.''

23 Another William Brennan—not the Justice—has reminded us of the terrible consequences that can follow when a nation rejects the sanctity of life ethic:

> The cultural environment for a human holocaust is present whenever any society can be misled into defining individuals as less than human and therefore devoid of value and respect.

24 As a nation today, we have *not* rejected the sanctity of human life. The American people have not had an opportunity to express their view on the sanctity of human life in the unborn. I am convinced that Americans do not want to play God with the value of human life. It is not for us to decide who is worthy to live and who is not. Even the Supreme Court's opinion in *Roe v. Wade* did not explicitly reject the traditional American idea of intrinsic worth and value in all human life; it simply dodged this issue.

25 The Congress has before it several measures that would enable our people to reaffirm the sanctity of human life, even the smallest and the youngest and the most defenseless. The Human Life Bill expressly recognizes the unborn as human beings and accordingly protects them as persons under our Constitution. This bill, first introduced by Senator Jesse Helms, provided the vehicle for the Senate hearings in 1981 which contributed so much to our understanding of the real issue of abortion.

26 The Respect Human Life Act, just introduced in the 98th Congress, states in its first section that the policy of the United States is ''to protect innocent life, both before and after birth.'' This bill, sponsored by Congressman Henry Hyde and Senator Roger Jepsen, prohibits the federal government from performing abortions or assisting those who do so, except to save the life of the mother. It also addresses the pressing issue of

infanticide which, as we have seen, flows inevitably from permissive abortion as another step in the denial of the inviolability of innocent human life.

27 I have endorsed each of these measures, as well as the more difficult route of constitutional amendment, and I will give these initiatives my full support. Each of them, in different ways, attempts to reverse the tragic policy of abortion-on-demand imposed by the Supreme Court ten years ago. Each of them is a decisive way to affirm the sanctity of human life.

28 We must all educate ourselves to the reality of the horrors taking place. Doctors today know that unborn children can feel a touch within the womb and that they respond to pain. But how many Americans are aware that abortion techniques are allowed today, in all 50 states, that burn the skin of a baby with a salt solution, in an agonizing death that can last for hours?

29 Another example: two years ago, the *Philadelphia Inquirer* ran a Sunday special supplement on "The Dreaded Complication." The "dreaded complication" referred to in the article—the complication feared by doctors who perform abortions—is the *survival* of the child despite all the painful attacks during the abortion procedure. Some unborn children *do* survive the late-term abortions the Supreme Court has made legal. Is there any question that these victims of abortion deserve our attention and protection? Is there any question that those who *don't* survive were living human beings before they were killed?

30 Late-term abortions, especially when the baby survives, but is then killed by starvation, neglect, or suffocation, show once again the link between abortion and infanticide. The time to stop both is now. As my Administration acts to stop infanticide, we will be fully aware of the real issue that underlies the death of babies before and soon after birth.

31 Our society has, fortunately, become sensitive to the rights and special needs of the handicapped, but I am shocked that physical or mental handicaps of newborns are still used to justify their extinction. This Administration has a Surgeon General, Dr. C. Everett Koop [author of "Ethical and Surgical Considerations in the Care of the Newborn with Congenital Abnormalities" in Part II of this book], who has done perhaps more than any other American for handicapped children, by pioneering surgical techniques to help them, by speaking out on the value of their lives, and by working with them in the context of loving families. You will not find his former patients advocating the so-called "quality of life" ethic.

32 I know that when the true issue of infanticide is placed before the American people, with all the facts openly aired, we will have no trouble deciding that a mentally or physically handicapped baby has the same intrinsic worth and right to life as the rest of us. As the New Jersey Supreme Court said two decades ago, in a decision upholding the sanctity of human life, "a child need not be perfect to have a worthwhile life."

33 Whether we are talking about pain suffered by unborn children, or about late-term abortions, or about infanticide, we inevitably focus on the humanity of the unborn child. Each of these issues is a potential rallying point for the sanctity of life ethic. Once we

as a nation rally around any one of these issues to affirm the sanctity of life, we will see the importance of affirming this principle across the board.

34 Malcolm Muggeridge, the English writer, goes right to the heart of the matter: ''Either life is always and in all circumstances sacred, or intrinsically of no account; it is inconceivable that it should be in some cases the one, and in some the other.'' The sanctity of innocent human life is a principle that Congress should proclaim at every opportunity.

35 It is possible that the Supreme Court itself may overturn its abortion rulings. We need only recall that in *Brown v. Board of Education* the court reversed its own earlier ''separate-but-equal'' decision. I believe if the Supreme Court took another look at *Roe v. Wade,* and considered the real issue between the sanctity of life ethic and the quality of life ethic, it would change its mind once again.

36 As we continue to work to overturn *Roe v. Wade,* we must also continue to lay the groundwork for a society in which abortion is not the accepted answer to unwanted pregnancy. Pro-life people have already taken heroic steps, often at great personal sacrifice, to provide for unwed mothers. I recently spoke about a young pregnant woman named Victoria, who said, ''In this society we save whales, we save timber wolves and bald eagles and Coke bottles. Yet, everyone wanted me to throw away my baby.'' She has been helped by Sav-a-life, a group in Dallas, which provides a way for unwed mothers to preserve the human life within them when they might otherwise be tempted to resort to abortion. I think also of House of His Creation in Coatesville, Pennsylvania, where a loving couple has taken in almost 200 young women in the past ten years. They have seen, as a fact of life, that the girls are *not* better off having abortions than saving their babies. I am also reminded of the remarkable Rossow family of Ellington, Connecticut, who have opened their hearts and their home to nine handicapped adopted and foster children.

37 The Adolescent Family Life Program, adopted by Congress at the request of Senator Jeremiah Denton, has opened new opportunities for unwed mothers to give their children life. We should not rest until our entire society echoes the tone of John Powell in the dedication of his book, *Abortion: The Silent Holocaust,* a dedication to every woman carrying an unwanted child: ''Please believe that you are not alone. There are many of us that truly love you, who want to stand at your side, and help in any way we can.'' And we can echo the always-practical woman of faith, Mother Teresa, when she says, ''If you don't want the little child, that unborn child, give him to me.'' We have so many families in America seeking to adopt children that the slogan ''every child a wanted child'' is now the emptiest of all reasons to tolerate abortion.

38 I have often said we need to join in prayer to bring protection to the unborn. Prayer and action are needed to uphold the sanctity of human life. I believe it will not be possible to accomplish our work, the work of saving lives, ''without being a soul of prayer.'' The famous British Member of Parliament, William Wilberforce, prayed with his small group of influential friends, the ''Clapham Sect,'' for *decades* to see an end to slavery in the British empire. Wilberforce led that struggle in Parliament, unflag-

gingly, because he believed in the sanctity of human life. He saw the fulfillment of his impossible dream when Parliament outlawed slavery just before his death.

39 Let his faith and perseverance be our guide. We will never recognize the true value of our own lives until we affirm the value in the life of others, a value of which Malcolm Muggeridge says: "... however low it flickers or fiercely burns, it is still a Divine flame which no man dare presume to put out, be his motives ever so humane and enlightened."

40 Abraham Lincoln recognized that we could not survive as a free land when some men could decide that others were not fit to be free and should therefore be slaves. Likewise, we cannot survive as a free nation when some men decide that others are not fit to live and should be abandoned to abortion or infanticide. My Administration is dedicated to the preservation of America as a free land, and there is no cause more important for preserving that freedom than affirming the transcendent right to life of all human beings; the right without which no other rights have any meaning.

Questions for Analysis

1. Although Reagan opposes the decision in *Roe v. Wade* (1973) and thus, by implication, all abortions, the examples he uses most often involve late-term fetuses or newborn infants (e.g., Baby Doe). Why does he do this? Is there a difference between an early-term fetus and a newborn, full-term baby?
2. In Paragraph 5, Reagan asserts that allowing abortion "diminish[es] the value of all human life." Do you agree with this conclusion?
3. In several places Reagan uses Mother Teresa as an authority to support his view on abortion and his repeated assertion that all human life is sacred. Explain his rhetorical strategy. While he was Governor of California and later as President, Reagan was a strong supporter of the death penalty. Is this position consistent with his stance on abortion? What do you think Mother Teresa would say?
4. Explain the distinction Reagan makes in Paragraph 19 between "the sanctity of life ethic and the 'quality of life' ethic."
5. In his discussion Reagan does not deal with what other writers call the "hard cases" (other than a very few references to handicapped infants) nor does he consider what rights a woman has over her body. Do these omissions help or hurt his argument?
6. In Paragraphs 36 and 37, Reagan mentions several agencies and individuals who help unwed mothers and unwanted children. What is the purpose of these paragraphs? Can these organizations and these individuals take care of all the unwanted children? What problems does Reagan overlook?
7. How would other writers in this section respond to Reagan's position? Consider especially Thomson, Kissling, and Wattleton.

Commonweal

Too Many Abortions

(1989)

Commonweal is a periodical sponsored by the Roman Catholic Church. This editorial appeared in the issue of August 11, 1989.

1 One-and-a-half million abortions a year is a national scandal. Most of these abortions fall outside even the broadest reading of our prevailing ethic that allows taking the life of an assailant in self-defense or the defense of another, that condemns to death individuals guilty of capital crimes, or that authorizes the killing of combatants in time of war or a just revolution. That much we allow the police, the courts, and the armed forces. Physicians and women are allowed greater latitude when it comes to the fetus. That's the law; but it is not moral.

2 The law rests on the Supreme Court's 1973 decision in *Roe v. Wade,* which ruled that most state laws restricting abortion were a violation of the personal liberty protected by the due process clause of the Fourteenth Amendment. Almost without exception subsequent Court decisions offered the broadest possible interpretation favoring abortion and limiting restrictions. Now many people think the Court's latest abortion decision, *Webster v. Reproductive Health Services,* will shift the balance in the opposite direction.

3 We are not so sure. First, the Court has not dismantled *Roe.* Second, whatever the law, there is an abortion ethic so deeply rooted in our culture that overturning or narrowing *Roe* may have minimal effect on the number of abortions. What was once unthinkable has become thinkable; indeed, as time passes, the abortion decision is increasingly treated as one almost not worth thinking about at all. A change in law will mean little without a transformation of minds and hearts.

4 One might argue that *Roe* engendered this abortion ethic—this unique exception to our general prohibition of killing innocent others. But in rereading *Roe,* it is hard to find the hard-edged thinking or absolutist language that has come to characterize the way we now speak individually and as a polity on the subject. For example, "abortion on demand" and "the absolute right to privacy" are catchphrases we hear often and loudly, phrases pro-choicers defend and against which pro-lifers rail. But back in 1973, the Court wrote: "Appellants . . . argue that the woman's right is absolute and that she is entitled to terminate her pregnancy at whatever time, in whatever way, and for whatever reason she alone chooses. With this we do not agree." The Court went on: "[T]he right of personal privacy includes the abortion decision, but . . . this right is not unqualified and must be considered against important state interests in regulation." Nor was the decision the woman's alone: "All these are factors [in the abortion decision] the woman and her responsible physician necessarily will consider in consultation." It is

not hard to find in these words justification for viability testing at twenty weeks as the Court did in upholding the Missouri law, or, for that matter, for upholding certain counseling and informed consent procedures that were not at issue in *Webster.*

5 We do not return to *Roe* in order to defend it; its usurpation of the political process in 1973 in favor of judicial fiat is indefensible. And if *Webster* is the prelude to a full, rational, political consideration of abortion at the state level, it is indeed welcome. But we harbor an unhappy premonition that it is not. While the Supreme Court teases the nation with a patch-work process of allowing some restrictions and turning down others, the acrimonious scramble for influence in fifty state houses and state legislatures by pro-life and pro-choice forces will be poisonous to our whole political system. Even worse, as we have suggested above, it is unlikely to help restore a moral perspective of a kind that will help actually to reduce the number of abortions, some of which, under the new dispensation, will be performed illegally. It is indeed a struggle for the minds and hearts of women—and men.

6 The best, but most difficult, place to begin is with the claim that the fetus is not nothing. *Roe* concluded that the fetus is not considered a ''person'' under the Fourteenth Amendment, and further on it declined to ''resolve the difficult question of when life begins.'' In most adult humans there arises a sound intuition that somewhere between the period of conception and implantation and a later period when the developing fetus has every aspect of a human being, this is a human being, a human being worthy of protection—and perhaps that sense is nowhere more fully developed than in the pregnant woman herself. Most of us would offer a seat on a crowded train to a pregnant woman; many would offer help if she collapsed on a street or rush to her aid if she was endangered by a speeding car or threatened with a beating. It is not just her comfort or her life that is at stake, but the life of another, our immediate sense is not of one human being deserving of protection, but two. The more obviously pregnant a woman is, the more surely we draw that conclusion. The fetus is something.

7 But so is the woman. And it is the woman contemplating an abortion who must be convinced that the fetus is something, indeed at a certain point becomes someone. Implanting and supporting this conviction has two possible starting points. The most immediate: A pregnant woman considering abortion should receive counseling that fully describes for her what we now know about fetuses and their development; if it is to be an abortion at eight weeks or at twelve weeks, she should see what such a fetus looks like and know its stage of development. Responsible counseling would also offer viable alternatives to the woman if she cannot raise the child; indeed a positive ethic of adoption and the ability of social workers to provide a woman with a serious adoption plan ought to be part of the counseling process. Does that unduly burden the abortion decision as the Court has previously ruled? Perhaps. But it is a burden that the gravity of an abortion decision warrants.

8 Another and more distant starting point for building the conviction that the fetus deserves maternal consideration and protection lies with a fuller development of the feminist insight that women themselves must take responsibility for their lives, the choices they make, their relationships with others—parallel to the kind of responsibility

men must also exercise. Moral agency entails a kind of autonomy, self-esteem, and responsibility in which women and men act instead of merely being acted upon. Feminist thought has generally treated the abortion decision as part and parcel of that exercise of autonomy, self-esteem, and responsibility, but the decision for abortion can be read in the opposite way.

9 Except in extreme cases, the decision to have an abortion can simply be the end point in a series of events in which a woman has failed to take responsibility for her sexual life and become pregnant in a situation in which no family life is possible, or she has allowed herself to be sexually exploited by a man who has no intention of sharing in the care of a child. This starting point for stemming the number of abortions depends on women becoming reproductively responsible moral agents by either saying no to men who will not or cannot share the responsibilities of parenthood or by women becoming effective users of contraception. This is not an ethic that fully expresses the Christian vision of human love, or the care that men and women should express toward one another. But it is a better ethic than the one now expressed in one-and-a-half million abortions. Pro-choice and pro-life advocates, at their best and most sensitive, recognize this: They see that along with the unborn no less victims of this dismal ethic are the women who have abortions. If the coming political struggle can be built on the sense that there are too many abortions, that women and fetuses alike are victims of a shabby ethic, then it will be a struggle that will end not only in better laws, but in a more tolerable moral standard.

Questions for Analysis

1. In Paragraph 3, the editors of *Commonweal* say that "whatever the law, there is an abortion ethic so deeply rooted in our culture that overturning or narrowing *Roe* may have minimal effect on the number of abortions." What is the ethic they have in mind? How would these editors say this ethic was generated?
2. Do the editors of *Commonweal* believe that the *Roe* v. *Wade* decision was good? Do they think it was legal?
3. Would you agree that the presentation in Paragraphs 8–9 assigns reproductive responsibility principally to women and implies that they must bear not only responsibility but blame if an abortion is necessary? Does this stance sound biased? Is it fair?
4. Reread the last paragraph in this editorial. Based on it and the opinions expressed earlier in the editorial, try to write in your own words the position the editors of *Commonweal* have taken.

Frances Kissling

Ending the Abortion War: A Modest Proposal

(1990)

Frances Kissling (b. 1943) is president of the Washington, DC-based organization Catholics for a Free Choice. This essay appeared in the February 21, 1990, issue of *The Christian Century* along with several other essays on abortion.

1 As we enter the 1990s with modest hopes for world peace, a particularly bitter and seemingly intractable domestic war continues unabated. The U.S. Supreme Court decision in *Webster v. Reproductive Health Services* has mobilized armies of supporters and opponents of legal abortion.

2 Explicitly, the court let stand a provision of a Missouri law that required testing to determine fetal viability in pregnancies of 20 weeks duration and longer (it should be noted that no such tests exist). The court further curtailed poor women's ability to choose abortion by substantially expanding its prior rulings on public funding. It ruled that states are free to prohibit abortions at any health-care facility that receives any public funding. Even private doctors who perform abortions on private patients with private funds will be affected by the ruling if their admission privileges happen to be at a hospital that receives public money or has contractual arrangements with state or local governments.

3 In a move troubling to most religious groups, the court also let stand the preamble to the Missouri law, which declared that life begins at conception, saying that the preamble represented a permissible value judgment by the state that would have no effect on the legality of abortion.

4 Implicitly, the five-justice plurality opinion warned that the court would no longer apply strict scrutiny to limitations on a woman's right to choose abortion. No longer would legislatures or regulatory bodies need to show a compelling state interest in order to intervene in women's decisions. The decision was interpreted by those who favor and those who oppose legal abortion as an open invitation to state legislatures to enact restrictive legislation designed to test further and possibly overturn *Roe*.

5 Both sides responded aggressively and passionately. Faye Wattleton, president of the Planned Parenthood Federation of America, declared, "Make no mistake about it. This is war." Kate Michelman, director of the National Abortion Rights Action League, told elected officials, "Take our rights, lose your jobs." Randall Terry, leader of the controversial Operation Rescue, said: "We're calling on thousands of pro-life Americans to peacefully blockade these killing centers with their bodies to prevent children from dying and we will launch an equal force against state legislatures to chip away at *Roe*." (By quoting Terry alongside Wattleton and Michelman, I do not mean to imply

any philosophical or strategic equivalence in their viewpoints or actions. It is simply that these were the voices most frequently heard and quoted in the last half of 1989).

6 By any reasonable measure, so far, my side, the side that favors legal abortion, is winning the war. On the electoral front, not only have candidates like Governor Douglas Wilder (Virginia) and Governor James Florio (New Jersey) made their pro-choice positions central to a winning strategy, but politicians considered pro-life are defecting to the pro-choice camp daily.

7 Perhaps more significant—and substantial—is that pro-choicers have partially shifted the terms of the debate from the question of whose rights will prevail, the woman's or the fetus's, to who will decide, women or the government. This is not to say that questions of rights or of the moral value of fetal life are insignificant in evaluating the act of abortion. However, to claim that the central conflict in the debate is between women and fetuses incorrectly and unfortunately casts a woman as the adversary of the fetus and in no way acknowledges her role as moral agent. Moreover, in light of the growing attempt to subordinate individual rights to a somewhat undefined "community," even opponents of legal abortion should exercise caution in making rights arguments paramount. In framing the question "who decides?" NARAL has moved subtly from the concept of "choice," a principle that has come to be seen as related to the trivial or selfish, to the concept of "decision making," which implies greater seriousness and complexity.

8 *Webster's* threat to legal abortion has also significantly increased the number of organizations, generally liberal to progressive, adding abortion to their portfolio of issues. The pro-choice coalition is bigger, stronger, more cohesive and better financed than ever before. It is convinced that given enough time and money it has the capacity to build the political machine necessary to win the war and preserve *Roe.*

9 Pro-life leaders, while stung by the losses of 1989, are equally committed to the long war and will surely win some victories in the next (or some subsequent) foray into the courts or state legislatures. The Catholic bishops have re-entered the political arena with a bang, declaring abortion—not the degradation of the planet, the economy or racism—their number one concern. Catholic legislators got a hint of the kind of political muscle the bishops are prepared to use when Bishop Leo T. Maher of San Diego announced in the midst of a special election for the California state senate that candidate Lucy Killea could no longer receive communion in the Roman Catholic Church because of her pro-choice position. Catholic legislators in Montana, Rhode Island, Washington, Connecticut and Minnesota have reported that their bishops have warned them that public pro-choice positions create "problems" for the church. With 28 professional statewide lobbying offices from Hartford to Sacramento, the bishops have a political machine capable of seriously restricting *Roe* at the state level.

10 How all this hardball political gamesmanship and bellicosity will contribute to sound, stable public policy on abortion remains to be seen. If the past 20 years are any model for the next 20, we can expect abortion to remain both an issue that is ideologically shaped and a problem that is unsolved.

11 One would hope, however, that this new moment in the abortion debate could be seen not only as a time of crisis by those of us who are pro-choice (and I speak only to that group, having neither the right nor the interest to suggest a course of action for the opposition) but as an opportunity to examine our own beliefs in light of the signs of the times and the experience of 17 years of legal abortion. Perhaps it is time, as one good friend so aptly put it, for those of us who are pro-choice to "take the high dive"; that is, to resist the temptation to think and act in 30-second sound bites and engage instead in serious moral discourse on abortion.

12 Perhaps we need to listen to the wisdom of more than 50 percent of our population. They hold in creative tension a basic sense of fair play in wanting women, with consultation, to make the decision about abortion or childbirth and a concern for the value of fetal life and the quality of women's decisions. Only then will we be in a position to advocate public policy that respects each individual woman and expresses our concern for human life and the community at large.

13 Abortion is not fundamentally a political question; it deals with people's deepest, most unconscious feelings about life, the power of creation and the survival of our species. Those in the so-called "muddled middle" understand this better than those at either end of the public opinion spectrum. They understand abortion—and reproduction—as both a private and a social phenomenon. They wait for one side or the other to answer such questions as: "How will we bring new life onto this planet?" "How will we treat the rest of life?" These elements are not unconnected. Just as we challenge pro-lifers to care about more than prenatal life, so must we challenge ourselves to talk about more than the life that is here. We must also talk with reverence of the life that is to come. Most important, this conversation cannot be viewed as a threat to the rights of women, but as an enhancement of the responsible exercise of those rights. We must not let our own justifiable fear of the opposition shape the dialogue.

14 Concretely, we must stop criticizing moderate pro-choice voices: public officials (like Governor Mario Cuomo) who speak of the "tragedy" of abortion; columnists (like Anna Quindlen of the *New York Times*) who express concerns about late-term abortions; and theologians (like Giles Milhaven of Brown University) who speak of women's sadness after abortion. All contribute a richness of spirit to the debate that needs to be encouraged, not crushed.

15 Our own inability to acknowledge the tragedy of abortion makes us suspect. Our continuous talk about *wanted* children does not inspire confidence but fear. We live in a world where our value is increasingly equated with wealth, brilliance or success. Many rightly perceive that they are powerless and unwanted. For the powerless, the fetus is a ready symbol of their own vulnerability—a symbol exploited by right-wing leaders.

16 Acknowledging fetal life as valuable and as an important factor in decision making about abortion need not be linked to a specific religious doctrine. The Christian respect for life has never required the absolute protection of life. It does not require conferring personhood or rights on the fetus, nor does it suggest limiting the legal rights of women to decide whether to bring new life into the world or to have an abortion.

17 On the other hand, an enhanced sense of the value of fetal life should move us beyond the status quo on abortion and beyond an absolutist interpretation of the fundamental rights articulated in *Roe v. Wade.* On both principled and practical grounds, pro-choice advocates need to see *Roe* as a framework for good policy on abortion, not as a fortress against policy.

18 By no means should the pro-choice movement abandon, at this time, the rights framework implicit in *Roe.* Given the unrelentingly punitive, hostile approach to women in our society, we continue to need the strongest legal protection available to enable our full and equal participation in society. This includes legal control over fertility.

19 An equally compelling reason for maintaining a rights framework is the unprecedented assault on individual rights mounted by the Reagan administration. Individual rights for women are inseparable from individual rights for people of color. Efforts in both progressive and conservative circles (from Stanley Hauerwas to George Will) to portray individual rights as a threat to the community must be resisted. Individual rights, once they include women and people of color, are a threat not to the whole community but to the community of white men.

20 A theory of community that places unequal burdens on women in welcoming and respecting new life is inherently unjust and doomed to fail. That injustice is obvious in our society and while lip service is paid to sharing the burden, there is little evidence that the architects of communitarian models or their admirers are moving toward a concrete embodiment of equality and responsibility.

21 Individual rights cannot, however, be slavishly pursued. Even the most fundamental rights are regulated under the Constitution. Many of us support even more regulation for any number of rights, such as the right to bear arms. Pro-choice advocates—not just those whose goal is prohibition—need to explore regulations that will enhance women's decision making in a manner that respects fetal life without making protection of fetal life absolute. (At the same time, we must strongly reject policy measures whose only purpose is to limit or prohibit access to legal abortion.) We must see that such regulations, once enacted, are enforced scrupulously and noncoercively and that penalties for deliberately misinforming, coercing or unfairly influencing a woman's ability to make good decisions are promulgated and used.

22 Finally, all regulations need to be looked at individually and cumulatively to ensure that they do not prevent the poor or people of color from exercising their right to act as decision makers. Walter Dellinger, professor of law at Duke University, pointed out recently in the *University of Pennsylvania Law Review:*

> A 48-hour waiting period, for example, may not be an "undue burden" for affluent professional women, and a hospitalization requirement may only serve to make her abortion more expensive. But for an 18-year-old girl in the rural South, unmarried, pregnant, hoping to finish school and build a decent life, who has little or no access to transportation, a hospitalization requirement can mean an abortion that will cost nearly $1,000 and involve a trip of hundreds of miles;

a waiting period can mean two long trips and an overnight stay in a strange and distant city. For such a woman, the burden would be absolute.

23 While it is premature to move from a brief exposition of some of the principles needed to inform public policy initiatives on abortion to a recommendation of specific measures, the state legislative season is upon us. Many legislators and advocates will not stop to reflect before running headlong to pass new laws. And it is important, as many rush to the "middle" on abortion, that those who seek to be consensus-builders or compromisers be held to a high standard of specificity. What do we think policy on abortion should be? Are we really listening to the middle or simply attempting to co-opt it?

24 Here, then, are some immediate guidelines and specific elements of a sound, stable public policy that can be implemented now and contribute to a balanced, long-term approach to the issue.

25 First, abortion laws need to acknowledge women's right—and need—to make reproductive health decisions free from coercion, as well as both women's and society's responsibility to create conditions for women to bring life into the world.

26 Either in the body of the law or by reference to other existing legislation, the community's reverence for life should be expressed in support of social and economic programs for children and families. A good model for this can be found in the legislative program of the Children's Defense Fund.

27 The balance between women's rights and reverence for life is best expressed by making resources available to assist women in good decision making and in preventing pregnancy. We should advocate a series of initiatives that signal government *involvement* as opposed to *intervention.* Among them: funding for voluntary nondirective, comprehensive and confidential counseling services for women and their partners who are contemplating abortion (no funds should be made available to groups that favor one decision over the other or that preclude any legal option from the range of choices offered); funding for more measures designed to prevent pregnancy, including contraceptive research and testing as well as contraceptive education and services; and equitably distributing funds for adoption, abortion, childbearing and child rearing.

28 These funding proposals represent a major shift in policy and would be a significant compromise for both sides of the debate. Pro-choice advocates will need to accept greater government involvement as an expression of community consensus; in turn, the community, through the government, will need to back up its involvement with resources.

29 Among the particularly thorny issues confronting legislatures this year are requirements for parental consent for minors' abortions, prohibitions on gender selection and postviability abortions, and so-called informed consent statutes. Critical to the pro-choice movement's ability to forge consensus on the general question of legal abortion will be its ability to respond rationally and concretely to these issues. Up to now, a fundamental rights approach and our fear of the "slippery slope" has led us to reject

outright all regulation in these areas. But a blanket No is simply not a sufficient response to these complex questions.

30 In the case of parental consent requirements, we need to acknowledge young women's special need for adult involvement. Indeed, we want to protect teens from either coercive abortion or coercive childbearing. Form letters mailed to parents do not adequately or effectively discharge our obligation to these women. Neither does the absence of policy.

31 Provisions for nondirective, confidential counseling by health-care workers, ministers and other qualified professionals would enhance decision making, and a record of such counseling could be kept as part of the medical file. Statutes similar to that passed in Maine, which demand involvement by a parent—or, when that is inappropriate, an adult family member, minister, teacher or counselor—should be applauded.

32 While there is no evidence that some women seek abortions solely for gender selection, pro-lifers have seized on this possibility as a convenient and gruesome example of the extremes to which abortion liberty will drive us. But in fact the devaluation of women in society is the cause of gender-selection abortion. The few reports of abortion in which gender was a factor point to those communities, primarily Asian and African, where male children are still considered a necessity. Indeed, in Africa a woman is called infertile if she does not produce boys, while some Asian wives are abused and abandoned. As odious as I would find the practice of gender selection even in these hard cases, I would be loathe to take responsibility for any prohibition that could cost these women dearly.

33 However, the notion that women would seek abortions in the mid to late second trimester because the nursery is painted blue or hubby's family has had firstborn boys for generations is ludicrous. It really deserves no response. It also deserves no defense. I would seek no laws to prevent that which does not happen, but I would not oppose such laws. This is an area for self-regulation, and one hopes that responsible providers of abortion would decline their services in such cases.

34 In a similar vein, I think the question of postviability abortions is of little practical significance and of enormous symbolic importance. In practice, it is extremely difficult to find a physician who will perform such abortions unless there is a serious, physical, life-threatening condition for the woman or the fetus is diagnosed with profound abnormalities. There is no evidence that the right to such abortions is necessary for women's well-being or full participation in society. These facts, combined with the growing sense that fetal life deserves increasing respect as it develops should lead pro-choice advocates to accept legislation limiting postviability abortions to life-threatening or disabling cases.

35 Another frequently cited set of regulations on abortions are those requiring "informed consent." Up to now, the court has struck down such measures. In the post-*Webster* climate they will once again be raised. Without exception, all past informed consent laws were drafted by opponents of legal abortion—not to assist in good decision making but to prevent abortion. The information mandated was often biased, inaccurate and simplistic: "life begins at conception," "the heart beats at eight weeks," "abortion

is dangerous and will make you sterile.'' Nondirective counseling is far more appropriate and respectful of women's capacity to make good decisions than existing informed consent approaches. Moreover, I cannot stress too strongly my belief that if the government is to be involved in the process of women's decision making, those who are entrusted with helping women need to be held to the highest standard of care.

36 For those whose interest is in outlawing abortion, the rather modest shift in both laws and values set forth here offers little. In the short run, these policy measures will not reduce the current number of abortions, which is troubling. It is important, however, that we not reduce abortion policy and values to a numbers game. The goal of caring people—eliminating all abortions—will require a radical transformation of society. We should focus our efforts on correcting the disease, not the symptom.

Questions for Analysis

1. Toward the beginning of her essay Kissling uses military words and phrases such as ''war,'' ''armies,'' ''winning the war,'' ''the pro-choice camp,'' ''victories,'' and so forth. Why does she use these words? Do they reflect her own attitudes?
2. One of Kissling's objectives in her essay is to encourage those speaking and writing about abortion to shift their grounds of argument and the terms they use. Several are listed below. Explain how each changes the nature of the debate, and assess the effect of each change based on your own opinions and those you have encountered:
   –The shift from whose rights will prevail, the woman's or the fetus's, to whose right is it to decide, the woman's or the government's;
   –The shift from the concept of ''choice'' to the concept of ''decision making'';
   –The shift from government intervention to government involvement.
3. One of Kissling's main points is that those who advocate abortions should ''resist the temptation to think and act in 30-second sound bites and engage instead in serious moral discourse on abortion'' (Paragraph 11). What would this discourse entail? In what ways might this discourse lead to moderation of extreme pro-choice positions? How might it lead to moderation of extreme antiabortion positions?
4. Although she does consider herself on the pro-choice side, Kissling does not allow that all abortions are moral or right. In what situations does she see moral problems? Would she advocate legislation to deal with these situations? Why or why not?
5. How would other authors in this section respond to Kissling's position?

Faye Wattleton

Reproductive Rights Are Fundamental Rights

(1991)

Faye Wattleton (b. 1943) was president of the Planned Parenthood Federation of America for over 12 years and in that capacity was one of the more outspoken pro-choice advocates. This essay, first published in *The Humanist,* was adapted from a speech presented by Ms. Wattleton to the International Platform Association when she accepted the 1990 Claude Pepper Humanitarian Award.

1 Today, the reproductive rights of women are imperiled as never before. In July 1989—16 years after *Roe* v. *Wade* recognized women's constitutional right to abortion—the Supreme Court retreated from that historic ruling. It cleared the way for laws that victimize poor women seeking abortions. And in two subsequent rulings in June 1990, the Court invited restrictions on teenagers' access to abortion.

2 It's easy to recognize *exactly* what the anti-choice zealots are doing. By attacking society's most vulnerable targets—the poor and the young—the anti-choice extremists are chipping away at the reproductive rights of *all* women. Plainly put, the recent Supreme Court rulings invite state governments to put fetuses first. And radicals in every state are trying to do just that. More than 200 anti-choice bills have been introduced in state legislatures since July 1989. Fortunately, the reenergized pro-choice majority has defeated most of them. But in Guam and Pennsylvania, extremists have pushed through bills that would virtually *abolish* legal abortion. And they're still trying in Louisiana.

3 Eventually, one of these laws (or a similar one) will bring this battle back to the Supreme Court—a Court that now teeters on the verge of radical imbalance. Already, four justices are ready to undermine *Roe* v. *Wade,* and President Bush is hoping for the critical fifth vote. He *claims* his choice of Judge David Souter had nothing to do with abortion rights. But only time will tell whether Judge Souter will uphold *all* our cherished constitutional rights.

4 Historically, we have counted on the Supreme Court to expand rights that were not explicit in the Constitution—rights for women, minorities, children, and the disabled. But today's Reagan-packed courts interpret the Constitution the way fundamentalists interpret the Bible—with a stubborn literalism. If a right wasn't spelled out by that first quill pen, it doesn't exist! In other words, "If you don't see it on the shelf, we don't carry it—and we won't order it!"

5 Step by horrifying step, our government is commandeering control of our bodies, our reproduction, our most private choices. Unless we act now, this dangerous trend won't stop at abortion. It won't even stop at eliminating contraception. Compulsory

pregnancy, forced caesareans, surveillance and detention of pregnant women—these are the chilling, *logical* outcome of laws that reduce women to instruments of the state.

6 If you think I'm being an alarmist, look at the history of Romania under Nicolae Ceaucescu. To boost the birthrate, the dictator banned contraception *and* abortion. Over time, birthrates were virtually unchanged—but the maternal death rate skyrocketed. Nearly 1,000 Romanian women died *each year* from illegal abortions—and those are just the ones who went to hospitals. Countless others, terrified of the law, chose to die at home. Today, in Bucharest alone, up to *30,000* women await hospital treatment for abortion complications. And *40,000* babies have been left orphaned or abandoned. This is the grisly legacy of a state that tried to control its citizens' reproduction. Women are *not* instruments of the state—in Romania, in the United States, or anywhere else in the world. We are *persons,* with human needs and human rights. Without reproductive autonomy, our other rights are meaningless. Our dignity is destroyed. And the first victims will be those among us who are already most vulnerable, those whose rights are already precarious, those whose access to health care is already limited: the young and the poor. And that usually means minorities.

7 But reproductive freedom is an issue that goes beyond the disadvantaged, beyond state boundaries, and far beyond abortion itself. It goes to the heart of what this country stands for: to the principles embodied in our Bill of Rights. The authors of that great document and its great defenders—such as Daniel Webster, Claude Pepper, and William Brennan—knew that certain fundamental freedoms must be *guaranteed*—insulated from public debate and immune to partisan politics.

8 For over 200 years, America has been "a light unto the nations." How disgraceful that, as the Berlin Wall came down and the Iron Curtain parted, the only barricade that began to crumble in *this* country was the precious wall protecting our private freedoms!

9 Those fundamental freedoms are the proudest heritage of our nation. But our heritage of Puritanism also remains deeply rooted. As a nineteenth-century humorist said, "The Puritans fled from a land of despotism to a land of freedom—where they could not only enjoy their own religion but where they could prevent everybody else from enjoying theirs!"

10 The flames of intolerance still burn brightly in this nation. And, like all fanatics, *today's* Puritans subscribe to their own moral code—a code that embraces far more brutality than morality. To "save lives," they burn clinics. To "defend womanhood," they taunt and threaten pregnant women. To "strengthen the family," they invade our privacy. Blinded by their disregard for the neediest of women, they insist that making abortion harder to get will make it go away.

11 Haven't these zealots learned *anything* from history? Throughout time, women with unwanted pregnancies have always ended them, regardless of the law, regardless of the risk to their lives. Throughout the world, women *and* men equate freedom and democracy with the right to make private reproductive decisions free from government intrusion!

12 Again, Romania provides a perfect example. When Ceaucescu was overthrown, two of the first acts of the new government were to decriminalize abortion and to deregulate

the private ownership of typewriters. The new regime clearly recognized that reproductive choice is as *fundamental* as freedom of speech.

13 If only our own government were so wise. On the contrary, our president has taken a jackhammer to the bedrock of our basic rights. He has repeatedly asked the Supreme Court to overturn *Roe* v. *Wade.* He has attacked the federal family planning program, which helps *prevent* half a million abortions each year. And in a recent Supreme Court brief, his administration attacked not only the right to abortion but the very concept of privacy that underlies our right to contraception!

14 It's nothing short of obscene that women are forced to expose themselves to politicians—to submit our private matters, our private decisions, and our private parts to *public* debate! Surely, America's politicians have more important things to do—like house the homeless, feed the hungry, and educate the ignorant. Like tackle the root cause of the abortion issue: unintended pregnancy.

15 Instead of compulsory ignorance, we need comprehensive education on human sexuality—in every home and in every school, from kindergarten through twelfth grade. Instead of laws that punish pregnant women, we need our government's commitment to develop better birth control. Instead of pontifications about the unborn, we need proper care for the children already born.

16 Finally, instead of state control of our reproduction, we need to be left alone by the government. We need to remove the abortion issue *forever* from the legislative arena. *We need a universal recognition that our civil liberties are off-limits to partisan debate!*

17 Our advocacy is vital to making these ideals a reality. Every one of us can and *must* make a difference. We must start at home, talking openly and often with our children about sexuality. We must activate our communities, promoting comprehensive sexuality education in local schools. We must activate our colleagues and return reproductive rights to their proper context. These are profound ethical, religious, and philosophical questions—to be debated and decided by individuals and families, *never* by politicians.

18 Finally, we must activate our elected officials—write to them, call them, lobby them. Tell them to stay out of our bedrooms and out of our family affairs! Tell them again and again that our reproductive rights are fundamental rights! Indivisible rights! *Non-negotiable* rights!

Questions for Analysis

1. At the beginning of Paragraph 2, Wattleton says that two recent court rulings have attacked "society's most vulnerable targets—the poor and the young" and that those attacks constitute a threat to all women. How have the "poor and young" been "attacked"? Is her concern for the reproductive rights of all women justified? In other words, is there really a "slippery slope" here?

2. Wattleton uses the history of Romania under and shortly after the rule of Nicolae Ceaucescu as a major source of evidence. What facts does she use? What conclusions does she draw? Are her points valid and effective?
3. In Paragraphs 9 and 10, Wattleton compares present-day opponents of abortion to the Puritans. Is her comparison valid? Is it effective? Explain.
4. Toward the end of her essay, Wattleton asserts that reproduction (including abortion and contraception) should not be approached as a political issue. Where does she suggest that government turn its attention and money?
5. This essay was originally prepared as a speech. Can you pick out phrases that seem to be intended more for the speech than for the printed essay?
6. The humanist movement and Christianity are often at odds. Compare this essay (which appeared in *The Humanist*) to Kissling's essay in *The Christian Century* and the editorial from *Commonweal.*

Don Wright

Woman

1991

Don Wright is political cartoonist for the *Palm Beach Post,* West Palm Beach, Florida.

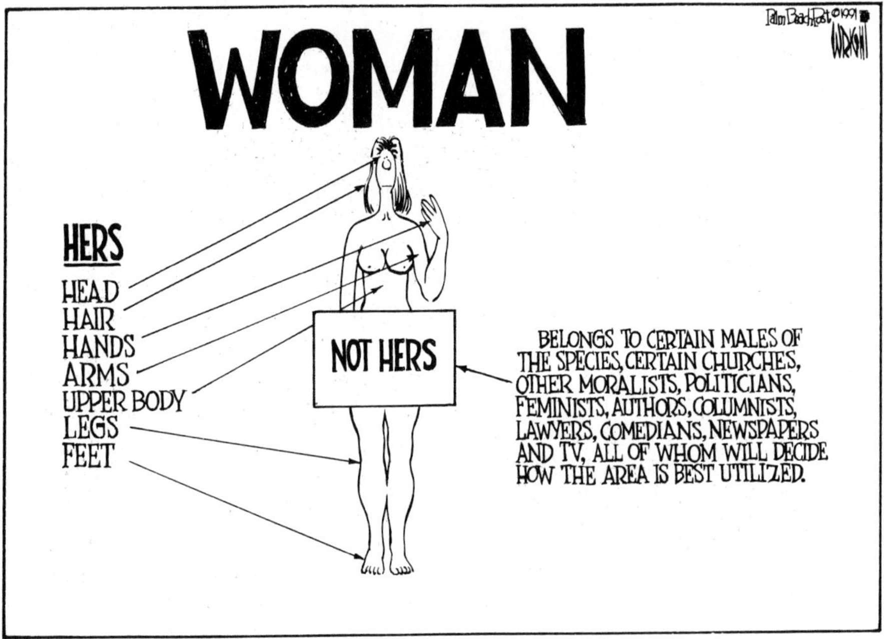

Don Wright, The Palm Beach Post.

Questions for Analysis

1. In his editorial cartoon ''Woman,'' Don Wright lists eleven groups ''all of whom will decide how the area [marked NOT HERS] is best utilized.'' Based on your reading in this book and elsewhere, what specific individuals or organizations could you place in each group? What is Wright's message about who decides a woman's rights?

Richard Seltzer

Abortion

(1974)

Trained as a physician and surgeon, Richard Seltzer (b. 1946) for many years practiced medicine and taught at Yale Medical School. The success of his short stories, essays, and books led him to set aside his medical career several years ago to devote himself full-time to his writing. This essay is taken from *Mortal Lessons,* a collection of essays and stories published in 1974.

1 Horror, like bacteria, is everywhere. It blankets the earth, endlessly lapping to find that one unguarded entryway. As though narcotized, we walk beneath, upon, through it. Carelessly we touch the familiar infected linen, eat from the universal dish; we disdain isolation. We are like the newborn that carry immunity from their mothers' wombs. Exteriorized, we are wrapped in impermeable membranes that cannot be seen. Then one day, the defense is gone. And we awaken to horror.

2 In our city, garbage is collected early in the morning. Sometimes the bang of the cans and the grind of the truck awaken us before our time. We are resentful, mutter into our pillows, then go back to sleep. On the morning of August 6, 1975, the people of 73rd Street near Woodside Avenue do just that. When at last they rise from their beds, dress, eat breakfast and leave their houses for work, they have forgotten, if they had ever known, that the garbage truck had passed earlier that morning. The event has slipped into unmemory, like a dream.

3 They close their doors and descend to the pavement. It is midsummer. You measure the climate, decide how you feel in relation to the heat and the humidity. You walk toward the bus stop. Others, your neighbors, are waiting there. It is all so familiar. All at once you step on something soft. You feel it with your foot. Even through your shoe you have the sense of something unusual, something marked by a special "give." It is a foreignness upon the pavement. Instinct pulls your foot away in an awkward little movement. You look down, and you see . . . a tiny naked body, its arms and legs flung apart, its head thrown back, its mouth agape, its face serious. A bird, you think, fallen from its nest. But there is no nest here on 73rd Street, no bird so big. It is rubber, then. A model, a . . . joke. Yes, that's it, a joke. And you bend to see. Because you must. And it is no joke. Such a gray softness can be but one thing. It is a baby, and dead. You cover your mouth, your eyes. You are fixed. Horror has found its chink and crawled in, and you will never be the same as you were. Years later you will step from a sidewalk to a lawn, and you will start at its softness, and think of that upon which you have just trod.

4 Now you look about; another man has seen it too. "My God," he whispers. Others come, people you have seen every day for years, and you hear them speak with strangely altered voices. "Look," they say, "it's a baby." There is a cry. "Here's another!" and

"Another!" and "Another!" And you follow with your gaze the index fingers of your friends pointing from the huddle where you cluster. Yes, it is true! There *are* more of these . . . little carcasses upon the street. And for a moment you look up to see if all the unbaptized sinless are falling from Limbo.

5 Now the street is filling with people. There are police. They know what to do. They rope off the area, then stand guard over the enclosed space. They are controlled, methodical, these young policemen. Servants, they do not reveal themselves to their public master; it would not be seemly. Yet I do see their pallor and the sweat that breaks upon the face of one, the way another bites the lining of his cheek and holds it thus. Ambulance attendants scoop up the bodies. They scan the street; none must be overlooked. What they place upon the litter amounts to little more than a dozen pounds of human flesh. They raise the litter, and slide it home inside the ambulance, and they drive away. You and your neighbors stand about in the street which is become for you a battlefield from which the newly slain have at last been bagged and tagged and dragged away. *But what shrapnel is this? By what explosion flung, these fragments that sink into the brain and fester there?* Whatever smell there is in this place becomes for you the stench of death. The people of 73rd Street do not then speak to each other. It is too soon for outrage, too late for blindness. It is the time of unresisted horror.

6 Later, at the police station, the investigation is brisk, conclusive. It is the hospital director speaking: ". . . fetuses accidentally got mixed up with the hospital rubbish . . . were picked up at approximately eight fifteen A.M by a sanitation truck. Somehow, the plastic lab bag, labeled HAZARDOUS MATERIAL fell off the back of the truck and broke open. No, it is not known how the fetuses got in the orange plastic bag labeled HAZARDOUS MATERIAL. It is a freak accident." The hospital director wants you to know that it is not an everyday occurrence. Once in a lifetime, he says. But you have seen it, and what are his words to you now?

7 He grows affable, familiar, tells you that by mistake, the fetuses got mixed up with the other debris. (Yes, he says other; he says debris.) He has spent the entire day, he says, trying to figure out how it happened. He wants you to know that. Somehow it matters to him. He goes on:

8 Aborted fetuses that weigh one pound or less are incinerated. Those weighing over one pound are buried at a city cemetery. He says this. Now you see. It *is* orderly. It *is* sensible. The world is *not* mad. This is still a civilized society.

9 There is no more. You turn to leave. Outside on the street, men are talking things over, reassuring each other that the right thing is being done. But just this once, you know it isn't. You saw, and you know.

10 And you know, too, that the Street of the Dead Fetuses will be wherever you go. You are part of its history now, its legend. It has laid claim upon you so that you cannot entirely leave it—not ever.

11 I am a surgeon. I do not shrink from the particularities of sick flesh. Escaping blood, all the outpourings of disease—phlegm, pus, vomitus, even those occult meaty tumors that terrify—I see as blood, disease, phlegm, and so on. I touch them to destroy them.

But I do not make symbols of them. I have seen, and I am used to seeing. Yet there are paths within the body that I have not taken, penetralia where I do not go. Nor is it lack of technique, limitation of knowledge that forbids me these ways.

12 It is the western wing of the fourth floor of a great university hospital. An abortion is about to take place. I am present because I asked to be present. I wanted to see what I had never seen.

13 The patient is Jamaican. She lies on the table submissively, and now and then she smiles at one of the nurses as though acknowledging a secret.

14 A nurse draws down the sheet, lays bare the abdomen. The belly mounds gently in the twenty-fourth week of pregnancy. The chief surgeon paints it with a sponge soaked in red antiseptic. He does this three times, each time a fresh sponge. He covers the area with a sterile sheet, an aperture in its center. He is a kindly man who teaches as he works, who pauses to reassure the woman.

15 He begins.

16 A little pinprick, he says to the woman.

17 He inserts the point of a tiny needle at the midline of the lower portion of her abdomen, on the downslope. He infiltrates local anesthetic into the skin, where it forms a small white bubble.

18 The woman grimaces.

19 That is all you will feel, the doctor says. Except for a little pressure. But no more pain.

20 She smiles again. She seems to relax. She settles comfortably on the table. The worst is over.

21 The doctor selects a three-and-one-half-inch needle bearing a central stylet. He places the point at the site of the previous injection. He aims it straight up and down, perpendicular. Next he takes hold of her abdomen with his left hand, palming the womb, steadying it. He thrusts with his right hand. The needle sinks into the abdominal wall.

22 Oh, says the woman quietly.

23 But I guess it is not pain that she feels. It is more a recognition that the deed is being done.

24 Another thrust and he has speared the uterus.

25 We are in, he says.

26 He has felt the muscular wall of the organ gripping the shaft of his needle. A further slight pressure on the needle advances it a bit more. He takes his left hand from the woman's abdomen. He retracts the filament of the stylet from the barrel of the needle. A small geyser of pale yellow fluid erupts.

27 We are in the right place, says the doctor. Are you feeling any pain? he asks.

28 She smiles, shakes her head. She gazes at the ceiling.

29 In the room we are six: two physicians, two nurses, the patient, and me. The participants are busy, very attentive. I am not at all busy—but I am no less attentive. I want to see.

30 *I see something!* It is unexpected, utterly unexpected, like a disturbance in the earth, a tumultuous jarring. I see a movement—a small one. But I have seen it.

31 And then I see it again. And now I see that it is the hub of the needle in the woman's belly that has jerked. First to one side. Then to the other side. Once more it wobbles, is *tugged,* like a fishing line nibbled by a sunfish.

32 Again! And I *know!*

33 It is the *fetus* that worries thus. It is the fetus struggling against the needle. Struggling? How can that be? I think: *that cannot be.* I think: the fetus feels no pain, cannot feel fear, has no *motivation.* It is merely reflex.

34 I point to the needle.

35 It is a reflex, says the doctor.

36 By the end of the fifth month, the fetus weighs about one pound, is about twelve inches long. Hair is on the head. There are eyebrows, eyelashes. Pale pink nipples show on the chest. Nails are present, at the fingertips, at the toes.

37 At the beginning of the sixth month, the fetus can cry, can suck, can make a fist. He kicks, he punches. The mother can feel this, can *see* this. His eyelids, until now closed, can open. He may look up, down, sideways. His grip is very strong. He could support his weight by holding with one hand.

38 A reflex, the doctor says.

39 I hear him. But I saw something in that mass of cells *understand* that it must bob and butt. And I see it again! I have an impulse to shove to the table—it is just a step—seize that needle, pull it out.

40 We are not six, I think. We are *seven.*

41 Something strangles *there.* An effort, its effort, binds me to it.

42 I do not shove to the table. I take no little step. It would be . . well, madness. Everyone here wants the needle where it is. Six do. No, five do.

43 I close my eyes. I see the inside of the uterus. It is bathed in ruby gloom. I see the creature curled upon itself. Its knees are flexed. Its head is bent upon its chest. It is in fluid and gently rocks to the rhythm of the distant heartbeat.

44 It resembles . . . a sleeping infant.

45 Its place is entered by something. It is sudden. A point coming. A needle!

46 A spike of *daylight* pierces the chamber. Now the light is extinguished. The needle comes closer in the pool. The point grazes the thigh, and I stir. Perhaps I wake from dozing. The light is there again. I twist and straighten. My arms and legs *push.* My hand finds the shaft—grabs! I *grab.* I bend the needle this way and that. The point probes, touches on my belly. My mouth opens. Could I cry out? All is a commotion and a churning. There is a presence in the pool. An activity! The pool colors, reddens, darkens.

47 I open my eyes to see the doctor feeding a small plastic tube through the barrel of the needle into the uterus. Drops of pink fluid overrun the rim and spill onto the sheet. He withdraws the needle from around the plastic tubing. Now only the little tube pro-

trudes from the woman's body. A nurse hands the physician a syringe loaded with a colorless liquid. He attaches it to the end of the tubing and injects it.

48 Prostaglandin, he says.

49 Ah well, prostaglandin—a substance found normally in the body. When given in concentrated dosage, it throws the uterus into vigorous contraction. In eight to twelve hours, the woman will expel the fetus.

50 The doctor detaches the syringe but does not remove the tubing.

51 In case we must do it over, he says.

52 He takes away the sheet. He places gauze pads over the tubing. Over all this he applies adhesive tape.

53 I know. We cannot feed the great numbers. There is no more room. I know, I know. It is a woman's right to refuse the risk, to decline the pain of childbirth. And an unwanted child is a very great burden. An unwanted child is a burden to himself. I know.

54 And yet . . . there is the flick of that needle. I *saw* it. I saw . . . I *felt*—in that room, a pace away, life prodded, life fending off. I saw life avulsed—swept by flood, blackening—then *out.*

55 There, says the doctor. It's all over. It wasn't too bad, was it? he says to the woman.

56 She smiles. It is all over. Oh, yes.

57 And who would care to imagine that from a moist and dark commencement six months before there would ripen the cluster and globule, the sprout and pouch of man?

58 And who would care to imagine that trapped within the laked pearl and a dowry of yoke would lie the earliest stuff of dream and memory?

59 It is a persona carried here as well as a person, I think. I think it is a signed piece, engraved with a hieroglyph of human genes.

60 I did not think this until I saw. The flick. The fending off.

61 Later, in the corridor, the doctor explains that the law does not permit abortion beyond the twenty-fourth week. That is when the fetus may be viable, he says. We stand together for a moment, and he tells of an abortion in which the fetus *cried* after it was passed.

62 What did you do? I ask him.

63 There was nothing *to* do but let it live, he says. It did very well, he says. A case of mistaken dates.

Questions for Analysis

1. "Horror" is the first word of this essay and at least begins to convey Seltzer's reaction to the events he describes. What is your reaction?

2. After you have acknowledged and expressed your emotional reaction—something we all should do before going on to an intellectual reaction when confronted with events like these—consider the purpose of Seltzer's essay. Why did he write it? What is his "argument"? How does the emotional—even perhaps physical—reaction he knows this essay will generate support his argument?
3. Why does Seltzer focus our attention on the hospital administrator's words as he tries to explain the mistakes that led to fetuses on the street?
4. How old is the fetus in the abortion that Seltzer observes? (See Paragraph 14.) Does knowing the age of the fetus make any difference in the way we react emotionally? Should the age of the fetus make any difference in our intellectual response and moral judgment? Would it make a difference (emotionally or intellectually) if we knew why this woman is getting an abortion?
5. Does this essay provide support for pro-choice or pro-life advocates? Could both sides use it? How would other writers you have read on abortion react to it?

A. J. Cronin

"Doctor, I Can't . . . I Won't Have a Child"

(1935)

A. J. Cronin (1886–1981) was an English physician and writer. "Doctor, I Can't . . . I Won't Have a Child" comes from *Adventures in Two Worlds* (1935), a collection of stories largely based on Cronin's experience practicing medicine.

1 "Doctor, I can't . . . I won't have a child."

2 It was four o'clock in the afternoon, the hour of my "best" consultations, and the woman who spoke so vehemently was tall, distinguished, and handsome, fashionably dressed in a dark grey costume, with an expensive diamond clip in her smart black hat.

3 I had just examined her, and now, having dried my hands methodically, I put away the towel and turned toward her. "It's a little late to make that decision now. You should have thought of it two months ago. You are exactly nine weeks pregnant. Your baby will be born toward the middle of July."

4 "I won't have it. . . . You've got to help me, Doctor. You simply must."

5 How often had I heard these words before. I had heard them from frightened little shopgirls in trouble; from a shamed spinster, aged thirty-five, who told me in a trembling voice, exactly like the heroine of old-time melodrama, that she had been "betrayed"; from a famous film actress defiantly resolved that her career should not be ruined; above

all had I heard them from selfish and neurotic wives, afraid of the pangs of childbirth, afraid of losing their figure, their health, their life, afraid—most specious pretext of all—of "losing their husband's love."

6 This case was somewhat different. I knew my patient, Beatrice Glendenning, socially; knew also her husband, Henry, and her two grown-up sons. They were wealthy people, with a town house in Knightsbridge and a large estate in Hampshire, where the pheasant shooting was excellent and where, indeed, I had spent several pleasant week ends.

7 "You understand . . . , it isn't just money, Doctor. . . . I must get out of this business, and to do so I'll give anything." She looked me full in the face.

8 There was no mistaking her meaning. Indeed, that same offer, indescribable in its implications, had been made to me before, though perhaps never so blatantly. It had been made by a young French modiste, estranged from her husband, who had compromised herself with another man and who, slim, elegant, and bewitching, with affected tears in her beautiful eyes, leaned forward and tried to take my hands in hers.

9 Doctors are only human, they have the same difficulty in repressing their instincts as other men. Yet, if not for moral reasons, from motives of sheer common sense, I had never lost my head. Once a doctor embarks upon a career as abortionist he is irretrievably lost.

10 There were, however, many such illicit practitioners in the vicinity, both men and women, plying their perilous undercover trade at exorbitant rates, until one day, inevitably, the death of some wretched girl brought them exposure, ruin, and a long term of imprisonment. Perhaps desperation blinded such patients as came to me, yet it always struck me as amazing how few of them were conscious of the infinite danger involved in illegal abortion. Under the best hospital conditions the operation holds a definite risk. Performed hastily in some backstairs room with a septic instrument by some brutal or unskilled practitioner, the result almost inevitably is severe hemorrhage, followed by infection and acute peritonitis.

11 There were others, too, among these women who believed it was within my power to relieve them of their incubus by such a simple expedient as an ergot pill or a mixture of jalap and senna. Others, too, who confessed to having tried the weirdest expedients, from boiling-hot baths to such eccentric gymnastics as descending the stairs backward, in a crouching position. Poor creatures, some were almost comic in their distress, and there were among them many who needed sympathy and comfort. This they got from me, with much good advice but nothing more.

12 Beatrice Glendenning, however, was neither comic nor ignorant, but a strong-minded, intelligent woman of the world who moved with considerable éclat in the best society.

13 My only possible attitude was not to take her seriously. So I reasoned mildly:

14 "I daresay it's rather inconvenient . . . , with these two grown-up sons of yours. And it'll spoil your London season. But Henry will be pleased."

15 "Don't be a fool, Doctor. Henry isn't the father."

16 Although I had half expected this, it silenced me.

17 During these country week ends I had met the inevitable family intimate, a close friend of Henry's, who went fishing and shooting with him, a sporting type, one of these "good fellows," whom I had disliked on sight and who obviously was on confidential terms with Henry's wife.

18 "Well," I said at last, "it's a bad business. But there's nothing I can do about it."

19 "You won't help me?"

20 "I can't."

21 There was a pause. The blood had risen to her cheeks and her eyes flashed fire at me. She drew on her gloves, took up her bag. A rejected woman is an enemy for life.

22 "Very well, Doctor, there's no more to be said."

23 "Just one thing before you go. . . . Don't put yourself in the hands of a quack. You may regret it."

24 She gave no sign of having heard, but swept out of the room without another word.

25 The interview left me not only with a bad taste in my mouth, but in a thoroughly bad mood. I felt that I had lost an excellent patient, an agreeable hostess, and the half dozen brace of admirable pheasants which I had come to regard as my annual autumnal perquisite. I never expected to see Mrs. Glendenning again. How wrong I was—how little I knew of that invincible woman's character!

26 About ten days later the telephone rang. It was Henry Glendenning himself. Beatrice, he told me, had a frightful cold, an attack of influenza, in fact. Would I be a dear chap and pop round to Knightsbridge as soon as convenient? Pleased by this rapprochement, I arrived within the hour at the Glendenning town house and was shown directly to Beatrice's room.

27 Attended by a nurse, a heavily built, middle-aged woman with a face like a trap, the patient was in bed. She appeared, at first sight, rather more ill than I had expected—fearfully blanched, with bloodless lips and every indication of a raging fever. Puzzled, I drew back the sheet . . ., and then the truth burst upon me. The thing had been done—botched and bungled—she was thoroughly septic and had been haemorrhaging for at least twelve hours.

28 "I have everything ready for you, Doctor." The nurse was addressing me in a toneless voice, proffering a container of swabs and gauze.

29 I drew back in a cold fury. I wanted, there and then, to walk out of the room. But how could I? She was in extremis. I must do something for this damned woman, and at once. I was fairly trapped.

30 I began to work on her. My methods, I fear, were not especially merciful, but she offered no protest, suffered the severest pangs without a word. At last the bleeding was under control. I prepared to go.

31 All this time, as she lay there, Mrs. Glendenning's eyes had never left my face. And now, with an effort, she spoke:

32 "It's influenza, Doctor. Henry knows it's influenza. I shall expect you this evening."

33 Downstairs, in the library, Henry had a glass of sherry ready for me, concerned, naturally, about his wife, whom he adored, yet hospitable, as always. He was in stature quite a small man, shy and rather ineffectual in manner, who had inherited a fortune from his father and spent much of it in making others happy. As I gazed at his open,

kindly face, all that I had meant to say died upon my tongue. I could not tell him. I could not.

34 "Nasty thing, this influenza, Doctor."

35 I took a quick breath.

36 "Yes, Henry."

37 "Quite a severe attack she has, too."

38 "I'm afraid so."

39 "You'll see her through, Doctor."

40 A pause.

41 "Yes, Henry, I'll see her through."

42 I called again that evening. I called twice a day for the next ten days. It was a thoroughly unpleasant case, demanding constant surgical attention. I suppose I did my part in maintaining the deception. But the real miracles of strategy were performed by Beatrice and the nurse. For Henry Glendenning, who lived all that time in the same house, who slept every night in the bedroom adjoining the sickroom, never for a moment suspected the true state of affairs. The thing sounds incredible, but it is true.

43 At the end of that month I made my final visit. Mrs. Glendenning was up, reclining on the drawing-room sofa, looking ethereal and soulful in a rose-coloured tea gown with pure white lace at cuff and collar. Flowers were everywhere. Henry, delighted, still adoring, was dancing attendance. Tea was brought, served by a trim maid—the grim-visaged nurse had long since departed.

44 Toying with a slice of teacake, Beatrice gazed at me with wide and wistful eyes.

45 "Henry is taking me to Madeira next week, Doctor. He feels I need the change."

46 "You do indeed, darling."

47 "Thank you, sweetheart."

48 Oh God, the duplicity, the perfidy of woman . . . the calm, deep, premeditated, and infernal cunning!

49 "We'll be alone together for the first week," she concluded, sweetly. "A second honeymoon. Then we expect George to join us. We're both very fond of George."

50 Her eye sought mine, held it, and did not for an instant falter.

51 "More tea, Doctor, dear? You must come and shoot with us when we get back."

52 When I rose to go, Henry saw me to the door, shook my hand warmly.

53 "Thank you for all you've done, Doctor." And he added, "Confoundedly nasty thing, that influenza."

54 I walked all the way home across Kensington Gardens, gritting my teeth and muttering, "That creature, oh that damned, that most damnable creature!"

55 But in September I got my half-dozen brace of pheasants. They were nice, tender birds!

Questions for Analysis

1. Cronin wrote this short story in 1935 when abortion was a criminal offense in Great Britain. Since he was a physician, the story is probably based on his personal

experience. Based on these facts how does this story illustrate the same point Faye Wattleton made when she described Romania under Ceaucescu?

2. How would you characterize the speaker's (the Doctor's) attitude toward women who wish to terminate their pregnancies? What is his attitude toward Mrs. Glendenning?
3. What do you think of Mrs. Glendenning? In your opinion, is her situation one in which an abortion is the best option? What would happen if she had the child?
4. This story is a study in character—Mrs. Glendenning, Henry Glendenning, George, the doctor. It is also a study of what people know, what they choose not to share, and what they guess about what others know. Are the deceptions that operate in this story—the doctor's, the wife's, and so on—justified? Discuss.
5. The Glendennings are rich and can afford the best medical treatment available. What might have happened in a poor family that faced this painful but not uncommon situation? For a poorer family, how would this scenario fit into the pro-choice arguments?

The Death Penalty: Justice? Legalized Murder? Deterrent?

As violent crime and our awareness of it have increased, the death penalty has been touted by many as a way to "get tough on crime." Supporters of the death penalty either assert or imply that the threat of death is a deterrent to murder and other capital crimes. However, as several of the following selections show, a deterrent effect is difficult, if not impossible, to establish. As a result, many supporters of the death penalty present other arguments for this form of punishment, including the need for retribution both to maintain human dignity and to affirm the social order.

Opponents of the death penalty, or abolitionists, point to the difficulties in the deterrence argument, assert that executions promote rather than discourage violence, show how the death penalty is arbitrarily and discriminatorily administered, and argue that it debases rather than affirms human dignity.

The death penalty is an issue that every citizen should consider carefully, for we all bear some measure of responsibility for each execution. The selections that follow reveal the range of opinions and arguments about capital punishment, show how arguments about it have evolved over more than two centuries of debate, and explore the issue from a personal perspective.

The first piece in this section is Steve Miller's cartoon depicting the "urge to kill" and the "urge to kill . . . via the death penalty" as essentially the same. The "urge to kill," however, is labeled "Bad," while the "urge to kill . . . via the death penalty" is labeled "Good," ironically suggesting that the morality of the death penalty might be a problem. Michael L. Radelet's "Introduction and Overview" from the book he edited, *Facing the Death Penalty: Essays on a Cruel and Unusual Punishment* (1989), explores our society's moral uncertainty over the death penalty. Radelet provides a quick but detailed summary of the key points in the debate, as well as an interesting review of the shifts in public opinion concerning the efficacy and morality of capital punishment.

Two pairs of pro–con essays follow next. Edward I. Koch's often-anthologized "Death and Justice" is a strong pro-death penalty statement. Its appearance in *The New Republic* (1985) inspired David Bruck, one of the most articulate opponents of capital punishment, to write a rebuttal that also appeared in *The New Republic* in 1985.

Both essays in the second pro–con pair deal with the effect of the death penalty on society. Walter Berns argues that the death penalty affirms human dignity and "the majesty of the moral order that is embodied in our law." John Cole Vodicka argues the opposite point of view. Using numerous examples, he asserts that the death penalty degrades society and humanity by promoting anger and violence and by postponing the healing process. William Hogarth's satirical engraving depicting an eighteenth-century execution reinforces Vodicka's key point: The death penalty has a brutalizing effect on all people.

The last two pieces in this section were chosen to engage your interest in a more personal way. The first of these is a statement by Willie Jasper Darden, Jr., a condemned prisoner who was executed in Florida in 1988. Darden's statement pushes us to confront the issue of capital punishment from the perspective of the condemned. Listening carefully and responding humanely in these cases is important for two reasons. First, statements such as Darden's introduce some possibility of human dignity into an event that can be exceptionally dehumanizing for all concerned. Second, Darden's statement and others like it carry unusual rhetorical emphasis because of the writer's impending death. They, therefore, offer the possibility of giving us a new perspective on the wisdom and justice of the death penalty. Of course, our response in these cases is complicated by many other factors including the pain caused by the crime, the remorse or lack of remorse displayed by the condemned prisoner, and any lingering questions of innocence.

The last piece in this section is Frank O'Connor's "Guests of the Nation." This short story, set in Ireland during its war to win independence from Great Britain, deals with the pain executions bring to those who come to understand and respect those who are condemned.

Steve Miller

The Urge to Kill

Steve Miller was editorial cartoonist for *The News and Observer,* Raleigh, North Carolina, in 1974.

'BAD' 'GOOD'

Miller/News & Observer, N.C./Rothco.

Michael L. Radelet

Introduction and Overview

(1989)

Michael L. Radelet (b. 1950) is Associate Professor of Sociology at the University of Florida. This essay comes from a collection of essays he edited, *Facing the Death Penalty: Essays on a Cruel and Unusual Punishment.*

1 Between 1930 and 1967 there were 3,859 executions carried out under state and civil authority in the United States (U.S. Department of Justice, 1986). The peak year, 1935, saw 199 executions, but not since 1951 has the annual figure surpassed 100. Between then and 1967 the pace of executions declined to the point where, in the decade of the 1960s, a total of 191 executions were carried out. After 1967, in fact, challenges to the constitutional validity of death penalty statutes led to a ten-year moratorium. Executions resumed in 1977 (with that of Gary Gilmore in Utah), and on 14 June 1988, Louisiana prisoner Edward Byrne became the hundredth inmate to be executed since the moratorium ended. By the end of 1988, another 2,182 men and women were living under a sentence of death (NAACP Legal Defense and Educational Fund, 1988). At the rate of one execution per week (that is, double the present execution rate), it would take 39 years, or until 2027, just to eliminate this backlog.

2 This situation raises a number of important questions. There are no comparable situations in which otherwise healthy men, women, and children are forced to spend years contemplating their intended demise. They do so with few resources, in a severely restricted physical environment and a less-than-supportive social atmosphere.

3 The scholars and practitioners contributing to this volume have studied the condemned population, handled their appeals, and/or assisted them in preparing for death. The authors include historians, attorneys, sociologists, anthropologists, criminologists, a minister, a philosopher, and three men sentenced to death. The chapters that follow, taken as a whole, present not only the struggles of the condemned and their families, but also those of a group of people who have dedicated themselves to working with the condemned or studying the death penalty and what it says about the society that uses it.

4 The primary goal of this book is not to debate the wisdom of capital punishment; several general overviews are already easily accessible (e.g., Bedau, 1982; Berns, 1979; Black, 1981; van den Haag and Conrad, 1983). Nor is it to generate sympathy for those convicted of horrible crimes. Our goal is instead to examine what life under a sentence of death is like for condemned inmates, how and why various professionals assist them in their struggles for life, and what these personal experiences with capital punishment tell us about the wisdom of this penal policy. Little support for capital punishment will be found in these pages. Few people close to the condemned count themselves as death penalty retentionists: even prison wardens have been known to call for universal abo-

lition (Duffy, 1962; Lawes, 1932). The interdisciplinary perspectives in this book will not resolve the death penalty debate, but they offer important and unique insights to all readers who wish to study the full effects of the penalty.

Death Penalty Litigation

5 In the 1972 case of *Furman v. Georgia* (408 U.S. 238), a divided U.S. Supreme Court ruled that the death penalty was arbitrarily applied and hence in violation of the Eighth Amendment's protection against cruel and unusual punishment. The vote was five to four, and each Justice wrote a separate opinion. In effect, all inmates then living under a sentence of death (633 in 32 states) had their sentences commuted to life imprisonment by this decision (Meltsner, 1973:292). Many believed the abolition would be permanent.

6 Today, however, 37 states and the U.S. military have operational death penalty statutes, and 34 states have prisoners living under a sentence of death (NAACP Legal Defense and Educational Fund, 1988). The movement to reinstate the death penalty was led by Florida, where, five months after the *Furman* decision, a special session of the legislature was called for the purpose of enacting a new capital statute (Ehrhardt and Levinson, 1973). Florida's law is an example of a "guided discretion" statute; it lists specific aggravating and mitigating circumstances that are intended to guide the judge and jury in their sentencing decisions. This law was approved by the U.S. Supreme Court in 1976 (*Proffitt v. Florida,* 428 U.S. 242); at the same time the Court ruled that mandatory death penalty statutes were unconstitutional (*S. Roberts v. Louisiana,* 428 U.S. 325). In later years the Court also invalidated mandatory death penalties for the murder of a police officer (*H. Roberts v. Louisiana,* 431 U.S. 633 [1977]) and for murders committed by inmates while serving a previous sentence of life imprisonment without the possibility of parole (*Sumner v. Schuman,* 107 S.Ct. 2716 [1987]).

7 Of the 34 states that at the end of 1988 housed condemned prisoners, five had death row populations of over one hundred: Florida (296), Texas (284), California (238), Illinois (119), and Georgia (106) (NAACP Legal Defense and Educational Fund, 1988). The primary reason for Florida's lead is that its statute, like Indiana's and Alabama's, allows a judge to sentence a defendant to death even if the jury has recommended a sentence of life imprisonment. While this override provision has been used infrequently in both Indiana and Alabama, in Florida it has been used in 20 percent of the 572 cases in which the death penalty has been imposed since 1972 (Mello and Robson, 1985; Radelet, 1985). Two men, Ernest Dobbert and Beauford White, have been executed in Florida after their trial jury's recommendation of life imprisonment was rejected and overridden by the judge. White's jury had voted unanimously for life.

8 Of the first 100 executions in America after the ten-year moratorium ended in 1977, 11 were "consensual": the inmate dropped his appeals and demanded immediate execution. All but one of the remaining executions occurred in the states of the former Confederacy, so that executions today remain almost exclusively a southern phenomenon. By the end of 1988, Texas led the country with 29 "post-*Furman*" executions, followed by 19 in Florida and 18 in Louisiana. One woman has been executed (Velma Barfield in North Carolina), as have three men whose crimes predated their eighteenth

birthdays. There are 31 others currently on death row for crimes committed when they were juveniles (NAACP Legal Defense and Educational Fund, 1988).

9 The death penalty is one of the most controversial issues in American politics. In this section I will briefly outline some of the major issues in contemporary death penalty debates, referring readers to sources for additional information (for a comprehensive bibliography, see Radelet and Vandiver, 1988). To see why Americans support or oppose the death penalty, we can use the *Gallup Report* of January 1986. Although some would argue that even in a democracy the life or death of a citizen should not be subject to a simple majority vote, opinion polls can give us important insights into the factual, mythical, and philosophical foundations of current attitudes.

10 The United States and South Africa stand alone among Western countries today in their use of capital punishment (Amnesty International, 1979). But despite the worldwide rejection of the death penalty, there is no question that at least in theory (the death penalty as it is actually applied is another matter), the majority of American citizens support its use. When asked "Are you in favor of the death penalty for persons convicted of murder," 70 percent voice support, and 22 percent stand opposed. Supporters are more likely to be male (74 percent versus 66 percent), white (73 versus 50 percent), and Republican (83 versus 62 percent). These figures stand in marked contrast to those of two decades ago; in 1966 only 42 percent of the public supported executions (Gallup, 1986). Interestingly, support declines when respondents are asked if they would still favor death if life imprisonment with no possibility of parole was an option (as it is in most states); in this case 55 percent support the death penalty, while 35 percent favor life imprisonment (Gallup, 1986). No data are available that measure support for use of the death penalty for crimes other than homicide; all inmates on death row today were convicted of murder (with the exception of a Mississippi man convicted of the rape of a minor). The Supreme Court struck down the use of the death penalty for the rape of an adult in 1977 (*Coker v. Georgia,* 433 U.S. 584).

11 Many notable groups are on record as opposing the death penalty, among them almost all Christian and Jewish denominations (National Interreligious Task Force on Criminal Justice, n.d.). The fight against capital punishment in the United States is being led by such groups as the American Civil Liberties Union, the NAACP Legal Defense and Educational Fund and Amnesty International (see, e.g., Amnesty International, 1987). Two Supreme Court Justices, Thurgood Marshall and William Brennan, stand opposed to its use in all cases. Popular opposition, however, is not (and never has been) represented on juries in capital trials, as prosecutors are permitted to exclude for cause from both the guilt and penalty phases of the trial all potential jurors who stand opposed to the death penalty (*Lockhart v. McCree,* 476 U.S. 162 [1986]).

12 The primary argument in support of the death penalty, and one not directly amenable to empirical research, is retribution. When a 1985 Gallup poll asked death penalty supporters to explain their position, 30 percent cited a desire for revenge and 18 percent said, "Murderers deserve punishment" (Gallup, 1985). Another 22 percent cited deterrence, 11 percent believed it was too costly to house prisoners for life, and 16 percent said it kept prisoners from killing again or removed a potential threat. Thirteen percent

gave other responses; 2 percent had no opinion (multiple responses were allowed). Those who opposed the death penalty offered these reasons: it is wrong to take a life (40 percent); wrongful convictions occur (15 percent); punishment should be left to God (15 percent); it does not deter crime (5 percent); rehabilitation is possible (5 percent); it is unfairly applied (3 percent). Seven percent gave other reasons; 16 percent had no opinion (Gallup, 1986).

13 The deterrence question is quite controversial among the lay public. Whereas many politicians argue that the death penalty is a deterrent, virtually no criminologist agrees. The 1986 Gallup poll found that 61 percent of the public believed the death penalty to be a deterrent; support for executions would decline from 70 percent to 56 percent if new evidence proved that it was not. Those who believe that public support for the death penalty is strong and solid will be surprised to learn that only 43 percent of the public would favor the death penalty, given the option of life imprisonment, if it were proved not to be a deterrent to murder (Gallup, 1986).

14 The argument that the death penalty is superior to long imprisonment in its deterrent effect receives its strongest support from a study conducted by Isaac Ehrlich that purported to show that each execution between 1933 and 1967 prevented approximately eight homicides (Ehrlich, 1975). This study has been criticized at length by several scholars, including a panel appointed by the National Academy of Sciences and headed by the 1980 Nobel laureate in economics, Lawrence Klein. This panel concluded: ''[I]t seems unthinkable to us to base decisions on the use of the death penalty on Ehrlich's findings'' (Klein et al., 1978:358). Other studies have found that the homicide rate actually increases after executions (Bowers and Pierce, 1980). A fair conclusion from this body of research is that if the death penalty does have a deterrent effect, it is so minuscule that the vast majority of researchers have failed to find it.

15 To the degree that the death penalty is a more severe punishment than is life imprisonment, an assertion that some would challenge, retribution is a solid pro-death penalty argument. Whether retribution should be a proper goal of state policy is more controversial. Clearly there are limits to the degree of retribution that can be permitted; we can all think of punishments worse than death (e.g., torture), and everyone agrees that they would be improper. The death penalty is superior to life imprisonment in its ability to incapacitate, as some convicted murderers (and other prisoners) will kill in prison if they are not put to death. The number of repeated murders prevented by the death penalty is quite small (Marquart and Sorensen, 1988; Wolfson, 1982), though some would argue that it would be worth executing dozens of murderers to incapacitate the one who would otherwise repeat his crime.

16 Also used to support the death penalty (though not probed in the Gallup surveys) is the argument that execution of the offender gives comfort and support to the family of the homicide victim. This argument is generally not foremost in the pro-death penalty position, however, since 98 percent of all homicide victims are not avenged with the death penalty, and the groups to which the victims' families most often turn for support—the churches—are also generally opposed to executions. By any measure, the needs of these families are not being met by the death penalty or any other public

policy, and regardless of our positions on the death penalty, we can all probably agree that attention to their agony is desperately needed in both scholarship and public policy. Among the best sources for information about these families are the recent works by Danto (1982), Magee (1983), and Rynearson (1984); Margaret Vandiver's essay in this volume (Chapter 9 [of *Facing the Death Penalty*]) compares the misery of the families of homicide victims and the misery of the equally innocent families of death row inmates.

17 Cost, though cited by 11 percent of the death penalty supporters in the *Gallup Report,* is actually a strong argument against the death penalty (Garey, 1985; Nakell, 1978). Homicide trials are more expensive if the death penalty is being sought, as are the costs in the executive and especially the judicial branches of government as the case is being appealed. Some, of course, will argue that costs would drop if we further restricted the appellate process in capital cases, although the Constitution presents strong barriers to such restrictions. Thus, for now and the foreseeable future, it is clear: each execution costs millions, several times more than the cost of incarcerating an offender for his or her natural life. This raises a question of growing importance: could not the millions we spend on executing our prisoners be better spent on more effective solutions to violence and more concrete assistance for the families of homicide victims?

18 Anti–death penalty citizens point out (correctly) that the execution of the innocent is inevitable (Bedau and Radelet, 1987). Death penalty retentionists now agree. As Ernest van den Haag, one of our country's most accomplished death penalty proponents, puts it: ''However rare, such miscarriages of justice are likely to occur'' (van den Haag and Conrad, 1983:55). He argues, however, that the benefits of the death penalty outweigh this definite liability. Abolitionists are also correct in stating that the problem of racial bias in sentencing has not been eliminated (Baldus et al., 1986; Bowers, 1984; Gross, 1985; Gross and Mauro, 1984; Nakell and Hardy, 1987; Radelet and Pierce, 1985), although it is noteworthy that only 3 percent of the abolitionists polled offer this rationale to support their position. Pre-*Furman* racial bias in the administration of the death penalty was particularly evident in the punishment for rape; 89 percent (405 out of 455) of the prisoners executed for rape since 1930 were black men whose victims were white (Wolfgang and Riedel, 1976). Today, the allegations of racial bias center on the race of the victim, as almost all of those on death row were condemned for murdering whites. In fact, when other predictive factors are controlled, having a white victim increases the probability of a death sentence by a greater amount than smoking increases the probability of heart disease (Gross, 1985). The Supreme Court acknowledges the validity of these conclusions, though in 1987 it failed (by one vote) to find in the statistics the type of *international* discrimination that would warrant relief (*McCleskey v. Kemp,* 107 S.Ct. 1756).

19 The lives of those condemned to death have been described (Gettinger, 1979; Johnson, 1981; Magee, 1980; Radelet et al., 1983), but rarely by those close to them. The families of the condemned must work frantically to deal with the inmates' needs. Furthermore, for obvious reasons, the condemned and their families rarely welcome the media when last-minute legal issues are being litigated and preparations for death are

being made. The essays collected for this volume attempt to fill this gap and help shed light on what the death penalty actually entails. . . .

It is hoped that this collection will offer readers a more personal glimpse of death row inmates and those who work with them, and some new ideas and perspectives that might enlighten contemporary death penalty debates. All of the essays, as I read them, support the argument that the death penalty as practiced today can only be considered a cruel, unusual, and unnecessary punishment. But it is hoped that even those readers who believe that the benefits of the death penalty outweigh these concerns will find some food for thought on what capital punishment does to the inmates, their families and attorneys, and our society as a whole.

Notes

Amnesty International. 1979. *The Death Penalty.* London: Amnesty International Publications.

———. 1987. *United States of America: The Death Penalty.* London: Amnesty International Publications.

Baldus, David C.; Charles A. Pulaski, Jr.; and George Woodworth. 1986. ''Arbitrariness and Discrimination in the Administration of the Death Penalty: A Challenge to State Supreme Courts.'' *Stetson Law Review* 15:133–261.

Bedau, Hugo Adam. 1982. *The Death Penalty in America.* 3d ed. New York: Oxford University Press.

Bedau, Hugo Adam, and Michael L. Radelet. 1987. ''Miscarriages of Justice in Potentially Capital Cases.'' *Stanford Law Review* 40:21–179.

Berns, Walter. 1979. *For Capital Punishment: Crime and the Morality of the Death Penalty.* New York: Basic Books.

Black, Charles L., Jr. 1981. *Capital Punishment: The Inevitability of Caprice and Mistake.* 2d ed. New York: W. W. Norton.

Bowers, William J. 1984. *Legal Homicide: Death As Punishment in America, 1864–1982.* Boston: Northeastern University Press.

Bowers, William J., and Glenn L. Pierce. 1980. ''Deterrence or Brutalization: What Is the Effect of Executions?'' *Crime and Delinquency* 26 (1980):453–84.

Danto, B. L. 1982. ''Survivors of Homicide.'' Pp. 85–97 in *The Human Side of Homicide,* edited by B. L. Danto, John Bruhns, and A. H. Kutscher. New York: Columbia University Press.

Duffy, Clinton T., with Al Hirshberg. 1962. *Eighty-eight Men and Two Women.* Garden City, N.Y.: Doubleday.

Ehrhardt, Charles W., and L. Harold Levinson. 1973. ''Florida's Legislative Response to *Furman:* An Exercise in Futility?'' *Journal of Criminal Law and Criminology* 64:10–21.

Ehrlich, Isaac. 1975. ''The Deterrent Effect of Capital Punishment: A Question of Life or Death.'' *American Economic Review* 65:397–417.

Gallup, George. 1985. ''The Death Penalty.'' *Gallup Report* 232–33 (Jan.–Feb.):3–11.

———. 1986. ''The Death Penalty.'' *Gallup Report* 244–45 (Jan.–Feb.):10–16.

Garey, Margot. 1985. ''The Cost of Taking a Life: Dollars and Sense of the Death Penalty.'' *University of California–Davis Law Review* 18:1221–73.

Gettinger, Stephen H. 1979. *Sentenced to Die: The People, the Crimes, and the Controversy.* New York: Macmillan.

Gross, Samuel R. 1985. ''Race and Death: The Judicial Evaluation of Evidence of Discrimination in Capital Sentencing.'' *University of California–Davis Law Review* 18:1275–325.

Gross, Samuel R., and Robert Mauro. 1984. ''Patterns of Death: An Analysis of Racial Disparities in Capital Sentencing and Homicide Victimization.'' *Stanford Law Review* 37:27–153.

Johnson, Robert. 1981. *Condemned to Die: Life Under Sentence of Death.* New York: Elsevier.

Klein, Lawrence R.; Brian Forst; and Victor Filatov. 1978. ''The Deterrent Effect of Capital Punishment: An Assessment of the Evidence.'' Pp. 336–60 in *Deterrence and Incapacitation: Estimating the Effects of Criminal Sanctions on Crime Rates,* edited by Alfred Blumstein, Jacqueline Cohen, and Daniel Nagin. Washington, D.C.: National Academy of Sciences.

Lawes, Lewis E. 1932. *Twenty Thousand Years in Sing Sing.* New York: Long and Smith.
Magee, Doug. 1980. *Slow Coming Dark: Interviews on Death Row.* New York: Pilgrim Press.
———. 1983. *What Murder Leaves Behind: The Victim's Family.* New York: Dodd, Mead.
Marquart, James W., and Jonathan R. Sorensen. 1988. ''Institutional and Postrelease Behavior of *Furman*-Commuted Inmates in Texas.'' *Criminology* 26:677–93.
Mello, Michael, and Ruthann Robson. 1985. ''Judge Over Jury: Florida's Practice of Imposing Death Over Life in Capital Cases.'' *Florida State University Law Review* 13:31–75.
Meltsner, Michael. 1973. *Cruel and Unusual: The Supreme Court and Capital Punishment.* New York: William Morrow.
NAACP Legal Defense and Educational Fund. 1988. ''Death Row, U.S.A.'' Unpublished compilation, available from 99 Hudson St., New York, N.Y., 10013.
Nakell, Barry. 1978. ''The Cost of the Death Penalty.'' *Criminal Law Bulletin* 14:69–80.
Nakell, Barry, and Kenneth A. Hardy. 1987. *The Arbitrariness of the Death Penalty.* Philadelphia: Temple University Press.
National Interreligious Task Force on Criminal Justice. N.d. *Capital Punishment: What the Religious Community Says.* New York: NITFCJ.
Radelet, Michael L. 1985. ''Rejecting the Jury: The Imposition of the Death Penalty in Florida.'' *University of California–Davis Law Review* 18:1409–31.
Radelet, Michael L., and Glenn L. Pierce. 1985. ''Race and Prosecutorial Discretion in Homicide Cases.'' *Law and Society Review* 19:587–621.
Radelet, Michael L., and Margaret Vandiver. 1988. *Capital Punishment in America: An Annotated Bibliography.* New York: Garland Press.
Radelet, Michael L.; Margaret Vandiver; and Felix M. Berardo. 1983. ''Families, Prisons, and Men with Death Sentences: The Human Impact of Structured Uncertainty.'' *Journal of Family Issues* 4:593–612.
Rynearson, E. K. 1984. ''Bereavement After Homicide: A Descriptive Study.'' *American Journal of Psychiatry* 141:1452–54.
U.S. Department of Justice. 1986. *Capital Punishment, 1984.* Washington, D.C.: U.S. Government Printing Office.
van den Haag, Ernest, and John P. Conrad. 1983. *The Death Penalty: A Debate.* New York: Plenum.
Wolfgang, Marvin E., and Mark Riedel. 1976. ''Rape, Racial Discrimination, and the Death Penalty.'' Pp. 99–121 in *Capital Punishment in the United States,* edited by Hugo Adam Bedau and Chester M. Pierce. New York: AMS Press.
Wolfson, Wendy Phillips. 1982. ''The Deterrent Effect of the Death Penalty Upon Prison Murder.'' Pp. 159–73 in *The Death Penalty in America,* 3d ed., edited by Hugo Adam Bedau. New York: Oxford University Press.

Cases Cited

Coker v. Georgia, 433 U.S. 584 (1977).
Ford v. Wainwright, 106 S.Ct. 2595 (1986).
Furman v. Georgia, 408 U.S. 238 (1972).
Lockhart v. McCree, 476 U.S. 162 (1986).
McCleskey v. Kemp, 107 S.Ct. 1756 (1987).
Proffitt v. Florida, 428 U.S. 242 (1976).
H. Roberts v. Louisiana, 431 U.S. 633 (1977).
S. Roberts v. Louisiana, 428 U.S. 325 (1976).
Sumner v. Schuman, 107 S.Ct. 2716 (1987).

Questions for Analysis

1. Radelet's ''Introduction and Overview'' is mainly a presentation of facts about the death penalty. What information did you find especially interesting or surprising?

2. In Paragraph 10, Radelet presents the results of two Gallup Polls that show a marked increase in support for the death penalty between 1966 (42 percent support) and 1986 (70 percent support). Radelet does not offer a reason to explain this dramatic shift in opinion. What reasons would you suggest? How would you support your suggestions?
3. In Paragraph 11, Radelet lists groups who oppose the death penalty and then points out that individuals who oppose the death penalty are not allowed on juries in capital trials. Why does he place these two pieces of information in the same paragraph?
4. In Paragraph 4, Radelet states that the goal of his book is to ''examine what life under a sentence of death is like.'' What is the purpose of this ''Introduction''? How is it different from the purpose of the book as a whole? If we look at the subtitle of the book (*Essays on a Cruel and Unusual Punishment*), we can safely say that it has a bias. Do you find evidence of bias in the ''Introduction''?
5. The captions ''Bad'' and ''Good'' in Steve Miller's cartoon, which appears before this reading, suggest that a moral distinction involving capital punishment has been made. Who made it? Does Miller agree with it? Would Radelet agree? Do you agree? Explain your answers.

Edward I. Koch

Death and Justice

(1985)

Ed Koch (b. 1924) has served as a Congressman and, for over a decade was Mayor of New York City. An outspoken, high-profile politician, Koch has written several books about his experience in politics. This essay appeared in *The New Republic* in 1985.

1 Last December a man named Robert Lee Willie, who had been convicted of raping and murdering an 18-year-old woman, was executed in the Louisiana state prison. In a statement issued several minutes before his death, Mr. Willie said: ''Killing people is wrong. . . . It makes no difference whether it's citizens, countries, or governments. Killing is wrong.'' Two weeks later in South Carolina, an admitted killer named Joseph Carl Shaw was put to death for murdering two teenagers. In an appeal to the governor for clemency, Mr. Shaw wrote: ''Killing is wrong when I did it. Killing is wrong when you do it. I hope you have the courage and moral strength to stop the killing.''

2 It is a curiosity of modern life that we find ourselves being lectured on morality by cold-blooded killers. Mr. Willie previously had been convicted of aggravated rape, aggravated kidnapping, and the murders of a Louisiana deputy and a man from Missouri. Mr. Shaw committed another murder a week before the two for which he was

executed, and admitted mutilating the body of the 14-year-old girl he killed. I can't help wondering what prompted these murderers to speak out against killing as they entered the death-house door. Did their newfound reverence for life stem from the realization that they were about to lose their own?

3 Life is indeed precious, and I believe the death penalty helps to affirm this fact. Had the death penalty been a real possibility in the minds of these murderers, they might well have stayed their hand. They might have shown moral awareness before their victims died, and not after. Consider the tragic death of Rosa Velez, who happened to be home when a man named Luis Vera burglarized her apartment in Brooklyn. ''Yeah, I shot her,'' Vera admitted. ''She knew me, and I knew I wouldn't go to the chair.''

4 During my 22 years in public service, I have heard the pros and cons of capital punishment expressed with special intensity. As a district leader, councilman, congressman, and mayor, I have represented constituencies generally thought of as liberal. Because I support the death penalty for heinous crimes of murder, I have sometimes been the subject of emotional and outraged attacks by voters who find my position reprehensible or worse. I have listened to their ideas. I have weighed their objections carefully. I still support the death penalty. The reasons I maintain my position can be best understood by examining the arguments most frequently heard in opposition.

5 (1) *The death penalty is ''barbaric.''* Sometimes opponents of capital punishment horrify with tales of lingering death on the gallows, of faulty electric chairs, or of agony in the gas chamber. Partly in response to such protests, several states such as North Carolina and Texas switched to execution by lethal injection. The condemned person is put to death painlessly, without ropes, voltage, bullets, or gas. Did this answer the objections of death penalty opponents. Of course not. On June 22, 1984, *The New York Times* published an editorial that sarcastically attacked the new ''hygienic'' method of death by injection, and stated that ''execution can never be made humane through science.'' So it's not the method that really troubles opponents. It's the death itself they consider barbaric.

6 Admittedly, capital punishment is not a pleasant topic. However, one does not have to like the death penalty in order to support it any more than one must like radical surgery, radiation, or chemotherapy in order to find necessary these attempts at curing cancer. Ultimately we may learn how to cure cancer with a simple pill. Unfortunately, that day has not yet arrived. Today we are faced with the choice of letting the cancer spread or trying to cure it with the methods available, methods that one day will almost certainly be considered barbaric. But to give up and do nothing would be far more barbaric and would certainly delay the discovery of an eventual cure. The analogy between cancer and murder is imperfect, because murder is not the ''disease'' we are trying to cure. The disease is injustice. We may not like the death penalty, but it must be available to punish crimes of cold-blooded murder, cases in which any other form of punishment would be inadequate and, therefore, unjust. If we create a society in which injustice is not tolerated, incidents of murder—the most flagrant form of injustice—will diminish.

7 (2) *No other major democracy uses the death penalty.* No other major democracy—in fact, few other countries of any description—are plagued by a murder rate such as that in the United States. Fewer and fewer Americans can remember the days when unlocked doors were the norm and murder was a rare and terrible offense. In America the murder rate climbed 122 percent between 1963 and 1980. During that same period, the murder rate in New York City increased by almost 400 percent, and the statistics are even worse in many other cities. A study at M.I.T. showed that based on 1970 homicide rates a person who lived in a large American city ran a greater risk of being murdered than an American soldier in World War II ran of being killed in combat. It is not surprising that the laws of each country differ according to differing conditions and traditions. If other countries had our murder problem, the cry for capital punishment would be just as loud as it is here. And I daresay that any other major democracy where 75 percent of the people supported the death penalty would soon enact it into law.

8 (3) *An innocent person might be executed by mistake.* Consider the work of Adam Bedau, one of the most implacable foes of capital punishment in this country. According to Mr. Bedau, it is "false sentimentality to argue that the death penalty should be abolished because of the abstract possibility that an innocent person might be executed." He cites a study of the 7,000 executions in this country from 1893 to 1971, and concludes that the record fails to show that such cases occur. The main point, however, is this. If government functioned only when the possibility of error didn't exist, government wouldn't function at all. Human life deserves special protection, and one of the best ways to guarantee that protection is to assure that convicted murderers do not kill again. Only the death penalty can accomplish this end. In a recent case in New Jersey, a man named Richard Biegenwald was freed from prison after serving 18 years for murder; since his release he has been convicted of committing four murders. A prisoner named Lemuel Smith, who, while serving four life sentences for murder (plus two life sentences for kidnapping and robbery) in New York's Green Haven Prison, lured a woman corrections officer into the chaplain's office and strangled her. He then mutilated and dismembered her body. An additional life sentence for Smith is meaningless. Because New York has no death penalty statute, Smith has effectively been given a license to kill.

9 But the problem of multiple murder is not confined to the nation's penitentiaries. In 1981, 91 police officers were killed in the line of duty in this country. Seven percent of those arrested in the cases that have been solved had a previous arrest for murder. In New York City in 1976 and 1977, 85 persons arrested for homicide had a previous arrest for murder. Six of these individuals had two previous arrests for murder, and one had four previous murder arrests. During those two years the New York police were arresting for murder persons with a previous arrest for murder on the average of one every 8.5 days. This is not surprising when we learn that in 1975, for example, the median time served in Massachusetts for homicide was less than two-and-a-half years. In 1976 a study sponsored by the Twentieth Century Fund found that the average time

served in the United States for first-degree murder is ten years. The median time served may be considerably lower.

10 (4) *Capital punishment cheapens the value of human life.* On the contrary, it can be easily demonstrated that the death penalty strengthens the value of human life. If the penalty for rape were lowered, clearly it would signal a lessened regard for the victims' suffering, humiliation, and personal integrity. It would cheapen their horrible experience, and expose them to an increased danger of recurrence. When we lower the penalty for murder, it signals a lessened regard for the value of the victim's life. Some critics of capital punishment, such as columnist Jimmy Breslin, have suggested that a life sentence is actually a harsher penalty for murder than death. This is sophistic nonsense. A few killers may decide not to appeal a death sentence, but the overwhelming majority make every effort to stay alive. It is by exacting the highest penalty for the taking of human life that we affirm the highest value of human life.

11 (5) *The death penalty is applied in a discriminatory manner.* This factor no longer seems to be the problem it once was. The appeals process for a condemned prisoner is lengthy and painstaking. Every effort is made to see that the verdict and sentence were fairly arrived at. However, assertions of discrimination are not an argument for ending the death penalty but for extending it. It is not justice to exclude everyone from the penalty of the law if a few are found to be so favored. Justice requires that the law be applied equally to all.

12 (6) *Thou Shalt Not Kill.* The Bible is our greatest source of moral inspiration. Opponents of the death penalty frequently cite the sixth of the Ten Commandments in an attempt to prove that capital punishment is divinely proscribed. In the original Hebrew, however, the Sixth Commandment reads, "Thou Shalt Not Commit Murder," and the Torah specifies capital punishment for a variety of offenses. The biblical viewpoint has been upheld by philosophers throughout history. The greatest thinkers of the 19th century—Kant, Locke, Hobbes, Rousseau, Montesquieu, and Mill—agreed that natural law properly authorizes the sovereign to take life in order to vindicate justice. Only Jeremy Bentham was ambivalent. Washington, Jefferson, and Franklin endorsed it. Abraham Lincoln authorized executions for deserters in wartime. Alexis de Tocqueville, who expressed profound respect for American institutions, believed that the death penalty was indispensable to the support of social order. The United States Constitution, widely admired as one of the seminal achievements in the history of humanity, condemns cruel and inhuman punishment, but does not condemn capital punishment.

13 (7) *The death penalty is state-sanctioned murder.* This is the defense with which Messrs. Willie and Shaw hoped to soften the resolve of those who sentenced them to death. By saying in effect, "You're no better than I am," the murderer seeks to bring his accusers down to his own level. It is also a popular argument among opponents of capital punishment, but a transparently false one. Simply put, the state has rights that

the private individual does not. In a democracy, those rights are given to the state by the electorate. The execution of a lawfully condemned killer is no more an act of murder than is legal imprisonment an act of kidnapping. If an individual forces a neighbor to pay him money under threat of punishment, it's called extortion. If the state does it, it's called taxation. Rights and responsibilities surrendered by the individual are what give the state its power to govern. This contract is the foundation of civilization itself.

14 Everyone wants his or her rights, and will defend them jealously. Not everyone, however, wants responsibilities, especially the painful responsibilities that come with law enforcement. Twenty-one years ago a woman named Kitty Genovese was assaulted and murdered on a street in New York. Dozens of neighbors heard her cries for help but did nothing to assist her. They didn't even call the police. In such a climate the criminal understandably grows bolder. In the presence of moral cowardice, he lectures us on our supposed failings and tries to equate his crimes with our quest for justice.

15 The death of anyone—even a convicted killer—diminishes us all. But we are diminished even more by a justice system that fails to function. It is an illusion to let ourselves believe that doing away with capital punishment removes the murderer's deed from our conscience. The rights of society are paramount. When we protect guilty lives, we give up innocent lives in exchange. When opponents of capital punishment say to the state: "I will not let you kill in my name," they are also saying to murderers: "You can kill in your *own* name as long as I have an excuse for not getting involved."

16 It is hard to imagine anything worse than being murdered while neighbors do nothing. But something worse exists. When those same neighbors shrink back from justly punishing the murderer, the victim dies twice.

Questions for Analysis

1. What is Koch's purpose in quoting two condemned killers in his opening paragraph? Koch obviously finds these statements irritating. Do you agree with him? Why or why not?
2. Explain the purpose of Paragraph 3. Is the logic Koch uses here valid? What do experts on criminal (human) behavior say about the assertion that the death penalty is a deterrent to crime?
3. In Paragraph 6, Koch sets up an analogy between the death penalty and attempts at curing cancer. Is this analogy logical and effective?
4. In response to the objections that no other major democracy uses the death penalty, Koch points out in Paragraph 7 that no other country has our murder rate. Is this a logical justification for the death penalty? Does it explain why 75 percent of our population supports the death penalty?
5. What is the rhetorical advantage of listing and numbering the objections Koch responds to?

6. In Paragraph 12, do you find Koch's response to the injunction "Thou shalt not kill" persuasive? Explain.
7. Koch ends his essay calling for us to assume the responsibility of "justly punishing the murderer. . . ." In your opinion can our society be more just and responsible with or without the death penalty? Do justice and responsibility depend on our using the death penalty?

David Bruck

The Death Penalty

(1985)

After graduating from Harvard College and the University of South Carolina Law School, David Bruck (b. 1949) began practicing law in South Carolina. Most of his professional time is spent defending those sentenced to death. He has published a number of essays on the death penalty, including a frequently anthologized piece that focuses on the racial bias inherent in the administration of the death penalty. The following response to Koch's essay appeared in *The New Republic* in 1985.

1 Mayor Ed Koch contends that the death penalty "affirms life." By failing to execute murderers, he says, we "signal a lessened regard for the value of the victim's life." Koch suggests that people who oppose the death penalty are like Kitty Genovese's neighbors, who heard her cries for help but did nothing while an attacker stabbed her to death.

2 This is the standard "moral" defense of death as punishment: even if executions don't deter violent crime any more effectively than imprisonment, they are still required as the only means we have of doing justice in response to the worst of crimes.

3 Until recently, this "moral" argument had to be considered in the abstract, since no one was being executed in the United States. But the death penalty is back now, at least in the southern states, where every one of the more than thirty executions carried out over the last two years has taken place. Those of us who live in those states are getting to see the difference between the death penalty in theory, and what happens when you actually try to use it.

4 South Carolina resumed executing prisoners in January with the electrocution of Joseph Carl Shaw. Shaw was condemned to death for helping to murder two teenagers while he was serving as a military policeman at Fort Jackson, South Carolina. His crime, propelled by mental illness and PCP, was one of terrible brutality. It is Shaw's last words ("Killing was wrong when I did it. It is wrong when you do it. . . .") that so outraged Mayor Koch: he finds it "a curiosity of modern life that we are being lectured on morality by cold-blooded killers." And so it is.

5 But it was not ''modern life'' that brought this curiosity into being. It was capital punishment. The electric chair was J. C. Shaw's platform. (The mayor mistakenly writes that Shaw's statement came in the form of a plea to the governor for clemency: Actually Shaw made it only seconds before his death, as he waited, shaved and strapped into the chair, for the switch to be thrown.) It was the chair that provided Shaw with celebrity and an opportunity to lecture us on right and wrong. What made this weird moral reversal even worse is that J. C. Shaw faced his own death with undeniable dignity and courage. And while Shaw died, the TV crews recorded another ''curiosity'' of the death penalty—the crowd gathered outside the death-house to cheer on the executioner. Whoops of elation greeted the announcement of Shaw's death. Waiting at the penitentiary gates for the appearance of the hearse bearing Shaw's remains, one demonstrator started yelling, ''Where's the beef?''

6 For those who had to see the execution of J. C. Shaw, it wasn't easy to keep in mind that the purpose of the whole spectacle was to affirm life. It will be harder still when Florida executes a cop-killer named Alvin Ford. Ford has lost his mind during his years of death-row confinement, and now spends his days trembling, rocking back and forth, and muttering unintelligible prayers. This has led to litigation over whether Ford meets a centuries-old legal standard for mental competency. Since the Middle Ages, the Anglo-American legal system has generally prohibited the execution of anyone who is too mentally ill to understand what is about to be done to him and why. If Florida wins its case, it will have earned the right to electrocute Ford in his present condition. If it loses, he will not be executed until the state has first nursed him back to some semblance of mental health.[1]

7 We can at least be thankful that this demoralizing spectacle involves a prisoner who is actually guilty of murder. But this may not always be so. The ordeal of Lenell Jeter—the young black engineer who recently served more than a year of a life sentence for a Texas armed robbery that he didn't commit—should remind us that the system is quite capable of making the very worst sort of mistake. That Jeter was eventually cleared is a fluke. If the robbery had occurred at 7 P.M. rather than 3 P.M., he'd have had no alibi, and would still be in prison today. And if someone had been killed in that robbery, Jeter probably would have been sentenced to death. We'd have seen the usual execution-day interviews with state officials and the victim's relatives, all complaining that Jeter's appeals took too long. And Jeter's last words from the gurney would have taken their place among the growing literature of death-house oration that so irritates the mayor.

8 Koch quotes Hugo Adam Bedau, a prominent abolitionist, to the effect that the record fails to establish that innocent defendants have been executed in the past. But this doesn't mean, as Koch implies, that it hasn't happened. All Bedau was saying was that doubts concerning executed prisoners' guilt are almost never resolved. Bedau is at work now on an effort to determine how many wrongful death sentences may have been imposed: his list of murder convictions since 1900 in which the state eventually *admitted* error is some four hundred cases long. Of course, very few of these cases involved

[1]AUTHOR'S NOTE: On June 26, 1986, the Supreme Court ruled against the State of Florida.

actual executions: the mistakes that Bedau documents were uncovered precisely because the prisoner was alive and able to fight for his vindication. The cases where someone is executed are the very cases in which we're least likely to learn that we got the wrong man.

9 I don't claim that executions of entirely innocent people will occur very often. But they will occur. And other sorts of mistakes already have. Roosevelt Green was executed in Georgia two days before J. C. Shaw. Green and an accomplice kidnapped a young woman. Green swore that his companion shot her to death after Green had left, and that he knew nothing about the murder. Green's claim was supported by a statement that his accomplice made to a witness after the crime. The jury never resolved whether Green was telling the truth, and when he tried to take a polygraph examination a few days before his scheduled execution, the state of Georgia refused to allow the examiner into the prison. As the pressure for symbolic retribution mounts, the courts, like the public, are losing patience with such details. Green was electrocuted on January 9, while members of the Ku Klux Klan rallied outside the prison.

10 Then there is another sort of arbitrariness that happens all the time. Last October, Louisiana executed a man named Ernest Knighton. Knighton had killed a gas station owner during a robbery. Like any murder, this was a terrible crime. But it was not premeditated, and is the sort of crime that very rarely results in a death sentence. Why was Knighton electrocuted when almost everyone else who committed the same offense was not? Was it because he was black? Was it because his victim and all 12 members of the jury that sentenced him were white? Was it because Knighton's court-appointed lawyer presented no evidence on his behalf at his sentencing hearing? Or maybe there's no reason except bad luck. One thing is clear: Ernest Knighton was picked out to die the way a fisherman takes a cricket out of a bait jar. No one cares which cricket gets impaled on the hook.

11 Not every prisoner executed recently was chosen that randomly. But many were. And having selected these men so casually, so blindly, the death penalty system asks us to accept that the purpose of killing each of them is to affirm the sanctity of human life.

12 The death penalty states are also learning that the death penalty is easier to advocate than it is to administer. In Florida, where executions have become almost routine, the governor reports that nearly a third of his time is spent reviewing the clemency requests of condemned prisoners. The Florida Supreme Court is hopelessly backlogged with death cases. Some have taken five years to decide, and the rest of the Court's work waits in line behind the death appeals. Florida's death row currently holds more than 230 prisoners. State officials are reportedly considering building a special ''death prison'' devoted entirely to the isolation and electrocution of the condemned. The state is also considering the creation of a special public defender unit that will do nothing else but handle death penalty appeals. The death penalty, in short, is spawning death agencies.

13 And what is Florida getting for all of this? The state went through almost all of 1983 without executing anyone: its rate of intentional homicide declined by 17 percent. Last

year Florida executed eight people—the most of any state, and the sixth highest total for any year since Florida started electrocuting people back in 1924. Elsewhere in the U.S. last year, the homicide rate continued to decline. But in Florida, it actually rose by 5.1 percent.

14 But these are just the tiresome facts. The electric chair has been a centerpiece of each of Koch's recent political campaigns, and he knows better than anyone how little the facts have to do with the public's support for capital punishment. What really fuels the death penalty is the justifiable frustration and rage of people who see that the government is not coping with violent crime. So what if the death penalty doesn't work? At least it gives us the satisfaction of knowing that we got one or two of the sons of bitches.

15 Perhaps we want retribution on the flesh and bone of a handful of convicted murderers so badly that we're willing to close our eyes to all of the demoralization and danger that come with it. A lot of politicians think so, and they may be right. But if they are, then let's at least look honestly at what we're doing. This lottery of death both comes from and encourages an attitude toward human life that is not reverent, but reckless.

16 And that is why the mayor is dead wrong when he confuses such fury with justice. He suggests that we trivialize murder unless we kill murderers. By that logic, we also trivialize rape unless we sodomize rapists. The sin of Kitty Genovese's neighbors wasn't that they failed to stab her attacker to death. Justice does demand that murderers be punished. And common sense demands that society be protected from them. But neither justice nor self-preservation demands that we kill men whom we have already imprisoned.

17 The electric chair in which J. C. Shaw died earlier this year was built in 1912 at the suggestion of South Carolina's governor at the time, Cole Blease. Governor Blease's other criminal justice initiative was an impassioned crusade in favor of lynch law. Any lesser response, the governor insisted, trivialized the loathsome crimes of interracial rape and murder. In 1912 a lot of people agreed with Governor Blease that a proper regard for justice required both lynching and the electric chair. Eventually we are going to learn that justice requires neither.

Questions for Analysis

1. In response to Koch's complaint about being "lectured on morality by cold-blooded killers," Bruck asserts that capital punishment provided the "platform" for this "curiosity." Explain the thrust of Bruck's argument and why he thought it important to point out that Shaw's words were uttered not in a plea to the governor, but seconds before his execution when all hope for his pardon had expired.

2. At the end of Paragraph 5, Bruck points out another "curiosity" associated with the death penalty—the crowd that gathers outside the death-house to "cheer on the executioner." How do you respond to this common occurrence at executions? Why does Bruck mention it?
3. In Paragraph 13, Bruck presents statistics that show what Florida is getting "for the money and time it invests in the death penalty." Has the death penalty worked to deter murder in Florida? Has it increased the murder rate? Can a cause–effect relationship be established between the number of executions and the number of murders? Explain.
4. What is the point of Bruck's final paragraph? What is his concept of justice and its requirement? How does it differ from Koch's?

Walter Berns

The Death Penalty Dignifies Society

(1979)

Walter Berns (b. 1919) is John M. Olin Distinguished Scholar at the American Enterprise Institute. His book *For Capital Punishment: Crime and the Morality of the Death Penalty* has been one of the most influential studies of this issue. The essay reprinted here is taken from that book.

1 Until recently, my business did not require me to think about the punishment of criminals in general or the legitimacy and efficacy of capital punishment in particular. In a vague way, I was aware of the disagreement among professionals concerning the purpose of punishment—whether it was intended to deter others, to rehabilitate the criminal, or to pay him back—but like most laymen I had no particular reason to decide which purpose was right or to what extent they may all have been right. I did know that retribution was held in ill repute among criminologists and jurists—to them, retribution was a fancy name for revenge, and revenge was barbaric—and, of course, I knew that capital punishment had the support only of policemen, prison guards and some local politicians. . . . The intellectual community denounced it as both unnecessary and immoral. It was the phenomenon of Simon Wiesenthal that allowed me to understand why the intellectuals were wrong and why the police, the politicians, and the majority of the voters were right: We punish criminals principally in order to pay them back, and we execute the worst of them out of moral necessity. . . .

Be Angry with Criminals

2 Why should anyone devote his life—more than thirty years of it!—exclusively to the task of hunting down the Nazi war criminals who survived World War II and escaped

punishment? Wiesenthal says his conscience forces him "to bring the guilty ones to trial." But why punish them? . . . We surely don't expect to rehabilitate them, and it would be foolish to think that by punishing them we might thereby deter others. The answer, I think, is clear: We want to punish them in order *to pay them back.* We think they must be made to pay for their crimes with their lives, and we think that we, the survivors of the world they violated, may legitimately exact that payment because we, too, are their victims. By punishing them, we demonstrate that there are laws that bind men across generations as well as across (and within) nations, that we are not simply isolated individuals, each pursuing his selfish interests and connected with others by a mere contract to live and let live. To state it simply, Wiesenthal allows us to see that it is right, morally right, to be angry with criminals and to express that anger publicly, officially, and in an appropriate manner, which may require the worst of them to be executed.

3 Modern civil-libertarian opponents of capital punishment do not understand this. They say that to execute a criminal is to deny his human dignity; they also say that the death penalty is not useful, that nothing useful is accomplished by executing anyone. Being utilitarians, they are essentially selfish men, distrustful of passion, who do not understand the connection between anger and justice, and between anger and human dignity.

4 Anger is expressed or manifested on those occasions when someone has acted in a manner that is thought to be unjust, and one of its origins is the opinion that men are responsible, and should be held responsible, for what they do. . . . And in holding particular men responsible, it pays them the respect that is due them as men. Anger recognizes that only men have the capacity to be moral beings and, in so doing, acknowledges the dignity of human beings. Anger is somehow connected with justice, and it is this that modern penology has not understood; it tends, on the whole, to regard anger as a selfish indulgence.

5 Anger can, of course, be that; and if someone does not become angry with an insult or an injury suffered unjustly, we tend to think he does not think much of himself. But it need not be selfish, not in the sense of being provoked only by an injury suffered by oneself. There were many angry men in America when President Kennedy was killed; one of them—Jack Ruby—took it upon himself to exact the punishment that, if indeed deserved, ought to have been exacted by the law. There were perhaps even angrier men when Martin Luther King, Jr., was killed, for King, more than anyone else at the time, embodied a people's quest for justice; the anger—more, the "black rage"—expressed on that occasion was simply a manifestation of the great change that had occurred among black men in America, a change wrought in large part by King and his associates in the civil-rights movement: the servility and fear of the past had been replaced by pride and anger, and the treatment that had formerly been accepted as a matter of course or as if it were deserved was now seen for what it was, unjust and unacceptable. King preached love, but the movement he led depended on anger as well as love, and that anger was not despicable, being neither selfish nor unjustified. On the contrary, it was a reflection of what was called solidarity and may more accurately be called a profound

caring for others, black for other blacks, white for blacks, and, in the world King was trying to build, American for other Americans. If men are not saddened when someone else suffers, or angry when someone else suffers unjustly, the implication is that they do not care for anyone other than themselves or that they lack some quality that befits a man. When we criticize them for this, we acknowledge that they ought to care for others. If men are not angry when a neighbor suffers at the hands of a criminal, the implication is that their moral faculties have been corrupted, that they are not good citizens.

Criminals Are Objects of Anger

6 Criminals are properly the objects of anger, and the perpetrators of terrible crimes—for example, Lee Harvey Oswald and James Earl Ray—are properly the objects of great anger. They have done more than inflict an injury on an isolated individual; they have violated the foundations of trust and friendship, the necessary elements of a moral community, the only community worth living in. A moral community, unlike a hive of bees or a hill of ants, is one whose members are expected freely to obey the laws and unlike those in a tyranny, are trusted to obey the laws. The criminal has violated that trust, and in so doing has injured not merely his immediate victim but the community as such. He has called into question the very possibility of that community by suggesting that men cannot be trusted to respect freely the property, the person, and the dignity of those with whom they are associated. If, then, men are not angry when someone else is robbed, raped, or murdered, the implication is that no moral community exists, because those men do not care for anyone other than themselves. Anger is an expression of that caring, and society needs men who care for one another, who share their pleasures and their pains, and do so for the sake of the others. It is the passion that can cause us to act for reasons having nothing to do with selfish or mean calculation; indeed, when educated, it can become a generous passion, the passion that protects the community or country by demanding punishment for its enemies. It is the stuff from which heroes are made. . . .

Criminal Law Must Be Awful

7 Capital punishment . . . serves to remind us of the majesty of the moral order that is embodied in our law, and of the terrible consequences of its breach. The law must not be understood to be merely a statute that we enact or repeal at our will, and obey or disobey at our convenience—especially not the criminal law. Wherever law is regarded as merely statutory, men will soon enough disobey it, and will learn how to do so without any inconvenience to themselves. The criminal law must possess a dignity far beyond that possessed by mere statutory enactment or utilitarian and self-interested calculations. The most powerful means we have to give it that dignity is to authorize it to impose the ultimate penalty. The criminal law must be made awful, by which I mean inspiring, or commanding "profound respect or reverential fear." It must remind us of the moral order by which alone we can live as *human* beings, and in America, now that the Supreme Court has outlawed banishment, the only punishment that can do this is capital punishment.

Questions for Analysis

1. Berns begins this piece with an account of his transition from one who did not have a well-developed opinion about the death penalty to one who strongly advocates it. Why is this personal account an effective way to begin his discussion of this issue?
2. Berns bases his argument here on our need as human beings to express anger in response to injustice. That anger, he asserts, is an expression of our human dignity, or sense of outrage when something offends that dignity. Compare Berns's attitude with the behavior Bruck describes outside the death house when Shaw was executed or similar incidents described by Vodicka, in the next selection. Was what went on in these situations (and it is not an uncommon occurrence) an expression of human dignity? How might Berns respond?
3. Berns mentions two murderers who invoked tremendous anger because of their crimes. Lee Harvey Oswald was killed by Jack Ruby before he could be brought to trial. James Earl Ray was sentenced to life in prison. Does the fact that neither of these men faced the death penalty weaken Berns's argument? Would our anger at the death of Martin Luther King, Jr., be lessened by Ray's death? Would his execution have allowed the venting of anger in a healthier way? Explain your answers.
4. In the final paragraph in this selection Berns argues that the death penalty invests the laws with an awesome dignity that "reminds us of the moral order." Although his argument grows out of recognition of the passion of anger and the need to validate that anger, is Berns simply renewing the argument that the death penalty is a deterrent to crime? Explain your answer.

John Cole Vodicka

The All-Embracing Effect of the Death Penalty

(1985)

John Cole Vodicka (b. 1948) has worked as an advocate for prisoners' rights in California, West Virginia, and Georgia and has been an active opponent of the death penalty in those states. He is currently with The Open Door, an organization in Atlanta, Georgia, that provides legal and other support services to prison inmates.

1 No matter how one feels about the death penalty, no matter what arguments one uses to bolster his or her position, one thing seems absolutely certain to me: State-

sanctioned executions expose more of the violence and injustice that are in us all. It is a dehumanizing ritual, one that brings more injury to each of us.

2 I have been a lifelong opponent of the death penalty. My opposition stems from a variety of reasons: Capital punishment does not deter; it is applied arbitrarily and in a discriminatory fashion; it is cruel and unusual punishment; it is irreversible; and it mocks the commandment, "Thou shalt not kill."

3 I also oppose the death penalty because in my work I have come to know the issue in human terms, in the names and faces of those involved or caught up in this grisly business. Some of these faces are of prisoners who have been executed; in the last 12 months I have lost six friends to the electric chair. Other faces are of the condemned prisoners' families, the families of their victims, of prison officials and guards, of chaplains, lawyers, judges, elected officials and witnesses to executions. And there are the angry faces of those who, out of frustration and fear, have told me they believe the death penalty, whether it "works" or not, is "just desert" for anyone convicted of murder. Countless faces and names, each in his or her own way, a victim of a degrading process that prohibits us from recognizing each other's humanity.

More Victims

4 On May 25, 1979, I stood with several hundred people in front of the Starke, Florida, penitentiary, where John Spenkelink was about to be executed. We were there to pray and to stand in opposition to the impending execution. Standing nearby, though, were several dozen people, a coffin perched atop their Winnebago, chanting "Go, Sparky, Go!" Some were wearing T-shirts that depicted an electric chair with the words, "1 down, 131 to go!"

5 On December 7, 1982, hundreds of college students gathered and gawked outside the Texas Penitentiary at Huntsville and celebrated the impending lethal-injection execution of Charlie Brooks, Jr. They ate popcorn and drank beer, taunting those of us gathered there standing in silent opposition. Some of the students held up handmade signs that read, "Kill Him in Vein" and "Put the Animal to Sleep."

6 On October 12, 1984, across the street from the Virginia Prison in Richmond, rowdy, beer-drinking death-penalty proponents gathered to cheer on the execution of Linwood Briley. They too displayed signs that conveyed a lynchmob mentality. "Fry, nigger, fry!" read one poster. "Burn, Briley, Burn," encouraged another. The demonstrators set off firecrackers when word finally came from the prison that Briley was dead.

7 And here in California earlier this year condemned prisoner Robert Harris lost another round of appeals, thereby temporarily clearing the way for his execution date to be set. The next day, I am told, the switchboard at San Quentin lit up, as dozens of people, including a Los Angeles County district attorney, phoned the warden's office requesting to be an official "witness" to the gassing of Robert Harris.

8 One of the callers was Steven Baker, the father of the child Robert Harris is accused of killing. Baker believes the death penalty will ease his pain, ease his anger. But listen: "Every time Harris files an appeal and his name gets in the papers, myself and the

families have to go through it all over again,'' Baker says. ''The longer this has dragged on the more my rage has been directed at the criminal justice system.''

Revenge and Retaliation

9 It is clear to me that the ritual of capital punishment brutalizes us all; it extends the violence, provokes anger, and hinders, rather than encourages, healing. The death penalty exposes a system which is based on revenge and retaliation. To the detriment of us all, it justifies lethal vengeance.

10 Virginia Governor Charles Robb, when asked about the pro-death penalty demonstration in Richmond on the night Linwood Briley was executed, called it ''inappropriate behavior.'' But my colleague and friend Marie Deans, who worked to halt Briley's electrocution and who is herself a family member of a murder victim, remarked that the crowd's behavior was ''no different than Governor Robb's allowing Briley to be executed, no more inappropriate than what occurred behind those prison walls.''

11 ''The ultimate result of this and every execution,'' Deans said, ''is nothing less than a total disregard for life.''

12 I am convinced that as we deny a death row prisoner his or her humanity, so do we lose a little more of our own.

13 Several years ago my friend Tim Baldwin faced imminent execution in Louisiana. Then, at the last hour, we were successful in obtaining a stay order from a panel of federal judges. A frustrated, vengeful public expressed its outrage. ''Killer Cheats Chair'' screamed one daily newspaper headline. And on one popular New Orleans radio talk show, the host suggested that not only should Baldwin have been electrocuted but that I should have been forced to sit in Baldwin's lap! (Tim Baldwin is one of those faces; he was ultimately executed on September 10, 1984.)

Circle of Tragedy

14 The death penalty doesn't end the suffering, it prolongs it. It doesn't limit the tragedy, it widens it. It doesn't abate the anger, it keeps the wounds open. Each execution draws dozens and dozens more people into its web. The circle of tragedy is always expanding and ultimately, all of us are affected.

15 During the periods of publicity and ritual surrounding executions in several Southern states, I have watched with sadness as victims' families and friends often become public spectacles. They are subjected to frequent indignities and damaging publicity at the time of trial. Healing is retarded as they are dragged through the experience again, usually years later, at the time of appeal and execution. ''For many,'' says Howard Zehr, director of the Mennonite Central Committee's Office of Criminal Justice, ''the ritual of the death penalty takes precedence over the ritual of mourning and remembrance.''

16 I know of at least one Southern prison warden who, when asked how an execution affected him personally, tearfully explained: ''This society makes me do its dirty work. I have to take care of these prisoners—one year, two years, maybe even 10 years. And then I have to kill them.''

17 The death penalty creates more victims.

18 Former San Quentin warden Lawrence Wilson, who participated in a number of executions, told Oakland freelance journalist Michael Kroll: ''You never get used to seeing [an execution]. You get sort of a sinking, sick feeling. After all, there's a guy in front of you, and he struggles to stay alive, but his life support system fails him. He expires before your eyes.''

19 The death penalty dehumanizes.

20 When Robert Wayne Williams was executed in Louisiana last December, Governor David Treen, who refused to grant clemency to Williams, broke down and cried. He called his decision not to spare Williams' life ''the most agonizing I've ever had to face.'' Sam Dalton, Williams' attorney, said, ''I felt like I had been amputated when I heard he had been executed. It was a loss that I just couldn't believe.''

21 The circle of tragedy grows.

22 And Howard Brodie, an artist for CBS News who witnessed the 1967 execution of Aaron Mitchell in California and the 1979 execution of John Spenkelink in Florida, called those experiences ''the most dehumanizing of my entire life.''

Extending the Pain

23 ''The death penalty only allows us to extend the pain,'' says Virginia activist Marie Deans. ''It allows us to continue to blame one another, to turn against one another, to learn to hate better.''

24 Yes, I have seen the full effects of capital punishment. It is measurable in the strain and stress of broken families, ill health, alcoholism, mental breakdown, hospitalization, and for those who survive these ills, in a brutalization born of desperation. It is a brutalization that mars not only the lives of prisoners but of all those touched by the death penalty.

25 Colin Turnbull, the noted anthropologist, has undertaken a study of the death penalty and its effect on society. And he concludes:

> Until we face the harsh facts of what happens on death row and in the execution room, in the witness room and in the offices and homes of the prison officials, lawyers and judges, we are not entitled to have an opinion on capital punishment and call it just. If we were really concerned with the well-being of society, there would be little or no need for the death penalty in the first place.

26 There's the rub. Are we really concerned with society's welfare or are we content in merely providing ourselves with the illusion that something is being done? Do we really believe we will be able to get rid of evil by defining it out of the human species? Or is it no more than revenge, the need to strike back, to get even?

No Right to Get Even

27 ''If it is vengeance, that's bad for society,'' says New York Governor Mario Cuomo, one of four current U.S. governors opposed to the death penalty. ''We don't have the right to get even. It reduces the value of life, and we've done that enough in past years.''

28 But will we ever learn? Will we ever admit to our past mistakes and begin to explore more constructive alternatives to the death penalty, alternatives that still convey firmly and clearly that murder is wrong? I hope so.

29 I know it is not easy for any of us to ward off bitterness and the desire for retaliation. But I also believe that for too long we have treated violence with violence and that's why it never seems to end.

30 Coretta Scott King has lost both a husband and mother-in-law to murder. Still, she speaks out powerfully against the death penalty, against killing people who kill people. Hers, too, is a face I cannot forget. Nor can I forget her words:

> 31 The truth is, we all pay for the death penalty because every time the state kills somebody, our society loses its humanity and compassion and we sow the seeds of violence. We legitimize retaliation as the way to deal with conflict. Yes, we all pay. And in this sense the death penalty means cruel and unusual punishment for not only the condemned prisoner but for the innocent as well, for all of us.

Questions for Analysis

1. Compare Vodicka's thesis in Paragraph 1 with Berns's in the previous selection and explain the differences between them. Try to explain why we see such a radical difference of opinion in two obviously intelligent, sensitive people.
2. Why does Vodicka in Paragraphs 4–6 describe what happened outside three different prisons when executions occurred? How do these descriptions support his thesis?
3. How do the words of Steven Baker in Paragraph 8 support Vodicka's thesis? Do you think he would agree with Vodicka?
4. How would you answer the question Vodicka raises in Paragraph 26?
5. Vodicka ends his essay by quoting Coretta Scott King. Is this an effective way to end? Explain.
6. Vodicka's essay depends heavily on quotes from other people. Is that strategy effective? Do you get from the essay a clear sense of Vodicka's position? Are there any examples or quotations that would have been better left out?

William Hogarth

The Idle 'Prentice Executed at Tyburn

(1747)

William Hogarth (1697–1764) was the most widely known British artist of his time. He made his living not by painting portraits of the rich (the usual path taken by eighteenth-century artists) but by painting scenes containing biting (but comic) social satire, then having them engraved in multiple copies for sale. His engravings are usually crowded with people engaged in a wide range of outrageous, foolish, sometimes vicious, but always very human acts. His painting *The Idle 'Prentice Executed at Tyburn* appears on the following page.

Questions for Analysis

1. One of the major justifications advanced for the death penalty is that it prompts people to reform themselves lest they begin the pattern of cruel, unlawful behavior that would lead them to the gallows. Examine Hogarth's painting of "The Idle 'Prentice Executed at Tyburn" carefully and describe what various people are doing. Are they profiting from the "lesson" of the execution? What do you think Hogarth is showing us about executions through this painting?

William Hogarth, 1697–1764, **The Idle 'Prentice Executed at Tyburn**.

Willie Jasper Darden, Jr.

An Inhumane Way of Death

(1988)

Willie Jasper Darden, Jr. (b. 1934), was executed by the State of Florida on March 15, 1988. His case had drawn wide attention in the media because of both evidence that he might have been innocent of the crime for which he was executed and indications that racial issues biased the prosecution. Both ABC ("20/20") and CBS ("West 57th Street") broadcast special reports on his situation.

1 Ironically, there is probably more hope on death row than would be found in most other places. Each of us has been convicted of murder. Some are guilty and a few are innocent. But the one thing we all have in common is that we await our demise side by side—the innocent and the guilty alike. We hope because it would be so easy for our fate to be changed. Hope is one thing we have in common with those stricken with a terminal illness.

2 Every person in our society is capable of murder. Who among us can say that they have never been so angry that they did foolish things, or that they have not wished for the death of one who destroyed their happiness? Isn't it true that those who advocate the use of capital punishment are just as guilty of homicide as the person executed? Isn't it dangerous for society to preach a message that some of its citizens deserve to die? Like those stricken with a terminal illness, I want to understand.

3 Before the Colosseum ''games'' of ancient Rome, the condemned gladiators stood before the royal podium and said, ''We who are about to die salute you, Caesar.'' Humans on death row do not have that immediacy of struggle or that intimacy with their impersonal foe on the field of battle. We are humans who face death because of the faulty wording of a legal appeal or the capriciously bad stomach of a judge or juror. If we executed all murderers, we would execute twenty thousand per year; we face execution because we are the scapegoats. Like those stricken with a terminal illness, I feel I was chosen at random. And, while morally it is no worse to execute the innocent than to execute the guilty, I will proclaim until the electric chair's current silences me that I am innocent of the charge that sent me here.

4 Our society executes as much ''for the person'' as ''for the crime.'' We execute for heresy—for being different, or for being at the wrong place at the wrong time. We execute for the traits of the person found guilty. If the person is black, uneducated, poor, outspoken, slightly retarded, eccentric, or odd, he stands a much higher chance of being executed than do those convicted of even worse crimes than he. Juries find it hard to convict one of their own, so middle-class whites are rarely in our ranks. Like those stricken with a terminal illness, I feel a tremendous sense of injustice. Unlike

others preparing to die, empirical studies have been conducted by the best minds in America that show I am right.

5 I have been on death row for 14 years and can honestly say that the only description of this place is hell. We send people to prisons to suffer, and prisons have been highly successful in achieving this goal. We live in a society that fosters the belief that inhumanity, revenge, and retribution are legitimate goals of the state. Like those stricken with a terminal illness, I fight my own anger.

6 Most, if not all, of the humans on death row have souls that can be made clean through love, compassion, and spirituality. However, to acknowledge this threatens our ability to execute, as we must dehumanize before we can kill in such a predetermined fashion. It takes concern and understanding to identify with one of God's own. Didn't Jesus glorify the shepherd who left his whole flock just to rescue one lamb? I believe it is the duty and obligation of all of God's children to save, heal, and repair the spirit, soul, mind, and body of others. When Jesus said, "Love your neighbor," I don't think he was talking about those whom it is easy to love. Like others preparing for death, I need community.

7 The one thing all humans want and need is to love and be loved. I often sit and just watch the men here. I watch them change. I watch, and I feel great pity for them. I feel shame, too. Shame because many of my Christian brothers and sisters in society allow this to continue in their names.

8 One of the most profound teachings of Jesus is, "Judge not that ye be not judged." I think that before we can hold up the lamp of understanding to others, we must hold it up to ourselves. That, I believe, is what death is all about.

Questions for Analysis

1. How do you react to Willie Darden's statement? Is his statement reasonable? Logical? Persuasive? Compelling?
2. How do you think Ed Koch would react to Darden's statement? Would he find it as offensive as those he mentioned in his essay? Why or why not?
3. Notice that in his statement Darden uses "we" frequently. What is the effect of his use of the first-person plural pronoun? What different groups are identified by his "we" in different places?
4. How would you characterize the tone of Darden's statement?
5. Does Darden say anything new about the death penalty? Does his situation—as a prisoner on death row about to be executed—give his message a special emphasis? Should that situation make us pay special attention to his comments? Does it? Explain your answers.

Frank O'Connor

Guests of the Nation

(1931)

Frank O'Connor (1903–1966, pen name of Michael O'Donovan) was born in Cork, Ireland. After fighting briefly with the Irish Republican Army during Ireland's struggle for independence, he worked as a librarian and theater director before achieving success as a short story writer. His stories, most of which focused on Irish issues, were published primarily in American magazines. He taught at Harvard and Northwestern universities. This story, set during Ireland's war of independence, is from his first collection of short stories.

I

1 At dusk the big Englishman, Belcher, would shift his long legs out of the ashes and say "Well, chums, what about it?" and Noble or me would say "All right, chum" (for we had picked up some of their curious expressions), and the little Englishman, Hawkins, would light the lamp and bring out the cards. Sometimes Jeremiah Donovan would come up and supervise the game and get excited over Hawkins's cards, which he always played badly, and shout at him as if he was one of our own "Ah, you divil, you, why didn't you play the tray?"

2 But ordinarily Jeremiah was a sober and contented poor devil like the big Englishman, Belcher, and was looked up to only because he was a fair hand at documents, though he was slow enough even with them. He wore a small cloth hat and big gaiters over his long pants, and you seldom saw him with his hands out of his pockets. He reddened when you talked to him, tilting from toe to heel and back, and looking down all the time at his big farmer's feet. Noble and me used to make fun of his broad accent, because we were from the town.

3 I couldn't at the time see the point of me and Noble guarding Belcher and Hawkins at all, for it was my belief that you could have planted that pair down anywhere from this to Claregalway and they'd have taken root there like a native weed. I never in my short experience seen two men to take to the country as they did.

4 They were handed on to us by the Second Battalion when the search for them became too hot, and Noble and myself, being young, took over with a natural feeling of responsibility, but Hawkins made us look like fools when he showed that he knew the country better than we did.

5 "You're the bloke they calls Bonaparte," he says to me. "Mary Brigid O'Connell told me to ask you what you done with the pair of her brother's socks you borrowed."

6 For it seemed, as they explained it, that the Second used to have little evenings, and some of the girls of the neighbourhood turned in, and, seeing they were such decent chaps, our fellows couldn't leave the two Englishmen out of them. Hawkins learned to dance "The Walls of Limerick," "The Siege of Ennis," and "The Waves of Tory"

as well as any of them, though, naturally, we couldn't return the compliment, because our lads at that time did not dance foreign dances on principle.

7 So whatever privileges Belcher and Hawkins had with the Second they just naturally took with us, and after the first day or two we gave up all pretence of keeping a close eye on them. Not that they could have got far, for they had accents you could cut with a knife and wore khaki tunics and overcoats with civilian pants and boots. But it's my belief that they never had any idea of escaping and were quite content to be where they were.

8 It was a treat to see how Belcher got off with the old woman of the house where we were staying. She was a great warrant to scold, and cranky even with us, but before ever she had a chance of giving our guests, as I may call them, a lick of her tongue, Belcher had made her his friend for life. She was breaking sticks, and Belcher, who hadn't been more than ten minutes in the house, jumped up from his seat and went over to her.

9 ''Allow me, madam,'' he says, smiling his queer little smile, ''please allow me''; and he takes the bloody hatchet. She was struck too paralytic to speak, and after that, Belcher would be at her heels, carrying a bucket, a basket, or a load of turf, as the case might be. As Noble said, he got into looking before she leapt, and hot water, or any little thing she wanted, Belcher would have it ready for her. For such a huge man (and though I am five foot ten myself I had to look up at him) he had an uncommon shortness—or should I say lack?—of speech. It took us some time to get used to him, walking in and out, like a ghost, without a word. Especially because Hawkins talked enough for a platoon, it was strange to hear big Belcher with his toes in the ashes come out with a solitary ''Excuse me, chum,'' or ''That's right, chum.'' His one and only passion was cards, and I will say for him that he was a good card-player. He could have fleeced myself and Noble, but whatever we lost to him Hawkins lost to us, and Hawkins played with the money Belcher gave him.

10 Hawkins lost to us because he had too much old gab, and we probably lost to Belcher for the same reason. Hawkins and Noble would spit at one another about religion into the early hours of the morning, and Hawkins worried the soul out of Noble, whose brother was a priest, with a string of questions that would puzzle a cardinal. To make it worse, even in treating of holy subjects, Hawkins had a deplorable tongue. I never in all my career met a man who could mix such a variety of cursing and bad language into an argument. He was a terrible man, and a fright to argue. He never did a stroke of work, and when he had no one else to talk to, he got stuck in the old woman.

11 He met his match in her, for one day when he tried to get her to complain profanely of the drought, she gave him a great come-down by blaming it entirely on Jupiter Pluvius (a deity neither Hawkins nor I had ever heard of, though Noble said that among the pagans it was believed that he had something to do with the rain). Another day he was swearing at the capitalists for starting the German war when the old lady laid down her iron, puckered up her little crab's mouth, and said: ''Mr. Hawkins, you can say what you like about the war, and think you'll deceive me because I'm only a simple poor countrywoman, but I know what started the war. It was the Italian Count that stole

the heathen divinity out of the temple in Japan. Believe me, Mr. Hawkins, nothing but sorrow and want can follow the people that disturb the hidden powers.''

12 A queer old girl, all right.

II

13 We had our tea one evening, and Hawkins lit the lamp and we all sat into cards. Jeremiah Donovan came in too, and sat down and watched us for a while, and it suddenly struck me that he had no great love for the two Englishmen. It came as a great surprise to me, because I hadn't noticed anything about him before.

14 Late in the evening a really terrible argument blew up between Hawkins and Noble, about capitalists and priests and love of your country.

15 ''The capitalists,'' says Hawkins with an angry gulp, ''pays the priests to tell you about the next world so as you won't notice what the bastards are up to in this.''

16 ''Nonsense, man!'' says Noble, losing his temper. ''Before ever a capitalist was thought of, people believed in the next world.''

17 Hawkins stood up as though he was preaching a sermon.

18 ''Oh, they did, did they?'' he says with a sneer. ''They believed all the things you believe, isn't that what you mean? And you believe that God created Adam, and Adam created Shem, and Shem created Jehoshaphat. You believe all that silly old fairytale about Eve and Eden and the apple. Well, listen to me, chum. If you're entitled to hold a silly belief like that, I'm entitled to hold my silly belief—which is that the first thing your God created was a bleeding capitalist, with morality and Rolls-Royce complete. Am I right, chum?'' he says to Belcher.

19 ''You're right, chum,'' says Belcher with his amused smile, and got up from the table to stretch his long legs into the fire and stroke his moustache. So, seeing that Jeremiah Donovan was going, and that there was no knowing when the argument about religion would be over, I went out with him. We strolled down to the village together, and then he stopped and started blushing and mumbling and saying I ought to be behind, keeping guard on the prisoners. I didn't like the tone he took with me, and anyway I was bored with life in the cottage, so I replied by asking him what the hell we wanted guarding them at all for. I told him I'd talked it over with Noble, and that we'd both rather be out with a fighting column.

20 ''What use are those fellows to us?'' says I.

21 He looked at me in surprise and said: ''I thought you knew we were keeping them as hostages.''

22 ''Hostages?'' I said.

23 ''The enemy have prisoners belonging to us,'' he says, ''and now they're talking of shooting them. If they shoot our prisoners, we'll shoot theirs.''

24 ''Shoot them?'' I said.

25 ''What else did you think we were keeping them for?'' he says.

26 ''Wasn't it very unforeseen of you not to warn Noble and myself of that in the beginning?'' I said.

27 ''How was it?'' says he. ''You might have known it.''

28 "We couldn't know it, Jeremiah Donovan," says I. "How could we when they were on our hands so long?"

29 "The enemy have our prisoners as long and longer," says he.

30 "That's not the same thing at all," says I.

31 "What difference is there?" says he.

32 I couldn't tell him, because I knew he wouldn't understand. If it was only an old dog that was going to the vet's, you'd try and not get too fond of him, but Jeremiah Donovan wasn't a man that would ever be in danger of that.

33 "And when is this thing going to be decided?" says I.

34 "We might hear tonight," he says. "Or tomorrow or the next day at latest. So if it's only hanging round here that's a trouble to you, you'll be free soon enough."

35 It wasn't the hanging round that was a trouble to me at all by this time. I had worse things to worry about. When I got back to the cottage the argument was still on. Hawkins was holding forth in his best style, maintaining that there was no next world, and Noble was maintaining that there was; but I could see that Hawkins had had the best of it.

36 "Do you know what, chum?" he was saying with a saucy smile. "I think you're just as big a bleeding unbeliever as I am. You say you believe in the next world, and you know just as much about the next world as I do, which is sweet damn-all. What's heaven? You don't know. Where's heaven? You don't know. You know sweet damn-all! I ask you again, do they wear wings?"

37 "Very well, then," says Noble, "they do. Is that enough for you? They do wear wings."

38 "Where do they get them, then? Who makes them? Have they a factory for wings? Have they a sort of store where you hands in your chit and takes your bleeding wings?"

39 "You're an impossible man to argue with," says Noble. "Now, listen to me—" And they were off again.

40 It was long after midnight when we locked up and went to bed. As I blew out the candle I told Noble what Jeremiah Donovan was after telling me. Noble took it very quietly. When we'd been in bed about an hour he asked me did I think we ought to tell the Englishmen. I didn't think we should, because it was more than likely that the English wouldn't shoot our men, and even if they did, the brigade officers, who were always up and down with the Second Battalion and knew the Englishmen well, wouldn't be likely to want them plugged. "I think so too," says Noble. "It would be great cruelty to put the wind up them now."

41 "It was very unforeseen of Jeremiah Donovan anyhow," says I.

42 It was next morning that we found it so hard to face Belcher and Hawkins. We went about the house all day scarcely saying a word. Belcher didn't seem to notice; he was stretched into the ashes as usual, with his usual look of waiting in quietness for something unforeseen to happen, but Hawkins noticed and put it down to Noble's being beaten in the argument of the night before.

43 "Why can't you take a discussion in the proper spirit?" he says severely. "You and your Adam and Eve! I'm a Communist, that's what I am. Communist or anarchist, it all comes to much the same thing." And for hours he went round the house, muttering

when the fit took him. "Adam and Eve! Adam and Eve! Nothing better to do with their time than picking bleeding apples!"

III

44 I don't know how we got through that day, but I was very glad when it was over, the tea things were cleared away, and Belcher said in his peaceable way: "Well, chums, what about it?" We sat round the table and Hawkins took out the cards, and just then I heard Jeremiah Donovan's footstep on the path and a dark presentiment crossed my mind. I rose from the table and caught him before he reached the door.

45 "What do you want?" I asked.

46 "I want those two soldier friends of yours," he says, getting red.

47 "Is that the way, Jeremiah Donovan?" I asked.

48 "That's the way. There were four of our lads shot this morning, one of them a boy of sixteen."

49 "That's bad," I said.

50 At that moment Noble followed me out, and the three of us walked down the path together, talking in whispers. Feeney, the local intelligence officer, was standing by the gate.

51 "What are you going to do about it?" I asked Jeremiah Donovan.

52 "I want you and Noble to get them out; tell them they're being shifted again; that'll be the quietest way."

53 "Leave me out of that," says Noble under his breath.

54 Jeremiah Donovan looks at him hard.

55 "All right," he says. "You and Feeney get a few tools from the shed and dig a hole by the far end of the bog. Bonaparte and myself will be after you. Don't let anyone see you with the tools. I wouldn't like it to go beyond ourselves."

56 We saw Feeney and Noble go round to the shed and went in ourselves. I left Jeremiah Donovan to do the explanations. He told them that he had orders to send them back to the Second Battalion. Hawkins let out a mouthful of curses, and you could see that though Belcher didn't say anything, he was a bit upset too. The old woman was for having them stay in spite of us, and she didn't stop advising them until Jeremiah Donovan lost his temper and turned on her. He had a nasty temper, I noticed. It was pitch-dark in the cottage by this time, but no one thought of lighting the lamp, and in the darkness the two Englishmen fetched their topcoats and said good-bye to the old woman.

57 "Just as a man makes a home of a bleeding place, some bastard at headquarters thinks you're too cushy and shunts you off," says Hawkins, shaking her hand.

58 "A thousand thanks, madam," says Belcher. "A thousand thanks for everything"—as though he'd made it up.

59 We went round to the back of the house and down towards the bog. It was only then that Jeremiah Donovan had told them. He was shaking with excitement.

60 "There were four of our fellows shot in Cork this morning and now you're to be shot as a reprisal."

61 "What are you talking about?" snaps Hawkins. "It's bad enough being mucked about as we are without having to put up with your funny jokes."

62 "It isn't a joke," says Donovan. "I'm sorry, Hawkins, but it's true," and begins on the usual rigmarole about duty and how unpleasant it is.

63 I never noticed that people who talk a lot about duty find it much of a trouble to them.

64 "Oh, cut it out!" says Hawkins.

65 "Ask Bonaparte," says Donovan, seeing that Hawkins isn't taking him seriously. "Isn't it true, Bonaparte?"

66 "It is," I say, and Hawkins stops.

67 "Ah, for Christ's sake, chum!"

68 "I mean it, chum," I say.

69 "You don't sound as if you meant it."

70 "If he doesn't mean it, I do," says Donovan, working himself up.

71 "What have you against me, Jeremiah Donovan?"

72 "I never said I had anything against you. But why did your people take out four of our prisoners and shoot them in cold blood?"

73 He took Hawkins by the arm and dragged him on, but it was impossible to make him understand that we were in earnest. I had the Smith and Wesson in my pocket and I kept fingering it and wondering what I'd do if they put up a fight for it or ran, and wishing to God they'd do one or the other. I knew if they did run for it, that I'd never fire on them. Hawkins wanted to know was Noble in it, and when we said yes, he asked us why Noble wanted to plug him. Why did any of us want to plug him? What had he done to us? Weren't we all chums? Didn't we understand him and didn't he understand us? Did we imagine for an instant that he'd shoot us for all the so-and-so officers in the so-and-so British Army?

74 By this time we'd reached the bog, and I was so sick I couldn't even answer him. We walked along the edge of it in the darkness, and every now and then Hawkins would call a halt and begin all over again, as if he was wound up, about our being chums, and I knew that nothing but the sight of the grave would convince him that we had to do it. And all the time I was hoping that something would happen; that they'd run for it or that Noble would take over the responsibility from me. I had the feeling that it was worse on Noble than on me.

IV

75 At last we saw the lantern in the distance and made towards it. Noble was carrying it, and Feeney was standing somewhere in the darkness behind him, and the picture of them so still and silent in the bogland brought it home to me that we were in earnest, and banished the last bit of hope I had.

76 Belcher, on recognizing Noble, said: "Hallo, chum," in his quiet way, but Hawkins flew at him at once, and the argument began all over again, only this time Noble had nothing to say for himself and stood with his head down, holding the lantern between his legs.

77 It was Jeremiah Donovan who did the answering. For the twentieth time, as though it was haunting his mind, Hawkins asked if anybody thought he'd shoot Noble.

78 “Yes, you would,” says Jeremiah Donovan.

79 “No, I wouldn't, damn you!”

80 “You would, because you'd know you'd be shot for not doing it.”

81 “I wouldn't, not if I was to be shot twenty times over. I wouldn't shoot a pal. And Belcher wouldn't—isn't that right, Belcher?”

82 “That's right, chum,” Belcher said, but more by way of answering the question than of joining in the argument. Belcher sounded as though whatever unforeseen thing he'd always been waiting for had come at last.

83 “Anyway, who says Noble would be shot if I wasn't? What do you think I'd do if I was in his place, out in the middle of a blasted bog?”

84 “What would you do?” asks Donovan.

85 “I'd go with him wherever he was going, of course. Share my last bob with him and stick by him through thick and thin. No one can ever say of me that I let down a pal.”

86 “We had enough of this,” says Jeremiah Donovan, cocking his revolver. “Is there any message you want to send?”

87 “No, there isn't.”

88 “Do you want to say your prayers?”

89 Hawkins came out with a cold-blooded remark that even shocked me and turned on Noble again.

90 “Listen to me, Noble,” he says. “You and me are chums. You can't come over to my side, so I'll come over to your side. That show you I mean what I say? Give me a rifle and I'll go along with you and the other lads.”

91 Nobody answered him. We knew that was no way out.

92 “Hear what I'm saying?” he says. “I'm through with it. I'm a deserter or anything else you like. I don't believe in your stuff, but it's no worse than mine. That satisfy you?”

93 Noble raised his head, but Donovan began to speak and he lowered it again without replying.

94 “For the last time, have you any messages to send?” says Donovan in a cold, excited sort of voice.

95 “Shut up, Donovan! You don't understand me, but these lads do. They're not the sort to make a pal and kill a pal. They're not the tools of any capitalist.”

96 I alone of the crowd saw Donovan raise his Webley to the back of Hawkins's neck, and as he did so I shut my eyes and tried to pray. Hawkins had begun to say something else when Donovan fired, and as I opened my eyes at the bang, I saw Hawkins stagger at the knees and lie out flat at Noble's feet, slowly and as quiet as a kid falling asleep, with the lantern-light on his lean legs and bright farmer's boots. We all stood very still, watching him settle out in the last agony.

97 Then Belcher took out a handkerchief and began to tie it about his own eyes (in our excitement we'd forgotten to do the same for Hawkins), and, seeing it wasn't big

enough, turned and asked for the loan of mine. I gave it to him and he knotted the two together and pointed with his foot at Hawkins.

98 "He's not quite dead," he says. "Better give him another."

99 Sure enough, Hawkins's left knee is beginning to rise. I bend down and put my gun to his head; then, recollecting myself, I get up again. Belcher understands what's in my mind.

100 "Give him his first," he says. "I don't mind. Poor bastard, we don't know what's happening to him now."

101 I knelt and fired. By this time I didn't seem to know what I was doing. Belcher, who was fumbling a bit awkwardly with the handkerchiefs, came out with a laugh as he heard the shot. It was the first time I heard him laugh and it sent a shudder down my back; it sounded so unnatural.

102 "Poor bugger!" he said quietly. "And last night he was so curious about it all. It's very queer, chums, I always think. Now he knows as much about it as they'll ever let him know, and last night he was all in the dark."

103 Donovan helped him to tie the handkerchiefs about his eyes. "Thanks, chum," he said. Donovan asked if there were any messages he wanted sent.

104 "No, chum," he says. "Not for me. If any of you would like to write to Hawkins's mother, you'll find a letter from her in his pocket. He and his mother were great chums. But my missus left me eight years ago. Went away with another fellow and took the kid with her. I like the feeling of a home, as you may have noticed, but I couldn't start again after that."

105 It was an extraordinary thing, but in those few minutes Belcher said more than in all the weeks before. It was just as if the sound of the shot had started a flood of talk in him and he could go on the whole night like that, quite happily, talking about himself. We stood round like fools now that he couldn't see us any longer. Donovan looked at Noble, and Noble shook his head. Then Donovan raised his Webley, and at that moment Belcher gives his queer laugh again. He may have thought we were talking about him, or perhaps he noticed the same thing I'd noticed and couldn't understand it.

106 "Excuse me, chums," he says. "I feel I'm talking the hell of a lot, and so silly, about my being so handy about a house and things like that. But this thing came on me suddenly. You'll forgive me, I'm sure."

107 "You don't want to say a prayer?" asks Donovan.

108 "No, chum," he says. "I don't think it would help. I'm ready and you boys want to get it over."

109 "You understand that we're only doing our duty?" says Donovan.

110 Belcher's head was raised like a blind man's, so that you could only see his chin and the tip of his nose in the lantern-light.

111 "I never could make out what duty was myself," he said. "I think you're all good lads, if that's what you mean. I'm not complaining."

112 Noble, just as if he couldn't hear any more of it, raised his fist at Donovan, and in a flash Donovan raised his gun and fired. The big man went over like a sack of meal, and this time there was no need of a second shot.

113 I don't remember much about the burying, but that it was worse than all the rest because we had to carry them to the grave. It was all mad lonely with nothing but a patch of lantern-light between ourselves and the dark, and birds hooting and screeching all round, disturbed by the guns. Noble went through Hawkins's belongings to find the letter from his mother, and then joined his hands together. He did the same with Belcher. Then, when we'd filled in the grave, we separated from Jeremiah Donovan and Feeney and took our tools back to the shed. All the way we didn't speak a word. The kitchen was dark and cold as we'd left it, and the old woman was sitting over the hearth, saying her beads. We walked past her into the room, and Noble struck a match to light the lamp. She rose quietly and came to the doorway with all her cantankerousness gone.

114 "What did ye do with them?" she asked in a whisper, and Noble started so that the match went out in his hand.

115 "What's that?" he asked without turning round.

116 "I heard ye," she said.

117 "What did you hear?" asked Noble.

118 "I heard ye. Do ye think I didn't hear ye, putting the spade back in the houseen?"

119 Noble struck another match and this time the lamp lit for him.

120 "Was that what ye did to them?" she asked.

121 Then, by God, in the very doorway, she fell on her knees and began praying, and after looking at her for a minute or two Noble did the same by the fireplace. I pushed my way out past her and left them at it. I stood at the door, watching the stars and listening to the shrieking of the birds dying out over the bogs. It is so strange what you feel at times like that that you can't describe it. Noble says he saw everything ten times the size, as though there were nothing in the whole world but that little patch of bog with the two Englishmen stiffening into it, but with me it was as if the patch of bog where the Englishmen were was a million miles away, and even Noble and the old woman, mumbling behind me, and the birds and the bloody stars were all far away, and I was somehow very small and very lost and lonely like a child astray in the snow. And anything that happened to me afterwards, I never felt the same about again.

Questions for Analysis

1. Why do Noble and Bonaparte react as they do to the executions of Hawkins and Belcher? Why is Donovan able to carry through on the executions? Do you believe that Noble and Bonaparte would have been able to conduct the executions on their own if they had received the orders? Explain.
2. How do Hawkins and Belcher react when they learn that they are to be executed? How is their behavior then characteristic of their earlier behavior? How is it different? Why do the different behaviors occur?
3. Why did O'Connor choose to write this piece in the first person?

4. This short story could have been included in Part IV's section on war. What does it show us about the people who go to war and their reasons for doing so?
5. At the very end of the story Bonaparte says that after the executions he felt that he "was somehow very small and very lost and lonely like a child astray in the snow." How does this visual image convey Bonaparte's feelings? How does it connect with other issues (religion and duty, for example) raised during the story?

Acid Rain: What Should We Do About It?

The debate over acid rain is a fascinating, complex, and sometimes frustrating blend of scientific and political rhetoric. (For example, acid rain should more accurately be called acid deposition since it includes all precipitation as well as dry, microscopic particles of acid-forming compounds.) Like many other environmental issues, it is complicated by very difficult scientific problems as well as by economic and political pressures.

Scientists know that a number of sources (including automobiles, heavy industry, and utilities) are emitting a tremendous volume of sulfate and nitrate compounds that combine with water in the atmosphere to form strong acids. However, because of the incredibly complex nature of atmospheric and ecological systems, researchers have only recently been able to pinpoint a few of the ways these acids affect our environment and thus to estimate with some precision the actual damage they do. This difficulty in determining the exact impact of acid rain on the environment has allowed businesses and interest groups to delay action by calling for additional scientific studies. These delays have saved businesses billions of dollars they would have had to invest to reduce or eliminate sources of pollution. However, the costs of these delays in terms of damage to our air, water, and ecological systems may be difficult, if not impossible, to recover.

The positions taken by politicians at the federal level, where most of the sweeping policy decisions must be made, have become predictable. Not surprisingly, politicians from states that either produce or burn large quantities of the fossil fuels responsible for acid rain argue that more studies are needed before laws that require costly changes are passed. Politicians from states where the damage from acid rains seems most serious argue that changes must be made quickly before irreparable harm is done. Division over acid rain is more along geographic lines than party lines: Republicans *and* Democrats both oppose and support stricter pollution-control laws.

Some of the readings in this section illustrate scientists' struggles to explain difficult processes and to draw conclusions they can defend based on the evidence available. Other examples show writers in the political arena attempting to diminish or enlarge on the scientific evidence to support their economic and political agendas.

This section begins and ends with editorial cartoons that set past against present and present against future. Robert Ariail's cartoon presents a new and disturbing set of images for us to set in stark contrast to those we have usually associated with "America the Beautiful." The first essay in this section is the March 1972 *Environment* article on acid rain by Gene E. Likens, F. Herbert Bormann, and Noye M. Johnson. One of the earliest essays that attempted to assess the potential damage done by acid rain, this piece presents the scientific evidence available in 1972 about the processes involved in acid-rain formation and the possible damage being done. Depending on their political or scientific stance, later writers either built on or questioned the evidence presented by Likens and his colleaques.

The next three selections, all published between 1984 and 1988, were written to question the seriousness of acid rain as an environmental threat and thus to slow implementation of policies that would be costly to utilities and other industries that are heavily dependent on fossil fuels. William M. Brown's essay in *Fortune* magazine (1984) argues that many other factors may have a greater effect on the acidity of certain New England lakes and streams than acid rain. The Reagan administration is right, he argued, to proceed slowly with controls until more evidence is in. Dixy Lee Ray's "The Great Acid Rain Debate" is a long, detailed attempt to counter environmentalists' arguments that new, very strict controls on air quality are needed to combat the effects of acid rain. Ray's approach questions both the reliability and validity of studies that suggest acid rain is a major destructive agent in the environment. She argues that acid rain and acid precursor compounds (sulfates and nitrates) in the atmosphere are natural phenomena. A report prepared by the National Acid Precipitation Assessment Program (NAPAP) follows. The NAPAP is a federal agency created by Congress in 1980 to "coordinate federally funded research and assessment activities to facilitate the timely development of a firm scientific basis for policy decisions that pertain to acid rain." The excerpts from this agency's 1986 and 1987 reports suggest that the effects of acid rain are not nearly as serious as many environmentalists first believed. Some observers have questioned these reports, suggesting that they may more accurately reflect the Reagan administration's bias than the conclusions suggested by the scientific evidence.

The final two essays in this section look at the problem of acid rain from a very different perspective. Volker A. Mohnen's *Scientific American* article on "The Challenge of Acid Rain" presents a case for acid rain as a threat to our ecosystem without denying the complexities and uncertainties inherent in the scientific evidence. Since he is writing more than 15 years after Likins, Bormann, and Johnson, Mohnen has access to more recent studies of the possible environmental impact of high acidity from precipitation. He also examines the new technologies that will enable utilities and other industries to reduce acidic emissions effectively and economically. Jon R. Luoma discusses "The Human Cost of Acid Rain" in an *Audubon* essay that examines how acidic chemicals in the air or fog can cause respiratory disease over a long period of time and even sudden death when concentrations are very high over a period of a few days.

Finally, Jeff McNelly's cartoon, "Earth Day 1990: A seedling takes root in a hostile environment," sets up a contrast between the present reality of industrial pollution and the frail hope that environmentalism can make a difference for the future. As you read these essays, notice how the same information is presented by different writers to support very different purposes. Together these essays demonstrate that even with scientific writing one's understanding of the significant facts depends as much on how those facts are presented as the facts themselves.

Robert Ariail

"America the Beautiful" (revised)

(1988)

Robert Ariail (b. 1955) is editorial cartoonist for *The State* newspaper, Columbia, South Carolina.

Robert Ariail, The State *(Columbia, S.C.).*

Gene E. Likens, F. Herbert Bormann, and Noye M. Johnson

Acid Rain

(1972)

At the time this article was published, Gene E. Likens (b. 1935) was Associate Professor in the Section of Ecology and Systematics at Cornell University; F. Herbert Bormann (b. 1922) was Professor of Forest Ecology in Yale University's School of Forestry; and Noye M. Johnson (b. 1930) was Professor of Earth Sciences at Dartmouth College. The article first appeared in the March 1972 issue of *Environment*.

1 European scientists have found that rain in northwestern Europe shows a trend toward increased acidity, particularly over the past fifteen years. The tendency appears linked to mounting levels of certain gaseous pollutants such as sulfur and nitrogen oxides, which can be converted chemically in the atmosphere to strong acids. Although the trend appears to pose no apparent threat to health, it can do considerable damage to man-made structures and equipment, and more importantly it has serious implications for ecological systems.

2 Data indicating this trend are expressed in what are called pH values. These values are a measure of hydrogen ion activity. Briefly, water slightly ionizes (is converted into ions, which are electrically charged particles), yielding hydrogen and hydroxyl ions. When the activity of these ions is equal, water is neither acid nor alkaline and is said to be neutral. This neutrality point is represented by the pH value 7, which actually varies slightly according to temperature. Water becomes increasingly acid at pH values below 7, increasingly alkaline at values above 7. There are tenfold differences between each unit. Thus, pH 6 is ten times more acid than pH 7, pH 5 is 100 times more acidic than pH 7, and so on.

3 Distilled water in contact with carbon dioxide in the air becomes slightly acid since carbon dioxide combines with water to form carbonic acid. Normally, the pH of rainwater, regulated only by carbon dioxide gas in the atmosphere, would be 5.7 or only slightly acid.[1] Recent European studies, however, have reported increasing quantities of much stronger acids in rain and snow, producing pH values between 3 and 5. The presence of these acids is presumably related to air pollution.

4 By burning fossil fuels, man releases large quantities of sulfur and nitrogen oxides to the atmosphere. These compounds are in addition to naturally occurring gaseous forms of sulfur and nitrogen. K. K. Bertine and E. D. Goldberg[2] estimate that about 3,740,000 tons of sulfur are released to the atmosphere each year by the combustion of fossil fuels. In 1968 man-made emissions from the United States contributed some 33.2 million tons of sulfur oxides and 20.7 million tons of nitrogen oxides to the atmosphere.[3] Sulfur dioxide and hydrogen sulfide are chemically changed (oxidized and hydrolyzed) in the atmosphere to sulfuric acid at varying rates depending upon environmental

conditions. Likewise, various nitrogen oxides are transformed into nitric acid. If these acids are not neutralized by alkaline substances also present in the atmosphere, they will ultimately fall to the land and waters in precipitation.

5 With unpolluted atmospheric conditions, the relatively weak acidity of carbonic acid in precipitation is one of the major factors in the chemical weathering of landscapes. (Weathering is the decomposition of rocks.) The chemical weathering process is in part responsible for the slow but steady leaching (removal) of nutrients from primary and secondary minerals in rocks and soils. By changing the acidity of precipitation, man's activities may have important modifying effects on these and other vital functions of natural ecosystems. Very little attention has been given to this problem in the literature.

6 Acid rain is not a new phenomenon although it may now be affecting large geographic regions. For example, C. Crowther and H. G. Rustan[4] report that substantial amounts of acid were added to the soil in the industrial city of Leeds, England, in rainfall during 1907–1908. Expressed as sulfuric acid, this amounted to 1.84 pounds of hydrogen ions per acre per year (sulfuric acid dissociates in water to release hydrogen and sulfate ions). By way of reference, one meter (about 40 inches) of rain per year at a pH of 4 would add 2.20 pounds of hydrogen ions per hectare (2.47 acres). At a pH of 5, the input would be 0.22 pounds per hectare, and at pH 3 it would be 22 pounds per hectare. The rain in Leeds was thus strongly acidic.

7 Increasing acidification of precipitation and the consequent ecological effects have received the most attention in Scandinavia.[5] There, it is estimated that more than 75 percent of the sulfur in the air is produced by human activity. Much of this sulfur apparently comes from distant industrialized regions, such as England and the Ruhr Valley. The average residence time for sulfur in the atmosphere is two to four days, and on the average it may be transported more than 620 miles before being deposited on the earth's surface.[6] Because of the availability of data from a network of sampling stations in Scandinavia, it is possible to map changes in acidity of precipitation in recent years. The results show that there has been a striking increase, with the acidity of rain in some parts of Scandinavia increasing more than 200-fold since 1956.[7] Values in rain as low as pH 2.8 have been recorded.[8]

8 E. Gorham has observed the relation between air pollution and the acidity of precipitation in the English Lake District, where the pH of rain averages less than 4.5 and occasionally may be less than 4.0.[9] A. V. Holden reports mean annual pH values of 5.08 to 4.74 to 4.40 in a southerly direction for three inland Scottish locations,[10] corresponding to increasing excess sulfate values and industrial atmospheric pollution. Even rain collected near Manaus in the center of the Amazon basin had pH values ranging between 4.0 and 5.4 during 1966–1968;[11] these values may be related to large-scale burning of forests in this area.[12] A few pH values for other localities in the world are summarized by D. Carroll.[13]

9 We first became aware of the problem of acid rain through our studies of biogeochemical cycles for the Hubbard Brook Experimental Forest in New Hampshire. Continuous measurement of pH in rain and snow samples since 1964 has clearly shown that precipitation in this rural, forested area is quite acid.[14] In fact, the hydrogen ion is

the predominant positively charged ion in precipitation, indicating the presence of strong acids such as sulfuric and nitric acids. The annual weighted average pH between 1965 and 1971 ranged between 4.03 and 4.19. (A weighted average takes into account the amount of rain as well as its composition.) Although there has been no apparent trend, 1971 is the only year in which the pH was less than 4.1. The lowest pH value recorded at Hubbard Brook was a surprisingly acid 3.0.

10 How acid is rainfall over the United States? Is the acidity changing and why? These questions are vital to considerations of environmental quality, but unfortunately answers are based on scanty information. However, from the few data that are available, it would appear that the acid precipitation is much more widespread than generally believed. We have attempted to assemble data to characterize the acidity of rain and snow in the United States, but there have been few comprehensive studies of precipitation chemistry, and pH values often are not detailed.[15] Most seriously, we can find no data to accurately describe long-term trends for the U.S.

11 Measurements recently completed in the central Finger Lakes Region of New York State show that rain and snow are equally as acid as that found in New Hampshire. . . . The annual pH, based upon samples collected during the twelve-month period 1970–1971, and weighted proportionally to the amount of water and pH during each period of precipitation, was 3.98 at Ithaca, New York; 3.91 at Aurora, New York; 4.02 at Geneva, New York; and 4.03 at Hubbard Brook, New Hampshire. Summertime values were lower for all four sites. Because local combustion of fossil fuels is greater during the winter, these variations may reflect different seasonal paths for regional air masses carrying sulfur or nitrogen derivatives from more distant industrialized areas. We have not yet completely analyzed our data in this regard, but it is noteworthy that major storm tracks and air masses generally differ between summer and winter seasons in central New York.[16] Current measurements over the entire state indicate that rain and snow are surprisingly and consistently acid (see Table 1). Based upon these data and those of F. J. Pearson, Jr. and D. W. Fisher,[17] it is apparent that the precipitation falling on most of the northeastern U.S. is characterized by high acidity. Weighted annual pH values of 4.27, 4.29, and 4.27 have been reported for New Durham, New Hampshire; Hubbardston, Massachusetts; and Thomaston, Connecticut. At Thomaston, the lowest monthly average pH, 3.9, was recorded at the height of the growing season.[18] In New Haven, Connecticut, pH values during the spring and summer of 1970 averaged 3.81, with a summer average of 3.62, and a low of 3.52. Killingworth, located 30 miles east of New Haven, recorded a pH of 4.31 in April 1970.

12 Although extensive data are available for New York on nitrogen and sulfur in precipitation during the first half of this century,[19] no concurrent published records of pH have been found. Apparently, prior to 1940, when most of this rainwater chemistry was done, only methyl orange was used to indicate acid or alkaline conditions in samples. Unfortunately, this indicator is of little use in describing the pH during this period since methyl orange changes color at a pH of 4.6, meaning that actual determinations of pH above or below this level could not be made. In the absence of data on pH, the large amounts of bicarbonate in rainwater samples taken at Geneva, New York during the

period 1919–1929[20] indicate much higher pH values than today. Bicarbonate, from carbonic acid, cannot coexist with the stronger acids found in today's rain. The presence of bicarbonate, therefore, would indicate that pH values in 1919–1929 were 5.7 or higher.

13 Available data on the pH of rain and snow in other parts of the U.S. help to define the problem. The acidity of rain and snow in the Pacific and eastern Gulf coastal regions of the U.S. is of particular interest in evaluating the localized effect of industrial air pollution, since prevailing air flow is onshore. The pH of rainfall at Corvallis, Oregon, in December 1969 and January 1970 ranged between 4.95 and 5.7.[21] R. F. Tarrant and his colleagues found that the pH of precipitation ranged between 5.7 and 6.3 (annual average of 6.1) during the period 1963–1964 in coastal Oregon forests.[22] The pH of glacial ice in the northern Cascade Mountains, which represents a historical composite of snow, has been measured at 5.6.[23] Rainwater values ranging from pH 5.4 to 8.5 in 1957–1958 and pH 4.9 to 6.8 in 1958–1959 at Menlo Park, California, have been reported.[24] P. L. Brezonik and his colleagues observed pH values between 5.3 and 6.8 during 1967–1968 in north central Florida.[25] Collectively, these pH values suggest a carbonic acid control for the precipitation of these areas, which by and large are meteorologically isolated from large industrial centers. (Carbonic acid control refers to acidity due to the carbonic acid rather than to stronger acids such as sulfuric acid.)

The Effects on Ecosystems

14 Simply stated, the problem is that water from rain and snow in many areas of the world is no longer characterized by the weak, although highly buffered (containing substances that prevent change in pH of a solution after the addition of either acid or alkali), carbonic acid, but instead is dominated by the stronger, although unbuffered, sulfuric and nitric acids, at a greatly reduced pH. The ecological effects of this change are as yet unknown, but potentially they are manifold and very complex. Effects may range from changes in leaching rates of nutrients from plant foliage, changes in leaching rates of soil nutrients, acidification of lakes and rivers, effects on metabolism of organisms, and corrosion of structures. These effects illustrate the dynamic and complex linkages between ecosystems.

15 Since most combustion of fossil fuels occurs in the mid-latitudes of the Northern Hemisphere, any consequent changes in acidity will be most evident here. However, there are separate and synergistic (combined) effects of other atmospheric and land-based pollutants such as sulfur dioxide, nitrogen oxides, and ozone. Thus, the effects of acid precipitation in ecosystems are often difficult to isolate from other man-induced changes that are also accelerating. The best data come from Scandinavia.

16 A trend of decreasing pH (increasing acidity) was observed during 1965–1970 in almost all lakes and rivers covered by a network of sampling stations in Scandinavia.[26] Acidity increased at a rate of 8 to 24 percent per year in Swedish rivers. This corresponds to the period of increasing acidity of rainfall for this area . . . but also must represent the effects of other pollutants dumped into aquatic ecosystems by man's activities. Significantly, unpolluted river systems also increased in acidity (in five years

Annual Weighted pH for Precipitation in New York State*
(The Range of Observed Values Is Given in Parentheses)

	1965–61†	1966–67	1967–68	1968–69
Mineola	—	4.42 (4.0–6.4)	4.45 (3.8–5.2)	4.57 (4.2–6.5)
Upton	(3.9–4.5)	4.46 (4.2–4.9)	4.33 (3.8–5.0)	4.11 (3.9–4.3)
Rock Hill	(4.3–5.6)	4.20 (4.0–4.8)	4.26 (4.0–5.0)	4.29 (4.0–4.8)
Albany	(4.2–4.4)	4.87 (4.3–6.5)	4.61 (4.2–6.6)	4.68 (4.3–6.8)
Hinckley	(4.1–4.6)	4.45 (4.2–6.9)	4.37 (4.0–6.4)	4.37 (4.1–4.7)
Allegany State Park	(6.1–6.5)	4.27 (4.0–7.2)	4.53 (4.1–6.0)	4.31 (4.1–7.0)
Mays Point	(4.1–4.3)	4.29 (4.0–4.8)	4.78 (4.2–7.1)	4.93 (4.3–7.0)
Canton	(4.3–4.4)	4.34 (4.0–5.0)	4.57 (4.3–5.9)	4.37 (4.1–5.5)
Athens, Pa.	(4.5–4.6)	4.34 (4.0–6.1)	4.25 (4.0–5.9)	4.28 (4.0–5.4)

*Calculated from U.S. Department of the Interior, Geological Survey, Water Resources Data for New York, Part II; Water Quality Records, 1966 through 1969, Albany, New York.

†August–October 1966.

the pH was lowered to 0.15 units, that is, the acidity increased 1.4 times); these changes were attributed directly to the acidification of precipitation.

17 The effects of increasing acidity on aquatic life may be very serious. According to M. Grande and E. Snekvik: "This fallout, which is particularly high in sulfur dioxide, has already so altered the pH of certain streams in southern Norway that salmon eggs can no longer develop and the salmon runs have been eliminated.[27] In most unpolluted, fresh water, the pH generally ranges between 6.5 and 8.5.[28]

18 Effects on soil fertility and biological productivity are intertwined and difficult to evaluate. Increased input of acid into soil may lead to increased leaching of calcium and other nutrient minerals. Such losses may not result in any significant short-term damage to arable land (land capable of producing crops), but they represent an added stress to the ecosystem. If it became necessary for man to replace chemicals lost from the soil as a result of acidification of rain, very large costs could be involved. In Sweden, it is thought that in the last fifteen years there has been an annual reduction in forest growth as a result of acid rainfall.[29]

19 Thus, these data indicate fundamental changes in land and water ecosystems resulting from acidified rainfall. This same phenomenon must be occurring in other parts of the world, but there is little cognizance of it, and it is often confounded by other sources of pollution. The eastern U.S., particularly New England, undoubtedly receives sulfur and nitrogen oxides from the West and Midwest, but large-scale changes and effects associated with increased inputs of these compounds and increased acidity of precipitation have been largely overlooked or ignored. Long-term records of water quality in lakes and rivers of the United States are scarce and difficult to interpret.[30] Similarly, any effects of acid rain on these ecosystems is at present unclear, but a few long-term observations are interesting and suggestive. C. L. Schofield, Jr.[31] reports that the water

chemistry of a relatively large clear-water, oligotrophic (deficient in plant nutrients and low in productivity) lake in the Adirondack Mountains of New York has changed appreciably since 1938: In December 1938, the alkalinity expressed as chemically equivalent concentrations of calcium carbonate ranged from 12.5 to 20.0 parts per million and the pH was 6.6 to 7.2, whereas during 1959–1960 the alkalinity ranged from 0 to 3.0 parts per million and the pH ranged from 3.9 to 5.8, demonstrating a sharp increase in acidity. Although the information prior to 1910 is scanty, it would appear that there was a significant jump in the sulfate content of Lake Michigan, the Illinois River, and possibly the Ohio River by 1920–1930, with a more gradual increase in concentration to the present time.[32] Significantly, in this regard, alkalinity values in Lake Michigan have decreased about 7 percent during the past years, suggesting increased acidity. A similar decrease in alkalinity of about 2 percent in the Mississippi River was observed between 1911 and 1968. The pattern in the Illinois and Ohio rivers is more complex, with periods of increase and decrease since the early 1900s. The interpretation of such data is very difficult, but changes in all of the environmental inputs must be considered and evaluated in assessing long-term fluctuations in environmental quality.

20 Sweden's case study for the U.N. Conference on Human Environment to be held in Stockholm in the summer of 1972 deals with ''air pollution across national boundaries.'' The early results clearly indicate that air pollution is an unpremeditated form of chemical warfare! Data collected on atmospheric pollutants and acid rain suggest a very serious problem in northern Europe. Existing data suggest that the problem in the United States, particularly in the Northeast, has already reached similar proportions. We urge consideration of these data in the establishment of air pollution standards and a massive effort to increase our understanding of this problem. Detailed ecological and geochemical studies are urgently needed on the separate and combined effects of additions of nitrogen and sulfur oxides and associated acidity on ecosystems.

Acknowledgments: This is contribution No. 48 of the Hubbard Brook Ecosystem Study. Financial support for the field study at Hubbard Brook was provided by the National Science Foundation, and was done through the cooperation of the Northeastern Forest Experiment Station, Forest Service, U.S. Department of Agriculture, Upper Darby, Pennsylvania. Support for studies of precipitation chemistry in the Finger Lakes Region of New York was provided by the U.S. Department of Interior, Office of Water Resources Research through the Cornell University Water Resources and Marine Sciences Center. Climatological data for New York were obtained from the U.S. Department of Commerce, Environmental Sciences Services Administration. We thank John S. Eaton, Cornell University, for computational assistance and Ray T. Oglesby, Cornell University, and C. A. Federer, U. S. Forest Service, for comments on the manuscript.

Notes

1. Barrett, E., and G. Brodin, ''The Acidity of Scandinavian Precipitation,'' *Tellus,* 7:251–257, 1955.
2. Bertine, K. K., and E. D. Goldberg, ''Fossil Fuel Combustion and the Major Sedimentary Cycle,'' *Science,* 173:233–235, 1971.
3. Massachusetts Institute of Technology, *Man's Impact on the Global Environment: Report of the Study of Critical Environmental Problems,* M.I.T. Press, Cambridge, Mass., 1970, p. 296.
4. Crowther, C., and H. G. Rustan, ''The Nature, Distribution and Effects upon Vegetation of Atmospheric Impurities in and near an Industrial Town,'' *J. Agric. Sci.,* 4:25–55, 1911.
5. For example, see: Odén, S., Nederbördens och Luftens Försurning-dess Orsaker, Förlopp och Verkan I Olida Miljöer, Statens Naturvetenskapliga Forskningsrad, Stockholm, Bull. No. 1, 1968, 86 pp. Odén,

S., and T. Ahl, Försurningen av skandinaviska vatten (The Acidification of Scandinavian Lakes and Rivers), Ymer, Ärsbok, 1970, pp. 103–122. Lundholm, B., ''Interactions Between Oceans and Terrestrial Ecosystems,'' in *Global Effects of Environmental Pollution,* S. F. Singer, ed., Springer-Verlag, New York, 1970, pp. 195–201. Reiquam, H., ''European Interest in Acidic Precipitation,'' in *Precipitation Scavenging,* R. J. Engelmann and W. G. N. Slinn, eds., U.S. Atomic Energy Symposium, Series 22, Division of Technical Information, Oak Ridge, Tennessee, 1970, pp. 289–292. Engström, A., ''Air Pollution Across National Boundaries, The Impact on the Environment of Sulfur in Air and Precipitation,'' Report of the Swedish Preparatory Committee for the U.N. Conference on Human Environment, Kungl. Boktryckeriet P. A. Norstedt et Söner, Stockholm, 1971, 96 pp.

6. Engström, *Ibid.*
7. Odén, *loc. cit.*
8. Odén, S., personal communication.
9. Gorham, E., ''Free Acid in British Soils,'' *Nature,* 181:106, 1958.
10. Holden, A. V., ''A Chemical Study of Rain and Stream Waters in the Scottish Highlands,'' *Freshwater and Salmon Fisheries Research,* 37:3–17, Dept. of Agriculture and Fisheries, Edinburgh, Scotland, 1966.
11. Ungemach, H., ''Chemical Rain Water Studies in the Amazon Region,'' in *Il Simposio y Foro de Biologia Tropical Amazonica,* J. M. Idrobo, ed., Editorial Pax, Bogota, Colombia, 1970.
12. Forman, R., personal communication.
13. Carroll, D., ''Rainwater as a Chemical Agent of Geological Processes—A Review,'' Geol. Surv. Water-Supply Paper 1535-G, 1962, 18 pp.
14. Fisher, D. W., et al., ''Atmospheric Contributions to Water Quality of Streams in the Hubbard Brook Experimental Forest, New Hampshire,'' *Water Resources Research,* 4:1115–1126, 1968.
15. Carroll, *loc. cit.* Junge, C. E., *Air Chemistry and Radioactivity,* Academic Press, New York, 1963, 382 pp. Lodge, J. R., Jr., et al., ''Chemistry of United States Precipitation,'' Final Report on the National Precipitation Sampling Network, National Center for Atmospheric Research, Boulder, Colorado, 1968, 66 pp. Pearson, F. J., Jr., and D. W. Fisher, ''Chemical Composition of Atmospheric Precipitation in the Northeastern United States,'' Geol. Surv.—Supply Paper 1535-P, 1971, 23 pp.
16. For example, see: Dethier, B. E., ''Precipitation in New York State,'' Cornell University Agric. Expt. Station, Ithaca, N.Y., Bull. 1009, 1966, 78 pp.
17. Pearson and Fisher, *loc. cit.*
18. Fisher, D. W., personal communication.
19. For example, see: Collision, R. C., and J. E. Mensching, ''Lysimeter Investigations: II. Composition of Rainwater at Geneva, N.Y. for a 10-year Period,'' New York Agric. Expt. Station, Tech. Bull. No. 193:3–19, 1932. Wilson, B. D., ''Nitrogen and Sulfur in Rainwater in New York,'' *J. Amer. Soc. Agron.,* 18:1108–1112, 1926. Leland, E. W., ''Nitrogen and Sulfur in the Precipitation at Ithaca, N.Y.,'' *Agron. Journal,* 44(4):172–175, 1952.
20. Collison and Mensching, *loc. cit.*
21. Malueg, K., personal communication.
22. Tarrant, R. F., et al., ''Nutrient Cycling by Throughfall and Stemflow Precipitation in Three Coastal Oregon Forest Types,'' USDA Forest Service, Research Paper PNW-54, Pacific Northwest Forest and Range Expt. Station, Portland, Oregon, 1968, 7 pp.
23. Reynolds, R. C., and N. M. Johnson, ''Chemical Weathering in the Temperate Glacial Environment of the Northern Cascade Mountains,'' *Geochim Gosmochim. Acta,* 1972.
24. Whitehead, H. C., and J. H. Feth, ''Chemical Composition of Rain, Dry Fallout, and Bulk Precipitation at Menlo Park, California, 1957–1959,'' *J. Geophys. Res.,* 69(16):3319–3333, 1964.
25. Brezonik, P. L., et al., *Eutrophication Factors in North Central Florida Lakes,* Florida, Engineering and Industrial Expt. Station, Gainesville, Bull. Series 134, Water Resources Research Center Publ. No. 5.
26. Odén and Ahl, *loc. cit.*
27. Grande, M., and E. Snekvik, ''Major Pollution Problems Affecting Inland Fisheries in Norway,'' Report of a Meeting of Representatives of the Norwegian Water and Hydro-Electricity Board, the Farmer's Association, The Institute for Water Research, and the Fish and Wildlife Service, Oslo, February 26, 1969 (quoted from Klein, D. R., ''Reaction of Reindeer to Obstructions and Disturbances,'' *Science,* 173:393–398, 1971).
28. Federal Water Pollution Control Administration, ''Water Quality Criteria,'' Report of the National Technical Advisory Committee of the Secretary of the Interior, Washington, D.C., 1968, 234 pp. 00–00.
29. Engström, *loc. cit.*
30. Wolman, M. G., ''The Nation's Rivers,'' *Science,* 174:905–918, 1971.

31. Schofield, C. L., Jr., "Water Quality in Relation to Survival of Brook Trout," *Salvelinus fontinalis* (Mitchill)," *Trans. Amer. Fisheries Soc.*, 94(3):227–235, 1965.
32. Ackermann, W. C., R. H. Harmeson, and R. A. Sinclair, "Some Long-Term Trends in Water Quality of Rivers and Lakes," *Trans. Amer. Geophys. Union,* 51:516–522, 1970.

Questions for Analysis

1. This article is generally recognized as the first major publication about acid rain in the United States. What do you notice about the way the article is written and organized that reflects earlier standards?
2. Analyze the rhetorical strategy used in Paragraph 10. What is the purpose of this paragraph? How does its rhetorical strategy help achieve that purpose?
3. What is the purpose of Paragraph 13? How do the data presented help the authors make their point?
4. Paragraphs 18 and 19 contain what are basically educated guesses about possible effects of acid rain. Are these paragraphs convincing even without supporting data? Do the authors have an alternative other than to speculate? Should they have omitted these paragraphs or should they feel and honor an obligation to point out these possibilities?
5. What is your overall reaction to this essay? Do you find it convincing and persuasive? What is the purpose of the article? Does it achieve this purpose?
6. Scientists and technical people are often accused of using a formal, indirect style that is characterized by passive and impersonal constructions. How would you evaluate the style these authors use? Is it difficult to follow? Look back and find passages you found difficult and try to determine if the difficulty is inherent in the subject matter or is caused by the style. Try to rewrite the passage if you believe the problem is caused by style. Find individual sentences in the article that are in the passive voice or contain impersonal constructions and rewrite them so that they are active and personal. Have you strengthened the sentences? Are they easier to read and understand?

William M. Brown

Maybe Acid Rain Isn't the Villain

(1984)

William M. Brown (b. 1935) is Director of Technological Studies at the Hudson Institute and a principal author of *The Great Acid Rain Mystery* published by the Hudson Institute. This article originally appeared in *Fortune* magazine.

1 The controversy over acid rain has political, economic, and scientific dimensions, but in a presidential election year it was doubtless inevitable that national politics would

drive the debate. So most of the disagreements we're reading about these days relate to federal policy. Why is President Reagan resisting an all-out attack on acid rain? (His latest budget proposes only modest amounts for further study of the problem.) Why is William Ruckelshaus, head of the Environmental Protection Agency, defending the President instead of pushing his own more aggressive program to control acid rain? Which of the numerous bills floating around Congress has a chance of passage? How should we deal with the maddening difficulty that the costs associated with many of the bills generally fall most heavily on Midwestern states (whose industry would have to spend huge sums to reduce emissions of sulfur dioxide) while the expected benefits generally accrue to other states, mostly in the East (whose lakes and forests would be less exposed to the acidified rain)?

2 The emphasis on the politics of the issue is especially unfortunate because the big news may be scientific. The standard scientific view of acid rain's effects may simply be wrong. It is too soon to state categorically that it's wrong, but some recent evidence suggests that we have at least good reason to pause. In a study of acid rain done at the Hudson Institute, my colleagues and I calculated that it could eventually cost Americans about $100 billion in today's dollars to achieve a major reduction in sulfur dioxide emissions. Before committing to any program of this magnitude, we should want to be more certain that acid rain is in fact a major threat to the country's environment.

3 The standard scientific view is easy enough to understand, intuitively plausible, and manifestly true—up to a point. It tells us that the Midwestern factories are spewing tons of sulfur dioxide into the atmosphere and that some of these and other pollutants combine with water vapor, become oxidized and acidic, are borne east by the prevailing winds, and finally rain down on the lakes and forests of New England, the mid-Atlantic states, and Canada. This is the part that's clearly true. It is based on compelling scientific evidence, much of it marshaled in a 1981 study performed by the National Academy of Sciences.

4 Since that study, however, we have been learning more about how rainwater filters into lakes and streams. Recent research by soil scientists, especially Edward C. Krug and Charles R. Frink of the Connecticut Agricultural Experiment Station, suggests that the portrait drawn in the National Academy study is incomplete. This is also the conclusion of the Hudson Institute study, which was finished last November. (Its title: *A Perspective on Current Acid Rain Issues.*) In it we reached conclusions substantially different from those of other investigations.

5 It is not surprising that there should be sharp disagreements about acid rain. The rain has been studied only for about six years, and scientists working in the field have been raising questions about acidified lakes faster than researchers can provide answers. Thus the view propounded in this article—in most respects a minority view—claims only to be a provocative hypothesis, not a proven reality.

6 Nevertheless, we now have grounds for suspecting that the following propositions are true: First, the pollutants in the rain are only a minor contributor to the high-level acidity found in some Eastern lakes and streams. Second, this acidity, which is indeed hostile to the existence of game fish and other aquatic creatures, is mostly natural rather than industrial in origin. Third, the popular notion that acid rain is threatening forests

in the Eastern U.S., and indeed all across the earth's Temperate Zone, is based less on substance than upon ill-informed conjecture and is probably wrong.

7 Obviously, the perspective afforded by these propositions has different policy implications from the National Academy study (which recommended a major reduction in sulfur dioxide emissions). The new perspective would not deny that industrial emissions should continue to be controlled in a reasonable manner, as required by the Clean Air Act. But it also tells us to focus on the possibility that the threats from these emissions may turn out to be largely illusory.

8 The most important argument used to justify a heavy spending war on acid rain is that it is entering our aquatic systems and threatening their populations. It has been shown, for example, that over 200 lakes in New York's Adirondack Mountains, along with the streams that feed them, are now devoid of fish, or at least of trout and other desirable game fish. Since the decline of the fish populations clearly derives from acidified water, many scientists have naturally come to view the problem somewhat as follows: (a) acidified precipitation falls onto the watershed, (b) it then runs into the streams and lakes, and (c) it kills the fish—at least, it does so unless the lake waters contain enough alkalies to neutralize the acid.

9 It is also natural for many scientists to fear that this process could eventually spread far beyond Adirondack lakes and, ultimately, produce a worldwide ecological disaster. If any such threat seemed genuine, then a $100 billion program to forestall it would clearly not be excessive in my judgment. However, the underlying reality appears at once more complex and less threatening.

10 Rainfall, whether acidic or not, gets into our aquatic systems by circuitous processes. Except for the very small fraction of rain that falls directly onto lakes, the precipitation that ends up in them passes through a series of filters in the watershed. Each of these filters affects the water's acidity in its own way. . . . At least one of these natural filters, the so-called mor humus, can put far more acid into the rainwater than could any anticipated amount of industrial pollution. Indeed this humus may contain as much as 1,000 times the acid that falls from the sky in a year. Regardless of its initial acidity or alkalinity, water percolating through mor humus emerges from it far more acidic than acid rain. In short, the forests of the Temperate Zones—especially coniferous forests—are *natural acid creators.*

11 These forests would long since have killed off the desirable game fish in most of the lakes and streams throughout the Temperate Zone but for another natural phenomenon. Other filters through which the rainwater passes are alkaline—that is, acid neutralizing. These deeper filters, mostly porous layers of mineral rock, are often several feet thick and generally contain substantial amounts of limestone and other alkaline substances. They not only neutralize the acid in water seeping into them but often generate natural buffers, such as alkaline bicarbonates, that neutralize any acids that might enter lakes from other sources—for example, from adjacent bogs or from the acid rain that falls directly onto the lakes.

12 However, these layers of acid-neutralizing rock are not found everywhere. In some parts of the Adirondacks and in a few other areas of the U.S., the deeper soil layers lack enough limestone or other alkaline minerals to neutralize the acidic water emerging from the humus above them. Might this lack explain all by itself why the fish of some Adirondack lakes have been in trouble? It might—except for one bothersome detail. The geology of the region hasn't changed lately, and yet the higher acidity levels of some lakes, and the related problems of their fish populations, are relatively recent events.

13 The possibility that our acidified lakes got that way naturally is hard for people to accept precisely because of this logical difficulty. If some of the fish are now in a more hostile environment than they were in earlier decades, then we must look to something new in the environment. Sulfur dioxide from heavy industry seems to be just the kind of suspect that makes sense. In fact, however, these emissions are not the only change in the forest environment. Another new feature is Smokey the Bear. Or, less metaphorically, the huge success of the United States in preventing forest fires during the past half-century or so.

14 Forest fires can have a tremendous impact on the acidity of adjacent lakes. The fires can totally destroy the acid-producing humus, replacing it with a layer of alkaline ash. When that happens, a naturally acidified lake within the burned area may become neutralized and temporarily—meaning for several decades—more hospitable to fish. Eventually, of course, the forest would be expected to regrow, the alkaline ash left by the fire would be used up, the acidic humus layer would be regenerated, and the fish would be in trouble again.

15 The possibility that fire prevention accounts for a major portion of the lakes' acidity still has to be viewed as just that—a possibility. It's another of the many fascinating hypotheses that are still too new to have been tested properly by field researchers undertaking controlled experiments. Meanwhile, all we know for sure is that the fires are far less prevalent than they once were.

16 Until early in this century they were normal all through the earth's Temperate Zone. Our ancestors in America, including the Pilgrims, set them deliberately and routinely because they were the simplest way to clear sizable tracts of land. Later, during the 18th and 19th centuries, rough-and-ready logging practices created large areas that were susceptible to forest fires in dry spells. There is essentially no virgin forest in the Eastern U.S. today—only regrown forest.

17 So it really is possible that one new element in the forest and lake environment of the East is the absence of forest fires. It is clear, in any case, that the forests of the Northeast have expanded remarkably during the past half-century. And, of course, their growth has been accompanied by sizable increases in the amount of humus and natural acidity in the soil.

18 If this is indeed the process by which the lakes have been acidified and the fish killed, it would appear to follow that the outlook for trout fishing is much less bleak. We can plausibly expect industrialization to keep spreading on the planet, so the acid rain hypothesis predicts that more and more lakes and streams will get in trouble. The

forest fire hypothesis predicts that relatively few lakes—those lacking the natural acid neutralizers—will be troubled. It is worth recalling that the acidified lakes in what New York State calls the Adirondack Ecological Zone constitute only a minority (19%, to be exact) of the lakes in the area and represent even less of the lakes' total surface area (4%) and volume (2%).

19 What about the widespread belief that acid rain represents a threat to the future of the forests? The evidence for this view turns out to be elusive. It is true, to be sure, that we occasionally find damage to clumps of trees in forests and often have no ready explanation of the damage. But it is not established that such damage is new, or growing, or, indeed, that similar damage couldn't have been observed a million years ago. Acid rain is simply not a likely suspect. The acid in Eastern rainfall is usually diluted to about four parts per million or less. Why should we believe that this relatively weak dose is the *likely* cause of the signs of stress observed in a few forest areas? If it is the cause, how do we explain that vast areas of Temperate Zone forest subject to similar precipitation have *not* been damaged?

20 Finally, why are so few forest ecologists, either in the U.S. or Europe, supporting the concept that acid rain is the villain identified in the media? Some of these scientists have publicly scorned the concept. Here, for example, is a summary statement on the subject by the respected British ecologist Kenneth Mellanby, writing last year in *Nature.* "Reports in the press and on television on the ill effects of acid rain have implied widespread damage to trees, directly caused by sulfur output from industry. But by the end of a recent international meeting . . . at which no less than 50 papers were delivered on the topic of acid precipitation, it was apparent that these simplistic views were neither accurate nor supported by scientific investigation."

21 All of which suggests that the Administration's much criticized current proposal on acid rain, which is to go slow and spend relatively little—the fiscal 1985 budget includes $55.5 million for study of the problem—makes a lot of sense. I certainly agree that less sulfur dioxide emissions are better than more. But less spending is also better than more, especially when there's a chance we're spending to solve the wrong problem. Before doing any spending, we need to start thinking of acid rain as a scientific rather than a political issue.

Questions for Analysis

1. In what ways does Brown's thesis echo the thesis presented by Likens, Bormann, and Johnson in the preceding reading? In what ways is it very different?
2. Does Brown have a political agenda that might influence how he looks at the scientific data? Where do you see evidence of this agenda?

3. As Brown points out, the highly acidic mor humus does add acidity to the rainwater passing through it. However, wouldn't the acidity of the rainwater going into the mor humus have an effect on the acidity of the water when it emerges? Why does Brown not mention this?
4. Brown confines his discussion to those lakes in the Adirondack Mountains that are naturally acidic and gives very little attention to other systems. Is this focus a problem? How would he respond to this statement as a criticism of his essay?
5. Does the fact that this essay was written for *Fortune* magazine have any effect on Brown's tone? Would readers of *Fortune* be more or less likely to be sympathetic to his position? Would readers of *Environment* be sympathetic?

Dixy Lee Ray

The Great Acid Rain Debate

(1987)

Dixy Lee Ray (b. 1914) has served in government at both the state level as governor of Washington and at the federal level as Chair of the Atomic Energy Commission. This essay on acid rain appeared in *The American Spectator* in 1987.

1 The Great Acid Rain Debate has been going on for more than a decade. Public alarm in the United States probably dates from a widely publicized 1974 report which concluded that "the northeastern U.S. has an extensive and severe acid precipitation problem." Does it? Probably not. Is rain really acidic? Yes. Does acid rain, or preferably, acid precipitation, really damage forests, lakes and streams, fish, buildings and monuments? Yes, in some instances, but not as the primary or only cause. Can the adverse environmental effects that have been attributed to acid rain—whatever the real cause—be mitigated by reducing the amount of sulfur dioxide emitted to the atmosphere from industrial sources? No, what evidence there is suggests that it cannot be. Is enough known, and understood, about acid precipitation to warrant spending billions of dollars of public funds on supposed corrective measures? Certainly not.

2 Clearly, the U.S. Environmental Protection Agency agrees with this assessment, for the agency's administrator, Lee M. Thomas, said in 1986: "Current scientific data suggest that environmental damage would not worsen materially if acidic emissions continued at their present levels for ten or twenty more years. Acid rain is a serious problem, but it is not an emergency."

3 That rain is acidic has been known for a long time. Among the first records are a reference to acid rain in Sweden in 1848 and a discussion on the chemistry of English

rain in 1872. Sulfur dioxide was established as a possible cause of damage to trees and other plants in Germany in 1867. The commonly repeated alarm that rainfall has become increasingly acidic over the past twenty-five years rests for its validity on an influential and oft-cited series of articles by G. E. Likens and his co-workers published in the 1970s. Careful evaluation by a group of scientists at Environmental Research and Technology Inc. reveals that Likens's research suffered from problems in data collection and analysis, errors in calculations, questionable averaging of some data, selection of results to support the desired conclusions, and failure to consider all the available data. In a more recent study, Vaclav Smil of the University of Manitoba reached similar conclusions. Besides analyzing Likens's methods of determining rain acidity, Smil examined maps of the distribution of acid precipitation in the eastern U.S. between the mid-1950s and the mid-1960s, prepared by Likens et al. and publicized as providing "unassailable proofs" of rising acidity. "In reality," Smil concludes, "the measurement errors, incompatibility of collection and analytical procedures, inappropriate extrapolations, weather effects and local interferences, make such maps very dubious."

4 Rain forms when molecules of water vapor condense on ice crystals or salt crystals or minute particles of dust in clouds and then coalesce to form droplets that respond to the force of gravity. As rain falls through the atmosphere it can "pick up" or "wash out" chemicals or other foreign materials or pollutants that may be present. Because water is such a good solvent, even in the cleanest air, rainwater dissolves some of the naturally present carbon dioxide, forming carbonic acid. Hence, rainwater is *always acidic* or if you like, acid rain is normal. There is no such thing as naturally neutral rainwater. Scientific studies generally distinguish between "acid rain," i.e., the acidity of rainwater itself, and "acid deposition," i.e., the fallout of sulfates, nitrates, and other acidic substances. Acid deposition may be "wet" if washed out of the atmosphere with rain, or "dry" if gases or particles simply settle out.

5 How acidic is pure water? Despite the fact that water molecules are very stable, with a chemical composition of two parts hydrogen to one part oxygen (H_2O), the molecular structure or architecture is somewhat asymmetrical; the molecules tend both to clump and to dissociate in response to intermolecular forces. Dissociation leads to a few hydrogen ions carrying a positive charge and an equal number of OH or hydroxyl ions with a negative charge. Under normal conditions, in pure distilled water only a few molecules are dissociated, in fact, about two ten-millionths of one percent. Now 2/10,000,000 of 1 percent is an awkward numerical expression. Therefore, for greater ease in expressing the number of dissociated molecules, which is the measure of relative acidity, a method called pH has been adopted. The pH of pure water is 7, the numerical expression of neutrality. Any pH measure below 7 is acidic, any above 7 is basic or alkaline. The pH scale is logarithmic (like the Richter scale for measuring intensity of earthquakes); therefore a change of one pH unit, for example, from pH 5 to pH 6, is a ten-fold change.

6 Water in the atmosphere normally contains some carbonic acid from dissolved carbon dioxide, and the pH of clean rainwater even in pristine regions of the earth is about pH 5.0 to 5.5.[1] Any lower pH is believed to be environmentally damaging. Lakes, streams, rivers, ponds, indeed all bodies of fresh water may and usually do receive

dissolved material, either acidic or alkaline, from runoff and from the soil or earthen basin in which the water stands or flows. Both acid and alkaline lakes are natural phenomena, and exist without intervention by humans.

7 Getting an accurate measure of the pH of rainwater is more difficult than it may at first seem. Certainly it is no simple litmus test; accurate procedures require careful laboratory analyses. For example, early work—that is, measurements taken before 1968—generally used soft glass containers; it is now known that even when the containers were carefully cleaned and when the analysis was done very soon after collection, the soft glass contributed alkalinity to the sample, and this increased with time in storage. Indeed the range of error attributable to the use of soft glass is sufficient so that it might account for the difference in pH measurements between 1955–56 and 1965–66 reported by Coghill and Likens. Rainwater collection made in metal gauges, a common procedure before the 1960s, also influenced the results. An experiment to test this difference, using a dilute solution of sulfuric acid with a pH of 4.39, gave a reading of pH 5.9 when held for a short time in a metal gauge.

8 It is also now known that a rainwater sample taken at the beginning of a storm will give a pH reading different from that taken during and at the end of the rainfall; that measurements may differ widely at different locales within a region; and that weather and climate affect the results. With regard to this last phenomenon, it may be that the more alkaline results reported by Likens for the northeast U.S. in the 1950s were related to the drought conditions that prevailed during those years. By contrast, the 1960s were rainy. When dry conditions persist, dust particles are more prevalent, and if they are present in the rain samples, they can neutralize some of the acidity and shift the pH toward the alkaline end of the scale.

9 For several reasons, then, it now appears that the historical data, on which so much of the alarm and worry has been based, are of insufficient quality and quantity to establish as indisputable a trend toward higher acidity in the rainfall of the northeastern United States.

10 Complicating the acid rain picture still further are results of samples recently collected from ice frozen in the geological past, and from rainfall in remote regions of the earth. These results suggest that the relationship between acidity and the industrial production of sulfur dioxide emissions is at best extremely tenuous.

11 Analysis of ice pack samples in the Antarctic and in the Himalayas indicates that precipitation deposited at intervals hundreds and thousands of years ago in those pristine environments had a pH value of 4.4 to 4.8. Some measurements were as low as 4.2. Examination of Greenland icepack samples shows that many times in the last 7,000 years the acidity of the rain was as high as pH 4.4. In some cases the periods of extremely high acidity lasted for a year or more. Coal burning utilities spewing out sulfur dioxide could not have been responsible, but these periods of high acidity do correspond to times of major volcanic eruptions. Also remarkable is the period of low acidity in the ice lasting from 1920 to 1960, when no major volcanic eruptions occurred but industrial pollution increased.

12 Recent measurements taken by the National Oceanic and Atmospheric Administration on Mauna Loa in Hawaii at 3,500 meters above sea level gave average pH values of 4.9 regardless of wind direction. Moreover, sampling at Cape Matatula on American Samoa, a monitoring site selected for its extreme cleanliness, resulted in measurements from pH 4.5 to 6.0 in the rainwater.

13 To gather more systematic data on the pH of rain in remote areas, a Global Precipitation Chemistry Project was set up in 1979. Samples of rainwater were tested from five sites: Northern Australia, Southern Venezuela, Central Alaska, Bermuda, and Amsterdam Island in the southern Indian Ocean halfway between Africa and Australia. The first results were published in 1982. Precipitation was everywhere acidic, pH values averaging between 4.8 and 5.0. Now it is possible to imagine that the Bermuda results could have been affected by long range transport of sulfate aerosols or other atmospheric pollution from the U.S., or that Alaskan atmosphere is polluted from coal burning in the Midwest, but that does not appear to be reasonable. At the remaining sites, including American Samoa, clearly man-made emissions could not have caused the measured acidity.

14 Conversely, in some areas where one might expect a low pH, actual measurements of the rainwater reveal higher than anticipated pH values. Twelve sites in Mexico, for example, measured pH 6.2 to 6.8; nine inland sites in India gave a median pH of 7.5 (range 5.8 to 8.9). It turns out that the expected natural acidity of the rain is neutralized by suspended alkaline particles, mainly dust from dry fields, unpaved streets, and so on.

15 In China seventy percent of the basic energy comes from burning coal; sulfur dioxide releases are very high, particularly in urban areas. Rainwater in Peking is nevertheless close to neutral, most values falling between pH 6.0 and 7.0. Interestingly, the same samples have heavy concentrations of sulfate and nitrate ions as well as suspended alkaline matter, probably dust blown from desert regions. The pH is determined by complex interaction among these aerosols, ions, and particles.

16 Acid rain can also be buffered or neutralized by soil conditions. Recent studies at nearly 200 sites in the United States show that in the northern Great Plains high levels of calcium and magnesium ions occur, along with ammonia associated with animal husbandry and fertilizers. These combine to neutralize acidic precipitation. In the western half of North America 75 to 96 percent of all acid anions are so neutralized. By way of contrast, in the northeastern U.S. 52 percent of all acid anions are not so neutralized.

17 It might be that lower levels of alkaline dust, especially in the northeast, are a consequence of successful air pollution control, resulting in the effective capture of particulate matter from industrial smoke. This possibility was investigated in 1985 by Smil, who reports a great loss of airborne alkaline material between the mid-1950s and mid-1960s. This loss resulted from large scale replacement of coal as fuel for homes, transportation, and industrial boilers, as well as highly efficient removal of fly ash from flue gases. Although exact and accurate calculations are not possible, reasonable estimates of the largely alkaline particulate emissions were about nine million tons annually

in the 1950s; this fell to about four million tons by 1975. Actually the total loss of man-made alkaline material over the northeast was probably much larger than the estimates indicate since emission controls were also applied to the iron, steel, and cement industries. And the amount of barren, dusty land shrank with advancing settlements, paved roads, lawns, and considerable re-growth of forests. Another contributing factor to loss of alkaline materials may have been the practice of prompt extinction of forest fires. Wildfires, when left to burn themselves out, result in an accumulation of alkaline ash, which, together with the minerals it contains, acts to buffer natural acidity in the soil and redress the mineral imbalance.

18 One final point should be made about natural acidity and alkalinity. Soils along the North Pacific coast tend to be quite acidic, a usual feature in areas that had been glaciated. Peat bogs are common; cranberries, huckleberries, blueberries, and Douglas Fir trees—all requiring acid soil—are abundant. For comparison, soils in the arid west and southwest are alkaline, and rarely measure a pH below 9.0. By contrast the soils in New England are among the most acid in the world. Representative Adirondack soil measures pH 3.4. Soils in southeast Canada are similar. That region also was glaciated, and the thin poor soil overlays acid granitic material. In other words, the soils of the northeast United States are by nature acidic, and always have been, environmentalist claims notwithstanding.

19 There is an extensive and growing body of scientific literature on atmospheric chemistry, much of it highly technical. Gradually, understanding is also growing, but many areas of uncertainty remain. Experts are divided on exactly how acids are formed in clouds, in rainwater, and upon deposition. There is some disagreement too on the relative amount and importance of acid precursors from man-made versus natural sources. Most knowledgeable scientists tend to take a middle view, that the amount of pollutants in the air, particularly of sulfates and nitrates, on a global scale comes about equally from natural and human sources, but even this is a supposition or educated guess.

Natural Sources

20 Sulfur and nitrogen compounds—the "acid" in acid rain—are produced naturally by the decay of organic matter in swamps, wetlands, intertidal areas, and shallow waters of the oceans. How much is contributed to the atmosphere from those sources is not known for certain, but it is considerable. Estimates of naturally produced sulfates and other sulfur compounds are from 35 percent to 85 percent of the total—a rather wide range!—and naturally occurring nitrogen compounds are generally believed to be 40 percent to 60 percent of the total. Some experts go further and claim that nature contributes over 90 percent of the global nitrogen. Considering the additional sulfur that emanates from volcanoes and fumaroles and hot springs and ocean spray, and the nitrogen fixed by lightning, the generally accepted contribution from natural sources may be underestimated.

21 The contribution of lightning to the acidity of rain is significant. Two strokes of lightning over one square kilometer (four-tenths of a square mile) produce enough nitric

acid to make eight-tenths of an inch of rain with a pH of 3.5. In fact, it has been estimated that lightning creates enough nitric acid so that annual rainfall over the world's land surfaces would average pH 5.0 even without taking into account other natural sources of acidity.

22 The contribution of volcanoes to atmospheric sulfur dioxide seems never to have been taken seriously; acknowledged, yes—but then dismissed as trivial. Perhaps this is related to the fact that volcanoes are studied by geologists and vulcanologists rather than by atmospheric scientists. Or perhaps it's because volcanic mountains tend to be where meteorologists are not. Predicting exactly when an eruption will occur is notoriously undependable, and obtaining direct measurements or samples of ejecta during eruptions is dangerous and can be fatal. During the daylong eruption of Mt. St. Helens on May 18, 1980, over four billion tons of material were ejected. Although large quantities of gases, including sulfur dioxide, were released to the atmosphere, no direct measurements could be made during the major eruption itself. Before May 18, in the period March 29 to May 14, spectroscopic measurements revealed about forty tons per day of sulfur dioxide. By May 25 measuring was resumed and showed 130 to 260 tons per day. On June 6 this increased abruptly to 1,000 tons per day. From the end of June through December of that year the rates of sulfur dioxide ranged from 500 tons per day to 3,400 tons per day. Sulfur dioxide, hydrogen sulfide, carbon disulfide, and other sulfur compounds continue to be released from the crater floor and dome, and arise also from fumaroles and the debris of pyroclastic flows.

23 El Chicon, an exceptionally acidic and sulfurous mountain in Mexico, erupted in early 1982, far more violently than Mt. St. Helens. Materials ejected reached the stratosphere and will probably affect the atmosphere for many years. Again no direct measurements were possible, but it is estimated that twenty million tons of sulfur dioxide were released. Also in the northern hemisphere, Mt. St. Augustine in Alaska erupted twice in 1986 with sulfur fumes detectable in Anchorage many miles away. Sulfur fumes continue to seep from both El Chicon and St. Augustine.

24 In 1973 two scientists, Stoiber and Jepson, reported data on sulfur dioxide emissions from Central American volcanoes, obtained both by remote sensing and by calculation. They conclude that 10,000 metric tons of sulfur dioxide are released to the atmosphere daily. Extrapolating worldwide, they calculate that volcanoes are responsible for emitting annually about 100 million metric tons of sulfur compounds. Thus nature is responsible for putting large quantities of sulfates and nitrates into the atmosphere.

Man-Made Sources

25 But so, of course, is man. Industrial activity, transportation, and burning fossil fuel for commercial and domestic purposes all contribute sulfate, nitrates, and other pollutants to the atmosphere. Since passage of the Clean Air Act in 1970 there has been an overall reduction of more than 40 percent in factory and utility sulfur dioxide production. But as sulfur dioxide emissions decrease, nitrogen emissions are increasing, primarily from oil burning and oil used in transportation. Industrial society also produces other air pollutants, including volatile organic compounds, ammonia, and hydrocarbons. Any of

these may contribute to the formation of acid rain, either singly or in combination. Further, some man-made pollutants can undergo photo-oxidation in sunlight, leading, for example, to the conversion of sulfur dioxide to highly toxic sulfur trioxide. But even this compound, should it be deposited over the ocean, loses its toxicity due to the extraordinarily high buffering capacity of sea water.

26 Another photo oxidant, ozone, is possibly the most damaging of all air pollutants derived from human activity. Ozone accumulates in quantities toxic to vegetation in all industrial regions of the world. Ozone is a product of photochemical oxidation between oxides of nitrogen and volatile organic substances. The latter may be unburned hydrocarbons (e.g., from automobile exhaust in cars not equipped with catalytic converters) or various organic solvents. Ozone is known to cause severe injury and even death to certain forest trees. The best known cases are the decline of white pine in much of eastern North America and ponderosa and Jeffrey pine in the San Bernardino Mountains of California. Ozone acts synergistically with other pollutants and has been shown to cause damage to agricultural crops when exposure occurs along with sulfur and nitrogen oxides.

27 Thus, singling out sulfur dioxide produced by human activities as the major cause of acid rain is not only a gross over-simplification, but probably wrong.

Effects on Forests

28 What about the dying forests? Here again the acid rain activists blame sulfur dioxide produced by industry.

29 Trees, like every other living thing, are not immortal. They too grow old and die. The decline of a forest may be part of the slow but natural process of plant succession, or it may be initiated by any of several stress-causing factors. Each forest and each tree species responds differently to environmental insults, whether natural or human. As Professor Paul D. Mannion of the State University of New York has said: "If one recognizes the complex array of factors that can contribute to the decline of trees, it is difficult to accept the hypothesis that air pollutants are the basis of our tree decline problems today . . . [although] to question the popular opinion on the cause of our decline problems is not to suggest that pollutants do not produce any effect."

30 Widespread mortality of forest trees has occurred at times and places where pollution stress was probably not a factor. Declines of western white pine in the 1930s and yellow birch in the 1940s and fifties, for example, were induced by drought, while secondary invasion by insects or other disease organisms is most often the ultimate cause of fatality.

31 Currently the most widely publicized forest decline problem in the U.S. is the red spruce forest in the northern Appalachian Mountains. Few people now cite the widespread mortality in red spruce between 1871 and 1890. The dieback occurred at roughly the same time in West Virginia, New York, Vermont, New Hampshire, Maine and New Brunswick, and was then attributed to the invasion of a spruce beetle that followed some other stress. What that was is not clear.

32 Today the dieback symptoms of the red spruce are most pronounced above 900 meters in an environment that is subject to natural stresses such as wind, winter cold, nutrient-poor soils, and possible high levels of pollutants, heavy metals, and acidity in the clouds that often envelop the forest. The relative importance of each of these stresses has not been rigorously investigated.

33 The affected trees grow in one of the windiest locations in North America. It is known that wind can dry out or even remove red spruce foliage, especially if rime ice has formed; it can also cause root damage by excessive tree movements. Tree ring analyses indicate a possible relation between recent cold winters and decline. The abnormal cold extending into spring may have caused the trees to be more susceptible to the adverse effects of pollutants. Arthur H. Johnson and Samuel B. MacLaughlin, who have studied tree rings and the red spruce forest decline, conclude in *Acid Deposition: Long Term Trends* (National Academy Press, 1986) that "there is no indication now that acidic deposition is an important factor in red spruce decline. . . . The abrupt and synchronous changes in ring width and wood density patterns across such a wide area seem more likely to be related to climate than to air pollution." Airborne chemicals might play a role, but they will have to be further assessed.

34 And then there are the dying forests of Germany. Whereas originally the focus was on acid precipitation and deposition of sulfur dioxide and to a lesser extent nitrogen oxides, emphasis has now shifted to the oxides of nitrogen, hydrocarbons, soil minerals such as aluminum and magnesium, and photo oxidants, chiefly ozone. Sulfur dioxide emissions have been declining in Germany since the mid-1970s, due mainly to the substitution of nuclear energy for coal burning in the production of electricity. But this decline was not accompanied by improvement in the health of forests, suggesting that other factors may be implicated. It is now believed that only in exceptional cases does sulfur dioxide cause direct damage to forests in Germany. But motor vehicle pollution from more than 27 million autos and trucks is among the highest in the world in density per area, and is considered to be a contributing factor to the formation of ozone. Indeed, ozone levels in Germany's damaged forests are often remarkably high. Long-term measurements indicate that the mean value of ozone concentration has increased by one-third over the last twenty years. And the investigators at the Norwegian Forest Research Institute have reached similar conclusions about the importance of ozone in forest declines.

35 The adoption of the catalytic converter for automobiles in America was primarily to control the release of unburned hydrocarbons in order to reduce the photochemical production of ozone. In this it has functioned well, although it has also led to formation of formaldehyde and larger amounts of acid, especially sulfuric acid. But there is another source of atmospheric hydrocarbons that has not been controlled—cows! American cows burp about fifty million tons of hydrocarbons to the atmosphere annually! There is no known control technology for these emissions. Whether they contribute to ozone formation is also not known, but their presence helps to emphasize the complexity of atmospheric chemistry.

Effects on Lakes and Fish

36 There are three kinds of naturally occurring acidic lakes: 1) those associated with inorganic acids in geothermal areas (i.e., Yellowstone Park) and sulfur springs (pH 2.0 to 3.0); 2) those found in peat lands, cypress swamps, and rain forests where the acidity is derived from organic acids leached from humus and decaying vegetation (pH 3.5 to 5.0); and 3) those located in areas of weather resistant granitic or silicious bedrock. Only the last-named are involved in the acid rain question. In these lakes and streams, the absence of carbonate rocks means little natural buffering capacity. This type of naturally acidic lake is common in large areas of eastern Canada and the northeastern United States, where glaciers exposed granitic bedrock during the last period of glaciation. The lakes are called ''sensitive'' because they may readily become further acidified with adverse impacts on aquatic organisms, of which fish are the most important to man. Indeed the most widely proclaimed complaint about the consequence of acid deposition is the reduction or elimination of fish populations in response to surface water acidification.

37 But again, this is not a recent phenomenon. Dead lakes are not new. A study by the New York State Department of Environmental Conservation reveals that the stocking of fish in twelve lakes was attempted and failed as early as the 1920s. Of course, many people did catch fish in the 1920s and 1930s in lakes where fish are not available today. But the fact is that during those years many of the Adirondack lakes were being stocked annually by the Fish and Game Commission; fish did not propagate, and the stocking program was discontinued about 1940.

38 In the United States 219 lakes have been identified as too acidic to support fish. Two hundred and six of these lakes are in the Adirondacks, but they account for only four percent of the lake surface of New York state alone. This, then, is hardly a national problem; it is local. The same applies to southeast Canada, where the highest percentage of acid lakes is located.

39 Uncertainty continues whether these acid lakes have always had a low pH or whether human activities have reduced the neutralizing capability of the waters, or the lake basin. A range of human activities could be to blame: use of chemical pesticides to control spruce budworm or black fly infestations, changes in fish hatchery production, change in angler pressure, lumbering, burning of watersheds. On the other hand, declining fish populations were noted in some New York lakes as early as 1918, and bottom sediments deposited eight hundred years ago in Scandinavian lakes are more acid than today's sediments.

40 To conclude that a decline in fish population is caused by atmospheric acid deposition, it must be established that the lake formerly supported a viable fish population; one or more species of fish formerly present has been reduced or lost; the lake is more acidic now than it was when the fish were present; the increased acid level was not caused by local factors; and other factors, e.g., toxic chemicals, are not present or are unimportant.

41 Such data are rare. Studies on three lakes in the Adirondacks—Panther, Sagamore, and Woods Lake, which are remote but close enough together to be affected by the

same rainfall—disclosed radically different degrees of acidity, large differences that can be accounted for by the varying geological makeup of the three lake beds and local, surrounding soils and vegetation.

42 Outside the Adirondack Mountains and New York state, many emotional claims have been made about fish kills in Canada, Norway, and Sweden. Most of the losses are reported in the spring; in Scandinavia fish kills have been reported annually in the springtime for more than one hundred years. This recurring natural phenomenon is likely due to oxygen depletion or to snow melt and rain runoff carrying sudden high concentrations of many materials into lakes and streams, and in fact, the acidity of most waters is greatest in the spring. Modern findings call into question the claim that distant sources of sulfur dioxide are responsible for the growing acidity of waters hundreds of miles away.

43 Using trace elements, Dr. Kenneth Rahn of the University of Rhode Island has found that it is local pollution sources, mostly residual fuel oil burned for domestic, commercial, and industrial purposes in New England, that are the main cause of added acidity in rain and snow. A meteorological team from the University of Stockholm cautioned the Swedish people not to blame acid rain on emissions from England; they found that local sources accounted for local acid rain. Great Britain, incidentally, has reduced sulfur dioxide emissions by more than 30 percent since 1970 with no effect whatever on the acidity of lakes or rain in Scandinavia. In New York City, EPA scientists traced elevated sulfur dioxide and sulfuric acid in the wintertime to the burning of oil in the 35,000 oil burners of the city's apartment houses. European scientists at the Organization for Economic and Cooperative Development in Paris have reached the same conclusion; the most revealing result of an extensive project is that every source region affects itself more than any other region.

Effects on Man-Made Structures

44 The impact of air borne pollutants and acid rain on deterioration of buildings, monuments, and man-made materials is also predominantly a local phenomenon. It is at least as complex as the effects on the natural environment. And, like forests and lakes, every site is specific and every material different. Few generalizations are possible; fewer still stand up under careful scrutiny. Of course metals corrode, marble and limestone weather, masonry and concrete deteriorate, paint erodes, and so on; but the conditions and substances that lead to loss of integrity vary widely. Perhaps the only statement that can be made is that moisture is essential, that deterioration results more from acid deposition than from acid rain, and that local sources are more important than possible long-range transport of pollutants.

45 Yet belief persists that acid rain from "someplace else" is destroying cultural monuments. Perhaps the most egregious example is the damage to the granite Egyptian obelisk, "Cleopatra's Needle," located since 1881 in New York City's Central Park. It has been claimed that "the city's atmosphere has done more damage than three and one half millennia in the desert, and in another dozen years the hieroglyphs will probably disappear." A careful study of the monument's complex history, however, makes

it clear that the damage can be attributed to advanced salt decay, the high humidity of the New York climate, and unfortunate attempts at preservation. There is no question but that acid deposition causes incremental damage to materials, but far more research is needed before reliable surface protection systems can be developed.

46 At the very least, the historical record of dramatic fluctuations in rain acidity, and episodes of environmental damage that cannot be attributed to industrial pollution; the evidence that natural events such as drought and abnormal cold can be important factors in environmental deterioration; the probability that compounds other than sulfur dioxide (e.g., ozone) are responsible for causing damage to plant life; the complex interactions among the many chemicals, aerosols, and other substances in the atmosphere and upon deposition; the likelihood that local sources are responsible for local effects; and the fact that there is no real, direct evidence that long distance transport of sulfur dioxide causes acid rain problems in New England, should make Congress very cautious about committing public funds to ill-conceived "solutions" to an ill-defined problem. At best, proposed federal programs constitute, in the words of Dr. S. Fred Singer of the National Advisory Committee on Oceans and Atmosphere, a multibillion dollar solution to a multimillion dollar problem.

47 One federal program that fits this description is a plan developed last summer by Drew Lewis and William Davis, special envoys for the United States and Canada, respectively. Under this plan, the U.S. will spend $2.5 billion of federal funds and $2.5 billion from U.S. industry to demonstrate how to burn high sulfur coal and release less sulfur dioxide to the atmosphere. Burning low sulfur coal was not proposed because that would "impose significant socio-economic costs on high sulfur coal miners, their families and their communities." According to EPA administrator Lee N. Thomas, the $5 billion program will be a proper "first step toward the goal of a solution to North America's acid rain problem."[2] There is no reason to believe that the proposed solution will solve or even contribute to solving the perceived problem.

48 Despite reports to the contrary in the popular press, the Committee on Atmosphere and Biosphere of the National Research Council–National Academy of Sciences did *not* conclude in its 1981 report that a 50 percent reduction in sulfur dioxide from factories and utilities in the Midwest would significantly reduce environmental problems attributed to acid rain in the northeast. This misinterpretation was pointed out in the 1983 NRC-NAS report for the Environmental Studies Board, which concluded: "The relative contributions of such long range effects and of more local regional effects are currently unknown and cannot be reliably estimated using currently available models." The only change since this position was reached is the growing evidence of the past three years that local sources predominantly influence local effects.

49 Nevertheless, industrial activities generally and coal burning in particular put pollutants into the atmosphere, and what goes up must come down—somewhere. It is reasonable therefore to require, as the Clean Air Act does, that emissions of sulfur dioxide and other pollutants be reduced. It is also reasonable to spend federal funds to collect accurate data and to continue efforts to understand the problem of acid deposition

in all its complexity. What is not reasonable is the requirement by a Congress impatient for immediate results that all coal-burning utilities must use expensive flue gas scrubbers regardless of whether the coal complies with federal standards or not. With even less reason the 1977 amendments to the Clean Air Act require that the sulfur content of all coal be reduced by the same specified percentage. It seems not to matter, under this law, that low sulfur western coal still goes into the scrubbers cleaner than high sulfur eastern coal comes out of them. What apparently does matter is that the top eight polluting states have large high sulfur coal reserves and high economic dependence on mining it. They are represented in the House of Representatives by about 105 votes. By contrast western, low sulfur coal is dominated by two states, Montana with two votes and Wyoming with one.

50 But even this pales to insignificance beside legislation considered by the 99th Congress, HR 4567. This bill had about 160 co-sponsors and was approved by the House Energy Subcommittee on Health and the Environment on July 20, 1986. It called for significant further reductions of sulfur dioxide emissions from utilities, industries, and motor vehicles, and nitrogen oxides were also to be reduced along with hydrocarbons, particulates, and carbon monoxide. The greatest burden would have fallen on utilities, and therefore the greatest effect would have been to drive up electricity rates. For this reason subsidies were to be provided to keep rates from rising more than 10 percent. Also proposed was a nationwide fee on all electrical generation. Department of Energy estimates put the cost of HR 4567 at a minimum of $2.5 billion to $8 billion annually. Others calculated that the costs could exceed $15 billion a year. TVA reported that the bill would drive up their electric rates by 12–14 percent, while Ohio Power's residential customers would pay 34 percent more and industry 44 percent more. The bill was opposed by the Administration, utilities, industry including coal mining, automobile manufacturers, and some members of Congress. Although the 99th Congress adjourned without taking action on this or other acid rain bills, the sponsors have vowed to try again when the new Congress convenes in January.

51 Department of Energy Secretary Herrington, in testimony before Congress in June 1986, pointed out (as have all responsible scientific reports) that "there is no evidence to suggest that the problem [of acid rain] is urgent or getting worse." Why then the big push to spend billions—not on research so that we may know what we're doing, but on supposed controls that no one can say will be effective? The Great Acid Rain Debate goes on . . . and on.

Notes

1. The pH of clean rainwater compares to that of carrots (pH 5.0), and lies between the acidity of spinach (pH 5.4) and bananas (pH 4.6). Rainwater is far less acidic, for example, than cola drinks (pH 2.2).
2. This statement, which appeared in the *EPA Journal* (June/July 1986), is particularly curious, since in the same article Mr. Thomas also says: "It is difficult, if not impossible, to predict with any certainty to what extent acid deposition in any specific area would be reduced by emission controls on any specific sources."

Questions for Analysis

1. Do you find Dixy Lee Ray's essay effective? What arguments do you find effective?
2. In Paragraph 4, Ray points out that "acid rain is normal." How does she use this fact to help her argument? What, if anything, does she leave out that might weaken her argument?
3. What is the purpose of Paragraphs 7–9?
4. Compare Ray's discussion of "Natural Sources" and "Man-Made Sources." Which source of acidity seems the more significant based on her discussion? Why does Ray list the many tons per day of acidic compounds put into the atmosphere by volcanoes and provide only the fact that factory- and utility-produced sulfur dioxide was reduced by 40 percent between 1970 and 1986? Has she used statistics in a misleading way? Explain.
5. At the end of Paragraph 46, Ray quotes Dr. S. Fred Singer's characterization of the proposed federal program to reduce acid rain as "a multibillion dollar solution to a multimillion dollar problem." Explain why this statement is rhetorically effective. What might an environmentalist say in response to it?

National Acid Precipitation Assessment Program (NAPAP)

The Latest Official Report on Acid Rain

(1988)

NAPAP was created by the United States Congress in 1980 to conduct and assess research on acid rain so that policy decisions made by the government could be based on scientific evidence. The piece below is a compilation by the editors of *Consumers' Research* based on excerpts from NAPAP reports of 1986 and 1987.

1 Acid rain in the amounts and concentrations that occur over the entire United States would appear to have no significant effects on the yield of most, if not all, agricultural crops.

2 Levels of sulfur dioxide and nitrogen dioxide gases (the two main ingredients of acid rain) that have been reported to cause crop damage in controlled studies rarely occur in the rural United States. The interactive effects of the two pollutants may cause damage to some crops in a few local situations such as near a smelter with uncontrolled emissions.

3 Acidic deposition at present levels may have a modest net benefit to cropland by providing needed nitrogen and sulfur to the soil.

4 According to data from the National Crop Loss Assessment Network (NCLAN), ozone at current levels in the United States reduces the yield of most agricultural crops compared to yields in charcoal-filtered air. National agricultural crop production is estimated to be reduced on average by at least 5% due to anthropogenically-produced ozone. According to the NCLAN Program, this translates to a loss of potential crop value on the order of $1 billion.

Effects on Forests

5 As with agricultural crops, there appears to be no significant foliar effect on seedlings. Because seedlings have, proportionally, more sensitive leaf or needle tissue than mature trees, foliar effects on mature trees would not be expected to be more severe than on seedlings. Therefore, forests are probably relatively unaffected by ambient acidity in rain on their foliage at low elevations or even in the mist of above-cloud-base forests. However, effects of acidic deposition mediated through soils have not been resolved.

6 Forests in the United States are probably stressed to some extent by ambient ozone levels. At low elevation, this may be reflected in growth suppression without visible injury. In the Northeast, growth reductions are reported for red spruce at lower elevations. Tree ring and standard plot studies of pines in coastal plain and piedmont provinces of the Southeast, and on hardwoods and conifers in large areas of the Northeast show a reduction of growth over the past few decades. There are differences of opinion whether this can be accounted for solely by natural processes or whether air pollution makes a contribution.

7 The growth of the loblolly pine seedlings is reduced by ozone, and the magnitude of this response varies among families. But generally, the height, diameter, and total biomass decreased as ozone concentrations increased.

8 The mountaintop forests in the Appalachians (above cloud base), which show obvious decline, experience a higher average daily ozone concentration than adjacent forests at low elevation. Further, the trees are enshrouded in mist about half the time. Experiments with crops have shown that ozone damage increases with average humidity, reaching a maximum with continuous nightly mist.

9 Hydrogen peroxide may cause additional significant stress contributing to the decline of the above-cloud-base in forests.

10 Historical data on high elevation spruce-fir forests of the Southeast show that major disturbances in the past were caused by railroad logging, windstorms, slash fires, grazing, and balsam woolly aphid. These disturbances can change species composition, age distribution, site quality, and forest health in general, depending on the time and location. The more that is known about each one and its effects, the clearer the role of air pollutants will be.

11 All low-elevation New England forest tree species investigated are growing at rates equal to or exceeding those prior to 1960, with the exception of the red spruce and balsam fir. Recent studies have identified a definite decline in basal area growth rates

of stands (60 to 75 years old) of red spruce and balsam fir starting about 1960. It once was suspected that the decline was associated with acid rain.

12 However, a recent analysis of tree ring data indicates that stand aging is playing a major role in these growth declines in low-elevation forests. These data showed that most low-elevation red spruce stands are functionally even-aged as the result of harvesting and spruce budworm infestations after the turn of the century. These stands have now attained an age when a natural reduction in growth rate is expected.

Effects on Lakes

13 The current chemical condition of Eastern lakes is now known on a broad regional scale for the first time. Based on the number of low pH (the lower the pH, the higher the acidity) in several subregions also receiving high sulfur deposition, it is expected that acidic deposition has played a role in their current condition. There is currently no evidence to suggest that regional scale chronic acidification has occurred in Western lakes.

14 There is increasingly clear evidence that sulfate deposition influences sulfate concentrations in surface waters. However, the relationship may be quite different in areas receiving similar deposition, for example, the Adirondacks versus the Southern Appalachians, suggesting the importance of watershed characteristics in controlling acidification.

15 Bedrock composition appears to be the major watershed property affecting surface water chemistry in five watersheds in western Maryland and Virginia. One small stream flowing on pure quartzite bedrock and overlying quartz sand soil showed the stream pH at 4.5 with average local rain at 4.2. For these watersheds, the less reactive the bedrock and associated soil, the more acidic a system will become under similar deposition levels.

16 Episodic inputs of acidic deposition from snowmelt or storm events can produce short-term pulses of reduced pH in streams and lakes. In well-buffered lake systems, these episodes may not be injurious to fish health. In other cases, the pH may be lowered enough for a sufficient period to reduce fish populations. Peaks due to heavy rainfall from naturally acid soil have also been observed and have caused fish mortality in a fish hatchery.

17 For lakes and streams with low pH, the chemical environment can be improved by periodic liming to provide a suitable habitat for brook trout and lake sports fish. Experiments in the United Kingdom and Scandinavia and model studies in Wisconsin have shown that liming a watershed has more long-term benefit to the condition of an acidic lake system than direct liming of the lakes. In most instances, healthy fish populations can be restocked.

Effects on Materials

18 A wide variety of man-made and naturally occurring materials are used in all types of building projects. These materials are subjected to fluctuating natural environmental

pH of West Deposition in 1986

Explanation
• pH at sample site
– Line of equal ph value

0 100 200 300 400 Miles

SOURCE: The National Acid Precipitation Assessment Program, Annual Report for 1987.

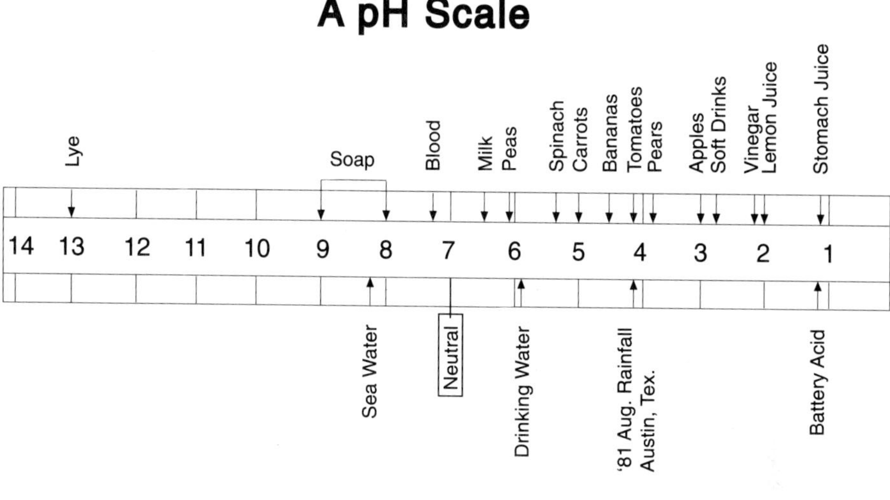

Courtesy of Dr. John J. McKetta, University of Texas, Austin, Texas.

factors, including temperature, wind, humidity, rain, dew, snow, and solar radiation, all of which may contribute to their gradual deterioration.

19 In addition, in many locations these materials are also subjected to variable quantities of man-made oxidants (such as ozone), acid precursor gases (such as oxides of sulfur and nitrogen), particulate matter, and acidic rainfall. Depending on their concentration, some of these pollutants may add a significant increment to the deterioration of certain materials.

20 The problem is first to measure quantitatively the incremental effect on a particular material and second, to determine if this effect causes a significant decrease in the normal time of replacement or repair. If this is the case, an economic value can be placed on the reduction of the pollutant. This process is a complicated one, and, to date, has not been completed for any material.

Acid Rain's Sources

21 Within the United States, sulfur dioxide (SO_2) and oxides of nitrogen (NO_x) are emitted mainly by electricity generation, transportation, and other fuel-burning processes. Transportation, petroleum refining, chemical manufacturing, and paint and solvent use are the major sources of volatile organic compounds (VOCs), some of which help transform sulfur dioxide and nitrogen oxides to acidic compounds in the atmosphere.

22 Natural sources such as soils, tidal areas, ocean waters, dust storms, and lightning discharges may also be important contributors to these emissions. Natural sources contribute significantly to the total VOC emissions, and possibly to NO_x emissions.

23 Sulfur dioxide emissions in the United States increased from about 10 million tons per year in 1900 to more than 20 million tons per year in 1925. After peaks in 1944

and the early 1970's, SO_2 emissions in 1986 are about the same as 1930—21 million metric tons per year.

24 Man-made emissions of SO_2 in the United States have decreased by about 28% since reaching a peak in 1973. Since 1975, national SO_2 emissions from coal-fired power plants have decreased by 10%, while coal consumption has increased by 70%. In the Northeast, these emissions have dropped by 19% while coal consumption has increased by 24%.

25 Seventy percent of SO_2 emissions come from the utility sector, and in 1980 about 94% of these emissions came from plants that were not subject to the EPA New Source Performance Standards (NSPS), which require use of lower sulfur flues or flue-gas desulfurization. As old power plants reach the end of their economic life and are repowered or replaced by new NSPS plants, the emissions of SO_2 will decrease.

Atmospheric Chemistry

26 The total amount of SO_2 derived from natural emissions is estimated to be about 2 million tons. In the Eastern United States, natural source contributions to the total emissions of sulfur are negligible (approximately 0.1%).

27 The total natural NO_x emissions are estimated to be about 3 million tons per year. At present, natural sources of NO_x are a minor contributor to the total in the Eastern United States. In more remote areas (e.g., the Northwest), natural sources of NO_x play a more important role.

28 Results of studies in Pennsylvania emphasized the influence of natural emissions, primarily of VOC, on the production of ozone at a rural site in the East. Most ozone in the lower atmosphere is produced through photochemical reactions that involve simultaneously both NO_x and VOC as the major precursors. Previous studies have established that anthropogenic emissions are the major source of NO_x over rural areas in the eastern United States.

29 The dominant source of hydrogen peroxide (H_2O_2) is photochemical reactions in the atmosphere. Hydrogen peroxide is a compound of considerable interest because it may affect tree growth and because of its role in the oxidation of SO_2 in cloud water. Hydrogen peroxide concentrations can be relatively high in summer, sometimes greater, sometimes less than sulfur dioxide concentrations. In winter, H_2O_2 concentrations are typically quite low.

30 In the Northeastern United States, the acidity of rain is two to three times greater in the summer than the winter due primarily to increased concentrations of hydrogen peroxide in the clouds. The nitric acid component of wet deposition is relatively constant through the seasons.

31 The annual average concentrations of SO_2 and NO_x in the urban environment are at least a factor of 10 greater than in rural areas. The average acidity of rain in the New York City area is about 50% greater than in surrounding rural areas, according to a recent study. This may be true for other cities as well.

Emissions by Source Category, 1980 and 1986

(In millions of metric tons per year)

	Source	1980	1986		Source	1980	1986
SO_2	Utility	15.9	14.4	NO_x	Utility	5.6	6.3
	Industrial Fuel Combustion	2.4	2.2		Industrial Fuel Combustion	3.0	2.6
	Comm./Institutional/ Residential	0.9	0.6		Comm./Institutional/ Residential	0.7	0.6
	Industrial Processes	3.5	3.0		Industrial Processes	0.7	0.6
	Other	0.9	0.8		Other	2.0	2.0
	TOTALS	**23.6**	**21.0**		**TOTALS**	**19.4**	**19.1**

SOURCE: The National Acid Precipitation Assessment Program, Annual Report for 1987.

Questions for Analysis

1. What is the overall conclusion of this report? What message would members of Congress who were considering clean-air legislation get from its information and conclusions?
2. Paragraph 4, the last paragraph in the section concerning effects on crops, focuses on ozone. What is the purpose of this paragraph? How does it operate rhetorically against the first three paragraphs in this section? Compare the discussion of ozone's effect on forests in Paragraphs 7 and 8 with that in Paragraph 4. Is ozone being presented as a more serious threat to the environment than the compounds that form acid rain? How does the way this information is presented affect the conclusions readers would draw? Is there any connection between the presence of ozone and compounds that cause acid rain?
3. What is the purpose of Paragraph 17? Is the liming of lakes or the liming of lakes' watersheds a reasonable solution to the problem of acid rain? Is it presented here as a solution? Why do the report writers present information on liming?
4. What is the conclusion presented in the section "Effects on Materials"?
5. How would you characterize the tone of this report? Do you come away from it with a clear sense of the report's purpose? Using only the information it provides, would you understand the effects of acid rain?
6. Evaluate the illustration entitled "A pH Scale." Why are almost all of the items listed as illustrations things we eat or drink?

Volker A. Mohnen

The Challenge of Acid Rain

(1988)

Awarded a Ph.D. from the University of Munich in 1966, Volker A. Mohnen (b. 1937) is Professor of Atmospheric Science at the State University of New York at Albany. An expert on atmospheric chemistry who has testified before Congress on acid rain, Mohnen is now studying the effect of the atmosphere on the health of forests. This article originally appeared in the *Scientific American*.

1 The atmosphere functions as a pool and chemical-reaction vessel for a host of substances. Many of the most important ones—oxygen, carbon dioxide and nitrogen and sulfur compounds, for example—are released by the activity of organisms. Often with the help of the water cycle, they pass through the atmosphere and are eventually taken up again into soil, surface water or organic matter. Through technology, human beings have added enormously to the atmospheric burden of some of these substances, with far-reaching consequences for life and the environment. The evidence is clearest in the case of acid rain: precipitation and particles that have been made acidic by air pollution.

2 The alarm over the increasing acidity of precipitation in Europe and eastern North America was first sounded in the 1960's. Since then the most attention has been focused on acid rain's effects, established and suspected, on lakes and streams, with their populations of aquatic life, and on forests, although the list of concerns is far broader. It includes contamination of groundwater, corrosion of manmade structures and, most recently, deterioration of coastal waters. Twenty years later, how much damage to the ecosystem, lakes and forests in particular, has been confirmed and measured? What has been learned about the processes that produce acid rain and underlie its effects? What does the knowledge imply for efforts to control the emissions—mainly sulfur dioxide from coal- and oil-burning power plants and oxides of nitrogen from motor vehicles and power plants—that cause acid rain?

3 The study of these questions has grown into a major scientific enterprise. Under the aegis of the National Acid Precipitation Assessment Program (NAPAP), enacted in 1980, many different agencies of the Federal Government sponsor research on the atmospheric processes that produce acid rain, its effects on the ecosystem and options for controlling it. In addition the Electric Power Research Institute, which is funded by the utility industry, supports studies of acid-rain effects and research on technologies for reducing power-plant emissions. The NAPAP will not issue a major report until 1990. Yet much evidence is already in hand—enough to make it clear that acid rain, or more correctly the pollutants that cause it, represents a large-scale interference in the biogeochemical cycles through which living things interact with their environment. Good global housekeeping demands an effort to protect the integrity of these cycles, and economical means of doing so are at hand.

4 Acid rain is a direct consequence of the atmosphere's self-cleansing nature. The tiny droplets of water that make up clouds continuously capture suspended particles and soluble trace gases. When precipitation coalesces from cloud water, it washes the impurities out of the atmosphere. Not all trace gases can be removed by precipitation, but sulfur dioxide (SO_2) and oxides of nitrogen emitted into the atmosphere are chemically converted into forms that are readily incorporated into cloud droplets: sulfuric and nitric acids.

5 The processes that convert the gases into acid and wash them from the atmosphere began operating long before human beings started to burn large quantities of fossil fuels; sulfur and nitrogen compounds are also released by natural processes such as volcanism and the activity of soil bacteria. But human economic activity has made the reactions vastly more important. They are triggered by sunlight and depend on the atmosphere's abundant supply of oxygen and water.

6 The reaction cycle is played out in the troposphere, the lowest 10 or 12 kilometers of the atmosphere. It begins as a photon of sunlight strikes a molecule of ozone (O_3), which may have mixed downward from the ozone layer in the stratosphere or may have been formed in the troposphere by the action of nitrogen- and carbon-containing pollutants. The result is a molecule of oxygen (O_2) and a lone, highly reactive oxygen atom, which then combines with a water molecule (H_2O) to form two hydroxyl radicals (HO). This scarce but active species transforms nitrogen dioxide (NO_2) into nitric acid (HNO_3) and initiates the reactions that transform sulfur dioxide into sulfuric acid (H_2SO_4).

7 The concentration of the hydroxyl radical in the atmosphere is less than one part per trillion, but it is practically inexhaustible: several of the oxidation processes it triggers end up by regenerating it. For example, one by-product of the initial oxidation of sulfur dioxide is the hydroperoxyl radical (HO_2), which reacts with nitric oxide (NO) to produce nitrogen dioxide and a new hydroxyl radical. In effect each hydroxyl radical can oxidize thousands of sulfur-containing molecules. As a result only the amount of pollutant in the air determines how much acid is ultimately produced.

8 The sulfuric and nitric acids formed from gaseous pollutants can easily make their way into clouds. (Some sulfuric acid is also formed directly in cloud droplets, from dissolved sulfur dioxide and hydrogen peroxide.) Nitric acid gas readily dissolves in existing cloud droplets. Sulfuric acid formed through gas-phase reactions condenses to form microscopic droplets, from roughly .1 to two micrometers (millionths of a meter) in diameter, which are one component of the summertime haze in the eastern U.S. Some of these sulfate particles settle to the ground in a process known as dry deposition. (Dry deposition also refers to the capture of sulfur dioxide gas by vegetation.) Most of them, however, are incorporated in clouds. Moisture readily condenses on an existing surface—a condensation nucleus—and sulfate particles are ideal condensation nuclei. They grow into cloud droplets containing dilute sulfuric acid.

9 The sulfuric and nitric acids in cloud droplets can give them an extremely low *p*H. Water collected near the base of clouds in the eastern U.S. during the summer typically has a *p*H of about 3.6, but values as low as 2.6 have been recorded. (A *p*H of 7 is

neutral; the lower the number, the stronger the acid it represents.) In the greater Los Angeles area the *p*H of fog has fallen as low as 2—about the acidity of lemon juice.

10 These very high acidities are found only near the base of clouds; the upper reaches are significantly cleaner. Soil and vegetation swathed in acidic clouds, as high-altitude forests can be, are directly exposed to the extremely acidic cloud base. Precipitation particles, however, combine water from much of a cloud's thickness. The resulting dilution of the acid lowers the concentration of sulfur and nitrogen compounds in precipitation by a factor of between three and 30 and the acidity by between one-half and one *p*H unit, to an average in the Northeast of about 4.2.

11 The acid rain may fall hundreds of miles from the pollution source. Wherever it lands, it undergoes a new round of physical and chemical alterations, which can reduce the acidity and change the chemical characteristics of the water that eventually reaches lakes and streams. Alkaline soils, such as soils rich in limestone, can neutralize the acid directly. In the slightly acidic soils typical of the evergreen forests exposed to acid rain in the U.S., Canada and Europe two other processes can blunt the effects of acid deposition. The acid can be immobilized as the soil or vegetation retains sulfate and nitrate ions (from sulfuric and nitric acids respectively). It can also be buffered through a process that is known as cation (positive ion) exchange.

12 In cation exchange the ions of calcium, magnesium and other metals found in many soils take the place of the acid's hydrogen ions. The source of the metal ions is rock weathering: the dissolution of minerals by precipitation and groundwater containing dissolved carbon dioxide, which releases the positive metal ions into the soil together with anions, or negative ions, of bicarbonate (HCO_3^-). Then, when sulfuric acid is added to the soil, the sulfate (SO_4^{2-}) of the acid can displace the calcium or magnesium ions. As the sulfate solution washes the metal cations from the soil, the hydrogen ions responsible for the acidity are left behind.

13 The extent to which retention and cation exchange take place in runoff or groundwater depends on the character of the watershed—its geology, vegetation and flow patterns, among other things. Soil processes cannot affect runoff from frozen or fully saturated ground or bare granite bedrock, and so the water that reaches the lake or stream remains about as acidic as the precipitation. Even when the rain does soak in, soil processes may be ineffective. Quartz, for example, is resistant to weathering and lacks the metals needed for cation exchange, and so percolation through quartz sand does little to buffer acid. In watersheds with deep soils capable of retaining large amounts of sulfate or nitrate, however, or soils rich in exchangeable cations, the release of acid to the lake or stream may be forestalled, at least until the retention or buffering capacity is used up.

14 What happens when acidified runoff or groundwater reaches a lake or a stream? A body of water may contain bicarbonate and other basic ions derived from rock weathering, which can neutralize an influx of acid, preventing the *p*H of the water from falling below a value of about 5. The water's content of such neutralizing ions is known as its acid-neutralizing capacity (ANC), and the value of the ANC provides one measure of a

lake's susceptibility to acidification. A lake with a very high ANC is protected against acid rain, at least for the moment; a lake with an ANC of zero may stay healthy if it lies far from acid rain. Otherwise any input of acid will acidify it directly.

15 An acidified lake is easy to spot. Its ANC is exhausted and its *p*H has fallen to well below 6; its waters are high in sulfate and other ions, such as aluminum, that are mobilized when acid percolates through soil, and it hosts an altered community of aquatic life (or no life at all). Forecasting the acidification of a lake with a low but still positive ANC is another matter. The retention or buffering of acid that is deposited in the watershed may slow the depletion of ANC for the time being. Moreover, a lake's budget of ANC is not fixed. Even as it is depleted by an influx of acid, it may be renewed by the weathering of minerals in the lake's surroundings. To predict how a lake will respond to a steady input of acid one must know not only its ANC but also how fast its ANC is replenished and how long that rate can be maintained.

16 These interacting processes in the watershed and the lake, then, determine whether a given lake will acidify, and how fast. They are still not thoroughly understood, and learning enough about a system to predict its behavior is difficult. There is no doubt about the overall trend, however: in areas where the soil is poor in weatherable minerals and acid deposition is heavy, lakes have been acidifying. In 1986 a committee of the National Academy of Sciences compiled measurements of *p*H and alkalinity (a measure of buffering ability similar to ANC) made between the 1920's and the 1940's in several hundred lakes in Wisconsin, New Hampshire and New York and compared the data with recent measurements. In the interim, the committee found, *p*H and alkalinity have on the average increased in the Wisconsin lakes and stayed largely unchanged for those in New Hampshire. In New York, however, and in particular in the Adirondack Mountains, the data for some lakes show a trend of acidification.

17 The NAS committee got a more complete picture of the trend from microorganisms preserved in lake-bottom sediments. As the *p*H of a lake changes, the assemblage of diatoms and golden-brown algae it hosts changes as well. Species of these minute plants can be distinguished by the form of their skeletons, which makes it possible to reconstruct changes with time in the community of species, and hence in water *p*H. Of the 11 Adirondack lakes for which such data were available, six had increased in acidity since the 1930's, falling to a *p*H of below 5.2; the acidification was fastest during the period ending in 1970. The committee could identify no cause for the *p*H change other than acid rain.

18 Acidification of lakes in the Adirondacks is a function of the region's highly acidic precipitation (rain collected nearby, in western New York, has an average *p*H of about 4.1, the lowest in the country) and the poor buffering ability of its granite-floored soil and lakes. The recent National Surface Water Survey examined other areas around the country where the ANC of lakes and streams tends to be low, leaving them vulnerable to acid rain. The survey found high percentages of acidic lakes in the Pocono Mountains of eastern Pennsylvania and on Michigan's Upper Peninsula—regions where rain is highly acidic. Acid rain is high on the list of suspected culprits for the relatively large

number of acidic lakes found in central and southern New England. Florida showed a strikingly high proportion of acidic lakes, but they are believed to reflect other circumstances, such as organic acids produced by decaying vegetation in swampy regions and fertilizer-rich runoff from agricultural land.

19 Maine has the lowest percentage of acidic lakes in the Northeast in spite of its poorly buffered soil and waters. Poorly buffered lakes surveyed in the upper Great Lakes region, the southern Blue Ridge Mountains and the mountainous West also were mostly healthy, showing a pH of more than 6. What sets those regions apart is their relative freedom from acid rain.

20 The evidence is not nearly as definitive for the other major environmental effect attributed to acid rain: forest decline. Since 1980 many forests in the eastern U.S. and parts of Europe have suffered a drastic loss of vitality—a loss that could not be linked to any of the familiar causes, such as insects, disease or direct poisoning by a specific air or water pollutant. The most dramatic reports have come from Germany, where scientists, stunned by the extent and speed of the decline, have called it *Waldsterben,* or forest death. Yet statistics for the U.S. are also unnerving.

21 The decline is most dramatic in high-elevation coniferous forests. For many sites lying above 850 meters in the Adirondacks, the Green Mountains in Vermont and the

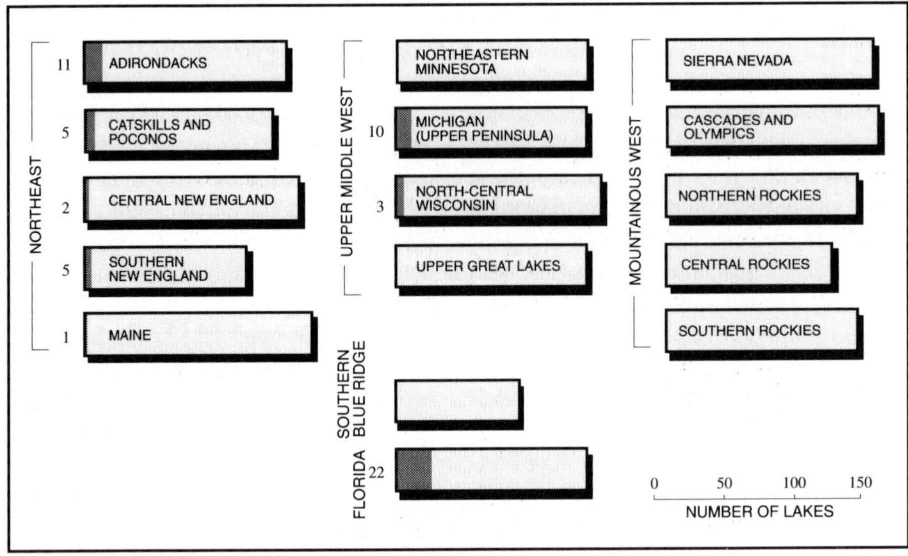

Acidified lakes are concentrated in the Northeast and the Upper Middle West. The graph shows results of the National Surface Water Survey. The segment of each bar in shading corresponds to the numbers of sampled lakes whose content of bicarbonate and other acid-neutralizing ions has been depleted; the number is also given as a percentage (darker shading). Such lakes usually have a low pH and changed aquatic life. Sulfuric and nitric acids from pollutants are thought to account for most such lakes, except in Florida, where they are thought to reflect such factors as organic acids from decaying vegetation and fertilizer runoff.

White Mountains in New Hampshire a comparison of historical records with current surveys shows that more than 50 percent of the red spruce have died in the past 25 years. At lower elevations injury to both softwoods and hardwoods has been documented.

22 In the forests at high elevations, at least, the dead timber is only the most dramatic evidence of a pervasive loss of tree vigor. Tree-ring records from high-elevation forests in the Northeast show sharply reduced annual growth increments beginning in the early 1960's. The declines occur in stands of many different ages, with different histories of disturbance or disease. What common factor could underlie the growth reductions?

23 The role of acid rain and other forms of air pollution is under intensive investigation. In spite of the dimensions of the forest damage, however, a firm causal link has proved to be elusive. One can get some idea of the difficulties by contrasting the recent forest decline with clear-cut cases of fumigation: forest poisoning by air pollutants. Smelters and chemical plants that emit sulfur dioxide, oxides of nitrogen or fluoride compounds are often girdled by dead timber. In such cases there is a clear correlation between tree damage, a specific pollution source and a threshold concentration of the pollutant. The forests that are now dying, in contrast, are far from any source and are exposed to pollutants in concentrations well below the levels previously reported to injure trees. If air pollution, and specifically acid rain, plays a part in forest decline, it probably does so less as a lethal agent than as a stress.

24 Many stresses, both biotic and abiotic, combine to affect the vigor of a forest. The trees' genetic endowment or age can be a source of stress: a stand may be genetically weak or senescent. Other stresses may take such forms as diseases, insects, parasitic fungi and seed plants, a shortage of light, water or essential nutrients and sporadic injury from events such as floods, high winds and ice storms. Stresses easily withstood in isolation can combine with debilitating or fatal effects. A fatal sequence of stresses may begin with a "predisposing" stress, such as a shortage of nutrients. The tree may then be seriously weakened by an "inciting" stress, such as a severe winter. It is then defenseless against a final, "contributing" stress—the actual cause of death—such as disease or insect attack.

25 Acid and other pollutants could add to the high level of abiotic stresses, including thin soil, low temperatures and desiccating winds, present in a high-elevation forest. That is, the pollutants might handicap the trees with one more predisposing stress as they face subsequent stresses. But what is the nature of the added stress?

26 Investigators, most of them in Europe, have put forward a number of hypothetical mechanisms, many of which would ultimately lead to nutrient deficiency in the tree. Several mechanisms would be played out in the soil. The aluminum released from soil minerals by acid might compete with calcium for binding sites on fine roots, reducing a tree's supply of calcium and slowing its growth. Alternatively, the soil itself might lose nutrients when vital elements such as calcium, magnesium and potassium are leached away by acid rain. The death of soil microorganisms is another possible source of nutrient stress. Low soil *p*H and high concentrations of aluminum can reduce populations of the bacteria that break down and release nutrients locked in decaying organic

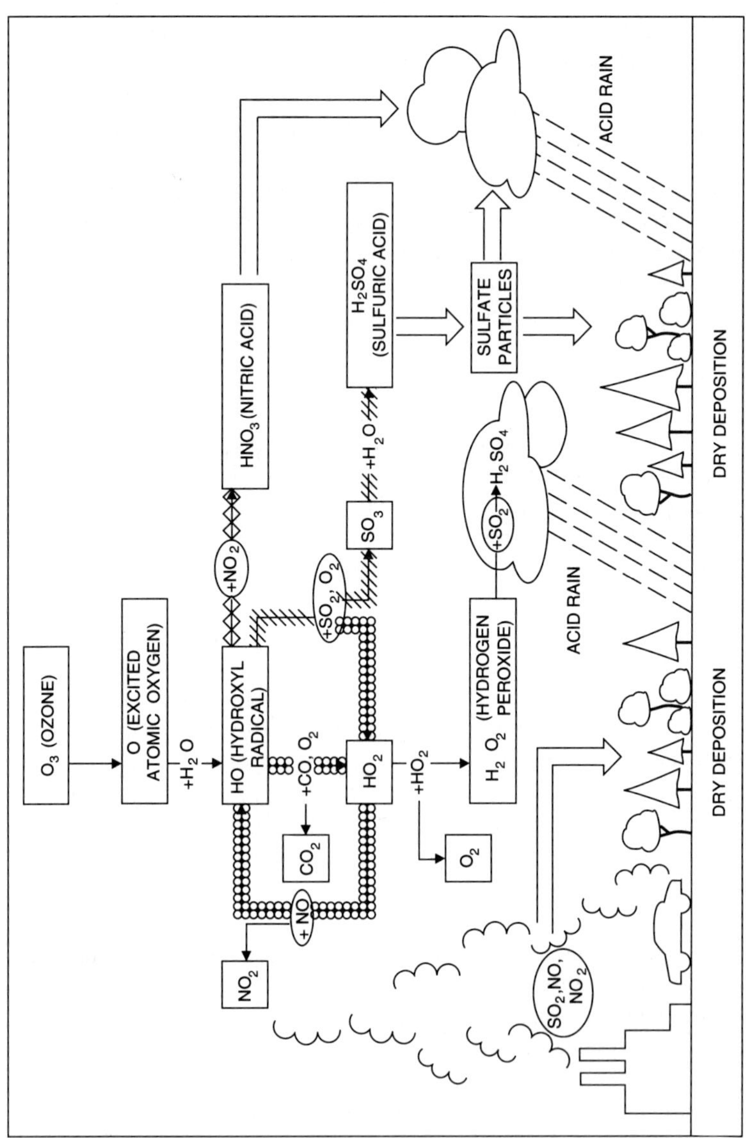

"The Challenge of Acid Rain" by Volker A. Mohnem © 1988 August, by Scientific American.

Atmospheric chemistry generates sulfuric and nitric acids from sulfur dioxide and oxides of nitrogen given off by industry and vehicles. The hydroxyl radical, formed when a molecule of ozone breaks apart and releases an oxygen atom that can react with water, is the major actor. It converts nitrogen dioxide into nitric acid (◇◇◇) and initiates the conversion of gaseous sulfur dioxide into sulfuric acid (/////). (A different reaction sequence forms sulfuric acid from sulfur dioxide and hydrogen peroxide dissolved in cloud water.) The hydroxyl radical is regenerated by reactions (○○○○○) involving nitric oxide, and the acids come to the earth as dry particles and in rain and other forms of precipitation.

material. In addition, high levels of nitrate from nitric acid deposition can injure the mycorrhizae, symbiotic fungi that live on the roots of conifers and help the trees to ward off disease and extract water and nutrients.

27 In other scenarios the pollutants would work their effects aboveground. Acid rain or, more likely, acidic cloud droplets intercepted by the needles of a conifer could leach out nutrients—magnesium, calcium and potassium in particular—faster than the tree's roots could replace them. An additional pollutant, ozone, might worsen nutrient leaching by degrading the water-resistant waxy coating of the needles. Still another hypothesis holds that ozone alone might lead to nutrient stress because it can damage chlorophyll, thereby impeding photosynthesis.

28 Finally, acid rain might augment the stress of low winter temperatures. In the fall a conifer ordinarily prepares for the freezing temperatures of winter by withdrawing water from its needles, a process known as cold hardening. The initiating signal for cold hardening ordinarily comes from the roots, in the form of a decreased supply of the nitrogen-bearing nutrients that are produced by soil microorganisms. As acid soaks into the needles, however, the nitrogen compounds it contains might in effect fertilize the tree. They might override the signal from the roots, delaying cold hardening and leaving the tree vulnerable to damage from ice formation in needle tissue. Ozone too might reduce a tree's resistance to freezing by damaging cell membranes in the foliage.

29 Laboratory tests are now under way to see which of these mechanisms (if any) might operate under the conditions of pollutant exposure in the afflicted forests. But only field studies, in the forests themselves, can show that a given mechanism is actually at work. The task is challenging: one is trying to track down what may be a relatively small increment of stress, superimposed on a complex set of natural stresses. That background of stresses may vary from stand to stand and even from tree to tree.

30 Whiteface Mountain in the Adirondacks provides a case in point. It displays some of the most dramatic forest decline in the U.S., but because of the dominance of several natural stresses only tentative conclusions about the role of pollutants can be drawn. The direct cause of forest decline, inferred from foresters' records and temperature data, seems to have been severe, repeated damage by desiccation or freezing during the winters in the early 1960's. Ozone may well have made the trees more vulnerable to frost damage: shielding tree limbs from the ambient ozone leads to changes in biochemistry that suggest ozone can indeed weaken the tree by attacking cell membranes in the foliage. The role of acid rain and acidic clouds has not yet been fully investigated, but it is conceivable that they also acted as a predisposing stress in some way.

31 Even though uncertainties surround acid rain's role in forest decline, its effects in the soil and water alone leave no question about the need to reduce the ambient burden of sulfur and nitrogen compounds and thereby lower the acidity of precipitation. Some progress has already been made. In the Northeast the sulfate content of rain and the concentration of airborne sulfur compounds have decreased in the past 15 years; the decreases reflect the pollution-control measures mandated by the Clean Air Act, enacted in 1975, and additional emission laws passed by individual states. The rate at which lakes in the Northeast are acidifying seems to have slowed as well. To actually reverse

the trend, however, acid deposition will have to be reduced much further, and many policymakers and scientists are now asking: How quickly? By how much?

32 For precise answers to those questions we need to know how long soil processes can continue to buffer or retain acid in the threatened regions and how fast lakes can renew their acid-neutralizing capacity. We also need to understand the relation between acid rain and forest decline. Some answers should be forthcoming in the 1990 NAPAP report. Certain scientists have already speculated, however, that to protect lakes and streams in sensitive areas such as the Adirondacks it will be necessary to reduce acid deposition to less than 50 percent of its current level.

33 Where and by how much will emissions have to be reduced to achieve such reductions in deposition? Guidance will come from two massive computer models of acid production, transport and deposition that are now being tested: the Regional Acid Deposition Model (RADM), supported by the U.S. Environmental Protection Agency, and the Acid Deposition and Oxidant Model (ADOM), supported by agencies of the Canadian and West German governments. The models take into account all the atmospheric chemistry and meteorological processes known to act on molecules containing sulfur, nitrogen and carbon. (Carbon-containing molecules are included because of their role in producing the oxidants that convert sulfur and nitrogen emissions into acids.)

34 Given a set of source locations, emission levels and atmospheric conditions, these models can forecast weather and atmospheric chemistry in order to predict, with a geographic resolution of better than 50 miles square, the amount of acid deposited across an entire region in the course of up to four days. By averaging results calculated for a variety of atmospheric conditions, the models can also predict the long-term pattern of deposition for a given emission pattern, which should make them invaluable for designing a strategy of emission reductions.

35 How might the cuts be made? The most direct way of controlling the pollutants that cause acid rain would be to burn less fossil fuel for transportation and energy generation. Expanded mass transit and fuel-efficient cars can reduce oil consumption in the transportation sector, but energy generation is less tractable. In spite of worthy strategies for conserving energy, consumption is likely to increase in the long run, and current alternatives to fossil-fueled power plants do not look promising. Hydroelectric power is limited by a scarcity of appropriate sites, and nuclear power is beset by economic problems and a crisis of public confidence in its safety.

36 The key to controlling acid rain, then, must be the reduction of emissions from fossil-fueled power plants, coal-burning plants in particular. The approach that has already led to reductions in sulfur emissions in the U.S., West Germany and Japan combines the use of coal that is naturally low in sulfur, or has been washed to remove sulfur and other contaminants, with flue-gas desulfurization (FGD). In FGD wet limestone is sprayed into the plant's hot exhaust gases, where it scavenges as much as 90 percent of the sulfur dioxide. The sulfur-containing waste can be difficult to dispose of, however, and FGD reduces the efficiency of a power plant, causing it to consume several percent more

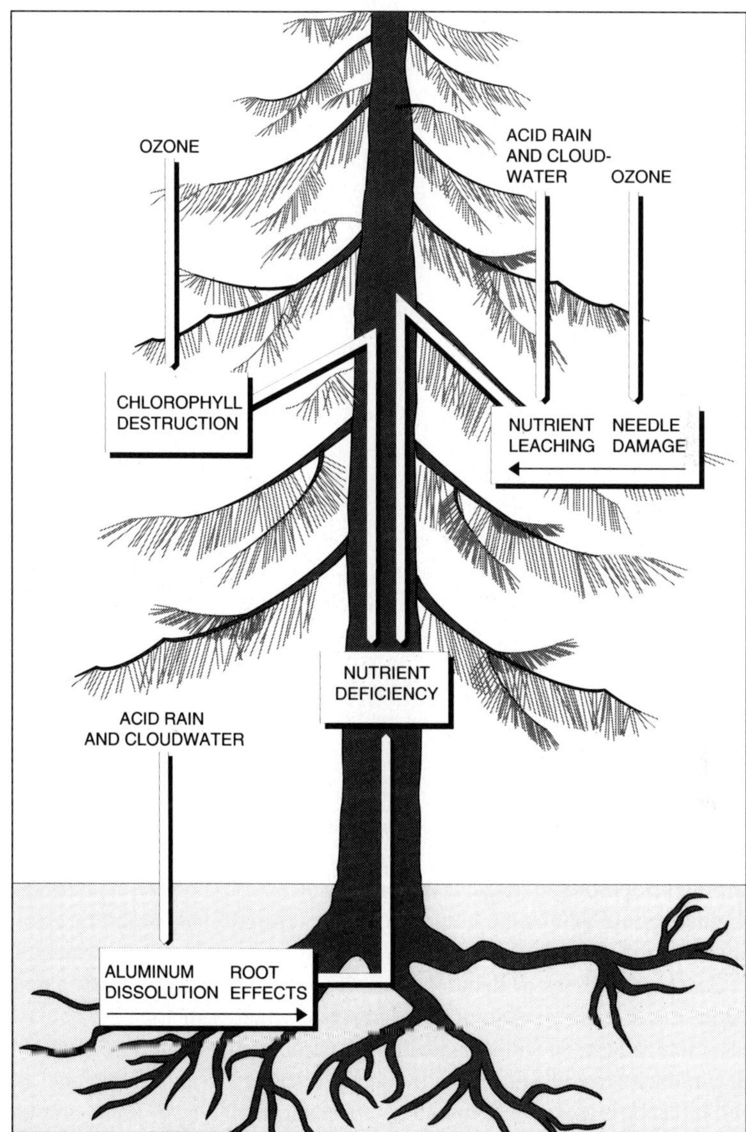

"The Challenge of Acid Rain" by Volker A. Mohnem © 1988 August, by Scientific American.

Acid rain and ozone together could lead to nutrient deficiency in a coniferous tree, according to a currently favored scenario for their possible role in forest decline. The ozone might act both by destroying chlorophyll (vital to photosynthesis) and by degrading the waxy coating of the needles. Acid rain or cloud water could then soak into needle tissue more readily and leach out nutrients. In the ground the acid rain might compound the nutrient deficiency by mobilizing aluminum, which could displace calcium from its binding sites on the tree's fine roots. Stressed by lack of nutrients, the tree would be vulnerable to destruction by insects, disease, or some other process.

coal for a given output. Furthermore, the process does nothing to reduce nitrogen oxide emissions.

37 The new power-plant technologies developed jointly by the Government and industry under the Clean Coal Demonstration Program, enacted in 1984, offer a more comprehensive solution. Three clean-coal technologies are already being demonstrated in full-size plants [see "Coal-fired Power Plants for the Future," by Richard E. Balzhiser and Kurt E. Yeager; *Scientific American,* September, 1987]. In the system known as atmospheric fluidized-bed combustion, a turbulent bed of pulverized coal and limestone is suspended by an upward blast of air; the combustion region is threaded with boiler tubes, which supply steam to the plant's turbines. The turbulent mixing of the coal and the air allows combustion to take place at a lower and more even temperature than it does in a conventional boiler, which reduces the formation of oxides of nitrogen. Meanwhile the limestone efficiently captures the sulfur dioxide. In a related technology known as pressurized fluidized-bed combustion the coal is burned in compressed air, which improves the plant's efficiency as well.

38 In the third technology, gasification/combined-cycle, coal is reacted with steam and air at high temperatures to produce a gas consisting mainly of hydrogen and carbon monoxide. The gas can then be burned, spinning a turbine; waste heat in the gas turbine's exhaust serves for generating steam, which drives a steam turbine to yield additional electricity. A gasification/combined-cycle plant operates much more efficiently than a conventional plant and gives off considerably less sulfur dioxide and nitrogen oxides.

39 Retrofitting existing plants with FGD offers the fastest way to reduce power-plant emissions. Almost half of the coal-fired plants in the U.S. were built before 1975 and have no controls for sulfur and nitrogen pollutants. Concentrated in the eastern half of the U.S., they account for most of the country's sulfur emissions. Adding conventional FGD to the plants could cut total emissions of sulfur dioxide from all power plants to less than half their present level, and the reduction could be accomplished within 15 years. Emissions of nitrogen oxides would not be affected, however. In addition, utilities object to the expense of installing and operating FGD equipment and the loss of plant efficiency it would cause.

40 Clean-coal technologies present an attractive alternative. Any effort to control acid rain must be focused on the aging plants, many of which will soon become candidates for retirement or refurbishment. Gradually replacing them with new conventional plants equipped with FGD would yield only modest reductions in emissions, and the cost of designing, building and getting regulatory approval for the new plants would be staggering. Instead most of the old plants—the 410 generating stations built between 1955 and 1975—could be "repowered": refurbished with a new combustion section incorporating one of the clean-coal technologies.

41 A repowered plant could preserve much of its existing equipment for handling coal and ash and most of its steam-cycle and electricity-generating hardware. The repowering of an existing plant would thus be quick and cheap compared with building a new one. The approach has an additional attraction for the utility industry: the new hardware

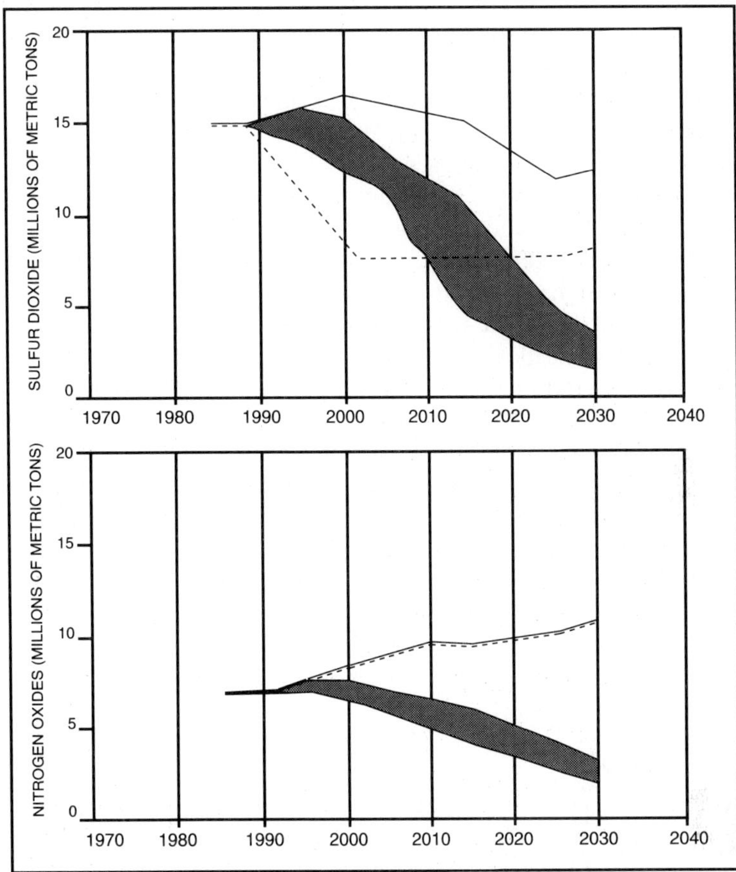

Expected reductions in annual emissions of sulfur dioxide (top) and oxides of nitrogen (bottom) from power plants vary depending on the choice of technology. Replacing plants as they reached 50 years of age with new ones incorporating flue-gas desulfurization (FGD) would reduce only sulfur dioxide, and the reductions would come slowly (solid line). Retrofitting all existing power plants with FGD on a 15-year schedule would yield much sharper reductions, again in sulfur dioxide alone (broken line). In both cases nitrogen oxide emissions would continue to climb as additional plants were built to satisfy growing demand for power. Refurbishing plants built between 1955 and 1975 with "clean coal" technologies such as fluidized-bed combustion (a strategy known as repowering) would eventually lead to the largest cuts in both kinds of pollutants. The shaded bands illustrate the range of reductions expected if the plants were refurbished when they reached an age of between 40 and 50 years.

could be added to a plant in modules, which would enable utilities to adjust generating capacity to the demand for power.

42 The repowering of aging plants promises ultimately the greatest emission reductions, affecting the full range of pollutants implicated in acid rain. The strategy could cut sulfur dioxide emissions by more than 80 percent and nitrogen oxide emissions by more

than 50 percent; the emission of fewer nitrogen compounds would in turn reduce the formation of ozone in the troposphere.

43 We now know that the term acid rain covers a host of phenomena. Oxides of nitrogen, for example, affect the chemical cycle that converts sulfur dioxide into sulfuric acid, and the ozone they help to produce may work in concert with acid rain to destroy forests. The nitrate ion as well as the acidity that accompanies it may affect the ecosystem, not just on land but also, it now appears, in coastal waters. The emission reductions that are promised by repowering could lessen all these effects.

44 The drawback is that the reductions, dramatic as they are, would be slow in coming. The recent declines in the sulfate content of air and precipitation in the Northeast and the slowing of lake acidification suggest that some breathing space remains. The nation can probably forgo the short-term solution of retrofitting pollution controls on existing plants in favor of the gradual but more comprehensive and economical approach of repowering. Yet Government intervention, in the form of a timetable, may still be needed to speed the pace. If utilities simply repower plants as the need arises—as the plants reach an age of 50 years or so—the process would not be completed until well into the next century.

45 Technology has leapfrogged science and presented us with an option for addressing the problem of acid rain that is likely to be attractive whatever the resolution of the remaining scientific uncertainties. The urgent need to reduce human interference in the complex chemistry of the biosphere is already painfully clear.

Questions for Analysis

1. In his article Mohnen describes processes that you have seen described in earlier essays. On the whole, are his explanations more or less effective than those in earlier essays? Why?
2. In Paragraphs 6 and 7, Mohnen discusses the role played by ozone in the transformation of nitrate and sulfate pollutants into acid rain. Compare Mohnen's discussion of ozone to those you found in Ray's essay and the NAPAP report. Which account is clearer and provides a fuller explanation? What is the full range of problems (based on what you have read) associated with high levels of ozone in the troposphere?
3. Does Mohnen's discussion of acid levels in clouds (Paragraphs 10 and 11) help clarify why environmentalists are concerned about the effects of nitrate and sulfate pollutants on forests in the higher elevations of the Eastern United States? Explain.
4. What are the conclusions Mohnen reaches in his essay? Do the facts and examples he provides support his conclusions? Is his essay more or less effective than those that argue a different position?

5. Why does Mohnen include information about the new technology available to cut down on pollution? In what ways (if at all) does this information help his argument?

Jon R. Luoma

The Human Cost of Acid Rain

(1988)

Jon R. Luoma (b. 1951) is a professional writer whose work focuses on wildlife and conservation. His *Crowded Ark: The Role of Zoos in Wildlife Conservation* examines the role of zoos in preserving natural habitat and rescuing endangered species. This essay originally appeared in *Audubon* magazine.

1 Take a deep breath. Some ten million times each year you ventilate about a pint of atmosphere deep into trachea, bronchi, bronchial tubes, bronchioles, and moist alveolar membranes for purposes of gas exchange—oxygen diffusing into blood, carbon dioxide diffusing out.

2 The majority of us don't pay much attention to the mechanics of it, vital of function though it be. But a significant minority must. According to the American Lung Association, breathing problems afflict about one out of every five of us noticeably and many more of us subtly, insidiously, and eventually. The obvious problems can range from an intermittent condition doctors call "twitchy lungs" to the chest tightness and wheezing of asthma, to chronic bronchitis, cystic fibrosis, and emphysema. The less obvious problems include diminished lung function and a slow alteration in lung architecture that can go unfelt and undiagnosed for years but can nevertheless lead to miseries ranging from moderate discomfort to difficulty in exercising or doing heavy work outdoors, to lost workdays, to considerable pain, to early death.

3 Some leading health experts warn that the same pollutants that cause acid rain can instigate or exacerbate these health problems. They also suggest that respiratory disease would almost certainly be diminished as a side benefit of any congressional action that attempts to protect lakes, streams, forests, fish, and wildlife by sharply reducing the pollutants responsible for acid rain.

4 Each year in the United States, largely while burning or refining fossil fuels for energy, we dump some 25 million tons of sulfur dioxide, a pollutant gas, into the air. The furnaces of coal-burning utilities and nonferrous metal smelters are the major sources of this pollution. Sulfur dioxide, at sufficiently high levels, has long been considered a threat to public health—irritating the lungs, stressing the heart, and lowering the body's resistance to respiratory infections.

5 In the eastern half of North America the gas also is the chemical precursor of about two-thirds of the acidity in acid rain—more properly called "acid deposition," since

it includes snow, fog, and even microscopic dry acidic particles called acid aerosols. The remainder of human-made acid deposition comes from nitrogen oxides, pollutant by-products of combustion in many types of engines and furnaces. Since many sources of sulfur dioxide spew their pollutants with little emission control, and since highly efficient control technologies are available, most proposed initial solutions to the acid deposition problem have focused on controlling this gas. Congress is considering bills to reduce emissions by 30 to 40 percent over periods of seven to ten years. Without these controls, sulfur dioxide emissions will increase.

6 A German scientist, M. Firket, was among the first to link sulfur dioxide and its acid by-products to public health threats. In 1931 Firket published a paper called "The Causes of Accidents Which Occurred in the Meuse Valley During the Fogs of December 1930." The accidents in question were deaths from the first medically chronicled "killer fog." In that month industrial and residential air pollution poured into a Meuse Valley atmosphere socked in by a temperature inversion, a sort of atmospheric lid over a piece of the Earth which prevents warm gases from escaping. Because of the inversion, pollutants could not rise out of the valley and instead accumulated close to the ground. Firket reckoned that sixty residents of the valley died from inhaling sulfur gases and acids during the episode, and several hundred more suffered lung irritation and asthma-like paroxysms. Autopsies on ten of the dead showed severe lung congestion. Firket further calculated that if a fog of that pollutant intensity ever settled over the city of London, there would be 3,179 attributable deaths. No one paid much notice.

7 Then, in October 1948, the Pennsylvania steel-mill town of Donora suffered a fog that lasted two days, killed eighteen of the small town's residents and left about 5,900, or 43 percent of the rest, gasping and wheezing. But the worst was yet to come. In December 1952 the Great Fog settled over London, and the intensely polluted air ended the lives of an estimated four thousand residents. Firket's estimates, it seems, had been on the sanguine side. Subsequent incidents in both London and New York City debilitated more victims.

8 Fear of such disasters helped bring about the Clean Air Act in 1970 and its renewal and revision in 1977. Environmental Protection Agency regulations flowing from the act attempt to limit sulfur dioxide gas levels in the air we breathe—the ambient air. But rather than strictly requiring factories and powerplants to limit their emissions, the early version of the act assumed that a diluted concentration of pollutant gunk was acceptable. Thus, each state was required to jump through an astonishing series of bureaucratic hoops to develop localized "implementation plans" so that pollution could be controlled, but not wastefully over-controlled. Later amendments required stricter emissions caps. But many sources of pollution, including dozens of huge coal-fired powerplants, were grandfathered by the amendments. Although today's scrubbers can remove 95 percent or more of the gas, dozens of huge plants remain scrubberless and can be expected to belch sulfur fumes into the atmosphere for another thirty years or more. And it's perfectly legal.

9 Sulfur dioxide levels did drop after passage of the Clean Air Act, but emissions are again increasing, and some sixty counties, including much of the urbanized Midwest and East, still violate minimal health standards. According to the American Lung Association, about 115 million Americans continue to be exposed to air pollution levels exceeding federal health standards. Moreover, there are no specific standards for acid aerosols, which are so tiny that they tend to be drawn deep into the lungs. EPA has only begun the laborious process of investigating whether acid aerosol standards should be adopted.

10 According to lobbyists from the automobile, coal, and coal-burning electric utility industries, the Clean Air Act is fully protecting public health. ''The Clean Air Act Is Working'' a headline in a recent utility public relations brochure happily reports, as if to suggest that the utilities themselves had drafted the act they once lobbied so vigorously against. But now, such prominent physicians' organizations as the American Lung Association, the American Academy of Pediatrics, and the American Public Health Association have begun to disagree. Current levels of sulfur dioxide and acid aerosols, they say, constitute a threat to public health.

11 Bailus Walker, a professor of public health at the State University of New York at Albany, former commissioner of public health for the State of Massachusetts, and president of the American Public Health Association, testified last year before Congress: ''Acid rain affects more than just fish or trees—it indirectly affects the health of people.''

12 The specific concerns are wide-ranging—from a long-standing worry that unregulated short-term doses of sulfur dioxide are causing asthma attacks to concern that microscopic acidic aerosols might be invading people's lungs. There is also troubling speculation that acid deposition, by leaching toxic metals into drinking water, may be linked to a range of localized maladies, including lead poisoning and Alzheimer's disease.

13 Despite the level of concern, there are gaps and uncertainties in existing research. To understand air pollution's effects on human health, a researcher can follow three lines of analysis: experiments on humans, experiments on animals, and epidemiological studies. Unfortunately, each method faces unavoidable limits that make it virtually impossible to establish a firm connection between health and pollution—the same sort of limits that have made it possible for the tobacco lobby to decry the overwhelming evidence of their products' potential hazards. But Dr. Thomas Godar, a practicing pulmonary disease specialist at the St. Francis Hospital in Hartford, Connecticut, and president of the American Lung Association, says, ''Knowing what we already know, we don't need to have people dropping dead in the streets to appreciate that long-term health effects are occurring and that there's reason to be concerned.''

14 Although long-term, lethal experiments on human subjects might provide the best proof, scientists obviously cannot carry out such experiments. Nor can they expose subjects to sublethal but permanent damage. ''Our clinical studies have to be designed so that they show only a minimal risk and only a reversible risk. You just don't conduct experiments that provoke an asthma attack or put a subject in the hospital,'' says Dr.

Mark Utell, a University of Rochester School of Medicine researcher who has conducted several highly regarded studies on human volunteers. In these studies a subject is placed into an airtight chamber or fitted with an inhalation mask and dosed with a measure of artificially polluted air for a few minutes. After the brief fumigation, subjects will huff and puff into monitoring gadgets that measure lung capacity and function. The idea is to look for what will amount to very tiny changes, such as reductions in lung function, from the brief exposure. Critics of the procedure can always argue, however, that any detected disruption of lung function is merely temporary and therefore of no particular consequence.

15 Although most research scientists lack similar ethical qualms about research on lab animals, studies on guinea pigs and other animals are equally limited. A critic of even the most meticulous animal research can always insist that guinea pigs aren't humans and that their respiratory systems may respond differently.

16 If this were a simple world, epidemiological investigation would be the best of the three approaches. It would be neat and orderly and would offer a precise statistical scope for looking at pollutant damage to large populations. A researcher could, for example, compile all the data for daily levels of sulfur dioxide collected by monitoring gadgets in, say, Peoria. This information, when it is correlated with chronological data about visits to doctors for respiratory ailments, cases of chronic lung disease, and early deaths should yield many answers. Do rates of illness or death rise or fall in relation to fluctuations in pollutant levels? How do data from Peoria compare with similar data from Gary, Indiana, or Lubbock, Texas?

17 But it isn't such a simple world. Those in Gary or Lubbock may have different smoking habits, may come from different educational and economic backgrounds, may have different health-care levels. They may have greater or lesser degrees of stress at home or on the job, or better diets. One city or another may have more or fewer smokers. There may be genetic differences among ethnic groups. The weather in one city may affect the transport or chemistry of the pollutant mix in the local atmosphere. In the end, sorting out the epidemiological signal amidst all the statistical background noise is a task for a Hercules among number-crunchers.

18 Yet, despite all the complications, Dr. Philip Landrigan, a pediatric lung specialist and professor of medicine at the Mount Sinai Medical Center in New York, insists that "converging lines of evidence" from all three research arenas now point in the same troubling direction. While none of the lines taken alone may be conclusive, and while there are gaps and contradictions, Landrigan and many of his colleagues agree that the evidence is now too compelling to ignore.

19 Low-dose laboratory studies on humans have shown that exposures to sulfur dioxide gas can indeed induce gasping and wheezing. In these experiments, those with normal, healthy lungs suffer only at sulfur dioxide levels exceeding those usually found in the air over the United States. However, and most significantly, some studies have shown that some mild asthmatics and others among the one-fifth of us with breathing problems experience chest tightness and wheezing symptoms at about 100 parts per billion of

sulfur dioxide administered for five minutes. That's a level found in the real world, where pollution lasts not for five minutes but for hours, days, or forever. Such levels are prevalent in many parts of the industrialized Midwest, where coal burners and refineries proliferate. In 1985 Ashtabula County, Ohio, and Jefferson County, Indiana, for example, *averaged* about four times that level. And sulfur dioxide emissions in Miami, Arizona, downwind from a smelter, averaged 1,500 ppb.

20 Medical science still knows little about the specific effects of sulfuric acid aerosols. But some short-exposure studies on humans have shown that these tiny particles can diminish both the sense of smell and respiratory function in mildly asthmatic human test subjects. Studies have also shown that tiny acid particles can interfere with the respiratory tract's rate of mucociliary clearance—the body's defense mechanism that rids the lungs of tiny particles and disease organisms.

21 Because their respiratory plumbing is so underdeveloped, small children, especially those under two years of age, might be as vulnerable as mild asthmatics. No small children have been subjected to this sort of respiratory experiment, and, for ethical reasons, most likely none ever will be. But Dr. Richard Narkewicz, president of the American Academy of Pediatrics, says that since both groups tend to respond similarly, the experiments with mild asthmatics can serve as a model for effects on young children. Obviously, a small child with asthma is even more susceptible.

22 Studies on animals have used pollutants for longer periods of time and often at higher doses. In one study guinea pigs showed symptoms of air-way constriction after exposure for as little as one hour to concentrations of 160 parts per billion of sulfur dioxide gas. Guinea pigs exposed to as little as 40 ppb of sulfuric acid aerosols showed similar signs of bronchial constriction. Not all the guinea pigs responded at that level. Differences in age and, presumably, genetic makeup meant that each animal, like each smoker, became ill at a different dosage. Predictably, the studies showed that as aerosol levels went up, more animals fell ill. Animal studies have shown that chronic exposure to acid aerosol pollutants increases the size and number of mucus secretory cells. In 1983 and 1987 studies with rabbits showed that exposure to 100 to 200 ppb of acid aerosols for only one hour per day, five days per week, can cause cell changes. The significance: Some of those changes occur in human smokers and appear to be early signs of chronic lung disease.

23 Fran du Melle, director of government relations for the American Lung Association, notes that the third avenue of investigation, epidemiology, is riddled with problems. "It allows you to look at very large populations. But there are a lot of confounding factors, lots of noise, and you're looking for what amounts to a very small signal. The only way you get an obvious body count is if you peak so high that you've got people lining up in the emergency room gasping for air."

24 Although many epidemiological studies show higher rates of premature deaths in polluted areas, the pollution lobby can marshal a few that show little or no effect. In total, however, a pattern emerges. Common sense suggests that mere sampling flaws or design errors would skew the results equally above and below the norm. Yet there

are no epidemiological studies showing *improvements* in premature death rates because of air pollution. Landrigan, the Mount Sinai professor, insists that the probabilities lean heavily toward the evidence of damage. In fact, the congressional Office of Technology Assessment deemed the epidemiology convincing enough to predict, in 1984, that current sulfate and other small particle levels were causing an estimated 50,000 premature deaths each year in North America. However, EPA, which once relied on epidemiology, has virtually abandoned it under the Reagan Administration.

25 Despite the complications and limitations, there are now some compelling studies that go further than mixing data into a pot to see what rises to the top. These studies reinforce the notion that sulfur pollutants are damaging public health. A long-term study by Harvard University scientists has compared air pollution and the day-to-day health of a sample of residents in six cities—ranging from the dirty-air Steubenville, Ohio, area to the clean-air Portage, Wisconsin, area—and has shown a strong relationship between total air pollution levels and such symptoms as chronic cough and bronchitis rates among children. Another study of a sample of families in four Utah communities showed increases in cough and phlegm in direct relationship to sulfur dioxide and sulfate levels. More recent studies in Canada, conducted at children's summer camps, have shown a statistically significant, positive correlation between breathing problems and the comings and goings of polluted air masses. Another Canadian study compared lung function among children in Tillsonburg, Ontario, where acid deposition levels are high, and children in Portage la Prairie, Manitoba, where levels are low. Not only did children in the more polluted area show greater rates of chest colds, respiratory allergies, and cough with phlegm, but the average lung function was down about two percent. That latter finding may not seem significant, but recall that it is an *average.* Because of individual variations, some subjects will show no change and others, inevitably, will show more. Notes Dr. Landrigan, "These are real, measurable changes. While they might not seem like much, if you apply them across large populations of millions of people you're going to find greater rates of asthma attacks. Any physician who's dealt with a child having a severe asthma attack wouldn't call that a small change."

26 For lack of adequate research, the indirect effects of acid deposition are still unknown, including the effect on humans of increased levels of toxic metals liberated from soil or plumbing by acid runoff or drinking water. Some scientists have speculated that more acidic waters can leach lead from the pipes or joints of older water systems. In a recent Ontario study, analysts found that tapwater that had been standing in plumbing contained levels of copper and lead exceeding recommended minimum health standards. Studies in the Adirondacks showed that about 11 percent of residential wells and about 22 percent of cisterns contained lead levels exceeding EPA standards. Lead has been linked to brain damage in children. Some researchers have suggested a link between aluminum and Alzheimer's disease. Aluminum, virtually omnipresent but normally harmlessly bound up in almost all soils, can be leached away by acid runoff. Acid rain has also been shown to liberate mercury in its most toxic form, methyl

mercury, which can then accumulate in the fatty tissue of fish and, eventually, in humans who eat the fish.

27 The weight of evidence seems at least great enough to lend considerable force to arguments for stringent sulfur dioxide controls. The American Lung Association's Du Melle suggests that some impressive economic studies also debunk much of the coal and electric utility lobbies' claims that sulfur dioxide regulations should remain frozen because of the high costs of emissions control. "It's easy for anyone to figure the cost of a doodad on a smokestack," she says. "It's less simple to calculate the toll pollution takes on public health. But some of the studies we've seen indicate that the costs of sulfur dioxide damage to health are far higher than the costs of control." A 1982 study showed that pollution reductions brought about by the Clean Air Act between 1970 and 1978 saved about $14 billion per year in costs associated with early death and another $2 billion annually in costs associated with illness. Another study commissioned by the European Economic Community showed that a 34 percent reduction in sulfur dioxide emissions would increase average life expectancies by about a year and a half and that savings from costs related to death and illness would approach $6 billion. And a 1979 study in the United States suggested that a 60 percent average reduction from 1978 particle and sulfur dioxide gas emission levels could save more than $40 billion yearly in illness and death costs. Costs, in these cases, include such cold factors as projected lost wages and medical bills. It's probably safe to assume that no one has pinned down a dollar value for pain, miserable health, or loss of a loved one.

28 In response to the physicians, and with echoes of the tobacco lobby, the Consolidation Coal Company of Pittsburgh submitted detailed testimony to the U.S. Senate, carefully picking apart each known study on sulfur dioxide and health for "uncertainties, inconsistencies, and unanswered questions." Landrigan finds efforts to debunk research on the problem to be "something like the old shell game at the carnival. But the other side is to say, who should bear the burden of proof? Considering that there's good evidence that these pollutants are causing permanent damage to vital functions, might it not make more sense to stop this since we have the means to do it? Go ahead and continue the research. If science can exonerate the pollutants, then go ahead and put them back into the air." As he told Congress, "I would argue that under the present circumstances EPA cannot afford to wait, possibly for several more years, for more precise research data on the adverse effects of acid air pollution on the lungs."

29 Said Godar on behalf of the American Lung Association, "I would point out that the death of a human is a rather severe endpoint when one looks at cause and effect."

Questions for Analysis

1. Explain the rhetorical purpose and strategy in Paragraph 1. Is it effective? Why?
2. Explain the purpose and effect of the examples and discussions in Paragraphs 6 and 7? Are those examples in themselves enough to justify action against sources of pollution? Explain.

3. Luoma admits to ''uncertainties'' and problems with all three lines of research that scientists use to determine the effects of acidic pollutants on human health. He nevertheless believes they all point to serious problems. Based on the evidence he presents, do you agree? What evidence do you find compelling? Does it help Luoma's argument that he admits ''uncertainties'' and problems?
4. How do the coal industry and other representatives of polluting industries respond to the work of scientists whose work suggests the need for strict controls?

Jeff McNelly

Earth Day 1990

(1990)

Jeff McNelly is editorial cartoonist for the *Chicago Tribune.*

EarthDay1990: A seedling takes root in a hostile environment.

Reprinted by permission: Tribune Media Services.

Questions for Analysis

1. Based on this cartoon, do you think McNelly is optimistic about the future of our environment? Why?
2. Are you optimistic or pessimistic about the future of our environment? Explain your answer.

Part IV

PERSISTENT HUMAN PROBLEMS

Civil Rights: A Historical Perspective on Current Problems

Social change is always difficult. It cannot be accomplished without an understanding of the accompanying tensions and their history or a clear sense of where the changes will lead. Most of the selections in this sub-section present the history of the Civil Rights Movement in the United States. A few focus on differences of opinion that are now emerging among members of the African-American community. One essay deals with the problems generated by racial separation and discrimination in South Africa.

The first selection is Maya Angelou's "Graduation," an autobiographical account of her experiences in an African-American school in Arkansas. She describes how her pleasure and sense of accomplishment in graduating from the eighth grade are undercut by the unannounced visit of the white politician in charge of the school. Her story poignantly reveals the physical and emotional limitations imposed on African Americans before the Civil Rights Movement.

Three documents essential to the history of the Civil Rights Movement follow: "Public Statement by Eight Alabama Clergymen," Martin Luther King, Jr.'s response to that statement in "Letter from Birmingham Jail," and King's "I Have a Dream" speech. These three selections together reveal the problems—political, legal, and personal—faced by the African-American leadership in the early 1960s. All three documents are arguments. Each illustrates how writers mold their arguments to fit special situations. King spoke for all African Americans but found his strongest following in southern Christian churches. Charles H. Turner's "Dream Deferred" expresses what that time was like for African Americans living in northern cities where the Black Muslims held greater appeal than King and other southern-based Christian leaders.

The next two essays are concerned with current problems faced by African Americans. In "Being Black and Feeling Blue," Shelby Steele candidly examines characteristics that limit the willingness and ability of many African Americans to take advantage of opportunities. In "To Blacks and Jews: Hab Rachmones," James A. McPherson dissects the complex, often contradictory relationship that has existed between African Americans and the Jewish community over the last few decades.

Although both Lance Morrow and Benjamin L. Hooks, the authors of the next two essays, are aware of how current difficulties have grown out of the past, their essays focus on problems of the 1990s. Morrow uses his review of the movie *Glory* to criticize the rhetoric and action used by the current civil-rights leadership. Hooks, Executive Director of the National Association for the Advancement of Colored People (NAACP), wrote his essay, "The Broader Issue of the Barry Case," in the summer of 1990 to clarify his position on Mayor Marion Barry's trial for drug possession. His essay answers those who have questioned the direction he and others in the NAACP have taken. Together these essays demonstrate the intellectual, political, and emotional complexity of debate on racial issues.

Alice Walker's "Everyday Use" is an amusing yet poignantly powerful story that captures the tensions between generations that the new ideas of the 1960s brought to many African-American families. Walker's story illustrates how much can be lost for the sake of progress and change if we are not careful.

The final essay in this subsection, Joseph Lelyveld's "Spiritual and Political Pilgrimage of Beyers Naudé," shifts the scene from America to South Africa and allows us to see the problems generated by racial separation and discrimination from another angle. Lelyveld's short study traces Beyers Naudé's transformation from being an influential member of the dominant Afrikaner social class to being one of the most outspoken opponents of apartheid. Naudé's story reveals how close people can live to racial discrimination without really recognizing, or allowing themselves to recognize, the dehumanizing conditions and attitudes that exist. The intellectual and moral imperative that drove Naudé to fight to rectify the problems brought on by apartheid is inspiring: He did what he knew was right even at the expense of losing his standing within his social group and ultimately his freedom to speak, write, and travel within his own country. His willingness to pursue truth, understanding, and tolerance can teach us much as we face, and *work through,* new racial tensions in the years ahead.

This subsection ends with Kevin Siers' cartoon "______ Was Here," a powerful and hopeful commentary dealing with political imprisonment and oppression.

Maya Angelou

Graduation

(1969)

Although she has attained success as a singer, actress, and dancer, Maya Angelou (b. 1928) is best known for her work as a writer. She has written several volumes of poetry, a number of plays for stage and screen, and at least five volumes of autobiographical short stories. "Graduation" comes from *I Know Why the Caged Bird Sings* (1969), her first volume of autobiographical stories. "Graduation" is set in Arkansas, where Angelou lived and attended public schools during her early childhood.

1 The children in Stamps trembled visibly with anticipation. Some adults were excited too, but to be certain the whole young population had come down with graduation epidemic. Large classes were graduating from both the grammar school and the high school. Even those who were years removed from their own day of glorious release were anxious to help with preparations as a kind of dry run. The junior students who were moving into the vacating classes' chairs were tradition-bound to show their talents for leadership and management. They strutted through the school and around the campus exerting pressure on the lower grades. Their authority was so new that occasionally if they pressed a little too hard it had to be overlooked. After all, next term was coming, and it never hurt a sixth grader to have a play sister in the eighth grade, or a tenth-year student to be able to call a twelfth grader Bubba. So all was endured in a spirit of shared understanding. But the graduating classes themselves were the nobility. Like travelers with exotic destinations on their minds, the graduates were remarkably forgetful. They came to school without their books, or tablets or even pencils. Volunteers fell over themselves to secure replacements for the missing equipment. When accepted, the willing workers might or might not be thanked, and it was of no importance to the pre-graduation rites. Even teachers were respectful of the now quiet and aging seniors, and tended to speak to them, if not as equals, as beings only slightly lower than themselves. After tests were returned and grades given, the student body, which acted like an extended family, knew who did well, who excelled, and what piteous ones had failed.

2 Unlike the white high school, Lafayette County Training School distinguished itself by having neither lawn, nor hedges, nor tennis court, nor climbing ivy. Its two buildings (main classrooms, the grade school and home economics) were set on a dirt hill with no fence to limit either its boundaries or those of bordering farms. There was a large expanse to the left of the school which was used alternately as a baseball diamond or a basketball court. Rusty hoops on the swaying poles represented the permanent recreational equipment, although bats and balls could be borrowed from the P. E. teacher if the borrower was qualified and if the diamond wasn't occupied.

3 Over this rocky area relieved by a few shady tall persimmon trees the graduating class walked. The girls often held hands and no longer bothered to speak to the lower

students. There was a sadness about them, as if this old woman was not their home and they were bound for higher ground. The boys, on the other hand, had become more friendly, more outgoing. A decided change from the closed attitude they projected while studying for finals. Now they seemed not ready to give up the old school, the familiar paths and classrooms. Only a small percentage would be continuing on to college—one of the South's A & M (agricultural and mechanical) schools, which trained Negro youths to be carpenters, farmers, handymen, masons, maids, cooks and baby nurses. Their future rode heavily on their shoulders, and blinded them to the collective joy that had pervaded the lives of the boys and girls in the grammar school graduating class.

4 Parents who could afford it had ordered new shoes and ready-made clothes for themselves from Sears and Roebuck or Montgomery Ward. They also engaged the best seamstresses to make the floating graduating dresses and to cut down secondhand pants which would be pressed to a military slickness for the important event.

5 Oh, it was important, all right. Whitefolks would attend the ceremony, and two or three would speak of God and home, and the Southern way of life, and Mrs. Parsons, the principal's wife, would play the graduation march while the lower-grade graduates paraded down the aisles and took their seats below the platform. The high school seniors would wait in empty classrooms to make their dramatic entrance.

6 In the Store I was the person of the moment. The birthday girl. The center. Bailey had graduated the year before, although to do so he had had to forfeit all pleasures to make up for his time lost in Baton Rouge.

7 My class was wearing butter-yellow piqué dresses, and Momma launched out on mine. She smocked the yoke into tiny crisscrossing puckers, then shirred the rest of the bodice. Her dark fingers ducked in and out of the lemony cloth as she embroidered raised daisies around the hem. Before she considered herself finished she had added a crocheted cuff on the puff sleeves, and a pointy crocheted collar.

8 I was going to be lovely. A walking model of all the various styles of fine hand sewing and it didn't worry me that I was only twelve years old and merely graduating from the eighth grade. Besides, many teachers in Arkansas Negro schools had only that diploma and were licensed to impart wisdom.

9 The days had become longer and more noticeable. The faded beige of former times had been replaced with strong and sure colors. I began to see my classmates' clothes, their skin tones, and the dust that waved off pussy willows. Clouds that lazed across the sky were objects of great concern to me. Their shiftier shapes might have held a message that in my new happiness and with a little bit of time I'd soon decipher. During that period I looked at the arch of heaven so religiously my neck kept a steady ache. I had taken to smiling more often, and my jaws hurt from the unaccustomed activity. Between the two physical sore spots, I suppose I could have been uncomfortable, but that was not the case. As a member of the winning team (the graduating class of 1940) I had outdistanced unpleasant sensations by miles. I was headed for the freedom of open fields.

10 Youth and social approval allied themselves with me and we trammeled memories of slights and insults. The wind of our swift passage remodeled my features. Lost tears

were pounded to mud and then to dust. Years of withdrawal were brushed aside and left behind, as hanging ropes of parasitic moss.

11 My work alone had awarded me a top place and I was going to be one of the first called in the graduating ceremonies. On the classroom blackboard, as well as on the bulletin board in the auditorium, there were blue stars and white stars and red stars. No absences, no tardinesses, and my academic work was among the best of the year. I could say the preamble to the Constitution even faster than Bailey could say it. We timed ourselves often: "WethepeopleoftheUnitedStatesinordertoformamoreperfect-union . . ." I had memorized the Presidents of the United States from Washington to Roosevelt in chronological as well as alphabetical order.

12 My hair pleased me too. Gradually the black mass had lengthened and thickened, so that it kept at last to its braided pattern, and I didn't have to yank my scalp off when I tried to comb it.

13 Louise and I had rehearsed the exercises until we tired out ourselves. Henry Reed was class valedictorian. He was a small, very black boy with hooded eyes, a long, broad nose and an oddly shaped head. I had admired him for years because each term he and I vied for the best grades in our class. Most often he bested me, but instead of being disappointed I was pleased that we shared top places between us. Like many Southern black children, he lived with his grandmother, who was as strict as Momma and as kind as she knew how to be. He was courteous, respectful and soft-spoken to elders, but on the playground he chose to play the roughest games. I admired him. Anyone, I reckoned, sufficiently afraid or sufficiently dull could be polite. But to be able to operate at a top level with both adults and children was admirable.

14 His valedictory speech was entitled "To Be or Not to Be." The rigid tenth-grade teacher had helped him write it. He'd been working on the dramatic stresses for months.

15 The weeks until graduation were filled with heady activities. A group of small children were to be presented in a play about buttercups and daisies and bunny rabbits. They could be heard throughout the building practicing their hops and their little songs that sounded like silver bells. The older girls (non-graduates, of course) were assigned the task of making refreshments for the night's festivities. A tangy scent of ginger, cinnamon, nutmeg and chocolate wafted around the home economics building as the budding cooks made samples for themselves and their teachers.

16 In every corner of the workshop, axes and saws split fresh timber as the woodshop boys made sets and stage scenery. Only the graduates were left out of the general bustle. We were free to sit in the library at the back of the building or look in quite detachedly, naturally, on the measures being taken for our event.

17 Even the minister preached on graduation the Sunday before. His subject was, "Let your light so shine that men will see your good works and praise your Father, Who is in Heaven." Although the sermon was purported to be addressed to us, he used the occasion to speak to backsliders, gamblers and general ne'er-do-wells. But since he had called our names at the beginning of the service we were mollified.

18 Among Negroes the tradition was to give presents to children going only from one grade to another. How much more important this was when the person was graduating

at the top of the class. Uncle Willie and Momma had sent away for a Mickey Mouse watch like Bailey's. Louise gave me four embroidered handkerchiefs. (I gave her three crocheted doilies.) Mrs. Sneed, the minister's wife, made me an underskirt to wear for graduation, and nearly every customer gave me a nickel or maybe even a dime with the instruction "Keep on moving to higher ground," or some such encouragement.

19 Amazingly the great day finally dawned and I was out of bed before I knew it. I threw open the back door to see it more clearly, but Momma said, "Sister, come away from that door and put your robe on."

20 I hoped the memory of that morning would never leave me. Sunlight was itself still young, and the day had none of the insistence maturity would bring it in a few hours. In my robe and barefoot in the backyard, under cover of going to see about my new beans, I gave myself up to the gentle warmth and thanked God that no matter what evil I had done in my life He had allowed me to live to see this day. Somewhere in my fatalism I had expected to die, accidentally, and never have the chance to walk up the stairs in the auditorium and gracefully receive my hard-earned diploma. Out of God's merciful bosom I had won reprieve.

21 Bailey came out in his robe and gave me a box wrapped in Christmas paper. He said he had saved his money for months to pay for it. It felt like a box of chocolates, but I knew Bailey wouldn't save money to buy candy when we had all we could want under our noses.

22 He was as proud of the gift as I. It was a soft-leather-bound copy of a collection of poems by Edgar Allan Poe, or, as Bailey and I called him, "Eap." I turned to "Annabel Lee" and we walked up and down the garden rows, the cool dirt between our toes, reciting the beautifully sad lines.

23 Momma made a Sunday breakfast although it was only Friday. After we finished the blessing, I opened my eyes to find the watch on my plate. It was a dream of a day. Everything went smoothly and to my credit I didn't have to be reminded or scolded for anything. Near evening I was too jittery to attend to chores, so Bailey volunteered to do all before his bath.

24 Days before, we had made a sign for the Store, and as we turned out the lights Momma hung the cardboard over the door-knob. It read clearly: CLOSED. GRADUATION.

25 My dress fitted perfectly and everyone said that I looked like a sunbeam in it. On the hill, going toward the school, Bailey walked behind with Uncle Willie, who muttered, "Go on, Ju." He wanted him to walk ahead with us because it embarrassed him to have to walk so slowly. Bailey said he'd let the ladies walk together, and the men would bring up the rear. We all laughed, nicely.

26 Little children dashed by out of the dark like fireflies. Their crepe-paper dresses and butterfly wings were not made for running and we heard more than one rip, dryly, and the regretful "uh uh" that followed.

27 The school blazed without gaiety. The windows seemed cold and unfriendly from the lower hill. A sense of ill-fated timing crept over me, and if Momma hadn't reached for my hand I would have drifted back to Bailey and Uncle Willie, and possibly beyond.

She made a few slow jokes about my feet getting cold, and tugged me along to the now-strange building.

28 Around the front steps, assurance came back. There were my fellow "greats," the graduating class. Hair brushed back, legs oiled, new dresses and pressed pleats, fresh pocket handkerchiefs and little handbags, all homesewn. Oh, we were up to snuff, all right. I joined my comrades and didn't even see my family go in to find seats in the crowded auditorium.

29 The school band struck up a march and all classes filed in as had been rehearsed. We stood in front of our seats, as assigned, and on a signal from the choir director, we sat. No sooner had this been accomplished than the band started to play the national anthem. We rose again and sang the song, after which we recited the pledge of allegiance. We remained standing for a brief minute before the choir director and the principal signaled to us, rather desperately I thought, to take our seats. The command was so unusual that our carefully rehearsed and smooth-running machine was thrown off. For a full minute we fumbled for our chairs and bumped into each other awkwardly. Habits change or solidify under pressure, so in our state of nervous tension we had been ready to follow our usual assembly pattern: the American national anthem, then the pledge of allegiance, then the song every Black person I knew called the Negro National Anthem. All done in the same key, with the same passion and most often standing on the same foot.

30 Finding my seat at last, I was overcome with a presentiment of worse things to come. Something unrehearsed, unplanned, was going to happen, and we were going to be made to look bad. I distinctly remember being explicit in the choice of pronoun. It was "we," the graduating class, the unit, that concerned me then.

31 The principal welcomed "parents and friends" and asked the Baptist minister to lead us in prayer. His invocation was brief and punchy, and for a second I thought we were getting back on the high road to right action. When the principal came back to the dais, however, his voice had changed. Sounds always affected me profoundly and the principal's voice was one of my favorites. During assembly it melted and lowed weakly into the audience. It had not been in my plan to listen to him, but my curiosity was piqued and I straightened up to give him my attention.

32 He was talking about Booker T. Washington, our "late great leader," who said we can be as close as the fingers on the hand, etc. . . . Then he said a few vague things about friendship and the friendship of kindly people to those less fortunate than themselves. With that his voice nearly faded, thin, away. Like a river diminishing to a stream and then to a trickle. But he cleared his throat and said, "Our speaker tonight, who is also our friend, came from Texarkana to deliver the commencement address, but due to the irregularity of the train schedule, he's going to, as they say, 'speak and run.' " He said that we understood and wanted the man to know that we were most grateful for the time he was able to give us and then something about how we were willing always to adjust to another's program, and without more ado—"I give you Mr. Edward Donleavy."

33 Not one but two white men came through the door offstage. The shorter one walked to the speaker's platform, and the tall one moved over to the center seat and sat down. But that was our principal's seat, and already occupied. The dislodged gentleman bounced around for a long breath or two before the Baptist minister gave him his chair, then with more dignity than the situation deserved, the minister walked off the stage.

34 Donleavy looked at the audience once (on reflection, I'm sure that he wanted only to reassure himself that we were really there), adjusted his glasses and began to read from a sheaf of papers.

35 He was glad "to be here and to see the work going on just as it was in the other schools."

36 At the first "Amen" from the audience I willed the offender to immediate death by choking on the word. But Amens and Yes, sir's began to fall around the room like rain through a ragged umbrella.

37 He told us of the wonderful changes we children in Stamps had in store. The Central School (naturally, the white school was Central) had already been granted improvements that would be in use in the fall. A well-known artist was coming from Little Rock to teach art to them. They were going to have the newest microscopes and chemistry equipment for their laboratory. Mr. Donleavy didn't leave us long in the dark over who made these improvements available to Central High. Nor were we to be ignored in the general betterment scheme he had in mind.

38 He said that he had pointed out to people at a very high level that one of the first-line football tacklers at Arkansas Agricultural and Mechanical College had graduated from good old Lafayette County Training School. Here fewer Amen's were heard. Those few that did break through lay dully in the air with the heaviness of habit.

39 He went on to praise us. He went on to say how he had bragged that "one of the best basketball players at Fisk sank his first ball right here at Lafayette County Training School."

40 The white kids were going to have a chance to become Galileos and Madame Curies and Edisons and Gauguins, and our boys (the girls weren't even in on it) would try to be Jesse Owenses and Joe Louises.

41 Owens and the Brown Bomber were great heroes in our world, but what school official in the white-goddom of Little Rock had the right to decide that those two men must be our only heroes? Who decided that for Henry Reed to become a scientist he had to work like George Washington Carver, as a bootblack, to buy a lousy microscope? Bailey was obviously always going to be too small to be an athlete, so which concrete angel glued to what county seat had decided that if my brother wanted to become a lawyer he had to first pay penance for his skin by picking cotton and hoeing corn and studying correspondence books at night for twenty years?

42 The man's dead words fell like bricks around the auditorium and too many settled in my belly. Constrained by hard-learned manners I couldn't look behind me, but to my left and right the proud graduating class of 1940 had dropped their heads. Every girl in my row had found something new to do with her handkerchief. Some folded the

tiny squares into love knots, some into triangles, but most were wadding them, then pressing them flat on their yellow laps.

43 On the dais, the ancient tragedy was being replayed. Professor Parsons sat, a sculptor's reject, rigid. His large, heavy body seemed devoid of will or willingness, and his eyes said he was no longer with us. The other teachers examined the flag (which was draped stage right) or their notes, or the windows which opened on our now-famous playing diamond.

44 Graduation, the hush-hush magic time of frills and gifts and congratulations and diplomas, was finished for me before my name was called. The accomplishment was nothing. The meticulous maps, drawn in three colors of ink, learning and spelling decasyllabic words, memorizing the whole of *The Rape of Lucrece*—it was for nothing. Donleavy had exposed us.

45 We were maids and farmers, handymen and washerwomen, and anything higher that we aspired to was farcical and presumptuous.

46 Then I wished that Gabriel Prosser and Nat Turner had killed all whitefolks in their beds and that Abraham Lincoln had been assassinated before the signing of the Emancipation Proclamation, and that Harriet Tubman had been killed by that blow on her head and Christopher Columbus had drowned in the *Santa María.*

47 It was awful to be Negro and have no control over my life. It was brutal to be young and already trained to sit quietly and listen to charges brought against my color with no chance of defense. We should all be dead. I thought I should like to see us all dead, one on top of the other. A pyramid of flesh with the whitefolks on the bottom, as the broad base, then the Indians and their silly tomahawks and tepees and wigwams and treaties, the Negroes with their mops and recipes and cotton sacks and spirituals sticking out of their mouths. The Dutch children should all stumble in their wooden shoes and break their necks. The French should choke to death on the Louisiana Purchase (1803) while silkworms ate all the Chinese with their stupid pigtails. As a species, we are an abomination. All of us.

48 Donleavy was running for election, and assured our parents that if he won we could count on having the only colored paved playing field in that part of Arkansas. Also—he never looked up to acknowledge the grunts of acceptance—also, we were bound to get some new equipment for the home economics building and the workshop.

49 He finished, and since there was no need to give any more than the most perfunctory thank-you's, he nodded to the men on the stage, and the tall white man who was never introduced joined him at the door. They left with the attitude that now they were off to something really important. (The graduation ceremonies at Lafayette County Training School had been a mere preliminary.)

50 The ugliness they left was palpable. An uninvited guest who wouldn't leave. The choir was summoned and sang a modern arrangement of "Onward, Christian Soldiers," with new words pertaining to graduates seeking their place in the world. But it didn't work. Elouise, the daughter of the Baptist minister, recited "Invictus," and I could have cried at the impertinence of "I am the master of my fate, I am the captain of my soul."

51 My name had lost its ring of familiarity and I had to be nudged to go and receive my diploma. All my preparations had fled. I neither marched up to the stage like a conquering Amazon, nor did I look in the audience for Bailey's nod of approval. Marguerite Johnson, I heard the name again, my honors were read, there were noises in the audience of appreciation, and I took my place on the stage as rehearsed.

52 I thought about colors I hated: ecru, puce, lavender, beige and black.

53 There was shuffling and rustling around me, then Henry Reed was giving his valedictory address, ''To Be or Not to Be.'' Hadn't he heard the whitefolks? We couldn't *be,* so the question was a waste of time. Henry's voice came out clear and strong. I feared to look at him. Hadn't he got the message? There was no ''nobler in the mind'' for Negroes because the world didn't think we had minds, and they let us know it. ''Outrageous fortune''? Now, that was a joke. When the ceremony was over I had to tell Henry Reed some things. That is, if I still cared. Not ''rub,'' Henry, ''erase.'' ''Ah, there's the erase.'' Us.

54 Henry had been a good student in elocution. His voice rose on tides of promise and fell on waves of warnings. The English teacher had helped him to create a sermon winging through Hamlet's soliloquy. To be a man, a doer, a builder, a leader, or to be a tool, an unfunny joke, a crusher of funky toadstools. I marveled that Henry could go through with the speech as if we had a choice.

55 I had been listening and silently rebutting each sentence with my eyes closed; then there was a hush, which in an audience warns that something unplanned is happening. I looked up and saw Henry Reed, the conservative, the proper, the A student, turn his back to the audience and turn to us (the proud graduating class of 1940) and sing, nearly speaking,

Lift ev'ry voice and sing
Till earth and heaven ring
Ring with the harmonies of Liberty . . .*

It was the poem written by James Weldon Johnson. It was the music composed by J. Rosamond Johnson. It was the Negro national anthem. Out of habit we were singing it.

56 Our mothers and fathers stood in the dark hall and joined the hymn of encouragement. A kindergarten teacher led the small children onto the stage and the buttercups and daisies and bunny rabbits marked time and tried to follow:

Stony the road we trod
Bitter the chastening rod
Felt in the days when hope, unborn, had died.
Yet with a steady beat

*''Lift Ev'ry Voice and Sing''—words by James Weldon Johnson and music by J. Rosamond Johnson. Copyright by Edward B. Marks Music Corporation. Used by permission.

Have not our weary feet
Come to the place for which our fathers sighed?

57 Every child I knew had learned that song with his ABC's and along with ''Jesus Loves Me This I Know.'' But I personally had never heard it before. Never heard the words, despite the thousands of times I had sung them. Never thought they had anything to do with me.

58 On the other hand, the words of Patrick Henry had made such an impression on me that I had been able to stretch myself tall and trembling and say, ''I know not what course others may take, but as for me, give me liberty or give me death.''

59 And now I heard, really for the first time:

We have come over a way that with tears has been watered,
We have come, treading our path through the blood of the slaughtered.

60 While echoes of the song shivered in the air, Henry Reed bowed his head, said ''Thank you,'' and returned to his place in the line. The tears that slipped down many faces were not wiped away in shame.

61 We were on top again. As always, again. We survived. The depths had been icy and dark, but now a bright sun spoke to our souls. I was no longer simply a member of the proud graduating class of 1940; I was a proud member of the wonderful beautiful Negro race.

62 Oh, Black known and unknown poets, how often have your auctioned pains sustained us? Who will compute the lonely nights made less lonely by your songs, or the empty pots made less tragic by your tales?

63 If we were a people much given to revealing secrets, we might raise monuments and sacrifice to the memories of our poets, but slavery cured us of that weakness. It may be enough, however, to have it said that we survive in exact relationship to the dedication of our poets (include preachers, musicians and blues singers).

Questions for Analysis

1. Although this autobiographical narrative is about what happened at her graduation, Angelou devotes almost half the essay (Paragraphs 1–28) to what happened in the hours, days, weeks, even years before the actual ceremony. Why did she choose to do this?
2. Look back over the first 28 paragraphs and notice the details and events Angelou spends time on. How do these details and events connect with what happens at graduation? Consider, for example, the details about her dress; the volume of Edgar Allan Poe's poetry Bailey gave her; the information about Henry Reed.

3. What is it about Donleavy's presence and especially his speech that undercuts the graduation ritual for Angelou? How did it make her feel? (Re-examine Paragraphs 44–54.)
4. What is the significance of the ''Negro National Anthem'' in the story? How has music served as a source of hope and support for African Americans as seen in this story, James Baldwin's ''Sonny's Blues,'' and in the remaining selections?
5. Angelou's story is set in the spring of 1940. How have things changed for African Americans since that time? How have they remained the same?
6. What is the thesis (or argument) of Angelou's story? What is she trying to help us understand about her life and growth as an individual? What is she trying to show us about the life of African Americans in Arkansas in 1940?

Public Statement by Eight Alabama Clergymen

(1963)

In 1963, eight prominent white Birmingham-area clergymen representing the Protestant and Jewish faiths asked that the African-American community cease its civil-rights demonstrations, obey the laws, and wait for change. Their statement, reprinted here, prompted the famous reply from the Reverend Martin Luther King, Jr., that appears on page 402.

1 We the undersigned clergymen are among those who, in January, issued ''An Appeal for Law and Order and Common Sense,'' in dealing with racial problems in Alabama. We expressed understanding that honest convictions in racial matters could properly be pursued in the courts, but urged that decisions of those courts should in the meantime be peacefully obeyed.

2 Since that time there had been some evidence of increased forbearance and a willingness to face facts. Responsible citizens have undertaken to work on various problems which cause racial friction and unrest. In Birmingham, recent public events have given indication that we all have opportunity for a new constructive and realistic approach to racial problems.

3 However, we are now confronted by a series of demonstrations by some of our Negro citizens, directed and led in part by outsiders. We recognize the natural impatience of people who feel that their hopes are slow in being realized. But we are convinced that these demonstrations are unwise and untimely.

4 We agree rather with certain local Negro leadership which has called for honest and open negotiation of racial issues in our area. And we believe this kind of facing of issues can best be accomplished by citizens of our own metropolitan area, white and Negro, meeting with their knowledge and experience of the local situation. All of us need to face that responsibility and find proper channels for its accomplishment.

5 Just as we formerly pointed out that "hatred and violence have no sanction in our religious and political traditions," we also point out that such actions as incite to hatred and violence, however technically peaceful those actions may be, have not contributed to the resolution of our local problems. We do not believe that these days of new hope are days when extreme measures are justified in Birmingham.

6 We commend the community as a whole, and the local news media and law enforcement officials in particular, on the calm manner in which these demonstrations have been handled. We urge the public to continue to show restraint should the demonstrations continue, and the law enforcement officials to remain calm and continue to protect our city from violence.

7 We further strongly urge our own Negro community to withdraw support from these demonstrations, and to unite locally in working peacefully for a better Birmingham. When rights are consistently denied, a cause should be pressed in the courts and in negotiations among local leaders, and not in the streets. We appeal to both our white and Negro citizenry to observe the principles of law and order and common sense.

Signed by:

C. C. J. Carpenter, D.D., LL.D., *Bishop of Alabama*
Joseph A. Durick, D.D., *Auxiliary Bishop, Diocese of Mobile, Birmingham*
Rabbi Milton L. Grafman, *Temple Emanu-El, Birmingham, Alabama*
Bishop Paul Hardin, *Bishop of the Alabama-West Florida Conference of the Methodist Church*
Bishop Nolan B. Harmon, *Bishop of the North Alabama Conference of the Methodist Church*
George M. Murray, D.D., LL.D., *Bishop Coadjutor, Episcopal Diocese of Alabama*
Edward V. Ramage, *Moderator, Synod of the Alabama Presbyterian Church in the United States*
Earl Stallings, *Pastor, First Baptist Church, Birmingham, Alabama*

Questions for Analysis

1. How would you describe the tone and argument of this letter? Reasonable? Impatient? Condescending? Realistic?

Martin Luther King, Jr.

Letter from Birmingham Jail

(1963)

One of the key leaders of the 1960s Civil Rights Movement, Martin Luther King, Jr. (1929–1968), is also one of the most influential figures in American history. The combination of his powerful oratory and insistence on nonviolent protest gave the Civil Rights Movement the energy and focus necessary to change some of the discriminatory laws and policies that had oppressed African Americans for more than a century. The two documents by King that are reprinted in this volume were written within a few months of each other in one of the most turbulent years in American history. King's "Letter from Birmingham Jail" was written in response to a public statement issued by prominent Birmingham clergymen (see page 400). It is a measured, rational defense and explanation of the Civil Rights Movement designed for an audience King knew well—other clergymen.

April 16, 1963

My Dear Fellow Clergymen:

1 While confined here in the Birmingham city jail, I came across your recent statement calling my present activities "unwise and untimely." Seldom do I pause to answer criticism of my work and ideas. If I sought to answer all the criticisms that cross my desk, my secretaries would have little time for anything other than such correspondence in the course of the day, and I would have no time for constructive work. But since I feel that you are men of genuine good will and that your criticisms are sincerely set forth, I want to try to answer your statement in what I hope will be patient and reasonable terms.

2 I think I should indicate why I am here in Birmingham, since you have been influenced by the view which argues against "outsiders coming in." I have the honor of serving as president of the Southern Christian Leadership Conference, an organization operating in every southern state, with headquarters in Atlanta, Georgia. We have some eighty-five affiliated organizations across the South, and one of them is the Alabama Christian Movement for Human Rights. Frequently we share staff, educational and financial resources with our affiliates. Several months ago the affiliate here in Birmingham asked us to be on call to engage in a nonviolent direct-action program if such were deemed necessary. We readily consented, and when the hour came we lived up to our promise. So I, along with several members of my staff, am here because I was invited here. I am here because I have organizational ties here.

3 But more basically, I am in Birmingham because injustice is here. Just as the prophets of the eighth century B.C. left their villages and carried their "thus saith the Lord" far beyond the boundaries of their home towns, and just as the Apostle Paul left his village of Tarsus and carried the gospel of Jesus Christ to the far corners of the Greco-Roman

world, so am I compelled to carry the gospel of freedom beyond my own home town. Like Paul, I must constantly respond to the Macedonian call for aid.

4 Moreover, I am cognizant of the interrelatedness of all communities and states. I cannot sit idly by in Atlanta and not be concerned about what happens in Birmingham. Injustice anywhere is a threat to justice everywhere. We are caught in an inescapable network of mutuality, tied in a single garment of destiny. Whatever affects one directly, affects all indirectly. Never again can we afford to live with the narrow, provincial "outside agitator" idea. Anyone who lives inside the United States can never be considered an outsider anywhere within its bounds.

5 You deplore the demonstrations taking place in Birmingham. But your statement, I am sorry to say, fails to express a similar concern for the conditions that brought about the demonstrations. I am sure that none of you would want to rest content with the superficial kind of social analysis that deals merely with effects and does not grapple with underlying causes. It is unfortunate that demonstrations are taking place in Birmingham, but it is even more unfortunate that the city's white power structure left the Negro community with no alternative.

6 In any nonviolent campaign there are four basic steps: collection of the facts to determine whether injustices exist; negotiation; self-purification; and direct action. We have gone through all these steps in Birmingham. There can be no gainsaying the fact that racial injustice engulfs this community. Birmingham is probably the most thoroughly segregated city in the United States. Its ugly record of brutality is widely known. Negroes have experienced grossly unjust treatment in the courts. There have been more unsolved bombings of Negro homes and churches in Birmingham than in any other city in the nation. These are the hard, brutal facts of the case. On the basis of these conditions, Negro leaders sought to negotiate with the city fathers. But the latter consistently refused to engage in good-faith negotiation.

7 Then, last September, came the opportunity to talk with leaders of Birmingham's economic community. In the course of the negotiations, certain promises were made by the merchants—for example, to remove the stores' humiliating racial signs. On the basis of these promises, the Reverend Fred Shuttlesworth and the leaders of the Alabama Christian Movement for Human Rights agreed to a moratorium on all demonstrations. As the weeks and months went by, we realized that we were the victims of a broken promise. A few signs, briefly removed, returned; the others remained.

8 As in so many past experiences, our hopes had been blasted, and the shadow of deep disappointment settled upon us. We had no alternative except to prepare for direct action, whereby we would present our very bodies as a means of laying our case before the conscience of the local and the national community. Mindful of the difficulties involved, we decided to undertake a process of self-purification. We began a series of workshops on nonviolence, and we repeatedly asked ourselves: "Are you able to accept blows without retaliating?" "Are you able to endure the ordeal of jail?" We decided to schedule our direct-action program for the Easter season, realizing that except for Christmas, this is the main shopping period of the year. Knowing that a strong

economic-withdrawal program would be the by-product of direct action, we felt that this would be the best time to bring pressure to bear on the merchants for the needed change.

9 Then it occurred to us that Birmingham's mayoral election was coming up in March, and we speedily decided to postpone action until after election day. When we discovered that the Commissioner of Public Safety, Eugene "Bull" Connor, had piled up enough votes to be in the run-off, we decided again to postpone action until the day after the run-off so that the demonstrations could not be used to cloud the issues. Like many others, we waited to see Mr. Connor defeated, and to this end we endured postponement after postponement. Having aided in this community need, we felt that our direct-action program could be delayed no longer.

10 You may well ask: "Why direct action? Why sit-ins, marches and so forth? Isn't negotiation a better path?" You are quite right in calling for negotiation. Indeed, this is the very purpose of direct action. Nonviolent direct action seeks to create such a crisis and foster such a tension that a community which has constantly refused to negotiate is forced to confront the issue. It seeks so to dramatize the issue that it can no longer be ignored. My citing the creation of tension as part of the work of the nonviolent-resister may sound rather shocking. But I must confess that I am not afraid of the word "tension." I have earnestly opposed violent tension, but there is a type of constructive, nonviolent tension which is necessary for growth. Just as Socrates felt that it was necessary to create a tension in the mind so that individuals could rise from the bondage of myths and half-truths to the unfettered realm of creative analysis and objective appraisal, so must we see the need for nonviolent gadflies to create the kind of tension in society that will help men rise from the dark depths of prejudice and racism to the majestic heights of understanding and brotherhood.

11 The purpose of our direct-action program is to create a situation so crisis-packed that it will inevitably open the door to negotiation. I therefore concur with you in your call for negotiation. Too long has our beloved Southland been bogged down in a tragic effort to live in monologue rather than dialogue.

12 One of the basic points in your statement is that the action that I and my associates have taken in Birmingham is untimely. Some have asked: "Why didn't you give the new city administration time to act?" The only answer that I can give to this query is that the new Birmingham administration must be prodded about as much as the outgoing one, before it will act. We are sadly mistaken if we feel that the election of Albert Boutwell as mayor will bring the millennium to Birmingham. While Mr. Boutwell is a much more gentle person than Mr. Connor, they are both segregationists, dedicated to maintenance of the status quo. I have hope that Mr. Boutwell will be reasonable enough to see the futility of massive resistance to desegregation. But he will not see this without pressure from devotees of civil rights. My friends, I must say to you that we have not made a single gain in civil rights without determined legal and nonviolent pressure. Lamentably, it is an historical fact that privileged groups seldom give up their privileges voluntarily. Individuals may see the moral light and voluntarily give up their unjust posture; but, as Reinhold Niebuhr has reminded us, groups tend to be more immoral than individuals.

13 We know through painful experience that freedom is never voluntarily given by the oppressor; it must be demanded by the oppressed. Frankly, I have yet to engage in a direct-action campaign that was "well timed" in the view of those who have not suffered unduly from the disease of segregation. For years now I have heard the word "Wait!" It rings in the ear of every Negro with piercing familiarity. This "Wait" has almost always meant "Never." We must come to see, with one of our distinguished jurists, that "justice too long delayed is justice denied."

14 We have waited for more than 340 years for our constitutional and God-given rights. The nations of Asia and Africa are moving with jetlike speed toward gaining political independence, but we still creep at horse-and-buggy pace toward gaining a cup of coffee at a lunch counter. Perhaps it is easy for those who have never felt the stinging darts of segregation to say, "Wait." But when you have seen vicious mobs lynch your mothers and fathers at will and drown your sisters and brothers at whim; when you have seen hate-filled policemen curse, kick and even kill your black brothers and sisters; when you see the vast majority of your twenty million Negro brothers smothering in an airtight cage of poverty in the midst of an affluent society; when you suddenly find your tongue twisted and your speech stammering as you seek to explain to your six-year-old daughter why she can't go to the public amusement park that has just been advertised on television, and see tears welling up in her eyes when she is told that Funtown is closed to colored children, and see ominous clouds of inferiority beginning to form in her little mental sky, and see her beginning to distort her personality by developing an unconscious bitterness toward white people; when you have to concoct an answer for a five-year-old son who is asking: "Daddy, why do white people treat colored people so mean?"; when you take a cross-country drive and find it necessary to sleep night after night in the uncomfortable corners of your automobile because no motel will accept you; when you are humiliated day in and day out by nagging signs reading "white" and "colored"; when your first name becomes "nigger," your middle name becomes "boy" (however old you are) and your last name becomes "John," and your wife and mother are never given the respected title "Mrs."; when you are harried by day and haunted by night by the fact that you are a Negro, living constantly at tiptoe stance, never quite knowing what to expect next, and are plagued with inner fears and outer resentments; when you are forever fighting a degenerating sense of "nobodiness"—then you will understand why we find it difficult to wait. There comes a time when the cup of endurance runs over, and men are no longer willing to be plunged into the abyss of despair. I hope, sirs, you can understand our legitimate and unavoidable impatience.

15 You express a great deal of anxiety over our willingness to break laws. This is certainly a legitimate concern. Since we so diligently urge people to obey the Supreme Court's decision of 1954 outlawing segregation in the public schools, at first glance it may seem rather paradoxical for us consciously to break laws. One may well ask: "How can you advocate breaking some laws and obeying others?" The answer lies in the fact that there are two types of laws: just and unjust. I would be the first to advocate obeying just laws. One has not only a legal but a moral responsibility to obey just laws.

Conversely, one has a moral responsibility to disobey unjust laws. I would agree with St. Augustine that "an unjust law is no law at all."

16 Now, what is the difference between the two? How does one determine whether a law is just or unjust? A just law is a man-made code that squares with the moral law or the law of God. An unjust law is a code that is out of harmony with the moral law. To put it in the terms of St. Thomas Aquinas: An unjust law is a human law that is not rooted in eternal law and natural law. Any law that uplifts human personality is just. Any law that degrades human personality is unjust. All segregation statutes are unjust because segregation distorts the soul and damages the personality. It gives the segregator a false sense of superiority and the segregated a false sense of inferiority. Segregation, to use the terminology of the Jewish philosopher Martin Buber, substitutes an "I—it" relationship for an "I—thou" relationship and ends up relegating persons to the status of things. Hence, segregation is not only politically, economically and sociologically unsound, it is morally wrong and sinful. Paul Tillich has said that sin is separation. Is not segregation an existential expression of man's tragic separation, his awful estrangement, his terrible sinfulness? Thus it is that I can urge men to obey the 1954 decision of the Supreme Court, for it is morally right; and I can urge them to disobey segregation ordinances, for they are morally wrong.

17 Let us consider a more concrete example of just and unjust laws. An unjust law is a code that a numerical or power majority group compels a minority group to obey but does not make binding on itself. This is *difference* made legal. By the same token, a just law is a code that a majority compels a minority to follow and that it is willing to follow itself. This is *sameness* made legal.

18 Let me give another explanation. A law is unjust if it is inflicted on a minority that, as a result of being denied the right to vote, had no part in enacting or devising the law. Who can say that the legislature of Alabama which set up that state's segregation laws was democratically elected? Throughout Alabama all sorts of devious methods are used to prevent Negroes from becoming registered voters, and there are some counties in which, even though Negroes constitute a majority of the population, not a single Negro is registered. Can any law enacted under such circumstances be considered democratically structured?

19 Sometimes a law is just on its face and unjust in its application. For instance, I have been arrested on a charge of parading without a permit. Now, there is nothing wrong in having an ordinance which requires a permit for a parade. But such an ordinance becomes unjust when it is used to maintain segregation and to deny citizens the First-Amendment privilege of peaceful assembly and protest.

20 I hope you are able to see the distinction I am trying to point out. In no sense do I advocate evading or defying the law, as would the rabid segregationist. That would lead to anarchy. One who breaks an unjust law must do so openly, lovingly, and with a willingness to accept the penalty. I submit that an individual who breaks a law that conscience tells him is unjust, and who willingly accepts the penalty of imprisonment in order to arouse the conscience of the community over its injustice, is in reality expressing the highest respect for law.

21 Of course, there is nothing new about this kind of civil disobedience. It was evidenced sublimely in the refusal of Shadrach, Meshach and Abednego to obey the laws of Nebuchadnezzar, on the ground that a higher moral law was at stake. It was practiced superbly by the early Christians, who were willing to face hungry lions and the excruciating pain of chopping blocks rather than submit to certain unjust laws of the Roman Empire. To a degree, academic freedom is a reality today because Socrates practiced civil disobedience. In our own nation, the Boston Tea Party represented a massive act of civil disobedience.

22 We should never forget that everything Adolf Hitler did in Germany was "legal" and everything the Hungarian freedom fighters did in Hungary was "illegal." It was "illegal" to aid and comfort a Jew in Hitler's Germany. Even so, I am sure that, had I lived in Germany at the time, I would have aided and comforted my Jewish brothers. If today I lived in a Communist country where certain principles dear to the Christian faith are suppressed, I would openly advocate disobeying that country's antireligious laws.

23 I must make two honest confessions to you, my Christian and Jewish brothers. First, I must confess that over the past few years I have been gravely disappointed with the white moderate. I have almost reached the regrettable conclusion that the Negro's great stumbling block in his stride toward freedom is not the White Citizen's Counciler or the Ku Klux Klanner, but the white moderate, who is more devoted to "order" than to justice; who prefers a negative peace which is the absence of tension to a positive peace which is the presence of justice; who constantly says: "I agree with you in the goal you seek, but I cannot agree with your methods of direct action"; who paternalistically believes he can set the timetable for another man's freedom; who lives by a mythical concept of time and who constantly advises the Negro to wait for a "more convenient season." Shallow understanding from people of good will is more frustrating than absolute misunderstanding from people of ill will. Lukewarm acceptance is much more bewildering than outright rejection.

24 I had hoped that the white moderate would understand that law and order exist for the purpose of establishing justice and that when they fail in this purpose they become the dangerously structured dams that block the flow of social progress. I had hoped that the white moderate would understand that the present tension in the South is a necessary phase of the transition from an obnoxious negative peace, in which the Negro passively accepted his unjust plight, to a substantive and positive peace, in which all men will respect the dignity and worth of human personality. Actually, we who engage in nonviolent direct action are not the creators of tension. We merely bring to the surface the hidden tension that is already alive. We bring it out in the open, where it can be seen and dealt with. Like a boil that can never be cured so long as it is covered up but must be opened with all its ugliness to the natural medicines of air and light, injustice must be exposed, with all the tension its exposure creates, to the light of human conscience and the air of national opinion before it can be cured.

25 In your statement you assert that our actions, even though peaceful, must be condemned because they precipitate violence. But is this a logical assertion? Isn't this like

condemning a robbed man because his possession of money precipitated the evil act of robbery? Isn't this like condemning Socrates because his unswerving commitment to truth and his philosophical inquiries precipitated the act by the misguided populace in which they made him drink hemlock? Isn't this like condemning Jesus because his unique God-consciousness and never-ceasing devotion to God's will precipitated the evil act of crucifixion? We must come to see that, as the federal courts have consistently affirmed, it is wrong to urge an individual to cease his efforts to gain his basic constitutional rights because the quest may precipitate violence. Society must protect the robbed and punish the robber.

26 I had also hoped that the white moderate would reject the myth concerning time in relation to the struggle for freedom. I have just received a letter from a white brother in Texas. He writes: "All Christians know that the colored people will receive equal rights eventually, but it is possible that you are in too great a religious hurry. It has taken Christianity almost two thousand years to accomplish what it has. The teachings of Christ take time to come to earth." Such an attitude stems from a tragic misconception of time, from the strangely irrational notion that there is something in the very flow of time that will inevitably cure all ills. Actually, time itself is neutral; it can be used either destructively or constructively. More and more I feel that the people of ill will have used time much more effectively than have the people of good will. We will have to repent in this generation not merely for the hateful words and actions of the bad people but for the appalling silence of the good people. Human progress never rolls in on wheels of inevitability; it comes through the tireless efforts of men willing to be co-workers with God, and without this hard work, time itself becomes an ally of the forces of social stagnation. We must use time creatively, in the knowledge that the time is always ripe to do right. Now is the time to make real the promise of democracy and transform our pending national elegy into a creative psalm of brotherhood. Now is the time to lift our national policy from the quicksand of racial injustice to the solid rock of human dignity.

27 You speak of our activity in Birmingham as extreme. At first I was rather disappointed that fellow clergymen would see my nonviolent efforts as those of an extremist. I began thinking about the fact that I stand in the middle of two opposing forces in the Negro community. One is a force of complacency, made up in part of Negroes who, as a result of long years of oppression, are so drained of self-respect and a sense of "somebodiness" that they have adjusted to segregation; and in part of a few middle-class Negroes who, because of a degree of academic and economic security and because in some ways they profit by segregation, have become insensitive to the problems of the masses. The other force is one of bitterness and hatred, and it comes perilously close to advocating violence. It is expressed in the various black nationalist groups that are springing up across the nation, the largest and best-known being Elijah Muhammad's Muslim movement. Nourished by the Negro's frustration over the continued existence of racial discrimination, this movement is made up of people who have lost faith in America, who have absolutely repudiated Christianity, and who have concluded that the white man is an incorrigible "devil."

28 I have tried to stand between these two forces, saying that we need emulate neither the "do-nothingism" of the complacent nor the hatred and despair of the black nationalist. For there is the more excellent way of love and nonviolent protest. I am grateful to God that, through the influence of the Negro church, the way of nonviolence became an integral part of our struggle.

29 If this philosophy had not emerged, by now many streets of the South would, I am convinced, be flowing with blood. And I am further convinced that if our white brothers dismiss as "rabble-rousers" and "outside agitators" those of us who employ nonviolent direct action, and if they refuse to support our nonviolent efforts, millions of Negroes will, out of frustration and despair, seek solace and security in black-nationalist ideologies—a development that would inevitably lead to a frightening racial nightmare.

30 Oppressed people cannot remain oppressed forever. The yearning for freedom eventually manifests itself, and that is what has happened to the American Negro. Something within has reminded him of his birthright of freedom, and something without has reminded him that it can be gained. Consciously or unconsciously, he has been caught up by the *Zeitgeist,* and with his black brothers of Africa and his brown and yellow brothers of Asia, South America and the Caribbean, the United States Negro is moving with a sense of great urgency toward the promised land of racial justice. If one recognizes this vital urge that has engulfed the Negro community, one should readily understand why public demonstrations are taking place. The Negro has many pent-up resentments and latent frustrations, and he must release them. So let him march; let him make prayer pilgrimages to the city hall; let him go on freedom rides—and try to understand why he must do so. If his repressed emotions are not released in nonviolent ways, they will seek expression through violence; this is not a threat but a fact of history. So I have not said to my people: "Get rid of your discontent." Rather, I have tried to say that this normal and healthy discontent can be channeled into the creative outlet of nonviolent direct action. And now this approach is being termed extremist.

31 But though I was initially disappointed at being categorized as an extremist, as I continued to think about the matter I gradually gained a measure of satisfaction from the label. Was not Jesus an extremist for love: "Love your enemies, bless them that curse you, do good to them that hate you, and pray for them which despitefully use you, and persecute you." Was not Amos an extremist for justice: "Let justice roll down like waters and righteousness like an ever flowing stream." Was not Paul an extremist for the Christian gospel: "I bear in my body the marks of the Lord Jesus." Was not Martin Luther an extremist: "Here I stand; I cannot do otherwise, so help me God." And John Bunyan: "I will stay in jail to the end of my days before I make a butchery of my conscience." And Abraham Lincoln: "This nation cannot survive half slave and half free." And Thomas Jefferson: "We hold these truths to be self-evident, that all men are created equal. . . ." So the question is not whether we will be extremists, but what kind of extremists we will be. Will we be extremists for hate or for love? Will we be extremists for the preservation of injustice or for the extension of justice? In that dramatic scene on Calvary's hill three men were crucified. We must never forget that all three were crucified

for the same crime—the crime of extremism. Two were extremists for immorality, and thus fell below their environment. The other, Jesus Christ, was an extremist for love, truth and goodness, and thereby rose above his environment. Perhaps the South, the nation and the world are in dire need of creative extremists.

32 I had hoped that the white moderate would see this need. Perhaps I was too optimistic; perhaps I expected too much. I suppose I should have realized that few members of the oppressor race can understand the deep groans and passionate yearnings of the oppressed race, and still fewer have the vision to see that injustice must be rooted out by strong, persistent and determined action. I am thankful, however, that some of our white brothers in the South have grasped the meaning of this social revolution and committed themselves to it. They are still all too few in quantity, but they are big in quality. Some—such as Ralph McGill, Lillian Smith, Harry Golden, James McBride Dabbs, Ann Braden and Sarah Patton Boyle—have written about our struggle in eloquent and prophetic terms. Others have marched with us down nameless streets of the South. They have languished in filthy, roach-infested jails, suffering the abuse and brutality of policemen who view them as "dirty nigger-lovers." Unlike so many of their moderate brothers and sisters, they have recognized the urgency of the moment and sensed the need for powerful "action" antidotes to combat the disease of segregation.

33 Let me take note of my other major disappointment. I have been so greatly disappointed with the white church and its leadership. Of course, there are some notable exceptions. I am not unmindful of the fact that each of you has taken some significant stands on this issue. I commend you, Reverend Stallings, for your Christian stand on this past Sunday, in welcoming Negroes to your worship service on a nonsegregated basis. I commend the Catholic leaders of this state for integrating Spring Hill College several years ago.

34 But despite these notable exceptions, I must honestly reiterate that I have been disappointed with the church. I do not say this as one of those negative critics who can always find something wrong with the church. I say this as a minister of the gospel, who loves the church; who was nurtured in its bosom; who has been sustained by its spiritual blessings and who will remain true to it as long as the cord of life shall lengthen.

35 When I was suddenly catapulted into the leadership of the bus protest in Montgomery, Alabama, a few years ago, I felt we would be supported by the white church. I felt that the white ministers, priests and rabbis of the South would be among our strongest allies. Instead, some have been outright opponents, refusing to understand the freedom movement and misrepresenting its leaders; all too many others have been more cautious than courageous and have remained silent behind the anesthetizing security of stained-glass windows.

36 In spite of my shattered dreams, I came to Birmingham with the hope that the white religious leadership of this community would see the justice of our cause and, with deep moral concern, would serve as the channel through which our just grievances could reach the power structure. I had hoped that each of you would understand. But again I have been disappointed.

37 I have heard numerous southern religious leaders admonish their worshippers to comply with a desegregation decision because it is the law, but I have longed to hear white ministers declare: ''Follow this decree because integration is morally right and because the Negro is your brother.'' In the midst of blatant injustices inflicted upon the Negro, I have watched white churchmen stand on the sideline and mouth pious irrelevancies and sanctimonious trivialities. In the midst of a mighty struggle to rid our nation of racial and economic injustice, I have heard many ministers say: ''Those are social issues, with which the gospel has no real concern.'' And I have watched many churches commit themselves to a completely otherworldly religion which makes a strange, un-Biblical distinction between body and soul, between the sacred and the secular.

38 I have traveled the length and breadth of Alabama, Mississippi and all the other southern states. On sweltering summer days and crisp autumn mornings I have looked at the South's beautiful churches with their lofty spires pointing heavenward. I have beheld the impressive outlines of her massive religious-education buildings. Over and over I have found myself asking: ''What kind of people worship here? Who is their God? Where were their voices when the lips of Governor Barnett dripped with words of interposition and nullification? Where were they when Governor Wallace gave a clarion call for defiance and hatred? Where were their voices of support when bruised and weary Negro men and women decided to rise from the dark dungeons of complacency to the bright hills of creative protest?''

39 Yes, these questions are still in my mind. In deep disappointment I have wept over the laxity of the church. But be assured that my tears have been tears of love. There can be no deep disappointment where there is not deep love. Yes, I love the church. How could I do otherwise? I am in the rather unique position of being the son, the grandson and the great-grandson of preachers. Yes, I see the church as the body of Christ. But, oh! How we have blemished and scarred that body through social neglect and through fear of being nonconformists.

40 There was a time when the church was very powerful—in the time when the early Christians rejoiced at being deemed worthy to suffer for what they believed. In those days the church was not merely a thermometer that recorded the ideas and principles of popular opinion; it was a thermostat that transformed the mores of society. Whenever the early Christians entered a town, the people in power became disturbed and immediately sought to convict the Christians for being ''disturbers of the peace'' and ''outside agitators.'' But the Christians pressed on, in the conviction that they were ''a colony of heaven,'' called to obey God rather than man. Small in number, they were big in commitment. They were too God-intoxicated to be ''astronomically intimidated.'' By their effort and example they brought an end to such ancient evils as infanticide and gladiatorial contests.

41 Things are different now. So often the contemporary church is a weak, ineffectual voice with an uncertain sound. So often it is an archdefender of the status quo. Far from being disturbed by the presence of the church, the power structure of the average community is consoled by the church's silent—and often even vocal—sanction of things as they are.

42 But the judgment of God is upon the church as never before. If today's church does not recapture the sacrificial spirit of the early church, it will lose its authenticity, forfeit the loyalty of millions, and be dismissed as an irrelevant social club with no meaning for the twentieth century. Every day I meet young people whose disappointment with the church has turned into outright disgust.

43 Perhaps I have once again been too optimistic. Is organized religion too inextricably bound to the status quo to save our nation and the world? Perhaps I must turn my faith to the inner spiritual church, the church within the church, as the true *ekklesia* and the hope of the world. But again I am thankful to God that some noble souls from the ranks of organized religion have broken loose from the paralyzing chains of conformity and joined us as active partners in the struggle for freedom. They have left their secure congregations and walked the streets of Albany, Georgia, with us. They have gone down the highways of the South on tortuous rides for freedom. Yes, they have gone to jail with us. Some have been dismissed from their churches, have lost the support of their bishops and fellow ministers. But they have acted in the faith that right defeated is stronger than evil triumphant. Their witness has been the spiritual salt that has preserved the true meaning of the gospel in these troubled times. They have carved a tunnel of hope through the dark mountain of disappointment.

44 I hope the church as a whole will meet the challenge of this decisive hour. But even if the church does not come to the aid of justice, I have no despair about the future. I have no fear about the outcome of our struggle in Birmingham, even if our motives are at present misunderstood. We will reach the goal of freedom in Birmingham and all over the nation, because the goal of America is freedom. Abused and scorned though we may be, our destiny is tied up with America's destiny. Before the pilgrims landed at Plymouth, we were here. Before the pen of Jefferson etched the majestic words of the Declaration of Independence across the pages of history, we were here. For more than two centuries our forebears labored in this country without wages; they made cotton king; they built the homes of their masters while suffering gross injustice and shameful humiliation—and yet out of a bottomless vitality they continued to thrive and develop. If the inexpressible cruelties of slavery could not stop us, the opposition we now face will surely fail. We will win our freedom because the sacred heritage of our nation and the eternal will of God are embodied in our echoing demands.

45 Before closing I feel impelled to mention one other point in your statement that has troubled me profoundly. You warmly commended the Birmingham police force for keeping "order" and "preventing violence." I doubt that you would have so warmly commended the police force if you had seen its dogs sinking their teeth into unarmed, nonviolent Negroes. I doubt that you would so quickly commend the policemen if you were to observe their ugly and inhumane treatment of Negroes here in the city jail; if you were to watch them push and curse old Negro women and young Negro girls; if you were to see them slap and kick old Negro men and young boys; if you were to observe them, as they did on two occasions, refuse to give us food because we wanted to sing our grace together. I cannot join you in your praise of the Birmingham police department.

46 It is true that the police have exercised a degree of discipline in handling the demonstrators. In this sense they have conducted themselves rather "nonviolently" in public. But for what purpose? To preserve the evil system of segregation. Over the past few years I have consistently preached that nonviolence demands that the means we use must be as pure as the ends we seek. I have tried to make clear that it is wrong to use immoral means to attain moral ends. But now I must affirm that it is just as wrong, or perhaps even more so, to use moral means to preserve immoral ends. Perhaps Mr. Connor and his policemen have been rather nonviolent in public, as was Chief Pritchett in Albany, Georgia, but they have used the moral means of nonviolence to maintain the immoral end of racial injustice. As T. S. Eliot has said: "The last temptation is the greatest treason: To do the right deed for the wrong reason."

47 I wish you had commended the Negro sit-inners and demonstrators of Birmingham for their sublime courage, their willingness to suffer and their amazing discipline in the midst of great provocation. One day the South will recognize its real heroes. They will be the James Merediths, with the noble sense of purpose that enables them to face jeering and hostile mobs, and with the agonizing loneliness that characterizes the life of the pioneer. They will be old, oppressed, battered Negro women, symbolized in a seventy-two-year-old woman in Montgomery, Alabama, who rose up with a sense of dignity and with her people decided not to ride segregated buses, and who responded with ungrammatical profundity to one who inquired about her weariness: "My feets is tired, but my soul is at rest." They will be the young high school and college students, the young ministers of the gospel and a host of their elders, courageously and nonviolently sitting in at lunch counters and willingly going to jail for conscience' sake. One day the South will know that when these disinherited children of God sat down at lunch counters, they were in reality standing up for what is best in the American dream and for the most sacred values in our Judaeo-Christian heritage, thereby bringing our nation back to those great wells of democracy which were dug deep by the founding fathers in their formulation of the Constitution and the Declaration of Independence.

48 Never before have I written so long a letter. I'm afraid it is much too long to take your precious time. I can assure you that it would have been much shorter if I had been writing from a comfortable desk, but what else can one do when he is alone in a narrow jail cell, other than write long letters, think long thoughts and pray long prayers?

49 If I have said anything in this letter that overstates the truth and indicates an unreasonable impatience, I beg you to forgive me. If I have said anything that understates the truth and indicates my having a patience that allows me to settle for anything less than brotherhood, I beg God to forgive me.

50 I hope this letter finds you strong in the faith. I also hope that circumstances will soon make it possible for me to meet each of you, not as an integrationist or a civil-rights leader but as a fellow clergyman and a Christian brother. Let us all hope that the dark clouds of racial prejudice will soon pass away and the deep fog of misunderstanding will be lifted from our fear-drenched communities, and in some not too distant tomorrow the radiant stars of love and brotherhood will shine over our great nation with all their scintillating beauty.

Yours for the cause of Peace and Brotherhood,
MARTIN LUTHER KING, JR.

Questions for Analysis

1. After reading King's letter, do you react differently to the eight clergymen's statement on page 400?
2. What is the effect you think King wanted to achieve in his first paragraph? Do you think it worked? Explain.
3. Examine Paragraphs 14, 23, 25, and 31. What rhetorical technique is common to each of these paragraphs? Explain how this technique works and what advantages and disadvantages it offers.
4. What kind of sources (writers and books) does King draw on to support his points? How effective would these sources be with his audience? Explain.
5. Explain King's logical and rhetorical strategy at the beginning of Paragraph 15.
6. King devotes a number of paragraphs to his disappointment with the white moderates (Paragraphs 23 ff.) and the church (Paragraphs 33 ff.). Since these paragraphs obviously deal with groups that would include the eight clergymen, why did King not begin with these criticisms? What is the basic organizational pattern of King's letter?
7. In Paragraph 48, King says that his letter is too long and explains why it is so. Others have called attention to the letter's length as a flaw. How could King have edited the letter to make it shorter? What would it gain from the shortening? What, if anything, would it lose?

Martin Luther King, Jr.

I Have a Dream

(1963)

"I Have a Dream" is perhaps the most famous speech of the Civil Rights Movement. With this speech, delivered in Washington, DC, at the Lincoln Memorial, Martin Luther King, Jr., helped millions of African Americans and other Americans find the strength and courage to fight discrimination. Three months after this speech, President John F. Kennedy was killed. In 1964 Martin Luther King, Jr., was awarded the Nobel Peace Prize. He was assassinated in Memphis, Tennessee, in 1968.

1 I am happy to join with you today in what will go down in history as the greatest demonstration for freedom in the history of our nation.

2 Five score years ago, a great American, in whose symbolic shadow we stand today, signed the Emancipation Proclamation. This momentous decree came as a great beacon light of hope to millions of Negro slaves who had been seared in the flames of withering

injustice. It came as a joyous daybreak to end the long night of their captivity. But one hundred years later, the Negro still is not free. One hundred years later, the life of the Negro is still sadly crippled by the manacles of segregation and the chains of discrimination. One hundred years later, the Negro lives on a lonely island of poverty in the midst of a vast ocean of material prosperity. One hundred years later, the Negro is still anguished in the corners of American society and finds himself in exile in his own land. And so we have come here today to dramatize a shameful condition.

3 In a sense we have come to our nation's capital to cash a check. When the architects of our republic wrote the magnificent words of the Constitution and the Declaration of Independence, they were signing a promissory note to which every American was to fall heir. This note was the promise that all men—yes, Black men as well as white men—would be guaranteed the inalienable rights of life, liberty, and the pursuit of happiness.

4 It is obvious today that America has defaulted on this promissory note insofar as her citizens of color are concerned. Instead of honoring this sacred obligation, America has given the Negro people a bad check, a check which has come back marked "insufficient funds." But we refuse to believe that the bank of justice is bankrupt. We refuse to believe that there are insufficient funds in the great vaults of opportunity of this nation; and so we have come to cash this check, a check that will give us upon demand the riches of freedom and the security of justice.

5 We have also come to this hallowed spot to remind America of the fierce urgency of *now*. This is no time to engage in the luxury of cooling off or to take the tranquilizing drug of gradualism. *Now* is the time to make real the promises of democracy. *Now* is the time to rise from the dark and desolate valley of segregation to the sunlit path of racial justice. *Now* is the time to lift our nation from the quicksands of racial injustice to the solid rock of brotherhood. *Now* is the time to make justice a reality for all of God's children.

6 It would be fatal for the nation to overlook the urgency of the moment. This sweltering summer of the Negro's legitimate discontent will not pass until there is an invigorating autumn of freedom and equality. Nineteen Sixty-three is not an end, but a beginning. And those who hope that the Negro needed to blow off steam and will now be content will have a rude awakening if the nation returns to business as usual. There will be neither rest nor tranquility in America until the Negro is granted his citizenship rights. The whirlwinds of revolt will continue to shake the foundations of our nation until the bright day of justice emerges.

7 But there is something that I must say to my people who stand on the warm threshold which leads into the palace of justice. In the process of gaining our rightful place, we must not be guilty of wrongful deeds. Let us not seek to satisfy our thirst for freedom by drinking from the cup of bitterness and hatred. We must forever conduct our struggle on the high plane of dignity and discipline. We must not allow our creative protest to degenerate into physical violence. Again and again we must rise to the majestic heights of meeting physical force with soul force. And the marvelous new militancy which has engulfed the Negro community must not lead us to a distrust of all white people; for

many of our white brothers, as evidenced by their presence here today, have come to realize that their destiny is tied up with our destiny, and they have come to realize that their freedom is inextricably bound to our freedom.

8 We cannot walk alone. And as we walk we must make the pledge that we shall always march ahead. We cannot turn back. There are those who are asking the devotees of civil rights, "When will you be satisfied?" We can never be satisfied as long as the Negro is the victim of the unspeakable horrors of police brutality. We can never be satisfied as long as our bodies, heavy with the fatigue of travel, cannot gain lodging in the motels of the highways and the hotels of the cities. We cannot be satisfied as long as the Negro's basic mobility is from a smaller ghetto to a larger one. We can never be satisfied as long as our children are stripped of their selfhood and robbed of their dignity by signs stating "For Whites Only." We cannot be satisfied as long as the Negro in Mississippi cannot vote and a Negro in New York believes he has nothing for which to vote. No, no, we are not satisfied, and we will not be satisfied until justice rolls down like waters and righteousness like a mighty stream.

9 I am not unmindful that some of you have come here out of great trials and tribulations. Some of you have come fresh from narrow jail cells. Some of you have come from areas where your quest for freedom left you battered by the storms of persecution and staggered by the winds of police brutality. You have been the veterans of creative suffering. Continue to work with the faith that unearned suffering is redemptive.

10 Go back to Mississippi, and go back to Alabama. Go back to South Carolina. Go back to Georgia. Go back to Louisiana. Go back to the slums and ghettos of our Northern cities, knowing that somehow this situation can and will be changed. Let us not wallow in the valley of despair.

11 I say to you today, my friends, even though we face the difficulties of today and tomorrow, I still have a dream. It is a dream deeply rooted in the American dream. I have a dream that one day this nation will rise up and live out the true meaning of its creed: "We hold these truths to be self-evident, that all men are created equal." I have a dream that one day, on the red hills of Georgia, sons of former slaves and the sons of former slave owners will be able to sit down together at the table of brotherhood. I have a dream that one day even the state of Mississippi, a state sweltering with the heat of injustice, sweltering with the heat of oppression, will be transformed into an oasis of freedom and justice. I have a dream that my four little children will one day live in a nation where they will not be judged by the color of their skin, but by the content of their character.

12 I have a dream today. I have a dream that one day down in Alabama—with its vicious racists, with its governor's lips dripping with the words of interposition and nullification—one day right there in Alabama, little Black boys and Black girls will be able to join hands with little white boys and white girls as sisters and brothers.

13 I have a dream today. I have a dream that one day every valley shall be exalted and every hill and mountain shall be made low, the rough places will be made plain and the crooked places will be made straight, and the glory of the Lord shall be revealed, and all flesh shall see it together.

14 This is our hope. This is the faith that I go back to the South with. And with this faith we will be able to hew out of the mountain of despair a stone of hope. With this faith we will be able to transform the jangling discords of our nation into a beautiful symphony of brotherhood. With this faith we will be able to work together, to play together, to struggle together, to go to jail together, to stand up for freedom together, knowing that we will be free one day.

15 And this will be the day—this will be the day when all of God's children will be able to sing with new meaning:

> My country, 'tis of thee,
> Sweet land of liberty,
> Of thee I sing;
> Land where my fathers died,
> Land of the Pilgrims' pride,
> From every mountainside
> Let freedom ring.

And if America is to be a great nation, this must become true.

16 And so let freedom ring from the prodigious hilltops of New Hampshire. Let freedom ring from the mighty mountains of New York. Let freedom ring from the heightening Alleghenies of Pennsylvania. Let freedom ring from the snow-capped Rockies of Colorado. Let freedom ring from the curvaceous slopes of California.

17 But not only that. Let freedom ring from Stone Mountain of Georgia. Let freedom ring from Lookout Mountain of Tennessee. Let freedom ring from every hill and molehill of Mississippi. "From every mountainside let freedom ring."

18 And when this happens—when we allow freedom to ring, when we let it ring from every village and every hamlet, from every state and every city—we will be able to speed up that day when all of God's children, Black men and white men, Jews and Gentiles, Protestants and Catholics, will be able to join hands and sing in the words of the old Negro spiritual: "Free at last! Free at last! Thank God Almighty. We are free at last!"

Questions for Analysis

1. In what ways is the "I Have a Dream" speech like the "Letter from Birmingham Jail"? In what ways is it different?
2. What differences in the "I Have a Dream" speech and the "Letter" are attributable to the different audiences? What differences may be attributed to the different rhetorical situations inherent in a speech and a letter?

3. Identify places in the "I Have a Dream" speech where King moves to emotional peaks. How does he achieve these peaks? What does he do immediately following these peaks to calm his audience and regain any control he may have lost?
4. What is the significance of music and song in this piece? How does their use compare to that in Maya Angelou's "Graduation"?

Charles H. Turner

A Dream Deferred

(1978)

A graduate of Harvard University, Charles H. Turner (b. 1936) was founding Director of the Afro Institute at Boston's Northeastern University, an organization devoted to supporting minorities in their search for jobs. The following speech was first presented in the African-American World Studies Program's 1978 summer institute at the University of Iowa and was reprinted 10 years later in the January/February 1988 issue of *The Black Scholar*.

1 I am very concerned about the situation of black people and the state of the nation. I think that any kind of in-depth perspective would demonstrate that black people, after 400 years in what Elijah Muhammad called "the wilderness of North America," are perhaps facing our darkest hour.

2 When we look at the situation that is confronting black educators, organizers and children, we see many indications of serious concern, namely, the demise of our leadership and the growing split between those of us who have received education and have achieved certain kinds of stature within the society and the masses of our people who have not.

3 This serious condition exists despite the fact that today we have more cars and more jobs than we ever had as black people. We have more homes and certainly more education in white institutions than anybody ever dreamed of, as well as more B.A.'s, M.A.'s, and Ph.D.'s. It is phenomenal to see, on the one side, all that mass of accomplishment, but to see on the other how bad off we are as a people. The last set of economic figures I saw indicated that the income gap between blacks and whites is widening again. At one point during the 1960s, it was beginning to be close.

Loss of Optimism

4 All these factors lead me to say that this is a dark period for black people in this country. What is darkest is that as we listen to other blacks talk and as we try to get a sense of the pulse of our diversified community, it seems as if a dynamic which has always sustained black people through some of our darkest days is not clearly in evidence.

5 As we examine our spirit and the spirit of our nation, the sense of vision and optimism for the future which any people must have if they are going to create a future of substance is not there. Given the surge of energy that we saw in the flames of conviction and desire for change that came out of the 1960s, how in the world did we wind up in the present situation just a few years after one of the most progressive outpourings of black energy, thought and activity that we have ever seen?

6 The pace in the sixties was a constant, fanatic motion, always driving, moving forward—being pushed back, sometimes—but always, somehow, finding energy to move into a new phase and level of struggle. What happened to that energy? Where is the faith that despite the darkness of the clouds, the light is going to shine?

7 As teachers of black studies, we must raise these kinds of cultural questions. Has not this been a fundamental aspect of our cultural history? Isn't this part of our church, street and musical life?

8 If we can't find that energy then we need to look at the 1960s to find out how and where we slipped. I certainly do not have the answers, but I think the responsibility for the serious exploration of these kinds of questions lies not only with us who have stayed in the streets, but also with those who have gone on to other kinds of attainments and have new kinds of tools to analyze and understand these issues.

Historical Roots

9 What I want to do is offer a few thoughts and personal reflections that came out of my experience in the 1950s, 60s and 70s that are important for me in terms of a sense of where I can go individually as a black person in the United States—in terms of my own energy flow—and where I would like to see black people think about going in this country.

10 I would like to focus my presentation on three poems by Langston Hughes. I think that we must root any kind of political, economic or social analysis in the poetic vision of who we are as a people, because our historical experience has been such that we miss our true dimensions if we define our experience only as a reflection of the white experience.

11 One poem is called ''Mother to Son'':

Well, son, I'll tell you:
Life for me ain't been no crystal stair.
It's had tacks in it,
And splinters,
And boards torn up,
And places with no carpet on the floor—
Bare.

But all the time
I'se been a-climbin' on,

And reachin' landin's,
And turnin' corners,
And sometimes goin' in the dark
Where there ain't been no light.
So boy, don't you turn back.
Don't you set down on the steps
'Cause you finds it's kin der hard.
Don't you fall now—
For I'se still goin', honey,
I'se still climbin'
And life for me ain't been no crystal stair.

12 In the poem called "Lenox Avenue Mural," Hughes asks, "What happens to a dream deferred?"

Does it dry up
like a raisin in the sun?
Or fester like a sore—
And then run?
Does it stink like rotten meat?
Or crust and sugar over—
like a syrupy sweet?

Maybe it just sags
like a heavy load.
Or does it explode?

13 And the last one, the one that thrills me, is "Dream Variation":

To fling my arms wide
In some place of the sun,
To whirl and to dance
Till the white day is done.
Then rest at cool evening
Beneath a tall tree
While night comes on gently,
    Dark like me—
That is my dream!

To fling my arms wide
In the face of the sun,
Dance! Whirl! Whirl!
Till the quick day is done.

Rest at pale evening . . .
A tall, slim tree . . .
Night coming tenderly
Black like me.

Family Heritage

14 I have chosen those three poems because Langston captures in them an essence of the struggle and some of the contradictions that played themselves out not only in the 1960s, but throughout our history.

15 In "Mother to Son," the feeling is that life is a struggle. It is a struggle, but you must evaluate where you have gone, and you must understand that you cannot stop—that there is just no stopping! That theme is an essence that came out of the sixties.

16 My brother Darwin and I talk sometimes about growing up in a relatively conservative family in Cincinnati, Ohio. Our family was well-educated and had various other kinds of attainments, but basically it exhibited the kind of conservatism identified with the black middle class. But there was always a sense of being of service to our people.

17 I remember the stories about our grandmother going down to the Ohio River to welcome black folks who were landing in boats from the South. There was no welfare system and no white folks who would go down to the boat to meet these people. That was the responsibility of black folks, to provide for other blacks. It was hard and it was tough, but it was part of life, part of the struggle to "just keep on going on."

Black Heritage

18 I sometimes wonder whether the story of my grandmother's work is one of the major forces that persuaded me that a Harvard education and an entree into the white world were not necessarily my role in life. Stories of her service taught me that I was part of a struggle that was not easy and certainly was not over, but I did not have any choice.

19 I did not have any choice because it was clear that my life was defined by and oriented around black people. Even though we lived in a neighborhood that was predominantly white, there was no doubt in my understanding that my life and future were rooted in blackness regardless of the kinds of degrees or opportunities I had.

20 That to me is the same feeling that caused many black students in the 1960s to come out of the schools in the South to risk what their families had struggled so hard to bring to them. That was a serious life choice those students made.

21 Consider the situation for many of them. After years of struggle, their mothers and fathers were still sacrificing to send their children to school. Suddenly the children say to them, "No, Mom. No, Dad. I have got to go out in the streets because it is more important to fight for my freedom and my people's freedom than just to get an education for myself."

Concept of Service

22 The 1960s proved to be a tremendously important kind of psychological nurturing ground for a new generation of blacks being trained to provide for the needs of our

people. We all know what the South was like with its beatings, lynchings and murder of blacks who defied the system. The students made very difficult choices, but not merely to rebel against their parents or to rebel against relatively conservative, middle-class school administrations.

23 I think their choices were rooted in the concept of service, a concept that has been a part of our historical tradition. If we do not understand that this concept was a force of the 1960s and if we do not hold that up to our youth, then we will not understand who we are or where our power was coming from in the 1960s.

24 The second poem that I have chosen for a text asks, ''What happens to a dream deferred?'' Many of us perhaps became familiar with the poem because of Lorraine Hansberry's play, *A Raisin in the Sun.* For me, that poem is a good perspective from which to examine the aftermath of the 1954 Supreme Court decision in Brown vs. the Topeka Board of Education.

Psychological Importance

25 1954 was a very significant year in our growth as a people. Certainly, the declaration that racial segregation in education is unconstitutional was a vindication of those who believed that it was through the power of education that blacks would gain equality of status in this country. But I believe that that decision gave us something even more important psychologically. Let me explain.

26 It hurts to be a black, Negro or colored person in America. It hurts in your heart. It hurts because it is frightfully difficult psychologically for any human being to be in a situation in which the laws, economic system and social patterns say to you, as a human being, that you are not worth as much as some other human beings. It is difficult to overcome that psychological pain whether we are teaching in white universities, serving on the boards of major corporations, or living on welfare.

27 It is very difficult to cope with the problem of living in a country that denies your existence. To do so, you must repress a certain amount of the natural human love of self, or you must affirm that natural love of self, perhaps explosively. I think that is essentially what Hughes was trying to say to America in his poem. If you have a person within your midst whom you refuse to treat as though they have human dignity, you must expect them to explode at some point.

28 The Supreme Court was a catalyst, in a sense, for our surge of energy of the 1960s. I wonder how many of the black folks in Montgomery and other places would have stood up if there had not been a decision by the Supreme Court saying that the law no longer defines blacks as being sub-human.

Growth of Civil Rights Movement

29 I would prefer to be able to look back on black history and say that that Supreme Court decision was a minor event because, in black families and black culture, we were unaffected by the attitudes of white bigots. I would like to believe that we were so secure in our sense of ourselves that we did not care what others called us. I would like to believe that blacks of the 1940s and 1950s had such a secure sense of self as that.

30 But the reality is that that was not our psychological situation in the South and generally not even in the North. The Supreme Court's saying that it was now legal for us to participate in the society energized the movement, Martin Luther King, Jr., the ministers in the Southern Christian Leadership Conference, the students at North Carolina A & T University and blacks nationwide as the movement spread. I would argue that it was the court's release of that positive energy that saved America from a possibly worse situation in the 1960s.

31 Granted, the 1960s seemed difficult and revolutionary, but I believe that the movement of the 1960s was characterized by significant rationality. Without the 1954 decision of the court, much greater destruction might have occurred in the 1960s, and America might have had an entirely different social situation.

32 The third poem I have chosen is called "Dream Variation." I chose it because the sense of struggle has always been a fundamental part of our life in America. Equally fundamental has been a dream of what it would be like to be free of the definition of being a "nigger," to live in a situation where your children would no longer be considered different.

Black Nationalism

33 When I read "Dream Variations," I do not merely hear the voices of Hughes, Baldwin and W.E.B. DuBois calling for total freedom of identification within this country. I also think of Elijah Muhammad, Malcolm X, Marcus Garvey and other black leaders who urged black nationalist separation because they did not believe that blacks could find freedom in white America.

34 Elijah, Malcolm and Garvey were not the first blacks to insist that blacks leave America in order to find themselves. They were part of a tradition. Think of the 300 or so blacks in Savannah, Georgia, who boarded ships in the 1890s to create a nation of free blacks in Liberia. Think of the stories told about blacks in Arkansas who helped build the railroad tracks just so that they could board trains to New York, where they could then board ships that would carry them back to Africa. Think of the African Methodist Episcopal Church that from the 1880s to the early 1900s was spearheading a Back-to-Africa movement.

35 When we look at the 1960s, therefore, we must not restrict our vision to King's dream of black freedom within a better America. We must look also at the nationalist dream represented by Elijah and Malcolm. We must see how these different currents of thought played against each other, particularly for young blacks of the 1960s. And we must consider the interplay of these two currents for black people of all ages today. Where should we go?

Differences between the North and South

36 For me, the situation of being a community organizer in the North was very different than it would have been if I had been an organizer in the South. Although I cannot speak definitely about black community organizers in the South because I did not work there, I believe that they were primarily concerned with achieving a dream of equal

rights, civil rights. They wanted to say, "We demand the freedom to go wherever we want—schools, libraries, restaurants, lunch counters, theaters—and to participate equally because we are human beings. We are going to be part of this society, and we are not going to be segregated as though we were inferior."

37 Now that cause was important, and that desire was important. But what about those of us in the North who already were tokens in integrated schools, who had equal access to the facilities of libraries, restaurants, theaters, and buses? How did that Southern projection of the civil rights struggle relate to us?

38 Many young Northern blacks had difficulty relating to that vision. We turned away from King and the SCLC, not only because we reacted against King's spirituality and creed of nonviolence, but even more because we did not comprehend how the Southern goals fit our needs. We knew that our struggle was not to sit down next to white people in restaurants or to integrate the toilets. We applauded the efforts of those blacks required to struggle at that level for human dignity.

Nation of Islam

39 But we young blacks in the North raised the question of the differences between the psychological situation of black people in the South and that of black people in the North. Blacks today need to consider the extent to which that dichotomy created a difference of approaches in the struggle and a tendency to lean toward different leaders.

40 I know that in a real way, Malcolm and Elijah may have saved my sanity because, believe me, Harvard was driving me crazy. There were four or five of us blacks in a class of 1,000. My grades were satisfactory, but I felt overwhelmed by the whiteness.

41 I remember that during my junior year, I went to the Nation of Islam Temple in Roxbury (Massachusetts), where I met Malcolm, who invited me to go along to Washington, D.C., to hear the Honorable Elijah Muhammad talk about "Freedom or Death." I had to go. I was fascinated by the power of Malcolm's conviction and belief and certainty that we were not the vassals of America, that our lives would not be played out as their servants, the step-children of this country. This belief compelled me to go to Washington.

Respect for Black Muslims

42 I remember that just outside Baltimore, the bus stopped at a luncheon stop. I saw a lot of black people from churches, social organizations and various groups getting off other buses. I was impressed by the contrast between the two groups. The Black Muslims seemed to know what they were doing. They were organized and had direction. When we reached D.C., I was even more convinced that I was in the company of a very well-directed, well-organized, and well-thought-out force of people. Regardless of what people thought about the politics of the Muslims, they were organized and respected.

43 I focus on this because in my own life, although I never formally joined the Nation, its writings, teachings and words remained important to me even after Malcolm left, because he had been the disciple of Elijah, carrying out Elijah's thoughts. Even after Malcolm died, Elijah's thought continued to capture for many of us a sense of dignity,

power and worth that we were not able to find in an image of bowing down before white people. Many young black men and women conceived of the nonviolent movement as one that led to bowing down before whites.

44 But we were coming of age, and we were coming of age in a time of conflict. Our question was, how do we face the tests brought on by the conflict?

Style of the 1960s

45 Style is one of our weaknesses, and it is also one of our strengths. We are so much into style. That is a very important concept to me when we talk about the 1960s, because the style that the Southern movement was offering to young blacks of the North was not an emotionally energizing style. It was not clear what we would win by doing that.

46 I remember a very interesting conference in Washington, D.C., in 1965. A lot of black and white people who were working in the North in community action projects came to D.C. in some kind of convention of unrepresented people. There was a decision to hold a workshop of black people from the South and North to see how we could synthesize some of the different currents of thought and propose some kind of collective analysis.

47 Some of the Northern brothers doubted whether they could talk with white people because in the South, blacks struggled against whites. Many Northern brothers and sisters said that "working with whites is not our thing."

48 Blacks struggled for two kinds of opportunities in the North in the early 1960s. One was general integration, but a more important struggle was that of finding jobs. In the North, as we were energized by the Southern struggle, we debated the question of where we fit into the struggle. Eventually our struggle in the North took on a more economic and nationalist character than did that in the South.

Dialectics of Change

49 I would suggest that despite the current praise of the improvement of opportunities for blacks in the South, we may be witnessing a periodic phenomenon in the South's development. Even though black people continue to leave the North and go to the South, in the next 10 or 15 years the "New South" may become the "Old South" again. Then those of us who have returned may complain, "O Lord, I'm home again and look what they have done to me—again."

50 These are the kinds of issues we need to analyze. Mao Tse-tung and others have said that thought plus action brings results. Then one must analyze the result, rethink it, take action again, and rethink it again. It is a constant dialectical process. If, in looking at the dialectic of the 1960s, we do not try to synthesize the two seemingly opposing currents of thought, then we will not be able, as thinkers and educators, to throw light to coming generations and to those around us now.

51 The main questions to answer are, "Where do we go from here as a people?" and "How do the 1960s relate to our thoughts about where we might go?"

52 I believe that at this present time, we must struggle to remake American society. We must begin that struggle by reshaping our own values and then seeking to form creative

alliances with others around this country. The U.S. is not a country of haves; it is a country of have nots. So, when you look at what is happening, you can see that the country is in turmoil.

Restructuring of Society

53 However, we must realize our greatness, strength, tenacity and the endurance of a people that we have had. We must teach our children to appreciate what it was like for our ancestors to survive after being torn out of the bosom of one kind of life and pulled to this country into an entirely different kind of life. Our children must appreciate that history and what a magnificent job our people have performed in overcoming stupendous odds.

54 Nevertheless, I tend to feel that black success is impossible in America. On one hand, I believe that there must be a struggle by black people to restructure America. I also believe, however, that King was right when he said that this restructuring cannot reach its full shape until black people fashion a new existence on a new piece of land, and use that new existence and new piece of land to energize struggles in this country and throughout the world.

55 Cuba is a very small land mass; yet if you look at the effect that Cuba has had on the world, it is staggering. The effect is staggering not because Cubans are communists, but because they do not see their survival as one limited to the survival of their little island alone. They see the entire world as their island and frame a foreign policy to relate Cuba to an international struggle.

56 Two questions that we all must look at are these: Do we believe that America, over the next 10 to 15 years, is going to fashion a positive existence for our youth? Do we think that the answer to our joblessness will be solved through more government programs?

Self-Help

57 I think that alliances between blacks, whites, Hispanics and Asians can overturn economic conditions eventually, but not in the short run. If we are committed to our people and to our youth, then we must fashion the economic and cultural strategies for the survival of our people. We must do that. White people have never done that for us in this country. We have always had to do it ourselves.

58 If the country will not solve the problem for us, then we must find ways to produce wealth and jobs. We must find ways to keep our children from destroying themselves in the frustration of being a people that have no home. Genocide is one thing, but suicide is another. What I see going on is a very subtle form of genocide. We seem to destroy ourselves while the white instigators of our destruction remain invisible.

59 Thoughts of trying new lands, seeking a new existence, and founding a nation are hard thoughts. But I call on educators not to turn away from the questions. Do we have a responsibility to search for the truth inside ourselves and to risk everything? Do we have any choice? Are we free? Are any of us free to live any way we want?

60 We need to look at the 1960s, but only as an exercise. We need to use our understanding of this period to empower our movement, because it is not finished. We must join intellectuals and educators with less educated blacks to create the analysis and thought that can provide a new vision.

Questions for Analysis

1. At the beginning of his lecture Turner describes the problems he sees within the African-American community in 1978. Why would *The Black Scholar* reprint his essay for its readers 10 years after it was written? What problems still exist? What new problems have emerged?
2. Turner builds a major part of his essay thematically and structurally around three poems by Langston Hughes. Explain how this approach works. Is it effective? Why?
3. Turner's lecture is a cultural history built largely around his own personal experience. Even with this personal element, does Turner's account come across as being objective? Does he provide a clear and believable sense of what was going on in the nation as a whole? Explain your responses.
4. How would you characterize Turner's outlook as expressed in the last two sections of his essay? In Paragraph 54 he states "black success is impossible in America." Do you agree? Explain. Is the answer to the problems Turner sees "a new existence on a new piece of land"? Is this alternative possible? Was it possible in 1978?

Shelby Steele

Being Black and Feeling Blue

(1989)

Shelby Steele (b. 1946) teaches English at San Jose State University. His many essays on the subject of race and his recent book, *The Recoloring of America,* have established him as one of the leading voices among African Americans. His positions are often at odds with the established civil-rights leadership. The following essay first appeared in *The American Scholar.*

1 In the early seventies when I was in graduate school, I went out for a beer late one afternoon with another black graduate student whom I'd only known casually before. This student was older than I—a stint in the army had interrupted his education—and

he had the reputation of being bright and savvy, of having applied street smarts to the business of getting through graduate school. I suppose I was hoping for what would be called today a little mentoring. But it is probably not wise to drink with someone when you are enamored of his reputation, and it was not long before we stumbled into a moment that seemed to transform him before my very eyes. I asked him what he planned to do when he finished his Ph.D., fully expecting to hear of high aspirations matched with shrewd perceptions on how to reach them. But, before he could think, he said with a kind of exhausted sincerity, "Man, I just want to hold on, get a job that doesn't work me too hard, and do a lot of fishing." Was he joking, I asked. "Hell no," he said with exaggerated umbrage. "I'm not into it like the white boys. I don't need what they need."

2 I will call this man Henry and report that, until five or six years ago when I lost track of him, he was doing exactly as he said he would do. With much guile and little ambition he had moved through a succession of low-level administrative and teaching jobs, mainly in black studies programs. Of course, it is no crime to just "hold on," and it is hardly a practice limited to blacks. Still, in Henry's case there was truly a troubling discrepancy between his ambition and a fine intelligence recognized by all who knew him. But in an odd way this intelligence was more lateral than vertical, and I would say that it was rechanneled by a certain unseen fear into the business of merely holding on. It would be easy to say that Henry had simply decided on life in a slower lane than he was capable of traveling in, or that he was that rare person who had achieved ambitionless contentment. But, if this was so, Henry would have had wisdom rather than savvy, and he would not have felt the need to carry himself with more self-importance than his station justified. I don't think Henry was uninterested in ambition; I think he was afraid of it.

3 It is certainly true that there is a little of Henry in most people. My own compulsion to understand him informs me that I must have seen many elements of myself in him. And though I'm sure he stands for a universal human blockage, I also believe that there is something in the condition of being black in America that makes the kind of hesitancy he represents one of black America's most serious and debilitating problems. As Henry reached the very brink of expanded opportunity, with Ph.D. in hand, he diminished his ambition almost as though his degree delivered him to a kind of semi-retirement. I don't think blacks in general have any illusions about semi-retirement, but I do think that, as a group, we have hesitated on the brink of new opportunities that we made enormous sacrifices to win for ourselves. The evidence of this lies in one of the most tragic social ironies of late twentieth-century American life—as black Americans have gained in equality and opportunity, we have also declined in relation to whites, so that by many socio-economic and other measures we are further behind whites today than before the great victories of the civil rights movement. By one report, even the black middle class, which had made great gains in the seventies, began to lose ground to its white counterpart in the eighties. Most distressing of all, the black underclass continues to expand rather than shrink.

4 Of course, I don't suggest that Henry's peculiar inertia singularly explains social phenomena so complex and tragic. I do believe, however, that blacks in general are susceptible to the same web of attitudes and fears that kept Henry beneath his potential, and that our ineffectiveness in taking better advantage of our greater equality and opportunity has much to do with this. I think there is a specific form of racial anxiety that all blacks are vulnerable to that can, in situations where we must engage the mainstream society, increase our self-doubt and undermine our confidence so that we often back away from the challenges that, if taken, would advance us. I believe this hidden racial anxiety may well now be the strongest barrier to our full participation in the American mainstream—that it is as strong or stronger even than the discrimination we still face. To examine this racial anxiety, allow me first to look at how the Henry was born in me.

5 Until the sixth grade, I attended a segregated school in a small working-class black suburb of Chicago. The school was a dumping ground for teachers with too little competence or mental stability to teach in the white school in our district. In 1956 when I entered the sixth grade, I encountered a new addition to the menagerie of misfits that was our faculty—an ex-Marine whose cruelty was suggested during our first lunch hour when he bit the cap off his Coke bottle and spit it into the wastebasket. Looking back I can see that there was no interesting depth to the cruelty he began to show us almost immediately—no consumptive hatred, no intelligent malevolence. Although we were all black and he was white, I don't think he was even particularly racist. He had obviously needed us to like him though he had no faith that we would. He ran the class like a gang leader, picking favorites one day and banishing them the next. And then there was a permanent pool of outsiders, myself among them, who were made to carry the specific sins that he must have feared most in himself.

6 The sin I was made to carry was the sin of stupidity. I misread a sentence on the first day of school, and my fate was sealed. He made my stupidity a part of the classroom lore, and very quickly I in fact became stupid. I all but lost the ability to read and found the simplest math beyond me. His punishments for my errors rose in meanness until one day he ordered me to pick up all of the broken glass on the playground with my bare hands. Of course, this would have to be the age of the pop bottle, and there were sections of this playground that glared like a mirror in sunlight. After half an hour's labor I sat down on strike, more out of despair than rebellion.

7 Again, cruelty was no more than a vibration in this man, and so without even a show of anger he commandeered a bicycle, handed it to an eighth grader—one of his lieutenants—and told the boy to run me around the school grounds "until he passes out." The boy was also given a baseball bat to "use on him when he slows down." I ran two laps, about a mile, and then pretended to pass out. The eighth grader knew I was playing possum but could not bring himself to hit me and finally rode off. I exited the school yard through an adjoining cornfield and never returned.

8 I mention this experience as an example of how one's innate capacity for insecurity is expanded and deepened, of how a disbelieving part of the self is brought to life and

forever joined to the believing self. As children we are all wounded in some way and to some degree by the wild world we encounter. From these wounds a disbelieving *anti-self* is born, an internal antagonist and saboteur that embraces the world's negative view of us, that believes our wounds are justified by our own unworthiness, and that entrenches itself as a lifelong voice of doubt. This anti-self is a hidden but aggressive force that scours the world for fresh evidence of our unworthiness. When the believing self announces its aspirations, the anti-self always argues against them, but never on their merits (this is a healthy function of the believing self). It argues instead against our worthiness to pursue these aspirations and, by its lights, we are never worthy of even our smallest dreams. The mission of the anti-self is to deflate the believing self and, thus, draw it down into inertia, passivity, and faithlessness.

9 The anti-self is the unseen agent of low self-esteem; it is a catalytic energy that tries to induce low self-esteem in the believing self as though it were the complete truth of the personality. The anti-self can only be contained by the strength of the believing self, and this is where one's early environment becomes crucial. If the childhood environment is stable and positive, if the family is whole and provides love, the schools good, the community safe, then the believing self will be reinforced and made strong. If the family is shattered, the schools indifferent, the neighborhood a mine field of dangers, the anti-self will find evidence everywhere with which to deflate the believing self.

10 This does not mean that a bad childhood cannot be overcome. But it does mean—as I have experienced and observed it—that one's *capacity* for self-doubt and self-belief are roughly the same from childhood on, so that years later when the believing self may have strengthened enough to control the anti-self, one will still have the same capacity for doubt whether or not one has the actual doubt. I think it is this struggle between our capacities for doubt and belief that gives our personalities one of their peculiar tensions and, in this way, marks our character.

11 My own anti-self was given new scope and power by this teacher's persecution of me, and it was so successful in deflating my believing self that I secretly vowed never to tell my parents what was happening to me. The anti-self had all but sold my believing self on the idea that I was stupid, and I did not want to feel that shame before my parents. It was my brother who finally told them, and his disclosure led to a boycott that closed the school and eventually won the dismissal of my teacher and several others. But my anti-self transformed even this act of rescue into a cause of shame—if there wasn't something wrong with me, why did I have to be rescued? The anti-self follows only the logic of self-condemnation.

12 But there was another dimension to this experience that my anti-self was only too happy to seize upon. It was my race that landed me in this segregated school and, as many adults made clear to me, my persecution followed a timeless pattern of racial persecution. The implications of this were rich food for the anti-self—my race was so despised that it had to be segregated; as a black my education was so unimportant that even unbalanced teachers without college degrees were adequate; and ignorance and cruelty that would be intolerable in a classroom of whites was perfectly all right in a

classroom of blacks. The anti-self saw no injustice in any of this, but instead took it all as confirmation of a racial inferiority that it could now add to the well of personal doubt I already had. When the adults thought they were consoling me—"Don't worry. They treat all blacks this way"—they were also deepening the wound and expanding my capacity for doubt.

13 And this is the point. The condition of being black in America means that one will likely endure more wounds to one's self-esteem than others and that the capacity for self-doubt born of these wounds will be compounded and expanded by the black race's reputation of inferiority. The anti-self will most likely have more ammunition with which to deflate the believing self and its aspirations. And the universal human struggle to have belief win out over doubt will be more difficult.

14 And, more than difficult, it is also made inescapable by the fact of skin color, which, in America, works as a visual invocation of the problem. Black skin has more dehumanizing stereotypes associated with it than any other skin color in America, if not the world. When a black presents himself in an integrated situation, he knows that his skin alone may bring these stereotypes to life in the minds of those he meets and that he, as an individual, may be diminished by his race before he has a chance to reveal a single aspect of his personality. By the symbology of color that operates in our culture, black skin accuses him of inferiority. Under the weight of this accusation, a black will almost certainly doubt himself on some level and to some degree. The ever-vigilant anti-self will grab this racial doubt and mix it into the pool of personal doubt, so that when a black walks into an integrated situation—a largely white college campus, an employment office, a business lunch—he will be vulnerable to the entire realm of his self-doubt before a single word is spoken.

15 This constitutes an intense and lifelong racial vulnerability and anxiety for blacks. Even though a white American may have been wounded more than a given black, and therefore have a larger realm of inner doubt, his white skin with its connotations of privilege and superiority will actually help protect him from that doubt and from the undermining power of his anti-self, at least in relations with blacks. In fact, the larger the realm of doubt, the more he may be tempted to rely on his white skin for protection from it. Certainly in every self-avowed white racist, whether businessman or member of the Klan, there is a huge realm of self-contempt and doubt that hides behind the mythology of white skin. The mere need to pursue self-esteem through skin color suggests there is no faith that it can be pursued any other way. But if skin color offers whites a certain false esteem and impunity, it offers blacks vulnerability.

16 This vulnerability begins for blacks with the recognition that we belong quite simply to the most despised race in the human community of races. To be a member of such a group in a society where all others gain an impunity by merely standing in relation to us is to live with a relentless openness to diminishment and shame. By the devious logic of the anti-self, one cannot be open to such diminishment without in fact being inferior and therefore deserving of diminishment. For the anti-self, the charge verifies the crime, so that racial vulnerability itself is evidence of inferiority. In this sense, the

anti-self is an internalized racist, our own subconscious bigot, that conspires with society to diminish us.

17 So when blacks enter the mainstream, they are not only vulnerable to society's racism but also to the racist within. This internal racist is not restricted by law, morality, or social decorum. It cares nothing about civil rights and equal opportunity. It is the self-doubt born of the original wound of racial oppression, and its mission is to establish the justice of that wound and shackle us with doubt.

18 Of course, the common response to racial vulnerability, as to most vulnerabilities, is denial—the mind's mechanism for ridding itself of intolerable possibilities. For blacks to acknowledge a vulnerability to inferiority anxiety, in the midst of a society that has endlessly accused us of being inferior, feels nothing less than intolerable—as if we were agreeing with the indictment against us. But denial is not the same as eradication, since it only gives unconscious life to what is intolerable to our consciousness. Denial reassigns rather than vanquishes the terror of racial vulnerability. This reassignment only makes the terror stronger by making it unknown. When we deny we always create a dangerous area of self-ignorance, an entire territory of the self that we cannot afford to know. Without realizing it, we begin to circumscribe our lives by avoiding those people and situations that might breach our denial and force us to see consciously what we fear. Though the denial of racial vulnerability is a human enough response, I think it also makes our public discourse on race circumspect and unproductive, since we cannot talk meaningfully about problems we are afraid to name.

19 Denial is a refusal of painful self-knowledge. When someone or something threatens to breach this refusal, we receive an unconscious shock of the very vulnerability we have denied—a shock that often makes us retreat and more often makes us intensify our denial. When blacks move into integrated situations or face challenges that are new for blacks, the myth of black inferiority is always present as a *condition* of the situation, and as such it always threatens to breach our denial of racial vulnerability. It threatens to make us realize consciously what is intolerable to us—that we have some anxiety about inferiority. We feel this threat unconsciously as a shock of racial doubt delivered by the racist anti-self (always the inner voice of the myth of black inferiority). Consciously, we will feel this shock as a sharp discomfort or a desire to retreat from the situation. Almost always we will want to intensify our denial.

20 I will call this shock "integration shock" since it occurs most powerfully when blacks leave their familiar world and enter into the mainstream. Integration shock and denial are mutual intensifiers. The stab of racial doubt that integration shock delivers is a pressure to intensify denial, and a more rigid denial means the next stab of doubt will be more threatening and therefore more intense. The symbiosis of these two forces is, I believe, one of the reasons black Americans have become preoccupied with racial pride, almost to the point of obsession over the past twenty-five or so years. With more exposure to the mainstream we have endured more integration shock, more jolts of inferiority anxiety. And I think we have often responded with rather hyperbolic claims of black pride by which we deny that anxiety. In this sense, our self-consciousness around pride, our need to make a point of it, is, to a degree, a form of denial. Pride

becomes denial when it ceases to reflect self-esteem quietly and begins to compensate loudly for unacknowledged inner doubt. Here it also becomes dangerous since it prevents us from confronting and overcoming that doubt.

21 I think the most recent example of black pride-as-denial is the campaign (which seems to have been launched by a committee) to add yet another name to the litany of names that blacks have given themselves over the past century. Now we are to be African-Americans instead of, or in conjunction with, being black Americans. This self-conscious reaching for pride through nomenclature suggests nothing so much as a despair over the possibility of gaining the less conspicuous pride that follows real advancement. In its invocation of the glories of a remote African past and its wistful suggestion of homeland, this name denies the doubt black Americans have about their contemporary situation in America. There is no element of self-confrontation in it, no facing of real racial vulnerabilities, as there was with the name "black." I think "black" easily became the name of preference in the sixties precisely because it was not a denial but a confrontation of inferiority anxiety, with the shame associated with the color black. There was honest self-acceptance in this name, and I think it diffused much of our vulnerability to the shame of color. Even between blacks, "black" is hardly the drop-dead fighting word it was when I was a child. Possibly we are ready now for a new name, but I think "black" has been our most powerful name yet because it so frankly called out our shame and doubt and helped us (and others) to accept ourselves. In the name African-American there is too much false neutralization of doubt, too much looking away from the caldron of our own experience. It is a euphemistic name that hides us even from ourselves.

22 I think blacks have been more preoccupied with pride over the past twenty-five years because we have been more exposed to integration shock since the 1964 Civil Rights Bill made equal opportunity the law of the land (if not quite the full reality of the land). Ironically, it was the inequality of opportunity and all the other repressions of legal segregation that buffered us from our racial vulnerability. In a segregated society we did not have the same accountability to the charge of racial inferiority since we were given little opportunity to disprove the charge. It was the opening up of opportunity—anti-discrimination laws, the social programs of the Great Society, equal opportunity guidelines and mandates, fair housing laws, Affirmative Action, and so on—that made us individually and collectively more accountable to the myth of black inferiority and therefore more racially vulnerable.

23 This vulnerability has increased in the same proportion that our freedom and opportunity have increased. The exhilaration of new freedom is always followed by a shock of accountability. Whatever unresolved doubt follows the oppressed into greater freedom will be inflamed since freedom always carries a burden of proof, always throws us back on ourselves. And freedom, even imperfect freedom, makes blacks a brutal proposition: if you're not inferior, prove it. This is the proposition that shocks us and makes us vulnerable to our underworld of doubt. The whispers of the racist anti-self are far louder in the harsh accountability of freedom than in subjugation where the oppressor is so entirely to blame.

24 The bitter irony of all this is that our doubt and the hesitancy it breeds now help limit our progress in America almost as systematically as segregation once did. Integration shock gives the old boundaries of legal segregation a regenerative power. To avoid the shocks of doubt that come from entering the mainstream, or plunging more deeply into it, we often pull back at precisely those junctures where segregation once pushed us back. In this way we duplicate the conditions of our oppression and re-enact our role as victims even in the midst of far greater freedom and far less victimization. Certainly there is still racial discrimination in America, but I believe that the unconscious replaying of our oppression is now the greatest barrier to our full equality.

25 The way in which integration shock regenerates the old boundaries of segregation for blacks is most evident in three tendencies—the tendency to minimalize or avoid real opportunities, to withhold effort in areas where few blacks have achieved, and to self-segregate in integrated situations.

26 If anything, it is the presence of new opportunities in society that triggers integration shock. If opportunity is a chance to succeed, it is also a chance to fail. The vulnerability of blacks to hidden inferiority anxiety makes failure a much more forbidding prospect. If a black pursues an opportunity in the mainstream—opens a business, goes up for a challenging job or difficult promotion—and fails, that failure can be used by the anti-self to confirm both personal and racial inferiority. The diminishment and shame will tap an impersonal as well as personal source of doubt. When a white fails, he alone fails. His doubt is strictly personal, which gives him more control over the failure. He can discover *his* mistakes, learn the reasons *he* made them, and try again. But the black, laboring under the myth of inferiority, will have this impersonal, culturally determined doubt to contend with. This form of doubt robs him of a degree of control over his failure since he alone cannot eradicate the cultural myth that stings him. There will be a degree of impenetrability to his failure that will constitute an added weight of doubt.

27 The effect of this is to make mainstream opportunity more intimidating and risky for blacks. This is made worse in that blacks, owing to past and present deprivations, may come to the mainstream in the first place with a lower stock of self-esteem. High risk and low self-esteem are hardly the best combination with which to tackle the challenges of a highly advanced society in which others have been blessed by history with very clear advantages. Under these circumstances opportunity can seem more like a chance to fail than a chance to succeed. All this makes for a kind of opportunity aversion that I think was behind the hesitancy I saw in Henry, in myself, and in other blacks of all class backgrounds. It is also, I believe, one of the reasons for the sharp decline in the number of black students entering college, even as many colleges launch recruiting drives to attract more black students.

28 This aversion to opportunity generates a way of seeing that minimalizes opportunity to the point where it can be ignored. In black communities the most obvious entrepreneurial opportunities are routinely ignored. It is often outsiders or the latest wave of immigrants who own the shops, restaurants, cleaners, gas stations, and even the homes and apartments. Education is a troubled area in black communities for numerous rea-

sons, but certainly one of them is that many black children are not truly imbued with the idea that learning is virtually the same as opportunity. Schools—even bad schools—were the opportunity that so many immigrant groups used to learn the workings and the spirit of American society. In the very worst inner city schools there are accredited teachers who teach the basics, but too often to students who shun those among them who do well, who see studying as a sucker's game and school itself as a waste of time. One sees in many of these children almost a determination not to learn, a suppression of the natural impulse to understand, that cannot be entirely explained by the determinism of poverty. Out of school, in the neighborhood, these same children learn everything. I think it is the meeting with the mainstream that school symbolizes that clicks them off. In the cultural ethos from which they come, it is always these meetings that trigger the aversion to opportunity behind which lies inferiority anxiety. Their parents and their culture send them a double message: go to school but don't really apply yourself. The risk is too high.

29 This same pattern of avoidance, this unconscious circumvention of possibility, is also evident in our commitment to effort—the catalyst of opportunity. Difficult, sustained effort—in school or career or family life—will be riddled with setbacks, losses, and frustrations. Racial vulnerability erodes effort for blacks by exaggerating the importance of these setbacks, by recasting them as confirmation of racial inferiority rather than the normal pitfalls of sustained effort. The racist anti-self greets these normal difficulties with an I-told-you-so attitude, and the believing self, unwilling to risk seeing that the anti-self is right, may grow timid and pull back from the effort. As with opportunity, racial vulnerability makes hard effort in the mainstream a high-risk activity for blacks.

30 But this is not the case in those areas where blacks have traditionally excelled. In sports and music, for example, the threat of integration shock is effectively removed. Because so many blacks have succeeded in these areas, a black can enter them without being racially vulnerable. Failure carries no implication of racial inferiority, so the activity itself is far less risky than those in which blacks have no record of special achievement. Certainly in sports and music one sees blacks sustain the most creative and disciplined effort, and they seize opportunities where one would have thought there were none. But all of this changes the instant racial vulnerability becomes a factor. Across the country thousands of young black males take every opportunity and make every effort to reach the elite ranks of the NBA or the NFL. But in the classroom, where racial vulnerability is a hidden terror, they and many of their classmates put forth the meagerest effort and show a virtual indifference to the genuine opportunity that education is.

31 But the most visible circumvention that results from integration shock is the tendency toward self-segregation that, if anything, seems to have increased over the last twenty years. Along with opportunity and effort, it is also white people themselves who are often avoided. I hear young black professionals say they do not socialize with whites after work unless at some "command performance" that comes with the territory of their career. On largely white university campuses where integration shock is

particularly intense, black students often try to enforce a kind of neo-separatism that includes black ''theme'' dorms, black student unions, Afro-houses, black cultural centers, black student lounges, and so on. There is a geo-politics involved in this activity, where race is tied to territory in a way that mimics the ''whites only''/''coloreds only'' designations of the past. Only now these race spaces are staked out in the name of pride.

32 I think this impulse to self-segregate, to avoid whites, has to do with the way white people are received by the black anti-self. Even if the believing self wants to see racial difference as essentially meaningless, the anti-self, that hidden perpetrator of racist doubt, sees white people as better than black people. Its mission is to confirm black inferiority, and so it looks closely at whites, watches the way they walk, talk, and negotiate the world, and then grants these styles of being and acting superiority. Somewhere inside every black is a certain awe at the power and achievement of the white race. In every barbershop gripe session where whites are put through the grinder of black anger, there will be a kind of backhanded respect—''Well, he might be evil, but that white boy is smart.'' True or not, the anti-self organizes its campaign against the believing self's faith in black equality around this supposition. And so, for blacks (as is true for whites in another way), white people in the generic sense have no neutrality. In themselves they are stimulants to the black anti-self, deliverers of doubt. Their color slips around the deepest need of blacks to believe in their immutable equality and communes directly with their self-suspicion.

33 So it is not surprising to hear black students on largely white campuses say that they are simply more comfortable with other blacks. Nor is it surprising to see them caught up in absurd contradictions—demanding separate facilities for themselves even as they protest apartheid in South Africa. Racial vulnerability is a species of fear, and, as such, it is the progenitor of countless ironies. More freedom makes us more vulnerable so that in the midst of freedom we feel the impulse to carve out segregated comfort zones that protect us more from our own doubt than from whites. We balk before opportunity and pull back from effort just as these things would bear fruit. We reconstitute the boundaries of segregation just as they become illegal. By averting opportunity and curbing effort for fear of awakening a sense of inferiority, we make inevitable the very failure that shows us inferior.

34 One of the worst aspects of oppression is that it never ends when the oppressor begins to repent. There is a legacy of doubt in the oppressed that follows long after the cleanest repentance by the oppressor, just as guilt trails the oppressor and makes his redemption incomplete. These themes of doubt and guilt fill in like fresh replacements and work to duplicate the oppression. I think black Americans are today more oppressed by doubt than by racism and that the second phase of our struggle for freedom must be a confrontation with that doubt. Unexamined, this doubt leads us back into the tunnel of our oppression where we re-enact our victimization just as society struggles to end its victimization of us. We are not a people formed in freedom. Freedom is always a call to possibility that demands an overcoming of doubt. We are still new to freedom, new to its challenges, new even to the notion that self-doubt can be the slyest enemy

of freedom. For us freedom has so long meant the absence of oppression that we have not yet realized that it also means the conquering of doubt.

35 Of course, this does not mean that doubt should become a lake we swim in, but it does mean that we should begin our campaign against doubt by acknowledging it, by outlining the contours of the black anti-self so that we can know and accept exactly what it is that we are afraid of. This is knowledge that can be worked with, knowledge that can point with great precision to the actions through which we can best mitigate doubt and advance ourselves. This is the sort of knowledge that gives the believing self a degree of immunity to the anti-self and that enables it to pile up little victories that, in sum, grant it even more immunity.

36 Certainly inferiority has long been the main theme of the black anti-self, its most lethal weapon against our capacity for self-belief. And so, in a general way, the acceptance of this piece of knowledge implies a mission: to show ourselves and (only indirectly) the larger society that we are not inferior on any dimension. That this should already be assumed goes without saying. But what "should be" falls within the province of the believing self where it has no solidity until the doubt of the anti-self is called out and shown false by demonstrable action in the real world. This is the proof that grants the "should" its rightful solidity, that transforms it from a well-intentioned claim into a certainty.

37 The temptation is to avoid so severe a challenge, to maintain a black identity, painted in the colors of pride and culture, that provides us with a way of seeing ourselves apart from this challenge. It is easier to be "African-American" than to organize oneself on one's own terms and around one's own aspiration and then, through sustained effort and difficult achievement, put one's insidious anti-self quietly to rest. No black identity, however beautifully conjured, will spare blacks this challenge that, despite its fairness or unfairness, is simply in the nature of things. But then I have faith that in time we will meet this challenge since this, too, is in the nature of things.

Questions for Analysis

1. Why does Steele move from the example of Henry to his own experience *before* he begins his analysis and explanation of one current racially related problem?
2. How does Steele define the difference and tension between the "anti-self" and the "believing self"?
3. The "anti-self" becomes, according to Steele, the "racist within." In what ways does this "racist within" operate to slow the progress of African Americans into the economic and social mainstream?
4. Steele contrasts the terms "African-American" and "black" to illustrate what he sees as "pride-as-denial." What is the distinction he makes between these terms? What strengths does he see in one, and what weaknesses does he see in the other?

5. In Paragraph 25, Steele introduces three tendencies that he believes regenerate "the old boundaries of segregation for blacks." Of these he says the most "visible" is self-segregation. His analysis is likely to generate controversy because he sees this tendency as a "pulling back" from opportunity. How would you support his assertion? How would you argue to assert that this pattern does *not* diminish opportunity?
6. In Paragraph 36, Steele ends his essay by asserting that knowledge "can point with great precision to the actions through which we can best mitigate doubt and advance ourselves." What actions do you think he has in mind for African Americans based on this knowledge? What can whites do to help African Americans? Or can whites only be fair, open, and patient?

James A. McPherson

To Blacks and Jews: Hab Rachmones

(1989)

James A. McPherson (b. 1943) is a Pulitzer Prize–winning writer of essays and short fiction who teaches English at the University of Iowa. His books include *Hue and Cry, Railroad,* and *Elbow Room.* This essay first appeared in the journal *Tikkum* and was reprinted in *The Best American Essays: 1990.*

1 About 1971, Bernard Malamud sent me a manuscript of a novel called *The Tenants.* Malamud had some reservations about the book. Specifically, he was anxious over how the antagonism between Harry Lesser, a Jewish writer, and Willie Spear, a Black writer, would be read. We communicated about the issue. On the surface, Malamud was worried over whether he had done justice to Willie Spear's Black idiom; but beneath the surface, during our exchange of letters, he was deeply concerned about the tensions that were then developing between Black intellectuals and Jewish intellectuals. I was living in Berkeley at the time, three thousand miles away from the fragmentation of the old civil rights coalition, the mounting battle over affirmative action, and most of the other incidents that would contribute to the present division between the Jewish and Black communities.

2 I was trying very hard to become a writer. As a favor to Malamud, I rewrote certain sections of the novel, distinguished Willie Spear's idiom from Harry Lesser's, and suggested several new scenes. I believed then that the individual human heart was of paramount importance, and I could not understand why Malamud had chosen to end his novel with Levenspiel, the Jewish slumlord who owned the condemned building in which the two antagonists lived, pleading with them *"Hab rachmones"* ("Have

mercy''). Or why Levenspiel begs for mercy 115 times. Like Isaac Babel, I felt that a well-placed period was much more effective than an extravagance of emotion. Malamud sent me an autographed copy of the book as soon as it was printed. Rereading the book eighteen years later, I now see that, even after the 115th plea for mercy by Levenspiel, there is no period and there is no peace.

3 Well-publicized events over the past two decades have made it obvious that Blacks and Jews have never been the fast friends we were alleged to be. The best that can be said is that, at least since the earliest decades of this century, certain spiritual elites in the Jewish community and certain spiritual elites in the Black community have found it mutually advantageous to join forces to fight specific obstacles that block the advancement of both groups: lynchings, restrictive housing covenants, segregation in schools, and corporate expressions of European racism that target both groups. During the best of times, the masses of each group were influenced by the moral leadership of the elites. From my reading of the writers of the extreme right wing, in whose works one can always find the truest possible expression of white racist sentiment, I know that the Black and Jewish peoples have historically been treated as ''special cases.'' The most sophisticated of these writers tend to examine the two groups as ''problems'' in Western culture. Both share incomplete status. Both are legally included in Western society, but for two quite different reasons each has not been fused into the ''race.''

4 Until fairly recently, Jews were considered a ''sect-nation,'' a group of people living within Western territorial states and committed to a specific religious identity. This extraterritorial status allowed Jews to convert and become members of a confessional community, as was often the case in Europe, or to drop any specific religious identification and become ''white,'' as has often been the case in the United States.

5 This second Jewish option is related, in very complex ways, to the special status of Black Americans and thus to the core of the present Black–Jewish problem. The romantic illusions of Black nationalism aside, Black Americans have not been Africans since the eighteenth century. Systematic efforts were made to strip Black slaves of all vestiges of the African cultures from which they came. The incorporation of European bloodlines, from the first generations onward, gave the slaves immunities to the same diseases, brought by Europeans to the Americas, that nearly decimated America's indigenous peoples. The slave ancestors of today's thirty or so million Black Americans took their ideals from the sacred documents of American life, their secular values from whatever was current, and their deepest mythologies from the Jews of the Old Testament. They were a self-created people, having very little to look back on. The one thing they could not acquire was the institutional protection, or status, that comes in this country from being classified as ''white.'' And since from its very foundation the United States has employed color as a negative factor in matters of social mobility, we Black Americans have always experienced tremendous difficulties in our attempts to achieve the full rewards of American life. The structure of white supremacy is very subtle and complex, but the most obvious thing that can be said about it is that it ''enlists'' psychologically those whites who view their status as dependent on it. It has the effect of encouraging

otherwise decent people to adopt the psychological habits of policemen or prison guards.

6 Given this complex historical and cultural reality, most Black Americans, no matter how wealthy, refined, or "integrated," have never been able to achieve the mobility and security available to whites. Jewish Americans, by contrast, have this option, whether or not they choose to exercise it. Blacks recognize this fact, and this recognition is the basis of some of the extreme tension that now exists between the two groups. While Jews insist that they be addressed and treated as part of a religious community, most Black Americans tend to view them as white. When Jews insist that Jewish sensitivities and concerns be recognized, Black Americans have great difficulty separating these concerns from the concerns of the corporate white community.

7 And yet, despite the radically different positions of the two groups, there has been a history of alliances. Perhaps it is best to say that mutual self-interest has defined the interaction between Blacks and Jews for most of this century. In her little-known study *In the Almost Promised Land,* Hasia R. Diner has traced the meeting and mutual assessment of the two peoples as presented in the Yiddish press to the two million Jewish immigrants from Eastern Europe and Russia who came to the United States during the first four decades of this century. Community papers like the *Tageblatt* and the *Forward* forged a socialistic language that brought together Jewish immigrants from different backgrounds, that helped them acculturate, and that advised them about the obstacles and opportunities they would find in America. These papers gave more attention to Black American life than to any other non-Jewish concern. They focused on Black marriage and family, on Black crime, on Black "trickery and deception," and on Black education, entertainment, and achievement. They linked Black suffering to Jewish suffering. Diner writes:

> The Yiddish papers sensed that a special relationship existed between blacks and Jews and because of this the press believed that the two groups were captivated by each other. . . . Jews believed that a history of suffering had predisposed Jews toward understanding the problems of blacks. ("Because we have suffered we treat kindly and sympathetically and humanly all the oppressed of every nation.")

The central theme was that Black people were America's Jews. Historical parallels were emphasized: the Black Exodus from the South was compared to the Jewish Exodus from Egypt and to the Jewish migration from Russia and Germany.

8 But there were much more practical reasons why the two groups—one called "white," the other defined by caste; one geared to scholarship and study, the other barely literate; one upwardly mobile, the other in constant struggle merely to survive—managed to find common ground during the first four decades of this century. There was the desperate Black need for financial, legal, and moral support in the fight against racism, lynchings, and exclusion from the institutions of American life. There was the Jewish

perception that many of the problems of exclusion faced by Black people were also faced by Jews. Diner writes:

> Black Americans needed champions in a hostile society. Jewish Americans, on the other hand, wanted a meaningful role so as to prove themselves to an inhospitable [society]. . . . Thus, American Jewish leaders involved in a quest for a meaningful identity and comfortable role in American society found that one way to fulfill that search was to serve as the intermediaries between blacks and whites. The Jewish magazines defined a mission for Jews to interpret the black world to white Americans and to speak for blacks and champion their cause.

9 Diner is describing the ''interstitial'' role, traditionally assumed by Jewish shopkeepers and landlords in Black communities, being extended into the moral sphere. Given the radical imbalance of potential power that existed between the two groups, however, such a coalition was fated to fail once American Jews had achieved their own goals.

10 For mutually self-interested reasons, I believe, the two groups began a parting of the ways just after the Six Day War of 1967. The rush of rationalizations on both sides—Jewish accusations of Black anti-Semitism, Black Nationalist accusations of Jewish paternalism and subversion of Black American goals—helped to obscure very painful realities that had much more to do with the broader political concerns of both groups, as they were beginning to be dramatized in the international arena, than with the domestic issues so widely publicized. Within the Black American community, even before the killing of Martin King, there arose a nationalistic identification with the emerging societies of newly liberated Africa. In the rush to identify with small pieces of evidence of Black freedom *anywhere* in the world, many Black Americans began to embrace ideologies and traditions that were alien to the traditions that had been developed, through painful struggle, by their earliest ancestors on American soil.

11 A large part of this romantic identification with Africa resulted from simple frustration: the realization that the moral appeal advocated by Martin King had authority only within those southern white communities where the remnants of Christian tradition were still respected. The limitations of the old civil rights appeal became apparent when King was stoned while attempting to march in Cicero, Illinois, in 1966. We Black Americans discovered that many ethnic Americans, not just southern whites, did not care for us. The retrenchment that resulted, promoted by the media as Black Nationalism, provided convenient excuses for many groups to begin severing ties with Black Americans. Expressions of nationalism not only alienated many well-meaning whites; they had the effect of discounting the Black American tradition of principled struggle that had produced the great leaders in the Black American community. To any perceptive listener, most of the nationalistic rhetoric had the shrillness of despair.

12 For the Jewish community, victory in the Six Day War of 1967 caused the beginning of a much more complex reassessment of the Jewish situation, one based on some of the same spiritual motivations as were the defeats suffered by Black Americans toward

the end of the 1960s. The Israeli victory in 1967 was a *reassertion* of the nationhood of the Jewish people. But, like the founding of Israel in 1948, this reassertion raised unresolved contradictions. My reading teaches me that, until the twentieth century, Zion to most Jews was not a tangible, earthly hope, but a mystical symbol of the divine deliverance of the Jewish nation. Zion was a heavenly city that did not yet exist. It was to be planted on earth by the Messiah on the Day of Judgment, when historical time would come to an end. But the Jewish experience in Europe seems to have transformed the dream of a heavenly city into an institution in the practical world. This tension has turned the idea of the Jews as a nation existing as the community of the faithful into the idea of Israel as a Western territorial sovereign. Concerned for its survival, Israel has turned expansionist; but the price it has paid has been the erosion of its ethical identity. It is said that the world expects more from the Jews than from any other people. This deeply frustrating misconception, I believe, results from the dual premise (religious and political) of the State of Israel. I also believe that American Jews are extraordinarily frustrated when they are unable to make non-Jews understand how sensitive Jews are to uninformed criticism after six thousand years of relentless persecution.

13 The majority of Black Americans are unaware of the complexity of the meaning of Israel to American Jews. But, ironically, Afro-Zionists have as intense an emotional identification with Africa and with the Third World as American Jews have with Israel. Doubly ironic, this same intensity of identification with a ''Motherland'' seems rooted in the mythologies common to both groups. In this special sense—in the spiritual sense implied by ''Zion'' and ''Diaspora'' and ''Promised Land''—Black Americans *are* America's Jews. But given the isolation of Black Americans from any meaningful association with Africa, extensions of the mythology would be futile. We have no distant homeland preparing an ingathering. For better or worse, Black Americans are *Americans*. Our special problems must be confronted and solved here, where they began. They cannot be solved in the international arena, in competition with Jews.

14 Related to the problem of competing mythologies is a recent international trend that, if not understood in terms of its domestic implications, will deepen the already complex crisis between Blacks and Jews. The period of European hegemony, mounted in the fifteenth century and consolidated in the nineteenth, imposed on millions of non-European people values and institutions not indigenous to their cultural traditions. One of these institutions was the nation-state. Since the end of World War II, the various wars of independence in India, Asia, Africa, and elsewhere have exposed the fact that a European invention does not always meet the mythological, linguistic, and cultural needs of different ethnic groups competing within artificial ''territorial states.'' We sometimes forget that it took many centuries for Europeans to evolve political forms suited to their own habits. Since the 1950s, colonized people have begun to assert their own cultural needs. The new word coined to define this process is ''devolutionism.'' While devolutionism is currently a Third World phenomenon, two of the most prominent groups within the territorial United States, because of their unique origins, can be easily drawn into this struggle: Black Americans, because of our African origins and

our sympathy for the liberation struggle currently taking place in South Africa; and Jews, because of their intense identification with Israel. Given the extent of Israeli involvement in South Africa, and given the sympathy many Black Americans feel for Black South Africans and Palestinians, it is only predictable that some Black Americans would link the two struggles. My deepest fear is that the dynamics of American racism will force Black Americans into a deeper identification with the Palestinians, thus incorporating into an already tense domestic situation an additional international dimension we just do not need. The resulting polarization may well cause chaos for a great many people, Blacks and Jews included.

15 I have no solutions to offer beyond my feeling that we should begin talking with each other again.

16 I remember walking the streets of Chicago back in 1972 and 1973, gathering information for an article on Jewish slumlords who had "turned" white neighborhoods and then sold these homes at inflated prices to poor Black people, recent migrants from the South, on installment purchase contracts. I remember talking with Rabbi Robert Marx, who sided with the buyers against the Jewish sellers; with Gordon Sherman, a businessman who was deeply disturbed by the problem; with Marshall Patner, a lawyer in Hyde Park; and with other Jewish lawyers who had volunteered to work with the buyers in an attempt to correct the injustice. I spent most of a Guggenheim Fellowship financing my trips to Chicago. I gave the money I earned from the article to the organization created by the buyers. And although the legal case that was brought against the sellers was eventually lost in federal district court, I think that all the people involved in the effort to achieve some kind of justice found the experience very rewarding. I remember interviewing poor Black people, the victims, who did not see the sellers as Jews but as whites. I remember interviewing Mrs. Lucille Johnson, an elderly Black woman who seemed to be the spiritual center of the entire effort. Her influence could get smart Jewish and Irish lawyers to do the right thing, as opposed to the legal thing. I asked her about the source of her strength. I still remember her reply:

> The bad part of the thing is that we just don't have what we need in our lives to go out and do something, white or black. We just don't have *love*. . . . But this ain't no situation to get hung up on color; getting hung up on some of God's love will bail us out. I think of "Love one another" and the Commandments. If we love the Lord our God with all our hearts and minds, and love our neighbors as ourselves, we done covered them Commandments. And "Let not your heart be troubled; he that believes in God believes also in me."

17 I think there was, a generation or two ago, a group of stronger and wiser Black and Jewish people. I think they were more firmly grounded in the lived mythology of the Hebrew Bible. I think that, because of this grounding, they were, in certain spiritual dimensions, almost one people. They were spiritual elites. Later generations have opted for more mundane values and the rewards these values offer. Arthur Hertzberg told me, "Anti-Semitism is the way Blacks join the majority. Racism is the way Jews join the

majority. Individuals in both groups have the capacity to package themselves in order to make it in terms the white majority can understand.''

18 Certain consequences of the Black–Jewish alliance cannot be overlooked. The spiritual elites within both groups recognized, out of common memories of oppression and suffering, that the only true refuge a person in pain has is within another person's heart. These spiritual elites had the moral courage to allow their hearts to become swinging doors. For at least six decades these elites contributed to the soul of American democracy. Their influence animated the country, gave it a sense of moral purpose it had not known since the Civil War. The coalition they called into being helped to redefine the direction of the American experience and kept it moving toward transcendent goals. With the fragmentation of that coalition, and with the current divisions among its principals, we have fallen into stasis, if not into decadence. Bernard Malamud's Levenspiel the landlord would like to be rid of his two troublesome tenants. I have no solutions to offer. But, eighteen years later, I want to say with Malamud: Mercy, Mercy, Mercy, Mercy, Mercy, Mercy, Mercy, Mercy, Mercy, Mercy.

19 I want to keep saying it to all my friends, and to all my students, until we are strong enough to put a period to this thing.

Questions for Analysis

1. What key characteristics and experiences have operated to create bonds as well as tensions between African Americans and Jews in America? Why have Jewish people had less difficulty with racism in America than African-American people?
2. McPherson sees the Six Day War of 1967 as a parting of the ways for African Americans and Jewish Americans. How does McPherson see Jewish identification with Israel and African-American identification with emerging Third-World nations causing tension?
3. In Paragraphs 10 and 11, McPherson discusses the rise of Black Nationalism as it relates to the ''old civil rights'' movement led by Martin Luther King, Jr. To which group would McPherson give allegiance? Why? Why does he suggest Black Nationalism became popular?
4. Paragraph 15 of McPherson's essay is one sentence: ''I have no solutions [to tensions between African Americans and Jews] to offer beyond my feeling that we should begin talking with each other again.'' What purpose and argument do you see in the four paragraphs that follow Paragraph 15?
5. Much of McPherson's essay is a history lesson that focuses on African American and Jews in this country, especially since the 1960s. Like Steele, he is arguing that knowledge can ''point'' to actions. How can this knowledge of history help African Americans, Jews, and whites get beyond racial tensions?

Lance Morrow

Manhood and the Power of *Glory*

(1990)

Lance Morrow (b. 1939) is a contributing editor for *Time* magazine, where this review of the movie *Glory* appeared in February 1990. You will find other essays by Morrow in this anthology.

1 The movie *Glory* is, as the historian James M. McPherson has written, the most powerful and historically accurate film ever made about the American Civil War. But *Glory,* which tells the story of one of the war's first black regiments, has deeper meaning. The movie addresses the most profound theme of race in America in 1990. *Glory* is about black manhood and responsibility.

2 The worst problems of the black underclass today—young black men murdering other young black men; young black males fathering children of females who are virtually children themselves; young blacks lost to crack and heroin—all connect directly to black manhood and responsibility.

3 Perhaps Marion Barry, Washington's mayor, and Benjamin Hooks, executive director of the National Association for the Advancement of Colored People, should celebrate Black History Month by watching *Glory.* When Barry was arrested for cocaine possession last month, Hooks' most visible reaction was that the mayor had been the victim of a plot by law enforcement to persecute black elected officials. Presumably, the mayor of the nation's capital (not exactly an unemployed ghetto youth, but, absurdly, a role model for unemployed ghetto youths) is not responsible for being in a hotel room with a fashion model, smoking crack. A white conspiracy must have put a pistol to his head and made him do it. Hooks' reaction harmonized with something the late Whitney Young said 23 years ago. Young, then the head of the Urban League, told white leaders, "You've got to give us some victories." But if a victory is "given," it is not a victory. It is a dole.

4 The freemen and runaway slaves of the 54th Massachusetts Infantry regiment were not given anything in 1863; certainly not victory. The blacks of the 54th were actual men who died actual deaths in a redemptive violence that they sought. The lesson that *Glory* teaches—and it is finding an audience—is this: it was not the Great White Paternalist alone who freed the slaves and made them American citizens. It was also blacks who freed themselves. These were the blacks who enlisted, trained, suffered, endured condescension and insult, disciplined themselves, fought for the right to fight and the opportunity to die in the pursuit of their freedom and manhood.

AUTHOR'S NOTE: James Munro McPherson, Professor of American History at Princeton University, has written extensively on the plight and activities of African Americans during the nineteenth century, especially during the Civil War and Reconstruction.

5 On July 18, 1863, the blacks of the 54th Massachusetts led a virtually suicidal assault upon Fort Wagner, a massive Confederate earthwork guarding the approach to Charleston, S.C., harbor. At a critical moment in *Glory's* version of the attack, Trip, the runaway slave-soldier played by Denzel Washington, seizes the American flag and runs forward with it to his death. His death says this: "I did not want your white man's flag; earlier I refused the "honor" of carrying it. But I will do it now, dying with other black men, because, understand me, we are citizens, we are Americans, not white Americans, but black Americans . . . but Americans!" In that historical proto-moment, at the instant of death, blacks become, incontrovertibly, Americans. They won it. It was—is—theirs.

6 Every generation forges its own conscience. *Glory* reaffirms an older, persistent moral theme in the black community that in the past 25 years seemed to go out of fashion, at least at the leadership level of the civil rights movement: self-determination, responsibility. This sterner theme, developed well before emancipation and repeated by Frederick Douglass, Booker T. Washington, Martin Luther King, Jr. and generation after generation of struggling black fathers and mothers, instructed the antidote to racism is excellence.

7 But after the Great Society, the emphasis on dignity, struggle and pride in accomplishment was replaced in the rhetoric of some black leaders by a toxic seepage of self-pity, of the victim theme. Passivity, grievance and denial became the psychic orthodoxy. The culture of victimization came to replicate in an eerie way the configurations of slave days—the Government functioning as benevolent slave master, dispenser of all things. Many blacks were trapped in ghettos as surely and hopelessly as slaves on plantations. Perhaps civil rights organizations, designed to battle discrimination and hardening over the years into institutional mind-sets, could not adjust to new realities and needs after the structure of Jim Crow had been torn down.

8 At worst, the Great Society turned the leaders into petitioners, even while thousands upon thousands of working-class blacks toiled in the hardest, dirtiest jobs rather than accept welfare.

9 Those who suggest that the solution to black problems lies in the minds and wills of blacks are always accused of blaming the victims. But that is a futile line. Forget blame. Presumably, black America long since abandoned the delusion (if it ever harbored it) that white America was going to ride to its rescue. The only authentic black fulfillment will be achieved by blacks.

10 Jesse Jackson is one black leader who over the years has consistently preached self-help. Now he warns, "Our failure to become introspective and responsible takes away our moral authority." Nelson Mandela worked the same vein last week: "All students must return to school and learn." The lesson of *Glory,* proceeding out of black history, is that blacks are not powerless in the face of racism or poverty. The battles fought and won by earlier generations of blacks were immensely more difficult than those that face most blacks today.

11 Once, in 1961, Martin Luther King, Jr. told some black college students about the Aristotelian bigot. This bigot, said King, constructed a syllogism: All men are made in the image of God; God, as everyone knows, is not a Negro; therefore, the Negro is not

a man. The black soldiers of the 54th Massachusetts, and 180,000 other blacks who served in the Civil War, took that syllogism and burned it to ashes.

Questions for Analysis

1. What is the problem Morrow sees within what he calls the African-American ''underclass'' today? What is the problem he sees in some African-American leaders?
2. What does Morrow see as the connection between the movie *Glory*—a movie about an African-American regiment in the Civil War—and contemporary racial issues?
3. In Paragraph 7, Morrow speaks of a shift in rhetoric that has occurred between the decade of the 1960s and today. What characterizes that shift? Would Shelby Steele agree with Morrow's assessment? How might that shift be the result of civil rights and Great Society institutions?
4. What is the overall argument of Morrow's essay? How effectively does he support it? Explain. How might one of the African-American leaders he has in mind—he mentions Benjamin Hooks, for example—respond to his criticism?

Benjamin L. Hooks

The Broader Issue of the Barry Case

(1990)

Benjamin L. Hooks (b. 1925) is a former Executive Director of the National Association for the Advancement of Colored People (NAACP). This letter appeared in the July 22, 1990 issue of *The Washington Post.*

1 For some, it is a relatively simple matter to determine the guilt or innocence of Mayor Marion S. Barry Jr. Indeed, there are persons all over Washington and throughout the nation who are absolutely and adamantly convinced of the outcome Barry's trial should have. For me, however, the trial's result is less significant than are some of the troubling issues raised by the case.

2 Because I have had the temerity to speak on those issues, I have been subjected to a barrage of inflammatory personal attacks. I have been branded a conspiracy-mongering demagogue, a paranoid, a spreader of ''falsehood,'' and charged with engaging in ''imitative incitement,'' to cite a few of the terms writers more interested in heat than light have used.

3 My attempt to defend not Barry, but our Anglo-American concepts of judicial fairness and restraint in the application of the state's awesome power against the citizen—to defend, in short, the Constitution, the Bill of Rights and truth, justice and the American way—has been met with ferocious attacks from an intellectual firing squad directing its fire against one who does not have the press's power to reply.

4 Most of these critics take exception to what they understand me to have said in my keynote address to the 81st annual convention of the NAACP in Los Angeles. I do not recall a single one of these attackers having attended the convention. Not one has sought an interview for elaboration or clarification or even a copy or recording of the speech.

5 In fact, that speech ran to more than 5,000 words and dealt with a number of issues: recent Supreme Court decisions that have gutted affirmative action, the push to get the Civil Rights Act of 1990 enacted, the need for heightened black self-help efforts, the S&L scandal—and the disproportionate and selective prosecution of black elected officials. A mere 38 words dealt indirectly with the Barry situation. Just how those 38 words could become such an albatross, I will never understand.

6 Here are some points from that speech that you may not have read about:

- "I'm calling today for a moratorium on excuses. I challenge black America—all of us to set aside our alibis."
- "We must take responsibility for our own lives; for our own destiny. We must not wallow in self-pity and blame someone else . . ."
- "We black Americans must rebuild the altars of strong family support, renovate community pride and unity, turn to each other and not against each other, say 'no' to dope and 'yes' to hope and renounce the insidious plea of dope dealers."
- "We must teach our young people that having babies without a job, education or marriage is not a sign of maturity, but a manifestation of irresponsibility . . ."

7 You may not know I said those things. If you only read sensation-seeking news accounts or inflammatory commentaries, you would believe that I and other black leaders spend our time in "the cultivation of the aura of victimization and the denunciation of victimizers," to quote one of my detractors.

8 At the same time, I apologize not one whit for demanding that the larger society meet its responsibilities. Government and the private sector have a clear duty to redress the unfair balance that their policies of discrimination against and exclusion of African-Americans have helped to create and sustain.

9 To return to Mayor Barry: Let me make it clear that I have expressed no opinion as to his guilt or innocence other than to remind Americans, from the perspective of one who has spent a lifetime in the law, that our legal system presumes the innocence of every accused person until guilt is established in court. Marion Barry's guilt or innocence will be decided, as it should be, by a jury.

10 For the record, should anyone care for the truth: At no time, in no forum, have I condoned drug use by Marion Barry or anyone else. At no time have I "defended"

Marion Barry. If the mayor is guilty, he must lie in the bed he made and accept his punishment.

11 However, after years as a public defender and criminal court judge, I understand that if prosecutors set out to ''get'' someone, they usually succeed in securing an indictment. I have told journalists that there exists among black Americans a perception that black elected officials are subjected to more intense scrutiny and greater harassment than are others. That feeling goes back at least 30 years to the days of Rep. Adam Clayton Powell (D-N.Y.). My critics, who use the Barry case to attempt to disprove any allegations of racism, are strangely silent about the way in which Andrew Young was put through the wringer or on the tribulations of Birmingham Mayor Richard Arrington.

12 The Barry case has been marked throughout its almost decade-long history by the expenditure of inordinate amounts of time, money and energy in the search for wrongdoing on Barry's part. Even if, as has been suggested, the government spent only $4 million on this investigation, that figure seems excessive in the pursuit of recreational drug abuse, which is the essence of the government's case.

13 I believe that the government's priorities have been out of kilter, and the money, time and energy invested in the Barry case have been disproportionate, especially in light of the government's claim at one point that it lacked resources to pursue and prosecute the connivers and thieves responsible for the $500-billion rip-off of the taxpayers in the savings and loan scandal, a fiasco that will cost every American thousands of dollars.

14 I challenge prosecutors to explain by what reasoning they decided to hunt this plagued man. There are in Washington alone, not to mention the rest of the nation, thousands of mid-level drug dealers and other traffickers. How can the government justify the expenditure of millions to catch one user, while the streets of the capital have become a drug bazaar and a killing ground?

15 Well, it is argued, Mayor Barry is a person of celebrity, a role model. So are the many rock singers, film actors, and athletes who in recent years have confessed drug use. Few if any such persons have been pursued and prosecuted as has Barry.

16 Even conceding that Barry's faults are many and troubling, anyone would be a bad role model who has been demonized as he has been through leaks from grand juries and investigative authorities. No hint or whisper of wrong doing by Marion Barry seems to have gone unshared with a press corps avid for such news.

17 Prosecutors have discretion in the crimes and offenders they will prosecute. How does the U.S. attorney's office justify its zealous pursuit of this one alleged user? Was it because prosecutors, try as they would, were unable to pin charges of official corruption—graft and abuse of office—on Barry and then took an ''any-stick-to-beat-a-dog'' approach?

18 There also is the question of the ''sting'' at the Vista Hotel. I and others have questioned the propriety of using a sexual lure in the operation. That is a tactic far better suited to police-state societies than to open and above-board law enforcement. I share the view expressed long ago by Justice Oliver Wendell Holmes:

19 "I think it less evil that some criminals should escape than that the government should play an ignoble part."

20 There is a moment in Robert Bolt's drama "A Man for All Seasons" when Thomas More asks his son-in-law, "Would you cut a great road through the law to get at the devil? Suppose the devil turned round on you, where would you flee, all the laws being flat? I'd give the devil benefit of law for my own safety's sake."

21 The thoughts are a tribute to the rule of law. That is what the NAACP has sought for 81 years.

22 The simple issue is Marion Barry and whether he used drugs and lied about the fact. A jury will decide that point. The broader and more complex issues are governmental priorities, the wisdom of allocating badly needed resources in the pursuit of one addict, and government tactics—the depths to which government will stoop—to conquer and catch whom they want.

23 All black Americans want is justice and equity, which America has not always given during 240 years of slavery and more than 100 years of Jim Crow. America would make a grave mistake, and a sad one, to assume that black America will stand idly by and let James Crow, Esquire, continue his grandfather's legacy in a more subtle and crafty way.

Questions for Analysis

1. Hooks is clearly responding to several specific criticisms in this letter. What are the major criticisms he is trying to counter? How successful is he at countering each criticism?
2. In Paragraph 7, Hooks might be responding to, among others, Lance Morrow. (See subsection's this previous essay by Morrow, Paragraph 3.) Does Hooks convince you that his message is more than "the cultivation of the aura of victimization"?
3. Is the point Hooks makes about Barry's treatment clear and well-supported?
4. How do you think Shelby Steele would respond to Hooks's essay? With what would he agree? With what would he disagree?

Alice Walker

Everyday Use

(1973)

For Your Grandmama

A native of Georgia educated at Sarah Lawrence College, Alice Walker (b. 1944) was active in the civil-rights movement and served as a case worker for the New York City welfare department before starting a career as a teacher of creative writing and African-American literature. Her best-known work is *The Color Purple* (1982), a novel that not only won both the Pulitzer Prize and the American Book Award, but also became the basis for a popular movie. "Everyday Use" is reprinted from her volume *In Love and Trouble.*

1 I will wait for her in the yard that Maggie and I made so clean and wavy yesterday afternoon. A yard like this is more comfortable than most people know. It is not just a yard. It is like an extended living room. When the hard clay is swept clean as a floor and the fine sand around the edges lined with tiny, irregular grooves, anyone can come and sit and look up into the elm tree and wait for the breezes that never come inside the house.

2 Maggie will be nervous until after her sister goes: she will stand hopelessly in corners, homely and ashamed of the burn scars down her arms and legs, eying her sister with a mixture of envy and awe. She thinks her sister has held life always in the palm of one hand, that "no" is a word the world never learned to say to her.

3 You've no doubt seen those TV shows where the child who has "made it" is confronted, as a surprise, by her own mother and father, tottering in weakly from backstage. (A pleasant surprise, of course: What would they do if parent and child came on the show only to curse out and insult each other?) On TV mother and child embrace and smile into each other's faces. Sometimes the mother and father weep, the child wraps them in her arms and leans across the table to tell how she would not have made it without their help. I have seen these programs.

4 Sometimes I dream a dream in which Dee and I are suddenly brought together on a TV program of this sort. Out of a dark and soft-seated limousine I am ushered into a bright room filled with many people. There I meet a smiling, gray, sporty man like Johnny Carson who shakes my hand and tells me what a fine girl I have. Then we are on the stage and Dee is embracing me with tears in her eyes. She pins on my dress a large orchid, even though she has told me once that she thinks orchids are tacky flowers.

5 In real life I am a large, big-boned woman with rough, man-working hands. In the winter I wear flannel nightgowns to bed and overalls during the day. I can kill and clean a hog as mercilessly as a man. My fat keeps me hot in zero weather. I can work outside all day, breaking ice to get water for washing; I can eat pork liver cooked over the open fire minutes after it comes steaming from the hog. One winter I knocked a bull calf

straight in the brain between the eyes with a sledge hammer and had the meat hung up to chill before nightfall. But of course all this does not show on television. I am the way my daughter would want me to be: a hundred pounds lighter, my skin like an uncooked barley pancake. My hair glistens in the hot bright lights. Johnny Carson has much to do to keep up with my quick and witty tongue.

6 But that is a mistake. I know even before I wake up. Who ever knew a Johnson with a quick tongue? Who can even imagine me looking a strange white man in the eye? It seems to me I have talked to them always with one foot raised in flight, with my head turned in whichever way is farthest from them. Dee, though. She would always look anyone in the eye. Hesitation was no part of her nature.

7 "How do I look, Mama?" Maggie says, showing just enough of her thin body enveloped in pink skirt and red blouse for me to know she's there, almost hidden by the door.

8 "Come out into the yard," I say.

9 Have you ever seen a lame animal, perhaps a dog run over by some careless person rich enough to own a car, sidle up to someone who is ignorant enough to be kind to him? That is the way my Maggie walks. She has been like this, chin on chest, eyes on ground, feet in shuffle, ever since the fire that burned the other house to the ground.

10 Dee is lighter than Maggie, with nicer hair and a fuller figure. She's a woman now, though sometimes I forget. How long ago was it that the other house burned? Ten, twelve years? Sometimes I can still hear the flames and feel Maggie's arms sticking to me, her hair smoking and her dress falling off her in little black papery flakes. Her eyes seemed stretched open, blazed open by the flames reflected in them. And Dee. I see her standing off under the sweet gum tree she used to dig gum out of; a look of concentration on her face as she watched the last dingy gray board of the house fall in toward the red-hot brick chimney. Why don't you do a dance around the ashes? I'd wanted to ask her. She had hated the house that much.

11 I used to think she hated Maggie, too. But that was before we raised the money, the church and me, to send her to Augusta to school. She used to read to us without pity; forcing words, lies, other folks' habits, whole lives upon us two, sitting trapped and ignorant underneath her voice. She washed us in a river of make-believe, burned us with a lot of knowledge we didn't necessarily need to know. Pressed us to her with the serious way she read, to shove us away at just the moment, like dimwits, we seemed about to understand.

12 Dee wanted nice things. A yellow organdy dress to wear to her graduation from high school; black pumps to match a green suit she'd made from an old suit somebody gave me. She was determined to stare down any disaster in her efforts. Her eyelids would not flicker for minutes at a time. Often I fought off the temptation to shake her. At sixteen she had a style of her own: and knew what style was.

13 I never had an education myself. After second grade the school was closed down. Don't ask me why: in 1927 colored asked fewer questions than they do now. Sometimes Maggie reads to me. She stumbles along good-naturedly but can't see well. She knows

she is not bright. Like good looks and money, quickness passed her by. She will marry John Thomas (who has mossy teeth in an earnest face) and then I'll be free to sit here and I guess just sing church songs to myself. Although I never was a good singer. Never could carry a tune. I was always better at a man's job. I used to love to milk till I was hooked[1] in the side in '49. Cows are soothing and slow and don't bother you, unless you try to milk them the wrong way.

14 I have deliberately turned my back on the house. It is three rooms, just like the one that burned, except the roof is tin; they don't make shingle roofs any more. There are no real windows, just some holes cut in the sides, like the portholes in a ship, but not round and not square, with rawhide holding the shutters up on the outside. This house is in a pasture, too, like the other one. No doubt when Dee sees it she will want to tear it down. She wrote me once that no matter where we "choose" to live, she will manage to come see us. But she will never bring her friends. Maggie and I thought about this and Maggie asked me, "Mama, when did Dee ever *have* any friends?"

15 She had a few. Furtive boys in pink shirts hanging about on washday after school. Nervous girls who never laughed. Impressed with her they worshiped the well-turned phrase, the cute shape, the scalding humor that erupted like bubbles in lye. She read to them.

16 When she was courting Jimmy T she didn't have much time to pay to us, but turned all her faultfinding power on him. He *flew* to marry a cheap city girl from a family of ignorant flashy people. She hardly had time to recompose herself.

17 When she comes I will meet—but there they are!

18 Maggie attempts to make a dash for the house, in her shuffling way, but I stay her with my hand. "Come back here," I say. And she stops and tries to dig a well in the sand with her toe.

19 It is hard to see them clearly through the strong sun. But even the first glimpse of leg out of the car tells me it is Dee. Her feet were always neat-looking, as if God himself had shaped them with a certain style. From the other side of the car comes a short, stocky man. Hair is all over his head a foot long and hanging from his chin like a kinky mule tail. I hear Maggie suck in her breath. "Uhnnnh," is what it sounds like. Like when you see the wriggling end of a snake just in front of your foot on the road. "Uhnnnh."

20 Dee next. A dress down to the ground, in this hot weather. A dress so loud it hurts my eyes. There are yellows and oranges enough to throw back the light of the sun. I feel my whole face warming from the heat waves it throws out. Earrings gold, too, and hanging down to her shoulders. Bracelets dangling and making noises when she moves her arm up to shake the folds of the dress out of her armpits. The dress is loose and flows, and as she walks closer, I like it. I hear Maggie go "Uhnnnh" again. It is her sister's hair. It stands straight up like the wool on a sheep. It is black as night and

AUTHOR'S NOTE: "Hooked" here means to be pierced by a cow's horn.

around the edges are two long pigtails that rope about like small lizards disappearing behind her ears.

21 “Wa-su-zo-Tean-o!” she says, coming on in that gliding way the dress makes her move. The short stocky fellow with the hair to his navel is all grinning and he follows up with “Asalamalakim,[2] my mother and sister!” He moves to hug Maggie but she falls back, right up against the back of my chair. I feel her trembling there and when I look up I see the perspiration falling off her chin.

22 “Don't get up,” says Dee. Since I am stout it takes something of a push. You can see me trying to move a second or two before I make it. She turns, showing white heels through her sandals, and goes back to the car. Out she peeks next with a Polaroid. She stoops down quickly and lines up picture after picture of me sitting there in front of the house with Maggie cowering behind me. She never takes a shot without making sure the house is included. When a cow comes nibbling around the edge of the yard she snaps it and me and Maggie *and* the house. Then she puts the Polaroid in the back seat of the car, and comes up and kisses me on the forehead.

23 Meanwhile Asalamalakim is going through motions with Maggie's hand. Maggie's hand is as limp as a fish, and probably as cold, despite the sweat, and she keeps trying to pull it back. It looks like Asalamalakim wants to shake hands but wants to do it fancy. Or maybe he don't know how people shake hands. Anyhow, he soon gives up on Maggie.

24 “Well,” I say. “Dee.”

25 “No, Mama,” she says. “Not ‘Dee,’ Wangero Leewanika Kemanjo!”

26 “What happened to ‘Dee’?” I wanted to know.

27 “She's dead,” Wangero said. “I couldn't bear it any longer, being named after the people who oppress me.”

28 “You know as well as me you was named after your aunt Dicie,” I said. Dicie is my sister. She named Dee. We called her “Big Dee” after Dee was born.

29 “But who was *she* named after?” asked Wangero.

30 “I guess after Grandma Dee,” I said.

31 “And who was she named after?” asked Wangero.

32 “Her mother,” I said, and saw Wangero was getting tired. “That's about as far back as I can trace it,” I said. Though, in fact, I probably could have carried it back beyond the Civil War through the branches.

33 “Well,” said Asalamalakim, “there you are.”

34 “Uhnnnh,” I heard Maggie say.

35 “There I was not,” I said, “before ‘Dicie’ cropped up in our family, so why should I try to trace it that far back?”

36 He just stood there grinning, looking down on me like somebody inspecting a Model A car. Every once in a while he and Wangero sent eye signals over my head.

37 “How do you pronounce this name?” I asked.

AUTHOR'S NOTE: “Asalamalakim” and “Wa-su-zo-Tean-o” are both phonetic representations of greetings used in African dialects.

38 "You don't have to call me by it if you don't want to," said Wangero.

39 "Why shouldn't I?" I asked. "If that's what you want us to call you, we'll call you."

40 "I know it might sound awkward at first," said Wangero.

41 "I'll get used to it," I said. "Ream it out again."

42 Well, soon we got the name out of the way. Asalamalakim had a name twice as long and three times as hard. After I tripped over it two or three times he told me to just call him Hakim-a-barber. I wanted to ask him was he a barber, but I didn't really think he was, so I didn't ask.

43 "You must belong to those beef-cattle peoples down the road," I said. They said "Asalamalakim" when they met you, too, but they didn't shake hands. Always too busy: feeding the cattle, fixing the fences, putting up salt lick shelters, throwing down hay. When the white folks poisoned some of the herd the men stayed up all night with rifles in their hands. I walked a mile and a half just to see the sight.

44 Hakim-a-barber said, "I accept some of their doctrines, but farming and raising cattle is not my style." (They didn't tell me, and I didn't ask, whether Wangero (Dee) had really gone and married him.)

45 We sat down to eat and right away he said he didn't eat collards and pork was unclean. Wangero, though, went on through the chitlins and corn bread, the greens and everything else. She talked a blue streak over the sweet potatoes. Everything delighted her. Even the fact that we still used the benches her daddy made for the table when we couldn't afford to buy chairs.

46 "Oh, Mama!" she cried. Then turned to Hakim-a-barber. "I never knew how lovely these benches are. You can feel the rump prints," she said, running her hands underneath her and along the bench. Then she gave a sigh and her hand closed over Grandma Dee's butter dish. "That's it!" she said. "I knew there was something I wanted to ask you if I could have." She jumped up from the table and went over in the corner where the churn stood, the milk in it clabber by now. She looked at the churn and looked at it.

47 "This churn top is what I need," she said. "Didn't Uncle Buddy whittle it out of a tree you all used to have?"

48 "Yes," I said.

49 "Uh huh," she said happily. "And I want the dasher, too."

50 "Uncle Buddy whittle that, too?" asked the barber.

51 Dee (Wangero) looked up at me.

52 "Aunt Dee's first husband whittled the dash," said Maggie so low you almost couldn't hear her. "His name was Henry, but they called him Stash."

53 "Maggie's brain is like an elephant's," Wangero said, laughing. "I can use the churn top as a centerpiece for the alcove table," she said, sliding a plate over the churn, "and I'll think of something artistic to do with the dasher."

54 When she finished wrapping the dasher the handle stuck out. I took it for a moment in my hands. You didn't even have to look close to see where hands pushing the dasher up and down to make butter had left a kind of sink in the wood. In fact, there were a

lot of small sinks; you could see where thumbs and fingers had sunk into the wood. It was beautiful light yellow wood, from a tree that grew in the yard where Big Dee and Stash had lived.

55 After dinner Dee (Wangero) went to the trunk at the foot of my bed and started rifling through it. Maggie hung back in the kitchen over the dishpan. Out came Wangero with two quilts. They had been pieced by Grandma Dee and then Big Dee and me had hung them on the quilt frames on the front porch and quilted them. One was in the Lone Star pattern. The other was Walk Around the Mountain. In both of them were scraps of dresses Grandma Dee had worn fifty and more years ago. Bits and pieces of Grandpa Jarrell's Paisley shirts. And one teeny faded blue piece, about the size of a penny matchbox, that was from Great Grandpa Ezra's uniform that he wore in the Civil War.

56 “Mama,” Wangero said sweet as a bird. “Can I have these old quilts?”

57 I heard something fall in the kitchen, and a minute later the kitchen door slammed.

58 “Why don't you take one or two of the others?” I asked. “These old things was just done by me and Big Dee from some tops your grandma pieced before she died.”

59 “No,” said Wangero. “I don't want those. They are stitched around the borders by machine.”

60 “That'll make them last better,” I said.

61 “That's not the point,” said Wangero. “These are all pieces of dresses Grandma used to wear. She did all this stitching by hand. Imagine!” She held the quilts securely in her arms, stroking them.

62 “Some of the pieces, like those lavender ones, come from old clothes her mother handed down to her,” I said, moving up to touch the quilts. Dee (Wangero) moved back just enough so that I couldn't reach the quilts. They already belonged to her.

63 “Imagine!” she breathed again, clutching them closely to her bosom.

64 “The truth is,” I said, “I promised to give them quilts to Maggie, for when she marries John Thomas.”

65 She gasped like a bee had stung her.

66 “Maggie can't appreciate these quilts!” she said. “She'd probably be backward enough to put them to everyday use.”

67 “I reckon she would,” I said. “God knows I been saving 'em for long enough with nobody using 'em. I hope she will!” I didn't want to bring up how I had offered Dee (Wangero) a quilt when she went away to college. Then she had told me they were old-fashioned, out of style.

68 “But they're *priceless*!” she was saying now, furiously; for she has a temper. “Maggie would put them on the bed and in five years they'd be in rags. Less than that!”
“She can always make some more,” I said. “Maggie knows how to quilt.”

69 Dee (Wangero) looked at me with hatred. “You just will not understand. The point is these quilts, *these* quilts!”

70 “Well,” I said, stumped. “What would *you* do with them?”

71 “Hang them,” she said. As if that was the only thing you *could* do with quilts.

72 Maggie by now was standing in the door. I could almost hear the sound her feet made as they scraped over each other.

73 "She can have them, Mama," she said, like somebody used to never winning anything, or having anything reserved for her. "I can 'member Grandma Dee without the quilts."

74 I looked at her hard. She had filled her bottom lip with checkerberry snuff and it gave her face a kind of dopey, hangdog look. It was Grandma Dee and Big Dee who taught her how to quilt herself. She stood there with her scarred hands hidden in the folds of her skirt. She looked at her sister with something like fear but she wasn't mad at her. This was Maggie's portion. This was the way she knew God to work.

75 When I looked at her like that something hit me in the top of my head and ran down to the soles of my feet. Just like when I'm in church and the spirit of God touches me and I get happy and shout. I did something I never had done before: hugged Maggie to me, then dragged her on into the room, snatched the quilts out of Miss Wangero's hands and dumped them into Maggie's lap. Maggie just sat there on my bed with her mouth open.

76 "Take one or two of the others," I said to Dee.

77 But she turned without a word and went out to Hakim-a-barber.

78 "You just don't understand," she said, as Maggie and I came out to the car.

79 "What don't I understand?" I wanted to know.

80 "Your heritage," she said. And then she turned to Maggie, kissed her, and said, "You ought to try to make something of yourself, too, Maggie. It's really a new day for us. But from the way you and Mama still live you'd never know it."

81 She put on some sunglasses that hid everything above the tip of her nose and her chin.

82 Maggie smiled; maybe at the sunglasses. But a real smile, not scared. After we watched the car dust settle I asked Maggie to bring me a dip of snuff. And then the two of us sat there just enjoying, until it was time to go in the house and go to bed.

Questions for Analysis

1. Walker reveals Mama's character through details about her past life, her physical appearance, and her physical abilities. Which of these details do you find most significant? Why is it important for Walker to establish Mama's character?
2. Central to the story are several important contrasts. The contrast between Maggie and Dee (Wangero) and how they would use the quilts is the most obvious. But also consider the contrast between Dee and Wangero. How do these contrasts help Walker make her point?
3. Most of us come away from the story feeling sympathy for Mama and Maggie. Why? Why do we feel less sympathy for Dee (Wangero)?

4. Why has Dee changed her name and lifestyle? What has she gained? What has she lost? In what ways is Wangero very much like the old Dee?
5. How does this story illustrate some of the problems discussed by Shelby Steele and James McPherson?

Joseph Lelyveld

The Spiritual and Political Pilgrimage of Beyers Naudé

(1985)

Joseph Lelyveld, (b. 1937) is a *New York Times* correspondent who has been posted in London, the United States, India, Hong Kong, and South Africa (twice). Following his last experience in South Africa, he wrote *Move Your Shadow: South Africa, Black and White,* a book that has received international praise as well as a Pulitzer Prize. "The Spiritual and Political Pilgrimage of Beyers Naudé" (my title) is an excerpt from that book.

1 Having just started parish work in the poorest of Durban's townships, Biko's heir said he didn't side with any one of the political sects fighting apartheid but with all of them. ''I recognize all good as my pursuit,'' he explained, laughing again from the chest, ''not just so-and-so's good.'' For that very reason there were some who now counted him as lost to ''the movement.''

2 In the same week that he had his last serious conversation with his friend Malusi Mpumlwana, who was then at the start of his own pilgrimage to the priesthood, Steve Biko had another long conversation with a white pastor, whose spiritual and political pilgrimage had been perhaps the most remarkable any South African had taken. The young black man, who had given himself to political struggle, talked to Biko about ''the role of God.'' The Reverend Christiaan Frederick Beyers Naudé, who was then in his seventh decade and only a few months away from being silenced by a banning order, had talked politics rather than theology. Near the end of an arduous quest, he had come to believe that for a white South African, especially an Afrikaner, doing God's will meant supporting black political initiatives. There is no way of knowing if Biko had time to reflect on the contrast, but a kind of parallax was occurring in his orbit. Where the young black was now inclined to seek a political fulfillment through religion, the older white sought a spiritual fulfillment through politics. Specifically Beyers Naudé was preoccupied then by the question of what could be done to harness the fractious black movements into something like a unified force.

3 The trajectory he had traveled to reach this point, where he was beyond any doubt a traitor and heretic in the eyes of most Afrikaners, had carried Beyers Naudé from one

end of the South African political firmament to the other. If he were to be compared to any contemporary figure of conscience, it would have to be the dissident Soviet physicist Andrei Sakharov. Naudé's apostasy, like Sakharov's, was especially galling and unforgivable because it had occurred at the very heart of a power elite. Once he had been the most highly regarded Afrikaner clergyman of his generation; any position his church or people had to offer could have been within his reach. Now, or so the top security officials contended, he was an agent of the underground. That charge had never been proved, but like the charge that Sakharov had illicit ties with the Americans, it could not be dismissed as altogether beyond belief. Contained within the smear was a germ of plausibility, for Beyers Naudé had unquestionably aligned himself with a cause most Afrikaners viewed as revolutionary. Not content to be merely a voice of conscience, he had crossed the invisible line that separates liberals from radicals in the eyes of most whites: He had sided with blacks. It did no good to argue that he was still more accurately described as a Calvinist than a Marxist, that he explained himself in terms of biblical injunctions and theological concepts of justice. Where he came from, a white who believed in black power had to be at least a Communist, if he was not even more depraved.

4 Yet the man was more remarkable than the story of his life. It wasn't only the distance he had traveled but his readiness at every stage to go on traveling, to find some new injunction in any new set of circumstances, that set him apart. From the outside it could appear as if his moral machinery were put together without a brake, as if the accelerator had got stuck, or, as if, in imbibing the stern sense of duty on which Afrikaners are supposed to be reared, he had overdosed. If that were all, if he had merely followed the dictates of his conscience, subjecting the primordial value of Afrikaner survival to earnest theological scrutiny, his entire journey could have been summed up in a sermon, and he would today be seen as an example, not as a threat. His principles only began the process of his detachment from his Afrikaner patriarchy. What did him in was his openness to experience, his readiness to step across the racial barrier and see for himself what it was really like over there.

5 Initially he had no appetite for confrontation or rebellion; when he was breaking with his people on issues they regarded as fundamental, he found ways to sidestep them in his preaching. He could tailor principles, like most preachers, but he could not deny facts. Starting in late middle age, he taught himself to embrace them. The urgency came from this openness; the more he knew, the more he felt was demanded of him. Even after he had been placed under a banning order and confined to a single district, he managed to travel deeper into the heart of South Africa than practically any other white, traveling with zest as well as zeal. Ostracized by Afrikaners, he sought a wider community, and yet, even after leaving his church so he could worship with blacks, he never ceased to be an Afrikaner dominee in his unfailing courtesy and pastoral manner, even in his grooming. The safari suits he wore in summer always looked freshly pressed; his hair always was neatly combed and never, it seemed, in need of cutting. His days were crammed with appointments, but he never allowed himself to seem rushed or distracted. Some worried that he was politically naïve or reckless; none could question

his courage. Yet whenever I spent an hour or two in his company, it was not so much his personal history or righteousness that struck me as his directness, his ability to fasten his attention on a person or issue. Being in politics, a risky branch of moral theology, especially for one who was under heavy surveillance, he could not afford to be entirely guileless. But he had overcome patriarchal aloofness, unbending and mellowing even as he became more intense. "You can always find something to laugh about in this country," he said to me once, "and you can always, always cry."

6 Beyers Naudé doesn't mention his father, a severe and distant figure in the patriarchal mode, as a model for the life he has led. But it is hard not to notice a rough symmetry between the journeys of father and son, although they traveled in opposite directions politically. The elder Naudé was never a man for easy compromises. Jozua François Naudé was one of only six out of sixty delegates who refused at the peace conference that ended the Boer War to affix their signatures to a treaty that gave the losing side a chance to win the peace under the Union Jack and the distant suzerainty of the British crown. In the face of certain defeat, he would have preferred to go on fighting. He then became a dominee but still wasn't resigned to the loss of Afrikaner sovereignty when, thirteen years later, in 1915, the fourth of his eight children and second son was born and named after another uncompromising Afrikaner. General C. F. Beyers, a Boer War hero, had died the year before in a brief rebellion provoked by the decision of some of his old comrades, who now held authority in Pretoria, to take South Africa into the World War on Britain's side. In the same period Jozua Naudé became one of the half dozen founders of a secret society that swore an oath to advance the cause of Afrikaner nationhood and dominance in all spheres of South African life. This was the Broederbond, which slowly amassed influence and power over the next three decades in what outsiders, including many Afrikaners, came to see as a sinister conspiracy. When Beyers Naudé, a half century after the founding of the Broederbond, broke with it to found an organization called the Christian Institute, his initial idea was that an elite group of idealistic Afrikaner clergymen could gradually change the outlook of their people through mutual consultation in private on the issues they faced. The Broederbond was quick to condemn the institute, and eventually it was banned. But different as his aims and methods would become, the son's instinct in searching for a way to return his people to the path of righteousness may have been nearer to that of his father at the outset than he or orthodox Afrikaners would have imagined.

7 So much for symmetry. What is striking about Beyers Naudé's formative years is not the indoctrination he received but his complete insulation from the issues he was later to accept as central to the moral existence of every South African. He has no recollection of hearing his father say anything about blacks. No one told him that blacks were inferior or culturally backward or unfathomably different or destined to play a subservient role. No one explained the reasons for their exclusion from society. All of this went without saying, all of it was there to be absorbed by osmosis. Years later Beyers Naudé discovered that Robert Sobukwe, the university lecturer who founded the Pan-Africanist Congress, was growing up in Graaff Reinet while he was living there in his parents' home. But then Sobukwe, nine years his junior, lived in the dusty African

"location," which Naudé cannot remember having visited. "It never entered my mind," he remarked, reflecting on his life up to the age of thirty, "that blacks were to be seen as a part of South Africa."

8 The issue of race grazed his consciousness for the first time in the form of a small, seemingly negligible question, provoked by the seemingly anomalous presence every Sunday of a handful of elderly coloreds at the rear of his father's church. The elder Naudé, who occasionally preached to a segregated colored congregation, explained that the old coloreds had been members of the white church before the traditional patterns of segregation had been found to be inadequate, before it was deemed necessary, in the interest of preserving the identity of Afrikaners as a white people, to set up an absolute bar to nonwhites' worshiping in the white church. The older coloreds, who had refused to relinquish their membership, were still allowed to sit apart at services, but their deaths would remove the last vestiges of racial laxity and perfect the exclusion of their people. The fact that it had once been a little different would then be conveniently forgotten, so the pattern of absolute separation could be elevated as the traditional way of life. Afrikaners did their duty to coloreds and blacks, the son was taught, by sending them missionaries.

9 That seemed to settle the business of race as far as he was then concerned. At the University of Stellenbosch, where he excelled in Hendrik Verwoerd's social science course, it never preoccupied him. There came another slight flutter of doubt when he started visiting a German mission station in the Cape called Genadendal after becoming engaged to a daughter of one of the missionaries. There coloreds and whites met in one another's homes on the basis of equality, the first such contacts across the color line he had experienced. Until then it had never occurred to him that this was possible; it was as if he had been reared in a teetotaling sect and had now allowed himself to sip a little wine. He was left with the guilty knowledge that it could be done, that there was a contradiction that probably needed some rationalizing between the kind of Christianity on which he had been reared and the kind practiced by his prospective in-laws, but it was nothing he allowed to burden his conscience.

10 To do so would have been to throw a shadow over his future, which seemed so tidily arranged. At the age of twenty-five, when he was serving his first congregation, he was approached in private by some of the elders and invited to join the Broederbond. Twenty-five was the minimum age for membership; the founder's son was right on course as one of the elect. The all-male monthly meetings of his "circle," or cell, became the main source of intellectual stimulation and fellowship in his life outside the church; here, too, he felt himself to be engaged in a sacred enterprise. Then, at thirty, he was called to a congregation near Pretoria, which meant moving to the Transvaal from the Cape, where the numerically predominant coloreds had seemed to blend into the landscape. In the Transvaal it was impossible not to notice that there was a huge black community physically present in the white heartland. For the first time, he acknowledged that there was a problem. It was something to think about, he thought—something to think about later.

11 The year 1948 comes, and Beyers Naudé votes for the National party and feels, when it squeaks into power on its apartheid platform, a deep sense of fulfillment tinged only by a filial regret that his dominee father, who died a few months before the election, had not lived to see this realization of his dreams. In the new government's first year, he becomes a minister in the Pretoria congregation that most of the Cabinet members attend, also a chaplain at Pretoria University, where, because even the most carefully indoctrinated students occasionally ask questions, he senses a need for the first time to have some answers on political issues. These he gets at Broederbond meetings, which in the capital now bring him into contact with key officials. If there is any injustice in the land, he feels confident, it is a reflection of man's sinful nature that can be addressed within the framework of apartheid. The vigor and obvious sincerity of his preaching win him a growing reputation, and he moves, with appropriate deference and decorum for one so young, in social circles that include the most powerful figures in the Afrikaner church and state. He is nearly forty before this picture starts to change significantly. Then, as a result of a half-year tour of Europe and North America as an emissary for the Dutch Reformed Church, he wakes up to the fact that his knowledge of what goes on in his own country is riddled with blanks. In Holland and England, Canada and the United States, churchmen ask him about the Defiance Campaign, which the congress movement has been waging. He has heard of it only vaguely and ignored what he has heard, so it is as remote to him as a report of a clash in Sumatra. Names of black leaders such as Albert Lutuli and Z. K. Matthews are mentioned in his presence; he avoids acknowledging, insofar as he can without actually lying, that he has never heard of them. He is asked what he thought of Alan Paton's *Cry, the Beloved Country,* which has had a secure reputation by then throughout the English-speaking world for five years. He confesses that he has heard of neither the author nor his book.

12 The trip teaches him a lesson about his own insularity; it also provokes him to undertake a private study of the biblical, theological, and historical justifications his church has advanced for the South African system. "It was a highly intellectual and academic exercise," he told me. "It had nothing to do with any personal experience." Yet the result is devastating. None of the justifications, he has to acknowledge to himself, can be honestly defended. He then widens his reading, allowing himself the forbidden fruit of studies of apartheid by English speaking writers who frame the issues of inequality and dispossession. Now, in his early forties, he finds himself burdened with an incubus of doubt on his ministerial and social rounds. It is invisible to his congregants, for he confines his preaching to pietistic and evangelical themes. It is even invisible to his wife and children, for he deliberately shields them from it and the problems it would instantly raise for them, should they be similarly infected, in their contacts in the community or at school. Very cautiously he voices some of the questions on his mind to fellow members of the Broederbond, who acknowledge the seriousness of the questions but urge him to be careful not to raise them in the wrong place, at the wrong time. The warning seems superfluous; the thought of voicing his doubts openly has yet to occur to him as a real possibility.

13 "I was afraid," he said. "I just couldn't face it." Then in a period of five years, which brings him to the age of forty-eight and his first experiences as a pariah, reality rapidly catches up with him. Two kinds of history are occurring, public and personal. As Beyers Naudé seeks to reconcile his secular and religious faiths, apartheid gets steadily harsher and more aggressive ideologically as a result of the ascent to power of his old teacher Verwoerd, and as most Afrikaners learn to march in lockstep, the consequences for those who stumble or break ranks on racial issues become clearer and more severe. At first these conspicuous trends are only a small cloud on his horizon, but then his reputation for integrity and his high position in the church—he has become acting moderator of his synod—make him a sounding board for the private anxieties of three white pastors who have been meeting rising resistance to their missionary efforts in black communities as a result of the sufferings imposed by Afrikanerdom's quasi-theocracy. At this point he makes his first misstep on the slippery slope of Christian action. Had he told his colleagues that he was troubled by their testimony, had he prayed with them or even offered to initiate a study group under some respected professor of theology at an Afrikaner seat of learning, Beyers Naudé would probably have satisfied their expectations and preserved the margin of safety his conscience required. Instead, saying he knows there are problems but cannot imagine that conditions are really so bad, he resolves to do the one thing that a shrewder, more self-protective man would avoid at all costs: to go and see for himself. In middle age, for the first time in his life, he enters black townships and the hostels reserved for migrant laborers. For the first time he allows himself to speak to blacks about what it is like to be black in white South Africa. These are not outspoken political people but the deferential, pathetically moderate elders of Dutch Reformed mission churches. Yet once he knows the circumstances of their lives, the weight of his doubt becomes almost too heavy to bear.

14 At this point his personal history starts to converge with the history of his times, for he is chosen as one of the representatives from his synod to an ecumenical conference on apartheid that brings the major denominations in South Africa together under the auspices of the World Council of Churches. Partly as the result of his efforts, the delegation from the Dutch Reformed Church manages to find common ground there on racial issues with the English-speaking churches, but that common ground is a retreat from apartheid and an affirmation that members of all racial groups have an equal right to share the "responsibilities, rewards and privileges" of citizenship. First Verwoerd and then the synods of Naudé's church repudiate the key resolutions. But when the time comes for him to recant, as the other delegates from his synod have done, Beyers Naudé refuses.

15 He has shown that he is undependable, a potential dissident, but he is not yet ostracized. In fact, he remains the senior minister of the most prestigious Dutch Reformed congregation in Johannesburg for two and one-half years and a member of the Broederbond. He is like a man on the ledge of a building high above a busy thoroughfare deciding whether he should leap, but he does not become an object of horror and pity. The shell of Afrikaner decorum never cracks; he loses his synodical office, of course, but viewed

from outside, his life proceeds as if nothing has happened. Individual brethren in the Broederbond take him aside for earnest discussion and entreaty, sometimes couched in idealistic or theological terms and sometimes more frankly menacing. He meets privately with a small group of dominees who are similarly troubled but in his preaching continues to avoid the issues that preoccupy him. Direct speech on social justice would inspire panic, turning instantly into resistance, he believes. His training has made him an instinctive elitist; to move his people, he feels, he must move their church, and to move their church, he must move its leaders. But his discussion group shrinks rather than expands as individual dominees, fearful of being typed as dissidents, swallow their doubts. Beyers Naudé, who still has not been able to face his family on these issues, finds something inside himself that needs to resist the gathering silence. He begins publication of a journal called *Pro Veritate* that addresses itself to the church's role in society and the questions it has evaded and finally gives up his pulpit to found his Christian Institute as an ecumenical movement aimed primarily at influencing the white churches. His own church condemns the institute, before it has had time to do anything, and subsequently proscribes it formally as an heretical organization.

16 Yet at this point, having overturned his life, he has merely broken ranks. He still has never talked politics with a black nationalist, still knows next to nothing of the history of black politics. In fact, he has not even had English-speaking friends or gone to dinner in a non-Afrikaan's home. He has traveled far, but if pressed at this point about his own politics, he still describes himself as a critical Nationalist. Nevertheless, by the age of fifty Beyers Naudé has been condemned as a traitor and almost wholly isolated within Afrikanerdom. In his family his motives and conduct are a source of bewilderment. Two sisters stop speaking to him, one permanently. Suddenly he has to learn to speak to his wife, his three sons, and his young daughter in a new way, not as the patriarch whose judgment on moral issues is final but as an equal trying to explain and persuade. Family love survives because he learns to accept debate, but that means accepting the reality that his elder sons will not follow him politically; only his wife, finally, manages to make that adjustment and go on making it as he blazes a new trail.

17 In this period, when his journey was still beginning, I encountered Beyers Naudé. It was 1965, and he was on the verge of liberalism. He still believed that initiatives for change would have to come from enlightened whites, that the Afrikaner people would not be able to go on negating the "voice of conscience." If the church moved, the people would follow, he said. Implicitly he was saying that he had managed to adjust his own position after discovering that his understanding of the racial situation was flawed and that other whites in growing numbers would manage to do the same; the churches could be the vehicle for clearing up what was basically a misunderstanding. My recollection is that there was something brittle and withheld in his conversation then, a point beyond which he could not be pressed, as if he recognized the weakness of his premise even as he stated it. He claimed that there were about 120 dominees in the Dutch Reformed Church who were silently sympathetic with his position. Soon it was only their silence, not their sympathy, that he experienced.

18 But he was now launched and reaching out to black and colored churchmen, and this introduced him to a basic law of South African social dynamics: The more a

movement for change seeks the serious involvement of blacks, the less it appeals to whites. It took only a few years for him to hurtle across the political spectrum, moving from critical Nationalist and reluctant dissident to active white supporter of black initiatives. Few black groups were too small and exotic for him to find within them seeds of promise and growth. The former leader of the white synod devoted himself to fostering the independence of its black missionary offspring. Moving farther afield, he prayed with the impoverished members of the despised Zionist and Ethiopian sects that resolutely held themselves apart from the white-led churches. "He was not pretending," a black man who accompanied him to these meetings told me, drawing a comparison between Naudé and other white clerics who had tried to get to know the members of these sects. "You could see this man. He understands what love means."

19 When Biko and other black students flaunted the banner of Black Consciousness and seemed to be turning their backs on white liberals, the Christian Institute was the one white-led organization that wasn't offended. On the contrary, it rushed to offer organizational support and to introduce this new black leadership to potential financial backers in Western churches. Beyers Naudé, like an explorer on uncharted seas, pressed ahead with a singular combination of earnestness and recklessness; one after another, the institute raised such high-voltage questions as civil disobedience, conscientious objection, boycotts, and economic sanctions. Inevitably, its white membership dwindled, liberal white businessmen stopped writing checks, and the authorities stepped up their pressure, seizing Naudé's passport and declaring the Christian Institute an "affected organization"—in effect, subversive—which meant it could no longer be the conduit for overseas funds for movements of South African resistance.

20 And still this was not the end of his journey. In 1976 the Christian Institute expressed its support for the aims of the "liberation" movements so long as these did not conflict with the gospel. A month after that, Naudé spent a night in jail for refusing to testify to an official commission that had advised the authorities to act against the Christian Institute on grounds that it promoted black dominance and socialism. Beyers Naudé by then had told an audience at the University of Cape Town that whites should seriously consider black criticism of the capitalist system and ask themselves whether economic justice might not be promoted under some homegrown form of "African socialism." What churchmen describe as his prophetic ministry had now carried him to an unabashedly radical stance, but he expressed himself that day in terms of moral urgency, not political jargon:

> If you truly love your country, then decide now—once and for all—what kind of country you wish to give yourself to and then commit yourself to see to it that you have a share in the way such a country is being created and built—even if it eventually has to be built from the ashes of a society which has destroyed itself through its own blindness, its avarice and its fear. For whatever is going to happen in between, one thing I know: A new South Africa is being born—a South Africa in which I wish to live . . . a South Africa in which I wish to give of myself to all the people of our land.

The next year, in the aftermath of Steve Biko's death, it became a criminal offense to print those words: The Christian Institute was banned as an organization, and Naudé was banned as an individual; that meant it was illegal for him to travel in the country, enter black areas, attend meetings, or be quoted in any publication.

21 And still that was not the end. Despite his restriction, which wasn't lifted until 1984, Beyers Naudé stayed in circulation, still maintaining, it seemed, a wider circle of contacts among black churchmen and activists than any other white in the country. If nothing else, his example demonstrated that it could be done. Younger Afrikaner renegades might never have seen him or heard him when they broke away—Dominee Eerlik and Frikkie Conradie hadn't—but they were intensely aware that they were walking in his footsteps. And as he went on, he showed them where these led. His political effectiveness was hard to assess and easy to belittle, but there was really no way of calculating how many lives he might have touched. For blacks he remained, Desmond Tutu wrote, "the most resplendent sign of hope in South Africa today." The authorities seemed to endorse this tribute, for they paid Beyers Naudé the unusual homage of declaring him to be, under their security laws, a "listed" as well as a "banned" person. At the age of sixty-eight, he was still regarded as dangerous; had his "listing" remained in force, it would have been illegal to quote his words even if he died. Scarcely a month later a political movement called the United Democratic Front came into existence, resurrecting the slogans and themes of the outlawed African National Congress. The new front named Christiaan Frederick Beyers Naudé as one of its patrons, along with the imprisoned Nelson Mandela.

22 It was easier to understand why blacks chose to honor Beyers Naudé than it was to see why the security police persisted in regarding him as a threat. Was their need to proscribe him explained simply by the old bitterness over his treason to the Broederbond? Or was there a touch here of ethnic pride, a sense that a little Afrikaner backbone was what the forces of resistance required to become really threatening? He rejected suggestions such as Bishop Tutu's that his personal history might in some sense prove to be prototypical, not just for a few spiritual misfits among Afrikaners but for his people as a whole. This was not Christian humility speaking but hard experience. He had tried to pierce the racial cocoon that the Afrikaner spins for his own protection and had acknowledged, long ago, that he had failed. So why couldn't his voice be heard? Whom would it move? It wasn't as if thousands of black youths were going to follow a near-septuagenarian Afrikaner dominee over the barricades.

23 This mystery was partly dispelled for me when, toward the end of my stay in South Africa, I finally heard Beyers Naudé preach. I had talked to him many times in his garden but had never actually heard the public voice that had been stilled. Then one afternoon, when I was busy working, I learned that he was due to show up at a vigil on the issue of resettlement in the homelands that was being conducted by the Black Sash, an organization of white women that seeks to serve blacks caught in the coils of apartheid. His name was not on the printed program, but I was told he would deliver what amounted to a sneak sermon, testing the limits of his banning order, as he occasionally did, by challenging the authorities to charge him for preaching on a biblical

text in the course of a worship service. I raced to get there in time and found myself listening to the emotional testimony of a white woman who had been shocked by what she had seen and heard on a visit to a "black spot" that was about to be cut out of the "white area" as if it were a malignancy. It was necessary to bring this to the "attention of the public," the good woman said, in a voice that sounded helpless with grief. She meant, of course, the white public, which had resolutely ignored the spectacle of the forced removal of blacks for more than three decades. I looked around the whitewashed chapel in which the vigil was being held. There were fewer than fifty persons, maybe thirty of them whites. There was also a press table, but it emptied before Beyers Naudé rose to speak; he still could not be quoted, so this was, strictly speaking, a nonevent. It was early evening in Johannesburg, and the reporters had deadlines; outside, offices and stores were emptying, sending whites and blacks scurrying to the separate buses that would take them to their separate group areas; escort agencies and restaurants were opening their doors on nearby streets in safe expectation of a better turnout than this. The organizers of the vigil had been recording the talks of all the other speakers, but now, as Naudé covered the short distance from his seat in the front row to the lectern in a few loping strides, his back bent slightly as if he were walking uphill, the tape recorder was switched off.

24 His text was I Kings 21, the story of Ahab, king of Samaria, who coveted the vineyard of Naboth the Jezreelite. Standing under a simple wooden cross, he read from his Bible only once, near the end of his narrative, which he related with the simplicity and immediacy of a fresh, cleanly told news report: how Ahab offered Naboth the choice of money for his vineyard or a better vineyard somewhere else; how Naboth replied that he couldn't surrender his patrimony; how Ahab then returned to his palace and sulked until his wife, Jezebel, promised to find a way to separate Naboth from his land; and how Jezebel then made illicit use of the royal seals to send an order to the elders of Jezreel so that Naboth would be hauled up on fabricated charges of blasphemy.

25 There was no straining after comparisons, but in Naudé's telling, Naboth's vineyard became as real as an agricultural enterprise as any small holding in the Transvaal, and Naboth emerged as a worthy cultivator whose love of his land was strong enough to overcome the temptation of silver. Jezebel's abuse of authority, her use of the royal seals and suborning of witnesses, was what he stressed. How did the queen, he asked, get Belial's sons to testify falsely against Naboth? "I don't know. It must have been," Naudé said, rubbing his thumb and forefinger together, "something like this." He didn't interrupt his narrative again to comment on the outrage of Naboth's death by stoning or the subsequent seizure of the vineyard; he let the story tell itself. It had probably been many Sundays since he had last preached, and at first, he kept poking the black rim of his eyeglasses up the bridge of his nose with an index finger in what seemed to be a slight gesture of nervousness. But his voice had a bright resonance, which carried through to the one passage that he read, in which the Lord—taking note of the penance of Ahab, who tears his clothes, puts on sackcloth, and goes on a fast—tells Elijah the Tishbite, "I will not bring the evil in his days: but in his son's days will I bring the evil upon his house."

26 The voice softened when the time came to reflect on the portion's meaning. The words "South Africa" and "resettlement" had yet to be spoken; there was no need to speak them now. There are many parallels in our land, Naudé said, but there are also differences. There it was just a case of Ahab and Jezebel's getting overcome by a greedy wish to own a particular vineyard; here it is a matter of state policy. In the same spare terms in which he had recounted the stoning of Naboth, he now described the agony and weeping of those who lost their land. In his telling, their suffering became a palpable fact, not a remote, subjective experience. As an Afrikaner, he continued, he was painfully aware that his people were largely responsible. How does this happen to a people? He spoke briefly of the power of ideology to stifle reason and compassion and then of a concept of self-interest—which he said Scripture and history both refute—that safety lies in grabbing and keeping.

27 "Why does God allow it?" he asked, putting the question speculatively, then restating it directly: "Why, God, do you allow it?" Naudé didn't wait for an answer or pretend that he had one already. "I don't know," he said, sounding briskly conversational, "but I know that sooner or later the Supreme Being that we call God ordains there must be justice. Is that day of judgment approaching in our land? I don't know, but we must pray and strive for liberation, and in the meantime, we all have our responsibilities and duties." He then ended by praying for migrant laborers, their families, those who make the policies that control their lives, those who carry them out, those who don't understand, and those who do understand but whose lives are ruled by fear.

28 It was very nearly a perfect homiletic exercise, I thought. It was also, I imagined, what Christians call a witness. There was nothing in the sermon that could be described as incitement, scarcely anything that could be called political. Its preoccupation was with scriptural themes from start to finish; the sense of urgency had come from Beyers Naudé's exposition and example. "We all have our responsibilities and duties," this Christian had said. I was neither Christian nor South African, but I thought, if I were South African, the experience of hearing that sermon could have changed my life. In what amounted to a moral Rorschach test, he had left it to each of his listeners to supply content to the words "responsibilities" and "duties." Their answers would come from themselves, not him. I could not imagine what this tiny audience, made up largely of middle-aged white women, might be thinking. But in that brief instant, it occurred to me that younger and darker South Africans might come up with an answer that was neither explicit nor implicit in Beyers Naudé's presentation. It occurred to me that they might think of guns.

Questions for Analysis

1. This excerpt from Lelyveld's book-length study of South Africa is a short biography. A biography, to be worth the reading, must be more than a series of facts

about one person's life—it should convey a point, a message, or an argument. What is the message in Lelyveld's short biography of Naudé?

2. Do you find it difficult to believe that Naudé lived in South Africa for over 40 years without really knowing the plight of South African blacks? Does this account of Naudé's experience help explain how discrimination can occur in this country and not be opposed by those who have the power and prestige to change things? Explain.
3. What qualities in Naudé enabled him to change his political affiliations so radically? In whose view was his change radical? Was it a radical move within his spiritual and moral framework? Explain.
4. Lelyveld ends his biography of Naudé with an account of a sermon Naudé delivered in the early 1980s. The short sermon was built around parallels between the story of Ahab, Jezebel, and Naboth (I Kings 21) and the situation in South Africa. Explain the parallels and then consider how Naudé used them. Lelyveld says that the sermon was not, explicitly or implicitly, an incitement, but that young blacks might upon hearing it "think of guns." How can an appeal for justice and peace also inspire thoughts of violence? Are the two inconsistent? Explain.
5. Compare what you know of Naudé's sermon to King's "I Have a Dream" speech and his "Letter from Birmingham Jail." How are they similar? How are they different?
6. Kevin Siers, in his cartoon "______ Was Here" (p. 470) includes the names of other people who were imprisoned or otherwise suppressed for seeking freedom from oppressive laws and governments. Who are these other people and what are their stories? After reading about Beyers Naudé, do you think his name deserves to be on the wall in Siers's cartoon? Can you think of other names that should be there?

Kevin Siers

____ Was Here

(1990)

Kevin Siers (b. 1954) is editorial cartoonist for *The Charlotte Observer,* Charlotte, North Carolina. This cartoon appeared soon after Nelson Mandela (b. 1918), President of the African National Congress (ANC), was freed after being held in prison for over 26 years because of his vigorous and open opposition to South Africa's apartheid system of racial segregation and oppression.

Kevin Siers, The Charlotte Observer.

Gender Issues

Our culture has experienced many dramatic changes during the 20th century, but few have been more far-reaching than the move toward legal and social equality for women. Various women's groups as well as other political and nonpolitical organizations have worked vigorously to provide women with the same opportunities and responsibilities traditionally given only to men. Although these changes are occurring throughout our society, they are having an especially profound effect in the workplace and in the home. Confining stereotypes about women—their rights, intellectual capabilities, emotional vulnerabilities, and biological characteristics—have been re-examined.

Our culture's re-examination of gender roles began by focusing on women and their experiences. In the process of re-evaluating women's roles, however, significant questions have arisen concerning men's roles in the work place and home as well. Although it has gained momentum only over the past five years or so, some men have started what might be called a Men's Movement. Because men in our society already have clearly defined political and financial powers, the Men's Movement has focused not on political or social action, which of necessity received much attention from women's groups, but on a detailed examination of traditional preconceptions about how men should behave and think.

Those who write on gender issues often call into question values and social structures that have determined for centuries how we deal with each other and how we define ourselves. It is easy in the face of these difficult, disturbing questions to feel a loss of emotional and intellectual stability and to rush blindly back to the traditional ways of thinking and acting. That approach, however, only avoids the issue and creates more problems. Our reassessment of gender issues and its promise of new freedoms for individuals of both sexes carries with it a need to reaffirm some old baselines of value and responsibility. The changes that have come and that are coming require careful scrutiny—they will influence how we, as individuals and as a culture, approach the everyday business of living.

The following selections give some sense of the questions that have been raised on gender issues. Although most of the selections in this section were first published within the past 10 years, the opening three were written long before the recent interest in women's rights. The first selection is a poem, "She Proves the Inconsistency of the Desires and Criticism of Men Who Accuse Women of What They Themselves Cause," written by Sor (Sister) Juana Inés de la Cruz. As the title suggests, Sor Juana is criticizing hypocritical male attitudes toward women and sex. Although three centuries have moderated attitudes somewhat, much of what Sor Juana saw and wrote about in the late seventeenth century is still true. The second selection moves us into the political arena in late nineteenth-century America. "On Women's Right to Suffrage" by Susan B. Anthony is a reasoned but passionate argument that American women should be given the right to vote, a right not granted until more than 50 years after Anthony wrote her plea.

Although it was written by a man, Warren Farrell's piece, ''The Masculine Value System: Men Defining Reality,'' was very important in the history of the Women's Movement. In it, Farrell analyzes how traditional masculine values permeate various aspects of our society (for example, business and politics) and suggests how the infusion of traditional feminine values might improve our institutions and culture.

The following two pieces were published in the early 1980s by women active in the feminist movement. In ''Sisterhood'' (originally published in 1972 and later reprinted in 1983) Gloria Steinem, founding editor of *Ms.* magazine, writes of her growing awareness of herself as a woman and of her bond with other women. Her essay is a definition of ''sisterhood'' that helps us understand the advent and growth of the Women's Movement. Susan Brownmiller's essay on ''Emotion'' examines different ways women and men respond to life's pressures as a way of affirming the positive value of women's emotional reactions.

Julie Matthaei's essay, ''Political Economy and Family Policy,'' provides an example of a radical feminist evaluation of the family. Matthaei looks at the traditional ''natural'' family, criticizes what she sees as its sexist economic structures, and suggests ''radical'' alternatives that she believes will work.

Two essays from very different sources are included to represent the Men's Movement. Augustus Napier's ''Heroism, Men and Marriage'' was written originally for professional marriage and family therapists and appeared later in the *Journal of Marital and Family Therapy.* Asa Baber's ''Call of the Wild'' originally appeared in *Playboy.* Both writers, however, are reassessing traditional male stereotypes and seeking new ways for men to define themselves. Both explore myth and the inner journey as ways for men to find and understand their manhood without losing masculine energy or resorting to aggressive, destructive actions.

Karen Peterson's *USA Today* article ''Debate: Does 'Wiring' Rule Emotion, Skill?'' helps us begin to think about whether physical differences in men and women determine differences in the way they react to the world. The article, based largely on interviews with professionals in medicine, science, and the social sciences, also illustrates the intense debate in those fields over gender issues. Accompanying the article in *USA Today* (and also reproduced here) is Suzy Parker's illustration titled ''Sex and the Brain.''

Finally, in her short story ''I Stand Here Ironing,'' Tilly Olsen presents the frustrations, heartaches, and second thoughts of a mother whose relationship with her daughter has been strained by years of economic and personal hardship. As the mother in Olsen's story thinks back over the experiences that shaped her life and her daughter's character, we get a powerfully clear perspective on some of the special burdens some women have had to bear.

Sor (Sister) Juana Inés De La Cruz

She Proves the Inconsistency of the Desires and Criticism of Men Who Accuse Women of What They Themselves Cause

(ca. 1680)

Perhaps the first outspoken advocate for women's rights in America, Sor Juana Inés De La Cruz (1648 or 1651–1695) was an illegitimate child born into a wealthy Mexican family. Educated under the direction of her grandfather, she possessed intellect, wit, and beauty that made her a favorite in the society and court of Mexico City. Even after she entered a convent, she continued to write, study, and maintain contact with her friends at court. However, in 1691 the Church forced her to give up all study and writing. She finally submitted, though not without protest. She died in 1695 while nursing victims of a plague.

Foolish men who accuse
women unreasonably,
you blame yet never see
you cause what you abuse.

You crawl before her, sad,
begging for a quick cure;
why ask her to be pure
when you have made her bad?

You combat her resistance
and then with gravity,
you call frivolity
the fruit of your intents.

In one heroic breath
your reason fails, like a wild
bogeyman made up by a child
who then is scared to death.

With idiotic pride
you hope to find your prize:
a regal whore like Thaïs

and Lucretia for a bride.
Has anyone ever seen
a stranger moral fervor:
you who dirty the mirror
regret it is not clean?

You treat favor and disdain
with the same shallow mocking voice: love you and you squawk,
demur and you complain.

No answer at her door
will be a proper part:
say no—she has no heart,
say yes—and she's a whore.

Two levels to your game
in which *you* are the fool:
one you blame as cruel,
one who yields, you shame.
How can one not be bad
the way your love pretends
to be? Say no and she offends.
Consent and you are mad.
With all the fury and pain
your whims cause her, it's good
for her who has withstood
you. Now go and complain!

You let her grief take flight
and free her with new wings.
Then after sordid things
you say she's not upright.

Who is at fault in all
this errant passion? She
who falls for his pleas, or he
who pleads for her to fall?

Whose guilt is greater in
this raw erotic play?
The girl who sins for pay
or man who pays for sin?

So why be shocked or taunt
her for the steps you take?
Care for her as you make
her, or shape her as you want,

but do not come with pleas
and later throw them in
her face, screaming of sin
when you were at her knees.

You fight us from birth
with weapons of arrogance.
Between promise and pleading stance,
you are devil, flesh, and earth.

Questions for Analysis

1. What is the "inconsistency" in men that Sor Juana says she will prove?
2. What proofs does she offer to support her assertion? Which of these proofs do you find most effective? Why?
3. Sor Juana's poem (and complaint) about the inconsistency of men was written in seventeenth-century Mexico. If she were alive and writing about men and women in late twentieth-century America, would her complaint be different or the same? Would some proofs need modification? Explain.
4. Sor Juana's complaint about men is in poetic form. How does the form help her make her argument? Would a prose statement be more or less effective? Explain.

Susan B. Anthony

On Women's Right to Suffrage

(1873)

Susan B. Anthony (1820–1906) began her career as a social reformer before the Civil War when she became active in the Abolitionist Movement. After the war she devoted more of her attention, time, and resources to securing the right to vote for women. Although she died 17 years before that right was gained, Anthony is recognized as one of the most persuasive of those who over many decades argued for that change. This speech was written after Anthony had been arrested for trying to exercise her right to vote.

1 Friends and fellow-citizens: I stand before you tonight under indictment for the alleged crime of having voted at the last Presidential election, without having a lawful

right to vote. It shall be my work this evening to prove to you that in thus voting, I not only committed no crime, but, instead, simply exercised my citizen's rights, guaranteed to me and all United States citizens by the National Constitution, beyond the power of any State to deny.

2 The preamble of the Federal Constitution says:

> We, the people of the United States, in order to form a more perfect union, establish justice, insure domestic tranquility, provide for the common defense, promote the general welfare, and secure the blessings of liberty to ourselves and our posterity, do ordain and establish this Constitution for the United States of America.

3 It was we, the people; not we, the white male citizens; nor yet we, the male citizens; but we, the whole people, who formed the Union. And we formed it, not to give the blessings of liberty, but to secure them; not to the half of ourselves and the half of our posterity, but to the whole people—women as well as men. And it is a downright mockery to talk to women of their enjoyment of the blessings of liberty while they are denied the use of the only means of securing them provided by this democratic-republican government—the ballot.

4 For any State to make sex a qualification that must ever result in the disfranchisement of one entire half of the people is to pass a bill of attainder, or an *ex post facto* law, and is therefore a violation of the supreme law of the land. By it the blessings of liberty are forever withheld from women and their female posterity. To them this government has no just powers derived from the consent of the governed. To them this government is not a democracy. It is not a republic. It is an odious aristocracy; a hateful oligarchy of sex; the most hateful aristocracy ever established on the face of the globe; an oligarchy of wealth, where the rich govern the poor. An oligarchy of learning, where the educated govern the ignorant, or even an oligarchy of race, where the Saxon rules the African, might be endured; but this oligarchy of sex, which makes father, brothers, husband, sons, the oligarchs over the mother and sisters, the wife and daughters of every household—which ordains all men sovereigns, all women subjects, carries dissension, discord and rebellion into every home of the nation.

5 Webster, Worcester and Bouvier all define a citizen to be a person in the United States, entitled to vote and hold office.

6 The only question left to be settled now is: Are women persons? And I hardly believe any of our opponents will have the hardihood to say they are not. Being persons, then, women are citizens; and no State has a right to make any law, or to enforce any old law, that shall abridge their privileges or immunities. Hence, every discrimination against women in the constitutions and laws of the several States is today null and void, precisely as is every one against Negroes.

Questions for Analysis

1. What is the rhetorical strategy Anthony uses in the first three paragraphs? Why does she quote from the Preamble to the Constitution?
2. What are the three basic arguments Anthony presents to support her claim that she should be allowed to vote?
3. In Paragraph 4, Anthony says that an oligarchy of learning or of race might be endured. Does this assertion—especially the reference to an oligarchy of race—undercut her argument today? Compare her willingness to endure an oligarchy of race to her statement in her final sentence and to the fact that she was an active supporter of the movement to abolish slavery.

Warren Farrell

The Masculine Value System: Men Defining Reality

(1974)

A sociologist, educator, and writer, Warren Farrell (b. 1940) has long been an active organizer of consciousness-raising groups for men as well as a member of the board of directors of the National Organization for Women and a contributor to such magazines as *Ms.* The following selection comes from *The Liberated Man,* an early and significant contribution to the Women's (and Men's) Liberation Movement.

1 The masculine value system is a series of characteristics and behaviors which men more than women in our society are *socialized* to adopt, especially outside of the home environment. Men are not born with masculine values. They are taught them by both men and women. But one lesson derived from the teaching is that it is more permissible for a man to lead and dominate than a woman. Since the dominant group in a society generally has its values adopted by the majority, masculine values have become the society's values in the public sphere. As they become society's most rewarded values, it is easy for both men and women to assume that masculine values (and therefore most men) are superior to traditionally feminine values (and therefore most women). . . .

Assumptions of Superiority

2 What are some of these masculine (now societal) values which we assume to be superior to traditional feminine values?

- a good talker and articulator *rather than a good listener*

- logic *as opposed to emotion*
- visible conflict and adventure *rather than behind-the-scenes incremental growth*
- self-confidence *in place of humility*
- quick decision-making *rather than thoughtful pondering*
- charisma and dynamism *more than long-term credibility*
- an active striving for power *rather than a general desire to achieve even if power does not accompany the achievement*
- politics or business as an end in itself *rather than a human concern as an end*
- a hard, tough and aggressive approach *instead of a soft, persuasive approach*
- a responsiveness to concrete results and to external and tangible rewards (money, trophies, votes) *rather than less concrete, more internal satisfactions, as the rewards of learning, of communicating, or of a good family life*
- sexuality *rather than sensuality*

3 There are some characteristics associated with men, such as sexual conquest and stoicism, which are not considered superior to feminine characteristics, but are still developed by men as a consequence of the other expectations of masculinity. . . .

4 In the real world, a man's world, the best of the feminine values, which are more humane values, are considered nice but unrealistic. Many of the traditional female values, though, are just the qualities politics and management are now discovering are missing. Politicians and business people have learned to talk their way in and out of anything, but thousands of companies are discovering that some of the salespersons who do best are the ones who listen. A customer will often have a need for something in the back of tes* mind, but it is not drawn out by the aggressive man in sales who is too ready just to sell his preplanned package. Research by Wyer, Weatherly and Terrell indicates that while aggressiveness is considered an important quality in the hiring of salespersons, when actual performance is measured, equally successful results are frequently achieved by persons of directly *opposite* personality traits.[1]

5 Once we are trained to look for one characteristic it takes considerable awareness to prevent ignoring others. Sheila Tobias, who heads the Women's Studies Program at formerly all-male Wesleyan University, says, "I never cease to be astounded at how readily male students will talk in class and how long it takes women students to respond. . . . A woman's questions are more subtle, her appreciations more complex. She digests a lecture slowly, referring to it or the reading weeks later." If Ms. Tobias had just assumed that those who responded immediately were her sharpest students (and many women who adopt the male or societal values make this assumption as readily as men), she would be discounting perceptive students and missing important contributions. The quick response of the men is rewarded over slow deliberation: an aggressive approach is praised more than a considered approach which seeks out subtleties.

**Te* = he or she; *tes* = his or her; *tlr* = him or her.

Masculine Values As Reality: The "News"

6 If Ms. Tobias gives her aggressive talker a higher grade and if the employer does hire a salesperson on the basis of aggressiveness, then the male system of values becomes the masculine system of realities. In almost every occupation realism is used as an excuse to fulfill masculine values. News reporting in the papers and on TV and radio is a prime example. News reporters contend they must report crimes to the extent they do because "crime is reality—to ignore it would be unrealistic." Yet reality is ignored all the time—the reality of *growth,* constructive and incremental growth. In education, for example, reporting reality would be reporting how students best learn or how effective teachers teach, not just how a few male union leaders conduct a strike once every two years. Yet the latter makes the front pages more than all the former put together. The strike is conflict and combat. Normal education is growth. The strike is male-conducted. Normal education is female-conducted.*

7 News reporters do not report reality because it is uneventful and doesn't sell papers to men or women. The public and the news reporters, both operating within the masculine value system, assume reality is found in the conflict that surfaces rather than within the events and nonevents beneath the surface. "Stories" mean conflict, and conflict gets "covered." *Goods news is no news. So we hear more about Watts during the few days it burst into flames than in the fifty years preceding this and the nine years since.* The masculine value system in news coverage reinforces the male socialization to create conflict by making it the only way to capture the attention necessary to create change. It also forces women who want change into the masculine value system. The Equal Rights Amendment, for example, sat in a House Committee for almost fifty years with millions of quiet supporters, but it took a women's liberation movement, with its concomitant sit-ins and demonstrations, to provide the atmosphere for its increased coverage. Careful arguments documenting injustices did not warrant coverage until the conflict atmosphere preceded it.

8 The masculine value system also limits news reporting by its focus on active decision-making, rather than the decisions which grow incrementally, that may in fact never be consciously made. For example, fascinating and crucial news such as how our everyday investments in Latin America force the U.S. government to support dictators are seldom reported until a situation erupts into conflict. The conflict can be tossed off as the product of rebels because the background events are seldom reported. The masculine value system, then, focuses on the biases which erupt into conflict, but rarely on the biases clouded in consensus or incremental growth.

9 Female-conducted conflict, the crises of romance magazines and soap operas, are not considered "news" worthy of coverage on the front pages of newspapers or by the Cronkites and Grimsbys of the media world. In fact, they are not worthy of front-page coverage. But neither is most of the male-conducted conflict which receives the coverage.

*Education becomes less female-conducted the more the status and income increase. Status and income are external rewards which men have learned to associate with their masculine role as breadwinner.

10 Journalists balk at the suggestion that crimes be listed in small type, as are obituaries; that an obituary page and a crime page be at the back of the paper. The protest goes "but obituaries do make the front page when an outstanding person dies." Crimes, though, make the front page when *any* person commits them, as long as the adventure, violence and blood are outstanding. The inherent value of crime is that very conflict and violence. With white-collar crimes, the participants must be important or the conflict value great before it is covered extensively. Watergate possessed both important participants and conflict value and was therefore covered extensively. With crimes of violence, though, the participants can be insignificant. Men's upbringing treats conflict and combat as the all-important processes of life. This is their reality. Women's upbringing treats growth as all-important. The humane value is clearly growth.

Masculine Values As Reality: Business

11 In business, men's attitudes and values force women to play the game by men's rules—unless they are willing to take "women's jobs." The woman is forced to take on a double load of the masculine value of aggressiveness to overcome the special barriers to success which are placed in her way. She then fulfills the male prophecy that "those women who make it are worse bitches than the men—what they really need is a good roll in the hay." If she continues to act aggressively, she provokes fear; if she returns to feminine values, she provokes laughter. She finds herself saddled with a burden of "proving herself" which is worse than any man's. In the meantime, the corporation and the men in it forfeit any of the human qualities women might otherwise have brought into the system.

12 When women do employ some of men's tactics, in addition to their "own," their effectiveness is often overlooked. For example, the direct power which men exert in business situations blinds them to the contributions of indirect power which women have traditionally made. In an article in the *Harvard Business Review,* Orth and Jacobs estimate that "in almost every company there is an informal power group of women that everyone knows about but no one overtly recognizes. The president's secretary eats lunch each day with a group of other senior women, and as a result, the group knows more about what is really happening in the company than do most of the senior officers."[2]

13 In my interviews with employers, I found many managers readily admitting, "I could not do my job without my secretary. She's invaluable, and actually, I'll tell you, she's highly competent." The "I'll tell you" is often said with an inclination of the head and a quick glance with the eyes to make sure no one is looking; and in a confiding manner which signals a "Now, don't tell anyone." Ironically, no one does tell anyone, and as Orth and Jacobs point out, even those women who do recognize their own competence and resent its lack of formal recognition hide their resentment and continue to channel their competence toward making the men feel good. While the managers are benefiting from their secretaries' luncheon discussions, they will often gaze benignly at the secretaries gathered at a table and consider their discussion "gossip." Their own

gossip, though, is considered ''realistic,'' ''a broadening of my information base'' or ''a deepening of the understanding of the way the company really works—its corporate politics.''

14 Women operating in a masculine value system are often overlooked for their effectiveness because their effectiveness just piles up credit for the men they are supporting. The indirect power of women has another limitation—its minimal scope. The woman is usually limited to influencing one man. She must choose to influence in the areas in which he chooses to have influence, according to his timetable (or that of more influential men), his priorities, but most importantly, his talents—meaning that her talents seldom get recognized in their most unique form. (Gloria Steinem might have been a talented assistant to a president, but not until she defined her own talents as editor, speaker and writer did she stand out in a way she could not have by doing someone else's bidding.) In business and in marriage the man recognizes ''the invaluable help'' he receives. Her true effectiveness, though, can never blossom as long as the focus is on his career and his ideas. On the job, in the home and in the bed she helps *him.* She is like a jockstrap—always supporting but never seen.

15 The validity of the argument that woman's focus is on the man should not cloud the lack of freedom which confronts the man. He also has little choice in the decisions he makes. He is caged by limitations imposed by his position within the corporation or factory and by the limited focus of the corporation itself. Yet the threatened man often complains about ''those women's lib ladies,'' instead of looking to the source of his own unhappiness—male-imposed corporate goals and bureaucratic power-seeking. Nor does he see how, when his own attaché* is sharing the responsibility for breadwinning, he becomes freer to question these goals, since if his questioning results in his being fired, his attaché provides a cushion of financial support, offering him the freedom to seek another position without panicking.

Masculine Values As Reality: Politics

16 In politics the integration of the more human-oriented of the traditional female values is most effectively repressed. Internal approval, satisfaction with one's self, and self-improvement for its own sake are sacrificed in politics for the masculine values of external approval and success depending upon another's failure. The politician's very existence is dependent on external approval. This is almost the definition of electoral politics. Internal satisfaction with seeking the truth is irrelevant unless it can be translated into external approval terms, and as most politicians know all too well, ''The truth never catches up with the lie (during the campaign).'' Success for the politician is dependent on the *failure* of everyone else. The politician cannot win unless all tes opponents lose. The politician cannot succeed unless everyone else fails *if* the politician defines success as obtaining office. The masculine value system has defined success that way; many women politicians also define success that way. Few seek the internal

**Attaché* = a person's ''mate''—male or female, hetero- or homosexual.

satisfactions of communicating or the rewards of the learning experience, or are satisfied with alternative paths of influence or the influence involved in the campaigning process itself.† It is not that winning office is inherently wrong. It is that society gives so much positive feedback for concrete success—and so little for a person losing with 49 percent of the vote—that only an exceptionally strong person can count the blessings of a loss.

17 The need to win is reinforced by the American winner-take-all political system, in which there is only one winner—the one with the most votes. This contrasts with the political system of many of the countries of Western Europe—the proportional representation system, in which, say, ten delegates will represent a larger area, with a party that receives only 20 percent of the vote still sending two of the ten delegates to represent that party in office. In addition, the fact that the focus is on the *party's* percentage of the total votes, rather than the individual's, means there is less personal ego at stake from an electoral loss. It means as well that the internal value of seeking the truth as one sees it, although it may only be convincing to 20 percent of the electorate, is still rewarded externally, thereby making the seeking of internal rewards a more realistic goal.‡

18 The masculine value system of success in politics is reinforced by the definition of success in capitalism. The competitiveness of business tends to make the electorate itself not only insensitive to the development of internal values but disdainful of them as not pragmatic in the "real world." The real world of the capitalist does conflict with the development of an inward-turning personality. The success of the salesperson (the backbone of business), like the success of the politician, is dependent on external rewards—the very definition of commission. External rewards such as money, power, votes and titles are the essence of business and politics. Most persons unconsciously evaluate themselves on the basis of their ability to outdo others in the accumulation of these rewards. Competition for success is so important that I have witnessed persons who, upon hearing of a friend's failure, react with a suppressed smile.

Masculine Values As Reality: The Bedroom

19 *Playgirl* is perhaps the perfect example of masculine values defining women's reality in bed.[3] It is produced by a man who views the bedroom as the domain of sexuality rather than sensuality. So *Playgirl* pictures a male nude—women "coming up to" men's standards of *sexuality.* If an attempt had been made to appreciate the feminine value system, the editors would have seen the focus in "women's magazines" on the senses—the smells of body oils and perfumes, the tastes of foods and spices, the touch of embroidered materials and fabrics. They might have translated this into close-ups of men's lips, earlobes, body hair; toe-touching, tongue-caressing, or men and women eating foods together in novel and sensuous ways. Of the Best Films of the New York

†Two exceptions are Shirley Chisholm and Harold Hughes.

‡The proportional representation system has many more advantages and disadvantages, but the purpose here is only to illustrate how the U.S. system reinforces the male value system.

Erotic Film Festival only one was made by a woman. It was an incredibly erotic film of the sectioning and peeling, the touching and eating, the squeezing, tormenting and fingering of an *orange*—done photographically so close up that it appeared as if it were the most intimate body part.

20 Men's magazines, though, view the bedroom as almost entirely sex-oriented and woman-oriented. If men are pictured, it is never being sensuous. The exceptions are so few they stand out. For example, the wrestling scene between two men in the film version of D. H. Lawrence's *Women in Love* was portrayed with great sensitivity. But it still contained all the male symbols of dark wood, trophies, thick red velvet, deep fireplaces and, of course, the wrestling.

21 The advertisements in men's magazines also deal with the power and status symbols associated with sex—sleek sports and racing cars, the Marlboro Man on horseback, ties, and gadgets from digital clocks to stereo systems.

22 Men learn to be more ''thing''-oriented—be it a gadget or a penis; women more total body- and sense-oriented. When men deal in senses—the taste of wine, Scotch, beer or gin—it's always surrounded in status. Finding the ''right wine,'' a status Scotch, a man's beer, an extra-dry martini. In the masculine value system, sensuality is distorted with the reinforcement of men's insecurities about their sexuality.

23 The assumption in the producing of *Playgirl* is that women will come up to men's concern with power, status and things—that they will be concerned with *sex* and *men* rather than sensual experiences with men, women, themselves or nature.

Her Place for Her Values

24 The masculine value system is like an exclusive WASP Wall Street brokerage firm which, upon admitting its first Jew, examines tir microscopically for any unrefined sign of greed. The masculine value system does this with women who attempt entry. The slightest lack of refinement brings accusations of ''karate types'' or ''Lesbians''; women are accused of flaunting their nudity as a way of showing their liberation. As one writer points out, ''It was all right when the girl in the *Playboy* centerfold was photographed naked, since that event was *arranged by and for men.* But let a woman initiate nudity, especially if it is for her own pleasure, and immediately men see the apocalypse upon us.''[4]

25 The masculine value system has another dimension—the assumption that certain general values, like creativity, are applied by men in ways that count, but are applied by women only in roles assigned to them. For example, men will compliment a woman for being creative in decorating, but will stop short of imagining how that creativity could also work in an employment situation. They will give a woman credit for being a disciplined student, but will never offer her the chance to apply this discipline in a bureaucratic setting, where constant distractions require such discipline. They praise women for their patience with children, but do not realize that the same patience could be applied gainfully to adults. Appreciation is shown for women's human concern as teachers, mothers and social workers, without recognizing that the same ability could be effective with customers.

26 If women were to twist their value system to eliminate men from certain areas, their argument might look like this:

Why We Oppose Votes for Men

1. Because man's place is in the army.
2. Because no really manly man wants to settle any question otherwise than by fighting about it.
3. Because if men should adopt peaceable methods women will no longer look up to them.
4. Because men will lose their charm if they step out of their natural sphere and interest themselves in other matters than feats of arms, uniforms, and drums.
5. Because men are too emotional to vote. Their conduct at baseball games and political conventions shows this, while their innate tendency to appeal to force renders them particularly unfit for the task of government.

—Alice Duer Miller, 1915

Notes

1. Robert S. Wyer, Donald Weatherly, and Glenn Terrell, ''Social Role, Aggression, and Academic Achievement,'' *Journal of Personality and Social Psychology,* Vol. 1, No. 6 (June 1965), pp. 645–648.
2. Charles D. Orth and Frederic Jacobs, ''Women in Management: Pattern for Change,'' *Harvard Business Review,* July–August 1971, p. 141.
3. Credit for this idea to Mimi Lobell, co-author of *John and Mimi* (New York: Bantam paperback, 1972).
4. Elizabeth Pochoda, ''Even the Sympathetic Ones Are Maddeningly Patronizing—It's Separatism or Complete Re-education, Says a Radical in Women's Lib—So Where Do Men Fit In?'' *Glamour,* July 1970, p. 142.

Questions for Analysis

1. Review the list of masculine/feminine oppositions in Paragraph 2. Are these stereotypes you have seen and experienced? Based on your observation and experience, are any false or misleading?
2. Farrell's argument is that ''men are not born with masculine values,'' but because men have been the dominant group ''masculine values have become the society's values. . . .'' Explain why you agree or disagree.
3. In his section on ''Masculine Values As Reality: The 'News,' '' Farrell argues that what is chosen for TV and radio reports and what appears on the front pages of newspapers reflect masculine values in their emphasis on ''conflict and combat'' rather than on growth. Does this emphasis reflect masculine values or the nature

of these media and human nature in general? Or is there a feminine alternative with an emphasis on growth that we have not yet seen in newspapers and TV? Discuss.

4. Farrell argues that even though masculine values are most visible in business, feminine values also operate in important ways. Do you agree with his analysis? Explain.
5. Evaluate Farrell's assessment of politics. Is expedient lying a fundamental part of politics? Is it necessarily a masculine trait? What alternatives to our political system would eliminate its winner-take-all influence and still get the business of government done?
6. Explain the ironic argument in Alice Duer Miller's "Why We Oppose Votes for Men." Why does Farrell end this section of his book with Miller's "reasons"?
7. Farrell's essay was written almost 20 years ago, in the early 1970s. How have realities in the news, politics, business, and the bedroom changed over that time? Are his basic points still valid? Explain.

Gloria Steinem

Sisterhood

(1972)

Founding editor of *Ms.* magazine in 1972, Gloria Steinem (b. 1934) is still one of the best known and most influential members of the women's movement. Her essay on "Sisterhood" originally appeared in *Ms.* and was reprinted in *Outrageous Acts and Everyday Rebellions* (1983), a collection of some of her essays.

1 A very, very long time ago (about three or four years), I took a certain secure and righteous pleasure in saying the things that women are supposed to say. I remember with pain—

"My work won't interfere with marriage. After all, I can always keep my typewriter at home." Or:

"I don't want to write about women's stuff. I want to write about foreign policy." Or:

"Black families were forced into matriarchy, so I see why black women have to step back and let their men get ahead." Or:

"I know we're helping Chicano groups that are tough on women, but *that's their culture.*" Or:

"Who would want to join a women's group? I've never been a joiner, have you?" Or (when bragging):

"He says I write like a man."

2 I suppose it's obvious from the kinds of statements I chose that I was secretly nonconforming. I wasn't married. I was earning a living at a profession I cared about.

I had basically—if quietly—opted out of the "feminine" role. But that made it all the more necessary to repeat the conventional wisdom, even to look as conventional as I could manage, if I was to avoid some of the punishments reserved by society for women who don't do as society says. I therefore learned to Uncle Tom with subtlety, logic, and humor. Sometimes, I even believed it myself.

3 If it weren't for the women's movement, I might still be dissembling away. But the ideas of this great sea-change in women's view of ourselves are contagious and irresistible. They hit women like a revelation, as if we had left a dark room and walked into the sun.

4 At first my discoveries seemed personal. In fact, they were the same ones so many millions of women have made and are continuing to make. Greatly simplified, they go like this: Women are human beings first, with minor differences from men that apply largely to the single act of reproduction. We share the dreams, capabilities, and weaknesses of all human beings, but our occasional pregnancies and other visible differences have been used—even more pervasively, if less brutally, than racial differences have been used—to create an "inferior" group and an elaborate division of labor. The division is continued for a clear if often unconscious reason: the economic and social profit of males as a group.

5 Once this feminist realization dawned, I reacted in what turned out to be predictable ways. First, I was amazed at the simplicity and obviousness of a realization that made sense, at last, of my life experience. I couldn't figure out why I hadn't seen it before. Second, I realized how far that new vision of life was from the system around us, and how tough it would be to explain this feminist realization at all, much less to get people (especially, though not only, men) to accept so drastic a change.

6 But I tried to explain. God knows (*she* knows) that women try. We make analogies with other groups that have been marked for subservient roles in order to assist blocked imaginations. We supply endless facts and statistics of injustice, reeling them off until we feel like human information retrieval machines. We lean heavily on the device of reversal. (If there is a male reader to whom all my *pre*realization statements seem perfectly logical, for instance, let him read each sentence with "men" substituted for "women"—or himself for me—and see how he feels: "My work won't interfere with marriage. . . ."; ". . . Chicano groups that are tough on men. . . ." You get the idea.)

7 We even use logic. If a woman spends a year bearing and nursing a child, for instance, she is supposed to have the primary responsibility for raising that child to adulthood. That's logic by the male definition, but it often makes women feel children are their only function, keeps them from doing any other kind of work, or discourages them from being mothers at all. Wouldn't it be just as logical to say that the child has two parents, therefore both are equally responsible for child rearing, and the father should compensate for that extra year by spending *more* than half the time caring for the child? Logic is in the eye of the logician.

8 Occasionally, these efforts at explaining actually succeed. More often, I get the feeling that most women are speaking Urdu and most men are speaking Pali.

9 Whether joyful or painful, both kinds of reaction to our discovery have a great reward. They give birth to sisterhood.

10 First, we share the exhilaration of growth and self-discovery, the sensation of having the scales fall from our eyes. Whether we are giving other women this new knowledge or receiving it from them, the pleasure for all concerned is enormous. And very moving.

11 In the second stage, when we're exhausted from dredging up facts and arguments for the men whom we had previously thought advanced and intelligent, we make another simple discovery: women understand. We may share experiences, make jokes, paint pictures, and describe humiliations that mean little to men, but *women understand.*

12 The odd thing about these deep and personal connections among women is that they often leap barriers of age, economics, worldly experience, race, culture—all the barriers that, in male or mixed society, seem so impossible to cross.

13 I remember meeting with a group of women in Missouri who, because they had come in equal numbers from the small town and from its nearby campus, seemed to be split between wives with white gloves welded to their wrists and students with boots who used words like ''imperialism'' and ''oppression.'' Planning for a child-care center had brought them together, but the meeting seemed hopeless until three of the booted young women began to argue among themselves about a young male professor. The leader of the radicals on campus, he accused all women unwilling to run Mimeograph machines of not being sufficiently devoted to the cause. As for child-care centers, he felt their effect of allowing women to compete with men for jobs was part of a dreaded ''feminization'' of the American male and American culture.

14 ''He sounds just like my husband,'' said one of the white-gloved women. ''He wants me to have bake sales and collect door-to-door for his Republican party.''

15 The young women had sense enough to take it from there. What difference did boots or white gloves make if they were all getting treated like servants and children? Before they broke up, they were discussing some subjects that affected them all (like the myth of the vaginal orgasm) and planning to meet every week. ''Men think we're whatever it is we do for men,'' explained one of the housewives. ''It's only by getting together with other women that we'll ever find out who we are.''

16 Even racial barriers become a little less formidable once we discover this mutuality of our life experiences as women. At a meeting run by black women domestics who had formed a job cooperative in Alabama, a white housewife asked me about the consciousness-raising sessions or ''rap groups'' that are often an organic path to feminism. I explained that while men, even minority men, usually had someplace—a neighborhood, a bar, a street corner, something—where they could get together and be themselves, women were isolated in their houses and families; isolated from other females. We had no street corners, no bars, no offices, no territory that was recognized as ours. Rap groups were an effort to create something of our own, a free place—an occasional chance for total honesty and support from our sisters.

17 As I talked about isolation, about the feeling that there must be something wrong with us if we aren't content to be housekeepers and mothers, tears began to stream

down the cheeks of this dignified woman—clearly as much of a surprise to her as to us. For the black women, some distance was bridged by seeing this white woman cry.

18 "He does it to us both, honey," said the black woman next to her, putting an arm around her shoulders. "If it's your own kitchen or somebody else's, you still don't get treated like people. Women's work just doesn't count."

19 The meeting ended with the housewife organizing a support group of white women who would extract from their husbands a living wage for domestic workers and help them fight the local authorities who opposed any pay raises; a support group without which the domestic workers felt their small and brave cooperative could not survive.

20 As for the "matriarchal" argument that I swallowed in prefeminist days, I now understand why many black women resent it and feel that it's the white sociologists' way of encouraging the black community to imitate a white suburban life-style. "If I end up cooking grits for revolutionaries," explained a black woman poet from Chicago, "it isn't my revolution. Black men and women need to work together: you can't have liberation for half a race." In fact, some black women wonder if criticism of the strength they were forced to develop isn't a way to keep half the black community working at lowered capacity and lowered pay, as well as to attribute some of black men's sufferings to black women, instead of to their real source—white racism. I wonder with them.

21 Looking back at all those male-approved things I used to say, the basic hang-up seems clear—a lack of esteem for women, whatever our race, and for myself.

22 This is the most tragic punishment that society inflicts on any second-class group. Ultimately the brainwashing works, and we ourselves come to believe our group is inferior. Even if we achieve a little success in the world and think of ourselves as "different," we don't want to associate with our group. We want to identify up, not down (clearly my problem in not wanting to join women's groups). We want to be the only woman in the office, or the only black family on the block, or the only Jew in the club.

23 The pain of looking back at wasted, imitative years is enormous. Trying to write like men. Valuing myself and other women according to the degree of our acceptance by men—socially, in politics, and in our professions. It's as painful as it is now to hear two grown-up female human beings competing with each other on the basis of their husband's status, like servants whose identity rests on the wealth or accomplishments of their employers.

24 And this lack of esteem that makes us put each other down is still the major enemy of sisterhood. Women who are conforming to society's expectations view the nonconformists with justifiable alarm. *Those noisy, unfeminine women,* they say to themselves. *They will only make trouble for us all.* Women who are quietly nonconforming, hoping nobody will notice, are even more alarmed because they have more to lose. And that makes sense, too.

25 The status quo protects itself by punishing all challengers, especially women whose rebellion strikes at the most fundamental social organization: the sex roles that convince half the population that its identity depends on being first in work or in war, and the other half that it must serve as docile, unpaid, or underpaid labor.

26 In fact, there seems to be no punishment inside the white male club that quite equals the ridicule and personal viciousness reserved for women who rebel. Attractive or young women who act forcefully are assumed to be either unnatural or male-controlled. If they succeed, it could only have been sexually, through men. Old women or women considered unattractive by male standards are accused of acting out of bitterness, because they could not get a man. Any woman who chooses to behave like a full human being should be warned that the armies of the status quo will treat her as something of a dirty joke. That's their natural and first weapon. She will *need* sisterhood.

27 All of that is meant to be a warning but not a discouragement. There are more rewards than punishments.

28 For myself, I can now admit anger and use it constructively, where once I would have submerged it and let it fester into guilt or collect for some destructive explosion.

29 I have met brave women who are exploring the outer edge of human possibility, with no history to guide them, and with a courage to make themselves vulnerable that I find moving beyond the words to express it.

30 I no longer think that I do not exist, which was my version of that lack of self-esteem afflicting many women. (If male standards weren't natural to me, and they were the only standards, how could I exist?) This means that I am less likely to need male values and approval and am less vulnerable to classic arguments. (''If you don't like me, you're not a real woman''—said by a man who is coming on. ''If you don't like me, you can't relate to other people, you're not a real person''—said by anyone who understands blackmail as an art.)

31 I can sometimes deal with men as equals and therefore can afford to like them for the first time.

32 I have discovered politics that are not intellectual or superimposed. They are organic. I finally understand why for years I inexplicably identified with ''out'' groups: I belong to one, too. And I know it will take a coalition of such groups to achieve a society in which, at a minimum, no one is born into a second-class role because of visible difference, because of race or of sex.

33 I no longer feel strange by myself or with a group of women in public. I feel just fine.

34 I am continually moved to discover I have sisters.

35 I am beginning, just beginning, to find out who I am.

Questions for Analysis

1. Why does Steinem begin her essay with statements she made a few years earlier that she remembers ''with pain'' as she wrote in 1972?
2. What does Steinem mean when she says in Paragraph 7 that ''logic is in the eye of the logician''? How does her statement apply to the discussion in her preceding paragraphs?

3. Steinem describes several women's groups she has attended. What points does she illustrate with these examples? Are they effective? Explain.
4. Why does Steinem end her essay with seven paragraphs that begin with ''I''?
5. Steinem's essay is in a sense a definition of ''sisterhood.'' Write a sentence definition of ''sisterhood,'' and then list the ways Steinem extends or expands this definition.

Susan Brownmiller

Emotion

(1984)

Susan Brownmiller (b. 1935) is a journalist and novelist whose writings, particularly her pieces on women's rights, have been widely anthologized. The following selection is from her 1984 book *Femininity*.

1 A 1970 landmark study, known in the field as *Broverman and Broverman,* reported that ''Cries very easily'' was rated by a group of professional psychologists as a highly feminine trait. ''Very emotional,'' ''Very excitable in a minor crisis'' and ''Feeling easily hurt'' were additional characteristics on the femininity scale. So were ''Very easily influenced,'' ''Very subjective,'' ''Unable to separate feelings from ideas,'' ''Very illogical'' and ''Very sneaky.'' As might be expected, masculinity was defined by opposing, sturdier values: ''Very direct,'' ''Very logical,'' ''Can make decisions easily,'' ''Never cries.'' The importance of *Broverman and Broverman* was not in nailing down a set of popular assumptions and conventional perceptions—masculine-feminine scales were well established in the literature of psychology as a means of ascertaining normality and social adjustment—but in the authors' observation that stereotypic femininity was a grossly negative assessment of the female sex and, furthermore, that many so-called feminine traits ran counter to clinical descriptions of maturity and mental health.

2 Emotional femininity is a tough nut to crack, impossible to quantify yet hard to ignore. As the task of conforming to a specified physical design is a gender mission that few women care to resist, conforming to a prepackaged emotional design is another imperative task of gender. To satisfy a societal need for sexual clarification, and to justify second-class status, an emblematic constellation of inner traits, as well as their outward manifestations, has been put forward historically by some of the world's great thinkers as proof of the ''different'' feminine nature.

3 ''Woman,'' wrote Aristotle, ''is more compassionate than man, more easily moved to tears. At the same time, she is more jealous, more querulous, more apt to scold and to strike. She is, furthermore, more prone to despondency and less hopeful than man, more void of shame or self-respect, more false of speech, more deceptive and of more

retentive memory. She is also more wakeful, more shrinking, more difficult to rouse to action, and she requires a smaller amount of nutriment.''

4 Addressing a suffrage convention in 1855, Ralph Waldo Emerson had kindlier words on the nature of woman, explicating the nineteenth-century view that her difference was one of superior virtue. ''Women,'' he extolled, ''are the civilizers of mankind. What is civilization? I answer, the power of good women. . . . The starry crown of woman is in the power of her affection and sentiment, and the infinite enlargements to which they lead.'' (In less elevated language, the Emersonian view was perhaps what President Reagan had in mind when he cheerfully stated, ''Why, if it wasn't for women, we men would still be walking around in skin suits carrying clubs.'')

5 A clarification is in order. Are women believed to possess a wider or deeper emotional range, a greater sensitivity, say, to the beauties of nature or to the infinite complexities of feeling? Any male poet, artist, actor, marine biologist or backpacker would strenuously object. Rather, it is commonly agreed that women are tossed and buffeted on the high seas of emotion, while men have the tough mental fiber, the intellectual muscle, to stay in control. As for the civilizing influence, surely something more is meant than sophistication, culture and taste, using the correct fork or not belching after dinner. The idealization of emotional femininity, as women prefer to see themselves affirmed, is more exquisitely romantic: a finer temperament in a more fragile vessel, a gentler nature ruled by a twin need to love and to be protected: one who appreciates—without urgency to create—good art, music, literature and other public expressions of the private soul; a flame-bearer of spiritual values by whose shining example the men of the world are inspired to redemption and to accomplish great things.

6 Two thousand years ago *Dominus flevit,* Jesus wept as he beheld Jerusalem. ''Men ceased weeping,'' proposed Simone de Beauvoir, ''when it became unfashionable.'' Now it is Mary, *Mater Dolorosa,* who weeps with compassion for mankind. In mystical visions, in the reliquaries of obscure churches and miraculous shrines, the figure of the Virgin, the world's most feminine woman, has been seen to shed tears. There are still extant cultures in which men are positively lachrymose (and kissy-kissy) with no seeming detriment to their masculine image, but the Anglo-Saxon tradition, in particular, requires keeping a stiff upper lip. Weeping, keening women shrouded in black are an established fixture in mourning rites in many nations. Inconsolable grief is a feminine role, at least in its unquiet representations. In what has become a stock photograph in the national news magazines, women weep for the multitudes when national tragedy (a terrorist bombing, an air crash, an assassination) strikes.

7 The catharsis of tears is encouraged in women—''There, there, now, let it all out''—while a man may be told to get a grip on himself, or to gulp down a double Scotch. Having ''a good cry'' in order to feel better afterward is not usually recommended as a means of raising the spirits of men, for the cathartic relief of succumbing to tears would be tempered by the uncomfortable knowledge that the loss of control was hardly manly. In the 1972 New Hampshire Presidential primary, Senator Edmund Muskie, then the Democratic front-runner, committed political suicide when he publicly cried during a campaign speech. Muskie had been talking about some harsh press comments

directed at his wife when the tears filled his eyes. In retrospect it was his watershed moment: Could a man who became tearful when the going got rough in a political campaign be expected to face the Russians? To a nation that had delighted in the hatless, overcoatless macho posturing of John F. Kennedy, the military successes of General Ike and the irascible outbursts of ''Give em hell'' Harry Truman, the answer was No. Media accounts of Muskie's all-too-human tears were merciless. In the summer of 1983 the obvious and unshakable grief displayed by Israeli prime minister Menachem Begin after the death of his wife was seized upon by the Israeli and American press as evidence that a tough old warrior had lost his grip. Sharing this perception of his own emotional state, perhaps, Begin shortly afterward resigned.

8 Expressions of anger and rage are not a disqualifying factor in the masculine disposition. Anger in men is often understood, or excused, as reasonable or just. Anger in men may even be cast in a heroic mold—a righteous response to an insult against honor that will preclude a manly, aggressive act. Because competitive acts of personal assertion, not to mention acts of outright physical aggression, are known to flow from angry feelings, anger becomes the most unfeminine emotion a woman can show.

9 Anger in a woman isn't ''nice.'' A woman who seethes with anger is ''unattractive.'' An angry woman is hard, mean and nasty; she is unreliably, unprettily out of control. Her face contorts into unpleasant lines: the jaw juts, the eyes are narrowed, the teeth are bared. Anger is a violent snarl and a hostile threat, a declaration of war. The endless forbearance demanded of women, described as the feminine virtue of patience, prohibits an angry response. Picture a charming old-fashioned scene: The mistress of the house bends low over her needlework, cross-stitching her sampler: ''Patience is a virtue, possess it if you can/Seldom seen in women, never seen in man.'' Does the needle jab through the cloth in uncommon fury? Does she prick her thumb in frustration?

10 Festering without a permissible release, women's undissolved anger has been known to seep out in petty, mean-spirited ways—fits of jealousy, fantasies of retaliation, unholy plots of revenge. Perhaps, after all, it is safer to cry. ''Woman's aptitude for facile tears,'' wrote Beauvoir, ''comes largely from the fact that her life is built upon a foundation of impotent revolt.''*

11 Beauvoir hedged her bet, for her next words were these: ''It is also doubtless true that physiologically she has less nervous control than a man.'' Is this ''doubtless true,'' or is it more to the point, as Beauvoir continues, that ''her education has taught her to let herself go more readily''?

12 Infants and children cry out of fear, frustration, discomfort, hunger, anxiety at separation from a parent, and rage. Surveying all available studies of crying newborns and little children, psychologists Eleanor Maccoby and Carol Jacklin found no appreciable sexual difference. If teenage girls and adult women are known to cry more than men—and there is no reason to question the popular wisdom in this regard—should the endocrine changes of adolescence be held to account? What of those weepy ''blue days''

*''Facile'' is the English translators' match for the French *facile,* more correctly rendered as ''easy.'' Beauvoir did not mean to ascribe a stereotype superficiality to women in her remark.

of premenstrual tension that genuinely afflict so many women? What about mid-life depression, known in some circles as "the feminine malady"? Are these conditions, as some men propose, a sign of "raging hormonal imbalance" that incapacitates the cool, logical functioning of the human brain? Or does feminine depression result, as psychiatrist Willard Gaylin suggests, when confidence in one's coping mechanism is lost?

13 Belief in a biological basis for the instability of female emotions has a notorious history in the development of medical science. Hippocrates the physician held that hysteria was caused by a wandering uterus that remained unfulfilled. Discovery in the seventeenth century that the thyroid gland was larger in women inspired that proposition that the thyroid's function was to give added grace to the feminine neck, but other beliefs maintained that the gland served to flush impurities from the blood before it reached the brain. A larger thyroid "was necessary to guard the female system from the influence of the more numerous causes of irritation and vexation" to which the sex was unfortunately disposed. Nineteenth-century doctors averred that womb-related disorders were the cause of such female complaints as "nervous prostration." For those without money to seek out a physician's care, Lydia E. Pinkham's Vegetable Compound and other patent medicines were available to give relief. In the 1940s and '50s, prefrontal lobotomy was briefly and tragically in vogue for a variety of psychiatric disorders, particularly among women, since the surgical procedure had a flattening effect on raging emotions. Nowadays Valium appears to suffice.

14 Beginning in earnest in the 1960s, one line of research has attempted to isolate premenstrual tension as a contributing cause of accidents, suicide, admittance to mental hospitals and the commission of violent crimes. Mood swings, irritability and minor emotional upsets probably do lead to more "acting out" by females at a cyclical time in the month, but what does this prove beyond the increasingly accepted fact that the endocrine system has a critical influence on the human emotional threshold? Suicide, violent crime and dangerous psychiatric disorders are statistically four to nine times more prevalent in men. Should we theorize, then, that "raging hormonal imbalance" is a chronic, year-round condition in males? A disqualifying factor? By any method of calculation and for whatever reason—hormonal effects, the social inhibitions of femininity, the social pleasure of the masculine role, or all of these—the female gender is indisputably less prone to irrational, antisocial behavior. The price of inhibited anger and a nonviolent temperament may well be a bucketful of tears.

15 Like the emotion of anger, exulting in personal victory is a harshly unfeminine response. Of course, good winners of either sex are supposed to display some degree of sportsmanlike humility, but the merest hint of gloating triumph—"Me, me, me, I did it!"—is completely at odds with the modesty and deference expected of women and girls. Arm raised in a winner's salute, the ritualized climax of a prizefight, wrestling match or tennis championship, is unladylike, to say the least. The powerful feeling that victory engenders, the satisfaction of climbing to the top of the heap or clinching a deal, remains an inappropriate emotion. More appropriate to femininity are the predictable tears of the new Miss America as she accepts her crown and scepter. Trembling lip and

brimming eyes suggest a Cinderella who has stumbled upon good fortune through unbelievable, undeserved luck. At her moment of victory the winner of America's favorite pageant appears overcome, rather than superior in any way. A Miss America who raised her scepter high like a trophy would not be in keeping with the feminine ideal.

16 The maidenly blush, that staple of the nineteenth-century lady's novel, was an excellent indicator of innocent virginal shyness in contrast to the worldliness and sophistication of men. In an age when a variety of remarks, largely sexual, were considered uncouth and not for the ears of virtuous women, the feminine blush was an expected response. On the other side of the ballroom, men never blushed, at least not in romantic fiction, since presumably they were knowledgeable and sexually practiced. Lowered eyes, heightened color, breathlessness and occasional swooning were further proofs of a fragile and innocent feminine nature that required protection in the rough, indelicate masculine world. (In the best-selling Harlequin and Silhouette books devoured by romance addicts who need the quick fix, the maidenly blush is alive and well.)

17 In a new age of relative sexual freedom, or permissiveness, at any rate, squeals and moans replace the blush and the downcast eye. Screaming bobbysoxers who fainted in the aisle at the Paramount Theater when a skinny young Frank Sinatra crooned his love ballads during the 1940s (reportedly, the first wave of fainting girls was staged by promoters) presaged the whimpering orgasmic ecstasy at rock concerts in huge arenas today. By contrast, young men in the audience automatically rise to their feet and whistle and shout when the band starts to play, but they seldom appear overcome.

18 Most emphatically, feminine emotion has gotten louder. The ribald squeal of the stereotypic serving wench in Elizabethan times, a supposed indicator of loose, easy ways, seems to have lost its lower-class stigma. One byproduct of our media-obsessed society, in which privacy is considered a quaint and rather old-fashioned human need, has been the reproduction of the unmistakable sounds of female orgasm on a record (Donna Summer's "Love to Love You Baby," among other hits). More than commercialization of sex is operative here. Would the sounds of male orgasm suffice for a recording, and would they be unmistakable? Although I have seen no studies on this interesting sex difference, I believe it can be said that most women do vocalize more loudly and uncontrollably than men in the throes of sexual passion. Is this response physiological, compensatory or merely symptomatic of the feminine mission to display one's feelings (and the corresponding masculine mission to keep their feelings under control)?

19 Feminine emotion specializes in sentimentality, empathy and admissions of vulnerability—three characteristics that most men try to avoid. Linking these traits to female anatomy became an article of faith in the Freudian school. Erik Erikson, for one, spoke of an "inner space" (he meant the womb) that yearns for fulfillment through maternal love. Helene Deutsch, the grande dame of Freudian feminine psychology, spoke of psychic acceptance of hurt and pain; menstrual cramps, defloration and the agonies of childbirth called for a masochistic nature she believed was innate.

20 Love of babies, any baby and all babies, not only one's own, is a celebrated and anticipated feminine emotion, and a woman who fails to ooh and ahh at the snapshot of a baby or cuddle a proffered infant in her arms is instantly suspect. Evidence of a maternal nature, of a certain innate competence when handling a baby or at least some indication of maternal longing, becomes a requirement of gender. Women with no particular feeling for babies are extremely reluctant to admit their private truth, for the entire weight of woman's place in the biological division of labor, not to mention the glorification of motherhood as woman's greatest and only truly satisfactory role, has kept alive the belief that all women yearn to fulfill their biological destiny out of a deep emotional need. That a sizable number of mothers have no genuine aptitude for the job is verified by the records of hospitals, family courts and social agencies where cases of battery and neglect are duly entered—and perhaps also by the characteristic upper-class custom of leaving the little ones to the care of the nanny. But despite this evidence that day-to-day motherhood is not a suitable or a stimulating occupation for all, the myth persists that a woman who prefers to remain childless must be heartless or selfish or less than complete.

21 Books have been written on maternal guilt and its exploitation, on the endemic feeling that whatever a mother does, her loving care may be inadequate or wrong, with consequences that can damage a child for life. Trends in child care (bottle feeding, demand feeding, not picking up the crying baby, delaying the toilet training or giving up an outside job to devote one's entire time to the family) illuminate the fear of maternal inadequacy as well as the variability or ''expert'' opinion in each generation. Advertising copy-writers successfully manipulate this feminine fear when they pitch their clients' products. A certain cereal, one particular brand of packaged white bread, must be bought for the breakfast table or else you have failed to love your child sufficiently and denied him the chance to ''build a strong body twelve ways.'' Until the gay liberation movement began to speak for itself, it was a commonplace of psychiatric wisdom that a mother had it within her power to destroy her son's heterosexual adjustment by failing to cut his baby curls, keep him away from dance class or encourage his interest in sports.

22 A requirement of femininity is that a woman devote her life to love—to mother love, to romantic love, to religious love, to amorphous, undifferentiated caring. The territory of the heart is admittedly a province that is open to all, but women alone are expected to make an obsessional career of its exploration, to find whatever adventure, power, fulfillment or tragedy that life has to offer within its bounds. There is no question that a woman is apt to feel most feminine, most confident of her interior gender makeup, when she is reliably within some stage of love—even the girlish crush or the stage of unrequited love or a broken heart. Men have suffered for love, and men have accomplished great feats in the name of love, but what man has ever felt at the top of his masculine form when he is lovesick or suffering from heartache?

23 Gloria Steinem once observed that the heart is a sex-distinctive symbol of feminine vulnerability in the marketing of fashion. Heart-shaped rings and heart-shaped gold pendants and heart-shaped frames on red plastic sunglasses announce an addiction to

love that is beyond the pale of appropriate design for masculine ornamentation. (A man does not wear his heart on his sleeve.) The same observation applies a little less stringently to flowers.

24 Rare is the famous girl singer, whatever her age, of popular music (blues, country, Top Forty, disco or rock) who is not chiefly identified with some expression of love, usually its downside. Torchy bittersweet ballads and sad, suffering laments mixed with vows of eternal fidelity to the rotten bastard who done her wrong communicate the feminine message of love at any cost. Almost unique to the female singer, I think, is the poignant anthem of battered survival, from Fanny Brice's "My Man" to Gloria Gaynor's "I Will Survive," that does not quite shut the door on further emotional abuse if her man should return.

25 But the point is not emotional abuse (except in extreme, aberrant cases); the point is feeling. Women are instructed from childhood to be keepers of the heart, keepers of the sentimental memory. In diaries, packets of old love letters and family albums, in slender books of poetry in which a flower is pressed, a woman's emotional history is preserved. Remembrance of things past—the birthday, the anniversary, the death—is a feminine province. In the social division of labor, the wife is charged with maintaining the emotional connection, even with the husband's side of the family. Her thoughtful task is to make the long-distance call, select the present and write the thank-you note (chores that secretaries are asked to do by their bosses). Men are busy; they move forward. A woman looks back. It is significant that in the Biblical parable it was Lot's wife who looked back for one last precious glimpse of their city, their home, their past (and was turned into a pillar of salt).

26 Love confirms the feminine psyche. A celebrated difference between men and women (either women's weakness or women's strength, depending on one's values) is the obstinate reluctance, the emotional inability of women to separate sex from love. Understandably. Love makes the world go round, and women are supposed to get dizzy—to rise, to fall, to feel alive in every pore, to be undone. In place of a suitable attachment, an unlikely or inaccessible one may have to do. But more important, sex for a woman, even in an age of accessible contraception, has reproductive consequences that render the act a serious affair. Casual sex can have a most uncasual resolution. If a young girl thinks of love and marriage while a boy thinks of getting laid, her emotional commitment is rooted not only in her different upbringing but in her reproductive biology as well. Love, then, can become an alibi for thoughtless behavior, as it may also become an identity, or a distraction, à la Emma Bovary or Anna Karenina, from the frustrations of a limited life.*

27 Christian houses of worship, especially in poor neighborhoods, are filled disproportionately by women. This phenomenon may not be entirely attributable to the historic

*The overwhelming influence of feminine love is frequently offered as a mitigating explanation by women who do unfeminine things. Elizabeth Bentley, the "Red Spy Queen" of the cold war Fifties, attributed her illegal activities to her passion for the Russian master spy Jacob Golos. Judith Coplon's defense for stealing Government documents was love for another Russian, Valentin Gubichev. More recently, Jean Harris haplessly failed to convince a jury that her love for "Scarsdale diet" Doctor Herman Tarnower was so great that she could not possibly have intended to kill him.

role of the Catholic and Protestant religions in encouraging the public devotions of women (which Judaism and Islam did not), or because women have more time for prayer, or because in the Western world they are believed to be more religious by nature. Another contributing factor may be that the central article of Christian faith, ''Jesus loves you,'' has particular appeal for the gender that defines itself through loving emotions.

28 Women's special interest in the field of compassion is catered to and promoted. Hollywood ''weepies,'' otherwise known as four-handkerchief movies, were big-studio productions that were tailored to bring in female box-office receipts. Columns of advice to the lovelorn, such as the redoubtable ''Dear Dorothy Dix'' and the current ''Dear Abby,'' were by tradition a woman's slot on daily newspapers, along with the coverage of society births and weddings, in the days when females were as rare in a newsroom as they were in a coal mine. In the heyday of the competitive tabloids, sob-sister journalism, that newsroom term for a human-interest story told with heart-wrenching pathos (usually by a tough male reporter who had the formula down pat), was held in contempt by those on the paper who covered the ''hard stuff'' of politics, crime and war. (Nathanael West's famous antihero labored under the byline of Miss Lonelyhearts.) Despite its obvious audience appeal, ''soft stuff'' was, and is, on the lower rungs of journalism—trivial, weak and unmanly.

29 In Government circles during the Vietnam war, it was considered a sign of emotional softness, of lily-livered liberals and nervous nellies, to suggest that Napalmed babies, fire-bombed villages and defoliated crops were reason enough to pull out American forces. The peace movement, went the charge, was composed of cowards and fuzzy thinkers. Suspicion of an unmanly lack of hard practical logic always haunts those men who espouse peace and nonviolence, but women, the weaker sex, are permitted a certain amount of emotional leeway. Feminine logic, after all, is reputedly governed by the heartstrings. Compassion and sentiment are the basis for its notorious ''subjectivity'' compared to the ''objectivity'' of men who use themselves as the objective standard.

30 As long as the social division of labor ordains that women should bear the chief emotional burden of caring for human life from the cradle to the grave while men may demonstrate their dimorphic difference through competitive acts of physical aggression, emblematic compassion and fear of violence are compelling reasons for an aversion to war and other environmental hazards. When law and custom deny the full range of public expression and economic opportunity that men claim for themselves, a woman must place much of her hopes, her dreams, her feminine identity and her social importance in the private sphere of personal relations, in the connective tissue of marriage, family, friendship and love. In a world out of balance, where men are taught to value toughness and linear vision as masculine traits that enable them to think strategically from conquest to conquest, from campaign to campaign without looking back, without getting sidetracked by vulnerable feelings, there is, and will be, an emotional difference between the sexes, a gender gap that may even appear on a Gallup poll.

31 If a true shape could emerge from the shadows of historic oppression, would the gender-specific experience of being female still suggest a range of perceptions and

values that differ appreciably from those of men? It would be premature to offer an answer. Does a particular emotion ultimately resist separation from its historic deployment in the sexual balance of power? In the way of observation, this much can be said: The entwining of anatomy, history and culture presents such a persuasive emotional argument for a "different nature" that even the best aspects of femininity collaborate in its perpetuation.

Questions for Analysis

1. What is Brownmiller's thesis? What is her purpose?
2. Outline Brownmiller's essay. At what points would you insert headings to help the reader see the structure, logic, and argument of the essay?
3. What is the point of Brownmiller's discussion of crying and anger? (See Paragraphs 6–12.)
4. Re-examine Paragraph 14. What is its point? Is the evidence she presents interesting and persuasive?
5. In Paragraph 15, Brownmiller generalizes about what are deemed "appropriate" male and female ways to respond to victory. Do you think her conclusion valid? Are her examples representative? Are there other reasons for the behaviors in her examples?
6. What is the point of Brownmiller's final paragraph? Does the biological experience of being a woman involve a "range of perceptions and values" that is fundamentally different from that experienced by men, or can we attribute the differences to cultural traditions?

Julie Matthaei

Political Economy and Family Policy

(1988)

An economics professor at Wellesley College, Julie Matthaei (b. 1951) has questioned traditional gender and family values from an economic perspective. She is author of *An Economic History of Women in America* and continues to write about the breakdown of the "natural" family, a theme she develops in the following essay, which is taken from *The Imperial Economy*, Book II: *Through the Safety Net* (1988).

1 *Our current, "natural" family system, based on biological similarities and differences, is in crisis. Not only are its institutions breaking down, they are also under attack*

as unjust, unequal, and unfree. The ''natural'' family system needs to be replaced by a consciously social family system; this means socializing parenting costs and pursuing policies which attack the sexual division of labor and better integrate economic and family life.

2 The family plays a central role in the distribution of income and wealth in our society, reproducing class, race, and gender inequalities. This paper will 1) present a radical and feminist analysis of the ''traditional'' family system, 2) discuss the recent breakdown of this system, 3) present a radical and feminist critique of the traditional family system, and 4) indicate social policies which would build a family system more consistent with the principles of equality, freedom, and social justice.

The "Natural" Family

3 The development of capitalism and wage labor in the nineteenth-century U.S. brought with it new familial institutions. The family continued to be patriarchal—ruled by the husband/father—but was less defined by and involved in commodity production, either as a family firm, or as a family enslaved to producing for others. The family emerged as an increasingly personal and feminine sphere, physically separate and distinct from the competitive and masculine economy (Matthaei 1982). Since, in the nineteenth century, ''scientific'' explanations of social life were replacing the former religious ones, the new familial institutions were viewed as ''natural,'' and stress was placed on their determination by biological similarities and differences. This ''natural''[1] family system has three, interconnected parts:

4 1. *''Natural'' Marriage.* Marriage is seen as a union of naturally different and complementary beings: men/males and women/females (biological sex and social gender are equated). Men and women are believed to be instinctually heterosexual; those who form homosexual liaisons are viewed as unnatural and perverted.[2] Men are seen as natural bread-winners, competing in the economy, and women as natural homemakers, caring for their husbands and children in the home, and segregated into dead-end, low paid ''women's jobs.'' Forced into this sexual division of labor, men and women need one another to be socially complete, and in order to undertake the essential function of marriage, which is seen as . . .

5 2. *''Natural'' Parenting.* Parenting is seen as the biological production of offspring, a process in which adults pass on their identities and wealth to their children, to ''their own flesh and blood.'' Children are seen as the responsibility and property of their parents. Women/females are seen as naturally endowed with special maternal instincts which make them more qualified than men/males for parenting.

6 3. *''Natural'' Community.* Connected to the view of family life as natural is a white racist view of society which divides people into races and views whites as the biologically superior race. Whites rationalize their political and economic domination

of people of color not only as natural but also as part of ''white man's burden to civilize the savages.''[3] Races and white supremacy are perpetuated as social entities by the prohibition of racial intermarriage; by the passing down of wealth or poverty, language and culture to one's children; and by racially segregated institutions such as housing and job markets.

The Breakdown of the "Natural" Family System

7 In the last fifteen years, the ''natural'' family system has been breaking down and coming under increasing attack by feminists and others.

8 1. *Married women have entered the labor force and ''men's jobs'' in growing numbers, challenging the ''natural'' sexual division of labor.* Now over half of married women are in paid jobs at any one time. Women are demanding entry into the better-paid ''men's jobs,'' and pressing their husbands to do ''women's work'' in the home. The ''natural'' marriage union between a bread-winning husband and a homemaking wife has become the exception rather than the rule, characterizing only 29% of husband/wife couples in 1985 (Current Population Reports March 1985).

9 2. *Married women's labor force participation has created a crisis in day care: there is a severe shortage of day care facilities, especially affordable ones.* In New York, for example, between 830,000 and 1.2 million preschool and school-age children vie for the fewer than 135,000 available licensed child care placements (Select Committee on Children 1987). The shortage of day care, combined with the absence of flexible jobs, forces parents to use make-shift arrangements: 2.1 million or 7% of 5–13 year olds whose mothers work outside the home are admittedly left unsupervised; actual numbers are much higher (Children's Defense Fund 1987).

10 3. *Growing numbers are not living in husband/wife families;* only 57% of all households include married couples. Adults are marrying later, spending more time living alone (23.4% of all households) or with friends or lovers. Homosexuality appears to be on the rise, and gays are coming out of the closet and demanding their rights. Marriages have become very unstable; divorce rates more than tripled between 1960 and 1982, more than doubling the number of female-headed households (1986 and 1987 Statistical Abstracts).

11 4. *''Natural'' parenting is on the wane.* Divorces create ''unnatural'' female-headed households, most with dependent children. Unwed mothering has increased to comprise 1 in 5 births and over half of all births among blacks (1987 Statistical Abstract). Remarriages create ''unnatural'' families, with step-parents and -siblings. More ''unnatural'' is the trend for sterile couples, gays, and singles to obtain children through artificial insemination, surrogate mothers, and inter-country inter-racial adoptions.

12 What do these trends mean? Members of the so-called Moral Majority interpret them as the breakdown of *the* family; their solution, embodied in the Family Protection Act of the late 1970s and early 1980s, is to put the ''natural'' family back together: encourage marriage; discourage divorce, unwed mothering, homosexuality; and get married women out of men's jobs and back into the home. The radical perspective is the opposite; the ''natural'' family is only one of many possible family systems, a very oppressive and ineffective one at that, as the next section will show. Growing numbers are rejecting the ''natural'' family system, and trying to create alternative family structures. What society needs is a radical family policy to focus and facilitate this process of dismantling of the old family system and constructing a new and more liberated one.

The Radical Critique of the "Natural" Family

13 The radical critique of the ''natural'' family has many prongs. All of these are underlain by a common claim—the ''natural'' family is not natural, necessary, or optimal, and a more adequate family system needs to be developed.

14 1. *The ''natural'' family system is not natural.* Biological differences in skin color or sex organs, and biological similarities between parent and child, do not necessitate a particular family form, or hierarchy and difference between the sexes and races. Past family systems have been very different from the ''natural'' family.[4] It is not nature but our society which is producing and reproducing the ''natural'' family, and its associated institutions of gender and race difference and inequality, through parenting practices, laws, labor market structures, and culture.

15 2. *The ''natural'' family system is classist and racist.* The conception of the ''natural'' family is generated by the dominant culture of upper-class, native-born whites, who then claim it applies to all. Since being a man means bread-winning and supporting a homebound homemaker and children, men without ''family wage'' jobs due to unemployment, class, or race discrimination are seen (and often see themselves) as less than manly. Black women, forced into the labor force to compensate for their husbands' lack of economic opportunity, are viewed as unfeminine, castrating ''matriarchs,'' and the extended and chosen family system which blacks have developed to combat poverty and economic insecurity is condemned as deviant (Stack 1974). The inability of the poor to properly parent their children because of their meager resources is seen as a fault in their characters, and they are criticized for having children at all, as if the poor do not have a right to parent.

16 3. *The ''natural'' family system impoverishes female-headed households.* Women and children face high risks of poverty. Married women are to specialize in unpaid homemaking and mothering, complementing their husbands' bread-winning. Divorce or widowhood leaves women with little access to income, but with major if not full emotional and financial responsibility for the children.[5] ''Women's jobs'' do not pay enough to cover child care and keep female households with young children out of

poverty. The present welfare system (Aid to Families with Dependent Children), structured to support the ''natural'' family system, does not even provide female-headed families with poverty-level income. The result: the majority of black and Hispanic female-headed families (50 and 53%, respectively), and 27% of white female-headed families, are poor. Children are penalized the most: 54% of children in such families are poor (Current Population Reports 1985).

17 4. *''Natural'' marriage creates inequality between the sexes.* Since wives are relegated to unpaid housework and low paid jobs, they are economically dependent upon their husbands. Fear of losing this financial support can force women into subservience to their husbands, and into staying in unsatisfying marriages. Indeed, some feminists see ''natural'' marriage as a struggle in which men have gained the upper hand by monopolizing the higher-paid jobs (Hartmann 1981). Whatever its origins, ''natural'' marriage is clearly unequal, making mutual love and respect difficult.

18 5. *''Natural'' parenting is oppressive and unjust.* Along with financial responsibility, parents are given almost total power over children. Children have no rights, and no system through which they can complain about mistreatment or find alternative parents (Rodham 1976). In a society where most men are under the power of bosses, and women under that of their husbands, parenting provides an arena where adults have total power and authority. It is easy to forget one's children's needs and use or abuse them to fill one's own needs. What results is not only an epidemic of child physical and sexual abuse,[6] but also the training of each child to accept and participate in hierarchical and authoritarian systems, from schools to workplaces to politics (Miller 1981).

19 6. *The ''natural'' family perpetuates inequality between families* through the generations, because parents pass down their economic position to their children. Inheritance keeps ownership of the means of production in the hands of a few, mostly white, families.[7] Children born into higher-income families receive better nutrition, housing, health care, and schooling than their poor counterparts, have the ''insurance'' of wealthy relatives to back them up and encourage risk-taking, and can expect to inherit wealth. On the other hand, 11 million children (one in five) must live without even the most basic goods and services (Current Population Reports 1985). This is not only unjust but also irrational: it is in society's interest to guarantee quality health care and education to its future workers and citizens.

20 7. *The ''natural'' family system discourages the formation of alternative families, while forcing many into unwanted ''natural'' families.* Its broad and virulent anti-gay discrimination—from education, employment, housing, and marriage laws to media images—makes it very difficult for people to love and share their lives with people of the same sex. It discriminates against couples who are unable to have children biologically by treating adoption and artificial insemination as ''unnatural'' and undesirable options. On the other hand, the ''natural'' family's equation of sex, reproduction, and

marriage creates unwanted children by creating opposition to sex education, birth control for unmarried teens, and abortion. Forty percent of all births are mistimed or unwanted—for those under 24, a disastrous 53%—forcing millions of women into premature or unwanted motherhood and/or marriages (1987 Statistical Abstract).

Conceptualizing a Social Family System

21 The ''natural'' family system is inadequate, oppressive, and is coming apart at the seams. At the same time, all need the love and warmth and sharing and parenting which family relationships provide.[8] Hence criticism is not enough; an *alternative* and better vision of family life needs to be delineated, along with a set of concrete policies to bring such a new family system into being.

22 The oppressiveness of the ''natural'' family system was accepted because its institutions were seen as natural and inevitable. Our new family system would be a *consciously* social one, its institutions developed through study, discussion, struggle and compromise, and continually criticized and improved so as to maximize freedom, equality, self-fulfillment, democracy, and justice. Here are some of the central principles of such a system; while it may appear utopian, many are living out parts of this vision now.

23 ***Social Marriage.*** Marriage would become a *symmetrical* relationship between whole, equal, and socially independent humanbeings, each participating in a similar range of familial, economic and political activities.[9] Its basis would be mutual love of the other, i.e., liking of, respect for, and sexual attraction to the person the other is, as providing the reason for intimate sharing of lives and living spaces and, if desired, parenting. Couples would not be expected to stay together ''for better or for worse . . . as long as ye both shall live''; nor would they need to, since each would have earnings.

24 ***Social Parenting.*** Parenting would be recognized as a quintessentially *social* activity which, by shaping our unconsciousnesses, bodies, and minds, shapes the future of our society. Society would ensure that each child is well cared for and educated, since the upbringing of children as physically and psychologically healthy, creative, educated, and socially-conscious citizens is essential both to society's well-being, and to our belief in equal opportunity. This would include providing children and their parents with economic and institutional support, as well as seeking out optimal parenting practices and educating prospective parents in them.

25 ***Social Community.*** Cultural and economic differences between groups of people would be acknowledged to be social rather than natural products. All human beings would be recognized as equally human citizens of the world, and a concept of basic human rights, both political and economic, developed. Intercultural marriages would be encouraged to further social understanding.

Bringing the Social Family into Being: A Policy Check-list

26 Although the "natural" family system is in decline, the social family system cannot replace it unless there are many changes in our economic and social institutions. Here are some of the policies which will help bring about these changes; many are now in place in other countries.

27 1. *Policies which socialize parenting*

a. *Policies which establish the right of all adults to choose when and if they wish to parent.* Universal sex education and parenting training for adolescents, as well as access of all to free, safe, 100% effective birth control, abortions, and adoption placement, are needed to make every child a wanted child. At the same time, society must recognize the right of those who are infertile, gay, or single to parent, and support the development of alternative modes of obtaining children from adoption to artificial insemination and in-vitro fertilization.[10] The right to parent must also be protected by programs to help low-income parents with the costs of child-rearing (see 1b). Finally, the right to parent must be seen as socially established, rather than inhering in the genetic connection between a parent and a child; parenting rights must be revocable if a parent neglects or abuses a child, and society should seek to prevent child abuse through an effective system of child advocates and parenting support and training.

28 b. *Policies which ensure a basic, social inheritance for every child.* The best way to ensure healthy and provided-for children is to ensure this health and income to all families through a system of national health insurance and a combination of anti-poverty measures, from full employment, to comparable worth, to a guaranteed annual income. In addition, since having children does increase a family's poverty risk, family allowances should be provided to parents according to need.[11] Furthermore, all children need to have access to high quality, free or sliding-scale education, from preschool day care when their parents are at work, to elementary and secondary school and college. This "social inheritance" program would be paid for by high inheritance taxes and very progressive income and/or luxury taxes. Such taxes would, in themselves, help reduce the present gross inequalities of opportunity among children.[12]

29 c. *Policies which socialize child-care costs: government- and business-subsidized day care.* Making quality child care available and affordable to all should be the joint financial responsibility of business and government, since it benefits both employers and society at large. A few trend-setting employers now provide child-care benefits to their workers, having found that these more than pay for themselves by decreasing worker absenteeism, increasing productivity, and attracting top workers (Blau and Ferber 1986). Current federal funding through Title 20 is woefully inadequate; many states are serving less than 30% of their eligible populations (Select Committee on Children 1987). One survey found that ¼ of all full-time homemakers, and ½ of all single parents, were kept from employment and training

programs by the unavailability of child care (Cal. Governor's Task Force on Child Care 1986). Again, Sweden provides the example to follow: the government pays 90% of the child-care costs of public day care centers, which are used by over half of children with employed mothers (Blau and Ferber 1986).

30 On the other hand, to permit parents with job commitments to spend more time with their children, especially their infants, a system of paid leaves from work without loss of one's job or seniority must be established. The U.S. does not even have laws guaranteeing prospective parents an *unpaid* leave when they have or adopt a child.[13] In a few states, women can use their temporary disability insurance to pay for 4 to 10 weeks of pregnancy/infant care leave (Kamerman et al. 1983). Again, Sweden is the model in this area, with 1) paid, year-long parental leaves, 2) up to 60 days a year paid leave to care for sick children, and 3) the right for all full-time employed parents with children under 8 to reduce their work weeks (with reduced pay) to 30 hours a week (Ginsberg 1983). Radicals have advocated a shorter work week without reduction in pay as a solution to unemployment and low productivity, for it would create more jobs, reduce unemployment, and increase output (Bowles, Gordon, and Weisskopf 1983); a consideration of the needs of parents makes such policies even more desirable. Other innovations which allow adults to combine work with parenting are flex-time and flex-place (working at home); the extension of health, pension, and other benefits to part-time workers; and the cafeteria benefit plan, which allows dual-career couples to eliminate doubly-covered benefits in favor of more of other benefits, such as leaves or child-care support (Farley 1983; Kamerman and Hayes 1982).

31 2. *Policies to support egalitarian, symmetrical marriages* in which partners participate equally in parenting, housework, the labor force, and political life.[14]

a. *Comparable worth, affirmative action, increased unionization.* Comparable worth would increase the pay of women's jobs to that of men's jobs requiring comparable skill, effort, and responsibility. Affirmative action encourages women to enter into traditionally masculine jobs. Women need to organize in unions to fight for the above, and for general wage increases; one platform is "solidarity wages," again practiced in Sweden, in which workers agree to take part of their wage increase to reduce inequalities among them. Together these policies would stop the segregation of women into low-paid, dead-end, less-satisfying jobs, reduce women's economic dependence upon men, and encourage more similar work and family participation by the sexes.

32 b. *Socialization of parenting* (see #1 above) would support symmetrical marriage, for it would allow adults to combine parenting with labor force commitments, reducing the pressure to specialize as in "natural" marriage.

33 c. *Repeal of the laws that discourage formation of "unnatural" marriages and non-traditional households.* This includes repealing sodomy laws and advocating legislation prohibiting discrimination against gays in employment, housing, insurance, foster parenting, adoption, and other areas.[15] Gay relationships must be

legitimized in marriage laws, to give spouses health insurance, pension, inheritance, and other benefits and rights enjoyed by heterosexual spouses.[16] The repeal of co-residence laws, which in many states prohibit the cohabitation of more than two unrelated adults, is needed to allow the formation of non-biologically–based extended families.

34 d. *Individual rather than joint taxation of married couples.* Our present income tax system is progressive and married couples are taxed on the basis of their combined incomes. This discourages wives from entering the labor force since, when a woman's earnings raise the household's tax bracket, much of her earnings are paid to the government in taxes.[17] Taxing adults individually (as is currently done in Sweden), rather than jointly, would instead encourage both members of a couple to participate in the labor force.

35 e. *Policies to aid the casualties of the ''natural'' marriage system.* Until the above changes are achieved, women and children will continue to face high poverty risks when they live in female-headed households. Many feminists advocate the strengthening of alimony and child-support laws; however, this both reinforces the ''natural'' marriage notion that husbands should be the main providers, and reproduces class and race inequality, because wives' and children's incomes depend on that of their husbands/fathers. Extensive welfare reform, combined with the policies above, is a better solution.

36 3. *Policies to create social community.* Labor market reforms (2a) must always aim at eliminating both race and sex segregation and discrimination. These, along with social inheritance policies, will go far in stopping the economic reproduction of racial inequality in the U.S. The decline of ''natural'' parenting views of children as ''one's own flesh and blood'' will foster, and in turn be fostered by, the decline of conceptions of race, as both are replaced by a view of a human community reproduced through social parenting.

Notes

1. Natural is in quotes because the ''natural'' family system is actually a social product.
2. In contrast, previous times viewed homosexual attractions as natural (and shared by all) but immoral and not to be acted on (Weeks 1979).
3. Similarly, whites in the Eugenics movement argued that poor whites had inferior genes, and worked to limit their reproduction (Gould 1981).
4. Among the Rangiroa, adopted children were given equal status and rights as biological offspring, and considered ''one belly'' (from the same mother) with one another and with their other siblings (Sahlins 1976). In the New England and Southern colonies, mothering among the wealthy was essentially biological, producing one's husband's children, who were then nursed and cared for by poor white or slave women. Mead (1935) found societies where men and women shared the early care of children. Many societies see polygamy as the norm for marriage; others have allowed females to live as men and take wives after having cross-sex dreams (Blackwood 1984). Among the ancient Greeks, the highest form of love for an adult man was homosexual love for a younger man.
5. In 1983, only 35% of mothers caring for their children with absent fathers received any child-support, and the average yearly payment was only $2,341; only 6% of separated or divorced women received any alimony (1987 Statistical Abstract).

6. The media have focussed on child abuse by strangers—on day care scandals and missing children—whereas the vast majority of children are abused by their parents or relatives (Eliasoph 1986).
7. The wealthiest 2.4% of households owns 65% of the income-producing wealth (Edwards, Reich, Weisskopf 1986).
8. Some feminists and gays have taken an "anti-family" position, as if the "natural" family is the only family form (Barrett and McIntosh 1982); however they usually advocate some alternative, family-like institutions.
9. If this seems far-fetched, an October 1977 CBS—*New York Times* National Survey found that 50% of 30–44 year olds, and 67% of 18–29 year olds, preferred a symmetrical marriage (of a man and woman who both had jobs, did housework, and cared for the children) over the traditional, complementary one.
10. Most doctors refuse to artificially inseminate single or lesbian women. The developing practice of surrogate mothering is very controversial among feminists and radicals. Since eggs can be fertilized outside of a womb, and embryos can be raised in incubators from the age of a few months, there are many other possibilities, including impregnating men, or even producing infants entirely outside of human bodies, as Marge Piercy (1976) and Shulamith Firestone (1970) have envisioned.
11. Sweden and France give housing allowances to parents (Kamerman and Kahn 1979); many European countries have national health insurance and family allowances. Swedish policy is to guarantee all citizens a minimum standard of living (Ibid.); in the U.S., the needy only receive support through "entitlement" programs, which require certain qualifications (such as being a female household head with children) other than being poor, and which do not, in any event, raise incomes up to the poverty level.
12. See Chester (1982) for a review of Western thought on inheritance.
13. Kamerman and Kingston (in Kamerman and Hayes 1982) found that paid maternity leave was available to fewer than one-third of all employed women in 1978, and averaged only about six weeks of benefits.
14. Cuba encourages such marriages through its "Family Code," adopted in 1975 (Randall 1981); however, it still discriminates against gay couples.
15. Sodomy laws, which outlaw forms of "unnatural sex" (e.g., anal intercourse and oral/genital sex, either heterosexual or homosexual), still exist in many states, and were recently upheld by the Supreme Court, although they are seldom enforced. Many cities and a few states have passed gay rights legislation, and more and more employers have extended their non-discrimination policy to include sexual preference or orientation.
16. In June 1987, the Swedish Parliament approved a bill which gave gay couples the same rights as heterosexuals married by common law; it will allow couples to sign housing leases as couples, regulate the division of property after a break-up, and grant lovers the right to inherit property in the absence of a will (*Gay Community News,* June 14–20, 1987).
17. Even though the recent tax reform reduced the progressivity of the tax system, and a 1983 reform exempted 10% of the income of the lower-earning partner from taxation, the "marriage penalty" persists (Blau and Ferber 1986).

Bibliography

Barrett, Michele, and McIntosh, Mary. 1982. *The Anti-Social Family.* London: New Left Books.

Blackwood, Evelyn. 1984. Sexuality and Gender in Certain Native Tribes: The Case of Cross-Gender Females. *Signs* 10(1):27–42.

Blau, Francine, and Ferber, Marianne. 1986. *The Economics of Women, Men, and Work.* Englewood Cliffs, N.J.: Prentice-Hall.

Bowles, Samuel, David M. Gordon, and Thomas E. Weisskopf. 1983. *Beyond the Wasteland: A Democratic Alternative to Economic Decline.* New York: Anchor/Doubleday.

Chester, Ronald. 1982. *Inheritance, Wealth, and Society.* Bloomington: Indiana University Press.

Children's Defense Fund. 1987. Unpublished paper.

Edwards, Richard, Reich, Michael, and Weisskopf, Thomas. 1986. *The Capitalist System.* Englewood Cliffs, N.J.: Prentice-Hall. Third Edition.

Eliasoph, Nina. 1986. Drive-In Mortality, Child Abuse, and the Media. *Socialist Review* #90, 16(6):7–31.

Farley, Jennie, ed. 1983. *The Woman in Management.* New York: ILR Press.

Firestone, Shulamith. 1970. *The Dialectic of Sex.* New York: Morrow.

Ginsberg, Helen. 1983. *Full Employment and Public Policy: The United States and Sweden.* Lexington, Mass.: D.C. Heath and Co.

Gould, Steven J. 1981. *The Mismeasure of Men.* New York: Norton.

Hartmann, Heidi. 1981. The Unhappy Marriage of Marxism and Feminism. In *Women and Revolution: A Discussion of the Unhappy Marriage of Marxism and Feminism,* Lydia Sargent (ed.), pp. 1–41. Boston: South End Press.

Kamerman, Sheila, and Kahn, Alfred. 1979. *Family Policy: Government and Families in Fourteen Countries.* New York: Columbia University Press.

Kamerman, Sheila, and Hayes, Cheryl (Eds.) 1982. *Families that Work: Children in a Changing World.* Washington: National Academy Press.

Kamerman, Sheila, et al. (Eds.) 1983. *Maternity Policies and Working Women.* New York: Columbia University Press.

Matthaei, Julie. 1982. *An Economic History of Women in America: Women's Work, the Sexual Division of Labor, and the Development of Capitalism.* New York: Schocken Books.

Mead, Margaret. 1935. *Sex and Temperament in Three Primitive Societies.* New York: William Morrow and Co.

Miller, Alice. 1981. *The Drama of the Gifted Child.* trans. by Ruth Ward. New York: Basic Books.

Piercy, Marge. 1976. *Woman on the Edge of Time.* New York: Fawcett.

Randall, Margaret. 1981. *Women in Cuba: Twenty Years Later.* New York: Smyrna Press.

Rodham, Hilary. 1976. Children under the Law. In *Rethinking Childhood,* Arlene Skolnick (ed.). Boston: Little, Brown and Co.

Sahlins, Marshall. 1976. *The Use and Abuse of Biology: An Anthropological Critique of Sociobiology.* Ann Arbor: University of Michigan Press.

Select Committee on Children, Youth and Families, U.S. House of Representatives. 1987. *Fact Sheet: Hearing on Child Care, Key to Employment in a Changing Economy.* March 10.

Stack, Carol. 1974. *All Our Kin.* New York: Harper & Row.

U.S. Bureau of the Census, Current Population Reports. 1985. Household and Family Characteristics: March 1985.

———. 1985. Money Income and Poverty Status of Families and Persons in the United States.

———. 1986. 1987. Statistical Abstract of the United States.

Weeks, Jeffrey. 1979. *Coming Out: Homosexual Politics in Britain, from the Nineteenth Century to the Present.* London: Quartet Books.

Questions for Analysis

1. What is the "natural" family system? Why does Matthaei put "natural" between quotation marks in this context?
2. In several places Matthaei says that the "natural" family is in trouble and uses terms such as "in crisis," "breaking down," or "coming apart at the seams." What evidence does she use to support her assertion? Do you agree with her assertion? Do you agree with her assessment? Do the problems she is able to document justify her evaluation and her suggestion of "radical" change?
3. How is Matthaei's critique of the "natural" family "radical"? Do you disagree with any of her critiques?
4. How do you react to the "Social Family System" and the "Policy Check-list" Matthaei presents? Do you find specific parts disturbing? Do you believe parts are unworkable or unfair? Explain.

5. Matthaei makes extensive use of headings (including letters and numbers—really an embedded outline) in her essay. Do you find this technique helpful? Did it help you read faster and with better comprehension? What, if anything, does she lose by using this technique?

Augustus Napier

Heroism, Men, and Marriage

(1989)

Augustus Napier (b. 1938) is a family and marriage therapist and Director of the Family Workshop in Atlanta, Georgia. He has written several books on the dynamics of marriage and family. The following essay was originally presented before the 1989 annual conference of the American Association of Marriage and Family Therapists and was reprinted in the *Journal of Marital and Family Therapy* in 1991.

1 As we approach the last decade of this waning century, my attempt to relate heroism, men, and marriage may seem misguided, if not a little foolish. Heroes, after all, defy dragons, raise the flag on Iwo Jima, scale Mt. Everest, walk the moon, go hand-to-hand with Darth Vader, or hit a home run for the Mets one week and score a touchdown for the Falcons the next. In our culture's mythology, this type of hero is still usually a man, and his conquests are in the great Out There, far from the humdrum concerns of marriage and the family.

2 But there is also something increasingly humdrum about these male Heroes. John Wayne looked tired thirty years ago, Chuck Yeager is selling spark plugs these days, and I slept through most of James Bond's latest exploits. Though there is still a place for male courage, this kind of male confrontation with external hardship and danger seems hackneyed to me, particularly in the face of the fresh and exciting adventures of today's women. As they break with the centuries-old strictures of their roles, the Shirley Valentines of today are the real news. Who wants to be wooden, work-bound, cro-magnon Joe, a man asleep at his role, awakened only by the prospect of losing his wife?

3 The fact is that the fresh winds of change blowing through the lives of so many women today are shaking up their partners, who are still mostly reacting—and reacting negatively—to these changes in women. Few men have a new sense of direction or purpose which is related to their roles. We men know the right words to say about equality these days, but we are clearly on the defensive; and we could use whatever is at hand to resist change: the pro-life movement, the mommy track, the appeal to

corporate loyalty. But justice as well as originality is on Shirley Valentine's side, and her cause will eventually prevail. In the meantime, she is having a hard time finding a male counterpart, a new kind of male hero.

4 Just beneath the business-as-usual surface, our culture is awash with cynicism and disillusionment with men, and for good reason. While we men have been widely known for many years for our capacities for warfare, murder, and pillage (skills sublimated of late into insider trading, arms for hostage trading, and the like), our reputation within the family, where once upon a time father knew best, has also suffered. In fact, on that wonderful forum on American absurdity, Saturday Night Live, a mythic pop psychology writer—dressed completely in black—was recently found promoting her book, "Woman Good, Man Bad," in which all her martyred heroines were the victims of men. At least we have Bill Cosby to remind us of the good old days.

5 What, for God's sake, would the ideal version of the man designed for something other than warfare, or for the conquest of the world's diminishing rain forests, or for staring into a computer screen—be like? Well, as a start, he should be able to live productively (translate cooperatively) in close proximity with men and women; and I believe he should hold himself equally responsible—with his wife—for raising their contribution to the next generation.

6 But whatever this new man's image is to be, a journey to find him needs to be undertaken by men, now. Not just for themselves, but for everyone. Like the late Joseph Campbell,[1] I believe that the modern hero's journey needs to be an internal one, into that often frightening world of the unconscious where the character of every person takes its definitive shape; and where the reformation of that person's life must ultimately occur.

7 According to Campbell, all heroic journeys—from those of the Greek Gods and Goddesses to the adventures of Han Solo—have certain similarities. The journey begins when some circumstance causes the hero to depart from the routines of everyday life. The "call to adventure" may begin as a simple blunder, a Freudian slip as it were, or a giving in to a tempting pursuit. While hunting a stag, King Arthur is drawn deeper and deeper into a primeval forest; he continues the pursuit until his horse dies from exhaustion; forced to rest, he falls into deep contemplation; and the real story begins.

8 For today's man, that separation from the familiar is usually begun by a life transition that challenges his sense of himself: he may pursue a risky new career; or an affair; he may become a parent. Many of us find ourselves pushed into new territory by the changes in our wives, changes which leave us feeling confused and threatened. If we are fortunate, we encounter a family therapist during this period; but all too many men begin the journey into themselves with the traumatic experience of divorce. Whether lured or forced, today's male sojourner finds himself in a strange, alien environment.

1. AUTHOR'S NOTE: Joseph Campbell (1903–1987) was one of the world's leading authorities on mythology and folklore. He produced a number of influential books and articles over a long and productive career as a teacher, scholar, and writer. His most accessible works include *A Hero with a Thousand Faces* (1949; revised 1980), *The Mythic Image* (1974), and (with Bill Moyers) *The Power of Myth* (1988). The last book is based on a six-part television series produced for the Public Broadcasting System in 1988.

Suddenly his life, as he has been taught to live it, is not working the way he thinks it should. This moment of confusion and doubt can be the first step on the heroic path.

9 Campbell finds that heroic journeys begin with an encounter with a powerful guide, a spirit figure who helps the hero negotiate the labyrinth ahead of him.

10 Among the American Indians of the Southwest, the favorite personage in this role is Spider Woman, a grandmotherly little woman who lives underground and who guides adventurers through their spiritual journeys. In classical myth, this figure is Hermes-Mercury; and in Christian mythology the part is played by the Holy Ghost.

11 Without this pivotal figure, the hero's journey is impossible; and in the lives of so many men today, there is no guide, no pilot, no shepherding figure to lead him into the vast and unfamiliar territory within himself, or to direct him toward the new behaviors which society needs him to learn. This lack of leadership and public support for change in men's lives is one of the greatest impediments to its occurring.

12 At the border of this new world—which we recognize as the land permeated by unconscious feelings and agendas—Campbell says that we should expect a shadow presence, a gatekeeper who guards this new world.

13 The Arcadian god Pan is a well-known Classical example of this dangerous presence. In those who accidentally ventured into his domain, he instilled panic and fear: a sudden groundless fright would flood the mind with imagined danger. In a frantic effort to escape from his own unconscious feelings, the victim often died.

14 For most men today, this ''threshold'' figure is likely to mutter seductively: ''Don't feel; don't know,'' which is of course a protection against such panicky self-awareness. The hero-aspirant must somehow defeat, or placate, or in some manner circumvent this symbol of repression and denial. Those of us who are the therapists to men know the formidable power of male denial of awareness of the inner self; often this denial must be forcefully confronted, or it can block the entire journey.

15 Once beyond the threshold, the hero enters a realm of unfamiliar but strangely intimate forces, many of which threaten him. Ahead lie a series of tests which try his strength and courage. Rising from this shadowy, anxiety-permeated landscape, these dangerous images could be seen as projective figures which represent the denied aspects of the self.

16 For all of us men, there is much to be faced here: the truth about us; the selves we don't want to admit. Defensiveness won't do us any good here; the demons must be confronted.

17 But we would be foolish to think that we men are eager to initiate these painful self-encounters. Most of us—and this was certainly true in my marriage—must be forcefully confronted by the consequences of our behavior; eventually our wives must stop protecting us and caretaking us; and if we are fortunate—as I was—they will confront us.

18 There are a number of familiar figures in this realm; and you can read all about them in the women's magazines at the checkout line. They aren't named Golem or Beezlebub there, but they might as well be for all the generosity or caring they display. And women didn't invent their cynicism about them.

1) There's the dominating, intimidating man. From General Noriega to the soft-voiced accountant in Scarsdale who makes his wife account for her pocket change, this guy is everywhere, and he is still in charge of most of the world's overt power. Like all authoritarians, he rules from fear of being dominated; and he binds his wife and children to him in a way that squelches their spirits and protects him from experiencing loss.
2) The intimidated, passive, passive-aggressive man. He's a nice guy; he may seem to be his dominant wife's victim, but he has a mean streak and may ultimately control his controlling partner. His inability to take a stand or to be there for his family drives his wife to distraction; and our practices are increasingly filled with these men—who have often had very little fathering—and their overfunctioning, frustrated partners. The marriage in which the woman is overfunctioning and the man underfunctioning may be universally unsatisfying (sociological research certainly labels it as such); it may also be on the way toward becoming the norm.

   Why can't we men share power equally with women? Why do we either bully women, or become little-boy-like in relation to them?
3) The unfaithful man. . . . [H]e may betray his friends in the name of ambition, his wife in the interest of freer sexuality; and his children for almost any reason. What happens to a boy that makes it so difficult for him to grow up to be faithful to his intimates? Intuitively, we know that he is the victim of betrayal by his childhood parents, but often it is difficult to see him as anybody's victim.
4) There's Virginia Satir's computer-man. He can be as ominous as Darth Vadar (and I know several) or as humorous as R2D2, but he is mechanical; and he wasn't born that way. His decision to live within the narrow zone of the intellect is created in childhood by experiences that make him feel terrified of emotion, and of intimacy. What are these experiences?
5) The dysfunctional, addicted man. Why are there so many of him? What forces in the family create such emotional emptiness, such human desolation that his only access to emotional warmth is through a chemical simulation of the experience? His loneliness touches every one of us.
6) The violent man, the lawbreaker. Why do we wait so late to see these men's desperation? Why must their ways of trying to solve their problems wait until they commit murder or rape to be noticed—when many of them can often be identified in elementary school? What is the human family doing to create so many male criminals?

19 I could go on; but there is a common thread in these men's problems: a pervasive self-focus, a narcissism of imperious habit (condoned by the culture) or of need (unmet in childhood) which makes it as difficult for these men to be emotionally giving and nurturing as it has been for women to learn self-assertion and self-enhancement. *Overcoming our narcissism may be the primary challenge for the new male ideal;* and indeed, Campbell finds that a willingness to transcend self-interest—in what he calls ''self-achieved submission''—is a marker of the hero.

20 Actually, this is a complex issue, because there are many self-sacrificing men: men who deny their emotional needs, who deplete themselves for their companies, their patients, their art. But all too often we sacrifice ourselves in a self-aggrandizing manner—if that makes any sense—and then we come home drained and depleted and ask "guess who?" to take care of us. What we need to do is to take better care of ourselves at work, and we need to develop supportive friendships outside the family, so that we can come home with lots to give to those who really matter. Our developing the capacity to nurture within the family demands that we find ways to be nurtured by a support system outside the family. And I don't mean an affair; I mean intimate male friendships.

21 It is a self-esteem issue to sacrifice those near to us while giving to those outside the family to an extreme degree; this pattern is really a reflection of our negative feelings about ourselves.

22 But large numbers of men—forming a collective of venturing spirits—need to go through a period of intense self-focus and self-exploration in order to address their problems—before they emerge with new resources for their families, and for the world. I am not referring to individual therapy for men—which is of course a useful experience—but to the kind of collective journey which women went through in the early days of the Women's Movement. We men must understand the male experience; or literally "stand under" the experience of the boys within men. Only through empathic, courageous self-confrontation can men discover the true humanity within themselves; and this is what the heroic journey is about.

23 At the heart of the journey, the hero faces ultimate challenges and threats; if he passes these tests, he may return to the world with much to teach. In the individual's journey, our personal tests are determined by the trials we were put through in our early years inside that charged and difficult container of the human spirit, what I have called the family crucible. But there are certain common experiences which we all share, and which shape the patterns of personal challenge.

24 From my view, the most obvious flaw in this family is the psychological and often physical absence of the father from the inner circle of the family; and especially from the process of child-rearing. With Dorothy Dinnerstein and Nancy Chodorow, I find this arrangement for rearing children destructive for everyone—girls, boys, and the men and women they become. And it is especially to men that I turn for a remedy.

25 In all the ways which feminist writers have described, this has truly been an unjust system for women: the tremendous emotional burden of children's needs, the social isolation, the lack of support from the children's father, the low status, the absence of overt power, the lack of intellectual satisfaction. As women have taken jobs and pursued careers outside the family, this situation has in certain respects become more unjust, not less, since women today have kept many of their old responsibilities, and simply added new ones. Current research tends to indicate that men have changed remarkably little, and may be doing only a little more child care—which is the critical issue—than their fathers.

26 In this environment, women are tempted—as Chodorow points out—to overidentify with their girl children, projecting onto them their needs, and perhaps overbonding to

them; while seeing their boy children as "other," different from them, and thereby subject to being the target for feelings about significant "others" in the mother's life—especially her husband and her father. The boy is set prematurely apart in the mother's consciousness, and he is inevitably the target of some of the adult needs which his mother should expect to be met by the boy's father, and the boy is also the target of some of the anger and frustration which she feels because of the failure of the boy's father to meet those needs.

27 And this is not her fault; she is in an impossible situation.

28 The father's absence places the young boy in a seductively important role in the young family; but the mother's needs, and her anger, make her a threatening figure for him. Soon enough, he decides that too much closeness to mother is dangerous, and that he must withdraw from her in preparation for becoming a man. And so at five or six, he becomes a Little Man, reaching for contact with father, whom he may idealize but doesn't know. According to Chodorow, he renounces his prematurely truncated needs for emotional support from his mother—and saves them for his future wife.

29 Few of us—girls or boys—ever reach father. He is the great cipher; and I believe that some boys model their behavior on him so slavishly in an effort to find out what he is like on the inside. If I do what he does, act like he acts, perhaps I can know what he feels like. This "identification with the lost object" may account for some of the difficulty men have in departing from or improving upon the literal, historical father's pattern. Even as men they are forever trying to reach father, and until—at least in some fashion—they do, it may be useless to attempt to get them to move away from his ways of living.

30 The basic pathology of the father's response is driven by his emotional distance from the inner circle of the family, and by his sense of unimportance within this sphere. The critical, dominating father may try to "connect" with his kids through the use of traditional male force; the passive father may become an indulgent, nonparental nice guy in order to gain favor with his kids; the unfaithful man may—in a terribly destructive move—sexualize his relationships with his daughters; the addicted man may maneuver to get his kids to feel sorry for him and to take care of him; and of course the violent man is often the one who feels the most isolated and the most insignificant, and his violence is a desperate attempt to gain power and influence in the family.

31 But what kids rarely get is an involved, strong, nurturant father who is there for them. Often, father's presence in the family is experienced as an aching, yearning sense of absence.

32 I agree with Chodorow that one of the tragedies of this system is its repetitiveness. The male who doesn't know his father—and thus doesn't know how to parent—and who fears emotional control by women, becomes a distancing figure during the early childhood years of his own family; and when he withdraws in fear and anxiety, his wife turns to her children for support; and the cycle begins again.

33 If our society could change this system, if we could insert a nurturing, involved, committed father into the everyday lives of his children, and if he could also become

a figure of emotional support directly to his wife, we could change the course of the human family.

34 But before that can happen, men need to face their childhood dilemmas within the early family. We need to see the truth of our own painful problems, and through reexperiencing the pain be reborn to our own denied feelings.

35 At the nadir of the hero's journey, he faces fearsome creatures; and if he overcomes or defeats them, he is often—according to Campbell—united with a powerful female figure, a Goddess who represents the primal life-force in the universe. According to Campbell, woman represents the totality of what can be known. This reunification with mother, or the female principle, is a necessity for many men who missed emotional support from their own mothers, and who have denied their own feminine, creative energies. This kind of resolution is often especially important to the traditional man who may have had a companionable, but nonintimate alliance with his father, but struggled with a distant relationship with his mother. Often it will be a good woman therapist who represents this redeeming figure in the literal life of the male sojourner.

36 The other pattern which Campbell finds at the heart of the heroic journey is a reconciliation with the primal father. And it is this resolution which many men who are on the softer side of the male continuum need to seek. As the poet Robert Bly has taught us, many men need contact with the strong, vital, magnetic animal presence which has characterized maleness throughout the ages. In this era of father absence, we need to rekindle the presence of father in the family; and father as a strong person, full of a beneficent power which he can give lovingly to his partner and to his children. No one, in the search for a new male hero, should want him to be weak and ineffectual. In this interest, it is imperative that men help men rediscover and maintain the best aspects of male power and male courage.

37 In reaching for traditional male traits like assertiveness and autonomy, women have tried to keep their warmth and gentleness and their capacity for nurturance; so do men in reaching for traditionally feminine traits need to keep the best aspects of their masculinity.

38 In fact, Campbell asserts that at the highest levels of heroic endeavor, in transcendent religious experience—which he also places within the context of world myth—the hero escapes the dualism of the world (a dualism which divides time and eternity, good and evil, subject and object, male and female, among others) and he finds unity with all things, and finds all things within himself. In world mythology, this transcendence is often represented as unification with an androgynous God: Bodhisattva, the female and male God-figure who holds the world (the lotus flower) in her and his hand.

39 And so, while there will always be differences which we will cherish, men and women are on the same quest, toward transcendence of the limiting aspects of the self and toward a greater wholeness of being in the world.

40 The man who makes this inward journey will have a perspective on what is truly heroic (and once again, it is not enough for individual men to do this; there must be a collective quest).

41 As he attempts to stand up to his fears of intimacy, he will know that he is doing something important and courageous, because he will understand the painful context in which the fears were acquired.

42 As he makes deep and lasting commitments to his wife and kids and manages to keep them, he will know that he is overcoming a sense of Oedipal betrayal in his childhood.

43 As he tries to be a more involved parent to his kids, he will realize the heroic nature of creating a role which was not given to him or taught to him.

44 As he does battle with the forces outside the family that attack and weaken its inner life, particularly as he stands up to the brutalizing forces in the workplace that encourage both men and women to abandon their children, he will know that he is on a righteous crusade.

45 Knowledge of the inner struggle will frame his experience, giving everyday victories the true significance they deserve. These are the very kinds of acts through which women's heroism has been exercised for so many centuries; and it is on this stage of ordinary life that it has taken place. Men need to seek, and emulate, this kind of unacknowledged, private, but vitally significant activity which involves caretaking and maintaining the more vulnerable moments and aspects of the human condition: especially our children.

46 *Let Us Now Praise Famous Men,* James Agee titles his study of tenant farmers during the Depression, taking a line from a passage from the Apocrypha which describes a variety of types of men of worldly power—the businessman, the scholar, the lawmaker—acknowledging that they have their rightful place in the human community. But the passage continues: ''And there are some that have no memorial, who have perished as though they had not lived; they have become as though they had not been born, and so have their children after them. But these were men of mercy, whose righteous deeds have not been forgotten; their posterity will continue forever, and their glory will not be blotted out. Their bodies were buried in peace, and their name lives to all generations.''

47 So let us look for this wise and more giving man in our midst as he returns from his journey. Like most such returned heroes he will look like an ordinary person. He will probably not have time to run for public office; nor is it likely that he will appear on television.

48 He'll talk about feeling torn between his work and his family. He will fight with the forces in his work life for time off to be with his kids; he will fiercely resist being transferred to another city; he will be willing to pass up a promotion if need be. He will actively seek support at his place of business for day care facilities; and he will show up at them as frequently as his wife does.

49 He will be like a friend of mine who was recently asked to serve on a committee at his kids' school, and who declined, saying that he only committed himself to activities that brought him into direct contact with his children.

50 He will doubtless be reaching out to other men for support in his new endeavors; he will have an active friendship network, and maybe a support group, among men with similar values.

51 And he will know what is going on in his wife's emotional life; and he will be a source of support and strength for her. He will actively support her life outside the family, however it is structured. He will be trying to think about her experience and attempting to find ways of facilitating it in exactly the same way she has been doing for him for so many years.

52 I hope we will see him at all his old haunts—playing softball, working under his car, jogging, taking pride in his maleness. But whatever he's doing, I hope he'll have his kids—daughters and sons—in tow—teaching them, helping them learn what he knows.

53 The question regarding what women can do in relation to our journey is a good one. You can be good "systems" thinkers and keep changing yourselves. Unfortunately, many of us men will not change unless the changes in our wives force us to.

54 As you continue on your journey, tell us more about what you need; and try to say it in ways that allow us to hear the vulnerability and stress of being a woman today. Tell us, in terms that we can hear, of the loneliness, the fatigue, the worry about the kids and about yourselves.

55 And ask us for help. Take the risk of believing we can be there for you (and for some this will be the first time in expecting real support from a man). If you can, be specific in your requests; we're a bit concrete, and it helps us to know particulars.

56 If you make agreements with us, try not to supervise us in helping you. Bite your fingernails and hope that we make it, and that the kids don't wander into traffic while we're learning. Assume that we will burn a lot of toast.

57 If the men today who are already on this journey are to escape their isolation, if they are to avoid giving up the quest in disillusionment and disappointment, if instead they are to find a voice, a direction, a plurality, they need the kind of outspoken, consciousness-raising leaders that the women's movement had; and these leaders need a new conceptual map which traces the evolution of the male personality from its difficult origins to its new heroic possibilities. The creation of this kind of "new map for masculinity" is a task which the family therapy community could undertake.

58 In our clinical work, we will have to keep confronting men, but we can also support them and help them expand their experience. As we work to understand the male experience, we can help our male clients form male support groups.

59 We ourselves can form more active interest groups focused on the male experience.

60 We could organize and fund a project focused on men's roles, something like the Fatherhood Project which the Bank Street College of Education has sponsored in recent years; and we could be much more public in attempting to attract media attention to these issues.

61 We could devote an entire conference of this organization to the problems of men in this society.

62 Whatever we do, we should make it very clear that when we go to Washington next year to talk about "Strengthening Families," we don't want to strengthen the same old family. We want to strengthen it by changing it.

63 Well, enough.

64 Let me read you what Joseph Campbell said about the hero's journey:

65 "The labyrinth is thoroughly known; we have only to follow the thread of the hero-path. And where we had thought to find an abomination, we shall find a god; where we had thought to slay another, we shall slay ourselves; where we had thought to travel outward, we shall come to the center of our own existence; where we had thought to be alone, we shall be with all the world."

References

Boszormenyi-Nagy, I., & Spark, G. M. (1973). *Invisible Loyalties.* New York: Harper & Row.

Bly, Robert. (1989). Male naivete and the loss of the Kingdom. *Pilgrimage: The Journal of Psycho-therapy and Personal Exploration* 15:2–16 September/October.

Bronstein, P., & Cowan, C. P. (Eds.). (1987). *Fatherhood Today,* New York: John Wiley & Sons.

Chodorow, N. (1978). *The Reproduction of Mothering.* Berkeley: University of California Press.

Gray-Little, B., & Burks, N. (1983). Power and satisfaction in marriage. *Psychological Bulletin, 933,* 513–538.

Lamb, M. E. (Ed.) (1981). *The Role of the Father in Child Development* (2nd ed.). New York: John Wiley & Sons.

Levinson, D. J. (1978). *The Seasons of a Man's Life.* New York: Alfred A. Knopf.

Miller, S. (1983). *Men and Friendship.* Boston: Houghton Mifflin.

Napier, A. Y. (1988). *The Fragile Bond.* New York: Harper & Row.

———. (1978). The rejection-intrusion pattern: A central family dynamic. *Journal of Marriage and Family Counseling,* Jan., 5–12.

Napier, A. Y., & Whitaker, C. A. (1978). *The Family Crucible.* New York: Harper & Row.

Questions for Analysis

1. Why does Napier include "Heroism" in his title? What different kinds of heroes does he have in mind?
2. Napier, among many others who write about the "new man," draws heavily on mythical stories. Here Napier focuses on the heroic journey. What is the pattern he lays out? What is the significance of that journey?
3. What does Napier see as the most obvious flaw in the contemporary family?
4. How do Napier's assessments of the problems men face and the healing processes they must go through parallel opinions expressed by feminists in previous essays?
5. Toward the end of his essay Napier outlines some things he would like to see in the "new man," the man who returns from the journey within. Review the characteristics he lists. What of them do you find appealing? Are these traits difficult to adopt? Why do most men lack them?
6. Compare the characteristics Napier would like to see with those presented by Warren Farrell in "The Masculine Value System." Have men made progress in the 20 years between these two essays? Is further progress possible? Explain.

Asa Baber

Call of the Wild

(1991)

A journalist and short-story writer, Asa Baber (b. 1936) is contributing editor for *Playboy* magazine, where this essay first appeared in 1991. A collection of his short stories, *Tranquility Base and Other Stories,* appeared in 1979.

1 This is about a revolution in male self-perception. Women have had their opportunity to create their cultural revolution. Now it is our turn. After too many years of allowing other people to define us, we are going to define ourselves.

2 Just for openers, do you remember when you first realized that men had their own problems in this culture? Was there a moment when you saw that sexism was as frequently targeted against men as against women?

3 When did you recognize that the formation of a solid male identity was not always easy to achieve in this society, that there were as many obstacles to growth and maturity *and equality* for men as there were for women?

4 And, finally, how long have you yearned to turn this feminized and prejudiced culture on its ear and assert your own identity and worth as a man?

5 Stick around; the next revolution is happening. Men—the average guy, not the *GQ* dandy, not the teacher's pet—are taking back the culture. It is a great time to be alive.

6 The seeds of my own revolution were planted early. The year was 1973. The place was Honolulu. At the time, I was losing custody of my two sons, Jim and Brendan, ages eight and five.

7 The sexism against men that I found in divorce court and its attendant provinces was overwhelming. In law offices, in courtrooms, in counseling sessions with the so-called experts who staffed the system, in classroom meetings with teachers and administrators, I was learning that the sexist bias against men in child-custody matters was intense and all-encompassing. The male in the divorce process was considered an irrelevant appendage to the nuclear family.

8 I fought hard for it, but I knew in my heart that I didn't have much of a chance of winning custody of Jim and Brendan. In those days, something like 95 percent of contested child custody cases were resolved in favor of the mother. (The figures are a little better today, but the system is still stacked against the father's rights.)

9 I had been a good father, a very involved father, a man who had spent at least as much time with his children as their mother had. But I lost custody of my sons, and the weight of that decision shattered me. I was losing the two most important people in my life, young sons who had taught me how to love, how to nurture, how to pare down my aggressive ego and place other human beings ahead of myself.

10 After the divorce, I went through several years of feeling unmanly and useless. Cut off from my sons—communications between us often obstructed, visitation frequently under threat of change and postponement—I had no pride in myself as a male.

11 All of these difficulties and failures were important things for me to experience, however. Without any preconceived plan, I started writing about the subject of men and the sexist prejudices they endure. At first, I wrote for myself, to explain things to myself. And then I got lucky. *Playboy* published an article of mine in December 1978 titled *Who Gets Screwed in a Divorce? I Do!* In that article, I talked about the difficult problems that men face in divorce and child-custody cases. I discussed the need for divorce reform. I also considered a larger subject (and one that is central to the next revolution): "How can we find identity and pride and self-worth *as men?*"

12 It was a simple but important question, and not many people were asking it publicly in those days. "Men must begin making a case for themselves," I wrote. "Manhood is an honorable condition. . . . It seems clear that men need help today perceiving themselves as men, and such help can come only from themselves." I outlined certain qualities that American males have in abundance but do not always advertise, including qualities such as courage, generosity, sensitivity, intellect, wit and humor. "Men have a job to do redefining our roles and reaching out for health and identity," I wrote.

13 My 1978 prediction about male resourcefulness turned out to be accurate. It took us a while, but here at the beginning of the Nineties, we are redefining our roles as men. That is what the next revolution is about: the establishment of a tough *and* loving male identity that cannot be obliterated by the sexism and prejudice under which we live.

14 We are aiming for the very best qualities of manhood. In pursuit of this goal, groups of men across the country are starting to meet on evenings and weekends to attend workshops, to think and explore and write and examine their roles as men. True, their efforts are occasionally awkward and improvisational and, yes, there are times when their methods could easily be mocked and misunderstood. But that does not discourage them. "For this is the journey that men make," wrote James Michener in *The Fires of Spring*. "To find themselves. If they fail in this, it doesn't matter what else they find."

15 In April 1982, I published my first *Men* column, "Role Models." In it, I talked about the way men learn and work and grow: "Men are by nature collegiate. We are convivial scavengers, patching our personalities together with chewing gum and baling wire. We collect traits from a million different sources."

16 The sources we are using to patch together our male revolution are likewise numerous and eclectic. They include the writings of Carl Jung, the poems, stories and interviews of Robert Bly, Bruno Bettelheim's theories about the uses of enchantment, fragments of fairy tales from the brothers Grimm, the work of Joseph Campbell, medieval legends about King Arthur's court, the perceptions and storytelling of the contemporary mythologist Michael Meade, the novels of D. H. Lawrence, the writings of William James, American Indian practices and rituals, segments of classical Greek myths, the writings and lectures of John Bradshaw on the origins and functions of shame in our culture, the insights of Jungian psychoanalyst Robert Moore and a host of other influences and properties.

17 Let's take a quick look at two men from the roster just listed: Joseph Campbell and Robert Bly.

18 A fundamental source for our next revolution is the work of the late scholar Joseph Campbell. His writings, including such books as *The Hero with a Thousand Faces* and *Myths to Live By,* and his interviews with Bill Moyers on PBS (published under the title *The Power of Myth*), have shown men how to take myths and stories from different ages and different cultures and make them useful in their own lives.

19 Myths are ''*models* for understanding your own life,'' Campbell says. ''Anybody going on a journey, inward or outward, to find values, will be on a journey that has been described many times in the myths of mankind.''

20 It is this idea of the journey inward, every man an explorer and hero as he faces his inner self, that suits us as men today. Our fathers and their fathers before them faced great hazards and overcame them with courage and persistence. And although their journeys were generally outward bound, not inner directed, the heroes of those ancient myths serve as examples as we confront our own difficulties and scrutinize the dynamics of our own male identity. Granted, it takes some grandiosity for the contemporary American male to see himself as an explorer embarking on a difficult expedition, but he is just that.

21 Under the fire of contemporary feminist scolding and sexism, the average man has been forced to question his identity and sexuality, and he has usually done so in isolation. But if he examines the myths of the past, he will learn that he is not as sequestered as he thought, that other men have traveled into treacherous territory before, experienced certain risks and come out of the labyrinth alive and well.

22 Take the tale of Aeneas. Wandering the world after the fall of Troy, Aeneas ventures into the underworld in search of his father, Anchises. Aeneas fords the dreadful river Styx, braves his way past Cerberus, the monstrous three-headed watchdog of Hades and finally manages to converse with the ghost of Anchises, who teaches Aeneas things he needs to know to continue his journey. Like most sons encountering a long-absent father, Aeneas tries to embrace his father, but his efforts are in vain; his father is a spirit and physically unavailable. However, Aeneas leaves Hades with his father's advice clear in his mind, bolstered by this visit into the unknown.

23 Most men can identify with the journey of Aeneas (which is recounted in Virgil's *Aeneid*). First, we understand the demands of the physical risks that Aeneas ran. Our lives, too, begin with boyhood quarrels and athletic competition that continue into vigorous adulthood (yes, boys are raised differently from girls). Second, we identify with Aeneas' loneliness, because our lives are frequently unsupported and isolated, in our homes as well as in the culture. Third, we understand the story of a man's going on a hazardous search for his father's spirit. We have all been there. Our fathers baffle us, intrigue us, haunt us. We never get away from them, and yet we are often fearful of confronting them, even after they have left us. The quest of Aeneas is our quest.

24 This search for our fathers is at the heart of male identity, and you will find no more emotional or difficult subject on the male agenda. We know we will travel where Aeneas has traveled. He is our brother, our contemporary, and he reminds us of how direct our link is to our forefathers.

25 No discussion of men and the next revolution can take place without consideration of Robert Bly, a major resource for men today. A highly respected poet, writer and lecturer, Bly is the foremost popularizer of the mythic approach to the male journey. In a recent issue of *New Age* magazine, he is saying much the same thing that he said there nine years ago in a pioneering interview with Keith Thompson. The subject centers on contemporary men and their struggles toward masculinity.

26 In that 1982 interview, Bly begins by citing the men of the past three decades who mark some kind of break in historical traditions of masculinity: "The waste and anguish of the Vietnam war made men [of the Sixties and Seventies] question what an adult male really is. . . . As men began to look at women and at their concerns, some men began to see their own feminine side and pay attention to it. That process continues to this day, and I would say that most young males are now involved in it to some extent."

27 Bly then sounds a note of caution. "The step of the male bringing forth his feminine consciousness is an important one—and yet I have the sense that there is something wrong. The male in the past twenty years has become more thoughtful, more gentle. But by this process, he has *not* become more free. He's a nice boy who now pleases not only his mother but also the young woman he is living with.

28 "I see the phenomenon," Bly continues, "of what I would call the 'soft male' all over the country today. . . . But something's wrong. Many of these men are unhappy. There's not much energy in them. They are life-preserving but not exactly *life-giving*."

29 For me, Bly presents a precise summation of what has happened to many men over the past three decades—when the feminist revolution has taken over the culture and told us how terrible we were as men and how much we needed to change. To be *macho* in any manner has been unfashionable. And yet, every man has an element of the *macho* in his genetic structure. To deny it and suppress it can be deadly to men (and to the culture). Such denial can leave us depressed, without energy or passion or identity.

30 As men, we have special gifts. One of those is the ability to be in touch with the Cro-Magnon man who lives somewhere deep inside our hearts and minds and calls to us. It is vital to remember that this man is not a savage. In no way is he an uncontrolled killer or evil oppressor. He is primordial but not barbaric, aboriginal but not vicious. He represents what is *best* in the spirit of manhood. Indomitable and invincible and wild, ready to protect and defend and compete, his instinct and perceptions necessary to ensure the survival of the human race, this primitive man at the center of our psyches must be allowed room to live and breathe and express himself. If this rudimentary part of us dies, male identity dies.

31 Bly, borrowing a term from *Iron John,* a tale written by the Grimm brothers in 1820, calls this primitive man "the wildman." It is not a bad name for him.

32 In *Iron John,* a young man on a difficult journey sees a large, hairy creature—the wildman—at the bottom of a pond that the young man is emptying, bucket by bucket. This discovery is frightening and intriguing. "What I'm proposing," says Bly, "is that every modern male has, lying at the bottom of his psyche, a large, primitive man covered with hair down to his feet. Making contact with this wildman . . . is the process that still hasn't taken place in contemporary culture. . . . Freud, Jung and Wilhelm Reich

are three men who had the courage to go down into the pond and accept what's there. . . . The job of modern males is to follow them down.''

33 Accepting what is dark down there—what he calls ''the shadow''—is another task that Bly assigns to any man who would discover his true male self and become an initiated male. Under Bly's urging, men are beginning to explore this shadow side of their personalities. Anger, aggression, grief, feelings of abandonment and rejection, rage, confusion—all the varied dark and shadowy forces that whirl around like demons in the male psyche—these are things that we have tried to deny or ignore in order to be acceptable and admired.

34 But we have tried much too hard to be nice and we have essentially handed over the job of self-definition to others. This turns out to have been self-destructive. We emasculate and feminize ourselves to gain female approval—and then we hope against all available evidence that our powerful masculine energies will leave us alone. But is that likely?

35 Face it: For most men, the hope that our energy will fade away is vain. Witness the fact that our sexuality emerges at a very early age—usually much earlier than the emergence of female sexuality—and carries with it a beautiful immediacy, from spontaneous erections to wet dreams to vivid fantasies. This immediacy of male sexuality lasts well into our adulthood, even into old age for many men. Are we really going to be able to suppress all of that energy? And why *should* we repudiate such a unique and wonderful drive?

36 To use a Bly analogy, ''The Widow Douglas wanted Huck Finn to be nice. And after he has floated down the river with a black man, Aunt Sally wants to adopt him and 'civilize' him. Huck says, 'I can't stand it. I been there before.' ''

37 Sounds familiar, doesn't it?

38 The wildman lives in every man. He is beautiful and divine. He has enormous, fundamental energy and a great love for the world. He is just as much a nurturer and protector and creator as any female figure, but he will do that nurturing and protecting in his own masculine way. It is time for the wildman in us to be celebrated without shame. That celebration is part of what our revolution is about. It is our job as men to know ourselves better so that we can contribute more to this world and be more honest with ourselves. We have a right to our revolution, in other words. An absolute right.

39 Cut to a damp and cold weekend in November 1988 at a lodge somewhere in Wisconsin. I am attending The New Warrior Training Adventure, one of the only programs in the country that emphasize male initiation as a necessary rite of passage. It is late at night, I have been here for a day and a half already and I am surrounded by a group of men who are asking me with focused energy to look deeply into my life. Who am I? What is my mission in life as a man? What is it that holds me back from completing my mission? What is my shadow, and how does it haunt me?

40 Understand that a number of things have occurred at this seminar before this moment, things that have pushed me and scared me and enlightened me and softened me up for the interrogation at hand. There have been some games, some questioning, there has

been a rendition of *Iron John,* a discussion of the shadow and what it means to men. I feel on the edge of a breakthrough. I am not sure that I like that feeling. I see myself as a man of containment and self-control, and yet here I am in emotional limbo. I feel like an astronaut on the moon.

41 I tell the men around me about what I perceive to be my shadow, my tendency toward aggression, my crazy childhood and difficult family life, how tough and defensive I became after early years of violence that seemed endemic in both my home and my neighborhood on Chicago's South Side, how combat-ready I always am, how I think that my turbulent mind-set interferes with my mission in life.

42 Rich Tosi, a former Marine and one of the founders of the New Warrior Training Adventure program, challenges me on my description of my shadow as that of the ferocious man. "Bullshit, Baber," he says. "I'm not worried about you and your violence. You've explored that. That's not your shadow, because you've faced it. You know the kind of guy who scares me? The man who has never confronted his violence, the passive-aggressive bastard who might freak out and lose control and get violent without any warning at all.

43 "Take a look. When are you going to admit to the grief you have for the men you've lost in your life? What about your father, for example, or your sons, when you lost custody of them, or the guys from your old neighborhood who never got out of there alive, or the Marines you knew who were killed? You've lost a lot of men, haven't you, Lieutenant? Pick one of the dead ones, any one, and talk to him now. Go on, do it!"

44 I felt all my defenses crumble and I faced my grief openly for the first time. I mourned, I raged, I pounded the floor, I went down into the dark pond of my psyche and dredged up the forces I had been containing for too many years, I bucketed out my rage and my grief under the guidance of good men.

45 Tosi and Dr. Ron Hering, another founder of The New Warrior Training Adventure, led me down into the grave of the man I happened to grieve for the most that evening, a Marine named Mike with whom I served and who was killed in a chopper crash in Laos in the mid-Sixties. Mike had been like a younger brother to me. His father had been like a father to me after my own father passed away in 1960. The secret war in Laos would kill Mike first, and Mike's death would kill his father a few years later. Losses? Mine were incalculable, and they had occurred in a very short time. *Two* fathers and many brothers dead in the space of a few years, and the additional specter of a full-scale war that had never been declared a war? I had not been able to handle the heartache of all that, so I had suppressed it, buried it. The heartache, you see, was my shadow.

46 Ron Hering and Rich Tosi and the other men working with me gave me room to grieve, let me explore my shadow, did not judge me or exploit me for my sadness, understood the losses that most men endure in self-imposed isolation, the denials we elaborately construct to hide from our grief.

47 Until then, I had always assumed that my physical survival was living proof of my cowardice and unmanliness. It was a certain kind of twisted male syllogism that is not uncommon: Men had died, I had not; therefore, I was undeserving of life; I should have

died before them, possibly thereby saving them. That is a classic case of survivor's guilt, of course, and I had it full-blown.

48 Hering and Tosi and my peers helped me see that the men who had died wanted me to carry on the best traditions of manhood for them. They—all my fathers and brothers and sons from the beginning of time—were handing me the golden ball of masculinity with all its energy and beauty, and they were asking me to preserve it, protect it and pass it on to the next generation of men. *That* was my mission in life.

49 With that realization, the shadow of guilt and grief that had dominated me faded in the light of my self-examination. I faced my shadow, battled it, tapped into my wildman energy and overcame it. Like Aeneas, I visited Hades and came away from the underworld with a little more wisdom.

50 In a very real sense, I was now an initiated male, a man ready to accept the joys and obligations of maturity.

51 "We are living at an important and fruitful moment now," Bly writes in his new book, *Iron John,* "for it is clear to men that the images of adult manhood given by the popular culture are worn out; a man can no longer depend on them. . . . [Men are] open to new visions of what a man is or could be."

52 New visions of masculinity: That is what our revolution is all about.

53 Welcome aboard.

Questions for Analysis

1. Baber's essay and the previous one by Augustus Napier are in some respects very similar—they both, for example, rely on the work of Joseph Campbell on myth. How do they differ in focus, tone, and purpose?
2. This essay originally appeared in *Playboy.* Does the definition of the new man Baber presents differ from the stereotypical man you associate with *Playboy?* In what ways?
3. Baber says in the first paragraph that "after too many years of allowing other people to define us, we are going to define ourselves." What does he mean? Who were the "other people" doing the defining? When he says "we are going to define ourselves," does he have in mind a group defining themselves as a group or individuals defining themselves as individuals?
4. Baber begins and ends his essay with personal accounts. How does this strategy both give his essay more authority, power, and appeal and yet limit our sense of how/what he says might apply to the experience of most other men?
5. Baber quotes from poet John Bly, who talks about the "soft male" and the "wildman." What are these two concepts? Why is each important? How do they work together?

6. Both Napier and Baber focus on the inner journey modern men must take to find and understand their manhood. The feminist writers in earlier readings touch briefly on the inner life of women and focus more directly on social change. What factors account for this difference in emphasis?

Karen S. Peterson

Debate: Does "Wiring" Rule Emotion, Skill?

(1991)

Suzy Parker

Sex and the Brain

(1991)

Karen S. Peterson is a writer and Suzy Parker a graphic artist for *USA Today,* where this story and illustration appeared July 8, 1991. Peterson's story is an overview of the reception among professional researchers of Anne Moir's book *Brain Sex: The Real Difference Between Men & Women,* published by Lyle Stuart in 1991.

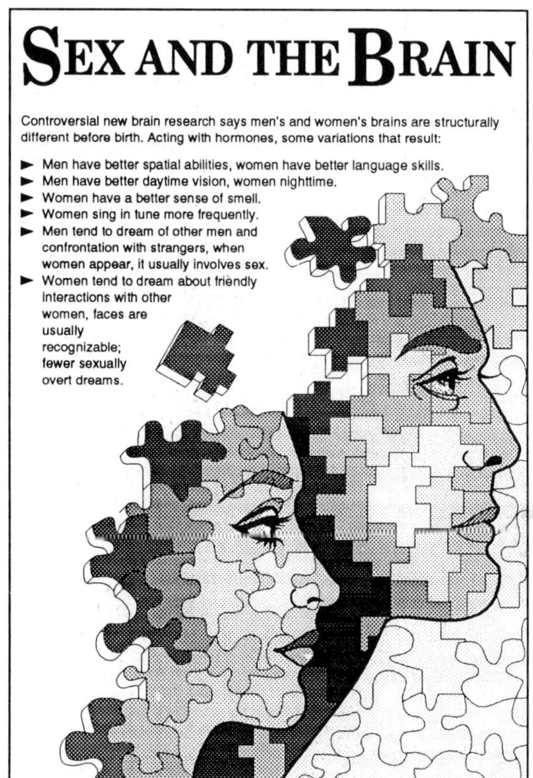

1 "Why can't you ever come to the point?" he asks. Her circumlocutions drive him crazy.

2 "Why won't you really talk to me?" she asks. His silence makes her back arch.

3 The real answers to such questions may be—literally—all in the mind. The newest scientific research shows men's and women's brains are "wired" differently. Each sex has a mind of its own.

4 Implications for relationships—why a woman can't be more like a man and vice versa—are mind-boggling. Not to mention controversial.

5 "The brain is differently constructed in men and in women," says Anne Moir, the latest to brainstorm the subject in *Brain Sex: The Real Difference Between Men & Women* (Lyle Stuart, $17.95).

6 In concert with hormones, men's and women's brains "process information in a different way, which results in different perceptions, priorities and behavior." Marriages suffer when the sexes refuse to acknowledge variations.

7 The message in Moir's hotly contested book: "Men are different from women. To maintain that they are the same in aptitude, skill or behavior is to build a society based on a biological and scientific lie."

8 The Englishwoman, the newest soldier in the battle of the sexes, holds a doctorate in genetics from Oxford. She's filming a three-part TV series, due in '92, based on her book.

9 "Her book is courageous," says anthropologist Helen Fisher, American Museum of Natural History in New York. "She says things Americans will not want to hear."

10 But brain researchers and social scientists have widely differing views about what the newest brain studies mean.

11 Two prominent brain experts, asked to review Moir's perspective, note:

- Ruben Gur, neuropsychologist, University of Pennsylvania. "I have some quibbles, but overall it is a commendable job. She went to the most eminent investigators in the field. In some ways you can't argue with it."
- Melissa Hines, biobehavioral scientist, University of California, Los Angeles. "There is no evidence that sex differences in the brain have anything to do with emotional responses. . . . This book is on the level of the *National Enquirer.*"

12 Roger Gorski, one of the field's most noted researchers, says he is "taken aback" by Moir's contention that men's and women's brains actually process information differently.

13 But "there are structural differences," says Gorski of UCLA's School of Medicine. "And it is logical to say there are potential differences in emotional responses." It's fair to claim understanding brain dissimilarities "can help us understand relationships better."

14 Scientists have found the corpus callosum—the mass of fibers connecting the brain's right and left hemispheres—is larger in proportion to brain weight in women than men.

Many now assume that means women have greater communication between the two hemispheres.

15 ''Women will see a problem from all angles,'' Moir says. ''They will read faces, body language'' that men won't. She also suggests the greater connections may account for ''women's intuition.''

16 While women's brains are diffusely organized, men's are wired to think in a linear way, many say. Men ''see A and B and arrive at C. They are not distracted,'' Moir notes.

17 Women are more apt to use both brain hemispheres to evaluate emotional messages, says Marian Diamond, University of California, Berkeley. ''Perhaps (that's why) males seem to have limited access to verbal codes for emotion.''

18 Gur's studies show women's brains have more gray matter than men's—nerve tissue that facilitates organizing and processing information locally in the brain. ''That could favor any work requiring depth in one specific area.''

19 But men have more white, connective tissue that facilitates sending information. ''Motor coordination in men probably benefits from this.''

20 He adds that conditioning is not the only reason men shed fewer tears. Their brains are wired so ''they are just biologically less disposed to cry.''

21 Virtually all scientists emphasize they are talking about averages, and there is much overlap between the sexes: Most men in a room will be taller than most women, but any woman may be taller than any man.

22 And none disagrees society and environment have a powerful role in shaping each individual. However, ''We've heard the cultural argument for generations,'' says Fisher. Moir's book is ''worth looking at carefully.''

23 Men's brains are wired to be ''measurably better than females at visual tasks, maps, mazes, three-dimensional rotation, and sense of direction; they also are better at orienting themselves in space,'' says Joe Tanenbaum, who writes about brain differences in *Male & Female Realities: Understanding the Opposite Sex* (Robert Erdman, $12.95).

24 Women, he says, ''are better at language skills: fluency, verbal reasoning, written prose and reading.''

25 The typical man will be better than the typical woman at a spatial game such as chess, says Glenn Wilson, a psychologist with London's Institute of Psychiatry. ''Men and women will do just as well at Scrabble. But in quiz games that rely on quick retrieval of verbal information, women will do better.''

26 Wilson says the evidence for Moir's book is ''incontrovertible and overwhelming.'' And he agrees with Moir's assertion—although others don't—that men's brains, more than women's, have been shaped by evolution to favor both physical aggression and sexual variety.

27 June Reinisch, co-founder of the Kinsey Institute, says she doesn't ''dichotomize nature-nurture the way (Moir) does.'' But, ''I would add that I'm starting to think sex is just a totally different phenomenon for men and women. Nobody has given that enough thought.''

28 Even the suggestion that men's and women's brains are different is heresy for many who believe differences can be used to justify discrimination. "I get outraged. . . . Moir is socially irresponsible," says Anne Fausto-Sterling, professor of medical science at Brown University. She believes brain differences are small, and many studies are flawed.

29 "Society is ill-equipped" to deal with differences, says Marie-Christine de Lacoste, neuroscientist at Yale University Medical School. "We have been trained since we were kids to believe that if two things are different, one has to be 'better.' "

30 But De Lacoste adds Moir is "running around making statements about research that is inconclusive."

31 Moir says that because the sexes' brains are different does not mean that any given woman isn't as qualified as any given man for a given job. "We have confused equality with sameness." But it does mean, she says, women may choose different fields from men.

32 And differences don't mean a man nurtures less or more than a woman. But his brain is wired so his "nurturing instinct will be expressed in action. He will lift little Johnny and toss him about, whereas Mom might try to chat things through."

33 And he'll tend to demonstrate devotion to his mate by "washing her car, bringing flowers," rather than expressing himself verbally.

34 Gorski emphasizes brain differences don't mean one sex is "better" than the other. And he makes a plea: "Let's do more work and find out what they really do mean."

Questions for Analysis

1. If Anne Moir's conclusions are based on measurable physiological differences that correspond to well-established behavioral differences in men and women, why did her book generate such radically different responses from professionals in medicine, science, and the social sciences?
2. Which responses seem most reasonable to you? Which seem based on preconceptions?
3. This piece is a review of Moir's book based on quotations from a number of different people whose careers are in the fields of scientific inquiry most affected by Moir's research and conclusions. In what ways do these quotations make this piece reliable? Based on this review, what can we conclude about the book? About opinions in the scientific community?
4. De Lacoste says that we have been taught to think that if two things are different, one has to be "better." Moir says "we have confused equality with sameness." Reread the passages these quotes come from. How are these two women saying the same thing yet making two very different points?

5. Does the possibility that men and women may be ''wired'' differently in any way undercut the admonitions by Augustus Napier, Asa Baber, and others that men should come to accept their feminine and emotional side? Does this possibility of ''wiring'' differences reinforce Susan Browmiller's point in the final paragraph of her essay about the special ''biological experience of a woman''? Discuss.
6. Why did graphic artist Suzy Parker draw her illustration as she did? Does her visual reinforce the issue addressed in the article? Explain.

Tillie Olsen

I Stand Here Ironing

(1956)

Although she began to write during the 1930s, Tillie Olsen (b. 1913) was not able to devote much time to her writing until the 1950s. Before then she had to spend most of her time working and raising her children. Her short stories, including "I Stand Here Ironing," are collected in *Tell Me a Riddle* (1961), and her essays in *Silences* (1978).

1 I stand here ironing, and what you asked me moves tormented back and forth with the iron.

2 ''I wish you would manage the time to come in and talk with me about your daughter. I'm sure you can help me understand her. She's a youngster who needs help and whom I'm deeply interested in helping.''

3 ''Who needs help.'' . . . Even if I came, what good would it do? You think because I am her mother I have a key, or that in some way you could use me as a key? She has lived for nineteen years. There is all that life that has happened outside of me, beyond me.

4 And when is there time to remember, to sift, to weigh, to estimate, to total? I will start and there will be an interruption and I will have to gather it all together again. Or I will become engulfed with all I did or did not do, with what should have been and what cannot be helped.

5 She was a beautiful baby. The first and only one of our five that was beautiful at birth. You do not guess how new and uneasy her tenancy in her now-loveliness. You did not know her all those years she was thought homely, or see her poring over her baby pictures, making me tell her over and over how beautiful she had been—and would be, I would tell her—and was now, to the seeing eye. But the seeing eyes were few or nonexistent. Including mine.

6 I nursed her. They feel that's important nowadays. I nursed all the children, but with her, with all the fierce rigidity of first motherhood, I did like the books then said. Though

her cries battered me to trembling and my breasts ached with swollenness, I waited till the clock decreed.

7 Why do I put that first? I do not even know if it matters, or if it explains anything.

8 She was a beautiful baby. She blew shining bubbles of sound. She loved motion, loved light, loved color and music and textures. She would lie on the floor in her blue overalls patting the surface so hard in ecstasy her hands and feet would blur. She was a miracle to me, but when she was eight months old I had to leave her daytimes with the woman downstairs to whom she was no miracle at all, for I worked or looked for work and for Emily's father, who "could no longer endure" (he wrote in his good-bye note) "sharing want with us."

9 I was nineteen. It was the pre-relief, pre-WPA world of the depression. I would start running as soon as I got off the streetcar, running up the stairs, the place smelling sour, and awake or asleep to startle awake, when she saw me she would break into a clogged weeping that could not be comforted, a weeping I can hear yet.

10 After a while I found a job hashing at night so I could be with her days, and it was better. But it came to where I had to bring her to his family and leave her.

11 It took a long time to raise the money for her fare back. Then she got chicken pox and I had to wait longer. When she finally came, I hardly knew her, walking quick and nervous like her father, looking like her father, thin, and dressed in a shoddy red that yellowed her skin and glared at the pockmarks. All the baby loveliness gone.

12 She was two. Old enough for nursery school they said, and I did not know then what I know now—the fatigue of the long day, and the lacerations of group life in the kinds of nurseries that are only parking places for children.

13 Except that it would have made no difference if I had known. It was the only place there was. It was the only way we could be together, the only way I could hold a job.

14 And even without knowing, I knew. I knew the teacher that was evil because all these years it has curdled into my memory, the little boy hunched in the corner, her rasp, "Why aren't you outside, because Alvin hits you? That's no reason, go out, scaredy." I knew Emily hated it even if she did not clutch and implore, "Don't go, Mommy" like the other children, mornings.

15 She always had a reason why we should stay home. Momma, you look sick. Momma, I feel sick. Momma, the teachers aren't there today, they're sick. Momma, we can't go, there was a fire there last night. Momma, it's a holiday today, no school, they told me.

16 But never a direct protest, never rebellion. I think of our others in their three-, four-year-oldness—the explosions, the tempers, the denunciations, the demands—and I feel suddenly ill. I put the iron down. What in me demanded that goodness in her? And what was the cost, the cost to her of such goodness?

17 The old man living in the back once said in his gentle way: "You should smile at Emily more when you look at her." What *was* in my face when I looked at her? I loved her. There were all the acts of love.

18 It was only with the others I remembered what he said, and it was the face of joy, and not of care or tightness or worry I turned to them—too late for Emily. She does not smile easily, let alone almost always as her brothers and sisters do. Her face is

closed and sombre, but when she wants, how fluid. You must have seen it in her pantomimes, you spoke of her rare gift for comedy on the stage that rouses a laughter out of the audience so dear they applaud and applaud and do not want to let her go.

19 Where does it come from, that comedy? There was none of it in her when she came back to me that second time, after I had had to send her away again. She had a new daddy now to learn to love, and I think perhaps it was a better time.

20 Except when we left her alone nights, telling ourselves she was old enough.

21 "Can't you go some other time, Mommy, like tomorrow?" she would ask. "Will it be just a little while you'll be gone? Do you promise?"

22 The time we came back, the front door open, the clock on the floor in the hall. She rigid awake. "It wasn't just a little while. I didn't cry. Three times I called you, just three times, and then I ran downstairs to open the door so you could come faster. The clock talked loud. I threw it away, it scared me what it talked."

23 She said the clock talked loud again that night I went to the hospital to have Susan. She was delirious with the fever that comes before red measles, but she was fully conscious all the week I was gone and the week after we were home when she could not come near the new baby or me.

24 She did not get well. She stayed skeleton thin, not wanting to eat, and night after night she had nightmares. She would call for me, and I would rouse from exhaustion to sleepily call back: "You're all right, darling, go to sleep, it's just a dream," and if she still called, in a sterner voice, "Now go to sleep, Emily, there's nothing to hurt you." Twice, only twice, when I had to get up for Susan anyhow, I went in to sit with her.

25 Now when it is too late (as if she would let me hold and comfort her like I do the others) I get up and go to her at once at her moan or restless stirring. "Are you awake, Emily? Can I get you something?" And the answer is always the same: "No, I'm all right, go back to sleep, Mother."

26 They persuaded me at the clinic to send her away to a convalescent home in the country where "she can have the kind of food and care you can't manage for her, and you'll be free to concentrate on the new baby." They still send children to that place. I see pictures on the society page of sleek young women planning affairs to raise money for it, or dancing at the affairs, or decorating Easter eggs or filling Christmas stockings for the children.

27 They never have a picture of the children so I do not know if the girls still wear those gigantic red bows and the ravaged looks on the every other Sunday when the parents can come to visit "unless otherwise notified"—as we were notified the first six weeks.

28 Oh it is a handsome place, green lawns and tall trees and fluted flower beds. High up on the balconies of each cottage the children stand, the girls in their red bows and white dresses, the boys in white suits and giant red ties. The parents stand below shrieking up to be heard and the children shriek down to be heard, and between them the invisible wall "Not To Be Contaminated by Parental Germs or Physical Affection."

29 There was a tiny girl who always stood hand in hand with Emily. Her parents never came. One visit she was gone. ''They moved her to Rose Cottage'' Emily shouted in explanation. ''They don't like you to love anybody here.''

30 She wrote once a week, the labored writing of a seven-year-old. ''I am fine. How is the baby. If I write my letter nicely I will have a star. Love.'' There never was a star. We wrote every other day, letters she could never hold or keep but only hear read—once. ''We simply do not have room for children to keep any personal possessions,'' they patiently explained when we pieced one Sunday's shrieking together to plead how much it would mean to Emily, who loved so to keep things, to be allowed to keep her letters and cards.

31 Each visit she looked frailer. ''She isn't eating,'' they told us.

32 (They had runny eggs for breakfast or mush with lumps, Emily said later, I'd hold it in my mouth and not swallow. Nothing ever tasted good, just when they had chicken.)

33 It took us eight months to get her released home, and only the fact that she gained back so little of her seven lost pounds convinced the social worker.

34 I used to try to hold and love her after she came back, but her body would stay stiff, and after a while she'd push away. She ate little. Food sickened her, and I think much of life too. Oh she had physical lightness and brightness, twinkling by on skates, bouncing like a ball up and down up and down over the jump rope, skimming over the hill; but these were momentary.

35 She fretted about her appearance, thin and dark and foreign-looking at a time when every little girl was supposed to look or thought she should look a chubby blonde replica of Shirley Temple. The doorbell sometimes rang for her, but no one seemed to come and play in the house or be a best friend. Maybe because we moved so much.

36 There was a boy she loved painfully through two school semesters. Months later she told me how she had taken pennies from my purse to buy him candy. ''Licorice was his favorite and I brought him some every day, but he still liked Jennifer better'n me. Why, Mommy?'' The kind of question for which there is no answer.

37 School was a worry to her. She was not glib or quick in a world where glibness and quickness were easily confused with ability to learn. To her overworked and exasperated teachers she was an overconscientious ''slow learner'' who kept trying to catch up and was absent entirely too often.

38 I let her be absent, though sometimes the illness was imaginary. How different from my now-strictness about attendance with the others. I wasn't working. We had a new baby, I was home anyhow. Sometimes, after Susan grew old enough, I would keep her home from school, too, to have them all together.

39 Mostly Emily had asthma, and her breathing, harsh and labored, would fill the house with a curiously tranquil sound. I would bring the two old dresser mirrors and her boxes of collections to her bed. She would select beads and single earrings, bottle tops and shells, dried flowers and pebbles, old postcards and scraps, all sorts of oddments; then she and Susan would play Kingdom, setting up landscapes and furniture, peopling them with action.

40 Those were the only times of peaceful companionship between her and Susan. I have edged away from it, that poisonous feeling between them, that terrible balancing of hurts and needs I had to do between the two, and did so badly, those earlier years.

41 Oh there are conflicts between the others too, each one human, needing, demanding, hurting, taking—but only between Emily and Susan, no, Emily toward Susan that corroding resentment. It seems so obvious on the surface, yet it is not obvious. Susan, the second child, Susan, golden- and curly-haired and chubby, quick and articulate and assured, everything in appearance and manner Emily was not; Susan, not able to resist Emily's precious things, losing or sometimes clumsily breaking them; Susan telling jokes and riddles to company for applause while Emily sat silent (to say to me later; that was *my* riddle, Mother, I told it to Susan); Susan, who for all the five years' difference in age was just a year behind Emily in developing physically.

42 I am glad for that slow physical development that widened the difference between her and her contemporaries, though she suffered over it. She was too vulnerable for that terrible world of youthful competition, of preening and parading, of constant measuring of yourself against every other, of envy, "If I had that copper hair," "If I had that skin. . . ." She tormented herself enough about not looking like the others, there was enough of the unsureness, the having to be conscious of words before you speak, the constant caring—what are they thinking of me? without having it all magnified by the merciless physical drives.

43 Ronnie is calling. He is wet and I change him. It is rare there is such a cry now. That time of motherhood is almost behind me when the ear is not one's own but must always be racked and listening for the child cry, the child call. We sit for a while and I hold him, looking out over the city spread in charcoal with its soft aisles of light. "*Shoogily,*" he breathes and curls closer. I carry him back to bed, asleep. *Shoogily.* A funny word, a family word, inherited from Emily, invented by her to say: *comfort.*

44 In this and other ways she leaves her seal, I say aloud. And startle at my saying it. What do I mean? What did I start to gather together, to try and make coherent? I was at the terrible, growing years. War years. I do not remember them well. I was working, there were four smaller ones now, there was not time for her. She had to help be a mother, and housekeeper, and shopper. She had to set her seal. Mornings of crisis and near hysteria trying to get lunches packed, hair combed, coats and shoes found, everyone to school or Child Care on time, the baby ready for transportation. And always the paper scribbled on by a smaller one, the book looked at by Susan then mislaid, the homework not done. Running out to that huge school where she was one, she was lost, she was a drop; suffering over the unpreparedness, stammering and unsure in her classes.

45 There was so little time left at night after the kids were bedded down. She would struggle over books, always eating (it was in those years she developed her enormous appetite that is legendary in our family) and I would be ironing, or preparing food for the next day, or writing V-mail to Bill, or tending the baby. Sometimes, to make me laugh, or out of her despair, she would imitate happenings or types at school.

46 I think I said once: "Why don't you do something like this in the school amateur show?" One morning she phoned me at work, hardly understandable through the weeping: "Mother, I did it. I won, I won; they gave me first prize; they clapped and clapped and wouldn't let me go."

47 Now suddenly she was Somebody, and as imprisoned in her difference as she had been in anonymity.

48 She began to be asked to perform at other high schools, even in colleges, then at city and statewide affairs. The first one we went to, I only recognized her that first moment when thin, shy, she almost drowned herself into the curtains. Then: Was this Emily? The control, the command, the convulsing and deadly clowning, the spell, then the roaring, stamping audience, unwilling to let this rare and precious laughter out of their lives.

49 Afterwards: You ought to do something about her with a gift like that—but without money or knowing how, what does one do? We have left it all to her, and the gift has as often eddied inside, clogged and clotted, as been used and growing.

50 She is coming. She runs up the stairs two at a time with her light graceful step, and I know she is happy tonight. Whatever it was that occasioned your call did not happen today.

51 "Aren't you ever going to finish the ironing, Mother? Whistler painted his mother in a rocker. I'd have to paint mine standing over an ironing board." This is one of her communicative nights and she tells me everything and nothing as she fixes herself a plate of food out of the icebox.

52 She is so lovely. Why did you want me to come in at all? Why were you concerned? She will find her way.

53 She starts up the stairs to bed. "Don't get me up with the rest in the morning." "But I thought you were having midterms." "Oh, those," she comes back in, kisses me, and says quite lightly, "in a couple of years when we'll all be atom-dead they won't matter a bit."

54 She has said it before. She *believes* it. But because I have been dredging the past, and all that compounds a human being is so heavy and meaningful in me, I cannot endure it tonight.

55 I will never total it all. I will never come in to say: She was a child seldom smiled at. Her father left me before she was a year old. I had to work her first six years when there was work, or I sent her home and to his relatives. There were years she had care she hated. She was dark and thin and foreign-looking in a world where the prestige went to blondeness and curly hair and dimples, she was slow where glibness was prized. She was a child of anxious, not proud, love. We were poor and could not afford for her the soil of easy growth. I was a young mother, I was a distracted mother. There were the other children pushing up, demanding. Her younger sister seemed all that she was not. There were years she did not want me to touch her. She kept too much in herself, her life was such she had to keep too much in herself. My wisdom came too late. She has much to her and probably little will come of it. She is a child of her age, of depression, of war, of fear.

56 Let her be. So all that is in her will not bloom—but in how many does it? There is still enough left to live by. Only help her to know—help make it so there is cause for her to know—that she is more than this dress on the ironing board, helpless before the iron.

Questions for Analysis

1. What events and circumstances have operated both to make the daughter who she is and to complicate the relationship between the mother and daughter? Why is the mother reluctant to take any action in response to the school official's request?
2. In a sense the mother is presenting a cause–effect argument. Is her argument sound? Does she gloss over her own responsibilities for her daughter's situation? Who is her audience? Whom is she trying to convince? Does she?
3. The mother begins her line of thought in response to a request from a school official. How have other authority figures and institutions operated to cause problems for the mother and daughter? What is the significance of ironing in this story? (Look especially at the last sentence of the story.)
4. In what ways does this story illustrate the special burden women must bear? How might a man's response and experience be different?
5. What parallels and differences do you see between "I Stand Here Ironing" and Alice Walker's "Everyday Use?"

War—
Reasons and Results: The Persian Gulf, Vietnam, and Before

Guernica is a small town in Spain, approximately 4,000 miles from Kuwait and Iraq. In 1937—about 54 years before the United States and its allies in the Persian Gulf began bombing targets there—the German Air Force bombed Guernica during the Spanish Civil War. Guernica thus became the first of many cities, towns, and villages that would be bombed during our century: London, Coventry, Berlin, Stalingrad (Vdgograd), Dresden, Hiroshima, Hanoi, Baghdad, Kuwait City.

This section begins with Picasso's famous painting, which captures the horror endured by the citizens of Guernica. It also conveys the artist's outrage that human beings could perpetrate such a cruel act against an unarmed and unwarned civilian population. Sadly, the nations of the world have not learned the lessons of art and history. They find themselves repeatedly engaged in war. Although the technology changes, the results do not—people, combatants and noncombatants alike, are killed, maimed, and wounded. Human beings seem to be irresistibly drawn into war—to be fascinated by it even as they are repelled. It is a crucible in which young men and women are tested and proven—if they live through it. War is often presented as the ultimate test of patriotism, duty, loyalty, courage, and honor. Oddly, however, behavior that would be dismissed as foolish at any other time is held up as demonstrating these virtues in time of war.

Nations send their citizens into war for many reasons:

- to protect themselves from an aggressor
- to help defend another country from an aggressor or oppressor
- to assert national—or personal—pride
- to acquire territory
- to gain control over rivals
- to protect vital interests
- to defend and advance political and social ideals and principles (freedom, democracy, communism, etc.)

Philosophers, political scientists, politicians, citizens, and soldiers constantly debate the morality of war. When are any of these reasons (or others) sufficiently strong to justify a war? Some say war is the only way to solve certain problems; others say alternative means are always preferable and available. The questions and answers about war are tied inextricably to questions about human nature and our ability (or inability) to work out our disagreements in nonviolent ways.

The selections in this subsection raise questions about why countries go to war, how people react to war, and what war does to people. The essay selections begin with articles about our country's most recent experience with war in the Persian Gulf. Subsequent selections move back in time as they deal with war and wars earlier in this century and in other periods.

The first essay, Lance Morrow's "A Moment for the Dead," originally appeared as an article in *Time* magazine on April 1, 1991, while people in the United States were still caught up in the euphoria of winning a war that cost so few American lives. Morrow asserts that as we celebrate our soldiers' safe return, our relief and pride should not allow us to forget that we killed 100,000 people. Martin E. Marty's "Lines for Impure Thinkers" was written a few months earlier as the air war in the Persian Gulf turned into the ground war. Marty maintains that individuals can support our troops even as they express reservations about the war.

The next four pieces were written or produced in August 1990 as the build-up of forces and preparations for war began in earnest. All deal with the justification or lack of justification for the war. Ellen Goodman's " 'Our Way of Life': Should We Die for It—Or Change It?" raises questions about the priorities and values which underlie a lifestyle that requires us to import tremendous amounts of oil from Persian Gulf countries. The essay by Warren Anderson, "Another Vietnam? Vital Interest Makes Involvements as Different as Desert and Jungle," demonstrates the differences between the Vietnam War and Operation Desert Storm. His emphasis on "vital interests," however, places him in a very different position from that expressed by Goodman or cartoonists Tom Toles and Kevin Siers. Their cartoons present their views in a graphic way.

Ralph Novak's "Coming to Terms with Nam" deals with one individual's adjustment to life in peaceful times and with the country's adjustment after the Vietnam War. Vietnam was probably the most politically divisive and psychically damaging of any war in our history. As Novak's essay suggests, our soldiers and citizens took almost two decades to find therapeutic ways of coming to terms with it; the healing process will go on for decades to come.

Even in wars waged for reasons that are widely acknowledged to be just, adjustment and healing are difficult, as William Manchester's "Okinawa: The Bloodiest Battle of All" very clearly shows. Manchester's burden in this essay is to explain why, despite the passage of almost 50 years since the end of World War II, his anger, guilt, and sorrow still move within him. An important part of his explanation is the vivid contrast he sets up between the romanticized version of war fed to the population through movies and other media, and the grim, grisly reality of combat.

The final selections are literary. Wilfred Owen's poem, "Dulce et Decorum Est," captures the human agony of World War I, the conflict believed by many at the time to be "the war to end all wars." An excerpt from Jonathan Swift's satirical masterpiece *Gulliver's Travels* shows the author's distaste for war and his contempt for those who, like Gulliver, can accept war seemingly without concern for the pain and destruction it brings.

Gulliver's account of gunpowder's qualities provides a fitting piece with which to end. Gunpowder brought us into the modern age of warfare in which thousands could be killed in a short time and from a great distance. Guernica and the Persian Gulf area experienced the destruction brought not only by gunpowder but also by more sophisticated technologies. Let us hope that we, unlike Gulliver, do not get so caught up in our fascination with how well these technologies work that we forget what happens to those on the ground when the video display records a hit. Peace, because it requires us to argue without fighting, is in many ways more difficult to wage than war. May we learn that it is worth the trouble.

Pablo Picasso
Guernica
(1937)

Pablo Picasso (1881–1973) was one of the most influential and most controversial artists of the twentieth century. Although best known for his paintings, he also worked as a sculptor, graphic artist, and ceramicist. Although he produced works in a number of different styles, he is chiefly remembered as the foremost of the Cubist painters. Picasso was born, studied, and began his career in Spain. He moved to France during the Spanish Civil War. In France, he sold paintings to support the Republican cause against Franco, the fascists, and their Nazi supporters. The most famous and powerful of his anti-war, anti-fascist works was *Guernica,* a huge painting (12 feet high and 26 feet long) produced for exhibition at the 1937 World's Fair in Paris. Picasso would not allow the painting to be exhibited in Spain while Franco was in power, and so for several years the painting was on loan to the Museum of Modern Art in New York City. In 1980, after Franco's death and the restoration of democracy in Spain, it was moved to the Prado in Madrid.

Lance Morrow

A Moment for the Dead

(1991)

Lance Morrow (b. 1939) is an editor for and frequent contributor to *Time* magazine. He also has written several nonfiction books, including *Chief,* a biography of his father. This essay appeared in *Time* on April 1, 1991.

1 The Pentagon ordered 16,099 body bags to be shipped to the Persian Gulf to bring home dead Americans. In the end, 15,773 of the bags were not necessary.

2 The Iraqi army would have needed—what? One hundred thousand body bags? More? No one knows or will ever know. No one has counted the Iraqi corpses. Many of them were buried in the sand, without ceremony; some have been taken care of by vultures.

3 That so few soldiers in the coalition died somehow seemed to Americans a vindication. It was even a return of their shining self, of Buffalo Bill, who (e.e. cummings wrote) could "ride a watersmooth-silver stallion and break onetwothreefourfivepigeonsjustlikethat." The unspoken text was this: the nation had recovered its immunity, its divine favor, or anyway its gift for doing things right. The victory was as satisfying as anything Americans have done together since landing on the moon.

4 Would it be seemly to have a moment of silence for the Iraqi corpses?

5 It is not inconsequential to kill 100,000 people. That much life suddenly and violently extinguished must leave a ragged hole somewhere in the universe. One looks for special effects of a metaphysical kind to attend so much death—the whoosh of all those souls departing. But many of them died ingloriously, like road kill, full of their disgrace, facedown with the loot scattered around them. The conquered often die ignominiously. The victors have not given them much thought.

6 Still, killing 100,000 people is a serious thing to do. It is not equivalent to shooting a rabid dog, which is, down deep, what Americans feel the war was all about, exterminating a beast with rabies. All those 100,000 men were not megalomaniacs, torturers and murderers. They did not all commit atrocities in Kuwait. They were ordinary people: peasants, truck drivers, students and so on. They had the love of their families, the dignity of their lives and work. They cared as little for politics, or less, than most people in the world. They were, precisely, not Saddam Hussein. Which means, since Saddam was the coalition's one true target in all of this, that those 100,000 corpses are, so to speak, collateral damage. The famous smart bombs did not find the one man they were seeking.

7 The secret of much murder and evildoing is to dehumanize the victim, to make him alien, to make him Other, a different species. When we have done that, we have prepared ourselves to kill him, for to kill the Other, to kill a snake, a roach, a pest, a Jew, a scorpion, a black, a centipede, a Palestinian, a hyena, an Iraqi, a wild dog, an Israeli . . . it's O.K.

8 If Saddam Hussein was a poisonous snake in the desert, and he had 1 million poisonous snakes arrayed around him, then it was good sense to drop bombs and kill 100,000 snakes and thus turn back the snake menace.

9 But, of course, the 100,000 Iraqis were not snakes.

10 To kill 100,000 people and to feel no pain at having done so may be dangerous to those who did the killing. It hints at an impaired humanity, a defect like a gate through which other deaths may enter, deaths no one had counted on. The unquiet dead have many ways of haunting—particularly in the Middle East, which has been accumulating the grievances of the dead for thousands of years.

11 In any case, there is not, or there should not be, such a thing as killing without guilt—especially not mass killings without guilt. When people kill without remorse, we call them insane. We call them maniacs, serial murderers.

12 Americans almost unconsciously regard the victory as a kind of moral cleansing: the right thing. But reality and horror have not been rescinded. All killing is unclean. It has upon it a stain that technology cannot annul or override. Americans are not omnipotent, not all virtuous, they should remind themselves, they do not bestride the world. Vainglory is one of the sillier postures: it invariably precedes the rude awakening. It is the sort of whooping glee that, in Daffy Duck cartoons, goeth before the fall.

13 Did the dead Iraqis need to be killed?

14 In the circumstances, yes.

15 Having killed them, how do the victors feel?

16 They feel great.

17 In Texas lore, there is a defense for murder that goes like this: ''He needed killing.'' Is there anything wrong with feeling great about killing 100,000 Iraqis who needed killing?

18 There is nothing wrong with feeling relieved. It is not required, it is not human nature, to mourn the soldiers who were arrayed to kill you. Killing the Iraqis meant that Americans and their partners did not have to face them on the battlefield and maybe die. As it was, the Iraqis who were left in the field surrendered almost without a fight.

19 Like some martial equivalent of the Reagan years, the victory in the gulf makes Americans feel better about themselves. It was splendid and necessary but also unreal—an action-adventure that, like most movies, was divided into three chapters, with decisive turning points: 1) the Iraqi invasion and the buildup of coalition forces; 2) the onset of the air war; and 3) the ground war and its denouement. The victory came with such merciless ease that on the winners' side, the deeper levels of experience (nobility, sacrifice, endurance and so on) were not engaged. The victors now celebrate mostly their relief that they have escaped what might have been. By the Fourth of July, the glorious moment will seem a long time ago.

20 The prospects going into the war were horrifying: the fourth largest army in the world, commanded by a thug whom we thought cunning at the time and even invested with satanic powers. Saddam was armed with chemical weapons and was working on the nuclear kind. All those dark possibilities gave the coalition, in effect, a license to kill. The killing was very well done. I hope it does not give us too much pleasure.

Questions for Analysis

1. What is the point of Morrow's essay? How do you think he would like his readers to react to the information and opinions he presents?
2. Did Morrow's essay cause you to rethink your reaction to the Persian Gulf war? If you did have that response to his essay (even if you did not ultimately change your opinion), what information or statement in Morrow's essay made you stop and think? Explain your reaction.
3. Do you think, as Morrow suggests, that the victory in the Gulf (or as he puts it, "the killing in the gulf") has brought Americans "too much pleasure"?
4. Morrow uses seven one-sentence paragraphs in this essay (Paragraphs 4, 8, 9, 13, 14, 15, and 16). In each case why does he use this strategy?
5. Explain the rhetorical strategy Morrow uses in his first paragraph.

Martin E. Marty

Lines for Impure Thinkers

(1991)

A Lutheran clergyman and a Professor of Church History at Chicago Divinity School, Martin Marty (b. 1928) is recognized by many as the leading authority on the history of the American Christian Church. Marty is a senior editor at *The Christian Century,* where this essay appeared in February of 1991.

I am an impure thinker. I am hurt, swayed, shaken, elated, disillusioned, shocked, comforted. . .

Eugen Rosenstock-Huessy

1 WE CAN SAY:

2 *I am an impure thinker.* With millions of fellow citizens, I think with my heart as well as my head this winter, as an air war turns to a ground war. I should remain detached, clear-headed, scholarly and objective. But I do not wish to join the pure thinkers, who dredge up millennium-old "criteria for a just war" and satisfy themselves that their opinions satisfy these criteria, and, pronouncing the conflict just, act as if it therefore becomes so.

3 *I am hurt* to think how quickly we let go of what we cherish in peace time. That we find it easy to follow the command to love our enemies until we have some. That we bless no peacemakers except those who would determine right through might. That we put our trust in princes and Patriots, and in "rulers who take counsel together," forgetting that in the face of such arrogations, "he that sitteth in the heavens shall laugh."

That we find in this war vindications of policies that will in the end certainly inspire us to beat our plowshares into swords.

4 *I am swayed* by those who, though they have family members on the desert front, still can empathize with and pray for sufferers in the enemies' camp. And by those who, knowing full well of the atrocities of the foe (whom until recently our nation strategically supported), look beyond him sympathetically to his tyrannized people, whom we must now fight and kill.

5 *I am shaken* to learn that tying yellow ribbons on anything is considered an automatic sign of patriotic virtue. That waving a flag before news cameras and raising the "We're Number One!" finger certifies one as a person of integrity—even if one is in no way inconvenienced by the war or makes no sacrifice for it.

6 *I am elated* to find that sometimes I can suppress my rage and my impulse to be sarcastic or cynical, and can let my weakness and my tears show. That I can find the company of other benumbed mumblers who seek words to express our sorrow. That together we can look for ways to be responsible, knowing that history might prove us, too, to have been wrong.

7 *I am disillusioned* to see that to question the starting of a war or to express mild reservation about any policy being enacted is seen as a political liability.

8 *I am shocked* to see how, once again, we who can find no funds to rebuild our cities can find plenty to destroy others. How while we cannot find means to shelter our homeless we can find means to increase the number of homeless elsewhere. How we make little of the fact that once again those who profit from sword-making stand to gain the most from the war. Again we give and will give moral *carte blanche* to those who pursue their own villainies by strategically allying with us. And then will cite them as being, with us, "overwhelmingly on the side of God."

9 *I am comforted* to find among our military leaders some people of intelligence and restraint, and many also of conscience, who do not resort to euphemism to describe the human cost of war, to the enemy and to us.

10 And, having in mind such leaders and those whom they command, during their living out what has now become "a tragic necessity," I am comforted to find that impure thinkers can identify at one point with the pure thinkers. With thoughts for military people far away: in empathy with them for their fears; in admiration for the courage they display while in harm's way; and knowing the reluctance so many of them have to be where they are and to do what they are called to do: "We support our troops in the Persian Gulf."

Questions for Analysis

1. Explain the distinction Marty makes between "pure thinkers" and "impure thinkers."

2. Why did Marty italicize the first few words in all but his final paragraph?
3. Why did Marty preface his whole statement with the phrase "WE CAN SAY:"? Why does he use "We" instead of "I" as he does at the beginning of Paragraphs 2–9? Why does he return to "We" in the final clause of his statement?
4. Would Lance Morrow consider himself a "pure" or an "impure" thinker? Why? Which are you? Why?
5. Which kind of thinkers would have the more difficult position in a discussion–debate over the Gulf War?

Ellen Goodman

"Our Way of Life": Should We Die For It—Or Change It?

(1990)

Ellen Goodman (b. 1941) is a syndicated columnist and associate editor of *The Boston Globe*. This essay was printed in newspapers around the country on or about August 28, 1990.

1 BOSTON—As I first turn the pages of the newsmagazines, I barely notice the ads. The cover stories are what I'm after, sober accounts of the near-war in the Mideast, grim details about the buildup to protect "our way of life," uneasy projections about oil and the economic future.

2 But gradually the subliminal message in the ads comes into focus as an odd and unsettling counterpoint to the news. They are selling cars: the symbols of "our way of life." Cars are a central character in this conflict that threatens that other American freedom: the freedom to drive.

3 This is what one carmaker promises in the tense summer of 1990: "That last-day-of-school feeling of exhilaration and independence you may have been missing for quite some time."

4 This is what another boasts while we send 50,000 soldiers to protect our supply line: "It not only looks like fun, it is fun. The undisputed king of the pleasure cruise."

5 This is what a third sells as we ship protective gear to guard against Iraq's chemical weapons: "In some ancient cultures, an Eclipse called for a sacrifice. Today it only calls for $10,919."

6 These messages already seem as anachronistic as the ads that once showed doctors recommending Camels. There is not a single mention of gas mileage. The words used

are comfort and performance, power and luxury. There are no warnings that cars may be hazardous to our health.

7 If the ad-makers are caught in a time lag, what can we make of our leaders? In these same weeks, the president has issued no statement about our four-wheeled dependence. He has uttered only the most casual words about conservation as he races his boat off Kennebunkport. Not one of his men has asked Americans to car-pool or even change our road map for Labor Day. The only concerted action in the nation's capital has been anger at the rising gas prices.

8 Bush is more at home in the uniform of a commander-in-chief than in the sweater Jimmy Carter donned in the oil crisis of the '70s. This oilman may not want to remind us that he was part of the problem during the deregulated decade, when the country was allowed to forget about energy and put our pedal to the metal.

9 Now, as environmentalist Barry Commoner puts it, "We have a military policy instead of an energy policy." America has driven itself into this desert conflict. We may make war over what we waste.

10 The ads before me are emblems of the era in which the all-American movie ends in a car chase and the all-American rite of passage is registering to drive, not to vote. They are emblems of an era in which we still believe what we were once told: What's good for General Motors is good for the country.

11 Today the United States uses 40% of the oil being produced in the world. Over 60% of that is for transportation. Our cars travel some 1,250 billion miles a year, almost as far as all the cars in the world put together. Half of the trips are made by a driver alone.

12 We built our suburbs for cars, deserted our cities by car, paved some 2% of our land for them and polluted the air for them. As the ad puts it: "Some cars make a statement. This one makes an exclamation." When Americans are also being asked to die for oil, that is indeed an exclamation point.

13 In the days since the young troops landed in Saudi Arabia, some have called for more drilling off our own shores, and others for nuclear energy. One would have us choose the pollution of our shores over conservation; another is sure we would prefer the dangers of nuclear waste to sacrifice.

14 It seems that Washington is still stuck in the stagnant, feel-good '80s, when we wasted time as well as energy—human and fossil. We knew the importance of cars that use less gas, cars that use renewable resources from crops to sun, cars that run on entirely different engines. We knew the value of mass transit. But our government behaved as if the oil would run forever.

15 The bugle from the Mideast sounds an unhappy wake-up call. Half a world away on desert sands, our men and women are expected to fight for access to inexpensive oil. But at home, our leaders remain reluctant to ask Americans what they can do and do without for their country.

16 So, "heartbeat of America" has a very different meaning these days. It's beginning to sound like cardiac arrest.

Questions for Analysis

1. Explain the rhetorical strategy Goodman uses in Paragraphs 3–5. Is her approach effective? What is the point she wants her readers to grasp?
2. Reread Paragraphs 8 and 9, and then identify and explain the contrast she creates. What is the point she makes in each paragraph?
3. What is the importance of Goodman's Paragraph 14, especially the phrases that begin with "we knew"? How does the information in these clauses help her argument?
4. At the end of Paragraph 15, Goodman says "our leaders remain reluctant to ask Americans what they can do and do without for their country." What famous quotation is she echoing here? What is her point and how does this phrasing (with its echo) help her make her point?
5. Explain the ironies and contrasts in Goodman's final paragraph. How do they help her make her point?

Warren Anderson

Another Vietnam? Vital Interest Makes Involvements as Different as Desert and Jungle

(1990)

Retired Army Lt. Col. Warren Anderson (b. 1935) had assignments in the military that included NATO headquarters in Europe and the Pentagon, where he was a member of a special study group that analyzed the Army's strategic posture. Since he retired, he has been a speech writer for banking executives. This essay originally appeared in *The Charlotte Observer* on August 25, 1990.

1 Just as I was passing Charlotte's Vietnam War Memorial, the newscaster on my car radio reported the addition of two squadrons of Marine FA-18 Hornets from Beaufort, S.C., to the rapidly growing list of Carolinas units deployed to the Mideast—a deployment that began with the 82nd Airborne division from Fort Bragg.

2 The news of increased Carolinas' forces to the Mideast, combined with the fading reflection of the Vietnam memorial in my rear-view mirror, called to mind the disquieting parallels being made between the '60s commitment of U.S. troops to Vietnam and the current deployment of forces to the Mideast. The most obvious parallel is that the United States was once again sending American forces to a foreign land to oppose aggression that was not aimed directly at American people or property.

3 But by the time my car had crossed Hawthorne Lane, I had begun to compare U.S. interests, options and risks between Vietnam and the Mideast from a more analytical view, ingrained from years of military planning in the Pentagon. The more dispassionate and practical approach made it obvious that the two commitments of U.S. forces are as different as the dense jungle and wet heat of Vietnam are from the barren sands and dry heat of Saudi Arabia.

4 Let's consider just four key areas for starters:

1. *Origin of Confrontation*

5 ■ **In Vietnam,** U.S. involvement began as just one more attempt to prop up a weak and corrupt government against a communist-supported war of national liberation in America's continuing effort to contain the Moscow-orchestrated spread of world communism. But what we realized too late was that by the mid-'60s the threat of centrally controlled world communism had all but disintegrated, and we were left embroiled in a regional Asian war with no U.S. vital interests at risk.

6 ■ **In the Mideast,** however, U.S. involvement broke out in reaction to a surprise act of unprovoked aggression, not only against an innocent nation, but against the U.S. vital interest of access to world oil supplies—a vital interest which is shared by the entire developed world.

7 With vital interests at stake, U.S. reaction had to be quick and dramatic. Although Hussein said he would not attack Saudi Arabia, he had already overrun and annexed one neighbor, and if he then continued his attack south could easily have overrun the weaker Saudi forces and gain control of vast Saudi oil reserves.

8 If he did so and succeeded, he would be in a far stronger position from which to fight or to negotiate a *fait accompli* peace that would leave him in control of an awesome portion of world *oil.*

2. *U.S. Vital Interests*

9 ■ **In Vietnam,** U.S. vital interests were not at stake, which became increasingly apparent to the American people. They were proven right when ultimately the enemy took the country and there was virtually no impact on the world power balance, on the American people or on the U.S. economy.

10 ■ **In the Mideast,** if Hussein is allowed to keep Kuwait and go no further, he would control 8.9% of U.S. oil imports (Iraq's included) and become a major influence on world supply. If he had been allowed to roll over the comparatively small Saudi forces to seize the vast reserves of Saudi Arabian oil, he would control another 15% of U.S. oil imports for a total of 23.9% and gain an immense influence over world oil supplies and prices.

11 This possibility—combined with allowing Hussein the capability of using oil to manipulate the world power equation—represents a critical challenge to America's vital interests.

3. *Enemy and Battlefield*

12 ■ **In Vietnam,** we were fighting a protracted guerrilla war in a land perfect for guerrilla warfare against a determined enemy who was *not* threatening our vital interests. (It seemed the ultimate paradox that we could not bring our massive firepower to bear against an enemy who chose when and where to fight and then dissolved into the jungle; it was like trying to drive off a mosquito with a mace and chain.)

13 ■ **In the Mideast,** we are deployed against a war-weary force, which fought for eight years to a virtual stalemate against an inferior Iranian force. It is led by an isolated aggressor threatening the vital interests of the United States and most advanced nations. If deterrence fails and war begins, it will be fought on terrain that favors sophisticated weapons technology and mobility. On the Arabian desert, superior forces can be decisively brought to bear and the weaker force can't run and can't hide.

14 In short, while Allied forces may have to fight a defensive holding action until sufficient heavy armor could be brought to bear, ultimate Allied victory in a matter of months, while costly, would be certain.

4. *World Support*

15 ■ **In Vietnam,** with token exceptions, we were the tone Western power, leaving the free world wondering why we were depleting our national will where our vital interests were not at stake.

16 ■ **In the Mideast,** we have, with the exception of a few outcast nations, the political support of the world, with a growing contribution of Arab and European military forces and the increasing support of the United Nations.

5. *Lessons from Vietnam*

17 But regardless of the marked differences between the two deployments, there are several key lessons that can be carried from our experience in Vietnam:

18 ■ The will of the American people is not inexhaustible, and our strategy cannot go beyond their forbearance.

19 ■ If—God forbid—fighting does break out, war should be declared by the Congress, sanctioned by the United Nations and executed as much as possible by a U.N. force.

20 ■ If war is declared, American forces should be expanded and supported with full and sacrificing commitment of the American people to include rapid mobilization, a fair and equitable draft and transition to a war-focused economy until it is won.

21 ■ And finally, the most perfect use of military force is where it protects our vital interests without ever firing a shot.

Questions for Analysis

1. What is the purpose of Anderson's essay? What does he want his readers to think about? How do you think he would like them to react?
2. Analyze the organizational structure of Anderson's essay. What is the purpose of Paragraphs 1–3? Are his points contrasting Vietnam and the Mideast clear? Effective? Do the visual elements (headings, boldfaced words, bullets) help? Why?
3. Based on this essay, what would you say Anderson's attitude toward war is? Does he want to see a war start? Explain.
4. Anderson uses the phrase "vital interests" a number of times. What does he mean by this term? Would Goodman agree that our interests in the Persian Gulf should be considered vital? Explain.
5. Based on your assessment of their cartoons, do you think that Tom Toles and Kevin Siers would agree with Anderson?
6. Carefully consider the attitude of the man being interviewed in Tom Toles's cartoon. How does this attitude reflect that of many Americans? Do you think this attitude was (and perhaps still is) typical? How is this man's attitude different from Anderson's?

Tom Toles

Now Wait a Minute

(1990)

Tom Toles (b. 1951) is editorial cartoonist for *The Buffalo News,* Buffalo, New York. This cartoon appeared in August of 1990, soon after Iraq invaded Kuwait.

Tom Toles in The Buffalo News.

Kevin Siers

Flag, Mom, Apple Pie, $1.01 9/10/gal.

(1990)

Kevin Siers (b. 1954) is editorial cartoonist for *The Charlotte Observer,* Charlotte, North Carolina. This cartoon appeared in the fall of 1990 as the buildup of United States forces in the Mideast continued and the likelihood of war increased.

Kevin Sears, The Charlotte Observer.

Ralph Novak

Coming to Terms with Nam

(1989)

A senior editor with *People Weekly,* Ralph Novak (b. 1943) writes on a broad range of subjects, including reviews of movies and books. This essay appeared in a special extra edition of *People Weekly* devoted to the 1980s. Novak focuses his essay on events in the 1980s which suggested that America was finally "coming to terms" with the Vietnam War and the divisions it caused within our country. Novak served with the 25th Infantry Division in Vietnam.

1 There are times, though it gets better, when anyone who has been touched by the war can close his eyes, hold out his hands and feel all the lost lives sifting through his fingers—the young Vietnamese and the young Americans, all alike now in this way.

2 The father had been home from the Vietnam War 10 years when his boy was born, on Christmas Day, 1979. The father had been lucky and came home unhurt, untraumatized, unashamed. So it had puzzled him that no one—not even his family and friends—had ever asked about the war. In their silence he had read a judgment: "You must have done terrible things. You must hate to think about it. It's best left alone." At times the father had wanted to grab people by the shoulders and confess: not to misdeeds but to having felt afraid, helpless amid the craziness, at times confused, at times convinced that by serving he had done the honorable thing.

3 The boy is 9 now, bright, open-minded, gentle. He could be a fine soccer player, but he doesn't seem to like the hard contact of it. He and his father are playing with toy soldiers. "You take these five," the boy says. "That way you get the one with the machine gun. I know you know how that works." He looks up at his father with what is clearly pride. The father is both touched and troubled, wanting his son to be proud of him, but not for the wrong reasons.

4 The years when Vietnam veterans were cursed and spat upon, when the Vietnam-vet-gone-berserk was a favorite cop-show premise, were still fresh in the father's mind. Back in 1979, at a Memorial Day gathering in New York to honor Vietnam servicemen, a paraplegic ex-marine named Robert Muller, a spokesman for a group of vets, had angrily confronted the crowd. "You people ran a number on us," he declared. "Your guilt, your hang-ups, your uneasiness, made it socially unacceptable to mention the fact that we were Vietnam veterans. Whenever we brought it up, you walked away from the conversation."

5 The veterans' sense of having been grossly mistreated was always exaggerated, the father knew, at least compared with Americans who had fought in other wars. After

all, once they had won, veterans of the Revolutionary and Civil wars had been forced to fight long, hard and often unsuccessfully for aid and pensions. Upwards of 25,000 Depression-ravaged World War I veterans descended on Washington, D.C., in 1932's Bonus March and stayed for two months. Korean War returnees were often scorned and, because of a few turncoats, their patriotism was questioned. Hailed and rewarded, the men who fought World War II were the exception, not the rule. But they cast a long shadow, one that fell across the entire Vietnam generation.

6 Still, in some ways Vietnam soldiers *were* unique, and not only because they had fought in a losing cause. By the late '70s, reports had begun to surface that veterans who had been exposed in Vietnam to American spraying of defoliants containing dioxin—Agent Orange—were suffering unusually high rates of cancer and their children seemed abnormally afflicted with birth defects. Post-Traumatic Stress Disorder was advanced as an explanation for the deranged behavior of some veterans.

7 Muller's outburst showed the depth of resentment the vets harbored. President Carter seemed to understand the need for a catharsis: the gathering that Muller addressed was part of a national Vietnam Veterans Week, which Congress had endorsed. "The nation," he had declared, "is ready to change its heart, its mind and its attitude about the men who fought in the war." But Carter was too divisive, not a man people could rally around. It remained for Ronald Reagan to catalyze the profound change of heart Carter had foreseen.

8 As often happened with Reagan, what he said mattered more than what he did. Veterans' organizations frequently castigated him for supporting cuts in federal benefits for ex-GIs, but the specific moral support he whole-heartedly offered helped crystallize a decade of reconciliation. At a Memorial Day ceremony in 1986, for instance, he singled out for praise "the boys of Vietnam, who fought a terrible and vicious war without enough support from home. . . . They chose to be faithful. They chose to reject the fashionable skepticism of their time; they chose to believe and answer the call of duty."

9 It seemed to the father that Americans were all too willing to jump on the feel-good bandwagon. In the mid-'80s frequent parades honored Vietnam soldiers. After a New York march in 1985 drew 25,000 participants and a million spectators (at least one of whom held up a sign reading YOU'RE OUR HEROES), one veteran said it was like "a gluttonous feast after years of starvation."

10 The father wondered whether the change in attitude was partially due to Americans' love of being proved right. The continuing exodus of Vietnamese refugees suggested that however misguided we were, our enemies could not have been such wholesome idealists themselves.

11 And what of the main domestic opponents of the war? Often the father would wonder: How important could the political opinions have been of a woman who would devote much of her time to devising video variations on bouncing and sweating, the better to cultivate her svelte self? Was it, perhaps, some sort of poetic justice delayed that Abbie Hoffman ended up doing bad stand-up comedy, Jerry Rubin hustling as a

Looking Back: Vietnam Reconsidered

People asked several individuals prominently associated with the Vietnam years to reflect on the war from the vantage point of 1989. Their replies:

I over-romanticized the Vietcong. If the U.S. was wrong, my attitude years ago was that the Vietcong were right. They seemed heroic in the amount of devastation they could take and keep coming back. They had the capacity to endure. But that endurance bred harshness and rigidity. They did damage to the South, to their own economy, their intellectual community and their standing in the world. Resilience has to make its presence in peace. I'm confident that in the long run Vietnam will find a way to make a more pluralistic society.

—**Tom Hayden,** *former Chicago Seven defendant and SDS leader*

This was the war that put to rest once and for all the myth that blacks will not fight as well as whites. So I find it painful to look at Vietnam movie after Vietnam movie and see no more than token participation by blacks, or worse. One day we're going to get a film that doesn't have to lie about Vietnam but can simply tell the truth: that blacks won medals of honor, that they commanded, that they tried to save Vietnamese people, that they tried to learn the language a little more than their white counterparts. And when that happens, I think black people will be able to accept their Vietnam veterans a little more than they have. You don't see as many blacks in the parades; you don't see as many blacks coming to the Memorial. I don't see them in the audiences when I speak at colleges, because they haven't caught up to everyone else—they're still skeptical.

—**Wallace Terry,** *author of Bloods: An Oral History of the Vietnam War by Black Veterans (1984)*

The changing of attitudes about the war are mainly of interest to those who indulge in and profit by endless examination and re-examination of the public's psyche. It is enough to state the facts. Vietnam, Cambodia and Laos are places where millions died and millions more suffer because the United States failed to do the job it set out to do: stop communist military aggression. Unless as a nation we finally come to realize that Vietnam was a noble cause, the 58,000 brave Americans who died there will truly have died in vain.

—**Richard M. Nixon,** *President of the United States, 1969–74*

The antiwar movement deserved then, and deserves now, to be seen as made up of people who loved this country at least as much as those who were blindly obeying the authorities. When I saw thousands of people in China holding their fingers in the 'V' sign—which is an old World War II sign that became the peace sign of the antiwar movement—I realized that people are still anxious to resist wrongful policy and that our movement didn't fail. I suspect there are people in China who find more inspiration in the example of the American antiwar movement than we do ourselves. I really do look forward to the day when there will be a memorial to the antiwar movement as there is to the veterans.

—**Daniel Ellsberg,** *former Rand Corp. analyst who leaked the Pentagon Papers in 1971*

The Vietnam War wall in Washington is an acceptable memorial, except for the statue. The soldiers in that statue are messy, they have no steel helmets, they aren't wearing proper combat uniforms. They look sloppy, and they weren't sloppy. At least mine weren't.

—**Gen. George S. Patton III,** *winner of the Distinguished Service Cross for heroism in Vietnam*

sorry yuppie pretender, Bobby Seale peddling cookbooks? The quintessential antiwar marriage, between Joan Baez and David Harris, broke up after Harris went to prison for draft evasion. Neither made a big impact on the '80s. George McGovern, who lost the 1972 presidential campaign disastrously, vanished as a moral or political force. By the '80s he seemed just a trivia answer.

12 But the father had no desire to gloat. Parades did not make it easier for him to play at toy soldiers with his son. Something was missing, unacknowledged. It was not until he visited the dark, downward-sloping Vietnam monument on the mall in Washington, D.C., that he understood what it was. Here, a 480-foot length of black marble became an altar—a place finally to grieve—and the engraved names of the 58,000 Americans who died became a litany.

13 The monument had been designed, fittingly, by the daughter of Asian immigrants, Maya Ying Lin, a young Yale architecture student. Between its dedication on Nov. 13, 1982, and mid-1989, 30 million people had come to visit the wall. They ranged from schoolchildren who asked each other, "What was Vietnam?" to veterans who didn't know they had lost a buddy until they saw his name engraved on the marble.

14 Like other veterans, the father looked for the less familiar but recognizable names—guys he'd met in Oakland or Long Binh or on an R&R bus in Singapore. And, of course, he tried to imagine what his own name would have looked like engraved in the wall, with the marble reflecting someone else's image. When the tears came, there was mourning for the dead, and frustration and bitterness. And there was a deep bewildering swirl of gratitude and doubt. He felt glad to be alive and unsure whether he deserved to be.

15 Standing at the wall, it was hard to identify with a character such as Rambo, so consumed by violence and hatred. The initial Rambo film, *First Blood,* was released the same year the wall was dedicated. In that film and its blockbuster 1985 sequel, Rambo was a Vietnam vet who had been maligned and mistreated at home. The character was sympathetic on the surface, the father thought, but only in the most dishonest, condescending way. The lampooned combat in the sequel seemed extravagant and ridiculous, demeaning the horror—and the nobility—of the real thing.

16 The father found Oliver Stone's *Platoon* (1987) and Stanley Kubrick's *Full Metal Jacket* (1988) more valid—an education for those who weren't there, a shared nightmare for those who were.

17 In 1983, PBS broadcast Stanley Karnow's 13-part series, *Vietnam: A Television History,* which the father found insightful. Maybe, he thought, little by little we remember, and everybody learns. Then, beginning with *Tour of Duty* on CBS in 1987 and *China Beach* on ABC in 1988, Vietnam came to prime time as entertainment. The father recognized this as a momentous change on some level. Still, the shows made the war seem too routine, too clean. He recalled an evening in 1969, coming back after an all-day patrol to a fire-support base dug in on the Cambodian border. In one bunker the men had tuned in AFVN-TV on battery-powered sets to watch reruns of *Combat* starring Vic Morrow. How distant, painless and fanciful World War II seemed in those images.

18 But, he thought, 10 years ago a TV series set in Vietnam would have been unthinkable. Maybe the pop-culturization of Vietnam does begin to redress the years when the war and its veterans were damned or ignored. And maybe the veteran's role is to accept that no one who wasn't there can ever fully comprehend the experience, and that the past can not all be made right. As he looked back over the decade, the father could not ignore the breadth of change, could almost hear hardened attitudes yielding, like the crack and groan of lake ice breaking up in the spring:

- The government agreed this year to reconsider Agent Orange's effect on veterans, offering the prospect of federal aid above the $180 million awarded to veterans in 1984 to settle a five-year suit against the companies that produced the defoliants.
- Phill Coleman, of Redondo Beach, Calif., started a Vietnam Data Resource and Electronic Library for use by veterans (for such purposes as pursuing benefit claims) as well as by scholars.
- The first American tourists landed in Vietnam in 1985.
- ''Vietnam: Reflexes and Reflections,'' a collection of art created by soldiers while in-country, toured the U.S.
- Congress passed a bill to fund a memorial to women veterans of the war.
- By one estimate, 393 courses on Vietnam are being taught at U.S. colleges and high schools, compared with 22 in 1980.
- In 1980 Geoffrey Steiner, a Cushing, Minn., vet, began planting a 100-acre forest that he hopes will eventually include one tree for every American who died in Vietnam. When he seemed about to run out of money, volunteers helped him raise funds to keep going. There are 143 major Vietnam memorials in the country now; there were two in 1980.

19 Yet it is clear as well that agonizing problems remain. Today 194 counseling centers continue to treat the psychological problems of Vietnam veterans. An American Division veteran in Nevada tries, still, to learn to live with the image inside his head of the day he fired a burst into a group of children to save his own life—one of the children was about to throw a grenade at him. The California Supreme Court invalidated the death sentence of a Vietnam veteran who killed two girls, 7 and 10, because his trial had excluded evidence that he had suffered a traumatic flashback. The Vietnam Veterans of America estimates that, of 2.8 million men who served in Vietnam, 83,000 are homeless.

20 During the 1988 presidential campaign, the controversy over Dan Quayle's military service showed how easily the wounds can be reopened. That Quayle had gone to considerable lengths to get himself into a National Guard unit seemed in the new climate of acceptance a clear offense. The father could understand people being upset, especially in light of Quayle's hawkishness. On the other hand, there were a lot of times when a lot of people would have loved to have access to the kind of deal he worked. Was he smarter than they were? Luckier? Less courageous?

21 Well, he thought, Quayle didn't make the war last a minute longer. He paid too. Let it go.

22 These phenomena are all symptoms of tragedies no mere decade can erase. Most Vietnam vets would probably agree that they are better off in 1989 than they were in 1979, to varying degrees. But a war is never over, finally, until every man and woman who fought in it has died.

23 The boy knows that there are popular movies and TV series about Vietnam and that some of those toy soldiers he plays with are described as veterans of the war. The father, wanting his son to be proud of him, has talked about being a soldier, has used words—*ambush, chopper, fire-fight*—that conjure excitement and triumph. And he has talked about the pain and fear that lived in everyone: "You know how you hate to get a shot and how much you think it hurts? Think of days and days of that. It's not a cartoon where the hero never gets hurt. It's a struggle, one where every minute you have to fight to keep from becoming someone you don't want to be.

24 "No father wants his son to have to go to war. But some day, when you're grown, you may have to go. If you do, I hope you will come back knowing that you didn't let your friends down, that you learned something and that you tried to do what is right.

25 "But, most of all, I hope you're one of those lucky enough to come back at all."

Questions for Analysis

1. Explain the purpose of Novak's essay. Can you distinguish between Novak's need to write for himself and the reason he wrote for his audience? Explain.
2. What is the purpose of Novak's first paragraph? How does it contribute to his purpose?
3. Why is the essay focused on a father and his son? Why is the relationship between the father and son presented in the third person? Is Novak the father? Explain.
4. Much of the evidence that Novak presents to support his thesis concerns events that occurred after the war. Explain how Novak uses these events to get across his message.
5. What is Novak's attitude toward war? How is that attitude conveyed in the father's words to his son?
6. The box "Looking Back: Vietnam Reconsidered" appeared with this essay. What attitudes toward war are conveyed by the opinions expressed? Do some seem more sensitive to the issues Novak and others raise about Vietnam and war? Explain.

William Manchester

Okinawa: The Bloodiest Battle of All

(1987)

William Manchester (b. 1922) is a journalist and novelist who has written extensively about the history of the twentieth century. His books often focus on famous people, including Douglas MacArthur, Winston Churchill, H. L. Menchen, and the Rockefellers. The following essay deals with his experience as a Marine in the South Pacific during World War II. This essay first appeared in the *New York Times Magazine* on June 14, 1987.

1 On Okinawa today, Flag Day will be observed with an extraordinary ceremony: two groups of elderly men, one Japanese, the other American, will gather for a solemn rite.

2 They could scarcely have less in common. Their motives are mirror images; each group honors the memory of men who tried to slay the men honored by those opposite them. But theirs is a common grief. After forty-two years the ache is still there. They are really united by death, the one great victor in modern war.

3 They have come to Okinawa to dedicate a lovely monument in remembrance of the Americans, Japanese and Okinawans killed there in the last and bloodiest battle of the Pacific war. More than 200,000 perished in the 82-day struggle—twice the number of Japanese lost at Hiroshima and more American blood than had been shed at Gettysburg. My own regiment—I was a sergeant in the 29th Marines—lost more than 80 percent of the men who had landed on April 1, 1945. Before the battle was over, both the Japanese and American commanding generals lay in shallow graves.

4 Okinawa lies 330 miles southwest of the southernmost Japanese island of Kyushu; before the war, it was Japanese soil. Had there been no atom bombs—and at that time the most powerful Americans, in Washington and at the Pentagon, doubted that the device would work—the invasion of the Nipponese homeland would have been staged from Okinawa, beginning with a landing on Kyushu to take place November 1. The six Marine divisions, storming ashore abreast, would lead the way. President Truman asked General Douglas MacArthur, whose estimates of casualties on the eve of battles had proved uncannily accurate, about Kyushu. The general predicted a million Americans would die in that first phase.

5 Given the assumption that nuclear weapons would contribute nothing to victory, the battle of Okinawa had to be fought. No one doubted the need to bring Japan to its knees. But some Americans came to hate the things we had to do, even when convinced that doing them was absolutely necessary; they had never understood the bestial, monstrous and vile means required to reach the objective—an unconditional Japanese surrender. As for me, I could not reconcile the romanticized view of war that runs like a

red streak through our literature—and the glowing aura of selfless patriotism that had led us to put our lives at forfeit—with the wet, green hell from which I had barely escaped. Today, I understand. I was there, and was twice wounded. This is the story of what I knew and when I knew it.

6 To our astonishment, the Marine landing on April 1 was uncontested. The enemy had set a trap. Japanese strategy called first for kamikazes to destroy our fleet, cutting us off from supply ships; then Japanese troops would methodically annihilate the men stranded ashore using the trench-warfare tactics of World War I—cutting the Americans down as they charged heavily fortified positions. One hundred and ten thousand Japanese troops were waiting on the southern tip of the island. Intricate entrenchments, connected by tunnels, formed the enemy's defense line, which ran across the waist of Okinawa from the Pacific Ocean to the East China Sea.

7 By May 8, after more than five weeks of fighting, it became clear that the anchor of this line was a knoll of coral and volcanic ash, which the Marines christened Sugar Loaf Hill. My role in mastering it—the crest changed hands more than eleven times—was the central experience of my youth, and of all the military bric-a-brac that I put away after the war, I cherish most the Commendation from General Lemuel C. Shepherd, Jr., U.S.M.C., our splendid division commander, citing me for "gallantry in action and extraordinary achievement," adding, "Your courage was a constant source of inspiration . . . and your conduct throughout was in keeping with the highest tradition of the United States Naval Service."

8 The struggle for Sugar Loaf lasted ten days; we fought under the worst possible conditions—a driving rain that never seemed to slacken, day or night. (I remember wondering, in an idiotic moment—no man in combat is really sane—whether the battle could be called off, or at least postponed, because of bad weather.)

9 *Newsweek* called Sugar Loaf "the most critical local battle of the war." *Time* described a company of Marines—270 men—assaulting the hill. They failed; fewer than 30 returned. Fletcher Pratt, the military historian, wrote that the battle was unmatched in the Pacific war for "closeness and desperation." Casualties were almost unbelievable. In the 22d and 29th Marine regiments, two out of every three men fell. The struggle for the dominance of Sugar Loaf was probably the costliest engagement in the history of the Marine Corps. But by early evening on May 18, as night thickened over the embattled armies, the 29th Marines had taken Sugar Loaf, this time for keeps.

10 Okinawa today, the ceremony will be dignified, solemn, seemly. It will also be anachronistic. If the Japanese dead of 1945 were resurrected to witness it, they would be appalled by the acceptance of defeat, the humiliation of their emperor—the very idea of burying Japanese near the barbarians from across the sea and then mourning them together. Americans, meanwhile, risen from their graves, would ponder the evolution of their own society, and might wonder, What ever happened to patriotism?

11 When I was a child, a bracket was screwed to the sill of a front attic window; its sole purpose was to hold the family flag. At first light, on all legal holidays—including

Election Day, July 4, Memorial Day and, of course, Flag Day—I would scamper up to show it. The holidays remain, but mostly they mean long weekends.

12 In the late 1920s, during my childhood, the whole town of Attleboro, Massachusetts, would turn out to cheer the procession on Memorial Day. The policemen always came first, wearing their number-one uniforms and keeping perfect step. Behind them was a two-man vanguard—the mayor and, at his side, my father, hero of the 5th Marines and Belleau Wood, wearing his immaculate dress blues and looking like a poster of a Marine, with one magnificent flaw: the right sleeve of his uniform was empty. He had lost the arm in the Argonne. I now think that, as I watched him pass by, my own military future was already determined.

13 The main body of the parade was led by five or six survivors of the Civil War, too old to march but sitting upright in open Pierce-Arrows and Packards, wearing their blue uniforms and broad-brimmed hats. Then, in perfect step, came a contingent of men in their fifties, with their blanket rolls sloping diagonally from shoulder to hip—the Spanish-American War veterans. After these—and anticipated by a great roar from the crowd—came the dough-boys of World War I, some still in their late twenties. They were acclaimed in part because theirs had been the most recent conflict, but also because they had fought in the war that—we then thought—had ended all wars.

14 Americans still march in Memorial Day parades, but attendance is light. One war has led to another and another and yet another, and the cruel fact is that few men, however they die, are remembered beyond the lifetimes of their closest relatives and friends. In the early 1940s, one of the forces that kept us on the line, under heavy enemy fire, was the conviction that this battle was of immense historical import, and that those of us who survived it would be forever cherished in the hearts of Americans. It was rather diminishing to return in 1945 and discover that your own parents couldn't even pronounce the names of the islands you had conquered.

15 But what of those who *do* remain faithful to patriotic holidays? What are they commemorating? Very rarely are they honoring what actually happened, because only a handful know, and it's not their favorite topic of conversation. In World War II, 16 million Americans entered the armed forces. Of these, fewer than a million saw action. Logistically, it took nineteen men to back up one man in combat. All who wore uniforms are called veterans, but more than 90 percent of them are as uninformed about the killing zones as those on the home front.

16 If all Americans understood the nature of battle, they might be vulnerable to truth. But the myths of warfare are embedded deep in our ancestral memories. By the time children have reached the age of awareness, they regard uniforms, decorations and Sousa marches as exalted, and those who argue otherwise are regarded as unpatriotic.

17 General MacArthur, quoting Plato, said: "Only the dead have seen the end of war." One hopes he was wrong, for war, as it had existed for over four thousand years, is now obsolete. As late as the spring of 1945, it was possible for one man, with a rifle, to make a difference, however infinitesimal, in the struggle to defeat an enemy who had attacked us and threatened our West Coast. The bomb dropped on Hiroshima made the man ludicrous, even pitiful. Soldiering has been relegated to Sartre's[1] theater of the

absurd. The image of the man as protector and defender of the home has been destroyed (and I suggest that that seed of thought eventually led women to re-examine their own role in society).

18 Until nuclear weapons arrived, the glorifying of militarism was the nation's hidden asset. Without it, we would almost certainly have been defeated by the Japanese, probably by 1943. In 1941 American youth was isolationist and pacifist. Then war planes from Imperial Japan destroyed our fleet at Pearl Harbor on December 7, and on December 8 recruiting stations were packed. Some of us later found fighting rather different from what had been advertised. Yet in combat these men risked their lives—and often lost them—in hope of winning medals. There is an old soldier's saying: "A man won't sell you his life, but he'll give it to you for a piece of colored ribbon."

19 Most of the men who hit the beaches came to scorn eloquence. They preferred the 130-year-old "Word of Cambronne." As dusk darkened the Waterloo battlefield, with the French in full retreat, the British sent word to General Pierre Cambronne, commander of the Old Guard. His position, they pointed out, was hopeless, and they suggested he capitulate. Every French textbook reports his reply as "The Old Guard dies but never surrenders." What he actually said was "*Merde.*"[2]

20 If you mention this incident to members of the U.S. 101st Airborne Division, they will immediately understand. "Nuts" was not Brigadier General Anthony C. McAuliffe's answer to the Nazi demand that he hoist a white flag over Bastogne. Instead, he quoted Cambronne.

21 The character of combat has always been determined by the weapons available to men when their battles were fought. In the beginning they were limited to hand weapons—clubs, rocks, swords, lances. At the Battle of Camlann in 539, England's Arthur—a great warrior, not a king—led a charge that slew 930 Saxons, including their leader.

22 It is important to grasp the fact that those 930 men were not killed by snipers, grenades or shells. The dead were bludgeoned or stabbed to death, and we have a pretty good idea how this was done. One of the facts withheld from civilians during World War II was that Kabar fighting knives, with seven-inch blades honed to such precision that you could shave with them, were issued to Marines and that we were taught to use them. You never cut downward. You drove the point of your blade into a man's lower belly and ripped upward. In the process, you yourself became soaked in the other man's gore. After that charge at Camlann, Arthur must have been half drowned in blood.

23 The Battle of Agincourt,[3] fought nearly one thousand years later, represented a slight technical advance: crossbows and long bows had appeared. All the same, Arthur would have recognized the battle. Like all engagements of the time, this one was short. Killing by hand is hard work, and hot work. It is so exhausting that even men in peak condition collapse once the issue of triumph or defeat is settled. And Henry V's spear carriers and archers were drawn from social classes that had been undernourished for as long as anyone could remember. The duration of medieval battles could have been measured in hours, even minutes.

24 The Battle of Waterloo, fought exactly four hundred years later, is another matter. By 1815, the Industrial Revolution had begun cranking out appliances of death, primitive by today's standards, but revolutionary for infantrymen of that time. And Napoleon had formed mass armies, pressing every available man into service. It was a long step toward total war, and its impact was immense. Infantrymen on both sides fought with single-missile weapons—muskets or rifles—and were supported by (and were the target of) artillery firing cannonballs.

25 The fighting at Waterloo continued for three days; for a given regiment, however, it usually lasted one full day, much longer than medieval warfare. A half century later, Gettysburg lasted three days and cost 43,497 men. Then came the marathon slaughters of 1914–1918, lasting as long as ten months (Verdun) and producing hundreds of thousands of corpses lying, as F. Scott Fitzgerald wrote afterward, "like a million bloody rugs." Winston Churchill, who had been a dashing young cavalry officer when Victoria was queen, said of the new combat: "War, which was cruel and magnificent, has become cruel and squalid."

26 It may be said that the history of war is one of men packed together, getting closer and closer to the ground and then deeper and deeper into it. In the densest combat of World War I, battalion frontage—the length of the line into which the 1,000-odd men were squeezed—had been 800 yards. On Okinawa, on the Japanese fortified line, it was less than 600 yards—about 18 inches per man. We were there and deadlocked for more than a week in the relentless rain. During those weeks we lost nearly 4,000 men.

27 And now it is time to set down what this modern battlefield was like.

28 All greenery had vanished; as far as one could see, heavy shellfire had denuded the scene of shrubbery. What was left resembled a cratered moonscape. But the craters were vanishing, because the rain had transformed the earth into a thin porridge—too thin even to dig foxholes. At night you lay on a poncho as a precaution against drowning during the barrages. All night, every night, shells erupted close enough to shake the mud beneath you at the rate of five or six a minute. You could hear the cries of the dying but could do nothing. Japanese infiltration was always imminent, so the order was to stay put. Any man who stood up was cut in half by machine guns manned by fellow Marines.

29 By day, the mud was hip deep; no vehicles could reach us. As you moved up the slope of the hill, artillery and mortar shells were bursting all around you, and, if you were fortunate enough to reach the top, you encountered the Japanese defenders, almost face to face, a few feet away. To me, they looked like badly wrapped brown paper parcels someone had soaked in a tub. Their eyes seemed glazed. So, I suppose, did ours.

30 Japanese bayonets were fixed; ours weren't. We used the knives, or, in my case, a .45 revolver and M1 carbine. The mud beneath our feet was deeply veined with blood. It was slippery. Blood is very slippery. So you skidded around, in deep shock, fighting as best you could until one side outnumbered the other. The outnumbered side would withdraw for reinforcements and then counterattack.

31 During those ten days I ate half a candy bar. I couldn't keep anything down. Everyone had dysentery, and this brings up an aspect of war even Robert Graves, Siegfried Sassoon, Edmund Blunden and Ernest Hemingway avoided. If you put more than a quarter million men in a line for three weeks, with no facilities for the disposal of human waste, you are going to confront a disgusting problem. We were fighting and sleeping in one vast cesspool. Mingled with that stench was another—the corrupt and corrupting odor of rotting human flesh.

32 My luck ran out on June 5, more than two weeks after we had taken Sugar Loaf Hill and killed the seven thousand Japanese soldiers defending it. I had suffered a slight gunshot wound above the right knee on June 2, and had rejoined my regiment to make an amphibious landing on Oroku Peninsula behind enemy lines. The next morning several of us were standing in a stone enclosure outside some Okinawan tombs when a six-inch rocket mortar shell landed among us.

33 The best man in my section was blown to pieces, and the slime of his viscera enveloped me. His body had cushioned the blow, saving my life; I still carry a piece of his shinbone in my chest. But I collapsed, and was left for dead. Hours later corpsmen found me still breathing, though blind and deaf, with my back and chest a junkyard of iron fragments—including, besides the piece of shinbone, four pieces of shrapnel too close to the heart to be removed. (They were not dangerous, a Navy surgeon assured me, but they still set off the metal detector at the Buffalo airport.)

34 Between June and November I underwent four major operations and was discharged as 100 percent disabled. But the young have strong recuperative powers. The blindness was caused by shock, and my vision returned. I grew new eardrums. In three years I was physically fit. The invisible wounds remain.

35 Most of those who were closest to me in the early 1940s had left New England campuses to join the Marines, knowing it was the most dangerous branch of the service. I remember them as bright, physically strong and inspired by an idealism and love of country they would have been too embarrassed to acknowledge. All of us despised the pompousness and pretentiousness of senior officers. It helped that, almost without exception, we admired and respected our commander in chief. But despite our enormous pride in being Marines, we saw through the scam that had lured so many of us to recruiting stations.

36 Once we polled a rifle company, asking each man why he had joined the Marines. A majority cited *To the Shores of Tripoli,* a marshmallow of a movie starring John Payne, Randolph Scott and Maureen O'Hara. Throughout the film the uniform of the day was dress blues; requests for liberty were always granted. The implication was that combat would be a lark, and when you returned, spangled with decorations, a Navy nurse like Maureen O'Hara would be waiting in your sack. It was peacetime again when John Wayne appeared on the silver screen as Sergeant Stryker in *Sands of Iwo Jima,* but that film underscores the point; I went to see it with another ex-Marine, and we were asked to leave the theater because we couldn't stop laughing.

37 After my evacuation from Okinawa, I had the enormous pleasure of seeing Wayne humiliated in person at Aiea Heights Naval Hospital in Hawaii. Only the most gravely wounded, the litter cases, were sent there. The hospital was packed, the halls lined with beds. Between Iwo Jima and Okinawa, the Marine Corps was being bled white.

38 Each evening, Navy corpsmen would carry litters down to the hospital theater so the men could watch a movie. One night they had a surprise for us. Before the film the curtains parted and out stepped John Wayne, wearing a cowboy outfit—ten-gallon hat, bandanna, checkered shirt, two pistols, chaps, boots and spurs. He grinned his aw-shucks grin, passed a hand over his face and said, "Hi ya, guys!" He was greeted by a stony silence. Then somebody booed. Suddenly everyone was booing.

39 This man was a symbol of the fake machismo we had come to hate, and we weren't going to listen to him. He tried and tried to make himself heard, but we drowned him out, and eventually he quit and left. If you liked *Sands of Iwo Jima,* I suggest you be careful. Don't tell it to the Marines.

40 And so we weren't macho. Yet we never doubted the justice of our cause. If we had failed—if we had lost Guadalcanal, and the Navy's pilots had lost the Battle of Midway—the Japanese would have invaded Australia and Hawaii, and California would have been in grave danger. In 1942 the possibility of an Axis victory was very real. It is possible for me to loathe war—and with reason—yet still honor the brave men, many of them boys, really, who fought with me and died beside me. I have been haunted by their loss these forty-two years, and I shall mourn them until my own death releases me. It does not seem too much to ask that they be remembered on one day each year. After all, they sacrificed their futures that you might have yours.

41 Yet I will not be on Okinawa for the dedication today. I would enjoy being with Marines; the ceremony will be moving, and we would be solemn, remembering our youth and the beloved friends who died there.

42 Few, if any, of the Japanese survivors agreed to attend the ceremony. However, Edward L. Fox, chairman of the Okinawa Memorial Shrine Committee, capped almost six years' campaigning for a monument when he heard about a former Japanese naval officer, Yoshio Yazaki—a meteorologist who had belonged to a four-thousand-man force led by Rear Admiral Minoru Ota—and persuaded him to attend.

43 On March 31, 1945, Yazaki-san had been recalled to Tokyo, and thus missed the battle of Okinawa. Ten weeks later—exactly forty-two years ago today—Admiral Ota and his men committed seppuku, killing themselves rather than face surrender. Ever since then Yazaki has been tormented by the thought that his comrades have joined their ancestors and he is here, not there.

44 Finding Yazaki was a great stroke of luck for Fox, for whom an Okinawa memorial had become an obsession. His own division commander tried to discourage him. The Japanese could hardly be expected to back a memorial on the site of their last great military defeat. But Yazaki made a solution possible.

45 If Yazaki can attend, why can't I? I played a role in the early stages of Buzz Fox's campaign and helped write the tribute to the Marines that is engraved on the monument.

But when I learned that Japanese were also participating, I quietly withdrew. There are too many graves between us, too much gore, too many memories of too many atrocities.

46 In 1978, revisiting Guadalcanal, I encountered a Japanese businessman who had volunteered to become a kamikaze pilot in 1945 and was turned down at the last minute. Mutual friends suggested that we meet. I had expected no difficulty; neither, I think, did he. But when we confronted each other, we froze.

47 I trembled, suppressing the sudden, startling surge of primitive rage within. And I could see, from his expression, that this was difficult for him, too. Nations may make peace. It is harder for fighting men. On simultaneous impulse we both turned and walked away.

48 I set this down in neither pride nor shame. The fact is that some wounds never heal. Yazaki, unlike Fox, is dreading the ceremony. He does not expect to be shriven of his guilt. He knows he must be there but can't say why. Men are irrational, he explains, and adds that he feels very sad.

49 So do I, Yazaki-san, so do I.

Notes

1. Jean Paul Sartre (1905–1980), existentialist philosopher, dramatist, and novelist.
2. Shit.
3. A famous battle (1914 A.D.) in which English archers decimated the French cavalry.

Questions for Analysis

1. Manchester begins his essay with two paragraphs that set up a tension between the ceremony often associated with the military and the grim reality of war. Why does Manchester begin with this tension? Where else in the essay do you encounter this or similar tensions?
2. How do the tensions mentioned in Question 1 operate to help Manchester make his argument? What is Manchester's argument?
3. In Paragraph 7, Manchester mentions the commendation he received from General Shepherd for his role in helping to capture Sugar Loaf Hill. Given Manchester's attitude toward war, why does he "cherish" and quote from this citation? Is Manchester's inclusion of this information a contradiction or a paradox? Explain.
4. In Paragraph 17, Manchester quotes Plato's observation that "Only the dead have seen the end of war." How does Manchester feel about this statement? Do you agree? What do you think other authors whose works appear in this section would say in response to Plato?
5. Why does Manchester give such a graphic account of the Battle of Okinawa in Paragraphs 27–33?

6. What is the purpose of Manchester's essay? How does his purpose differ from his argument?

Wilfred Owen

"Dulce et Decorum Est"

(1917–1918)

Wilfred Owen (1893–1918) worked as a lay assistant to an Anglican vicar, and then as a teacher of English in France before joining the British Army to fight in World War I. He served with distinction as an officer for five months in 1917 before being brought home for treatment of shell shock. He had written poetry earlier, but his wartime experience and the advice and encouragement of new friends led him to produce a number of excellent poems including *"Dulce et Decorum Est."* After recuperating, he returned to the front and was killed in action one week before the end of the war.

Bent double, like old beggars under sacks,
Knock-kneed, coughing like hags, we cursed through sludge,
Till on the haunting flares we turned our backs,
And towards our distant rest began to trudge.
Men marched asleep. Many had lost their boots,
But limped on, blood-shod. All went lame, all blind;
Drunk with fatigue; deaf even to the hoots
Of gas-shells dropping softly behind.

Gas! GAS! Quick, boys!—An ecstasy of fumbling,
Fitting the clumsy helmets just in time,
But someone still was yelling out and stumbling
And flound'ring like a man in fire or lime.—
Dim through the misty panes and thick green light,
As under a green sea, I saw him drowning.

In all my dreams before my helpless sight
He plunges at me, guttering, choking, drowning.

If in some smothering dreams, you too could pace
Behind the wagon that we flung him in,
And watch the white eyes writhing in his face,
His hanging face, like a devil's sick of sin,
If you could hear, at every jolt, the blood

Come gargling from the froth-corrupted lungs
Bitter as the cud
Of vile, incurable sores on innocent tongues,—
My friend, you would not tell with such high zest
To children ardent for some desperate glory,
The old lie: *Dulce et decorum est*
Pro patria mori.[1]

Questions for Analysis

1. What is the picture Owen wants the reader to see in the first stanza? How does he create that picture? Is it effective?
2. Why does Owen use the word *ecstasy* in line 9? How do our first associations with that word help him convey his message?
3. Why does Owen use the third-person in line 1–12, the first-person singular in lines 13–16, and the second person in lines 17–29?
4. *"Dulce et decorum est pro patria mori"* is a famous line from a poem by the Roman poet Horace. It translates to "How sweet and fitting it is to die for one's country." What is the argument of the poem and how does Horace's line fit into it?

1. AUTHOR'S NOTE: "It is sweet and fitting to die for one's country."

Jonathan Swift

Gulliver Offers Gunpowder to the King of Brobdingnag

(1726)

Jonathan Swift (1667–1745), the famous eighteenth-century poet and satirist, produced some of the most biting and on-target criticism in the English language on the subject of human nature and society. Although he wrote with eighteenth-century Britain in his mind and before his eyes, his insights still apply, and *Gulliver's Travels,* despite its clear references to events of his time, is still an accessible work that applies to many twentieth-century problems. This passage is from Part II of *Gulliver's Travels* in which Gulliver gives his account of a visit with the Brobdingnaggians, a race of people 12 times bigger than Gulliver. Despite their size, the Brobdingnaggians are a peaceful people with strong, simple institutions. They have human foibles, even some vices, but on the whole, they are good and gentle. They have not had wars in several centuries. The king is interested in Gulliver's account of Britain and Europe, but is appalled by the stories of war, corruption, and greed that Gulliver must tell to present the history of his country and European civilization.

1 But great allowances should be given to a king who lives wholly secluded from the rest of the world, and must therefore be altogether unacquainted with the manners and customs that most prevail in other nations: the want of which knowledge will ever produce many prejudices, and a certain narrowness of thinking, from which we and the politer countries of Europe are wholly exempted. And it would be hard indeed, if so remote a prince's notions of virtue and vice were to be offered as a standard for all mankind.

2 To confirm what I have now said, and further to show the miserable effects of a confined education, I shall here insert a passage which will hardly obtain belief. In hopes to ingratiate my self farther into his Majesty's favour, I told him of an invention discovered between three and four hundred years ago, to make a certain powder, into an heap of which the smallest spark of fire falling, would kindle the whole in a moment, although it were as big as a mountain, and make it all fly up in the air together, with a noise and agitation greater than thunder. That a proper quantity of this powder rammed into an hollow tube of brass or iron, according to its bigness, would drive a ball of iron or lead with such violence and speed as nothing was able to sustain its force. That the largest balls, thus discharged, would not only destroy whole ranks of an army at once, but batter the strongest walls to the ground, sink down ships, with a thousand men in each, to the bottom of the sea; and when linked together by a chain, would cut through masts and rigging, divide hundreds of bodies in the middle, and lay all waste before them. That we often put this powder into large hollow balls of iron, and discharged them by an engine into some city we were besieging, which would rip up the pavement, tear the houses to pieces, burst and throw splinters on every side, dashing out the brains

of all who came near. That I knew the ingredients very well, which were cheap, and common; I understood the manner of compounding them, and could direct his workmen how to make those tubes of a size proportionable to all other things in his Majesty's kingdom, and the largest need not be above two hundred foot long; twenty or thirty of which tubes, charged with the proper quantity of powder and balls, would batter down the walls of the strongest town in his dominions in a few hours, or destroy the whole metropolis, if ever it should pretend to dispute his absolute commands. This I humbly offered to his Majesty as a small tribute of acknowledgment in return of so many marks that I had received of his royal favour and protection.

3 The King was struck with horror at the description I had given of those terrible engines, and the proposal I had made. He was amazed how so impotent and groveling an insect as I (these were his expressions) could entertain such inhuman ideas, and in so familiar a manner as to appear wholly unmoved at all the scenes of blood and desolation, which I had painted as the common effects of those destructive machines, whereof he said, some evil genius, enemy to mankind, must have been the first contriver. As for himself, he protested, that although few things delighted him so much as new discoveries in art or in nature, yet he would rather lose half his kingdom than be privy to such a secret, which he commanded me, as I valued my life, never to mention any more.

4 A strange effect of narrow principles and short views! that a prince possessed of every quality which procures veneration, love, and esteem; of strong parts, great wisdom and profound learning, endued with admirable talents for government, and almost adored by his subjects, should from a nice unnecessary scruple, whereof in Europe we can have no conception, let slip an opportunity put into his hands, that would have made him absolute master of the lives, the liberties, and the fortunes of his people. Neither do I say this with the least intention to detract from the many virtues of that excellent king, whose character I am sensible will on this account be very much lessened in the opinion of an English reader: but I take this defect among them to have risen from their ignorance, by not having hitherto reduced politics into a science, as the more acute wits of Europe have done!

Questions for Analysis

1. The object of Swift's satire here is the European attitude toward war, its destruction, and the technology that enables it. Gulliver is the spokesman for European values. How does Swift use Gulliver to reveal these values? What values do you see reflected in the King of Brobdingnag?
2. Why does Gulliver offer gunpowder to the King in the first place? (Remember Gulliver's size relative to the Brobdingnaggians.) What does Swift suggest about the reasons some people and nations go to war?

Intercultural Understanding

Our culture determines in large measure how we think, how we deal with other people, and how we view the world. Culture, received through our families and other social units, is our greatest teacher about life and how we are expected to live it. Cultural indoctrination can also provide blind spots. We can become so focused on our own culture, so accustomed to the ways of living and values inherent in it, that we fail to understand and appreciate other cultures. That failure potentially can lead to misunderstanding, insult (intentional or unintentional), tension, conflict, and, more often than we would like, war.

Americans are especially susceptible to cultural chauvinism because our political and economic systems have been successful and because we have lived for so long in relative isolation. We tend to think that what works for us should work for people in any other country. We often do not take the time to consider that people from other cultures differ from us in how they think and in how they assign value. We, therefore, sometimes have difficulty seeing that their social structures might be best for them even though they are very different from our own. In many parts of the world, we have earned the reputation of "ugly Americans." However, an innocence and openness congruent with our democratic outlook still exists that often makes winning friends and crossing cultural barriers relatively easy. Furthermore, we are learning from our experiences around the world. For these and other reasons, we are "getting better" at cross-cultural understanding. Still, we have a long way to go. The readings in this section may provide a start in that direction.

The first selection compares cultural phenomena across several different cultures. William N. Ellis and Margaret McMahon Ellis's "Cultures in Transition" examines a number of Third-World countries for alternative approaches to reforming our own culture.

The remaining essays deal with cultural contrasts between the West (usually the United States) and specific countries or regions. The Middle East is represented by two essays. In "Islam against the West?" Lance Morrow examines the centuries-old conflicts between Islam and Western (usually Christian) cultures. He analyzes the dynamics surrounding the Iran Hostage Crisis of 1979—an analysis that is still valuable in the wake of the Persian Gulf War. In "Proxemics in the Arab World," Edward T. Hall describes in detail some fundamental differences in the ways people from Arab and Western cultures deal with spacial relationships in social contexts. His analysis helps explain why people from these cultures often feel uncomfortable or slighted in each other's presence.

The economic and technical competition between the United States and Japan continues to generate debate and analysis in the media. At the heart of the Japanese success (and American decline) in these areas are the differences between the Japanese and

American approaches to education. In ''Japanese Education: How Do They Do It?'' Merry White provides a detailed comparison that not only points out the strengths and weaknesses of the Japanese educational system relative to America's but also deals with the cultural attitudes that lead to successful Japanese adaptations of educational patterns picked up from Western countries.

Closer to home, three essays deal with the differences between Hispanic and Anglo culture in the United States. Arthur L. Campa's ''Anglo vs. Chicano: Why?'' sets up a vivid series of historical, social, and linguistic contrasts that reveal the differences between two closely related cultures. In ''La Raza Cosmica'' Marilyn Berlin Snell's record of her conversation with Richard Rodriguez calls attention to the special cultural identity problems still faced by recent Mexican immigrants. Robert Coles's brief essay ''Hispanic Dreams/American Dreams'' brings many of these problems into vivid focus by reporting on the experiences and dreams of one Hispanic boy growing up in Texas.

The relationship among language, education, and culture that Rodriguez and Coles deal with in their examinations of Hispanics in the United States is addressed in a very different light in Ngũgĩ wa Thiong'o's ''Decolonising the Mind.'' For reasons that reflect his country's long status as a British colony, Thiong'o argues that children in his country should be taught in their native language, not in English. Whereas Rodriguez wants Hispanic children to learn English in school so they can ''swallow'' American culture and remake it, Thiong'o wants Nigerian children to study in their native language so they can retain their culture and way of life.

The last two selections in this section describe the collision between the cultures of the white European settlers and Native Americans. The first selection is a speech by Chief Seattle made in response to a proposal by the United States government that his people sell a large portion of land. In ''A Change in Worlds'' is a short, almost poetic statement about the interdependence of human beings and their environment. Chief Seattle asserted, among other things, that the land is not something that can be sold. Realizing that the white people did not understand his people's way of life and thinking, Chief Seattle repeatedly called attention to the differences he saw between the ways of white men and the ways of Native Americans, perhaps hoping that he could persuade whites to see the mystery, beauty, and holiness in the land.

''Buffalo,'' a short story by Barry H. Lopez, is about the pressure exerted by increasing numbers of white settlers on both the buffalo and Native Americans. Lopez's story is also about the dramatic differences in thinking between the Native Americans, who speak and think about nature in a metaphoric, mystical way, and white settlers and scholars, who speak of and try to analyze natural phenomena in an objective, scientific manner. Lopez shows us the truth the Native Americans saw and expressed—a truth almost entirely missed by whites, despite their emphasis on empiricism and accuracy. Sadly, the story records the beginning of the end of a culture—an end Chief Seattle saw coming as well. ''My people,'' he said, ''are ebbing away like a fast receding tide that will never flow again.''

William N. Ellis
and Margaret McMahon Ellis

Cultures in Transition

(1989)

Margaret McMahon Ellis (b. 1923), an anthropologist, and William N. Ellis (b. 1920), a physicist, are co-founders and chief staff persons of TRANET, an organization that facilitates international exchange of ideas and information on cultural alternatives and change. This essay originally appeared in the March–April 1989 issue of *The Futurist*.

1 World problems such as poverty, pollution, war, and hunger are inherent in the current system of world order based on nation-states and economic competition. They can be solved if people know and understand one another on a global, grass-roots basis. By developing people-to-people linkages irrespective of national borders, we can start to ameliorate global tensions and inequities.

2 All this is little more than a truism now accepted by most of the people concerned with global problems. But the intercultural knowledge needed to solve world problems is more than that of the cultural tourist, development specialist, or even the anthropologist/scholar.

3 We need to understand other cultures so that we can understand and reform our own culture. We need to re-think our concepts of health, resource conservation, ownership, family, clan, universe, person, etc., from a non-Western viewpoint.

4 We need to use intercultural understanding to provide us with a platform from which we can see ourselves. There is much in other cultures that fits well with our current attempts to design a better future for ourselves. There are ''new future'' concepts already conceived and still practiced by various peoples around the world that we need to understand, adapt, and adopt.

5 This idea was brought home to us during a 1983 visit to an ''appropriate-technology center'' in Papua New Guinea. The center has been most successful in designing small-scale technologies and promoting them by developing cottage industries in remote villages. But the day we arrived, the native director of the center was back in his jungle village because a number of his relatives had died under somewhat suspicious circumstances. It turned out that the relatives had been killed by the local witch doctor at the urging of the village elders.

6 The victims had become successful entrepreneurs, building small businesses and gaining personal wealth. One was sending shredded coconut to Port Moresby, one was exporting cane furniture, another solar-dried tropical fruits, and another was selling hemp rope. But the village elders only saw the innovations as creating individualism, and they believed that the ''successful'' individuals were no longer contributing to the common good. This Papua New Guinea society was based on community and coop-

eration; the newly introduced economic system was based on individualism and competition.

7 Ironically, ''appropriate'' small-scale foreign aid may be destroying concepts in the Third World that many of us in Western nations are trying to foster in our own society. Erik Dammann's *The Future in Our Hands,* Alvin Toffler's *The Third Wave,* James Robertson's *Sane Alternative,* John Naisbitt's *Megatrends,* E. F. Schumacher's *Small Is Beautiful,* and other books have suggested that Western society is approaching a major paradigm shift toward an outlook that is more cooperative, participatory, holistic, and anticipatory.

8 But the thinking in these books, and our own individual ideas as well, comes from our history, our families, our institutions, from which we cannot escape. The only way to properly assess our own life and thought processes is by searching other, non-Western cultures for paradigms different from those in which we are enmeshed.

Community and Cooperation

9 In a more recent visit to People Development Organizations throughout the Pacific, we ran into a number of other examples of cultural concepts showing how intercultural contacts could open new vistas for all of us.

10 We were most impressed by various expressions of ''community'' and ''cooperation'' we found still extant. One village we visited in Fiji was harvesting, drying, and exporting sea cucumbers to Japan. But all of the proceeds of the co-op went to the village elders for community projects. A dance group performing for the posh tourist hotel in Tonga did the same with all proceeds from an evening of entertaining tourists. None of the participants personally received anything for the work done. In Papua New Guinea, roads were maintained by the ''youth clubs,'' all young men who had reached puberty but were not yet married. Payment did not go to the workers but to the common house in which they lived together and was spent for the common good.

11 Not many publications have yet explored in any depth this concept of community and cooperation in indigenous cultures. One that makes a start is *Cultural Transition* (Routledge & Kegan Paul, 1986), a collection of papers edited by Merry White [also author of an essay in this section] and Susan Pollak. In one essay, Richard Katz compares the ''synergistic'' economy of the African !Kung with the ''scarcity'' economy of Westerners. The !Kung function as guardians, not possessors, of resources and are guided by the motivation of service to others. Rather than assuming that resources are scarce and individuals must compete to gain access to them, the !Kung assume that resources are interrelated and that a greater whole is created through synergy. Collaboration rather than competition makes more available to all.

12 In another essay, Sumiko Iwao notes that the Japanese place more emphasis on good human relationships than on money. Whereas ''in American culture, achievement and affiliation are seen as antagonistic, in Japan the two are joined,'' writes Iwao. And B.K. Ramanujam describes the Hindu concept of the individual as being a ''field'' of relationships. A change for the individual results only from a change of the ''field.'' The individual's goal is then to integrate into society and to improve society.

13 While *Cultural Transition* is limited to ''social transformation in the Third World and Japan,'' the studies suggest an area of research relevant to the social evolution of modern industrial society. Our own survival depends on a major cultural transition away from the individualistic, materialistic, militaristic, nationalistic culture that has formed us. The book's editors and the 11 collected essays hold that culture is the major obstacle to development for the Third World. But this ''obstacle to development'' is a two-edged sword: The book has as much to say to those interested in the transition of Western culture as it has to students of the transition of the cultures of the developing countries.

14 Folk healing is generally seen as an obstacle to the dissemination of Western medical care, and the modern school as the only means for socializing children; it would require ''a major departure from conventional development thinking'' not to view traditional cultural values as obstacles to ''progress,'' the editors state. This can be said of our attempts to transform the Third World, but it is even more true of our need to transform our own culture. ''Western medical care'' and ''schooling'' are obstacles to the development of more-holistic wellness and learning paradigms.

15 As social critic Ivan Illich shows in *Medical Nemesis,* the concept of health in the West has moved from one of wholeness and well-being to one of drugs, knives, and professionalism—to the detriment of our health. And in *Deschooling Society,* he shows that in the past children ''learned'' by participating with their parents in the community; now they are ''educated'' to sit quietly for eight hours a day under the control of authoritarian ''teachers'' in preparation for a role in the fading industrial society.

Options for Our Future

16 Historical analysis gives us one perspective from which we can explore the options for our future. For instance, in *Tahiti: A Paradise Lost,* David Howarth examines the transition of Tahiti's indigenous culture in the eighteenth century. By carefully reading the logs and diaries of early ''discoverers'' of Tahiti, Howarth reconstructs the culture of 100,000 people crowded on a small island before the influx of Westerners.

17 For the indigenous islanders, what was needed for living was freely given and openly taken. Food, housing, sexual favors, tools, boats, and skills were available for all without question. They saw nothing wrong in taking anything brought ashore by the visiting sailors, nor in showering on visitors a bountiful share of their favors and possessions. But the culture of paradise, which had been stable for many centuries, was destroyed in a few decades by the excesses of the visitors, whose cultural paradigms were based on ''scarcity'' rather than ''enoughness.''

18 A second perspective for exploring our future options could come from comparing our Western cultural paradigms with those of other cultures. For example, the Australian aborigines have no concept of land ownership. They are the ''ownees'' of the land—the land owns them. The land is not only the soil and territory, but also the holy places, the spirits of their ancestors, the environment, the cosmos, and all else that has created them. They are part of the land and cannot conceive of being separated from it.

19 In Papua New Guinea, there is yet another concept of land. Different people have different rights on the same land. One may hold ceremonial rights, another fishing, another hunting, another netting bats, another dwelling rights, and another the right of passage. No one owns land. The idea that land is something that can be owned by an individual is almost unique to Western culture.

20 Many “economic” concepts are similarly unique to the West. In Ghana, “trade,” “barter,” or any other Western form of “economic exchange” is not practiced except where introduced by the colonials. Ghanaians merely give with no measure of what might be returned but know that the more they give the more will be given to them.

21 The Ghanaians' beliefs are similar to those of the Native Americans of the Pacific Northwest, who felt that “poverty” was the “insurance” policy and meant “wealth.” The more they gave away, the more esteem they gained for themselves and their family and the more was society beholden to them. Those who failed to contribute to the community or who hoarded material goods would not be helped in times of emergency and were the outcasts and the “poor” of society.

22 Our future culture will no more resemble our current one than this one resembles the age of hunter-gatherers. We have the opportunity to design our own future. To seize that opportunity, we must find ways to escape the biases inherent in our current cultural paradigms and institutions. Studies of other cultures could open our eyes to the options for a more positive future.

Questions for Analysis

1. In Paragraph 3, William Ellis and Margaret McMahon Ellis say that “we need to understand other cultures so that we can understand and reform our own culture.” Is this a reasonable and desirable goal? Can it be seen as a radical or revolutionary goal? Explain your answer.
2. What is the point of the story in Paragraphs 5 and 6 about the killing of cottage-industry entrepreneurs in Papua New Guinea?
3. Explain the “major paradigm shift” the authors foresee in Western culture. Do you agree with this forecast? Do you think the “new paradigm” would work in Western countries?
4. Explain the distinction between “synergistic” and “scarcity” economies (see Paragraph 11), and the distinction between “scarcity” and “enoughness” (see Paragraph 17).
5. Which of the non-Western cultural attitudes or practices do you find most appealing, and which do you find least attractive? Do you think they might be adapted to become a part of our culture? How? What changes would we need to make in our culture to accommodate adapted versions of these attitudes or practices?

6. What is the purpose of the article? Is it an argument for specific changes? What assumptions are made about the audience's attitude toward cultural change?

Lance Morrow

Islam Against the West?

(1979)

Lance Morrow (b. 1939) is a consulting editor with *Time* magazine. This essay appeared in that periodical a few months after fundamentalist Muslim followers of the Ayatollah Khomeini took over the American Embassy in Iran and held over 100 American citizens hostage. The Iran Hostage Crisis, which lasted over a year and was partially responsible for President Carter's failure to be re-elected, put in dramatic contrast many basic differences between Islamic and Western cultures. Although Khomeini is now dead, and we recently fought with Islamic countries against Iraq in the Persian Gulf War, Morrow's essay is still valuable: despite our military alliances and economic interdependence, tensions and misunderstandings between Islamic cultures and the West continue.

Whenever they kindle a fire for war, Allah extinguishes it. And they strive to create disorder in the earth, and Allah loves not those who create disorder.

—The Koran

1 The West and the world of Islam sometimes resemble two different centuries banging through the night on parallel courses. In full raucous cultural panoply, they keep each other awake. They make each other nervous. At times, as now, they veer together and collide: up and down the processions, threats are exchanged, pack animals and zealots bray, bales of ideological baggage spill onto the road. Embassies get burned, hostages taken. Songs of revenge rise in the throat.

2 Are these collisions inevitable? The mutual misunderstandings of the West and the Islamic world have a rich patina of history. Jews, Christians and Muslims, all "People of the Book," draw much of their faith from the same sources. Yet from the time of the Muslim conquests and the Crusades. West and Islam have confronted each other by turns in attitudes of incomprehension, greed, fanaticism, prurient interest, fear and loathing. The drama has lost none of its historic tension in the stagecraft of the Ayatullah Khomeini. "This is not a struggle between the United States and Iran," he has told the faithful. "It is a struggle between Islam and the infidel." At such moments, the Imam takes on the wild and grainy aspect of a dire Mohammedan prophet by DeMille.

3 Khomeini may even wish to transcend Iranian nationalism and export his fundamentalist Islamic revival. The prospect of such contagious piety disturbs other Muslim leaders, the Saudi royal family, for example. But it also raises apprehension and a certain amount of bewilderment in the West. When Mahdist Saudi zealots took over the mosque in Mecca last month, the Islamic world displayed a disconcerting readiness to believe

Khomeini's incendiary report that the attack had been the work of Zionists and U.S. imperialists. "The Americans have done it again," many Muslims told themselves reflexively. Some Americans have responded by asking with a truculent innocence: "What did we ever do to them?"

4 If the question is disingenuous, the answers are complex.

5 The U.S. never colonized Islamic countries, as, for example, Britain and France did. The U.S. has no large Islamic minority and thus, unlike the Soviet Union, has no record of bitter internal relations with Muslims. Besides (as some Muslim leaders know), Communism is far more inimical to Islam than capitalism. But in the past 30 years, the U.S. has been a chief participant in a cultural encounter that is in some ways even more traumatic to the world of Islam than colonialism: the full onslaught of secular, materialist modernization, 20th century civilization sweeping into the timeless Muslim villages. The vast apparatus of Western progress, a machine overwhelmingly vigorous, profoundly tempting and yet decadent by all the disciplines of the Prophet, has threatened Muslim identity.

6 Western science and technology have wounded the deep pride of Islam. The success of the unvirtuous, the infidel unfavored of Allah, is psychologically confusing. "Seen through Muslim eyes," writes Berkeley Historian Peter Brown, "the emergence of [the West] as the temporary master of the world remains an anomaly in the natural unfolding of the course of history." Muslims have recoiled from modernization in exact proportion to the force of its temptation for them. They have been attracted by secular materialism, have tried it in the guise of both capitalism and Marxism, but they have often been disappointed by it, have associated it with the colonial masters who introduced them to it. They have found it dangerously, almost radioactively, corrupt.

7 Some Muslims, of course, insist that Islam and modernization are perfectly compatible. Many Islamic countries supply the oil that is, for now, the indispensable ingredient of modernization, and they have tried to use their staggering and sudden wealth to buy the machines of progress without the devils that often inhabit them. Conservative Saudi leaders, for example, pursue a selective strategy regarding the technological riches of the West: they seek to modernize without the garish libertine free-for-all that Western secular individualism has promoted.

8 But for Muslims, the dilemma remains: if they are to develop economically, they must import Western technology. To master Western technology, they must send their young to be educated in the West. And that invariably means diluting their culture. Progress means better medicine and other mitigations of life's harshness, of course, but it also means the young women returning from Paris or Palo Alto in short skirts instead of *chadors:* it means 30% inflation, pollution, an open door to all the depressing vitality of the junk culture: it means the young leaving the villages and becoming infested with all kinds of Hefnerian tastes for hi-fis and forbidden pleasures. It is sometimes difficult for a Westerner to understand that to a Muslim, the cultural dismantling of Islam, the governing apparatus of his life and civilization, is a tragedy that amounts to a form of annihilation.

9 The sort of Muslim fundamentalism evident in Iran or Muammar Gaddafi's Libya may confirm a remark by Frantz Fanon, the philosopher of Third World uprisings: the native response to imperial domination is to fall back on what is authentic, what is resistant to modernization. The mosque becomes a symbolic safe haven.

10 Islam is not inherently or inevitably anti-Western, despite the often bloody encounters of the past. Muslims have historically occupied a geographically vulnerable position, which may account for their militant touchiness. But the religion has become the vehicle for certain anti-Western, anti-American resentments and antipathies. In some ways, the specifically Islamic religious component is almost incidental: Islam is, as much as anything else, the repository for grievances, envies and hatreds that Third World have-nots harbor for the privileged of the globe. Islam gives cohesion to complaints about the injustices of the world. The Muslim tradition provides the language and symbolism to express a wide social message: it is not necessarily a religious phenomenon. It is not anti-Christian. In fact, Muslims really regard modern Westerners as a species of pagan. Ironically, some of the resentment has been aroused by the emergence of oil-rich classes within the Islamic countries themselves. With that wealth came a widening gap between rich and poor, a dangerous ambivalence of rising expectations and an anxiety that old ways might be endangered. The resentment of modernization is not anything so simply and piously self-abnegating as a wish to avoid luxury; it is also a bitterness at being forced to live adjacent to a wealth one cannot possess.

11 Iran embodies both the essence of the Islamic complaint against the West and unique historical grievances of its own. By race (Aryan), language (Persian), religion (Shi'ite Muslim) and historical tradition (ancient Persia was conquered by Muslims in the 8th century), Iran is different from the rest of Middle Eastern Islam. It was never colonized, in the usual sense of the word, by the West. And yet the penetration of Western ideas was deeper in Iran than in some other parts of the Middle East and came to be seen in a considerably more sinister light.

12 While leaders in other Muslim states (Saudi Arabia and Libya, for example) have moderated Western influences, the Shah embraced the West with (as it turned out) a heedless enthusiasm. He set up a secular state, destroying the classic and crucial unity in Islam between church and government. Under the Pahlavis, women were liberated from the traditional chador, permitted to vote and divorce their husbands. The Shah made the mistake of ignoring the mullahs (priests). The U.S., in turn, embraced him, and even had the CIA engineer a coup to restore him to power in 1953. Corruption, dislocations of life and profoundly disorienting social change all accompanied his rule; so did political suppression and the tortures of SAVAK, his secret police. The U.S. was inextricably implicated in the career of this potentate—Ozymandias and Faust—and shared the people's judgment of him when it came.

13 Anti-Western, and specifically anti-American, sentiment in Iran is therefore not surprising or irrational, whatever irrational forms it has taken. The deep social anger at the Shah and the U.S. that supported him has assumed an air of fanaticism in its Shi'ite expression. Shi'ites, who make up 10% of Islam, tend toward a passionate, activist religious life and flirtation with martyrdom (they have been known to commit suicide

accidentally by bashing and mutilating themselves in mourning for their founder, Husain, the slaughtered grandson of the Prophet). Shi'ites also prefer charismatic leaders: they are forever parading the portrait of the Imam Khomeini.

14 The special ferocity and condensation of the will that are evident in the Iranian revolution owe much to this tendency toward the cult of personality. (One ironic aspect is that Khomeini may not, strictly speaking, be a very good Muslim at all. He not only condoned the violation of Islam's protection of foreign emissaries, but also made inflammatory, groundless claims about the American responsibility for the Mecca attack. He has deliberately fomented violence, which the Koran forbids.)

15 The distinction between Sunnis and Shi'ites is, according to some scholars of Islam, much greater than that between, say, Roman Catholics and Protestants. It is one of the most basic of many differences that make it not only inadvisable but impossible to generalize about Islam as if it were a single, coherent bloc. Just as the Communist world includes antagonists (U.S.S.R. and China, Viet Nam and Cambodia), the Islamic world is very much fragmented. Morocco and Algeria are fighting in the western Sahara. The Middle East is a psychodrama of the paranoiac fears entertained by Arabs for one another. North and South Yemen were at war earlier this year. Moderate Arab states like Saudi Arabia and Jordan fear a radical trend that might become uncontrollable. It is important to notice that for all the incendiary mobs that have eddied around American outposts in the past few weeks, none has ever got out of control of the governing authorities; when the government said stop, the rioting stopped. That suggests that the mobs might be viewed more as a form of demonstrative Muslim rhetoric (dangerous and expensive rhetoric, of course) rather than as any tidal force of history.

16 Furthermore, the world of Islam extends far beyond the Middle East. The largest single concentration of Muslims in the world exists in Indonesia, where there is virtually no Islamic outcry against the West or America. Says former Malaysian Premier Tunku Abdul Rahman: "It is a shame to think that Iran, one of the progressive Muslim countries, has literally speaking, gone to the dogs."

17 One inexhaustible source of anti-Americanism in Muslims is U.S. support of Israel and the question of a Palestinian homeland, issues that blend with the Third World prejudice against the privileged. But, says French Sociologist Jacques Berque, "any hopes or fears that the entire Muslim world will unite against the West amount to a romantic vision of pan-Islamism."

18 Muslims have aggressively sought the material wonders of the West, yet are ambivalent in their souls. Berque locates the central dilemma of Islam: If Islam is ever to become an economic and political competitor of capitalism and Marxism, it must embrace a progress that may forever weaken its ethical and spiritual structures, just as other religions have been drained by the secularization of the Western world. So far, Islam has not proved itself a vehicle of social change, a program to confront the modern world.

19 Still, oil has convinced the Islamic world—or half-convinced it—of its worth and power. The presence of oil in the complicated psychology of anti-Westernism makes

the volatility of the Islamic world especially perilous. It is an interesting point of Muslim psychology that the Arabs who grow unimaginably rich off Western payments for oil (and squander their petrodollars on Rodeo Drive in Beverly Hills, Calif., on Rolls-Royces and golden bathroom fixtures) have still in them enough desert asceticism to be contemptuous of the West's energy addictions. So here the old relation is reversed: the West is dependent on the East, and is learning something about the frustration that dependence brings.

20 In this encounter of East and West, the rage on either side has a way of spiraling up in a murderous double helix: the anger of the Muslims may feed on itself, and the countering anger of the West may further ignite the anger of Islam. So great is the mutual incomprehension that international relations degenerate rapidly to the chaotic psychology of the mob. Although U.S. reactions have been, all things considered, remarkably mild, the Iranian crisis has legitimized among Americans a new stereotype of the demented Muslim. Says University of Wisconsin Historian Kemal H. Karpat: "Khomeini has done more harm to the Islamic image in one month than all the propaganda of the past 15 years."

21 It should be possible for Americans to preserve an intelligent sympathy for the Islamic perspective without feeling vaguely guilt-stricken by the past. Anti-Americanism—the specific, sharper focus of anti-Westernism—is in some ways the Islamic world's excuse for its own failures, confusions and periodic collapses into incoherence. It is more convenient morally to blame the West than to gaze steadily at the Islamic dilemma, easier to devise revenge for the past than ideas for the future. Khomeini, with his absolutist pretensions and aggressive fantasies of *jihad* (holy war) against the West, demeans Islam; he gives it the aspect of a bizarre, dangerous but spiritually trivial cult. To the extent that Muslims support Khomeini, they share in the image of Islam that he has created.

Questions for Analysis

1. Explain the metaphor Morrow sets up in his first paragraph. How does it both get our attention and help prepare us for the rest of the essay? Morrow wrote this essay in December of 1979, a few months after the Iran Hostage Crisis started. Given your knowledge of America's experience in the Persian Gulf War, explain how the metaphor he uses in the first paragraph is still valid.
2. What is the purpose of Morrow's essay? Is he arguing a position? Raising questions? Presenting information? Explain your answer.
3. Is Morrow's depiction of Islam balanced? Does he call attention to both its strengths and weaknesses? Explain.
4. Does Morrow bring to his analysis too strong a Western bias? Is the West responsible for many of the collisions between Islam and the West? To which side does Morrow most often seem to assign blame? Explain.

5. What, according to Morrow, is the chief source of tension and conflict between the West and Islam? Where does he think changes in the attitudes must first come, Islam or the West?
6. Is the criticism of Islam in Morrow's final paragraph directed at all Muslims? Explain.
7. In what ways did Saddam Hussein try to use Islamic loyalties during and before the Persian Gulf War?

Edward T. Hall

Proxemics in the Arab World

(1966)

A professor of Anthropology at Northwestern University, Edward T. Hall (b. 1914) is a student of *proxemics* (from the Latin *proximus,* which means "nearest"), the study of how people deal with and respond to spatial relationships. This essay on proxemic differences between Arab and Western cultures comes from his book *The Hidden Dimension*. Hall's most recent publication is *An Anthropologist's Everyday Life: An Autobiography* (1992), a personal account of his life as a scientist.

1 In spite of over two thousand years of contact, Westerners and Arabs still do not understand each other. Proxemic research reveals some insights into this difficulty. Americans in the Middle East are immediately struck by two conflicting sensations. In public they are compressed and overwhelmed by smells, crowding, and high noise levels; in Arab homes Americans are apt to rattle around, feeling exposed and often somewhat inadequate because of too much space! (The Arab houses and apartments of the middle and upper classes which Americans stationed abroad commonly occupy are much larger than the dwellings such Americans usually inhabit.) Both the high sensory stimulation which is experienced in public places and the basic insecurity which comes from being in a dwelling that is too large provide Americans with an introduction to the sensory world of the Arab.

Behavior in Public

2 Pushing and shoving in public places is characteristic of Middle Eastern culture. Yet it is not entirely what Americans think it is (being pushy and rude) but stems from a different set of assumptions concerning not only the relations between people but how one experiences the body as well. Paradoxically, Arabs consider northern Europeans and Americans pushy, too. This was very puzzling to me when I started investigating these two views. How could Americans who stand aside and avoid touching be

considered pushy? I used to ask Arabs to explain this paradox. None of my subjects was able to tell me specifically what particulars of American behavior were responsible, yet they all agreed that the impression was widespread among Arabs. After repeated unsuccessful attempts to gain insight into the cognitive world of the Arab on this particular point, I filed it away as a question that only time would answer. When the answer came, it was because of a seemingly inconsequential annoyance.

3 While waiting for a friend in a Washington, D.C., hotel lobby and wanting to be both visible and alone, I had seated myself in a solitary chair outside the normal stream of traffic. In such a setting most Americans follow a rule, which is all the more binding because we seldom think about it, that can be stated as follows: as soon as a person stops or is seated in a public place, there balloons around him a small sphere of privacy which is considered inviolate. The size of the sphere varies with the degree of crowding, the age, sex, and the importance of the person, as well as the general surroundings. Anyone who enters this zone and stays there is intruding. In fact, a stranger who intrudes, even for a specific purpose, acknowledges the fact that he has intruded by beginning his request with "Pardon me, but can you tell me . . . ?"

4 To continue, as I waited in the deserted lobby, a stranger walked up to where I was sitting and stood close enough so that not only could I easily touch him but I could even hear him breathing. In addition, the dark mass of his body filled the peripheral field of vision on my left side. If the lobby had been crowded with people, I would have understood his behavior, but in an empty lobby his presence made me exceedingly uncomfortable. Feeling annoyed by this intrusion, I moved my body in such a way as to communicate annoyance. Strangely enough, instead of moving away, my actions seemed only to encourage him, because he moved even closer. In spite of the temptation to escape the annoyance, I put aside thoughts of abandoning my post, thinking, "To hell with it. Why should I move? I was here first and I'm not going to let this fellow drive me out even if he is a boor." Fortunately, a group of people soon arrived whom my tormentor immediately joined. Their mannerisms explained his behavior, for I knew from both speech and gestures that they were Arabs. I had not been able to make this crucial identification by looking at my subject when he was alone because he wasn't talking and he was wearing American clothes.

5 In describing the scene later to an Arab colleague, two contrasting patterns emerged. My concept and my feelings about my own circle of privacy in a "public" place immediately struck my Arab friend as strange and puzzling. He said, "After all, it's a public place, isn't it?" Pursuing this line of inquiry, I found that an Arab thought I had no rights whatsoever by virtue of occupying a given spot; neither my place nor my body was inviolate! For the Arab, there is no such thing as an intrusion in public. Public means public. With this insight, a great range of Arab behavior that had been puzzling, annoying, and sometimes even frightening began to make sense. I learned, for example, that if *A* is standing on a street corner and *B* wants his spot, *B* is within his rights if he does what he can to make *A* uncomfortable enough to move. In Beirut only the hardy sit in the last row in a movie theater, because there are usually standees who want seats and who push and shove and make such a nuisance that most people give up and leave.

Seen in this light, the Arab who "intruded" on my space in the hotel lobby had apparently selected it for the very reason I had: it was a good place to watch two doors and the elevator. My show of annoyance, instead of driving him away, had only encouraged him. He thought he was about to get me to move.

6 Another silent source of friction between Americans and Arabs is in an area that Americans treat very informally—the manners and rights of the road. In general, in the United States we tend to defer to the vehicle that is bigger, more powerful, faster, and heavily laden. While a pedestrian walking along a road may feel annoyed he will not think it unusual to step aside for a fast-moving automobile. He knows that because he is moving he does not have the right to the space around him that he has when he is standing still (as I was in the hotel lobby). It appears that the reverse is true with the Arabs who apparently *take on rights to space as they move.* For someone else to move into a space an Arab is also moving into is a violation of his rights. It is infuriating to an Arab to have someone else cut in front of him on the highway. It is the American's cavalier treatment of moving space that makes the Arab call him aggressive and pushy.

Concepts of Privacy

7 The experience described above and many others suggested to me that Arabs might actually have a wholly contrasting set of assumptions concerning the body and the rights associated with it. Certainly the Arab tendency to shove and push each other in public and to feel and pinch women in public conveyances would not be tolerated by Westerners. It appeared to me that they must not have any concept of a private zone outside the body. This proved to be precisely the case.

8 In the Western world, the person is synonymous with an individual inside a skin. And in northern Europe generally, the skin and even the clothes may be inviolate. You need permission to touch either if you are a stranger. This rule applies in some parts of France, where the mere touching of another person during an argument used to be legally defined as assault. For the Arab the location of the person in relation to the body is quite different. The person exists somewhere down inside the body. The ego is not completely hidden, however, because it can be reached very easily with an insult. It is protected from touch but not from words. The dissociation of the body and the ego may explain why the public amputation of a thief's hand is tolerated as standard punishment in Saudi Arabia. It also sheds light on why an Arab employer living in a modern apartment can provide his servant with a room that is a boxlike cubicle approximately 5 by 10 by 4 feet in size that is not only hung from the ceiling to conserve floor space but has an opening so that the servant can be spied on.

9 As one might suspect, deep orientations toward the self such as the one just described are also reflected in the language. This was brought to my attention one afternoon when an Arab colleague who is the author of an Arab-English dictionary arrived in my office and threw himself into a chair in a state of obvious exhaustion. When I asked him what had been going on, he said: "I have spent the entire afternoon trying to find the Arab equivalent of the English word 'rape.' There is no such word in Arabic. All my sources, both written and spoken, can come up with no more than an approximation, such as

'He took her against her will.' There is nothing in Arabic approaching your meaning as it is expressed in that one word.''

10 Differing concepts of the placement of the ego in relation to the body are not easily grasped. Once an idea like this is accepted, however, it is possible to understand many other facets of Arab life that would otherwise be difficult to explain. One of these is the high population density of Arab cities like Cairo, Beirut, and Damascus. According to the animal studies described [elsewhere], the Arabs should be living in a perpetual behavioral sink. While it is probable that Arabs are suffering from population pressures, it is also just as possible that continued pressure from the desert has resulted in a cultural adaptation to high density which takes the form described above. Tucking the ego down inside the body shell not only would permit higher population densities but would explain why it is that Arab communications are stepped up as much as they are when compared to northern European communication patterns. Not only is the sheer noise level much higher, but the piercing look of the eyes, the touch of the hands, and the mutual bathing in the warm moist breath during conversation represent stepped-up sensory inputs to a level which many Europeans find unbearably intense.

11 The Arab dream is for lots of space in the home, which unfortunately many Arabs cannot afford. Yet when he has space, it is very different from what one finds in most American homes. Arab spaces inside their upper middle-class homes are tremendous by our standards. They avoid partitions because Arabs *do not like to be alone.* The form of the home is such as to hold the family together inside a single protective shell, because Arabs are deeply involved with each other. Their personalities are intermingled and take nourishment from each other like the roots and soil. If one is not with people and actively involved in some way, one is deprived of life. An old Arab saying reflects this value: ''Paradise without people should not be entered because it is Hell.'' Therefore, Arabs in the United States often feel socially and sensorially deprived and long to be back where there is human warmth and contact.

12 Since there is no physical privacy as we know it in the Arab family, not even a word for privacy, one could expect that the Arabs might use some other means to be alone. Their way to be alone is to stop talking. Like the English, an Arab who shuts himself off in this way is not indicating that anything is wrong or that he is withdrawing, only that he wants to be alone with his own thoughts or does not want to be intruded upon. One subject said that her father would come and go for days at a time without saying a word, and no one in the family thought anything of it. Yet for this very reason, an Arab exchange student visiting a Kansas farm failed to pick up the cue that his American hosts were mad at him when they gave him the ''silent treatment.'' He only discovered something was wrong when they took him to town and tried forcibly to put him on a bus to Washington, D.C., the headquarters of the exchange program responsible for his presence in the U.S.

Arab Personal Distances

13 Like everyone else in the world, Arabs are unable to formulate specific rules for their informal behavior patterns. In fact, they often deny that there are any rules, and they

are made anxious by suggestions that such is the case. Therefore, in order to determine how the Arab sets distances, I investigated the use of each sense separately. Gradually, definite and distinctive behavioral patterns began to emerge.

14 Olfaction occupies a prominent place in the Arab life. Not only is it one of the distance-setting mechanisms, but it is a vital part of a complex system of behavior. Arabs consistently breathe on people when they talk. However, this habit is more than a matter of different manners. To the Arab good smells are pleasing and a way of being involved with each other. To smell one's friend is not only nice but desirable, for to deny him your breath is to act ashamed. Americans, on the other hand, trained as they are not to breathe in people's faces, automatically communicate shame in trying to be polite. Who would expect that when our highest diplomats are putting on their best manners they are also communicating shame? Yet this is what occurs constantly, because diplomacy is not only "eyeball to eyeball" but breath to breath.

15 By stressing olfaction, Arabs do not try to eliminate all the body's odors, only to enhance them and use them in building human relationships. Nor are they self-conscious about telling others when they don't like the way they smell. A man leaving his house in the morning may be told by his uncle, "Habib, your stomach is sour and your breath doesn't smell too good. Better not talk too close to people today." Smell is even considered in the choice of a mate. When couples are being matched for marriage, the man's go-between will sometimes ask to smell the girl, who may be turned down if she doesn't "smell nice." Arabs recognize that smell and disposition may be linked.

16 In a word, the olfactory boundary performs two roles in Arab life. It enfolds those who want to relate and separates those who don't. The Arab finds it essential to stay inside the olfactory zone as a means of keeping tab on changes in emotion. What is more, he may feel crowded as soon as he smells something unpleasant. While not much is known about "olfactory crowding," this may prove to be as significant as any other variable in the crowding complex because it is tied directly to the body chemistry and hence to the state of health and emotions. It is not surprising, therefore, that the olfactory boundary constitutes for the Arabs an informal distance-setting mechanism in contrast to the visual mechanisms of the Westerner.

Facing and Not Facing

17 One of my earliest discoveries in the field of intercultural communication was that the position of the bodies of people in conversation varies with the culture. Even so, it is used to puzzle me that a special Arab friend seemed unable to walk and talk at the same time. After years in the United States, he could not bring himself to stroll along, facing forward while talking. Our progress would be arrested while he edged ahead, cutting slightly in front of me and turning sideways so we could see each other. Once in this position, he would stop. His behavior was explained when I learned that for the Arabs to view the other person peripherally is regarded as impolite, and to sit or stand back-to-back is considered very rude. You must be involved when interacting with Arabs who are friends.

18 One mistaken American notion is that Arabs conduct all conversations at close distances. This is not the case at all. On social occasions, they may sit on opposite sides of the room and talk across the room to each other. They are, however, apt to take offense when Americans use what are to them ambiguous distances, such as the four- to seven-foot social-consultative distance. They frequently complain that Americans are cold or aloof or ''don't care.'' This was what an elderly Arab diplomat in an American hospital thought when the American nurses used ''professional'' distance. He had the feeling that he was being ignored, that they might not take good care of him. Another Arab subject remarked, referring to American behavior, ''What's the matter? Do I smell bad? Or are they afraid of me?''

19 Arabs who interact with Americans report experiencing a certain flatness traceable in part to a very different use of the eyes in private and in public as well as between friends and strangers. Even though it is rude for a guest to walk around the Arab home eying things, Arabs look at each other in ways which seem hostile or challenging to the American. One Arab informant said that he was in constant hot water with Americans because of the way he looked at them without the slightest intention of offending. In fact, he had on several occasions barely avoided fights with American men who apparently thought their masculinity was being challenged because of the way he was looking at them. As noted earlier, Arabs look each other in the eye when talking with an intensity that makes most Americans highly uncomfortable.

Involvement

20 As the reader must gather by now, Arabs are involved with each other on many different levels simultaneously. Privacy in a public place is foreign to them. Business transactions in the bazaar, for example, are not just between buyer and seller, but are participated in by everyone. Anyone who is standing around may join in. If a grownup sees a boy breaking a window, he must stop him even if he doesn't know him. Involvement and participation are expressed in other ways as well. If two men are fighting, the crowd must intervene. On the political level, *to fail to intervene* when trouble is brewing is to take sides, which is what our State Department always seems to be doing. Given the fact that few people in the world today are even remotely aware of the cultural mold that forms their thoughts, it is normal for Arabs to view *our* behavior as though it stemmed from *their* own hidden set of assumptions.

Feelings about Enclosed Spaces

21 In the course of my interviews with Arabs the term ''tomb'' kept cropping up in conjunction with enclosed space. In a word, Arabs don't mind being crowded by people but hate to be hemmed in by walls. They show a much greater overt sensitivity to architectural crowding than we do. Enclosed space must meet at least three requirements that I know of if it is to satisfy the Arabs: there must be plenty of unobstructed space in which to move around (possibly as much as a thousand square feet); very high ceilings—so high in fact that they do not normally impinge on the visual field; and, in addition, there must be an unobstructed view. It was spaces such as these in which the Americans referred to earlier felt so uncomfortable. One sees the Arab's need for a

view expressed in many ways, even negatively, for to cut off a neighbor's view is one of the most effective ways of spiting him. In Beirut one can see what is known locally as the "spite house." It is nothing more than a thick, four-story wall, built at the end of a long fight between neighbors, on a narrow strip of land, for the express purpose of denying a view of the Mediterranean to any house built on the land behind. According to one of my informants, there is also a house on a small plot of land between Beirut and Damascus which is completely surrounded by a neighbor's wall built high enough to cut off the view from all windows!

Boundaries

22 Proxemic patterns tell us other things about Arab culture. For example, the whole concept of the boundary as an abstraction is almost impossible to pin down. In one sense, there are no boundaries. "Edges" of towns, yes, but permanent boundaries out in the country (hidden lines), no. In the course of my work with Arab subjects I had a difficult time translating our concept of a boundary into terms which could be equated with theirs. In order to clarify the distinctions between the two very different definitions, I thought it might be helpful to pinpoint acts which constituted trespass. To date, I have been unable to discover anything even remotely resembling our own legal concept of trespass.

23 Arab behavior in regard to their own real estate is apparently an extension of, and therefore consistent with, their approach to the body. My subjects simply failed to respond whenever trespass was mentioned. They didn't seem to understand what I meant by this term. This may be explained by the fact that they organize relationships with each other according to closed social systems rather than spatially. For thousands of years Moslems, Marinites, Druses, and Jews have lived in their own villages, each with strong kin affiliations. Their hierarchy of loyalties is: first to one's self, then to kinsman, townsman, or tribesman, co-religionist and/or countryman. Anyone not in these categories is a stranger. Strangers and enemies are very closely linked, if not synonymous, in Arab thought. Trespass in this context is a matter of who you are, rather than a piece of land or a space with a boundary that can be denied to anyone and everyone, friend and foe alike.

24 In summary, proxemic patterns differ. By examining them it is possible to reveal hidden cultural frames that determine the structure of a given people's perceptual world. Perceiving the world differently leads to differential definitions of what constitutes crowded living, different interpersonal relations, and a different approach to both local and international politics.

Questions for Analysis

1. Analyze the structure and strategy Hall follows in his first six paragraphs. Pay particular attention to his movement from general to particular (or his moves up and down in level of abstraction).

2. In the section of his essay on ''Concepts of Privacy,'' Hall uses several language-based examples to illustrate Arab concepts of self and space. Explain these examples and how they illustrate the power of language to both reflect and maintain a cultural outlook.
3. Could the linguistic examples and behavioral patterns Hall presents in ''Concepts of Privacy'' just as easily reflect Arab attitudes toward women as concepts of self and space? Explain your answer.
4. In his final paragraph, Hall asserts that different perceptions of the world (seen, for example, through a study of proxemics) can lead to ''a different approach to both local and international politics.'' How might these characteristics affect politics? Should Hall have provided additional examples or discussion to support this assertion? What further examples or points might he make?

Merry White

Japanese Education: How Do They Do It?

(1984)

Merry White (b. 1941) is a sociologist who administered Harvard University's East Asian Studies Program before moving to Boston University. Her book *The Japanese Educational Challenge* was published in 1987. This essay appeared in the Summer 1984 issue of *The Public Interest.*

1 Japan has become the new reference point for the developing nations and the West, and comparisons with Japan cause increasing wonder and sometimes envy. Travel agents continue to profit from the curiosity of Americans, particularly businessmen, who take regular tours of Japan seeking the secrets of Japanese industry. They come back with photographs and full notebooks, convinced they have learned secrets that can be transplanted to their own companies.

2 Even the Japanese have entered the pop-sociological search for the secrets of their own success; their journalists suggest that they emphasize problem *prevention* while Americans make up for their lack of prescience and care through *remediation* (in the case of cars, recalls for flawed models). The explanation given by a European Economic Community report—that the Japanese are workaholics willing, masochistically, to live in ''rabbit hutches'' without complaint—was met with amused derision in Japan. But it seems that those who do not look for transportable ''secrets'' are nonetheless willing to believe that the source of Japanese success is genetic, and thus completely untransferable. There are alternatives to these positions, and an examination of Japanese education provides us with a backdrop for considering them.

The Social Consensus

3 The attention given to the decline of both American industry and American education has not yet led to an awareness here of the close relationship between the development of people and the development of society, an awareness we see everywhere in Japanese thought and institutions, and whose effects we can see in the individual achievements of Japanese children. If Americans realized how powerful the relationship is between Japanese school achievement and social and economic successes we might see the same kind of protectionist language aimed at the Japanese educational system that we see directed at their automobile industry. ("The Japanese must stop producing such able and committed students because *it isn't fair.*")

4 The Japanese understand how important it is to have not just a high level of literacy (which they have had since well before modernization), but also a high level of education in the whole population. It has been said that the Japanese high school graduate is as well educated as an American college graduate, and indeed it is impressive that any worker on the factory floor can be expected to understand statistical material, work from complex graphs and charts, and perform sophisticated mathematical operations. This consensus that education is important, however simple it may sound, is the single most important contributor to the success of Japanese schools. Across the population, among parents, at all institutional and bureaucratic levels, and highest on the list of national priorities, is the stress on excellence in education. This is not just rhetoric. If the consensus, societal mobilization, and personal commitment—all focused on education—are not available to Americans, the reason is not genetic, nor are we locked in an immutable cultural pattern. We simply have not mobilized around our children.

5 There are clear advantages to being a Japanese child: a homogeneous population focused on perpetuating its cultural identity; an occupational system where selection and promotion are based on educational credentials; a relatively equal distribution of educational opportunities; a universal core curriculum; highly trained and rewarded teachers; and families, especially mothers, devoted to enhancing the life chances of children and working cooperatively with the educational system. Finally, there are high standards for performance in every sector, and a carefully graded series of performance expectations in the school curriculum.

6 It is clear from these assertions that the measurable cognitive achievements of Japanese education represent only part of the picture. The American press stresses these achievements and accounts for them in terms of government expenditures, longer school years, and early use of homework. While the International Association for the Evaluation of Educational Achievement (IEA) test scores certainly indicate that Japanese children are testing higher than any children in the world (especially in math and science), and while some researchers have even claimed that Japanese children on average score 11 points more than American children on IQ tests, the social and psychological dimensions of Japanese education are similarly impressive and are primary contributors to cognitive achievement. The support given by family and teachers to the emotional and behavioral development of the child provides a base for the child's acquisition of knowledge and problem-solving skills. But beyond this, the Japanese think a major

function of education is the development of a happy, engaged, and secure child, able to work hard and cooperate with others.

Inside the Japanese School

7 In order to understand the context of the Japanese educational system, some basic information is necessary:

8 1. Education is compulsory for ages six to 15, or through lower secondary school. (Age is almost always correlated with grade level, by the way, because only rarely is a child "kept back" and almost never "put ahead.") Non-compulsory high school attendance (both public and private) is nearly universal, at 98 percent.

9 2. There is extensive "non-official" private education. Increasing numbers of children attend pre-schools. Currently, about 95 percent of the five-year-olds are in kindergarten or nursery school, 70 percent of the four-year-olds and 10 percent of three-year-olds. Many older children attend *juku* (after school classes) as well. These are private classes in a great variety of subjects; but most enhance and reinforce the material to be learned for high school or college entrance examinations. There are also *yobiko* (cram schools) for those taking an extra year between high school and college to prepare for the exams.

10 3. While competition for entrance to the most prestigious universities is very stiff, nearly 40 percent of the college-age group attend college or university. (The rates are slightly higher for women, since many attend two-year junior colleges.)

11 4. Japanese children attend school 240 days a year, compared to 180 in the U.S. Many children spend Sundays in study or tutoring, and vacation classes are also available. Children do not necessarily see this as oppressive, and younger children often ask their parents to send them to *juku* as a way of being with their friends after school. Homework starts in first grade, and children in Japan spend more time in home study than children in any other country except Taiwan. In Japan, 8 percent of the high school seniors spend less than five hours per week on homework, compared to 65 percent of American seniors.[1]

12 5. Primary and lower secondary schools provide what we would call a core curriculum: a required and comprehensive course of study progressing along a logical path, with attention given to children's developmental levels. In elementary and lower secondary school, language learning dominates the school curriculum, and takes up the greatest number of classroom hours, particularly from second to fourth grade. The large number of characters to be learned requires an emphasis on memorization and drill that is not exhibited in the rest of the curriculum. Arithmetic and math are next in number of class hours, followed by social studies. The curriculum includes regular physical education and morning exercise as part of a "whole-child" program. In high school all students take Japanese, English, math, science, and social studies each year, and all students have had courses in chemistry, biology, physics, and earth sciences. All high school students take calculus.

13 6. Computers and other technology do not play a large role in schools. The calculator is used, but has not replaced mental calculations or, for that matter, the abacus. There is no national program to develop high technology skills in children. Americans spend much more money on science and technology in the schools; the Japanese spend more on teacher training and salaries.

14 These features should be seen in the context of a history of emphasis on education in Japan. To begin with, an interest in mass (or at least widespread) education greatly antedated the introduction of Western schools to Japan. Literacy, numeracy, and a moral education were considered important for people of all classes. When Western style universal compulsory schooling was introduced in 1872, it was after a deliberate and wide-ranging search throughout the world that resulted in a selection of features from German, French, and American educational systems that would advance Japan's modernization and complement her culture. While uniform, centralized schooling was an import, it eventually brought out Japan's already refined powers of adaptation—not the ability to adapt to a new mode as much as *the ability to adapt the foreign mode to Japanese needs and conditions.*

15 Also striking was the rapidity with which Japan developed a modern educational system and made it truly universal. In 1873, one year after the Education Act, there was 28 percent enrollment in primary schools, but by 1904 enrollment had already reached 98 percent—one percent less than the current rate. The rush to educate children was buttressed both by the wish to catch up with the West and by a cultural interest in schooling.

A Truly National System

16 Tradition, ideology, and international competition are not, however, the only motive forces in Japanese education: other factors are as significant. First, Japan has a relatively homogeneous population. Racially and economically there is little variety. Minority groups, such as Koreans and the former out-castes, exist and do suffer some discrimination, but all children have equal access to good schooling. Income is more evenly distributed in Japan than in America and most people (96 percent in a recent Prime Minister's Office poll) consider themselves middle class. There are few remaining regional differences that affect the educational system, except perhaps local accents.

17 Second, educational financing and planning are centralized. While American educational policy sees the responsibility for schooling as a local matter, Japanese planners can rely on a centralized source of funding, curriculum guidance, and textbook selection. In terms of educational spending as a percentage of total GNP, the U.S. and Japan are not so far apart: The U.S. devotes 6.8 percent of its GNP to education, and Japan devotes 8.6 percent. But in Japan about 50 percent of this is national funding, while in the U.S. the federal government provides only 8 percent of the total expenditure on education, most of which is applied to special education, not to core schooling. Moreover, in the U.S. there exist no national institutions to build a consensus on what and how our children are taught. The most significant outcome of centralization in Japan is

the even distribution of resources and quality instruction across the country. National planners and policymakers can mobilize a highly qualified teaching force and offer incentives that make even the most remote areas attractive to good teachers.

18 Third (but perhaps most important in the comparison with the United States), teachers enjoy respect and high status, job security, and good pay. More than in any other country, teachers in Japan are highly qualified: Their mastery of their fields is the major job qualification, and all have at least a bachelor's degree in their specialty. Moreover, they have a high degree of professional involvement as teachers: 74 percent are said to belong to some professional teachers' association in which teaching methods and curriculum are actively discussed.[2]

19 Teachers are hired for life, at starting salaries equivalent to starting salaries for college graduates in the corporate world. Elementary and junior high school teachers earn $18,200 per year on the average, high school teachers $19,000. Compared to other Japanese public sector workers, who earn an average of $16,800, this is a high salary, but it is less than that of managers in large companies or bureaucrats in prestigious ministries. In comparison with American teachers, whose salaries average $17,600, it is an absolutely higher wage. The difference is especially striking when one considers that over all professions, salaries are lower in Japan than in the U.S. In fact, American teachers' salaries are near the bottom of the scale of jobs requiring a college degree. Relative status and prestige correlate with salary in both countries. Japanese teachers' pay increases, as elsewhere in Japan, are tied to a seniority ladder, and older "master teachers" are given extra pay as teacher supervisors in each subject.[3]

20 Japanese teachers see their work as permanent: Teaching is not a waystation on a path to other careers. Teachers work hard at improving their skills and knowledge of their subject, and attend refresher courses and upgrading programs provided by the Ministry of Education. While there are tendencies, encouraged by the Teachers' Union, to downplay the traditional image of the "devoted, selfless teacher" (since this is seen as exploitative), and to redefine the teacher as a wage laborer with regular hours, rather than as a member of a "sacred" profession, teachers still regularly work overtime and see their job's sphere extending beyond classroom instruction. Classes are large: The average is about 40 students to one teacher. Teachers feel responsible for their students' discipline, behavior, morality, and for their general social adjustment as well as for their cognitive development. They are "on duty" after school hours and during vacations, and supervise vacation play and study. They visit their students' families at home, and are available to parents with questions and anxieties about their children. The Teachers' Union protests strongly against this extensive role, but both teachers and parents reinforce this role, tied as it is to the high status of the teacher.

21 Fourth, there is strong ideological and institutional support for education because the occupational system relies on schools to select the right person for the right organization. Note that this is not the same as the "right job" or "slot": A new company recruit, almost always a recent graduate, is not expected to have a skill or special identity, but to be appropriate in general educational background and character for a company. The company then trains recruits in the skills they will need, as well as in

the company style. Of course, the basic skill level of the population of high school and college graduates is extremely high. But the important fact is that the social consensus supports an educational system that creates a committed, productive labor force. And although the emphasis seems to be on educational credentials, the quality of graduates possessing these credentials is indisputably high.

Mom

22 The background I have presented—of national consensus, institutional centralization, and fiscal support—alone does not explain the successes of Japanese education. There are other, less tangible factors that derive from cultural conceptions of development and learning, the valued role of maternal support, and psychological factors in Japanese pedagogy, and which distinguish it from American schooling.

23 The role of mothers is especially important. The average Japanese mother feels her child has the potential for success: Children are believed to be born with no distinguishing abilities (or disabilities) and can be mobilized to achieve and perform at high levels. Effort and commitment are required, and, at least at the beginning, it is the mother's job to engage the child. One way of looking at Japanese child development is to look at the words and concepts related to parental goals for their children. A "good child" has the following, frequently invoked characteristics: He is *otonashii* (mild or gentle), *sunao* (compliant, obedient, and cooperative), *akarui* (bright, alert), and *genki* (energetic and spirited). *Sunao* has frequently been translated as "obedient," but it would be more appropriate to use "open minded," "non-resistant," or "authentic in intent and cooperative in spirit." The English word "obedience" implies subordination and lack of self-determination, but *sunao* assumes that what we call compliance (with a negative connotation) is really cooperation, an act of affirmation of the self. A child who is *sunao* has not yielded his personal autonomy for the sake of cooperation; cooperation does not imply giving up the self, but in fact implies that working with others is the appropriate setting for expressing and enhancing the self.

24 One encourages a *sunao* child through the technique, especially used by mothers and elementary school teachers, of *wakaraseru,* or "getting the child to understand." The basic principle of child rearing seems to be: Never go against the child. *Wakaraseru* is often a long-term process that ultimately engages the child in the mother's goals, and makes her goals the child's own, thus producing an authentic cooperation, as in *sunao.* The distinction between external, social expectations and the child's own personal goals becomes blurred from this point on. An American might see this manipulation of the child through what we would call "indulgence" as preventing him from having a strong will of his own, but the Japanese mother sees long-term benefits of self-motivated cooperation and real commitment.

25 Japanese mothers are active teachers as well, and have a real curriculum for their pre-school children: Games, teaching aids, ordinary activities are all focused on the child's development. There are counting games for very small babies, songs to help children learn new words, devices to focus the child's concentration. Parents buy an average of two or three new books every month for their preschoolers, and there are

about 40 monthly activity magazines for preschoolers, very highly subscribed. The result is that most, at least most urban children, can read and write the phonetic syllabary before they enter school, and can do simple computations.

26 Maternal involvement becomes much more extensive and "serious" once she and the child enter the elementary school community. In addition to formal involvement in frequent ceremonies and school events, PTA meetings and visiting days, the mother spends much time each day helping the child with homework (sometimes to the point at which the teachers joke that they are really grading the mothers by proxy). There are classes for mothers, called *mamajuku,* that prepare mothers in subjects their children are studying. Homework is considered above all a means for developing a sense of responsibility in the child, and like much in early childhood education, it is seen as a device to train character.

27 The Japanese phenomenon of maternal involvement recently surfaced in Riverdale, New York, where many Japanese families have settled. School teachers and principals there noted that each Japanese family was purchasing two sets of textbooks. On inquiring, they found that the second set was for the mother, who could better coach her child if she worked during the day to keep up with his lessons. These teachers said that children entering in September with no English ability finished in June at the top of their classes in every subject.

28 The effort mothers put into their children's examinations has been given a high profile by the press. This is called the *kyoiku mama* syndrome—the mother invested in her children's progress. In contrast to Western theories of achievement, which emphasize individual effort and ability, the Japanese consider academic achievement to be an outgrowth of an interdependent network of cooperative effort and planning. The caricature of the mother's over-investment, however, portrays a woman who has totally identified with her child's success or failure, and who has no separate identity of her own. The press emphasizes the negative aspects of this involvement with accounts of maternal nervous breakdowns, reporting a murder by a mother of the child next door, who made too much noise while her child was studying. But the press also feeds the mother's investment by exhorting her to prepare a good work environment for the studying child, to subscribe to special exam-preparation magazines, to hire tutors, and to prepare a nutritious and exam-appropriate diet.

29 High-schoolers from outlying areas taking entrance exams in Tokyo come with their mothers to stay in special rooms put aside by hotels. They are provided with special food, study rooms, counselors, and tension-release rooms, all meant to supply home-care away from home. The home study-desk bought by most parents for their smaller children symbolizes the hovering care and intensity of the mother's involvement: All models have a high front and half-sides, cutting out distractions and enclosing the workspace in womb-like protection. There is a built-in study light, shelves, a clock, electric pencil sharpener, and built-in calculator. The most popular model includes a push-button connecting to a buzzer in the kitchen to summon mother for help or for a snack.

"How Do You Feel About Cubing?"

30 Not much work has been done yet to analyze the relationship between the strongly supportive learning atmosphere and high achievement in Japan. In the home, mothers train small children in a disciplined, committed use of energy through what Takeo Doi has called the encouragement of "positive dependency"; in the schools as well there is a recognition that attention to the child's emotional relationship to his work, peers, and teachers is necessary for learning.

31 A look at a Japanese classroom yields some concrete examples of this. Many Westerners believe that Japanese educational successes are due to an emphasis on rote learning and memorization, that the classroom is rigidly disciplined. This is far from reality. An American teacher walking into a fourth grade science class in Japan would be horrified: children all talking at once, leaping and calling for the teacher's attention. The typical American's response is to wonder, "who's in control of this room?" But if one understands the content of the lively chatter, it is clear that all the noise and movement is focused on the work itself—children are shouting out answers, suggesting other methods, exclaiming in excitement over results, and not gossiping, teasing, or planning games for recess. As long as it is the result of this engagement, the teacher is not concerned over the noise, which may measure a teacher's success. (It has been estimated that American teachers spend about 60 percent of class time on organizing, controlling, and disciplining the class, while Japanese teachers spend only 10 percent.)

32 A fifth grade math class I observed reveals some elements of this pedagogy. The day I visited, the class was presented with a general statement about cubing. Before any concrete facts, formulae, or even drawings were displayed, the teacher asked the class to take out their math diaries and spend a few minutes writing down their feelings and anticipations over this new concept. It is hard for me to imagine an American math teacher beginning a lesson with an exhortation to examine one's emotional predispositions about cubing (but that may be only because my own math training was antediluvian).

33 After that, the teacher asked for conjectures from the children about the surface and volume of a cube and asked for some ideas about formulae for calculation. The teacher asked the class to cluster into its component *han* (working groups) of four or five children each, and gave out materials for measurement and construction. One group left the room with large pieces of cardboard, to construct a model of a cubic meter. The groups worked internally on solutions to problems set by the teacher and competed with each other to finish first. After a while, the cubic meter group returned, groaning under the bulk of its model, and everyone gasped over its size. (There were many comments and guesses as to how many children could fit inside.) The teacher then set the whole class a very challenging problem, well over their heads, and gave them the rest of the class time to work on it. The class ended without a solution, but the teacher made no particular effort to get or give an answer, although she exhorted them to be energetic. (It was several days before the class got the answer—there was no deadline but the excitement did not flag.)

34 Several characteristics of this class deserve highlighting. First, there was attention to feelings and predispositions, provision of facts, and opportunities for discovery. The teacher preferred to focus on process, engagement, commitment, and performance rather than on discipline (in our sense) and production. Second, the *han:* Assignments are made to groups, not to individuals (this is also true at the workplace) although individual progress and achievement are closely monitored. Children are supported, praised, and allowed to make mistakes through trial and error within the group. The group is also pitted against other groups, and the group's success is each person's triumph, and vice versa. Groups are made up by the teacher and are designed to include a mixture of skill levels—there is a *hancho* (leader) whose job it is to choreograph the group's work, to encourage the slower members, and to act as a reporter to the class at large.

35 Japanese teachers seem to recognize the emotional as well as the intellectual aspects of engagement. Japanese pedagogy (and maternal socialization) are based on the belief that effort is the most important factor in achievement, and that the teacher's job is to get the child to commit himself positively and energetically to hard work. This emphasis is most explicit in elementary school, but persists later as a prerequisite for the self-discipline and effort children exhibit in high school.

36 American educational rhetoric does invoke "the whole child," does seek "self-expression," and does promote emotional engagement in "discovery learning." But Japanese teaching style, at least in primary schools, effectively employs an engaging, challenging teaching style that surpasses most American attempts. In the cubing class, I was struck by the spontaneity, excitement, and (to American eyes) "unruly" dedication of the children to the new idea, and impressed with the teacher's ability to create this positive mood. It could be a cultural difference: We usually separate cognition and emotional affect, and then devise artificial means of reintroducing "feeling" into learning. It is rather like the way canned fruit juices are produced—first denatured by the preserving process and then topped up with chemical vitamins to replace what was lost.

The Role of Competition

37 The frequent accusation that Japanese education involves children in hellish competition must also be examined. In the elementary school classroom, competition is negotiated by means of the *han.* The educational system tries to accommodate both the ideology of harmony and the interest in hierarchy and ranking. The introduction of graded, competitive Western modes of education into societies where minimizing differences between people is valued has often produced severe social and psychological dislocation (as in Africa and other parts of the Third World). In Japan, the importance of the modern educational system as a talent selector and the need to preserve harmony and homogeneity have produced complementary rather than conflicting forces. The regular classroom is a place where the individual does not stick out, but where individual needs are met and goals are set. Children are not held back nor advanced by ability: the cohesion of the age group is said to be more important. Teachers focus on pulling up the slower learners, rather than tracking the class to suit different abilities. For the most part, teachers and the school system refuse to engage in examination preparation hysteria.

Part of the reason for this is pressure from the Teachers' Union, a very large and powerful labor union which consistently resists any moves away from the egalitarian and undifferentiating mode of learning. Turning teachers into drill instructors is said to be dehumanizing, and the process of cramming a poor substitute for education.

38 So where is the competitive selection principle served? In the *juku. Juku* are tough competitive classes, often with up to 500 in one lecture hall. The most prestigious are themselves very selective and there are examinations (and preparation courses for these) to enter the *juku.* Some *juku* specialize in particular universities' entrance exams, and they will boast of their rate of admission into their universities. It is estimated that one third of all primary school students and one half of all secondary school students attend *juku,* but in Tokyo the rate rises to 86 percent of junior high school students. The "king of *juku,*" Furukawa Noboru, the creator of a vast chain of such classes, says that *juku* are necessary to bridge the gap of present realities in Japan. He says that public schools do not face the fact of competition, and that ignoring the reality does not help children. The Ministry of Education usually ignores this non-accredited alternative and complementary system, and permits this functional division to take the pressure off the public schools. While there is considerable grumbling by parents, and while it is clear that the *juku* introduce an inegalitarian element into the process of schooling (since they do cost money), they do, by their separation from the regular school, permit the persistence of more traditional modes of learning, while allowing for a fast track in the examinations.

39 It is important to note that in Japan there really is only one moment of critical importance to one's career chances—the entrance examination to college. There are few opportunities to change paths or retool. Americans' belief that one can be recreated at any time in life, that the self-made person can get ahead, simply is not possible in Japan—thus the intense focus on examinations.

The Problems—in Context

40 This rapid tour through the Japanese educational system cannot neglect the problems. However, two things must be kept in mind when considering these well-publicized difficulties: One is that although problems do exist, the statistical reality is that, compared to the West, Japan still looks very good indeed. The other is that the Japanese themselves tend to be quite critical, and educational problems are given attention. But this attention should be seen in context: Not that people are not truly concerned about real problems, but that the anxiety seems related to a sense of national insecurity. The Japanese focus on educational issues may emanate from a sense of the importance of intellectual development in a society where there are few other resources. Any educational problem seems to put the nation truly at risk.

41 Japanese parents are critical and watchful of the schools and are not complacent about their children's successes. There was a telling example of this in a recent comparative study of American and Japanese education. Mothers in Minneapolis and in Sendai, roughly comparable cities, were asked to evaluate their children's school experiences. The Minneapolis mothers consistently answered that the schools were fine and that their children were doing well, while the Sendai mothers were very critical of their

schools and worried that their children were not performing up to potential. Whose children were, in objective tests, doing better? The Sendai group—in fact so much better that the poorest performer in the Japanese group was well ahead of the best in the American group. Mothers in Japan and the U.S. have very different perspectives on performance: Japanese mothers attribute failure to lack of effort while American mothers explain it as lack of ability. Japanese children have an external standard of excellence to which they can aspire, while an American child normally can only say he will "do his best."

42 Problems have surfaced, of course. Psychotherapists report a syndrome among children related to school and examination pressure. School phobia, psychosomatic symptoms, and juvenile suicide are most frequently reported. Japan does lead the world in school-related suicides for the 15- to 19-year-old age group, at about 300 per year. Recently, the "battered teacher" and "battered parent" syndromes have received much attention. There are cases where teenagers have attacked or killed parents and teachers, and these have been related to examination pressure. The numbers involved in these cases are very small—at least in comparison with American delinquency patterns and other juvenile pathologies. Dropouts, drug use, and violent juvenile crimes are almost non-existent in Japan. The crimes reported in one year among school-age children in Osaka, for example, are equal to those reported in one day in New York.

43 Criticism leveled at Japanese education by Western observers focuses on what they regard as a suppression of genius and individuality, and a lack of attention to the development of creativity in children. The first may indeed be a problem—for the geniuses—because there is little provision for tracking them to their best advantage. There has been discussion of introducing tracking so that individual ability can be better served, but this has not been implemented. The superbright may indeed be disadvantaged.

44 On the other hand, creativity and innovation *are* encouraged, but their manifestations may be different from those an American observer would expect. We must look at our own assumptions, to see if they are too limited. Americans see creativity in children as a fragile blossom that is stifled by rigid educational systems or adult standards. Creativity involves a necessary break with traditional content and methods, and implies the creation of a new idea or artifact. Whether creativity is in the child or in the teaching, and how it is to be measured, are questions no one has answered satisfactorily. Why we emphasize it is another question, probably related to our theories of progress and the importance we attach to unique accomplishments that push society forward. The fact is that, if anything, our schools do less to encourage creativity than do the Japanese, especially in the arts. All children in Japan learn two instruments and how to read music in elementary school, have regular drawing and painting classes, and work in small groups to create projects they themselves devise. It is true, though, that if everyone must be a soloist or composer to be considered creative, then most Japanese are not encouraged to be creative.

45 It is not enough to claim that the Japanese have been successful in training children to take exams at the expense of a broader education. And it is not at all appropriate to

say that they are unable to develop children's individuality and create the geniuses who make scientific breakthroughs. The first is untrue and the second remains to be shown as false by the Japanese themselves, who are now mobilizing to produce more scientists and technologists. In fact, the scales are tipped in favor of Japan, and to represent it otherwise would be a distortion.

46 The success of the Japanese model has led to its use in other rapidly developing countries, including South Korea, Taiwan, and Singapore. There, education is seen as the linchpin for development, and attention to children has meant the allocation of considerable resources to schools. The results are similar to those seen in Japanese schools: highly motivated, hard-working students who like school and who have achieved very high scores on international achievement tests.

Seeing Ourselves through Japanese Eyes

47 What *America* can learn from Japan is rather an open question. We can, to begin with, learn more *about* Japan, and in doing so, learn more about ourselves. Japanese advancements of the past 20 years were based on American principles of productivity (such as ''quality control''), not on samurai management skills and zen austerities. Looking for Japanese secrets, or worse, protesting that they are inhuman or unfair, will not get us very far. They have shown they can adjust programs and policies to the needs and resources of the times; we must do the same. We need to regain the scientific literacy we lost and reacquire the concrete skills and participatory techniques we need. We should see Japan as establishing a new standard, not as a model to be emulated. To match that standard we have to aim at general excellence, develop a long-term view, and act consistently over time with regard to our children's education.

Notes

1. Thomas Rohlen, *Japan's High Schools* (Berkeley: University of California Press, 1983), p. 277.
2. William Cummings, *Education and Equality in Japan* (Princeton: Princeton University Press, 1980), p. 159.
3. There is a debate in Japan today concerning rewarding good teachers with higher pay: Professor Sumiko Iwao, of Keio University, reports that when quality is measured in yen, the commitment of teachers to good teaching declines.

Questions for Analysis

1. In her final paragraph, Merry White says, ''We should see Japan as establishing a new standard, not as a model to be emulated.'' What is the ''new standard'' White has in mind?
2. Make a list of the key differences White sees in Japanese and American education. For each difference you list, consider whether the difference has a cultural or non-

cultural basis. For each Japanese practice or attitude, consider whether America can or should change its policies, objectives, or values to follow the Japanese pattern.

3. In Paragraph 14, White emphasizes that Japan has "refined powers of adaptation—not the ability to adapt to a new mode as much as *the ability to adapt the foreign mode to Japanese needs and conditions.*" What are some of these adaptations? How have the Japanese taken, for example, some Western mode and made it fit the Japanese situation?
4. What are the problems inherent in Japanese education? Does White present them clearly and fairly? Does she think these problems are serious? Why?

Arthur L. Campa

Anglo vs. Chicano: Why?

(1973)

Born the son of missionary parents in Guaymas, Mexico, Arthur L. Campa (1905–1978) studied at the University of New Mexico and at Columbia University before beginning a long and distinguished career in higher education. He eventually became Chair of the Department of Modern Languages at the University of Denver. Campa also served in the Department of State as a cultural affairs officer and as Director of Training Projects for the Peace Corps. His scholarship focused on Hispanic culture, particularly in the American Southwest. This essay first appeared in *Western Review* (Spring 1972) and then was condensed for publication in *Intellectual Digest* in 1973. The condensed version is reprinted here.

1 The cultural differences between Hispanic and Anglo-American people have been dwelt upon by so many writers that we should all be well informed about the values of both. But audiences are usually of the same persuasion as the speakers, and those who consult published works are for the most part specialists looking for affirmation of what they believe. So, let us consider the same subject, exploring briefly some of the basic cultural differences that cause conflict in the Southwest, where Hispanic and Anglo-American cultures meet.

2 Cultural differences are implicit in the conceptual content of the languages of these two civilizations, and their value systems stem from a long series of historical circumstances. Therefore, it may be well to consider some of the English and Spanish cultural configurations before these Europeans set foot on American soil. English culture was basically insular, geographically and ideologically; was more integrated on the whole, except for some strong theological differences; and was particularly zealous of its racial

purity. Spanish culture was peninsular, a geographical circumstance that made it a catchall of Mediterranean, central European and north African peoples. The composite nature of the population produced a market regionalism that prevented close integration, except for religion, and led to a strong sense of individualism. These differences were reflected in the colonizing enterprise of the two cultures. The English isolated themselves from the Indians physically and culturally; the Spanish, who had strong notions about *pureza de sangre* [purity of blood] among the nobility, were not collectively averse to adding one more strain to their racial cocktail. Cortés led the way by siring the first *mestizo* in North America, and the rest of the conquistadores followed suit. The ultimate products of these two orientations meet today in the Southwest.

3 Anglo-American culture was absolutist at the onset; that is, all the dominant values were considered identical for all, regardless of time and place. Such values as justice, charity, honesty were considered the superior social order for all men and were later embodied in the American Constitution. The Spaniard brought with him a relativistic viewpoint and saw fewer moral implications in man's actions. Values were looked upon as the result of social and economic conditions.

4 The motives that brought Spaniards and Englishmen to America also differed. The former came on an enterprise of discovery, searching for a new route to India initially, and later for new lands to conquer, the fountain of youth, minerals, the Seven Cities of Cibola and, in the case of the missionaries, new souls to win for the Kingdom of Heaven. The English came to escape religious persecution, and once having found a haven, they settled down to cultivate the soil and establish their homes. Since the Spaniards were not seeking a refuge or running away from anything, they continued their explorations and circled the globe 25 years after the discovery of the New World.

5 This peripatetic tendency of the Spaniard may be accounted for in part by the fact that he was the product of an equestrian culture. Men on foot do not venture far into the unknown. It was almost a century after the landing on Plymouth Rock that Governor Alexander Spotswood of Virginia crossed the Blue Ridge Mountains, and it was not until the nineteenth century that the Anglo-Americans began to move west of the Mississippi.

6 The Spaniard's equestrian role meant that he was not close to the soil, as was the Anglo-American pioneer, who tilled the land and built the greatest agricultural industry in history. The Spaniard cultivated the land only when he had Indians available to do it for him. The uses to which the horse was put also varied. The Spanish horse was essentially a mount, while the more robust English horse was used in cultivating the soil. It is therefore not surprising that the viewpoints of these two cultures should differ when we consider that the pioneer is looking at the world at the level of his eyes while the *caballero* [horseman] is looking beyond and down at the rest of the world.

7 One of the most commonly quoted, and often misinterpreted, characteristics of Hispanic peoples is the deeply ingrained individualism in all walks of life. Hispanic individualism is a revolt against the incursion of collectivity, strongly asserted when it is felt that the ego is being fenced in. This attitude leads to a deficiency in those social qualities based on collective standards, an attitude that Hispanos do not consider

negative because it manifests a measure of resistance to standardization in order to achieve a measure of individual freedom. Naturally, such an attitude has no *reglas fijas* [fixed rules].

8 Anglo-Americans who achieve a measure of success and security through institutional guidance not only do not mind a few fixed rules but demand them. The lack of a concerted plan of action, whether in business or in politics, appears unreasonable to Anglo-Americans. They have a sense of individualism, but they achieve it through action and self-determination. Spanish individualism is based on feeling, on something that is the result not of rules and collective standards but of a person's momentary, emotional reaction. And it is subject to change when the mood changes. In contrast to Spanish emotional individualism, the Anglo-American strives for objectivity when choosing a course of action or making a decision.

9 The Southwestern Hispanos voiced strong objections to the lack of courtesy of the Anglo-Americans when they first met them in the early days of the Santa Fe trade. The same accusation is leveled at the *Americanos* today in many quarters of the Hispanic world. Some of this results from their different conceptions of polite behavior. Here too one can say that the Spanish have no *reglas fijas* because for them courtesy is simply an expression of the way one person feels toward another. To some they extend the hand, to some they bow and for the more *íntimos* there is the well-known *abrazo.* The concepts of ''good or bad'' or ''right and wrong'' in polite behavior are moral considerations of an absolutist culture.

10 Another cultural contrast appears in the way both cultures share part of their material substance with others. The pragmatic Anglo-American contributes regularly to such institutions as the Red Cross, the United Fund and a myriad of associations. He also establishes foundations and quite often leaves millions to such institutions. The Hispano prefers to give his contribution directly to the recipient so he can see the person he is helping.

11 A century of association has inevitably acculturated both Hispanos and Anglo-Americans to some extent, but there still persist a number of culture traits that neither group has relinquished altogether. Nothing is more disquieting to an Anglo-American who believes that time is money than the time perspective of Hispanos. They usually refer to this attitude as the ''*mañana* psychology.'' Actually, it is more of a ''today psychology,'' because Hispanos cultivate the present to the exclusion of the future; because the latter has not arrived yet, it is not a reality. They are reluctant to relinquish the present, so they hold on to it until it becomes the past. To an Hispano, nine is nine until it is ten, so when he arrives at nine-thirty, he jubilantly exclaims: ''¡Justo!'' [right on time]. This may be why the clock is slowed down to a walk in Spanish, while in English, it runs. In the United States, our future-oriented civilization plans our lives so far in advance that the present loses its meaning. January magazine issues are out in December; 1973 cars have been out since October; cemetery plots and even funeral arrangements are bought on the installment plan. To a person engrossed in living today the very idea of planning his funeral sounds like the tolling of the bells.

12 It is a natural corollary that a person who is present oriented should be compensated by being good at improvising. An Anglo-American is told in advance to prepare for an "impromptu speech," but an Hispano usually can improvise a speech because *"Nosotros lo improvisamos todo"* [we improvise everything].

13 Another source of cultural conflict arises from the difference between *being* and *doing*. Even when trying to be individualistic, the Anglo-American achieves it by what he does. Today's young generation decided to be themselves, to get away from standardization, so they let their hair grow, wore ragged clothes and even went barefoot in order to be different from the Establishment. As a result they all ended up doing the same things and created another stereotype. The freedom enjoyed by the individuality of *being* makes it unnecessary for Hispanos to strive to be different.

14 In 1963 a team of psychologists from the University of Guadalajara in Mexico and the University of Michigan compared 74 upper-middle-class students from each university. Individualism and personalism were found to be central values for the Mexican students. This was explained by saying that a Mexican's value as a person lies in his *being* rather than, as is the case of the Anglo-Americans, in concrete accomplishments. Efficiency and accomplishments are derived characteristics that do not affect worthiness in the Mexican, whereas in the American it is equated with success, a value of highest priority in the American culture. Hispanic people disassociate themselves from material things or from actions that may impugn a person's sense of being, but the Anglo-American shows great concern for material things and assumes responsibility for his actions. This is expressed in the language of each culture. In Spanish one says, *"Se me cayó la taza"* [the cup fell away from me] instead of "I dropped the cup."

15 In English, one speaks of money, cash and all related transactions with frankness because material things of this high order do not trouble Anglo-Americans. In Spanish such materialistic concepts are circumvented by referring to cash as *efectivo* [effective] and when buying or selling as something *al contado* [counted out], and when without it by saying *No tengo fondos* [I have no funds]. This disassociation from material things is what produces *sobriedad* [sobriety] in the Spaniard according to Miguel de Unamuno, but in the Southwest the disassociation from materialism leads to *dejadez* [lassitude] and *desprendimiento* [disinterestedness]. A man may lose his life defending his honor but is unconcerned about the lack of material things. *Desprendimiento* causes a man to spend his last cent on a friend, which when added to lack of concern for the future may mean that tomorrow he will eat beans as a result of today's binge.

16 The implicit differences in words that appear to be identical in meaning are astonishing. Versatile is a compliment in English and an insult in Spanish. An Hispano student who is told to apologize cannot do it, because the word doesn't exist in Spanish. *Apologia* means words in praise of a person. The Anglo-American either apologizes, which is a form of retraction abhorrent in Spanish, or compromises, another concept foreign to Hispanic culture. *Compromiso* means a date, not a compromise. In colonial Mexico City, two hidalgos once entered a narrow street from opposite sides, and when they could not go around, they sat in their coaches for three days until the viceroy ordered them to back out. All this because they could not work out a compromise.

17 It was that way then and to some extent now. Many of today's conflicts in the Southwest have their roots in polarized cultural differences, which need not be irreconcilable when approached with mutual respect and understanding.

Questions for Analysis

1. What is the purpose of Campa's essay? Do you think that he achieves it? Can reading and thinking about a few reasons for differences between cultures help bring the "mutual respect and understanding" Campa mentions in his final paragraph?
2. As you examine the differences between Anglo and Chicano cultures presented by Campa, which do you find most interesting and significant in helping you understand current tensions between Hispanics and Anglos?
3. How does the contrast between being and doing that Campa presents in Paragraph 14 parallel the point Richard Rodriguez makes at the beginning of "La Raza Cosmica" (his paragraphs 1–10) about present vs. future time?
4. Who is Campa's primary audience for this essay—Anglos or Chicanos? What evidence can you present to support your choice?

Richard Rodriguez
with Marilyn Berlin Snell

La Raza Cosmica

(1991)

Pacific News Service journalist Richard Rodriguez (b. 1944) has written frequently about convergence and conflict between Hispanic and American culture. He has often, as he does in this interview, voiced his ideas about language education for Hispanic children in American public schools. The following essay was based on a conversation with Marilyn Berlin Snell, a managing editor with *New Perspectives Quarterly*, where this piece first appeared in the Winter 1991 issue.

1 There is an extraordinary sign scrawled on a wall near the point where hundreds of Mexicans make their escape from Tijuana across the border into the US every night. It says: "Vete pero non me olvidas" — Go, but do not forget me—and it captures a particularly haunting dilemma for the Mexican emigrant: in order to survive, he must forsake his culture, which is based on memory and intimacy—a mother, an embrace, a

family name, an ancestral cemetery, a patch of sky—and enter a culture of amnesia, a culture that is almost totally constructed on the future and the first-person singular pronoun.

2 As the Mexican makes his way across the border, he assures himself that he is not going to forget Mexico, that he is not going to become a "gringo." He is only going for the job. The problem with this formulation is that the job is key to the identity that the US will offer him. When the Mexican starts earning more money than his father ever dreamed of earning, the culture of memory loses its authority to the culture of possibility—the culture of individuality and initiative which we call the United States. The Mexican suddenly finds himself immersed in a culture where people do not ask about his family name; they want to know what he does for a living. Then slowly, haltingly, he begins to have American expectations: that he can really escape his father's fate; that he can put away his father's eyes; that he can become someone new.

3 Gradually, the Mexican begins to change and is bewildered by the change. He goes back to Mexico, taking money back to his family as he promised, but he is no longer at ease. He is living out an ancient drama: the struggle of a man caught between two impulses. In this case, the struggle between the future tense of America and the past tense of Mexico.

Troubled People in Between

4 Mexico and the US are more or less agreed that Mexican migrants to the US are "troubled people in between." The US takes note of the fact that for many Mexicans, their first act in America is a criminal act. They steal into the US under the cover of night.

5 Mother Mexico's feelings are more ambivalent. On the one hand, migrants to the US have long been given a protective regard by the Mexican government which has not hesitated to voice her concern over the Mexicans' working conditions in the US, their harassment by US immigration authorities, etc. Yet Mexican travelers to the US have also been traditionally regarded by Mexico as a kind of peasant class—people who could not "make it" in their homeland.

6 Though much has been written—both positively and negatively—about the Mexican migrants' influence on the US, their enormous influence on Mexico is rarely noted. Yet for years and from hundreds of Mexican villages, men have been leaving for US cities and towns, and these same men have returned with their seductive stories. The grandfather returns and then takes his sons and grandsons, who then return with their own tales. And so the path between the two countries has been well worn over time. Mexicans have left Mexico with dreams and have returned with stereo equipment, t-shirts and dollars. In the process, we have unsettled Mexico.

7 In the state of Michoacán there is a village called Jaripo. Each year men and women who work in Stockton and Hollister or in the San Fernando Valley return to Jaripo. They pack their suitcases with black suits and evening gowns and each night in Jaripo they have a procession at sunset—the factory worker in an elegant suit, his teenage daughters and wife in prom gowns and high heels.

8 In an obvious way, the journey to Jaripo is an homage to memory. But in a more subtle way it is also a showing off of the US to Mexico. They come back to Mother Mexico and say, "Look at what we have accomplished." And their procession creates a foreign glamor in Jaripo, with its old plaza and its dusty streets. The ostensible homage to memory is at least also an homage to America's culture of desire. Perhaps most importantly, it is an homage to change.

9 In a very real way, these Mexicans who have travelled to America embody in blood and soul what the Mexican philosopher Jose Vasconcelos called "*La Raza Cosmica*"—the Cosmic Race. Most Mexicans are people of mixed race; Mexico's culture is a culture of mixture. In her official nationalism, however, Mexico has denied her own richness. Mexico has been afraid of the invader; since Independence, Mexican nationalists have portrayed Mexico as raped mother—put upon by Spain, by France, and of course by the US. Poor Mexico!

10 But this is nonsense. Mexico is not to be pitied. Mexico has been, since the 18th century, the first modern country of the world. Mexico has torn down the borders of the old world. Mexicans carry the blood of at least two continents. Mexico's true genius, her survival, has been due to her absorbancy. Indeed, if the Mexican is famous, it is not for giving up his gods but for taking the enemy's gods as his own. Mexico is a place of rape which became marriage, European intrigue which became romance. And so I—who carry Mexico's blood—I come out looking five shades darker than my brother who is mistaken in California for being Italian.

La Raza Reviled

11 The tragedy of Mexico was not her rape. The tragedy of Mexico has been that she does not have an idea of herself as rich as her blood. When I go to Mexico, even the waitress lets me know with her voice that I displease her because I don't speak Spanish well. I have betrayed Mother Mexico; I have betrayed memory.

12 On this side of the border, there is the same Mexican resistance to mixture by people who are the creatures of mixture. The Chicano movement of recent decades has become famous for its resistance to assimilation, the idea of the melting pot. And in the US I am accused by all sorts of people of having "lost my culture." My answer: Culture is not static. If I am not my father, it is because I did not grow up in Mexico. I did not grow up speaking Spanish into my adulthood.

13 My detractors seem to think I somehow "left my culture" at the Greyhound bus station; I forgot it somewhere. I lost it as though it were something independent of me. But one doesn't lose one's culture. I am my culture. Lucille Ball is my culture. And Walt Disney is my culture. A California freeway is my culture.

14 A Mexican-American bishop in Sacramento once pointed to a mosaic of Our Lady of Guadalupe—the Virgin Mary in the guise of an Indian Maiden—and said, "That is what I am and I want America to be. We are pieces of glass and we combine to make a beautiful mosaic." I disagree. I am not a piece of glass. I am not static. I have a soul. And souls are not static. We are not stone. We are fluid; we are human; we are experience. And within that experience we are transformed by our contact with each other.

I am Chinese because I live in San Francisco, a Chinese city. I became Irish in America. I became Portuguese in America.

15 Of course, many Mexicans don't feel the way I do. Indeed, I don't believe any group scolds its own more than the Mexicans. We brood over our children and tell them that they are going to lose their culture; that they must not be ashamed of their culture; that they must hold onto their culture. There are all kinds of historical reasons why we do this in the US, since Mexico has been mocked and trivialized here for a very long time. Nevertheless, in our admonitions against change, we turn our children against their culture in very deep ways. We should be telling them, "Don't be afraid of becoming Chinese. Go to France next year and don't apologize for learning French. Don't apologize for becoming what you always have been—children of assimilation. Assimilation is what your ancestors did, and that is how the Indians not only survived but flourished to the point where we frighten the environmentalists of North America with our "overpopulation."

16 In the end, we trivialize Mexico by proclaiming ourselves separate from the US mainstream. By insisting on our unique heritage, we deny our heritage.

17 Looking back on the Chicano movement of the sixties, I believe that if Mexican Americans had really wanted to be revolutionary in Protestant America, they would have asserted themselves as a culture of marriage and union, a Catholic culture of half-breeds, a culture rich in all the things puritan America most feared.

18 Individuality and separatism are North American traits, not Mexican traits. Americans, not wanting to admit that we create one another, continue to insist on the primacy of individuality. The rejection of the "we" has been particularly destructive to Mexican Americans because in denying Mexico's genius, we end up a puzzle to ourselves. As second- and third-generation Americans, we do not know why we are so Americanized when we don't want to be. We do not understand that our wanting to be Mexican is, in fact, a perversion of Catholic Mexico and of our Indian heritage.

Discovering the Discoverers

19 The problem is that we haven't made up our minds about the Indian. We don't understand who the Indian was or is. We don't understand the Indian's genius. We accept the white writers of Latin America—with their French wives and their brittle continental wit—as being the voice of the Indian. But they are not the voice of the Indian.

20 I believe I heard it once. I was travelling earlier this year throughout Mexico, working on a documentary for the BBC. For days we travelled, the London crew getting pink under the Mexican sun. Finally, one day, we arrived in an Indian village around noon and we heard singing from the inside of a church. As we approached we could see a group of dark old women, who looked like Greek furies singing at the foot of the altar. They were singing in Spanish but with a voice, a calm that translated the European words into an Indian temperament. They were reforming the language of Europe as they sang, and they were making Spanish an Indian language.

21 Now the great world is preparing for 1992—the 500th anniversary of the Columbus voyage. And the neo-Marxists and the effete liberal Europeans and the American

environmentalists are already organizing themselves to remember the ''shame'' of the Conquest. Once again the Indian will be required to play the role of victim. And the European will be the actor who tramples through the Americas, stealing the Indian's language and stealing the Indian's gods and ravishing innocence.

22 Such a view of history fails to give any stature to the Indian. My own view is that the Indian was at least curious when Columbus approached. European vocabularies do not have a rich enough word to describe this curiosity—the active principle within contemplation. Asia would probably better understand the Indian because the Indian is kin to Asia. What Columbus and his activist European tradition met when he arrived in ''India'' was an absorbing glance that swallowed him up.

23 I regard my own insistent curiosity about the US as an Indian curiosity, not a Spanish one. I see this quality coming from a Mexican rather than a Spanish inheritance. Indeed, as an educated Mexican-American I am engaged exactly as the Indian of the 16th century was engaged—in the discovery of the new world. I want nothing less than the world. I warn the US that if you think you are going to get tacos and nachos from me, you are going to be very surprised. I want the United States of America. I want to swallow you up. I have already swallowed your language and now it is mine.

24 In Shakespeare's *Tempest* there is a prophetic description of the Mexican—of me—in the figure of the Indian, Caliban. Shakespeare understood that if the European, Prospero, let Caliban loose, Caliban would turn and steal Prospero's books. Caliban was always plotting to get Prospero's books because he understood that those books would give him power. And now I have stolen your books, I have stolen Prospero's language, I have stolen his power.

The Price of Change

25 I wish I could tell Mexican children that they have nothing to lose by acquiring a new culture. But in some very basic and often tragic way, the child who comes from Mexico to Los Angeles must change, must move away from the language of parents and grandparents, the intimate pronoun of *tu*—toward the stranger's world, the realm of *usted.*

26 The popular educational ideology of the movement (masquerading as bilingual education) encourages children to imagine that there is no price to be paid. It is said you can speak your ''family language'' in the classroom while you learn English. But this is nonsense! Family language exists only within the family. What children need to learn in a classroom is public language and unless they learn it, they will miss the point of the classroom.

27 Mexicans come from a culture that prizes intimacy. But finally, in the Los Angeles classroom, the dilemma faced by the Mexican-American child is no different than that faced by children in Appalachia or in Bedford Stuyvesant. The child returns home after having heard public language in school and hears another language being spoken by family members. In that instant, the child knows that there is a difference between the public language of school and family language.

28 The bilingualism I care about is the ability to speak to two very different societies, public and private. The problem for many working-class Hispanic children in the US is that they speak neither a public Spanish nor a public English. They lack a public imagination of themselves.

29 I understood language very well as a child. At home I heard my father speak differently than my teacher. I was well aware of the implications of that difference. At school I knew I was being called to a different identity. The Irish nun at my Catholic elementary school in Sacramento said, "Richard, speak in a loud voice, repeat your name after me." She was asking me to use language publicly—the first lesson in school. And it wasn't that I could not say what she asked, that I could not make those sounds. I didn't want to make those sounds. I didn't want to speak her language, your language. I didn't want to speak to "all the boys and girls."

30 Language must always be the beginning of any discussion of education. The question is how children understand the language they are using and what that language is doing to their souls. The psychic, cultural and familial price a working-class child must pay, necessarily pay, for the transition from private to public language is very high. In California, 50 percent of Hispanics drop out of high school.

America's Forgotten Canon

31 I am concerned by the renewed movement toward a 60s-style ethnic separatism on the college campus. Higher education is retreating from the notion that there is an American canon. In a cruel way, American educators betray their newest non-white students.

32 It is very important for the university to say to the newcomer that there is a history here. It is crucial that the newcomer understand that America exists. And there is a difference between knowing about Plymouth Rock and knowing about Santa Fe. Something happened at Plymouth Rock that implicates the immigrant and will make him quite unlike his Confucian grandmother. The immigrant will become the new Protestant, the new Puritan. That is why he needs to know more about a mad British king of the 18th century than about Mexican revolutionaries of the 19th century. As an American, I have more to do with Paul Revere and Thomas Jefferson than with Benito Juarez.

33 The notion that there is nothing here, that the immigrant can bring his culture whole and set up his own private tent, is foolishness. America exists, and the professors who don't want to admit this fact are those same people who are most afraid of having to deal with the immigrant's inclusion in the American landscape. Easier to say: "Do your own thing."

34 At a time of spectacular ethnic diversity in this country, higher education is unable to come to terms with the common identity of Americans. Ultimately, those who will be blamed for this travesty will be the so-called ethnic radicals, but this is not where blame belongs. It belongs primarily with the distinguished, graying faculty members of Stanford and Harvard and all the other institutions of higher learning who can no longer define what it is we know or what we should know in common.

Questions for Analysis

1. To be effective, a first paragraph must get the reader's attention and preview in some significant way the content and purpose of the essay. Explain how the first paragraph in this essay does or does not meet this goal.
2. Rodriguez uses the town of Jaripo to illustrate the problems and potential inherent in Mexican immigration to the United States. Explain this point.
3. How does the concept of "La Raza Cosmica" fit with Rodriguez's attitude toward what should happen when two cultures come into conflict? How does his reaction to the bishop's statement of the mosaic of Our Lady of Guadalupe as a metaphor for cultural integrity indicate Rodriguez's attitude?
4. In Paragraphs 19–23, Rodriguez explains how the Indians of Mexico have "discovered their discoverers." Does his explanation here fit what happened in Mexico? In the United States? Explain.
5. In Paragraphs 25–30, Rodriguez takes a controversial position on language study and use that many Hispanics find objectionable. Explain his position and his reasoning. How would his critics respond?
6. In Paragraphs 31–34, Rodriguez takes another controversial position—this time about what books should be read and discussed in our classrooms. In his zeal to maintain the American tradition, would he disallow all reading in and study of other cultures? Would this be good or bad? Is there a middle ground he and those who argue for more cultural diversity in the schools might be able to find? Define it.

Robert Coles

Hispanic Dreams/American Dreams

(1988)

A professor of psychiatry and medical humanities at Harvard University, Robert Coles (b. 1929) is writing a five-volume study entitled *Children in Crisis.* The fourth volume in that series will be *Chicanos, Indians, Eskimos.* This essay appeared in *Change: The Magazine of Higher Learning* in an issue devoted to Hispanics in higher education (May/June 1988).

1 In the early 1970s I spent a lot of time talking with Spanish-speaking children and their parents—in San Antonio; in various towns scattered along the Rio Grande Valley; in Albuquerque, New Mexico, where we were living; and in other parts of that state. I was trying to learn how such children grow up—their particular way of learning at school, their hopes and expectations, their fears and worries, their everyday experiences

as they gave shape to their lives. In Albuquerque I got to know especially well a 10-year-old boy who was called "Franco" by his parents and brothers and sisters, and Frank at school. His legal name was Francisco. At first, as such details came to my attention, I thought of Spain's Civil War and the dictator who, alas, triumphed in that war; but this Franco was not headed for any great success, so his fourth grade teacher kept telling me: "He's a dreamy boy. His mind is always elsewhere." She offered no more and seemed annoyed that a visitor had further questions.

2 But I knew the boy fairly well, and in fact wanted to let her know where the pupil's mind went during those "dreamy" spells she kept noticing. Once, a couple of months later, we sat down and read some edited and condensed transcriptions of remarks made by Franco. The teacher was surprised, perplexed. How is it that someone who has so little to say in an elementary school classroom can be so voluble under other circumstances?

3 I had no answer of my own to that question, though I was convinced that Franco had already answered it, and so I suggested we read and reread his words and ponder them: "I want to be bigger. I don't like being someone those Anglo-teachers think is small. I know I'm not [I had commented that he wasn't small], but they treat me like I am, and then you become the way they see you." A long pause after that observation, uninterrupted by the all-too-quick reassurance I was often anxious to offer. Now it was the boy's turn to be puzzled, and to ask a question or two: "You seem as 'dreamy' as she [the teacher] tells me I am! What are you thinking? Are you wishing you were back in your hometown?"

4 I demur; I insist that I love being where I am. Franco watches me intently, doesn't seem convinced, decides to make a generalization, followed by a question: "If you're not where people are friendly, you try to find another place. Is that what you are thinking?" I tell him no, but I haven't the heart to throw his comment, his inquiry back at him. Besides, he is on to my ping-pong ways with him, those return serves (new questions) meant always to sound him out. Abruptly he changes the subject, or seems to do so. "I dreamt of that teacher the other day." Now I am all ears. Now I want him to remember, to say all that comes into his head. I try, though, to appear calm; I even consciously pretend a certain indifference—a calculation that he wants to tell me something, but would back off quickly if I were to press the matter. He offers nothing, though. I really do want to hear what he has dreamed, however, so I gather my courage, try to keep my cool—indeed, reach for all the "cool" I can find within myself, and ask about his dream: "What about that dream with your teacher in it?" He responds: "I was riding my bike [in the dream]. It was getting dark. I was going up Chavez [a street near his home], and I was hoping to get near the river [the Rio Grande]. I like to look at the water, even though there's not as much down here as up where my grandparents live [north of Santa Fe, in Truchas]. I've never seen an ocean, but I'd like to see one, and I'd like to join the navy and work on a submarine. I saw on TV what you can do; you can be an engineer and make the boat go. In the dream, I was looking at the houses and trying to get that bike to go as fast as my legs would push, push, push. The people were lighting up their *candelaria* [a Spanish custom at Christmas, to light

a candle in the windows, or these days, turn a switch to do so], and I was looking at them.

5 ''All of a sudden my teacher was coming down the street from the opposite direction. She was riding a bike. The only thing—she had one hand on the bike, but she was carrying a candle in the other hand. I think it was her right hand. [I had asked.] I thought she'd just keep going, but she didn't. She came right toward me, and so I speeded up. I wanted to show her I wasn't lazy. I said hello and I kept moving. Then she changed directions. She started following me. I didn't know what to do. I kept moving. So did she. The next thing I knew, she was up to me, and then she was saying something, and holding that candle, and I didn't know what she was saying, and no, she wasn't smiling, she wasn't friendly, I could tell. [I had asked what he thought the teacher intended, and about her mood, her attitude toward him.] I think she was being like herself. She was trying to tell me I was doing something wrong—and when she got ahead of me, she tried to stop me, and I was afraid I'd hit her, and I did stop, and that's when I woke up.''

6 As it is put in the South: there is no point in ''making a federal case'' out of one child's rather unsettling dream. Yet Franco was telling himself something in the middle of that Christmas season night—about a child's search for a kind of life that mixes his family's heritage (the candles, the river) with his nation's heritage (the navy, the submarine). The teacher has her own notion of what kind of ''light'' is ''right'' for that child (the candle in her hand). In the dream she is coming at him as an adversary of sorts, a sad outcome for both of them. Nor did Franco need some hifalutin Boston-trained expert in dream interpretation to explain what his mind had visualized and presented to him. His dream had its own language—a silent one of symbolic pictures that took direct aim at a cultural impasse as it was being enacted in a school. The dream, in a way, was a *third* language—summoned to make sense of the bilingual educational difficulties a boy knew all too well.

7 No question that Franco's dilemma—and that of his teacher—is shared by millions of other Spanish-speaking Americans who very much want to be part of a country, yet who also want to hold on to their own values and customs, not to mention their language. Certainly we ought to ask our Francos to learn to ride other streets than those they know so well; to seek other directions than the familiar ones; to be ''practical'' and ''realistic'' as well as ''dreamy,'' whether in school or at home. But certainly we ought to do some analysis not only of ''them''—their ways of living, their dreams—but ourselves: how it is we appear to those children in Texas and New Mexico and California, and in so many other states too. Children who feel themselves regarded as wrong, as inhabitants of an unenlightened world, as ''disadvantaged,'' will soon enough have dreams of disappointment or fear or stubborn rage; will soon enough remark to themselves at midnight that school is a futile, demeaning chase of sorts.

Questions for Analysis

1. What is the answer to the question raised by Franco's teacher at the end of Paragraph 2? Explain how that question is answered in both Franco's words in Paragraph 3 and in the dream he describes in Paragraph 4.
2. What are the Hispanic and American dreams referred to in this short essay? Do these dreams go beyond the dream Franco described?
3. Does the story of Franco and his dream work for or against Richard Rodriguez's argument (in the previous essay) for emphasis in schools on one public language (English) for Hispanic children? Do you think Coles would agree with Rodriguez? Do you think Rodriguez would agree with Coles's conclusion in Paragraph 7?

Ngũgĩ wa Thiong'o

Decolonising the Mind

(1986)

A native of Kenya, Ngũgĩ wa Thiong'o (b. 1938) is a highly respected and influential African author. Thiong'o's early novels, *Weep Not, Children* (1964) and *The River Between* (1965), were written in English. However, his later work, including *Ciataani Mũtharavá-Ini* (*Devil on the Cross,* 1982), has been written in his native language, Gĩkũyũ. Thiong'o taught at the University of Nairobi until he was arrested for political activism in 1977. He was released after an international outcry over his imprisonment. The following essay was taken from *Decolonising the Mind: The Politics of Language in African Literature* (1986). Since Thiong'o's book appeared, the situation in Kenyan schools has improved slightly: Children are now taught in their native languages during their first three years of school, but after that time English is the only language used.

1 I was born into a large peasant family: father, four wives and about twenty-eight children. I also belonged, as we all did in those days, to a wider extended family and to the community as a whole.

2 We spoke Gĩkũyũ as we worked in the fields. We spoke Gĩkũyũ in and outside the home. I can vividly recall those evenings of story-telling around the fireside. It was mostly the grown-ups telling the children but everybody was interested and involved. We children would re-tell the stories the following day to other children who worked in the fields picking the pyrethrum flowers, tea-leaves or coffee beans of our European and African landlords.

3 The stories, with mostly animals as the main characters, were all told in Gĩkũyũ. Hare, being small, weak but full of innovative wit and cunning, was our hero. We identified with him as he struggled against the brutes of prey like lion, leopard, hyena.

His victories were our victories and we learnt that the apparently weak can outwit the strong. We followed the animals in their struggle against hostile nature—drought, rain, sun, wind—a confrontation often forcing them to search for forms of co-operation. But we were also interested in their struggles amongst themselves, and particularly between the beasts and the victims of prey. These twin struggles, against nature and other animals, reflected real-life struggles in the human world.

4 Not that we neglected stories with human beings as the main characters. There were two types of characters in such human-centred narratives: the species of truly human beings with qualities of courage, kindness, mercy, hatred of evil, concern for others; and a man-eat-man two-mouthed species with qualities of greed, selfishness, individualism and hatred of what was good for the larger co-operative community. Co-operation as the ultimate good in a community was a constant theme. It could unite human beings with animals against ogres and beasts of prey, as in the story of how dove, after being fed with castor-oil seeds, was sent to fetch a smith working far away from home and whose pregnant wife was being threatened by these man-eating two-mouthed ogres.

5 There were good and bad story-tellers. A good one could tell the same story over and over again, and it would always be fresh to us, the listeners. He or she could tell a story told by someone else and make it more alive and dramatic. The differences really were in the use of words and images and the inflexion of voices to effect different tones.

6 We therefore learnt to value words for their meaning and nuances. Language was not a mere string of words. It had a suggestive power well beyond the immediate and lexical meaning. Our appreciation of the suggestive magical power of language was reinforced by the games we played with words through riddles, proverbs, transpositions of syllables, or through nonsensical but musically arranged words. So we learnt the music of our language on top of the content. The language, through images and symbols, gave us a view of the world, but it had a beauty of its own. The home and the field were then our pre-primary school but what is important, for this discussion, is that the language of our evening teach-ins, and the language of our immediate and wider community, and the language of our work in the fields were one.

7 And then I went to school, a colonial school, and this harmony was broken. The language of my education was no longer the language of my culture. I first went to Kamaandura, missionary run, and then to another called Maanguuũ run by nationalists grouped around the Gĩkũyũ Independent and Karinga Schools Association. Our language of education was still Gĩkũyũ. The very first time I was ever given an ovation for my writing was over a composition in Gĩkũyũ. So for my first four years there was still harmony between the language of my formal education and that of the Limuru peasant community.

8 It was after the declaration of a state of emergency over Kenya in 1952 that all the schools run by patriotic nationalists were taken over by the colonial regime and were placed under District Education Boards chaired by Englishmen. English became the language of my formal education. In Kenya, English became more than a language: it was *the* language, and all the others had to bow before it in deference.

9 Thus one of the most humiliating experiences was to be caught speaking Gĩkũyũ in the vicinity of the school. The culprit was given corporal punishment—three to five strokes of the cane on bare buttocks—or was made to carry a metal plate around the neck with inscriptions such as I AM STUPID OR I AM A DONKEY. Sometimes the culprits were fined money they could hardly afford. And how did the teachers catch the culprits? A button was initially given to one pupil who was supposed to hand it over to whoever was caught speaking his mother tongue. Whoever had the button at the end of the day would sing who had given it to him and the ensuing process would bring out all the culprits of the day. Thus children were turned into witch-hunters and in the process were being taught the lucrative value of being a traitor to one's immediate community.

10 The attitude to English was the exact opposite: any achievement in spoken or written English was highly rewarded; prizes, prestige, applause; the ticket to higher realms. English became the measure of intelligence and ability in the arts, the sciences, and all the other branches of learning. English became *the* main determinant of a child's progress up the ladder of formal education.

11 As you may know, the colonial system of education in addition to its apartheid racial demarcation had the structure of a pyramid: a broad primary base, a narrowing secondary middle, and an even narrower university apex. Selections from primary into secondary were through an examination, in my time called Kenya African Preliminary Examination, in which one had to pass six subjects ranging from Maths to Nature Study and Kiswahili. All the papers were written in English. Nobody could pass the exam who failed the English language paper no matter how brilliantly he had done in the other subjects. I remember one boy in my class of 1954 who had distinctions in all subjects except English, which he had failed. He was made to fail the entire exam. He went on to become a turn boy in a bus company. I who had only passes but a credit in English got a place at the Alliance High School, one of the most elitist institutions for Africans in colonial Kenya. The requirements for a place at the University, Makerere University College, were broadly the same: nobody could go on to wear the undergraduate red gown, no matter how brilliantly they had performed in all the other subjects unless they had a credit—not even a simple pass!—in English. Thus the most coveted place in the pyramid and in the system was only available to the holder of an English language credit card. English was the official vehicle and the magic formula to colonial elitedom.

12 Literary education was now determined by the dominant language while also reinforcing that dominance. Orature (oral literature) in Kenyan languages stopped. In primary school I now read simplified Dickens and Stevenson alongside Rider Haggard. Jim Hawkins, Oliver Twist, Tom Brown—not Hare, Leopard and Lion—were now my daily companions in the world of imagination. In secondary school, Scott and G. B. Shaw vied with more Rider Haggard, John Buchan, Alan Paton, Captain W. E. Johns. At Makerere I read English: from Chaucer to T. S. Eliot with a touch of Graham Greene.

13 Thus language and literature were taking us further and further from ourselves to other selves, from our world to other worlds.

14 What was the colonial system doing to us Kenyan children? What were the consequences of, on the one hand, this systematic suppression of our languages and the literature they carried, and on the other the elevation of English and the literature it carried? To answer those questions, let me first examine the relationship of language to human experience, human culture, and the human perception of reality.

15 Language, any language, has a dual character: it is both a means of communication and a carrier of culture. Take English. It is spoken in Britain and in Sweden and Denmark. But for Swedish and Danish people English is only a means of communication with non-Scandinavians. It is not a carrier of their culture. For the British, and particularly the English, it is additionally, and inseparably from its use as a tool of communication, a carrier of their culture and history. Or take Swahili in East and Central Africa. It is widely used as a means of communication across many nationalities. But it is not the carrier of a culture and history of many of those nationalities. However in parts of Kenya and Tanzania, and particularly in Zanzibar, Swahili is inseparably both a means of communication and a carrier of the culture of those people to whom it is a mother-tongue.

16 Language as communication has three aspects or elements. There is first what Karl Marx once called the language of real life, the element basic to the whole notion of language, its origins and development: that is, the relations people enter into with one another in the labour process, the links they necessarily establish among themselves in the act of a people, a community of human beings, producing wealth or means of life like food, clothing, houses. A human community really starts its historical being as a community of co-operation in production through the division of labour; the simplest is between man, woman and child within a household; the more complex divisions are between branches of production such as those who are sole hunters, sole gatherers of fruits or sole workers in metal. Then there are the most complex divisions such as those in modern factories where a single product, say a shirt or a shoe, is the result of many hands and minds. Production is co-operation, is communication, is language, is expression of a relation between human beings and it is specifically human.

17 The second aspect of language as communication is speech and it imitates the language of real life, that is communication in production. The verbal signposts both reflect and aid communication or the relations established between human beings in the production of their means of life. Language as a system of verbal signposts makes that production possible. The spoken word is to relations between human beings what the hand is to the relations between human beings and nature. The hand through tools mediates between human beings and nature and forms the language of real life: spoken words mediate between human beings and form the language of speech.

18 The third aspect is the written signs. The written word imitates the spoken. Where the first two aspects of language as communication through the hand and the spoken word historically evolved more or less simultaneously, the written aspect is a much later historical development. Writing is representation of sounds with visual symbols, from the simplest knot among shepherds to tell the number in a herd or the hieroglyphics

among the Agĩkũyũ gicaandi singers and poets of Kenya, to the most complicated and different letter and picture writing systems of the world today.

19 In most societies the written and the spoken languages are the same, in that they represent each other: what is on paper can be read to another person and be received as that language which the recipient has grown up speaking. In such a society there is broad harmony for a child between the three aspects of language as communication. His interaction with nature and with other men is expressed in written and spoken symbols or signs which are both a result of that double interaction and a reflection of it. The association of the child's sensibility is with the language of his experience of life.

20 But there is more to it: communication between human beings is also the basis and process of evolving culture. In doing similar kinds of things and actions over and over again under similar circumstances, similar even in their mutability, certain patterns, moves, rhythms, habits, attitudes, experiences and knowledge emerge. Those experiences are handed over to the next generation and become the inherited basis for their further actions on nature and on themselves. There is a gradual accumulation of values which in time become almost self-evident truths governing their conception of what is right and wrong, good and bad, beautiful and ugly, courageous and cowardly, generous and mean in their internal and external relations. Over a time this becomes a way of life distinguishable from other ways of life. They develop a distinctive culture and history. Culture embodies those moral, ethical and aesthetic values, the set of spiritual eyeglasses, through which they come to view themselves and their place in the universe. Values are the basis of a people's identity, their sense of particularity as members of the human race. All this is carried by language. Language as culture is the collective memory bank of a people's experience in history. Culture is almost indistinguishable from the language that makes possible its genesis, growth, banking, articulation and indeed its transmission from one generation to the next.

21 Language as culture also has three important aspects. Culture is a product of the history which it in turn reflects. Culture in other words is a product and a reflection of human beings communicating with one another in the very struggle to create wealth and to control it. But culture does not merely reflect that history, or rather it does so by actually forming images or pictures of the world of nature and nurture. Thus the second aspect of language as culture is as an image-forming agent in the mind of a child. Our whole conception of ourselves as a people, individually and collectively, is based on those pictures and images which may or may not correctly correspond to the actual reality of the struggles with nature and nurture which produced them in the first place. But our capacity to confront the world creatively is dependent on how those images correspond or not to that reality, how they distort or clarify the reality of our struggles. Language as culture is thus mediating between me and my own self; between my own self and other selves; between me and nature. Language is mediating in my very being. And this brings us to the third aspect of language as culture. Culture transmits or imparts those images of the world and reality through the spoken and the written language, that is through a specific language. In other words, the capacity to speak, the

capacity to order sounds in a manner that makes for mutual comprehension between human beings is universal. This is the universality of language, a quality specific to human beings. It corresponds to the universality of the struggle against nature and that between human beings. But the particularity of the sounds, the words, the word order into phrases and sentences, and the specific manner, or laws, of their ordering is what distinguishes one language from another. Thus a specific culture is not transmitted through language in its universality but in its particularity as the language of a specific community with a specific history. Written literature and orature are the main means by which a particular language transmits the images of the world contained in the culture it carries.

22 Language as communication and as culture are then products of each other. Communication creates culture: culture is a means of communication. Language carries culture, and culture carries, particularly through orature and literature, the entire body of values by which we come to perceive ourselves and our place in the world. How people perceive themselves affects how they look at their culture, at their politics and at the social production of wealth, at their entire relationship to nature and to other beings. Language is thus inseparable from ourselves as a community of human beings with a specific form and character, a specific history, a specific relationship to the world.

23 So what was the colonialist imposition of a foreign language doing to us children?

24 The real aim of colonialism was to control the people's wealth: what they produced, how they produced it, and how it was distributed; to control, in other words, the entire realm of the language of real life. Colonialism imposed its control of the social production of wealth through military conquest and subsequent political dictatorship. But its most important area of domination was the mental universe of the colonised, the control, through culture, of how people perceived themselves and their relationship to the world. Economic and political control can never be complete or effective without mental control. To control a people's culture is to control their tools of self-definition in relationship to others.

25 For colonialism this involved two aspects of the same process: the destruction or the deliberate undervaluing of a people's culture, their art, dances, religions, history, geography, education, orature and literature, and the conscious elevation of the language of the coloniser. The domination of a people's language by the languages of the colonising nations was crucial to the domination of the mental universe of the colonised.

26 Take language as communication. Imposing a foreign language, and suppressing the native languages as spoken and written, were already breaking the harmony previously existing between the African child and the three aspects of language. Since the new language as a means of communication was a product of and was reflecting the 'real language of life' elsewhere, it could never as spoken or written properly reflect or imitate the real life of that community. This may in part explain why technology always appears to us as slightly external, *their* product and not *ours*. The word 'missile' used to hold an alien far-away sound until I recently learnt its equivalent in Gĩkũyũ, *ngu-*

rukuhĩ, and it made me apprehend it differently. Learning, for a colonial child, became a cerebral activity and not an emotionally felt experience.

27 But since the new, imposed languages could never completely break the native languages as spoken, their most effective area of domination was the third aspect of language as communication, the written. The language of an African child's formal education was foreign. The language of the books he read was foreign. The language of his conceptualisation was foreign. Thought, in him, took the visible form of a foreign language. So the written language of a child's upbringing in the school (even his spoken language within the school compound) became divorced from his spoken language at home. There was often not the slightest relationship between the child's written world, which was also the language of his schooling, and the world of his immediate environment in the family and the community. For a colonial child, the harmony existing between the three aspects of language as communication was irrevocably broken. This resulted in the disassociation of the sensibility of that child from his natural and social environment, what we might call colonial alienation. The alienation became reinforced in the teaching of history, geography, music, where bourgeois Europe was always the centre of the universe.

28 This disassociation, divorce, or alienation from the immediate environment becomes clearer when you look at colonial language as a carrier of culture.

29 Since culture is a product of the history of a people which it in turn reflects, the child was now being exposed exclusively to a culture that was a product of a world external to himself. He was being made to stand outside himself to look at himself. *Catching Them Young* is the title of a book on racism, class, sex, and politics in children's literature by Bob Dixon. 'Catching them young' as an aim was even more true of a colonial child. The images of this world and his place in it implanted in a child take years to eradicate, if they ever can be.

30 Since culture does not just reflect the world in images but actually, through those very images, conditions a child to see that world in a certain way, the colonial child was made to see the world and where he stands in it as seen and defined by or reflected in the culture of the language of imposition.

31 And since those images are mostly passed on through orature and literature it meant the child would now only see the world as seen in the literature of his language of adoption. From the point of view of alienation, that is of seeing oneself from outside oneself as if one was another self, it does not matter that the imported literature carried the great humanist tradition of the best in Shakespeare, Goethe, Balzac, Tolstoy, Gorky, Brecht, Sholokhov, Dickens. The location of this great mirror of imagination was necessarily Europe and its history and culture and the rest of the universe was seen from that centre.

32 But obviously it was worse when the colonial child was exposed to images of his world as mirrored in the written languages of his coloniser. Where his own native languages were associated in his impressionable mind with low status, humiliation, corporal punishment, slow-footed intelligence and ability or downright stupidity, non-intelligibility and barbarism, this was reinforced by the world he met in the works of

such geniuses of racism as a Rider Haggard or a Nicholas Monsarrat; not to mention the pronouncement of some of the giants of western intellectual and political establishment, such as Hume ('. . . the negro is naturally inferior to the whites . . .'), Thomas Jefferson ('. . . the blacks . . . are inferior to the whites on the endowments of both body and mind . . .'), or Hegel with his Africa comparable to a land of childhood still enveloped in the dark mantle of the night as far as the development of self-conscious history was concerned. Hegel's statement that there was nothing harmonious with humanity to be found in the African character is representative of the racist images of Africans and Africa such a colonial child was bound to encounter in the literature of the colonial languages. The results could be disastrous.

33 In her paper read to the conference on the teaching of African literature in schools held in Nairobi in 1973, entitled 'Written Literature and Black Images', the Kenyan writer and scholar Professor Mĩcere Mũgo related how a reading of the description of Gagool as an old African woman in Rider Haggard's *King Solomon's Mines* had for a long time made her feel mortal terror whenever she encountered old African women. In his autobiography *This Life* Sydney Poitier describes how, as a result of the literature he had read, he had come to associate Africa with snakes. So on arrival in Africa and being put up in a modern hotel in a modern city, he could not sleep because he kept on looking for snakes everywhere, even under the bed. These two have been able to pinpoint the origins of their fears. But for most others the negative image becomes internalised and it affects their cultural and even political choices in ordinary living.

Questions for Analysis

1. What is Thiong'o's argument about the relationship among language, culture, and colonization?
2. Explain the purpose of Paragraphs 1–7. Why did Thiong'o provide these details about his early life and experience with Gĩkũyũ?
3. Look carefully at Thiong'o's definition of culture in Paragraphs 20 to 22. How does his concept of culture apply to his argument in this essay? How does it compare to the concepts offered in other essays on culture that you have read?
4. Explain Thiong'o's point where he says "Learning, for a colonial child, became a cerebral activity and not an emotionally felt experience."
5. What is Thiong'o's point in his final paragraph? How do the examples of experiences by Mũgo and Poitier support Thiong'o's argument? Poitier is an African American, but he was not born or educated in Africa. Does that fact weaken Thiong'o's argument?
6. Contrast Thiong'o's emphasis on teaching native African languages in African schools to Richard Rodriguez's argument that Hispanic children in American schools should be taught in English. Are their arguments contradictory?

Chief Seattle

A Change in Worlds

(1854)

Chief Seattle (1786–1866) was a Native-American leader from the Suquamish tribe, a people who lived in what is now the Puget Sound region of Washington state. In his native Lushootseed language Seattle's name was See-ahth, a word English-speaking settlers could not easily pronounce and thus changed to Seattle. This speech, translated by Dr. Henry Smith in 1887, was given to the Suquamish people and the representatives of the United States government sent by President Franklin Pierce. The United States government was offering to provide a reservation for the Suquamish people in return for most of the land on which Seattle, Washington, now stands. The treaty was signed in 1855. In 1865, one year before Chief Seattle died, the city of Seattle passed a law making it illegal for American-Indians to live there.

1 Yonder sky that has wept tears of compassion upon our fathers for centuries untold, and which to us looks eternal, may change. Today is fair, tomorrow it may be overcast with clouds.

2 My words are like the stars that never set. What Seattle says, the Great Chief at Washington can rely upon with as much certainty as our paleface brothers can rely upon the return of the seasons.

3 The son of the White Chief says his father sends us greetings of friendship and good will. This is kind, for we know he has little need of our friendship in return because his people are many. They are like the grass that covers the vast prairies, while my people are few and resemble the scattering trees of a storm-swept plain.

4 The Great, and I presume, also good, White Chief sends us word that he wants to buy our lands but is willing to allow us to reserve enough to live on comfortably. This indeed appears generous, for the Red Man no longer has rights that he need respect, and the offer may be wise also, for we are no longer in need of a great country.

5 There was a time when our people covered the whole land as the waves of a wind-ruffled sea covers its shell-paved floor. But that time has long since passed away with the greatness of tribes now almost forgotten. I will not mourn over our untimely decay, nor reproach my paleface brothers for hastening it, for we, too, may have been somewhat to blame.

6 When our young men grow angry at some real or imaginary wrong, and disfigure their faces with black paint, their hearts, also, are disfigured and turn black, and then their cruelty is relentless and knows no bounds, and our old men are not able to restrain them.

7 But let us hope that hostilities between the Red Man and his paleface brothers may never return. We would have everything to lose and nothing to gain.

8 True it is that revenge with our young braves is considered gain, even at the cost of their own lives, but old men who stay at home in times of war, and mothers who have sons to lose, know better.

9 Our great father Washington, for I presume he is now our father as well as yours, since George has moved his boundaries to the North—our great and good father, I say, sends us word by his son, who, no doubt, is a great chief among his people, that if we do as he desires he will protect us.

10 His brave armies will be to us a bristling wall of strength, and his great ships of war will fill our harbors so that our ancient enemies far to the northward—the Simsiams and Hydas—will no longer frighten our women and old men. Then he will be our father and we will be his children.

11 But can that ever be? Your God is not our God! Your God loves your people and hates mine! He folds His strong arms lovingly around the white man and leads him as a father leads his infant son—but He has forsaken his red children, he makes your people wax strong every day and soon they will fill all the land; while my people are ebbing away like a fast receding tide that will never flow again. The white man's God cannot love His red children or He would protect them. They seem to be orphans who can look nowhere for help.

12 How, then, can we become brothers? How can your father become our Father and bring us prosperity and awaken in us dreams of returning greatness?

13 Your God seems to us to be partial. He came to the white man. We never saw Him, never heard His voice. He gave the white man laws, but had no word for His red children whose teeming millions once filled this vast continent as the stars fill the firmament.

14 No. We are two distinct races, and must ever remain so, there is little in common between us.

15 The ashes of our ancestors are sacred and their final resting place is hallowed ground, while you wander away from the tombs of your fathers seemingly without regrets.

16 Your religion was written on tablets of stone by the iron finger of an angry God, lest you might forget it. The Red Man could never remember nor comprehend it.

17 Our religion is the traditions of our ancestors—the dreams of our old men, given to them by the Great Spirit, and the visions of our Sachems, and is written in the hearts of our people.

18 Your dead cease to love you and the homes of their nativity as soon as they pass the portals of the tomb. They wander far away beyond the stars, are soon forgotten and never return.

19 Our dead never forget the beautiful world that gave them being. They still love its winding rivers, its great mountains and its sequestered vales, and they ever yearn in tenderest affection over the lonely hearted living, and often return to visit and comfort them.

20 Day and night cannot dwell together. The Red Man has ever fled the approach of the white man, as the changing mist on the mountainside flee before the blazing morning sun.

21 However, your proposition seems a just one, and I think that my folks will accept it and will retire to the reservation you offer them, and we will dwell apart and in peace, for the words of the Great White Chief seem to be the voice of Nature speaking to my

people out of the thick darkness that is fast gathering around them like a dense fog floating inward from a midnight sea.

22 It matters little where we pass the remainder of our days. They are not many. The Indian's night promises to be dark. No bright star hovers above his horizon. Sad-voiced winds moan in the distance. Some grim Nemesis of our race is on the Red Man's trail, and wherever he goes he will still hear the sure approaching footsteps of the fell destroyer and prepare to meet his doom, as does the wounded doe that hears the approaching footsteps of the hunter.

23 A few more moons, a few more winters, and not one of all the mighty hosts that once filled this broad land or that now roam in fragmentary bands through these vast solitudes or lived in happy homes, protected by the Great Spirit, will remain to weep over the graves of a people once as powerful and as hopeful as your own!

24 But why should I repine? Why should I murmur at the fate of my people? Tribes are made up of individuals and are no better than they. Men come and go like the waves of a sea. A tear, a tamanamus, a dirge and they are gone from our longing eyes forever. Even the white man, whose God walked and talked with him as friend to friend, is not exempt from the common destiny. We may be brothers after all. We shall see.

25 We will ponder your proposition, and when we have decided we will tell you. But should we accept it, I hare and now make this the first condition, that we not be denied the privilege, without molestation, of visiting at will the graves of our ancestors and friends.

26 Every part of this country is sacred to my people. Every hillside, every valley, every plain and grove has been hallowed by some fond memory or some sad experience of my tribe. Even the rocks, which seem to lie dumb as they swelter in the sun along the silent shore in solemn grandeur, thrill with memories of past events connected with the fate of my people; the very dust under your feet responds more lovingly to our footsteps than to yours, because it is the ashes of our ancestors, and our bare feet are conscious of the sympathetic touch, for the soil is rich with the life of our kindred.

27 The sable braves, and fond mothers, and glad-hearted maidens, and the little children who lived and rejoiced here and whose very names are now forgotten, still love these solitudes and their deep fastnesses at eventide grow shadowy with the presence of dusky spirits.

28 And when the last Red Man shall have perished from the earth and his memory among white men shall have become a myth, these shores will swarm with the invisible dead of my tribe and when your children's children shall think themselves alone in the field, the store, the shop, upon the highway, or in the silence of the woods, they will not be alone. In all the earth there is no place dedicated to solitude.

29 At night, when the streets of your cities and villages shall be silent and you think them deserted, they will throng with the returning hosts that once filled and still love this beautiful land.

30 The white man will never be alone. Let him be just and deal kindly with my people, for the dead are not powerless.

31 Dead—did I say? There is no death. Only a change in worlds!

Questions for Analysis

1. In Paragraph 14, Chief Seattle speaks of the white men and the Red Man as "two distinct races." What are the major cultural differences mentioned by Chief Seattle that support this conclusion?
2. Recently Chief Seattle has been singled out by environmentalists as an early defender of the environment. Several groups have even distributed a distorted version of this speech in which additional, even inaccurate, information was included to emphasize environmentalist themes. What do you find in this version of Chief Seattle's speech that would make it attractive to use in this way?
3. Chief Seattle mentions in several places the dwindling numbers and strength of his people. Although he is obviously disturbed by the prospect of his people dying out, he nevertheless feels that he should not "repine" or "murmur" if this is to be their fate. How does he reconcile himself to this very real possibility? In what specific ways does his view of nature help his reconciliation? Whom does he blame for the "untimely decay" of his people? Is this dying out of cultures an inevitable result of "progress"? Should it be inevitable? Where else has it happened?
4. Do you find Chief Seattle's speech effective? What specific aspects of the speech do you respond to positively? What parts do you find less effective? Why? This translation was made by Dr. Henry Smith in 1887, around 33 years after the speech was originally given. Identify passages that seem to you likely to be particularly close to Chief Seattle's language and philosophy. What passages seem strongly influenced by the elaborate prose style that characterized nineteenth-century American writing? Explain why you chose these examples to illustrate each culture's use of language.

Barry H. Lopez

Buffalo

(1982)

Barry H. Lopez (b. 1945) is an award-winning writer whose works focus on the nature and folklore of western North America from the Arctic to the desert. "Buffalo," a short story that reads like an essay, first appeared in Lopez's book *Winter Count.* This piece is built on the attempt of a white writer (narrator) to understand Native-American stories about the impact of white civilization on the Western environment (especially the buffalo) and thus the Native Americans' way of life. As you read, you should notice that the white narrator of this piece is a character in the story and not Lopez.

1 In January 1845, after a week of cold but brilliantly clear weather, it began to snow in southern Wyoming. Snow accumulated on the flat in a dead calm to a depth of four

feet in only a few days. The day following the storm was breezy and warm—chinook weather. A party of Cheyenne camped in a river bottom spent the day tramping the snow down, felling cottonwood trees for their horses, and securing game, in response to a dream by one of them, a thirty-year-old man called Blue Feather on the Side of His Head, that they would be trapped by a sudden freeze.

2 That evening the temperature fell fifty degrees and an ice crust as rigid, as easily broken, as sharp as window glass formed over the snow. The crust held for weeks.

3 Access across the pane of ice to game and pasturage on the clear, wind-blown slopes of the adjacent Medicine Bow Mountains was impossible for both Indian hunters and a buffalo herd trapped nearby. The buffalo, exhausted from digging in the deep snow, went to their knees by the thousands, their legs slashed by the razor ice, glistening red in the bright sunlight. Their woolly carcasses lay scattered like black boulders over the blinding white of the prairie, connected by a thin cross-hatching of bloody red trails.

4 Winds moaned for days in the thick fur of the dead and dying buffalo, broken by the agonized bellows of the animals themselves. Coyotes would not draw near. The Cheyenne camped in the river bottom were terrified. As soon as they were able to move they departed. No Cheyenne ever camped there again.

5 The following summer the storm and the death of the herd were depicted on a buffalo robe by one of the Cheyenne, a man called Raven on His Back. Above the scene, in the sky, he drew a white buffalo. The day they had left camp a man was supposed to have seen a small herd of buffalo, fewer than twenty, leaving the plains and lumbering up the Medicine Bow River into the mountains. He said they were all white, and each seemed to him larger than any bull he had ever seen. There is no record of this man's name, but another Cheyenne in the party, a medicine man called Walks Toward the Two Rivers, carried the story of the surviving white buffalo to Crow and Teton Sioux in an effort to learn its meaning. In spite of the enmity among these tribes their leaders agreed that the incident was a common and disturbing augury. They gathered on the Box Elder River in southeastern Montana in the spring of 1846 to decipher its meaning. No one was able to plumb it, though many had fasted and bathed in preparation.

6 Buffalo were never seen again on the Laramie Plains after 1845, in spite of the richness of the grasses there and the size of the buffalo herds nearby in those days. The belief that there were still buffalo in the Medicine Bow Mountains, however, survivors of the storm, persisted for years, long after the disappearance of buffalo (some 60 million animals) from Wyoming and neighboring territories by the 1880s.

7 In the closing years of the nineteenth century, Arapaho and Shoshoni warriors who went into the Medicine Bow to dream say they did, indeed, see buffalo up there then. The animals lived among the barren rocks above timberline, far from any vegetation. They stood more than eight feet at the shoulder; their coats were white as winter ermine and their huge eyes were light blue. At the approach of men they would perch motionless on the granite boulders, like mountain goats. Since fogs are common in these high valleys in spring and summer it was impossible, they say, to tell how many buffalo there were.

8 In May 1887 a Shoshoni called Long Otter came on two of these buffalo in the Snowy Range. As he watched they watched him. They began raising and lowering their hooves, started drumming softly on the rocks. They began singing a death song, way back in the throat like the sound of wind moaning in a canyon. The man, Long Otter, later lost his mind and was killed in a buckboard accident the following year. As far as I know this is the last report of living buffalo in the Medicine Bow.

9 It is curious to me that in view of the value of the hides no white man ever tried to find and kill one of these buffalo. But that is the case. No detail of the terrible storm of that winter, or of the presence of a herd of enormous white buffalo in the Medicine Bow, has ever been found among the papers of whites who lived in the area or who might have passed through in the years following.

10 It should be noted, however, by way of verification, that a geology student from Illinois called Fritiof Fryxell came upon two buffalo skeletons in the Snowy Range in the summer of 1925. Thinking these barren heights an extraordinary elevation at which to find buffalo, he carefully marked the location on a topographic map. He measured the largest of the skeletons, found the size staggering, and later wrote up the incident in the May 1926 issue of the *Journal of Mammalogy.*

11 In 1955, a related incident came to light. In the fall of 1911, at the request of the Colorado Mountain Club, a party of Arapaho Indians were brought into the Rocky Mountains in the northern part of the state to relate to white residents the history of the area prior to 1859. The settlers were concerned that during the years when the white man was moving into the area, and the Indian was being extirpated, a conflict in historical records arose such that the white record was incomplete and possibly in error.

12 The Arapaho were at first reluctant to speak; they made up stories of the sort they believed the whites would like to hear. But the interest and persistence of the white listeners made an impression upon them and they began to tell what had really happened.

13 Among the incidents the Arapaho revealed was that in the winter of 1845 (when news of white settlers coming in covered wagons first reached them) there was a terrible storm. A herd of buffalo wintering in Brainard Valley (called then Bear in the Hole Valley) began singing a death song. At first it was barely audible, and it was believed the wind was making the sound until it got louder and more distinct. As the snow got deeper the buffalo left the valley and began to climb into the mountains. For four days they climbed, still singing the moaning death song, followed by Arapaho warriors, until they reached the top of the mountain. This was the highest place but it had no name. Now it is called Thatchtop Mountain.

14 During the time the buffalo climbed they did not stop singing. They turned red all over; their eyes became smooth white. The singing became louder. It sounded like thunder that would not stop. Everyone who heard it, even people four or five days' journey away, was terrified.

15 At the top of the mountain the buffalo stopped singing. They stood motionless in the snow, the wind blowing clouds around them. The Arapaho men who had followed

had not eaten for four days. One, wandering into the clouds with his hands outstretched and a rawhide string connecting him to the others, grabbed hold of one of the buffalo and killed it. The remaining buffalo disappeared into the clouds; the death song began again, very softly, and remained behind them. The wind was like the singing of the buffalo. When the clouds cleared the men went down the mountain.

16 The white people at the 1911 meeting said they did not understand the purpose of telling such a story. The Arapaho said this was the first time the buffalo tried to show them how to climb out through the sky.

17 The notes of this meeting in 1911 have been lost, but what happened there remained clear in the mind of the son of one of the Indians who was present. It was brought to my attention by accident one evening in the library of the university where I teach. I was reading an article on the introduction of fallow deer in Nebraska in the August 1955 issue of the *Journal of Mammalogy* when this man, who was apparently just walking by, stopped and, pointing at the opposite page, said, "This is not what this is about." The article he indicated was called "An Altitudinal Record for Bison in Northern Colorado." He spoke briefly of it, as if to himself, and then departed.

18 Excited by this encounter I began to research the incident. I have been able to verify what I have written here. In view of the similarity between the events in the Medicine Bow and those in Colorado, I suspect that there were others in the winter of 1845 who began, as the Arapaho believe, trying to get away from what was coming, and that subsequent attention to this phenomenon is of some importance.

19 I recently slept among weathered cottonwoods on the Laramie Plains in the vicinity of the Medicine Bow Mountains. I awoke in the morning to find my legs broken.

Questions for Analysis

1. What puzzle is the narrator of this story trying to solve? How does he go about it?
2. What is the basic pattern inherent in all the stories told by Native American tribes about the white buffalo? Do you believe the events described as happening in the winter of 1845 actually happened? Does it matter whether they actually happened?
3. In Paragraph 16, the "white people" who heard the Arapaho version of the white buffalo story said they did not understand the "purpose of telling such a story." Why did they not understand? In your opinion, what is the purpose of the story?
4. Do you think the narrator really understood the purpose of these stories? What is the difference in the way the narrator thinks and the way the Native Americans think? When he wakes up after camping on the Laramie Plains, why are both of the narrator's legs broken? (Remember that the narrator in this case is a character in the story—not the author himself.)

Appendix A Writing Arguments: An Overview

The ability to write effectively and persuasively is not dependent on an intimate knowledge of formal logic. However, being familiar with a few concepts and terms can help you identify problems with logic in what you read and can also help you clarify your own thinking and writing. This appendix provides a brief discussion of claims, appeals, and common fallacies. Your instructor may also have you study fuller discussions of argument and writing that include formal logic and, more likely, Toulmin logic. Before you begin to study the brief presentation here or even more comprehensive treatments of argument, you should remember that persuasive writing finally depends on your persistent asking and honest answering of a few important questions. Try to ask and answer the following questions as you plan, write, and revise:

1. Have I presented *enough* evidence to support my thesis?

   This question obviously applies to your entire essay as well as to each section within it. Each point you make must be backed up with reasons, examples, and illustrations. Writing that is not persuasive usually contains assertions that the author did not support.

2. Have I presented my evidence so that the reader *sees* and *understands* how it supports the thesis?

   Your burden as a writer is to explain how evidence supports assertions. If you continually question whether you have clearly connected evidence and thesis, you will find it much easier to locate and correct problems in logic (fallacies) and weak support. Persuasive writing is mainly a matter of applied common sense and clear thinking.

3. Have I anticipated questions, objections, needs, or reservations the reader might have?

   Anticipation is one of the key words in persuasive writing. Anticipate the questions that an antagonistic reader might raise. Think not only about challenges that your readers might offer to your argument, evidence, and reasoning, but also about what you can do and say to meet your reader's needs and to find common ground.

Claims

Basically, a *claim* is the proposition or thesis a writer, speaker, or artist tries to prove. A claim can be explicit or implicit. Most essays have explicit claims that appear as thesis statements or conclusions. In most poetry, fiction, or visual art, and in some essays, the claim is implicit: The writer or artist presents information (evidence) that should lead the reader or observer to the implied claim of the work.

Claims in essays can include one or more of the following three forms: claim of fact, claim of value, or claim of policy.

Claim of Fact. A *claim of fact* is an assertion that some thing or some condition has existed, now exists, or will exist; or that one condition or set of conditions has caused or will cause another condition or set of conditions.

Some claims of fact involve commonplace information (''The sun rises in the East'') or easily verifiable information (''The capital of Kenya is Nairobi''), and therefore do not require supporting evidence. Most claims of fact, however, do require supporting evidence in the form of examples, statistics, or authoritative testimony. Your burden as a writer or speaker is to present to the reader *enough* evidence that clearly and logically supports each claim of fact you make.

Some of the most obvious claims of fact in this anthology are found in the section on acid rain. For example, in ''The Challenge of Acid Rain'' Volker A. Mohnen provides a detailed explanation of the chemical and meteorological processes that support his first claim of fact: Acid rain exists. He then must describe another series of interconnected chemical and biological processes (with ample examples, statistics, and authoritative testimony to support individual claims of fact as he goes) that support his *claim (of fact)* that acid rain harms the environment in many different ways. This claim then leads to a *claim of value:* Acid rain does enough damage to the environment to justify the expense and trouble of reducing the emissions that cause elevated acid levels in precipitation.

Claim of Value. A *claim of value* is an assertion about the quality, morality, or worth of a condition, belief, action, or object. Claims of value are difficult to support because they are based on opinions that often differ from one person to another, one group to another, or one culture to another. They are, however, essential to make: We constantly desire or need to assert the relative value of what we find and do in our world. In aesthetics we have differing standards of taste and opinion for visual art, music, architecture, and physical beauty. Different standards of morality and ethics mean that we do not all agree about what constitutes acceptable or unacceptable behavior in specific circumstances.

Furthermore, we make decisions in our private and public lives based on our estimates of the relative worth of many different objects, practices, conditions, and policies. In our private lives we must decide about such things as whether to buy a new car or take a vacation; whether to spend leisure time working for a charity or with our family; whether to take a higher-paying job in a distant city or remain in a lower-paying job close to family or friends. All these choices involve making decisions about the relative worth of two or more alternatives. If we felt the need to justify our decision in one of these or a similar situation, we would be making a claim of value. Claims of value made in a public context are potentially very difficult and important because they frequently affect large numbers of people physically, financially, or emotionally. Decisions about where to build roads or schools, how to protect special natural environments, or whether to cut or expand social or educational programs all involve claims of value. They all require those of us involved in the decision to argue that one alternative has greater worth than another.

In his essay on acid rain Mohnen is presenting a claim of value when he asserts that the damage being done to the environment by acidified precipitation justifies the expense of dramatically reducing the amount of pollutants put into the atmosphere. Other people (someone employed by one of the polluting industries, for example) might disagree with his argument and offer another claim of value, arguing that the additional money needed to reduce the pollution from industrial sources would cost people jobs. Still others might agree with Mohnen's claim of value and yet disagree with the *claim of policy* he presents: that new technologies are available and should be used to reduce the levels of highly acidic rain.

Claim of Policy. A *claim of policy* is an argument advocating that a particular course of action or a particular policy be adopted. To be persuasive, claims of policy require the writer or speaker to outline clearly the proposed policy and to support that policy with the reasons it should be implemented.

In an open society like ours, important issues are constantly being debated in public arenas. Most include claims of policy. However, arguments that support claims of policy must include both claims of fact and claims of value. For example, Mohnen first establishes that certain conditions do exist (a *claim of fact*) and then argues that it is important to respond to these conditions (a *claim of value*) before he argues for a specific proposal (a *claim of policy*).

Appeals

An *appeal* is a rhetorical strategy used by a writer (or speaker) to persuade a reader (or listener) to respond positively to the information or argument presented. An appeal is thus a way of trying to get agreement or assent. Appeals, however, are not direct requests; they are instead strategies inherent in the kind of information presented and in the way that information is presented. Appeals are rhetorical because they involve attempts on the part of the writer to find and take advantage of common ground with the reader. The success of an appeal depends both on the writer's skill with language and the writer's ability to anticipate a reader's wants, needs, and interests. Arguments that use appeals may fail because the writer misjudges the audience, chooses an ineffective appeal, or misuses an appeal.

Familiarity with the basic kinds of appeals will help you understand the strategies used in the essays you read and will help you plan and carry out your own writing. The three basic kinds of appeals are *logos* appeals, *ethos* appeals, and *pathos* appeals.

Logos Appeals. *Logos appeals* are those you should use most often because they most directly involve the information you present and your reasoning about it. *Logos* appeals are rhetorical in that they depend on the writer and reader agreeing about which information (statistics, examples, testimony) is important and which ways of presenting and analyzing that information (analogies, quotations, pictures, definitions) are effective. And, as you might expect, *logos* refers to the logic or reasoning used to connect ideas and facts to one another and to the conclusions the writer presents.

Consider again the example of "The Challenge of Acid Rain" in which the author relies almost entirely on *logos* appeals. Mohnen presents several types of information including the results of scientific studies; descriptions of chemical, meteorological, and biological processes; definitions; detailed illustrations; and explanations of how new technologies work. His assumption is that all this information and the logic with which he connects it will be accepted by (or appeal to) his readers as adequate support for his conclusions.

Although *logos* appeals often rely heavily on the factual data presented, their success depends on the abilities of the writer. If, for example, statistics are not clearly presented and their conclusions not logically connected, readers will question them. The appeal of the data and the writer's conclusions will then be lost. Readers must feel confident about the accuracy of the data and about the ability of the writer to evaluate that data fairly and logically. Therefore, *logos* appeals depend in part on the writer's *ethos.*

Ethos Appeals. *Ethos appeals* are designed to persuade readers that a writer's argument should be accepted or at least carefully considered because of that writer's experience, knowledge, or character. Most ethos appeals establish the expertise or experience that makes the writer especially well qualified to argue the position presented in the essay. For example, the facts that Volker A. Mohnen is a Professor of Atmospheric Science who has testified before Congress, and is also Project Director of the U.S. Environmental Protection Agency's Cloud Chemistry Program give him and thus his essay more credibility. This information is presented in a short biographical sketch that appeared with the original essay in *Scientific American.*

Although it is common to see biographical sketches accompanying essays in periodicals and newspapers, most writers do not (and should not) rely entirely on that information to establish their credibility. Most writers include information to establish their knowledge of a subject or the circumstances that justify their being given special attention in their writing. Early in his "Letter from Birmingham Jail" Martin Luther King, Jr., reminds his primary audience (Birmingham-area church leaders) that he, too, is a clergyman who shares their beliefs, concerns, and ideals. The ethos he thus establishes would also work well for his secondary audience (white and African-American citizens of the city of Birmingham, the state of Alabama, and the southern United States) because these readers are for the most part Christians who share his beliefs and his value system, even if they do not agree with his immediate goals.

There are almost as many approaches to establishing *ethos* as there are writers and subjects. In "Refocusing Animal Rights" Sneed B. Collard, III, provides a brief history of his conflicts with animal rights activists to make his reconciliatory position seem more reasonable and appealing. In ''I'd Rather Smoke than Kiss'' Florence King presents amusing personal anecdotes that establish her *ethos* as a human being with a sense of humor whose patience and rights as a smoker are being pushed to the limit by ''health Nazis.'' Once you become aware that writers garner credibility and sympathy through the information they present about themselves and the attitude they project through their words, you will notice the many ways *ethos* can be established and how effective—even vital—it can be. The most common way of establishing *ethos* (and the strategy you will probably employ most of the time) is through the balanced, clear presentation of information. This approach suggests to the reader that the writer is an honest, reasonable person writing to intelligent readers.

As is the case with any appeal, *ethos* can be misused. This occurs most often when someone tries to use experience or knowledge in one area to establish *ethos* for an argument in another area. For example, Mohnen's excellent credentials in atmospheric science do *not* qualify him to speak as an expert when writing an essay advocating, for example, that health workers be required to take tests for the AIDS virus at frequent intervals. Although listing his scientific credentials may suggest that he has special authority in this matter because science is involved, the radically different fields really give him little more credibility as an authority discussing AIDS than the average lay person. However, knowing something of his work and, therefore, of his character and intellectual habits might mean that we can assume that his position on this question will be thoughtful and thorough. Sometimes credentials can be very misleading. Do the credentials of Duane T. Gish as a scientist and researcher establish an *ethos* that gives his advocacy of scientific creationism special weight? Many readers would say no, arguing that scientific creationism is a religious belief, not a scientific theory. Others might say that his credentials do strengthen his argument.

Celebrity endorsements are the most obvious form of *ethos* appeals. If Magic Johnson writes to advocate the training program he followed to develop skills in basketball (even if it were radically different from established programs), we would be justified in giving his program special attention. However, if we see Johnson promoting a particular brand of soft drink or clothing or advocating strict enforcement of gun controls, we should scrutinize the products or ideas he supports as we would those of any other less-well-known person. However, when Johnson speaks out about the importance of safe sex as a way of preventing the spread of AIDS, we do (and probably should) give his comments special attention and weight. The fact that he is a celebrity who has tested positively for the AIDS virus gives him a special *ethos* and thus adds emphasis to what he has to say. We feel sympathy for him and his plight and, therefore, pay closer attention to his words. Our response is based on our perception of him as a celebrity and our propensity as human beings to allow our emotions to guide our thinking. In this case, an *ethos* appeal comes very close to being a *pathos* appeal.

Pathos Appeals. *Pathos appeals* are designed to elicit an emotional response from the audience. Our emotional response is not to the author (which would technically make it *ethos*), but to the subject matter in an essay or speech. We react emotionally to many things, including people, ideas, and symbols, but we react most intensely and predictably to the plights of individual human beings. For example, several essays in this book's section on ''Intercultural Understanding'' discuss the problems faced by people, particularly children, who are caught between two cultures. In ''Hispanic Dreams/American Dreams,'' Robert Coles uses his interviews with a young Hispanic boy, Franco, to reveal the conflicting emotional and intellectual pressures felt by children in this situation. As we read about Franco and his dreams, we feel his discomfort, his tensions, his fears, and his frustrations, and we are able to see Coles's argument more easily and perhaps to agree with it. A study of 1000 children like Franco complete with a demographic and statistical analysis might make the same points, but it might not be as persuasive and certainly would not be as memorable because it would not have the same emotional impact.

Pathos appeals can be used in many ways on both sides of an issue. For example, in the current debate over abortion, those who oppose it will often talk of performing an abortion as ''killing a baby.'' Those who argue that abortions should be legal point to the large numbers of women who have died (and by implication will die) from illegal abortions. Even the choice of words used in discussing this and other issues is often calculated with emotional impact (or lack of it) in mind. The anti-abortion forces use words like *killing, butcher,* or *murder;* they use *baby* instead of *fetus* to evoke highly emotional reactions. Those on the other side will shift attention away from the act of abortion itself and focus on the women who are in distress and who might die from illegal abortions. Those on this side of the issue do not say they are ''pro-abortion''—they say they are ''pro-choice.'' When they do have to talk about the act of abortion itself, they speak of ''fetal material'' and avoid words that might provoke emotional responses.

Words and phrases that stimulate an emotional reaction because they either evoke or challenge our loyalty to ideals and principles (for example, *family, country, religion, friendship, honor,* or *freedom,*) can be found for use in connection with most topics. *Pathos* appeals can thus be ways of bringing out the best in people. They can also be abused; they can be manipulated (either intentionally or unintentionally) to encourage people to do certain things or to support certain causes because of emotional reactions.

Being emotionally aroused by the language or ideas that someone presents does not mean that you must agree with that person's suggestions. When you see emotional appeals in what you read, you should seek and carefully consider other more logical appeals that should accompany the emotional appeals. When you use an emotional appeal, be sure to supplement it with logical appeals. Furthermore, be careful not to overdo it: Overdone emotional appeals become too obvious and work against you. Emotional appeals can thus become *fallacies*—arguments that may deceive or mislead the reader and ultimately work against the writer.

Fallacies

Fallacies are arguments that contain misleading or deceptive reasoning. Fallacies can take many forms: conclusions may be based on insufficient evidence; connections between points may be unclear; language may be used inaccurately or deceptively; appeals to emotion may contradict or sidestep reasonable thinking.

Scholars who study logic and argumentation have long lists of fallacies and many different schemes for classifying them. For our purposes such elaborate frameworks are not necessary. Being aware of those fallacies that occur most often in writing will help you recognize them in what you read and avoid them as you write. Notice as you read the following descriptions that avoidance of each fallacy is really a matter of applying common sense and not thinking too narrowly. Since we discussed how *ethos* appeals can often be fallacious, we will start the list here with two additional forms of emotional fallacies and then provide further example of other types of fallacies.

Appeal to Tradition. The fallacy of *appeal to tradition* appeals to our loyalty to a long-established way of doing things or thinking about things. Basically, the argument is "we should continue to think this way or to do things this way because we have done so for a long time and to change would violate this tradition." This argument appeals to an emotional attachment to the status quo and thus diverts attention from the merits of the proposal being debated. Many of the rights now held by individuals and groups (e.g., civil rights, women's rights, etc.) were achieved only after their proponents had overcome arguments of this kind from opponents to change.

Appeal to the People *(ad populum)*. This appeal is based on the common desire to be a part of a larger group whose ideals, beliefs, and objectives we share. Politicians frequently use, and abuse, this appeal, making it a fallacy when they rely on patriotic statements that stress the greatness of our nation (or state, or city) and neglect substantive issues that the government must address. This kind of appeal (and fallacy) is closely akin to what some call the "bandwagon" fallacy, which is essentially an argument to do something because everyone else is doing it.

Argument to the Person *(ad hominum)*. *Argument to the person,* or *ad hominum arguments* are attempts to undercut the character or authority *(ethos)* of the opponent so that the audience will not seriously consider his or her arguments. *Ad hominum* arguments can range from simple distortions ("He won't do anything to help the poor; he's a Republican" or "He will overload the budget with wasteful social programs because he's a Democrat") to out-and-out character assassination (accusations of criminal activity, sexual misconduct, or other irresponsible behavior). Allegations against a person are fallacies only if they have nothing to do with the issue at hand. In certain situations (for example, politics), a person's character probably should be considered. However, the question of what aspects of a person's life are appropriate for discussion in a public forum as part of the political process is still a hotly debated question.

Hasty Generalization. *Hasty generalizations* are conclusions based on insufficient evidence. Prejudices are usually based on hasty generalizations. We have unpleasant experiences with a few people from a certain place or group and, therefore, generalize that everyone from that place or group will be like the few we have met. Researchers seek to avoid hasty generalization. Scientists who conduct empirical experiments carefully record their procedures so that they and other scientists can repeat them and verify the results. Social scientists have elaborate checks to make sure that their samples are large enough to provide a true picture of reality. The most famous recent instance of a hasty generalization in science occurred when two researchers in Utah announced that they were able to produce "cold fusion." Attempts by many scientists to duplicate their results have failed, strongly suggesting that the original conclusion was a hasty generalization.

***Post Hoc Ergo Propter Hoc* (After this, therefore, because of this).** *Post hoc ergo propter hoc* is Latin for "after this, therefore, because of this" and is used to refer to a faulty cause–effect relationship. The fact that one event occurs after another does not mean that the first caused the second. *Post hoc ergo propter hoc* reasoning also occurs when people accept superstition. If you have a freak accident shortly after seeing a black cat, *post hoc ergo propter hoc* reasoning might lead you to conclude that the cat is to blame. We can avoid this fallacy by insisting on logical and usually simple explanations about the relationships between cause and effect.

Slippery Slope. *Slippery slope* is used to describe the argument that if one condition is allowed, it will inevitably lead to a second undesirable condition. Often slippery-slope arguments assume a series of events that will connect the first undesired condition and the last even less desirable condition. The argument becomes a fallacy when the writer does not or cannot provide clear evidence or a cogent argument that connects the two conditions. Since these arguments are about the future, the burden of proof is very heavy. In his argument against withholding treatment from newborns, C. Everett Koop asserts that allowing this practice will eventually lead us to accept euthanasia as a common response to difficult medical problems in people of all ages. He even calls his argument a "slippery slope." He clearly believes that his slippery-slope argument is valid. Others might disagree and call his argument fallacious.

Either/Or (or False Dilemma). In the *either/or fallacy* the writer or speaker asserts that only two options (usually extremes) exist and insists that the reader must choose between the two. Obviously, in most situations many possibilities exist between the extremes. False-dilemma statements are common on bumper stickers: "Better Dead than Red," "When Guns Are Outlawed, Only Outlaws Will Have Guns." Others sound more sophisticated but limit possibilities just as radically: "We as a country must choose between vigorously continuing the war on drugs or facing the complete breakdown of society because of a population stoned on drugs." Clearly, more options than the two presented here are available.

Faulty Analogy. Analogies can often make certain complex issues or questions more concrete and accessible and thus strengthen arguments. However, they must be chosen and presented carefully. If the reader sees that we are comparing two things that do not match up logically (''comparing apples and oranges,'' as the old saying goes), then it is a *faulty analogy* that will not work. Even when comparisons seem to match up well, we must be careful in what we claim about them. Every situation is different, even when the parallels between it and another situation seem remarkably similar. Any comparison you set up should not distort or oversimplify the information or situation. For example, during the 1960s the domino theory was used to justify our increasing military role in Vietnam. The argument was that if the spread of Communism was not stopped in Vietnam, it would move through the rest of Southeast Asia, into the Philippines, and beyond. The analogy was that the fall of these countries would proceed like a line of dominoes, one knocking over the next and so on. Obviously, a line of dominoes grossly over-simplifies the situation in Southeast Asia. A quick look at the history of the area shows that war and social turmoil had existed for years because of European colonization, ethnic conflicts, and religious differences. The unique circumstances in each country should have been taken into account. These countries were not uniformly vulnerable as the domino analogy suggested.

***Non Sequitur* (It does not follow.).** *Non sequitur* describes the breakdown in logic between statements in sequence when one is presented as a conclusion based on the other. Consider an example: ''Professor Jones must be an excellent teacher; his students always make high grades in his class.'' This statement is a *non sequitur* because a teacher's effectiveness cannot be measured simply by the grades his students earn or are given. We can, however, say, ''Professor Jones must be an excellent teacher: Most of his students not only do well in his course but also perform well in other courses that build on the material his course covers.'' Although *non sequitur* is used to describe this specific cause–effect problem, it can also be used to describe the faulty thinking involved in most fallacies.

Straw Man. The *straw man fallacy* involves the misrepresentation of someone else's argument or claim to provide an easier target for attack. The misrepresentation then becomes the ''straw man'' and the attack on the ''straw man'' a diversion used to draw attention away from the substantive issues in the argument. For example, an opponent of gun-control laws might say, ''Those who advocate strict controls on handguns and semi-automatic weapons are obviously out to confiscate all guns and will inevitably take shotguns and rifles out of the hands of hunters. Those of us who hunt for recreation and food will thus lose a fundamental right and a tradition passed down from father to son for over three centuries. We must fight all gun-control laws.'' In this passage the shift to hunting guns is the straw man. That shift diverts attention from the real issue (cheap handguns and weapons designed to kill people) to another consideration. The substitute issue is one that will allow the writer to appeal to a very large group of people. (Notice that this example also illustrates several fallacies: slippery slope, *non sequitur,* appeal to tradition, and appeal to emotion.)

Appendix B: Working with Sources

The Researched Essay

Researched essays are common assignments in many composition courses, especially courses that emphasize reading and argument. A researched essay may be a "term-paper" length assignment or a shorter essay based on your opinions and some additional reading. In either case, examining information and essays written by others on your topic and using them in your essay can be very helpful. Reading information and opinions that expand your understanding of the issue can enhance your ability to define and support your own opinions. This reading will allow you to place your own opinions in the context of a larger, broader conversation about the issue.

Reading can also help you form your opinion. (Not having an opinion at the beginning is all right, by the way.) Your reading may also lead you to change your opinion. Reading and evaluating presentations that question conventional or previously held beliefs, values, and concepts are key to the present strength and continued viability of our culture. Information, opinions, and ideas from sources strengthen your argument in four ways:

1. They permit you to include additional evidence.
2. They permit you to include the opinions of experts who support your position.
3. They enable you to present and refute the opinions and arguments of those who disagree with you.
4. They enable you to place your argument in a larger context, thus building your readers' confidence in you as a knowledgeable writer on the subject.

It is very important that the information you present be accurate (i.e., true to the author's words and intent) and that the source of the information be documented. Clear, accurate documentation is essential in researched papers. Properly acknowledging sources is the responsibility of every writer.

Effective documentation is much more than just getting bibliographic details correct in the final draft (though that is an important factor); it also requires careful, thoughtful work from the time you begin taking notes until you produce your final draft. For this reason the following discussion will begin with a review of three note-taking strategies, move to an examination of how you incorporate source information into your text, and then end with a brief overview of the MLA documentation style.

Three Note-taking Strategies

There are many ways of keeping track of your research. You must find the strategy that suits your way of working as well as the purpose and size of your research project.

Three ways of taking notes are described below. Depending on your needs, work habits, and the requirements of your instructor, you may wish to choose one of the systems described or devise your own variation. Remember, any note-taking system is only as effective as you are thorough.

Note Cards. The *note-card system* requires two sets of cards: bibliography cards and note cards. On a bibliography card, record the *full* bibliographic citation for each source you refer to and a word, phrase (usually the author's last name or a key word from the title), or number that is unique to each source. Transcribe the information from the source on the note cards. Limit this information to one basic idea or a closely related group of facts on each card. Clearly indicate the source by using the unique word or phrase entered on the corresponding bibliography card. Always indicate on each card the page(s) from which the information came and be sure to indicate quoted material.

When you have finished your research, sort and arrange your note cards into groups that roughly correspond to your outline. Eliminate any cards with information that does not serve your purpose. After you organize the cards and revise your outline to reflect any changes or additions, begin to write your essay, using the cards as source material.

A note-card system offers a very detailed picture of your information. From that picture you can organize information by subject independent of the source. However, the size of note cards offers some disadvantages. Taking notes on cards with one idea to a card tends to fragment sources, making it difficult to reconstruct the overall sense of a source. Because of the limited space on the cards, your reactions to the information and opinions in the source must be written in the margins, on additional cards, and/or in your outline instead of on the note card with the source information.

If you will be using several sources and only a limited amount of information from each source, then note cards are the most logical system for you to choose. If your paper will require you to analyze your sources in some detail, you might wish to consider a different note-taking method.

Loose-Leaf Notebook. The *loose-leaf notebook* method uses 8 ½″ × 11″ loose-leaf notebook paper. The larger amount of space available on a piece of notebook paper helps you follow a source's flow of logic more coherently within your notes. It also allows you more space to record your responses to the source.

Record complete bibliographic information for each source at the top of a loose-leaf sheet. Below that entry, record the facts, opinions, and ideas that you find pertinent. Use only the right-hand two-thirds of each sheet for notes from the source so that the information will be easy to retrieve later and so that you will have room to record your reactions in the left margin. Try to divide your notes on the source into blocks that reflect changes in subject matter. Be sure to indicate quoted material and to record page numbers accurately. These notes may help you recognize key ideas or similar or opposing ideas from other sources. At the bottom of your last page of notes on the source, comment on your overall reaction and indicate how you might be able to use that source's information in your essay.

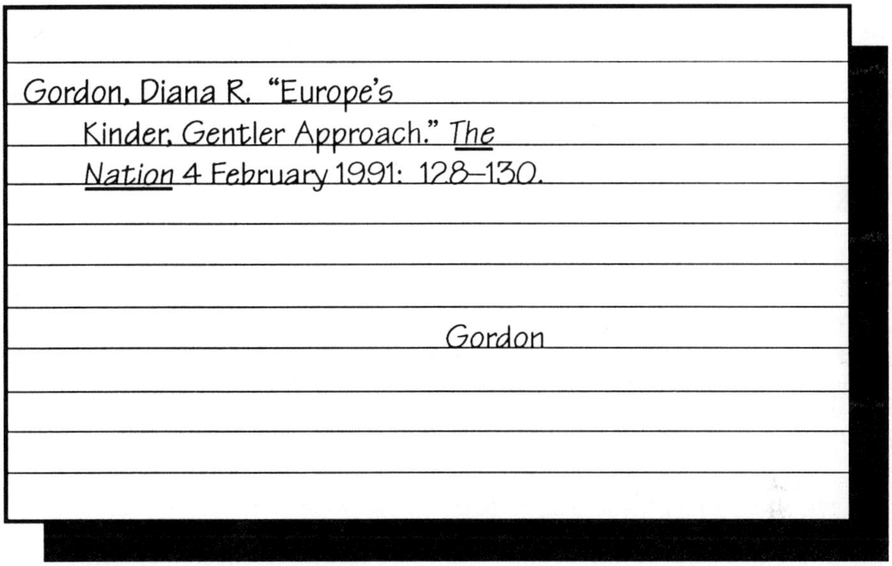

Gordon, Diana R. "Europe's
Kinder, Gentler Approach." *The*
Nation 4 February 1991: 128–130.

Gordon

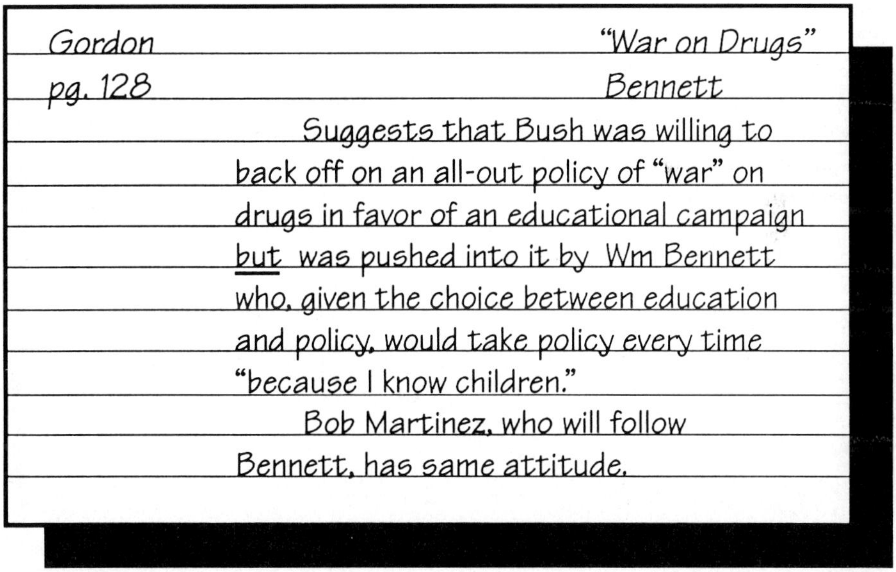

Gordon	"War on Drugs"
pg. 128	Bennett

Suggests that Bush was willing to back off on an all-out policy of "war" on drugs in favor of an educational campaign but was pushed into it by Wm Bennett who, given the choice between education and policy, would take policy every time "because I know children."

Bob Martinez, who will follow Bennett, has same attitude.

Loose-leaf notes allow you to maintain that source's logical coherence. You can also review your notes and source materials easily. The opportunity to record your reactions to the source material through notes in the left-hand margin not only improves your ability to remember and understand information, but also encourages you to state in

Diana R. Gordon. "Europe's Kinder, Gentler Approach."
The Nation. 4 February 1991: 128–130.

pg 128

	• Suggests that Bush was willing to back off an all out policy of "war" on drugs in favor
An interesting point given fact that Bennett was Secretary of Education!	of an education compaign but was pushed into it by William Bennett who given the choice between education and policy would take policy every time "because I know children." Bob Martinez, who will follow Bennett, has same attitude.
	• Gordon visited European countries to see if their approach is "as incoherent and cynical as ours." She found strict laws but a more relaxed attitude.
Good quote to use and set against Bennett's essay. →	". . . behind whatever policies are being adopted and implemented, there is less moral fundamentalism about drug taking and less demonization of drug takers than in the United States."
	• Gordon found several attractive approaches:
"harm reduction" →	For example, "harm reduction," which is based on the knowledge that many users cannot or will not stop. The strategy:
Impt. concept. p. 129 →	Lead them to get off drugs if possible, but if they can't get off, lead them "to drug use that is safer for them and for society as a whole."

your own words why you agree or disagree with what the author says. The process of writing your paper (of finding your own words and ideas) can start in the margin. This system places more importance on generating a detailed outline. Without an outline, you will spend a lot of time trying to find information. This system is especially effective if you must analyze and react to several sources—for example, when you are writing an explicitly argumentative essay drawing on the work of several writers who have published their opinions.

Photocopies. Modern technology allows you to get data and take it home—so why not use it? *Photocopying* is especially valuable when you have a few short sources and limited time to spend in the library. When you copy from a source, be sure to record full bibliographic information. Double-check each sheet to insure that the entire page, including the page number, was copied.

Highlight or underline passages that might be useful in your essay. Use the margins for notes about the content of the article and your reactions to it. If the margins on your copy are too narrow for comments, attach a cover sheet to the article and list the key passages (by page number or your own numbering system) along with your reactions to them.

Photocopying saves time and insures that you do not transcribe information incorrectly or omit important information. The larger format (more text per sheet), and variations in typeface and layout from source to source in this method can help you remember what you have read and where it is. Perhaps the most important advantage with photocopies is that the entire article is in hand and you are not limited to the information you thought would be important when you first read the source. Since the use of photocopies encourages skimming (which can lead to misunderstanding or missed information) instead of careful reading, try to read photocopies carefully at least the first time through. As with the loose-leaf notebook method, this approach requires close attention to outlining. Photocopies cost more money—the trade-off is in time saved.

As a rule, using a note-taking system built entirely on photocopies is best reserved for relatively short projects that use only a few sources. If your project is large, it is easy to get overwhelmed with information and paper. In those cases consider supplementing photocopies with a card system or loose-leaf notes.

All three of these note-taking strategies (or variations on them) can work well. Choose the method that suits you best. No matter what method you choose, be systematic and thorough.

Incorporating Sources Using the MLA Style

The discussion and examples provided below are in Modern Language Association (MLA) documentation style. MLA is the documentation system most often used in English and foreign-language departments. Other disciplines may use other documentation styles, but the basic principles that you will learn using the MLA style will apply to all documentation styles.

When you use outside sources in your paper, begin thinking about how they will fit into your text from the time you begin taking notes. As you begin to develop your initial outline, consider where and how you will weave information from other sources smoothly into your first draft.

Remember that the paper you write is your place for saying and justifying what you think about a topic. The sources you use should help you in that task. They should not take over the paper. The best way to control your sources is to mark very clearly for yourself and your reader what material is coming from sources. This marking also insures that you will not unintentionally plagiarize ideas or words that come from one of your sources. The marking system (documentation system) being suggested here uses two kinds of ''flags'': a verbal flag and a numerical flag.

The *verbal flag* introduces the source. It usually includes the author's name and the title of the publication the piece originally appeared in. It may also include the date it appeared and the title of the piece. The verbal flag alerts the reader that the information is from an outside source. The *numerical flag* follows the information from the source and includes the page number the cited information came from in the source.

The verbal flag and the numerical flag do two important things:

> First, they *bracket* the information that comes from the outside source, making it clear what is from the source and what is the writer's introduction and assessment.
>
> Second, along with the data in the Bibliography or Works Cited list, they tell readers exactly where the information comes from so that they can verify it if they wish.

If you consistently use verbal and numerical flags, there can be no question about how you are using your sources. Furthermore, you can use your sources as adjuncts to your argument.

The following short passages, which might have come from a paper on the legalization of drugs, illustrate how the system works. After each passage, you will find in brackets an explanation of what that passage demonstrates. The verbal and numerical flags in the passages are indicated in boldface type.

> In the **August 1990** issue of ***The Christian Century*, Walter Wink** attacks George Bush's war on drugs, saying that we have already lost it for ''spiritual reasons.'' According to **Wink,** ''Forcible resistance to evil simply makes it more profitable'' **(736).** Although his argument is unusual because of its ''spiritual'' orientation, Wink does join a growing number of people from differing political and intellectual camps who call for legalization.

[In this passage the verbal flag provides extensive information about the source because the writer thought that the additional information (the author's name, the time and place of publication) would help establish the author's credibility. Since the author's name appears in the text, it does not need to be repeated in the parenthetical numerical flag.]

William Bennett, who for several years was **President Bush's "Drug Czar,"** responded to the calls for legalization in his typical biting style:

> Like addicts seeking immediate euphoria, the legalizers want peace at any price, even though it means the inevitable proliferation of a practice that degrades, impoverishes, and kills **(506).**

[In this passage the writer did not think it necessary to include the publication information: The information about his government experience helps orient the reader to Bennett's perspective. Notice that since the quotation is fairly long (it covers at least three lines of text), it is set off from the main text of the paper.]

> Among so many articles and essays intensely arguing for or against legalization of drugs in the United States, **Diana Gordon's** analysis of what she calls **"Europe's Kinder, Gentler Approach"** is refreshing and enlightening. Although she takes no stand for or against legalization, she does call attention to the dangers inherent in our tendency to polarize ourselves with inflammatory rhetoric and the need for Americans to learn from Europeans and begin to treat addicts more as people afflicted with problems than as criminals who threaten us **(128–30).** Perhaps we should listen to her suggestions. . . .

[Here the information from Gordon's essay covers several pages in sequence, so we use a dash in the numerical flag to join the beginning and ending page numbers. If that information had come from two pages not in sequence, we would use a comma to separate the two page numbers, for example (128, 130).]

> The amount of cocaine seized by the authorities as they prosecute the war on drugs is often impressive. Within one week in late September 1989 over 36 tons of cocaine were intercepted and destroyed. Its street value was set at an astounding $11 billion **(Wink 737).**

[In this passage the writer is only presenting factual information and, therefore, did not think it was necessary to provide information about the source in a verbal flag. In this case and any situation in which you do not provide the author's name in the text, it must appear in the numerical flag so that the reader can easily find the source in the Works Cited list.]

> One powerful argument that runs through the writings of those who oppose the government's approach to the drug problem is that it does not adequately or sympathetically deal with addicts **(Gordon 128–130; Lapham 48; Wink 739).**

[Here the writer used several sources to support a point. Each source is given in the numerical flag separated by a semicolon.]

You may encounter several other situations that will require you to present additional or different information in the numerical flag. Examples of three of these follow.

When the source has both volume and page numbers: Provide the volume number followed by a colon and then the page number. This holds true whether the work uses arabic numbers or roman numerals for its volumes. For example:

(Jackson I:202–203)

(Jackson 3:410)

When the source does not give the name of the author: If you cannot find the author's name for a source, use the title of the essay or document. For example, if you used in your text a quotation or information from a *Time* magazine article called "Prospects for High School Graduates" and no author was listed, you would insert a shortened form of the title (say, "Graduates") in the numerical flag where you would usually put the author's name. (In the case of an anonymous book, however, you would use "Anonymous" instead of a shortened form of the title.)

When you use more than one source from the same author: In the case of using more than one source from the same author, instead of citing only the author's name, simply add a short version of the title so that the reader can go to the "Works Cited" and easily find which of the sources by this author is the one you are citing. For example, suppose that John Jones has written a book called *The U.S. Economy* and an article called "The Coming Recession." Here's how you cite the two in your numerical flag:

(Jones, **Economy** 176)

(Jones, "**Recession**" 101)

The Works Cited Page

The information on the Works Cited page corresponds with the verbal and numerical flags in the text of your paper. Here you list the *full* citation information for *all* of the sources you use in your paper. As its title suggests, you should list here only those works you actually cite within the text of the paper.

Organize the list alphabetically by author (or by title if the author of a piece is unknown). Each entry should include the title, the publication information, and, when appropriate, page numbers. (Titles that you underline if working on a typewriter will be in italics if you prepare your list on a word processor.) The first line of each entry should be flush with the left margin. Each additional line of the entry should be indented five spaces to the right. This allows readers to scan down the left side of the list of sources and find the name or title they are looking for.

A sample Works Cited listing appears below.

Works Cited

Adams, Suzanne. Having It All: Motherhood and Career. New York: Macmillan, 1991.

———. "What I Learned About Having a Career and Raising a Family in the Nineties." Time 4 July 1992: 67–72.

Dean, Stanley, and Maria Kuntz. The Evolution of the Nuclear Family in Modern American Society. Chicago: U of Chicago P, 1989.

Ford, Henrietta. "Helping Our Children by Helping Ourselves." The Modern American Family. Ed. Irene C. Buchanan. Los Angeles: Dodd, 1975.

Gardiner, Darryl. A History of Juvenile Delinquency in American Society. 3 vols. Baltimore: Johns Hopkins U P, 1981.

"Living for Family of Four Tighter than Ever." New York Times. 21 March 1992: 12A.

Miller, Evelyn. Family, Homelife, and Moral Rectitude. New York: n.p., n.d.

Stuyvesant, Derrick. "Optimal Environmental Conditioning in the Post-Nuclear Family." Journal of the American Psychological Institute 60 (Spring 1990): 41–66.

Sample Works Cited Entries with Explanations

The following examples illustrate the most common types of Works Cited entries. An entry in a list of works cited has three divisions: author, title, and publisher. Each division is separated by a period and two spaces.

Book

Adams, Suzanne. Having It All: Motherhood and Career. New York: Macmillan, 1991.

[Be sure to include all the publication information (author, title, place, publisher, and date) in your entry.]

Book with more than one volume

Gardiner, Darryl. A History of Juvenile Delinquency in American Society. 3 vols. Baltimore: Johns Hopkins U P, 1981.

[The number of volumes is placed between the title and the publication information.]

Books with more than one author

Dean, Stanley, and Maria Kuntz. The Evolution of the Nuclear Family in Modern American Society. Chicago: U of Chicago P, 1989.

[Both authors' names should be given in the entry. List the authors in the order in which they appear in the source.]

Essay that is included in a collection of essays

Ford, Henrietta. "Helping Our Children by Helping Ourselves." The Modern American Family. Ed Irene C. Buchanan. Los Angeles: Dodd, 1975.

[Always cite the *person who wrote the words or ideas you are using,* not the name of the person who edited the book. For example, even though Irene C. Buchanan edited the book *The Modern American Family,* the entry refers to information *within* the book. This information was written by Ms. Ford. It is Ford's words or ideas you are using, not Buchanan's.]

Essay from a magazine

Adams, Suzanne. "What I Learned About Having a Career and Raising a Family in the Nineties." Time 4 July 1992: 67–72.

[The information for periodicals is always provided in this order: author, title of article, publication, date, pages.]

Newspaper article

"Living for Family of Four Tighter than Ever." New York Times 21 March 1992: 12A.

[The sequence of information provided is the same for newspapers as for magazines. The format of the page number information, however, will probably be different. Newspapers often have sections as well as page numbers. Be sure to give both the section and page numbers, so your readers will not have to search.]

Articles with no author given

"Dual Career Families: An Economic Necessity," Family Today 23 March 1991: 32.

[Give all the information you can, and list the piece alphabetically according to its title as shown in the example for a newspaper article.]

Articles with continuous pagination, as in scholarly journals

Stuyvesant, Derrick. "Optimal Environmental Conditioning in the Post-Nuclear Family." Journal of the American Psychological Institute 60 (Spring 1990): 41–66.

[Many scholarly or technical journals number pages consecutively through the several issues of their volumes (e.g., the November issue may end with page 400 and the December issue may begin with page 401). With these, give the volume number, the issue date in parentheses followed by a colon, and the page numbers. The issue date may be a month ("November 1992") or a quarter ("Spring 1991").]

Sources that do not provide complete information

Miller, Evelyn. Family, Homelife, and Moral Rectitude. New York: n.p., n.d.

[Give as much information as you can, and use the abbreviation "n.p." for "no publisher listed" or "no place listed" and the abbreviation "n.d." for "no date listed." In the example above, no publisher or date of publication is given with this source. Be sure to check the copyright page of a book (the opposite side of the title page) before you assume that the information is not given.]

Two works by the same author

Adams, Suzanne. Having It All: Motherhood and Career. New York: Macmillan, 1991.

———. "What I learned About Having a Career and Raising a Family in the Nineties." Time 4 July 1992: 67–72.

[With the first work listed, provide the full name of the author. With each subsequent work by that same author, provide three dashes followed by a period ("———.") before listing the source itself.]

Credits and Acknowledgments

Joshua Adler, ''Our Alarmist Society'' from *The Humanist* by Joshua Adler. Copyright © 1991 and reprinted by permission of The American Humanist Association.

Cleveland Amory, ''Needless Cruelty to Animals'' from *The New York Times* by Cleveland Amory. Copyright © 1989 by *The New York Times.* Reprinted by permission.

Warren Anderson, ''Another Vietnam? Vital Interest Makes Involvement As Different As Desert and Jungle'' from *The Charlotte Observer* by Warren Anderson. Copyright © 1990 and reprinted by permission of Warren Anderson.

Maya Angelou, excerpted from *I Know Why The Caged Bird Sings* by Maya Angelou. Copyright © 1969 by Maya Angelou. Reprinted by permission of Random House, Inc.

Asa Barber, ''Call of The Wild'' from *Playboy* by Asa Barber. Copyright © 1991 and reprinted by permission of Playboy Enterprises, Inc.

James Baldwin, ''Sonny's Blues'' from *Going to Meet The Man* by James Baldwin. Copyright © 1957 by James Baldwin. Reprinted by permission of Doubleday, a division of Bantam Doubleday Dell Publishing Group.

Tom L. Beauchamp and James F. Childress, ''The Distinction Between Killing and Letting Die'' from *Principles of Biomedical Ethics*, 2/e, by Tom L. Beauchamp and James F. Childress. Copyright © 1983 by Tom L. Beauchamp and James F. Childress. Reprinted by permission of Oxford University Press.

Mary Field Belenky, et al., ''Toward An Education for Women'' from *Women's Ways of Knowing* by Mary Field Belenky, et al. Copyright © 1986 by Basic Books, Inc. Reprinted by permission of Basic Books, a division of HarperCollins Publishers.

William Bennett, ''Should Drugs Be Legalized?'' from *The Reader's Digest* by William Bennett. Copyright © 1990 by The Reader's Digest Assn., Inc. Reprinted with permission from the March 1990 Reader's Digest.

Walter Berns, ''The Death Penalty Dignifies Society'' from *For Capital Punishment: Crime and The Morality of The Death Penalty* by Walter Berns. Copyright © 1979 and reprinted by permission of Walter Berns.

Ray Bradbury, ''Summer Rituals'' from *Dandelion Wine* by Ray Bradbury. Copyright © 1953, renewed 1981 by Ray Bradbury. Reprinted by permission of Don Congdon Associates, Inc.

Anne Marie Brennan, ''Biblical Fundamentalism Versus Scientific Ones: The Creationism Controversy'' Copyright © 1982 by The Commonweal Foundation. Reprinted by permission of the Commonweal Foundation.

William M. Brown, ''Maybe Acid Rain Isn't the Villan'' from *Fortune* by William M. Brown. Copyright © 1984 by Time, Inc. Reprinted by permission of Fortune Magazine. All rights reserved.

Susan Brownmiller, ''Emotion'' from *Feminity* by Susan Brownmiller. Copyright © 1984 by Susan Brownmiller. Reprinted by permission of Linden Press, a division of Simon & Schuster, Inc.

David Bruck, ''The Death Penalty'' from *The New Republic* by David Bruck. Reprinted by permission of *The New Republic.* Copyright © 1985 by The New Republic, Inc.

Arthur Campa, ''Anglo Versus Chicano: Why?'' from *The Intellectual Digest* by Arthur Campa. Copyright © 1973 and reprinted by permission of Arthur Campa.

Robert Coles, ''Hispanic Dream/American Dreams'' from *Change: The Magazine of Higher Learning,* Volume 20, Number 3, pages 12–13, by Robert Coles. Reprinted with permission of the Helen

Dwight Reid Educational Foundation. Published by Heldref Publications, 1319 Eighteenth St., N.W., Washington, D.C. 20036–1802. Copyright © 1988.

Sneed B. Collard III, "Refocusing Animal Rights," originally appeared in July/August 1990 issue of *The Humanist* by Sneed B. Collard III. Copyright © 1990 and reprinted by permission of *The Humanist.*

Norman Cousins, "How to Make People Smaller Than They Are" from *Saturday Review* by Norman Cousins. Copyright © 1978 by Omni Publications International, LTD.

A. J. Cronin, excerpted from *Adventures In Two Worlds* by A. J. Cronin. Copyright © 1935, 1937, 1938, 1939, 1943, 1946, 1948, 1949, 1950, 1951, 1952 by A. J. Cronin. Reprinted by permission of Little, Brown, and Company.

Willie Jasper Darden, "An Inhumane Way of Death" from *Facing The Death Penalty: Essays on a Cruel and Unusual Punishment* by Willie Jasper Darden. Copyright © 1989 by Temple University Press. Reprinted by permission of Temple University Press.

Joan Didion, excerpt from "Los Angeles Notebook" from *Slouching Towards Bethlehem* by Joan Didion. Copyright © 1967, 1968 by Joan Didion. Reprinted by permission of Farrar, Straus, & Giroux, Inc.

William N. Ellis and Margaret McMahon, "Cultures in Transition" from *The Futurist* by William N. Ellis and Margaret McMahon. Copyright © 1989 and reprinted with permission from *The Futurist*, published by The World Future Society, 7910 Woodmont Ave., Suite 450, Bethesda, MD 20814.

Warren Farrell, excerpts from *The Liberated Man* by Warren Farrell. Copyright © 1974 by Warren Farrell. Reprinted by permission of Random House, Inc.

Duane T. Gish, "A Reply to Gould" from *Discover*, August 1981 by Duane T. Gish. Copyright © 1981 by and reprinted by permission of the author.

Ellen Goodman, "Our Way of Life: Should We Die For It—Or Change It?" from *The Charlotte Observer* by Ellen Goodman. Copyright © 1990 and reprinted by the permission of The Boston Globe Newspaper Company/Washington Post Writers Group.

Diana R. Gorden, "Drug Wars Over There: Europe's Kinder, Gentler Approach" from *The Nation* by Diane R. Gordon. Copyright © 1991 and reprinted by permission of The Nation Magazine/ The Nation Company, Inc.

Stephen Jay Gould, "Evolution as Fact and Theory" from *Discover*, August 25, 1990 by Stephen Jay Gould. Copyright © 1990 by and reprinted by permission of the author.

Edward T. Hall, "Proxemics in The Arab World" from *The Hidden Dimension* by Edward T. Hall. Copyright © 1966, 1982 by Edward T. Hall. Reprinted by permission of Doubleday, a division of Bantam Doubleday Dell Publishing Group, Inc.

Garret Hardin, "Lifeboat Ethics: The Case Against Helping The Poor" from *Psychology Today* by Garret Hardin. Copyright © 1974 and reprinted with permission from Psychology Today Magazine/Sussex Publishers, Inc.

Benjamin L. Hooks, "The Broader Issue of The Barry Case" from *The Washington Post* by Benjamin L. Hooks, Copyright © 1990 and reprinted by permission of Benjamin L. Hooks.

John G. Hubbell, "The 'Animal Rights' War On Medicine" from *The Reader's Digest* by John G. Hubbell. Copyright © 1990 by The Reader's Digest Assn., Inc. Reprinted with permission from *The Reader's Digest*, June 1990.

Gene E. Likens, F. Herbert Bormann, and Noye M. Johnson, "Acid Rain" from *Environment*, March 1972, Volume 1972, Number 14, Number 2, pages 33–40, by Gene E. Kikens, F. Herbert Bormann, and Noye M. Johnson. Reprinted with permission of the Helen Dwight Reid Educational Foundation. Published by Heldred Publications, 1319 Eighteenth St., N.W., Washington, D.C. 20036–1802. Copyright © 1972.

Florence King, ''I'd Rather Smoke Than Kiss'' from *National Review* by Florence King. Copyright © 1990 by National Review, Inc., 150 East 35th Street, New York, NY 10016. Reprinted with permission.

Martin Luther King, Jr., ''I Have A Dream'' by Martin Luther King, Jr. Copyright © 1963 by Martin Luther King, Jr., renewed by Coretta Scott King 1991. Reprinted by permission of Joan Daves Agency. ''Letter From Birmingham Jail'' from *Why We Can't Wait* by Martin Luther King, Jr. Copyright © 1963, 1964 by Martin Luther King, Jr. Reprinted by permission of HarperCollins Publishers.

Frances Kissling, ''Ending The Abortion War: A Modest Proposal'' from *The Christian Century* by Frances Kissling. Copyright © 1990 by The Christian Century Foundation. Reprinted by permission from the February 21, 1990 issue of *The Christian Century.*

Edward J. Koch, ''Death and Justice'' from *The New Republic* by Edward J. Koch. Copyright © 1985 by *The New Republic.* Reprinted by permission of *The New Republic.*

C. Everett Koop, ''Ethical and Surgical Considerations in the Care of the Newborn with Congenital Abnormalities'' from *Infanticide and The Handicapped Newborn* by C. Everett Koop. Copyright © 1982, Americans United for Life, 343 Dearborn Street, Suite 1804, Chicago, IL 60604. Reprinted with permission.

Lewis Lapham, ''A Political Opiate: The War on Drugs is a Folly and a Menace'' from *Harper's Magazine* by Lewis Lapham. Copyright © 1989 by *Harper's Magazine.*

''The Last Official Report On Acid Rain'' from *The Consumers' Research.* Reprinted with permission of *Consumers' Research* magazine, Vol. 71, No. 10, pp. 16–19. Copyright © 1988 by Consumers' Research, Inc.

Joseph Lelyveld, excerpts from *Move Your Shadow: South Africa, Black And White* by Joseph Lelyveld. Copyright © 1985 by Joseph Lelyveld. Reprinted by permission of Times Books, a division of Random House.

Barry Lopez, ''Buffalo'' from *Winter Count* by Barry Lopez. Copyright © 1981 by Barry Lopez. Reprinted by permission of Charles Scribner's Sons, an imprint of MacMillan Publishing Company.

Jon R. Luoma, ''The Human Cost of Acid Rain'' from *Audubon* by Jon R. Luoma. Copyright © by Jon R. Luona. Reprinted by permission.

William Manchester, ''Okinawa: The Bloodiest Battle of Them All'' from *The New York Times Magazine* by William Manchester. Copyright © 1987 by William Manchester. Reprinted by permission of Don Congdon Associates, Inc.

Martin E. Marty, ''Lines For Impure Thinkers'' from *The Christian Century* by Martin E. Marty. Copyright © 1991 by Christian Century Foundation. Reprinted by permission from the February 27, 1991 issue of *The Christian Century.*

Julie Matthaei, ''Political Economy and Family Policy'' from *The Imperiled Economy, Book II: Through The Safety Net* by Julie Matthaei. Copyright © 1988 and reprinted by permission of Julie Matthaei.

John McPhee, excerpt from ''The Woods from Hog Wallow'' from *The Pine Barrens* by John McPhee. Copyright © 1967, 1968 by John McPhee. Reprinted by permission of Farrar, Straus, & Giroux, Inc.

James A. McPherson, ''To Blacks and Jews: Hab Rachmones'' from *Tikkun* by James McPherson. Copyright © 1990 and reprinted with permission of *Tikkun,* a bimonthly Jewish critique of politics, culture, and society based in Oakland, CA. (800) 877-5231.

Marianne Means, ''Legalization Holds No Answer to Drugs'' from *Kings Features* by Marianne Means. Copyright © 1989 and reprinted by permission of King Features Syndicate.

Volker A. Mohnen. ''The Challenge of Acid Rain'' from *Scientific American* by Volker A. Mohnem.

Copyright © 1988 by Scientific American, Inc. All rights reserved.

Lance Morrow, "A Moment For The Dead" from *Time* by Lance Morrow. Copyright © 1991 by The Time Inc. Magazine Company. Reprinted by permission. "Islam Against The West?" from *Time* by Lance Morrow. Copyright © 1979 by The Time Inc. Magazine Company. Reprinted by permission. "Kidnapping the Brainchildren" and "Manhood and the Power of *Glory*" from *Time* by Lance Morrow. Copyright © 1990 by The Time Inc. Magazine Company. Reprinted by permission.

Augustus Napier, "Heroism, Men, and Marriage" from *Journal of Marital and Family Therapy* by Augustus Napier. Copyright © 1991 and reprinted by American Association for Marriage and Family Therapy, Inc.

Ralph Novak, "Coming to Terms With Nam" from *People Weekly* by Ralph Novak. Copyright © 1989 The Time Co. Magazine Company. Reprinted with permission.

Frank O'Connor, "Guests of The Nation" from *Collected Stories* by Frank O'Connor. Copyright © 1981 by Harriet O'Donovan Sheehy, Executrix of the Estate of Frank O'Connor. Reprinted by permission of Alfred A. Knopf, Inc.

Tillie Olson, "I Stand Here Ironing" from *Tell Me A Riddle* by Tillie Olson. Copyright © 1956, 1957, 1960, 1961 by Tillie Olson. Used by permission of Delcorte Press/Seymour Lawrence, a division of Bantam Doubleday Dell Publishing Group, Inc.

James Ostrowski, "Thinking About Drug Legalization" from *The Cato Institute* by James Ostrowski. Copyright © 1989 and reprinted with permission from The Cato Institute.

Wilfred Owen, "Dulce et Decorum Est" from *The Collected Poems of Wilfred Owen* by Wilfred Owen. Copyright © 1963 by Chatto & Windus, Ltd. Reprinted by permission of New Directions Publishing Corporation.

Peter Passell, "Lotto is Financed by the Poor and Won by the States" from *The New York Times* by Peter Passell. Copyright © 1989 by The New York Times Company. Reprinted by permission.

Karen S. Peterson, "Sex and The Brain/Debate: Does 'Wiring' Rule Emotion, Skill?" from *USA Today* by Karen S. Peterson. Copyright © 1991, *USA Today*. Reprinted with permission.

Michael Pollan, "Why Mow?" from *Second Nature* by Micheal Pollan. Copyright © 1991 by Michael Pollan. Used here with the permission of Atlantic Monthly Press.

James Rachels, "Active and Passive Euthanasia" from *The New England Journal of Medicine,* January 9, 1975, Volume 20, Number 3, pages 12–13 by James Rachels. Copyright © 1975 by *The New England Journal of Medicine.* Reprinted by permission.

Michael Radelet, "Introduction and Overview" from *Facing The Death Penalty: Essays on a Cruel and Unusual Punishment* by Michael Radelet. Copyright © 1989 by Temple University. Reprinted by permission of Temple University Press.

Dixy Lee Ray, "The Great Acid Rain Debate" from *The American Spectator* by Dixy Lee Ray. Copyright © 1987 and reprinted by permission from the January 1987 edition of *The American Spectator*, Arlington, VA.

Ronald Reagan, "Abortion And The Conscience of The Nation" from *Abortion and The Conscience of The Nation* by Ronald Reagan. Copyright © 1984 and reprinted by the permission of Thomas Nelson, Inc.

Richard Rodriguez and Marilyn Snell, "La Raza Cosmica" from *New Perspectives Quarterly* by Richard Rodriguez and Marilyn Snell. Reprinted with permission © *New Perspectives Quarterly*, Vol. 8, No. 1, Winter 1991.

Richard Selzer, "Abortion" from *Mortal Lessons* by Richard Selzer. Copyright © 1974, 1975, 1976 by Richard Selzer. Reprinted by permission of Simon & Schuster.

Earl E. Shelp, excerpt from *Born To Die: Deciding The Fate of Critically Ill Newborns* by Earl E. Shelp. Copyright © 1986 by The Free Press. Reprinted with the permission of The Free Press, a division of MacMillan, Inc.

Peter Singer, "Famine, Affluence, and Morality" from *Philosophy and Public Affairs* by Peter Singer. Copyright © 1972 by Princeton University Press. Reprinted by permission of Princeton University Press.

James Shreeve, "Machiavellian Monkeys" from *Discover* by James Shreeve. Copyright © 1991 and reprinted by permission of Discover Magazine/Walt Disney Productions.

Gloria Steinem, "Sisterhood" from *Outrageous Acts and Everyday Rebellions* by Gloria Steinem. Copyright © 1983 by Gloria Steinem, 1984 by East Toledo Productions, Inc. Reprinted by permission of Henry Holt and Company, Inc.

Shelby Steele, "Being Black and Feeling Blue: Black Hesitation on the Brink" from *The American Scholar* by Shelby Steele. Copyright © 1989 by Shelby Steele. Reprinted by permission of *The American Scholar*, Volume 58, Number 4, Autumn 1989.

Ngũgĩ wa Thiongo, Excerpt from *Decolonising The Mind: The Politics of Language in African Literature* by Ngũgĩ wa Thiongo. Reprinted with permission from Ngũgĩ wa Thiongo: *Decolonising The Mind: The Politics of Language in African Literature* (Heinemann Educational Books, Portsmouth, NH, 1968).

Judith Jarvis Thompson, "A Defense of Abortion" from *Philosophy and Public Affairs* by Judith Jarvis Thompson. Copyright © 1971 by Princeton University Press. Reprinted by permission of Princeton University Press.

Lewis Thomas, "The Medusa and the Snail" from *The Medusa and the Snail* by Lewis Thomas. Copyright © 1977 by Lewis Thomas. Reprinted by permission of Viking Penguin, a division of Penguin Books USA Inc.

Article, "Too Many Abortions" from *Commonweal.* Copyright © 1989 by Commonweal Foundation. Reprinted by permission of the Commonweal Foundation.

Charles A. Turner, "A Dream Deferred" from *The Black Scholar* by Charles A. Turner. Copyright © 1988 and reprinted by permission of *The Black Scholar*, Volume 19, Number 1, January/February 1988.

John Cole Vodicka, "The All-Embracing Affect of The Death Penalty" from *The California Prisoner* by John Cole Vodicka. Copyright © January 1985 by *The California Prisoner.* Reprinted with permission.

Alice Walker, "Everyday Use" from *In Love & Trouble* by Alice Walker. Copyright © 1973 by Alice Walker. Reprinted by permission of Harcourt Brace Jovanovich.

Richard A. Watson, "Reason and Morality in a World of Limited Food" from *World Hunger and Moral Obligation* by Richard A. Watson. Copyright © 1977 and reprinted by permission of Richard A. Watson.

Faye Wattleton, "Reproductive Rights Are Fundamental Rights" from *The Humanist* by Faye Wattleton. First appeared in the Jan/Feb 1991 issue of *The Humanist.* Reprinted with permission.

E. B. White, "Once More to the Lake" from *One Man's Meat* by E. B. White. Copyright © 1983 by and reprinted by permission of HarperCollins Publishers.

Merry White, "Japanese Education: How Do They Do It?" from *The Public Interest* by Merry White. Copyright © 1984 by Merry White. Reprinted by the permission of the author and National Affairs, Inc.

James Q. Wilson, "Against The Legalization of Drugs" from *Commentary* by James Q. Wilson. Copyright © 1990 by James Q. Wilson. Reprinted by permission of the author and *Commentary Magazine.*

Walter Wink, ''Biting The Bullet: The Case for Legalizing Drugs'' from *The Christian Century* by Walter Wink. Copyright © 1990 Christian Century Foundation. Reprinted by permission from the August 8–15, 1990 issue of *The Christian Century*.

Robert L. Wolke, ''A Message to Students: 'If You Have a Lawyer Handy, Go Ahead and Cheat Like Crazy'' from *The Chronicle of Higher Education* by Robert L. Wolke. Copyright © 1991 and reprinted by permission of Robert L. Wolke.

Index